V&R Academic

Edmund Schlink Works

Edited by

Matthew L. Becker

Volume 1

Vandenhoeck & Ruprecht

Edmund Schlink
Ecumenical and Confessional
Writings

Volume 1

The Coming Christ and Church Traditions
After the Council

Edited by Matthew L. Becker

Translated by Matthew L. Becker and Hans G. Spalteholz

Vandenhoeck & Ruprecht

Bibliographic information published by the Deutsche Nationalbibliothek
The Deutsche Nationalbibliothek lists this publication in the Deutsche Nationalbibliografie;
detailed bibliographic data available online: http://dnb.d-nb.de.

ISBN 978-3-525-56028-0

You can find alternative editions of this book and additional material on our Website:
www.v-r.de

Originally published as *Schriften zu Ökumene und Bekenntnis. Band 1*, edited by
Klaus Engelhardt © 2004, Vandenhoeck & Ruprecht GmbH & Co. KG, Theaterstraße 13,
D-37073 Göttingen/Vandenhoeck & Ruprecht LLC, Bristol, CT, U.S.A.

Typesetting by Konrad Triltsch GmbH, Ochsenfurt
Printed and bound by Hubert & Co GmbH & Co. KG, Robert-Bosch-Breite 6, D-37079 Göttingen.

Printed on aging-resistant paper.

Contents

Foreword to the German Edition

Whoever reads Edmund Schlink's writings discovers their abiding significance and contemporary relevance. When the Vatican's Congregation for the Doctrine of the Faith published the declaration *Dominus Iesus* three years ago[i] and the ecumenical dialogue with the Roman Catholic Church became much more difficult, Schlink's book on the council was an important discussion resource for me. His chapter on the Decree on Ecumenism from Vatican II serves as a knowledgeable guide to Roman Catholic ecclesiology and provides criteria for the critical examination needed for it. What becomes clear, above all, is that the prerequisite for a serious ecumenical dialogue is the willingness, at the very start, to be open, for the time being at least, to God's activity in the other churches, rather than from the start to be judgmental about them. This remains one of the strongest ecumenical driving forces which accompanied Schlink throughout his life. One finds it again and again in the most diverse contributions he made from completely different periods of his life.

Edmund Schlink promoted the relation of theology to other fields of study. He appropriated insights from psychology and philosophy, from the natural sciences, and from cultural studies. As a systematic theologian he made frequent reference to the exegetical disciplines and to the history of dogma in the ancient church. The diversity of issues within and beyond the discipline of theology gave his thought a breadth that makes it especially attractive. The diversity of his thought, moreover, is just as evident as the inner coherence of the topics treated from various fields of study. There is a red thread that runs through Schlink's numerous publications, from the early dissertation, *The Human Being in the Preaching of the Church*, to the *Ecumenical Dogmatics*, which appeared shortly before he died. The question, "What is a human being?" [*Was ist der Mensch?*], was his great theme, perhaps even his life's theme. What he wrote in an insightful personal remembrance about Julia von Bodelschwingh, the wife of the director of the Bethel Institutions, Friedrich von Bodelschwingh, characterizes not only the outline of his theological anthropology but also his ecclesiology and his passionate interest in ecumenical matters: "In her thinking she was never satisfied with the established and the familiar, but in a surprisingly original and unbiased way she inquired into why things are the way they are. While staying entirely focused on Bethel, she nevertheless at the same time went above and beyond what was already occurring there. Devoting herself entirely to the people at Bethel, she sought for what was not yet a reality in their lives."[ii] Schlink wanted likewise to be devoted to the separated churches and to discern in them a fullness which was not yet realized in an actual confessional form. It was precisely the Lutheran Confession, so he was convinced, that enables the separated churches to seek and discover one another as churches of Jesus Christ, and to come to live in the full breadth of the church of Jesus Christ.

This first volume of Edmund Schlink's works brings together two books, *The Coming Christ and Church Traditions: Essays for the Dialogue among the Separated Churches* and *After the Council*. They belong together even though they were originally published separately. The essays in the first book are more than preliminary studies for the *Ecumenical Dogmatics*, and the second book on the Second Vatican Council is more than the formal report of the official German Protestant observer at that council. What is needed for productive ecumenical dialogue is substantive scholarship in dogmatics and the history of dogma. This is just what these multifaceted texts provide. Beyond that, Edmund Schlink himself was convinced: If the goal of uniting the separated churches is in earnest, then no church can remain as it is now. For that reason, at the very start of every ecumenical endeavor—at the global, regional, or local level—there must be repentance for each church body's intransigence and the widespread sense of ecclesiological entitlement. In one of the last chapters of his book on the Second Vatican Council, Schlink speaks of "anxious Christendom" [*ängstlichen Christenheit*]. Ecumenical zeal is good, but it does not overcome that angst. That can only happen through "the mercy of Christ." Here beats the very heart of Schlink's theology. It is from the action of Christ that we need to come really to know our own church and the other churches. Schlink will then later speak, in the *Ecumenical Dogmatics*, of the "Copernican revolution in the consideration of Christendom." Christ—and not one's own church—must be the criterion for truly perceiving and evaluating the other churches.

This first volume makes accessible the important essay, "The Structure of the Dogmatic Statement as an Ecumenical Issue." As Edmund Schlink worked on this in 1957, he entered into new territory. He allowed anthropological criteria, such as modes of thinking and forms of language, as well as insights from linguistics and the psychology of thinking, to shed light on dogmatic and ecumenical reflection. He understood the differences within the New Testament—for example, between the Pauline and Johannine writings—not only as "differences in conceptuality and historical context, but also as differences in their author's modes of thinking."

The book *After the Council* describes the four periods of the Second Vatican Council, together with its hopes and surprises, its breakthroughs and setbacks. It is a small compendium of Roman Catholic ecclesiology. One learns what constitutes the difference between an assembly of the World Council of Churches and a council of the Roman Catholic Church. One learns what constitutions, decrees, and declarations are. One is astonished at the bold scale and intensity with which the official observers from the other churches were involved in the preparation of important texts and resolutions.

In controversial theological discussions with the Roman Catholic Church, the question is often raised: "Well, what has come of your council with its ecumenical openness?" Whoever reads Schlink's book on the council carefully will not stop with this question, for it must likewise be asked: "How have we in our own church responded to the council? Are we merely sitting back, or are we challenged toward our own renewal?" At the end of the book Schlink writes, "Beyond that, however, it is correct to say that none of the churches can remain exactly as it is; in every case, a renewal and an unfolding of catholicity, that is, a return to God and a turning toward the other churches, is needed." These are important driving forces in the ecumenical theology of Edmund Schlink, on which we are still dependent even after forty years.

On 6 March 2003 Edmund Schlink would have been 100 years old. A group of his students is preparing a multi-volume edition of the most important works that are either out of print or difficult to acquire. The edition will contain the following volumes: *Ecumenical and Confessional Writings*; *Ecumenical Dogmatics*; *The Doctrine of Baptism*; *The Theology of the Lutheran Confessions*; and *Sermons and Essays*. Each volume will contain an introduction that identifies aspects of the historical influence of the works published in that volume. In this first volume Jochen Eber has provided a biographical introduction.[iii] He situates the most important works by Edmund Schlink in relation to the course of Schlink's life and the context in which they originated, their life-setting [*Sitz im Leben*].

Karlsruhe, April 2003   Klaus Engelhardt

Editor's Notes

[i] Joseph Cardinal Ratzinger, Cardinal Prefect of the Congregation for the Doctrine of the Faith, "Dominus Iesus: On the Unicity and Salvific Universality of Jesus Christ and the Church" (Vatican City: Congregation for the Doctrine of the Faith, August 6, 2000), available on the Vatican's website, accessed on 22 April 2014, Vatican.va, vatican.va/roman_curia/congregations/cfaith/documents.

[ii] Edmund Schlink, "Erinnerungen an eine jugendliche Gestalt (Julia von Bodelschwingh)" [Memories of a Youthful Woman], *Frauen in Bethel: Acht Frauengestalten aus vergangener Zeit*, ed. Gottfried Michaelis (Melle: Knoth, 2000), 7.

[iii] See Jochen Eber, "Edmund Schlink 1903–1984: Ein Leben für die Einheit der Kirche," in *Schriften zu Ökumene und Bekenntnis*, vol. 1 (*Der kommende Christus und die kirchlichen Traditionen*; *Nach dem Konzil*), ed. Klaus Engelhardt (Göttingen: Vandenhoeck & Ruprecht, 2004), xi–xxii. This excellent German introduction served as the principal resource for the editor's introduction that is included in the present volume.

Preface to the American Edition

In 2004 Vandenhoeck & Ruprecht marked the centennial anniversary of the birth of Edmund Schlink and the twentieth anniversary of his death by publishing the first of five volumes that contain his principal theological writings, *Schriften zu Ökumene und Bekenntnis*. The final volume appeared in 2010.

In January 2012 Jörg Persch, the editorial director for theology and religion at Vandenhoeck & Ruprecht, invited me to begin an American edition of these volumes. I am grateful to him and to the Schlink family for entrusting me with this important project. I am also grateful to the editors of the German edition: Klaus Engelhardt, Günther Gassmann, Rolf Herrfahrdt, Michael Plathow, Ursula Schnell, and Peter Zimmerling.

Although nearly all of Edmund Schlink's writings in this first volume of the American edition have been available in English for several decades, the publication of the new German edition offered a significant impetus for providing a fresh and more accurate translation of them. Key terms are now translated consistently. Infelicitous and misleading renderings of Schlink's language into English, which more or less happened in the earlier versions, have been corrected. Technical theological terms and concepts received special attention so that their English equivalents are as accurate as possible. Sentences, footnotes, and entire paragraphs that, for whatever reason, were omitted have now been restored. Unlike the abridged English edition of *Der kommende Christus und die kirchlichen Traditionen*, which was published in 1967, this new edition includes all of the essays that appeared in the original book, published in 1961.

Working with Dr. Hans Spalteholz, emeritus professor of English and theology at Concordia University, Portland, Oregon, has been a great joy and privilege and not merely a collaborative labor of love. As a native German speaker, who also served for thirty-five years as a pastor to a German-speaking congregation in Portland, Prof. Spalteholz brought crucial, invaluable expertise to this project. I am truly grateful for the help he has provided me. I do, however, take full responsibility for the finished product.

We have attempted to be as faithful to Schlink's original language and polished style as context and word usage permitted. In general, we have tried to be "as literal as possible" and "as free as necessary." On occasion, we have not hesitated to borrow felicitous phrases and apt expressions from earlier translations of Schlink's works and those of other German writers. We have employed gender-inclusive language to the extent that such use was possible without misrepresenting what the author communicated or forcing his language to fit later church developments (for example, regarding the ordination of women to the pastoral ministry; cf. sec. 4 of chap. 8 ["Apostolic Succession"] in Book One below). We believe that were Dr. Schlink alive today he would use such inclusive language, given his strong emphasis on the inclusivity of the whole church within the one body of Christ.

Unless otherwise noted, all Scripture quotations are from the New Revised Standard Version Bible. Where Schlink's versification from Luther's Bible differs from the NRSV's, I have placed the latter's verse numbers in brackets. All quotations from the official documents of the Second Vatican Council are based on the English versions that appear on the official website of the Vatican (Vatican.va). Nevertheless, I have also freely made use of the Latin and English versions that appear in Denzinger and Tanner.[1] Where Schlink's German translations of these documents differ significantly from the online English versions, I have compared the German and all available English renderings with the Latin and made whatever adjustments were necessary.

The only material not included here is the biographical essay by Dr. Jochen Eber, which was published in the first volume of the German edition. That essay has been replaced by my own introduction, which is partly based on Dr. Eber's very helpful research.

Footnotes by Schlink appear as normal footnotes in the text (identified by plain superscripted arabic numerals), in a sequence that is identical to the German original (unless otherwise noted). On rare occasions where an incorrect or incomplete title or date appears in the footnotes, these have been corrected and missing publication information supplied. The other, infrequent mistakes in the original citations have been silently rectified. Whenever possible, references to existing English translations of works cited by Schlink are included. If a German work has not been published in English, a translation of its title is placed in brackets immediately after the German title. All translations of quoted German works are mine, unless otherwise noted. Notes added in their entirety in the American edition appear at the end of each chapter and are identified in the text by superscripted roman numerals in brackets. On occasion, an editorial insertion will be included in the body of the text or within one of Schlink's footnotes. These editorial insertions are placed in brackets and marked at the end with the abbreviation "Ed.," to make clear that they are my notes, not Schlink's. Numbers that appear in brackets, either in the text or in footnotes, refer to the page number(s) from the English translation of a given work. Each volume contains indexes of Scripture references, names, and subjects.

---

1 Henrich Denzinger, ed., *Enchiridion symbolorum: definitionum et declarationum de rebus fidei et morum/Compendium of Creeds, Definitions, and Declarations on Matters of Faith and Morals*, 43rd ed., ed. Peter Hünermann, Robert Fastiggi, and Anne Englund Nash (San Francisco: Ignatius Press, 2012); Norman P. Tanner, ed., *Decrees of the Ecumenical Councils*, 2 vols. (Washington, D. C.: Georgetown, 1990). I have followed Tanner's lead in using gender-inclusive language whenever possible.

The layout of the American edition retains Schlink's divisions of chapters, sections, and paragraphs. All Greek and Latin terms have been kept in the text and an English translation of the less familiar ones appears in brackets. On occasion Schlink's original German term or phrase is placed in brackets immediately after the English translation, usually because the word or phrase is a technical expression or its etymological roots are significant. I have maintained most instances where Schlink placed quotation marks around certain German words and phrases (and have usually then placed the original word or phrase in brackets after the translation). Where Schlink refers to a word as a word, I have placed that word in italics, not in quotation marks. Material placed in parentheses, either in the body of the text or in footnotes, unless otherwise noted, is original to Schlink's text.

A few remarks on certain specifics of the translation may be of some help to the reader. Normally *church* with a small-case *c* refers to "the one, holy, catholic, and apostolic church" or "the church of Jesus Christ," which cannot be strictly identified with any one church body or denomination. (The Latin designation for this, the *una sancta* confessed in the Latin form of the Nicene Creed, will likewise be small-case.) When *Church* appears with a large-case *C*, this term refers to a specific church body (for example, the Roman Catholic Church), a church tradition (for example, the Eastern Orthodox Church), or to a federation of churches (for example, The Protestant Church in Germany).

The word *Anfechtung* is an important term in the Lutheran theological tradition. Luther occasionally used it to translate the Latin term *tentatio*, that is, "spiritual crisis" or "turmoil" or "trial." Luther understood it also in the sense of "being attacked" or "being assailed" by forces opposed to Christ, the gospel, and the church. In such a context, one is being tempted to reject faith in Christ and to despair of God and oneself. So the term can also be translated as "temptation," although that lacks the aspect of "attack." The term will occasionally be left untranslated (as in the seventh chapter of Book One below, where Schlink defines it), or it will be rendered as "spiritual attack and trial." The antidote to such attack, according to both Luther and Schlink, is solely the gospel promise and the comfort it brings to the one who trusts it in faith.

While it would be nice to preserve Martin Luther's use and understanding of the term *evangelisch* (that is, oriented toward the *evangel* or *good news* of Jesus Christ), this word has come to mean something quite different in the United States from what it originally meant to sixteenth-century "evangelicals." Therefore, to avoid misunderstanding, this German adjective will normally be translated as "Protestant" or "Evangelical-Lutheran," depending on the context.

When used in reference to the worship service, the word *Ordnung* will be translated as "order," since it typically refers to the order of service in the liturgy. When used to refer to the organization and administration of those who serve in a given ministry of the church, this word will be translated as "ordering," since it typically refers here to the ordering or arranging of ministerial offices (as, for example, in the context of discussions about "faith and *order*"). When modified by the adjective *kirchenrechtlich*, the word *Ordnung* can refer to "canon law" (as in both the Eastern and Western Christian traditions), "church law" (as in the organization and administration of a given Protestant territorial church), or even "church regulations" (as in a church constitution, its ordinances and bylaws, as well as its formal agreements and legal obligations).

Given the confused and weakened state of Christian ecumenism today, which some have described as an "ecumenical winter," one might hope that a re-examination of the key theological writings of one of the great ecumenists of the twentieth century might assist efforts at renewing the ecumenical movement, especially regarding issues of "faith and order" which have been marginalized in recent decades. Since many of the theological issues with which Schlink wrestled are still pressing upon us today, our own thinking about them might be benefited by his. His reflections on the Second Vatican Council, among the first to be published in the wake of that historic event, are still apropos, more than fifty years after their appearance. His incisive, yet respectful theological criticism of the Roman Church (his preferred way of referring to that church body) seems as relevant today as it did in the late-1960s.

Finally, I wish to thank my wife and son for their loving support and for their patience during the time I worked on this project.

Valparaiso University   Matthew L. Becker
Feast of Pentecost 2016

Edmund Schlink (1903–1984):
An Ecumenical Life[1]

Matthew L. Becker

An influential teacher, pastor, and professor, and a leading participant in numerous official ecumenical dialogues for more than forty years, Edmund Schlink was one of the most significant Christian theologians of the twentieth century. The author of a weighty dogmatics text, five additional important books, and numerous essays, sermons, and addresses, this second-generation "ecumenical pioneer of the 20th Century" was the central systematic and historical theologian at Heidelberg University between 1946 and his death in 1984.[2] Lauded as a "teacher of the church," as a "forerunner of the Ecumenical Movement in the 20th Century," and as "a quiet reformer" who "lived his life for the unity of the church," Schlink's contribution to the development of ecumenical theology in the second half of the twentieth century was considerable.[3] In the words of one of his most well-known students, "By connecting such ecumenical breadth with a forceful emphasis on the abiding authority of the apostolic confession of Christ, the theological works of Edmund Schlink, and especially his *Ecumenical Dogmatics*, are still exemplary guides today."[4] The recent publication of these principal writings in a new German edition offers a further reason to re-examine Schlink's life and literary output, especially given the fact that many English-speaking students of

---

1 The following includes material from my essay, "Edmund Schlink (1903–1984)," in *Twentieth-Century Lutheran Theologians*, ed. Mark Mattes (Göttingen: Vandenhoeck & Ruprecht, 2013), 195–222.

2 Günther Gassmann, "Edmund Schlink–An Ecumenical Pioneer of the 20th Century," *Ecumenical Trends* 33 (2004), 6–10.

3 Michael Plathow, "Edmund Schlink–Lehrer der Kirche: Doxologische und poetische Theologie," *Badische Pfarrerblätter* (March 2003), 61–65 (here 61); Christoph Schwöbel, "Ökumenische Dogmatik: Zum 100. Geburtstag von Edmund Schlink am 6. März 2003," *Ökumenische Rundschau* 52 (2003), 244–58 (here 254); Eugene M. Skibbe, *A Quiet Reformer: An Introduction to Edmund Schlink's Life and Ecumenical Theology* (Minneapolis: Kirk House Publishers, 1999); and Jochen Eber, "Edmund Schlink 1903–1984: Ein Leben für die Einheit der Kirche," SÖB 1:xi–xxi (here xi). For additional biographical information on Schlink, see especially Eber's doctoral dissertation, *Einheit der Kirche als dogmatisches Problem bei Edmund Schlink*, Forschungen zur systematischen und ökumenischen Theologie, vol. 67, ed. Wolfhart Pannenberg and Reinhard Slenczka (Göttingen: Vandenhoeck & Ruprecht, 1993), 18–50; and Klaus Engelhardt, "Biographische Reminiszenz zu Edmund Schlink," *Ökumenische Rundschau* 52 (2003), 242–44.

4 Wolfhart Pannenberg, Foreword to the *Ecumenical Dogmatics*, ÖD ix.

religious studies, including younger American theologians, may be unfamiliar with this important German Protestant.

Early Years and Education

Edmund Schlink was born on 6 March 1903 in Darmstadt, the capital city of Hessen, south of Frankfurt. His only other sibling, Klara (1904–2001), was born one year later.[5] His mother, Ella (1877–1969), came from a family that had been heavily influenced by Herrnhuter Pietism. His father, Prof. D. Dr. Wilhelm Schlink (1875–1968), who had been raised Roman Catholic but then became Lutheran, was a professor of mechanics and aeronautical technology at the Technical College (*Hochschule*) of Darmstadt, later at the Technical College of Braunschweig, where he also served as rector, and finally back at Darmstadt (after 1921). As a child and young student, Edmund Schlink was interested in literature, philosophy, and music. In Braunschweig he attended the *Wilhelm Gymnasium* (preparatory high school) and also took violin lessons. He even directed a student orchestra there.[6] In her spiritual autobiography Klara recalls how she and her brother enjoyed browsing local bookstores in search of answers to their deepest questions. They spent much time reading such philosophers as Arthur Schopenhauer (1788–1860) and Friedrich Nietzsche (1844–1900).[7]

After completing his university entrance exam in 1922, he studied one term at the University of Tübingen before transferring to the University of Munich (1922–24) where, like his father, he initially concentrated on mathematics and the natural sciences (especially physics). He also studied philosophy, art, and psychology. Following the German custom of listening to the best professors in one's field at several universities before writing one's dissertation, he then studied at Kiel (1924), Vienna (1924–25), and Marburg (1925–27). Eventually he completed his Ph.D. dissertation in psychology and submitted it to the faculty of Marburg in 1927.[8] This work explores personality changes in those

---

5 After her initial education in schools in Braunschweig and Darmstadt, Klara studied at the Fröbel Seminary in Kassel and "the Inner Missions" (*Inneremission*) school for girls in Berlin. In 1929 she became a teacher in the Mission House Malche in Bad Freienwalde. She then studied psychology, philosophy, and art history at the universities of Berlin and Hamburg. In 1947 she and Erika Madauss (1904–99) established The Evangelical Sisterhood of Mary in Darmstadt. At her ordination as a nun Klara took the name Mother Basilea. Later she wrote several devotional books, including a spiritual autobiography, *Wie ich Gott erlebte..., Sein Weg mit mir durch sieben Jahrzehnte* [How I Experienced God..., His Way with Me through Seven Decades], 3rd ed. (Darmstadt: Ev. Marienschwesternshaft, 1980).

6 Eber, *Einheit*, 18.

7 Klara (Mutter Basilea) Schlink, *Wie ich Gott erlebte*, 26.

8 Edmund Schlink, *Persönlichkeitsänderung in Bekehrungen und Depressionen: Eine empirisch-religionspsychologische Untersuchung. Nebst kasuistischen Beiträgen zur Psychologie des Gotteserlebens als Anhang* [Personality Change in Conversions and Depression: An Empirical Study in

who experience a religious conversion and in those who suffer clinical depression. Partly as a result of this study, which also explores issues in natural religion, he was promoted to lecturer in philosophy at Marburg on 27 June 1929, although he never actually taught there.

A year prior to the completion of this initial dissertation, he himself underwent a religious conversion after suffering a crisis of faith.[9] Although he rarely spoke about this experience, even to his family, in his retirement he recounted that period of his life to some students who had asked him about it:

We young people after the First World War were disturbed by questions like: What is life? What meaning does life have? One would read a lot of Dostoevsky and Friedrich Nietzsche, great influences on my restless generation. Restless in this way, and wanting somehow to answer the question about the meaning of life, I sat in on some lectures on medicine and law, and also on the history of religions, disturbed by the question, "Why live at all?"—because I hoped in this way to get an answer to the question about the meaning of life. But in my case it was this way: the longer I studied philosophy, the further I was from an answer, and because of that I entered into a genuine existential crisis of meaning. For that reason, I took a year off and worked as a hired hand on a Silesian farm. Out of this crisis, then, I found my way to Christian faith and decided to study theology.[10]

During his time off from the university, he came into close contact with Christians who had been influenced by the Lutheran mystic Jakob Böhme (1575–1624). In particular, a conversation with Pastor Dr. Carl Eichhorn (1855–1934), who in his retirement served a Christian convalescent home, was also instrumental in helping Schlink to overcome his crisis and to steer him in the direction of Christian faith and theology.[11] That spring, in 1926, he returned to Darmstadt, resumed his studies at Marburg (where he also began to study theology more intensively), completed his dissertation in religious psychology under the direction of Eric Rudolf Jaensch (1883–1940), and then turned his full attention toward seeking to understand the Christian faith.

After a short period of study at Bethel Seminary, near Bielefeld in Westphalia, he transferred to the University of Münster in late 1927 in order to

---

the Psychology of Religion with an Appendix Containing Casuistic Contributions toward the Psychology of the Experience of God] (Phil. diss., University of Marburg, 1927). A portion of this 211-page dissertation was published under the same title in *Archiv für die gesamte Psychologie* 70 (1929), 1/2:81–118. Klara also wrote her Ph.D. dissertation on a religious-psychological theme, namely, the significance of the consciousness of sin in the religious struggles of adolescent girls.

9 Eber, *Einheit*, 19. Schlink's sister had also experienced a religious conversion in August 1922. See Klara (Mutter Basilea) Schlink, *Wie ich Gott erlebte*, 30.

10 Edmund Schlink, "Vortrag von Prof. Edmund Schlink im Ökumenischen Studentenheim am 'Hausabend' des Heims," tape-recorded by H. Plathow (6 May 1979) and transcribed by Irmgard Schlink (the translation here differs slightly from that by Skibbe, *A Quiet Reformer*, 137).

11 Eber, "Edmund Schlink 1903–1984," xi.

listen to the most well-known European theologian of the time, Karl Barth (1886–1968). Here Schlink encountered his first ecumenical problems, as he heard the Reformed theologian lecture on ethics and theological anthropology—and criticize elements in the Lutheran dogmatic tradition, especially in the area of Christology. After four semesters of study and research in Münster, where he also heard lectures by Roman Catholic theologians, he completed his theological dissertation in 1930 under Barth's direction. This second of his doctoral dissertations explores "emotional experiences of God" as "an empirical-psychological contribution to the issue of natural religion."[12] Upon completing this work and passing his theological examinations in Münster and Darmstadt (he received the rare mark of "excellent" [*vorzüglich*] on his first exam and was awarded *summa cum laude* after the oral portion), he was promoted to lecturer in Münster in February 1931. On this occasion he delivered a public lecture on the concept of teleology and its continuing significance for Christian theology, later published in the principal journal of German systematic theology.[13]

Initial Teaching and Pastoral Activities

After finishing his second dissertation but before he was promoted to lecturer in Münster, Schlink chose to enter the "preachers' seminary" (*Predigersemi-nar*) at Friedberg in order to prepare himself for pastoral ministry. In December 1931 he was ordained and began immediately to serve as an assistant pastor to two congregations near Frankfurt. Here he had his first run-in with the Nazi Party because he refused to transport the *Winterhilfswerk* that had been entrusted to him by the Party.[14] A year later he began serving as a campus pastor at the Technical College in Darmstadt, the same place where his father had taught for so many years. In addition to giving lectures to students and faculty on the fundamental questions and issues of the Christian faith, he also discussed with them such matters as the relation of Christ to technology and the problems of German nationalism.

While serving in Darmstadt he kept in close contact with the theology faculty at Giessen, and in 1933 he was invited to become a teaching assistant (*Repentent*) there in order to complete a *third* dissertation (his second

12 Edmund Schlink, *Emotionale Gotteserlebnisse: Ein empirisch-psychologischer Beitrag zum Problem der natürlichen Religion* [Emotional Experiences of God: An Empirical-Psychological Contribution on the Issue of Natural Religion], Abhandlungen und Monographien zur Philosophie des Wirklichen 5 (Leipzig: J. A. Barth, 1931).

13 Edmund Schlink, "Zum Begriff des Teleologischen und seiner augenblicklichen Bedeutung für die Theologie" [On the Concept of the Teleological and Its Present Significance for Theology], *Zeitschrift für systematische Theologie* 10 (1933), 94–125.

14 Eber, *Einheit*, 21. *Winterhilfswerk* was a Nazi project of public aid for poor people, which was partly instituted to present a positive image of the Nazis within German society.

theological thesis, the *Habilitationsschrift*) that would allow him to become an official professor of theology in a German university. This post-doctoral thesis in theological anthropology examines how human beings have been understood in the preaching of the church.[15] It was submitted to the Giessen faculty in July 1934, and thus it paved the way for him to be called to that faculty as an un-established university lecturer (*Privatdozent*) of dogmatic and practical theology. Due to pressure from the Nazi secret police (Gestapo), however, which was exerted against him because of his activity in the Confessing Church and because he had publicly criticized the racist leaders of the *Deutsche Christen* (DC) in a sermon, he was removed from this teaching position after only one semester (winter 1934–35).[16]

A positive outcome of this time in Giessen, however, was the life-long friendship that began there with his fellow faculty member, the systematic theologian Peter Brunner (1900–81), with whom he had taught a course on the Lutheran Confessions. Like Schlink, Brunner had also been removed from his university position as a consequence of his opposition to the activities of the DC. As the pastor of a small congregation near Giessen, he had opposed the efforts of the DC to take over the congregation. As a result of his words and actions, he was denounced as anti-Nazi, and eventually spent four months in the Dachau concentration camp in 1935. When Brunner returned from prison to resume his pastorate, Schlink kept the DC pastor who had been sent by the Nazified church administration from entering the congregation and assuming leadership.[17] During these difficult years, he and Brunner, like several others,

---

15 Edmund Schlink, *Der Mensch in der Verkündigung der Kirche* [The Human Being in the Proclamation of the Church: A Dogmatic Investigation] (Hab. diss., University of Giessen, 1934). This work forms the first part of an expanded, three-part book that Schlink later published under the same title: Edmund Schlink, *Der Mensch in der Verkündigung der Kirche: Eine dogmatische Untersuchung* (München: Chr. Kaiser, 1936).

16 Eber, *Einheit*, 21; Skibbe, *A Quiet Reformer*, 28. At the end of May 1934, the Synod that met in Barmen issued its *Theological Declaration* (the so-called "Barmen Declaration"). This document, initially drafted by Barth and then edited and augmented by several Lutheran theologians, spoke against the *Deutsche Christen* (DC), namely, those German Christians who wanted to control the twenty-eight regional Protestant churches in Germany, to bring them into alignment with the racist and nationalist ideology of the Nazis, and to organize them into a single imperial church (*Reichskirche*) under the authority of a single bishop appointed by Hitler. See Martin Heimbucher and Rudolf Weth, eds., *Die Barmer Theologische Erklärung: Einführung und Dokumentation*, 7th ed. (Göttingen: Neukirchener, 2009). Those who supported the "Barmen Declaration" later organized into "the Confessing Church," of which Schlink was a participant. His sermon, "Pflicht und Versuchung christlichen Bekennens" [The Duty and Temptation in Christian Confessing], was published in *Bekennende Kirche und Welt: Vorträge und Predigten aus den Jahren 1934 bis 1945* [Confessing Church and World: Essays and Sermons from the Years 1934 to 1945], Das christliche Deutschland 1933 bis 1945: Dokumente und Zeugnisse, ed., Arbeitsgemeinschaft katholischer und evangelischer Christen, Evangelische Reihe, vol. 10 (Tübingen: Furche, 1947), 9–26 (reprinted in AB 13–34).

17 For this account, see Peter Brunner, "Bericht von Prf Brunner," in *Jahrbuch der Hessischen Kirchengeschichtlichen Vereinigung* 32 (1981), 495–503; Albrecht Peters, "Ringen um die einigende Wahrheit" [Striving for the Unifying Truth], *Kerygma und Dogma* 29 (1983), 202; and

were forced back to the Confessions of the Lutheran Church as the authoritative witness to church doctrine, especially in a time of church conflict, and they found in them the means for theological resistance against the DC. After the war, the two theologians became close colleagues and friends in Heidelberg.

In the wake of Schlink's removal from the Giessen faculty, he was invited by the director of Bethel Institutions, Friedrich von Bodelschwingh the Younger (1877–1946), who had received positive reports about Schlink's theology and scholarship, to become an assistant professor (*Dozent*) of systematic theology at the seminary in Bethel, where Schlink had also briefly been a student.[18] He began his work there on 1 April 1935, following the departure of Hans-Wilhelm Schmidt (1903–91), the one theology faculty member there to have belonged to the Nazi Party. All of the newly called *Dozenten* at that time were members of the Confessing Church. At the Bethel Seminary Schlink worked alongside such notable individuals as Günther Bornkamm (1905–90), who taught New Testament, Georg Merz (1892–1959), who taught practical theology, and Robert Frick (1901–90), who taught church history. Offering courses and seminars on dogmatics, the Lutheran Confessions, ethics, philosophy, and issues in practical theology, Schlink also regularly preached at least three Sundays a month in local congregations or at the Bethel Hospital.[19] He later wrote that "praise of the Creator from the mouths of epileptics in the *Zionskirche* at Bethel opened for me new dimensions of theological thought."[20] A product of his preaching during these years was a little book of sermons, *Der Erhöhte spricht*, which was the first of his writings to be translated into English.[21] He served in Bethel until March 1939, when the seminary was closed by the Gestapo.

Edmund Schlink, "Predigt in der Trauerfeier für D. Peter Brunner: Professor der Theologie, gehalten am Sonntag Rogate, dem 24. Mai 1981," *Kerygma und Dogma* 28 (1982), 4.

18 For Schlink's activities at the Bethel seminary in the years 1935–39 and 1945–46, see Frank-Michael Kuhlemann, *Die kirchliche Hochschule Bethel. Grundzüge ihrer Entwicklung 1905–2005* [The Seminary Bethel. Principles of its Development 1905-2005], Schriften des Instituts für Diakonie- und Sozialgeschichte an der kirchlichen Hochschule Bethel, vol. 13, ed. Matthias Benad (Bielefeld: Bethel-Verlag, 2005), 53–55, 59–60, 74–81; and Gottfried Michaelis and Andreas Lindemann, *Lehren und Studieren in Bethel 1934 bis 1946* [Teaching and Studying in Bethel 1934 to 1946] (Bielefeld: Bethel-Verlag, 1999), 9–49.

19 Gottfried Michaelis, "Edmund Schlink's Jahre in Westfalen" [Edmund Schlink's Years in Westphalia], in *Lehren und Studieren in Bethel 1934 bis 1946*, ed. Michaelis and Lindemann, 15–19.

20 Quoted by Klaus Engelhardt in his sermon, "Trauergottesdienst für Edmund Schlink am 25. Mai 1984 in der Versöhnungskirche Heidelberg-Ziegelhausen gehalten von Landesbischof Dr. Klaus Engelhardt," 6 (typescript; translated by Skibbe, *A Quiet Reformer*, 29). Dr. Engelhardt is Edmund Schlink's son-in-law and had been his student. He is the retired president of the EKD.

21 Edmund Schlink, *Der Erhöhte spricht: Eine Auslegung der sieben Worte Jesu am Kreuz und ausgewählter Worte des Auferstandenen* (Berlin: Furche, 1939; 2d ed., Tübingen: Furche, 1948; 3rd ed., Hamburg: Furche, 1954). ET of the third edition: *The Victor Speaks*, trans. Paul F. Koehneke (St. Louis: Concordia Publishing House, 1958).

During his years in Bethel he was also active as a theological advisor to the leaders of the Confessing Church in Westphalia and Hessen-Nassau. Toward this end, he had participated as a delegate in the meetings of the Confessing Church at Augsburg (1935) and Bad Oeynhausen (1936). In the struggle against the DC, Schlink and other pastors in the Confessing Church found themselves resisting Nazi ideas and practices in the church, while at the same time taking care not to be accused of overt political resistance against the Nazi regime. While many of the pastors in the Confessing Church had been able to avoid making an oath of loyalty to Hitler in 1934, they could not elude doing so in 1938, at least not if they wanted to stay in office and to provide for their families and congregations.[22] Schlink and the other leaders in their regional Confessing Church advised their pastors to make the oath.[23] Surely they did so, however, with the understanding (made clear in Barth's oath controversy), that the reference to "God" in the oath implied the subordination of the German Leader to the authority of the First Commandment. Despite having made the oath in 1938, Schlink was required to make a second oath to Hitler in December 1941, because of continued political suspicions about his activities.[24]

These years were especially difficult for him, not merely because of the church struggle against the DC and their ideology but also because of the death of his first wife, Elisabeth Winkelmann, who had been a fellow theology student in Münster. They had married in April 1932, but she died from an apparent heart attack in May 1936. After her devastating death, he had to care

---

22 In 1934 the national Bishop Ludwig Müller tried but failed to demand that all Protestant pastors in Germany make an oath of loyalty to Hitler. Four years later (April 1938) Friedrich Werner, the president of the Protestant High Church Council in Berlin, was able to order all pastors to make such an oath. Each pastor was required to say the following. "I swear: I will be faithful and obedient to Adolf Hitler, the leader of the German empire and people, that I will conscientiously observe the laws and carry out the duties of my office, so help me God" (see Angelika Gerlach-Praetorius, *Die Kirche vor der Eidesfrage: die Diskussion um den Pfarrereid im "Dritten Reich"* [The Church Faces the Issue of the Oath: Discussion of the Pastors' Oath in the "Third Reich"] [Göttingen: Vandenhoeck & Ruprecht, 1967], 69).

23 It should be noted that in August 1934 Karl Barth also agreed to make the oath of loyalty to Hitler (identical in content to the 1938 oath) that was then required of all civil servants (e. g., university professors), provided he could add a phrase that limited his obedience "to the extent" that he could "be responsible as a Protestant Christian." After this request was rejected, and Barth had been suspended from teaching at Bonn, he made public the reason for his addition to the oath, namely, that no government is above the First Commandment. When the Reformed Alliance in Germany (a federation of Reformed churches in Germany) declared that for Christians the oath's reference to God "excluded any action that would be contrary to God's command as attested in Scripture," and when other members of the Confessing Church had publicly made the same point, Barth then agreed that he could make the oath without any qualification. By this time (Dec. 1934), however, his actions had raised suspicion among his superiors and he was dismissed from his university position by the Cologne administrative court. Cf. Eberhard Busch, *Karl Barth: His Life from Letters and Biographical Texts*, trans. John Bowden (Philadelphia: Fortress), 255–58.

24 Cf. Skibbe, *A Quiet Reformer*, 44.

for their two young daughters, Johanna (b. 1933) and Dorothea (b. 1935). Two years later, in October 1938, he married Irmgard Ostwald (1914–2006), a former student of his who had also previously studied with Barth in her native Basel.[25] After her arrival at Bethel, Schlink had asked her if she would agree to type the first draft of the book he was then completing, on the theology of the Lutheran Confessions. She agreed and stayed on through the following summer to finish that project. (For relaxation she accompanied him on the piano, while he played his violin.) Toward the end of their collaboration he asked her to marry him. Together they had two children, Wilhelm (b. 1939) and Bernhard (b. 1944).[26] For almost fifty years Frau Schlink would give her husband invaluable theological counsel and support.

After the closure of the seminary in Bethel, Schlink became an official regional church counsellor (*Visitator*) of congregations in the Confessing Church in Hessen-Nassau. Many congregations there were without pastors, and so he was called upon to preach and care for several of them. Within a few months, however, his preaching had put him at odds again with the Gestapo and he was thus banned from speaking in public.[27] After a short stint as a missionary in Schleswig-Hostein, he returned to Westphalia, where he was called to serve as a wartime substitute pastor and a pastoral administrator to two congregations in Dortmund. During this time, he and his family lived in the household of the systematic theologian, Hans Joachim Iwand (1899–1960), who had been director of the Confessing Church's seminary in Blöstau and later in Bielefeld. Because of the frequent allied bombing raids, Frau Schlink and the children returned to Bethel after a few months. A short time later Schlink was called and appointed pastor of a congregation in Bielefeld, but the church authorities in Berlin, all members of the DC, blocked the appointment.[28] Nevertheless, the elders of that Confessing Church congregation, the *Neustädter Marienkirche*, asked him to remain, despite the illegality of such an action. This he did through the end of the war.

Particularly strong and influential memories from this period were of experiences that brought him into close contact with Christians from other confessional traditions. "I could not forget the humble faces of the Orthodox female forced-laborers from Ukraine, who in Bielefeld stepped to the altar of the evangelical-Lutheran St. Mary's Church and to whom I could not deny the Sacrament."[29] He also could not forget the experience of officiating at funeral

---

25 Skibbe, *A Quiet Reformer*, 30.

26 While Wilhelm is an emeritus professor of art history at the University of Freiburg, Bernhard is an emeritus professor of law at Humboldt University, Berlin, and a world-famous novelist. See Bernhard Schlink, *Der Vorleser* (Zurich: Diogenes, 1995; translated as *The Reader*, trans. Carol Brown Janeway [New York: Vintage, 1997]). This novel has been adapted into the award-winning film of the same title.

27 Eber, *Einheit*, 25.

28 Skibbe, *A Quiet Reformer*, 43.

29 Edmund Schlink, "Persönlicher Beitrag" [Personal Contribution] in *Männer der Ev. Kirche in*

services with the local Roman Catholic priest, as together they stood before the mass graves, after a devastating bombing raid. Reflecting later on these various experiences, Schlink wrote:

Was that only the experience of an extreme situation [*Grenzsituation*, lit. "a border situation"], which is meaningless for normal church life and for the dogmatic understanding of the church? Or was it even a mistake? Or is there not much more the responsibility to think about that which in those days broke open for us in an elementary way with every sign of a truly spiritual inevitability, and to do so with thorough care for its ecclesiological significance and to maintain awareness of it in the engagement with the Confessions? What shines as the truth in extreme situations in the church cannot become false in normal situations, even if it cannot be repeated in the same way.[30]

Schlink would set forth similar thoughts in his book of postwar reflections about "the outcome of the church struggle":

In the crisis of oppression Christians sought out other Christians, not only in one's home congregation, but also among those scattered about in prisons and in open fields. That a person could be Christ to another, that Christ was present in the mutual consolation of the brothers and sisters, that was the rediscovery of the church…. This discovery was not limited to one's own church confession…. In this discovery of sisters and brothers in other Christian confessions, the differences between them were not annulled, but the accents were shifted and oppositions disappeared over against the reality of the Lord, who is greater than our understanding and more gracious than any dogma of grace. Greater than the differences was the power of the name of Jesus Christ we witnessed to together. We will never be able to forget, that in great need of the gospel's consolation, we heard it from brothers and sisters who belonged to churches in which the pure teaching of the gospel is obscured…. We began… to listen to each other and learn from each other in new ways, to admonish and to warn each other. And it became increasingly clear that none of us could speak and act from one's own confessional position without carefully thinking through and really listening to the voices of the brothers and sisters from the other confession.[31]

While serving in Bielefeld, he was also called to be the director of studies at the *Thomasstift* in Strasbourg, where the Lutheran Church in Alsace educated its pastors. From May 1943 until the Allied armies captured the city in September 1944, he spent half of a month teaching seminary students there and the other half ministering to his congregation 250 miles away. Not surprising, the

Deutschland. Eine Festschrift für Kurt Scharf zum 60. Geburtstag, ed. Heinrich Vogel (Berlin und Stuttgart: Lettner, 1962), 206.

30 Schlink, "Persönlicher Beitrag," 206–7 (cf. Eber, "Edmund Schlink 1903–84," xiii–xiv; the translation here differs slightly from that of Skibbe, *A Quiet Reformer*, 49).

31 Edmund Schlink, *Der Ertrag des Kirchenkampfes* [The Outcome of the Church Struggle], 2d ed. (Gütersloh: C. Bertelsmann, 1947), 19–20, and 39. This essay has been reprinted in AB 69–121.

students were "amazingly alert and focused on what was most essential."[32] Several months earlier he had discussed his situation with Dietrich Bonhoeffer (1906–45) in a meeting in Berlin.[33] Bonhoeffer informed him that individuals in the German Military High Command had concluded that Germany could not win the war. He advised Schlink not to take up residence in Strasbourg. Only after the war would Schlink learn of Bonhoeffer's involvement in the circle of conspirators in the German Military Intelligence Office (*Abwehr*) who had attempted to assassinate Hitler.

Although Schlink opposed the actions of the DC and was a member of the Confessing Church, he also sought to remain a responsible German citizen *and* a faithful Christian pastor in the context of a totalitarian dictatorship. From the perspective of the present, given what people now know about the Third Reich and its nihilistic, destructive, and evil actions, it is difficult to understand the problems, complexities, and burdens that Schlink and other pastors in the Confessing Church faced between 1934 and the end of the war. Contrary to the above statement by Schlink that the "church struggle" (*Kirchenkampf*) forced Christians to listen carefully to others from differing confessional traditions, the Confessing Church was never very united theologically, let alone politically. The pressure and power that the Nazi regime exerted against its citizenry through its state security and the ever present threat of public denunciation and imprisonment certainly had their effect as well. Still, some today may wonder why Schlink and other pastors in the Confessing Church did not more openly criticize a government they had come to deplore. Clearly his decision not to pursue political resistance against the Nazi state put him in a different place from the course that Bonhoeffer and few others took. Schlink's primary concerns were to continue Christ's ministry of word and sacrament to the people who had called him to be their pastor and to stand with the true church of Christ over against the false (the *Nicht-Kirche*). The concern for his young family also had to have been a factor in guiding his words and actions in this difficult, turbulent period.

After the war, Schlink was among those who preached a strong word of national and ecclesial repentance:

Just as great as the guilt of the political leadership is the guilt of those church leaders and pastors, who like the false prophets of the Old Testament cried, "God is with us," when God had already long been against us, and who proclaimed God's blessing when they should have threatened God's judgment, who applauded when they should have been silent, and who were silent when they should have given warning. They accommodated God's commandments to the totalitarian claims of political power, whose commands were proclaimed as God's commands and whose actions as God's

---

32 Edmund Schlink, "Vortrag von Prof. Edmund Schlink im Ökumenischen Studentenheim am 'Hausabend,'" 7; quoted in Skibbe, *A Quiet Reformer*, 46. For Schlink's activities in Strasbourg, see also Michaelis, "Edmund Schlinks Jahre in Westfalen," 23–24.

33 Skibbe, *A Quiet Reformer*, 45–46.

actions. They perceived an arbitrary independence in political actions, the administration of justice, and the waging of war that does not belong to them, and they have failed to measure them clearly and openly against the norm of the divine Word. I am speaking here not only of those German Christians who mixed up Christ and Hitler in the most amazing way, who persecuted the true church by denouncing its preachers and congregation members, and who helped to make possible the persecution of Jews by rejecting the Old Testament. I am thinking here also of the others who thought they could preach the gospel without proclaiming the divine law, who thought they could nurture a pious inwardness, without calling out publicly from the rooftops God's claim on all, and who still excused and hoped when the stones already cried out for God's thundering fist. I am thinking of the many whose highest principle was to preserve the church and their own office by compromise and silence, who in secret rejected National Socialism, but in public "joyfully affirmed" it. They have falsely interpreted Romans 13 and kept secret the wisdom, "We must obey God rather than any human authority" (Acts 5:29).[34]

Schlink's self-critical attitude toward the church would remain an essential feature of his theology for the rest of his life.

Heidelberg

After the end of the war, Schlink briefly served as the Director of the preacher's seminary in Brackwede, also near Bielefeld, and taught one course ("The Doctrine of the Church") and two seminars ("Justification" and "Luther's *Freedom of the Christian*") in the reopened Bethel Seminary. He also published a little work on "the theological problem of music."[35] By this time he had become well known in German theological circles, not merely because of his actions against the DC but also as a result of the publication of his first major work, *The Theology of the Lutheran Confessions*, which has been a standard introduction to these writings right up to the present day.[36] This work as a whole stresses the importance of confessing the faith in the midst of spiritual attacks and trials (*Anfechtungen*) and the persecution of the church. It clearly underscores the centrality of the distinction between law and gospel for the articulation of *all* of the articles of faith. Every essential doctrine of the Christian faith dare not be taught independently of this distinction, that is,

---

34 Schlink, *Bekennende Kirche und Welt*, 117–18. During the Second World War German soldiers wore belt buckles that stated *"Gott mit uns,"* God with us.

35 Edmund Schlink, *Zum Theologischen Problem der Musik* [On the Theological Issue of Music] (Tübingen: J. C. B. Mohr [Paul Siebeck], 1945; 2d. ed., 1950; reprinted in AB 147–69).

36 Edmund Schlink, *Theologie der lutherischen Bekenntnisschriften* (München: Chr. Kaiser Verlag, 1940; 2d. ed. 1946; 3rd ed. 1948; 4th ed. 1954; ET of the third edition: *Theology of the Lutheran Confessions*, trans. Paul F. Koehneke and Herbert J. A. Bouman [Philadelphia: Fortress Press, 1961, reprinted by Concordia Publishing House, 2003]). The fourth edition has been reprinted in SÖB, vol. 4 (abbreviated hereafter as TLB).

independently of faith in the gospel. The political context of the book needs to be underscored as well, since the author analyzed the Lutheran Confessions as the church's faithful exposition of the doctrinal content of the Scriptures, often over against the false understanding of Christian faith as presented by the DC.

Schlink's return to the Lutheran Confessions was not for the sake of fostering a sectarian denominationalism; rather, he discovered in them a basic motivation for seeking church unity:

> ...[S]trong impulses toward ecumenical activity must go out from the Church of the Augsburg Confession, for its Confession permits and orders the Lutheran Church to seek and find assemblies of believers also in those areas where no one is pledged to the Augsburg Confession. At the same time, however, this ecumenical activity must remain inexorable in a decisive respect, namely, that it may recognize the unity of churches only where the one gospel is preached and believed.[37]

While already in July 1945 Schlink had been extended a call to teach at the University of Heidelberg, he did not officially accept this call until February of the following year, largely because of the difficult situation of the Westphalian churches and seminaries at that time.[38] He began serving as professor of dogmatic and ecumenical theology at Heidelberg on 15 June 1946. During the previous winter, as a part of an initial reconnaissance, he had lodged with Hans von Campenhausen (1903–89), who had earlier accepted a call to teach church history there. "The hospitality shown him in the situation of poverty after the war and the lively conversation with [von Campenhausen] regarding the tasks of a theological faculty in the intellectual reconstruction of post-war Germany made the decision easy for him to go to Heidelberg."[39] He saw the call to this old medieval city, located along the Neckar River in the shadow of its picturesque castle—a university town famous for its "poets and thinkers" [*Dichter und Denker*]—as a great opportunity to engage the other academic disciplines from his perspective as a Christian systematic and historical theologian.

Together with his fellow theologians, Martin Dibelius (1883–1947), von Campenhausen, and Peter Brunner, Schlink helped to rebuild the theology faculty and make it a major center of theological debate in post-war Europe.[40]

---

37 Schlink, TLB, 172. Schlink would develop this theme further in "Die Weite der Kirche Augsburger Konfession" [The Expanse of the Church of the Augsburg Confession], *Lutherische Weltrundschau* 1 (1949), 1–13; and in "Die ökumenische Charakter und Anspruch des Ausburgischen Bekenntnisses" [The Ecumenical Character and Claim of the Augsburg Confession], in *The Augsburg Confession in Ecumenical Context*, LWF Report 6/7, ed. Harding Meyer (Stuttgart: Kreuz Verlag, 1980), 1–28.

38 Eber, *Einheit*, 30.

39 Engelhardt, "Biographische Reminiszenz zu Edmund Schlink," 242. Cf. Eber, "Edmund Schlinks Beitrag zum interdisziplinären Dialog," 159.

40 The Ruprecht-Karls-Universität is the oldest university in Germany. Founded in the late fourteenth century, it soon became a leading intellectual center in Europe, especially for the study of theology and law. The much-vaunted "spirit of Heidelberg," especially embodied later in the

Heidelberg soon developed into "the best balanced faculty in Europe" and housed "the strongest Lutheran-oriented faculty anywhere at a public university."[41] "The work being done there was well-grounded, energetic, and relevant."[42] Within a few years, Heinrich Bornkamm (1901–77), Gerhard von Rad (1901–71), Günther Bornkamm (Schlink's former Giessen colleague and Heinrich's brother), Wilhelm Hahn (1909–96), and Claus Westermann (1909–2000) had also joined the faculty.[43] Each of these theologians of the so-called "alte Heidelberger Fakultät" had been active, leading pastors in the Confessing Church during the Kirchenkampf. It is not surprising that they regularly preached in the revitalized Peterskirche, the university parish:

So it was self-evident not only for Schlink but really for the entire "old faculty" that theology and church, scholarship and faith belong together, and that confession is not a matter of historical interpretation but a matter of public and ecclesial witness, also over against other ideologies in the moment of Anfechtung and persecution. That the university worship services in the Peterskirche, which were led alternately by the professors, were frequently overflowing with worshippers, was a living testimony to this attitude of "the old faculty."[44]

Their published sermons and other writings also helped to attract a fairly consistent flow of students from foreign countries, including many who had graduated from the principal Lutheran seminaries in the United States.[45]

One facet of the theology faculty's collegiality with one another was the formation of a society in which they regularly met to discuss a topic of

scholarly activities of the social scientist Max Weber (1864–1920) and the philosopher Karl Jaspers (1883–1969), suffered demise when the Nazis took control of the university in the mid-1930s. Following the Second World War and a process of internal and external renewal, it was officially reopened in 1946. Dibelius, who was particularly important in helping to rebuild the university after the Nazi period, had taught New Testament there since 1915. The systematic theologian Brunner joined the faculty in 1947, a year after the patristics scholar von Campenhausen. The latter had already been called to the faculty in 1936 but had to give up this call a year later, due to his support of the Confessing Church.

41 Skibbe, A Quiet Reformer, 67.
42 Skibbe, A Quiet Reformer, 73.
43 Heinrich Bornkamm, who taught historical theology (Reformation), joined the faculty in 1948. The Old Testament scholar von Rad and the New Testament scholar Günther Bornkamm came the following year. Hahn, who taught homiletics, liturgics, and catechetics, arrived in 1950, and Westermann, who taught Old Testament, joined the faculty in 1958. In addition to the above theologians, one should note that the theologically oriented philosophers Hans-Georg Gadamer (1900–2002) and Karl Löwith (1897–1973) also taught at Heidelberg in those post-war years.
44 Reinhard Slenczka, letter to the author, 22 January 2009.
45 In addition to Skibbe, the American Lutheran theologian Walter Bouman (1929–2005) completed his doctorate under Schlink's direction in the early 1960s. See Walter H. Bouman, The Unity of the Church in 19th-c. Confessional Lutheranism (Ph.D. diss., Heidelberg University, 1962). He was the first to publish a study of Schlink's theology in any language, a short piece that he wrote for the student journal of his alma mater, Concordia Seminary, St. Louis: "Edmund Schlink and the Unity of the Church," Seminarian 48 (1957), 10–15. Many other American students attended lectures by Schlink, including Carl Braaten, Robert W. Jenson, and Paul Maier.

importance. "Here one could experience to what level technical discussion, even concerning controversial topics, could be led. As a newly habilitated faculty member, one would first keep the protocol of the meetings and then be received into the group after giving a lecture."[46]

Within a year of the reopening of the *Ruperto-Carola*, Schlink established an ecumenical institute there, the first of its kind in Germany. (The Ecumenical Institute in Bossey, Switzerland, was formed in the same year.) The Ecumenical Institute of Heidelberg University, which was initially housed in the building of the Heidelberg Academy of Sciences, offered a program of lectures and seminars on themes of ecumenical importance. Participants sought "to examine carefully the consonance and differences among Christian churches and the numerous efforts toward Christian unity in our time."[47] Through gifts and grants, especially from individuals in the United States, the Ecumenical Institute was able to build and dedicate a separate building in 1957. This allowed the Institute to provide housing to approximately thirty international students who came to the Institute to study issues of ecumenical theology. Schlink's inspiration to combine student housing with the Institute is compelling: ecumenical teaching and ecumenical life belong together so that theory and praxis can be mutually beneficial to each other. Students from around the world and from different cultural and religious backgrounds could live in close proximity to each other, pray daily in the chapel, and reflect together on their differences and their commonalities.[48] Schlink served as director of the Institute and overseer (*Ephorus*) of the students' living quarters (*Studentenwohnheim*) until his retirement in 1971.

Characteristic of Schlink's own work and a further way in which he influenced the revitalization of Heidelberg University was the encouragement he gave to interdisciplinary research. This encouragement was already evident in his inaugural lecture as professor, wherein he used the scepter of the university as a symbol for a particular relationship between "Christ and the faculties."[49] The image of the twelve-year-old Jesus teaching four figures that represent the four faculties (philosophy, law, medicine, and theology) depicts Bonaventure's vision of truth, knowledge, and wisdom, according to which the

---

46 Reinhard Slenczka, letter to the author, 22 January 2009.

47 Edmund Schlink, "Der Neubau des Ökumenischen Instituts und Studentenwohnheims der Universität Heidelberg" [The New Building of the Ecumenical Institute and Student Dormitory at the University of Heidelberg], *Ruperto-Carola* 23 (1958), 4. Cf. Reinhard Slenczka, "Ökumenisches Institut der Universität Heidelberg," *Ökumenische Rundschau* 14 (1965), 64–65.

48 Michael Plathow, "Das Ökumenische Institut/Studentenwohnheim der Universität Heidelberg: Eine Einheit von Lehre, Forschung und Leben" [The Ecumenical Institute/Student Dormitory of Heidelberg University: A Unity of Teaching, Researching, and Living] *Heidelberger Jahrbücher* 22 (1978), 117–18, 122–23.

49 Edmund Schlink, "Das Szepter der Universität Heidelberg: Christus und die Fakultäten" [The Scepter of Heidelberg University: Christ and the Faculties] in *Aus Leben und Forschung der Universität 1947/1948*, ed. W. Kunkel (Heidelberg: Springer, 1947), 31–50 (reprinted in AB 125–46).

crucified and risen Christ is the true teacher of all the faculties. In light of this vision, Schlink was deeply convinced that the public truth of Christian theology ought to be in critical dialogue with all of the disciplines of the modern university. Thus he sought creative ways to bring theology into just such interdisciplinary conversation. Among the most important of these efforts was the annual *Dozententag* in February, a day-long conference for faculty that was hosted by the theology professors and that fostered interdisciplinary discussion about wide-ranging topics of interest, for example, theology and the natural sciences, the problem of nuclear weapons, grace and law, and human rights.[50] Whatever the chosen topic, a theologian and a professor from one of the other faculties always presented formal papers that were then discussed. "Since his call to the university, Schlink was undoubtedly the one who initiated this new alignment of the faculty and frequently supported it as professor and during his time as rector."[51]

Partly in recognition of his positive interaction with non-theological faculty, he was elected rector of the university by the faculty senate in 1953–54. His rector's speech, delivered on 29 March 1953 and published as the lead essay in the inaugural volume of *Kerygma und Dogma*, focused on the contrast between "wisdom and foolishness" as set forth in Luther's *Heidelberg Disputation* of 1518.[52] In this address Schlink criticized commonly held notions of truth and rationality in favor of a radically alternative view that is grounded in Christian freedom and humility. In response to the central question of the university, namely, "What is a human being?" (*Was ist der Mensch?*), he set forth the Pauline-Lutheran paradox: in the crucified and risen Jesus Christ a human being is both saint and sinner. Faith in Christ frees the scholar to see the world in all of its complexity and to trust that ultimately all truth, including all lasting scientific knowledge, has its unity only in God.[53]

Former students remember Schlink as an engaging teacher, whose occasional sharp gaze revealed an even sharper mind. A person "of medium height and genteel demeanor, with penetrating eyes," he lectured softly in "a

---

50 Reinhard Slenczka, letter to the author, 22 January 2009.
51 Reinhard Slenczka, letter to the author, 22 January 2009.
52 Edmund Schlink, "Weisheit und Torheit" [Wisdom and Foolishness], *Kerygma und Dogma* 1 (1955), 1–22.
53 For further analysis of Schlink's understanding of the relation of theology to the other university faculties, see Dietrich Ritschl, "Theologie als Erkenntnis: Edmund Schlinks Verständnis von Wahrheit vor dem Hintergrund der Theologen seiner Generation" [Theology as Recognition: Edmund Schlink's Understanding of Truth against the Background of the Theologians of His Generation], *Ökumenische Rundschau* 34 (1985), 287–98. It is important to note, too, that the question, "What is a human being?", is also raised in the first article of the Roman Catholic Declaration on the Church's Relation to the Non-Christian Religions (*Nostra aetate*), which Schlink drew attention to in the first subsection of chap. 7 of *After the Council*. This question is also raised in the tenth article of the Pastoral Constitution on the Church in the Contemporary World (*Gaudium et spes*), which Schlink analyzed in the eighth chapter of his book on the council.

voice pitched slightly higher and thinner than usual.... A person might easily
have conflicting impressions: that he was aloof, almost icy, and at the same
time that he was fully open and caring.... Although he always spoke quietly,
students knew that he expected work only at the highest level."[54]

Over the course of two to three years he offered lectures on the principal
doctrines of the Christian faith that collectively entailed a complete dogmatics.
These included courses and seminars on "Prolegomena," "The Doctrine of the
Church," "The Doctrine of Justification," "The Self-understanding of Jesus,"
and "The Doctrine of Baptism in the Main Denominations/Churches and the
Unity of Baptism." He developed these lectures at his desk, beneath a reprint of
the risen Christ from the Isenheim Altarpiece by Matthias Grünewald, the
same image that was hung above Barth's desk. "Enterprising students with
short-hand skills soon made mimeographed copies of those lectures available
for a German mark or two."[55] On other occasions, visitors from foreign
countries were invited to give guest lectures that expanded the horizons of the
students.

Personally I received the strongest impressions of Schlink in his seminars, especially
in the special seminars and working groups for doctoral candidates, when I was a
student and later his assistant. These educational meetings were very carefully
prepared and, it must be added, naturally the assistants also had to do their part.
There was a clear program, certain tasks with reading, reports, and protocols, and the
participants themselves had to be very carefully prepared, which perhaps not all
enjoyed. The level of discussion was also correspondingly high. In any case, one could
not allow oneself to engage in idle chatter. Schlink was a firm and precise seminar
leader who formulated matters sharply and summarized them precisely. On occasion
visitors from the larger ecumenical world were introduced in these seminars, for
example, very prominent ones, such as Cardinals Bea or Willebrands who were
friends of Schlink.[56] In this way I was also able to meet Hans Küng when he was still
the assistant to Ernst Volk in Münster (Volk would later become the Cardinal and
Bishop of Mainz) and had been invited by Schlink to a seminar on justification. The
themes of these seminars were far-reaching and focused on texts from the history of
theology, again and again from the whole ecumenical world, but also texts from
philosophy. A special experience for all seminar participants was the regular seminar
invitation to visit the Schlink house that was specially prepared with much love and
care by Frau Schlink. The Schlinks had an open, hospitable home, and in retrospect it

---

54 Skibbe, *A Quiet Reformer*, 71.
55 Dale Krueger, letter to the author, 5 January 2009.
56 Augustin Cardinal Bea (1881–1968) was a German Jesuit who served as the first president of the
    Secretariat for Promoting Christian Unity (later called "The Pontifical Council for Promoting
    Christian Unity"), the Curial organization that is charged with the ecumenical affairs of the
    Roman Catholic Church. Johannes Gerardus Maria Willebrands (1909–2006) was a Dutch priest
    who also served as president of the Pontifical Council for Promoting Christian Unity (1969–89).
    He later was the Archbishop of Utrecht (1975–83).

is astonishing to me how many guests from foreign countries and churches came to visit them and how in this way a more lively and in many respects more stimulating exchange was thus cultivated.[57]

Ecumenical Activities

Without question Schlink's most significant extra-curricular concern was his ecumenical work. During the initial post-war years he participated in discussions and debates about how best to reconstitute church government in the German churches. For more than three years he served as a crucial mediator between the two conflicted groups, the Council of Brethren of the Confessing Church, led by Martin Niemöller (1892–1984), and the Lutheran Council, led by two key Lutheran bishops, Theophil Wurm (1868–1953) of Württemberg and Hans Meiser (1881–1956) of Bavaria. The Council of Brethren wanted structural unity that was also based on accepting the Theological Declaration from the Barmen Synod ("The Barmen Declaration") as an official confessional text, whereas the Lutheran Council was opposed to a structural union and did not want to include this Declaration as a part of the EKD's official confessional basis. Schlink's proposal for a broad unity in church life that also maintained the confessional integrity of the various Lutheran and Reformed churches in the new Protestant Church in Germany (EKD) was eventually accepted by both parties and helped to pave the way for the articulation of the constitution of that federation of German Protestant churches.[58]

Another of Schlink's early ecumenical activities was to help organize the first working group of Roman Catholic and Protestant theologians in the world. Begun in the same year that the Institute began (1946), this bilateral dialogue was ground-breaking, since no such other one then existed and the heads of the respective church bodies were not so ecumenically inclined at the time. It is also the longest lasting such dialogue in history. Originally called the Jäger-Stählin Group and then the Ecumenical Working Group of Protestant and Catholic Theologians, it helped to pave the way for Lutheran churches in the Lutheran World Federation and the Roman Catholic Church to become more involved in the modern ecumenical movement.[59] More importantly, this

---

57 Reinhard Slenczka, letter to the author, 22 January 2009.
58 Skibbe, A Quiet Reformer, 53–65.
59 For a history of this group, see Barbara Schwahn, Der Ökumenische Arbeitskreis evangelischer und katholischer Theologen von 1946 bis 1975 [The Ecumenical Working Group of Evangelical and Catholic Theologians from 1946 to 1975] (Göttingen: Vandenhoeck & Ruprecht, 1996); and Eduard Lohse, "Fünfzig Jahre Ökumenischer Arbeitskreis evangelischer und katholischer Theologen" [Fifty Years of the Ecumenical Working Group of Evangelical and Catholic Theologians], Kerygma und Dogma 42 (1996), 177–85. Schlink read a scholarly paper before this group on ten occasions between 1946 and 1984, more times than any other theologian. The next

working group provided Schlink with an important ecumenical venue in which to discuss his ideas, which proved especially helpful as he began working on his dogmatics. In recognition of his ecumenical leadership in the years immediately after the end of the war, the University of Mainz presented him with his first honorary doctorate in 1947. The University of Edinburgh bestowed a similar degree on him in 1953.

A third concern in Schlink's ecumenical work was his efforts to communicate ecumenical ideas and developments to the German-speaking world. He was a co-founder and co-editor of the important ecumenical journals *Ökumenische Rundschau* (Ecumenical Review) (1952–1984)—the first of its kind in Germany—and *Kerygma und Dogma* (1955–1984). Two years before the appearance of the inaugural issue of *Ökumenische Rundschau*, he had assisted Walter Freytag (1899–1959), professor of missiology at Hamburg, in co-founding the German Ecumenical Studies Commission (*Deutschen Ökumenischen Studienausschuss* or DÖSTA), a further venue for engaging ecumenical issues and problems within the German context.

A fourth ecumenical focus was Schlink's involvement in the World Council of Churches (more so than in the Lutheran World Federation). Here he sought to highlight the contributions that the Lutheran Church could make to the larger ecumenical world. In addition to participating in the inaugural assembly of the WCC in Amsterdam (1948), he delivered a key lecture at the Third World Conference for Faith and Order in Lund (1952) and one of the two major addresses at the Second Assembly of the WCC in Evanston (1954), "Christ—the Hope for the World."[60] This latter address provoked some controversy by sharply contrasting Christian hope and the hopes of the modern world for an abiding future. The former is grounded in the coming Christ who also brings the end of the world: "We will then only speak rightly of Christ as the hope of the world if we humble ourselves under God and rightly acknowledge God as the Judge of the world." "…We do not in truth hope for [Christ] as Savior of the world if we do not at the same time await him as Judge of the world. Just as little, however, do we fear him in truth as Judge, if we do not await him as Savior." According to Schlink, "the first action of hope is to

---

highest number was given by Karl Rahner (1904–84), who served as a reader (*Referent*) on eight occasions. The group almost dissolved in the wake of the 1950 papal promulgation of the dogma regarding the bodily assumption of Mary. At that time Schlink authored "an evangelical opinion" that provided a strong critique of the new dogma, which Schlink and other Protestant theologians thought was neither Scriptural nor based on authentic apostolic teaching. Nevertheless, despite the controversy regarding this Marian dogma, the group of Protestant and Roman Catholic theologians was able to continue working in subsequent decades and was a principal venue for discussions leading to the formation and acceptance of the *Joint Declaration on the Doctrine of Justification* in 1999. Cf. Gassmann, "Edmund Schlink," 7.

60 For the bibliographical information on these essays, see the initial footnote in each of the pertinent chapters in *The Coming Christ and Church Traditions*.

proclaim the gospel to the whole world." The "second action of hope is to work for the just ordering of this world."[61] The first action of hope is, however, crucial for properly grounding the second action. Schlink later participated in the WCC assemblies at New Dehli in 1961 and at Uppsala in 1968.

For nearly three decades he made significant, influential contributions to the work of the WCC's Commission on Faith and Order. During several of these years he served as the Commission's vice moderator and a member of its working committee. Through his papers and presentations he provided "decisive impulses and orientations for ecumenical thinking and method-ology."[62] For example, he articulated new approaches to such issues as altar fellowship, the eschatological dimension of Christian unity, ecumenical methodology, and conciliarity, and he brought a measure of clarity to them that was very helpful.[63] In 1959 he participated in the official meeting between representatives of the EKD and the Russian Orthodox Church, the so-called Arnoldshainer Dialogue, which focused on the theme of "tradition and justification by faith" and which helped to make possible the entrance of the Russian Orthodox Church into the WCC.[64] That Schlink was chosen to participate in this historic conference was no surprise since he had been a participant in informal meetings with Orthodox theologians since the early

---

61 The other major plenary address, by Robert L. Calhoun (1896–1983), who was at that time professor of systematic theology at Yale University and also a member of the WCC's Commission on Faith and Order, set forth an "Anglo-Saxon Approach" that seemed to many observers to contrast sharply with Schlink's presentation. Calhoun stressed the realization of Christ and his Kingdom within earthly, historical structures and the importance of Christian moral and social action in the present moment. Cf. Robert L. Calhoun, "Christ the Hope of the World," *Ecumenical Review* 7 (1955): 140–50. While the positions of Schlink and Calhoun seemed to be in irreconcilable tension with each other, they were actually more complementary than contradictory at the substantive level. Whereas the major accent in Schink's address was on the future, eschatological judgment of God, he also acknowledged that the *eschaton* is already a present reality for the Christian, something that Calhoun also acknowledged. While the latter accented the present realization of Christ as the boundary of human existence, he also bore witness to the contingency of human beings before God, which was a principal concern of Schlink's. Cf. esp. Conrad Simonson, *The Christology of the Faith and Order Movement* (Leiden: Brill, 1972), 78–83.

62 Gassmann, "Edmund Schlink – An Ecumenical Pioneer of the 20th Century," 8.

63 Cf. also Edmund Schlink, "Herrenmahl oder Kirchenmahl" [The Lord's Supper or the Church's Supper], *Der christliche Student* 24 (1950), 10–20 (translated as "Lord's Supper or Church's Supper," *The Student World* 43 [1950], 46–58, and republished under the same title in *Intercommunion*, ed. Donald Baillie [London: SCM, 1952], 296–302; idem, "The Nature of Christian Hope," *Ecumenical Review* 4 (1951/52), 284–90; idem, "Die Struktur der dogmatischen Aussage als ökumenisches Problem" [The Structure of the Dogmatic Statement as an Ecumenical Issue] *Kerygma und Dogma* 3 (1957), 251–306. For the significance of Schlink's specific ecumenical contributions, see Günther Gassmann, "Schlink, Edmund," in *Ökumene-Lexikon*, 2d ed., ed. Hanfried Krüger et al. (Frankfurt: Lembeck, 1987), 1085.

64 For the official report on the 1959 meeting, see *Tradition und Glaubensgerechtigkeit.* Studienheft Nr. 3, ed. Aussenamt der EKD (Witten: Luther-Verlag, 1961). Schlink participated in additional official ecumenical dialogues between the EKD and the Russian Orthodox Church in 1963, 1967, 1969, 1971, and 1973.

1950s. Already in 1948, he had offered a seminar on "The Church between East and West." In subsequent years he became an even more astute scholar of Eastern traditions of theology. The additional essays he published on Eastern Orthodoxy during this period testify to this.[65] His official trips on behalf of the WCC to Russia and Greece were important events in his ongoing engagement with the Eastern churches and their forms of spirituality. At the meeting of the WCC's Central Committee in Rhodes in 1959, he presented a paper on the significance of Eastern and Western theological traditions for the abiding, essential content of the Christian faith. Here he stressed the legitimacy of the diversity of spiritual and theological forms of expression within the wider ecumenical world and how they ought to complement each other. (One should keep in mind that this ecumenical work took place in the context of the Cold War between the West and the Soviet Union.) In recognition of his engagement with the Orthodox tradition, the Institute of Orthodox Theology in Paris, Saint-Serge, bestowed a third honorary doctorate upon him in 1962.

A fifth ecumenical focus for Schlink, which was also the high point of his ecumenical work, was his service as the EKD's official observer to the Second Vatican Council. For two years prior to the start of that historic council, Schlink had been in and out of Rome, assisting the Secretariat for the Promotion of Christian Unity as it made plans for inviting official observers to the council. Shortly after one of his meetings with Cardinal Bea in Rome and nearly eight months before the opening session of this historic council, he gave an address at the Ecumenical Institute at Bossey in which he stated:

All these [Christian] traditions are contained in Jesus Christ, both the Christ who has already come and the one who is to come. He came as the friend of sinners and the enemy of Pharisees and those learned in the Scriptures. He will come as the judge, not only of the world but also of the church—see, for example, the message of the Apocalypse—this is common knowledge. The first step towards the unification of the church will be when we not only know this, but when we are all moved to the depth of our hearts and accept the fact that the Lord of the church makes us all radicals and doubters. Then we shall no longer pride ourselves on the history of our church and its decisions, and face divine justice assured of their certainty, but we shall devote ourselves to penitence, which will show us that the life of our church, its doctrines and

---

65 Cf. several of the essays included in the third part of *The Coming Christ and Church Traditions*. In addition, cf. Edmund Schlink, "Wandlungen im protestantischen Verständnis der Ostkirche" [Transformations in the Protestant Understanding of the Eastern Church], *Ökumenische Rundschau* 6 (1957), 153–64 (reprinted in KC 221–31 and translated as "Changes in Protestant Thinking about the Eastern Church" in *Ecumenical Review* 10, 386–400); idem, "Zur neuesten ökumenische Stellungnahme des Moskauer Patriarchats" [On the Most Recent Ecumenical Opinion by the Patriarch of Moscow] *Ökumenische Rundschau* 7 (1958), 127–40; and idem, "Der ökumenische Beitrag der russisch-orthodoxen Kirche" [The Ecumenical Contribution of the Russian Orthodox Church], *Kerygma und Dogma* 4 (1958), 191–212 (translated as "The Ecumenical Contribution of the Russian Orthodox Church," *Scottish Journal of Theology* 12 [1959], 41–67).

its institutions only partially correspond to the fullness of the kingdom of God in Christ. Let us not seek in our penitence to justify and defend ourselves against other churches, but let us, together with them, see ourselves and our need for grace, and in view of that need let us seek no longer to point out the defects in other churches but rather to participate in whatever God has confided to them.[66]

This is the perspective that Schlink had when he witnessed the opening of the Second Vatican Council on 11 October 1962. From that day until the closing of the council on 8 December 1965 he never missed a session. He sat in a tribune reserved especially for the official observers, "right under the statue of St. Longinus, nearer to the presiders' table than even the cardinals were"—among the best seats in the *aula* of St. Peter's.[67]

The decision to admit non-Catholic observers as an integral body was not only unique in the annals of ecumenical councils but also allowed the deliberations of the council to be reviewed by scholars and churchmen who did not share many of the basic assumptions upon which Catholic doctrine and practice were based. As events proved, this decision stimulated a more searching scrutiny of the deliberations and decisions, and it was important for not allowing the attention of the council to focus on issues of concern only to Roman Catholics—or only to Roman Catholic prelates.[68]

At the start of the first session he was elected by the official non-Catholic observers to serve as one of the leaders of a small committee, which also included Bernard Pawley (1911–81) of the Church of England and Lukas Vischer (1926–2008) of the World Council of Churches.[69] According to Douglas Horton (1891–1968), who kept a diary during the council, this committee "was to take care of any matters that might come up, such as the appointment of people to reply for the observers at public meetings."[70] This committee met frequently with the council's officials, especially Cardinal Bea and Cardinal Willebrands, but also with the media. When Bea hosted a

---

66 Edmund Schlink, "Shaken Spirituality?," delivered to the Ecumenical Institute of the WCC in Bossey, Switzerland, in April 1962. This address was later published as "Pneumatische Er-shütterung? Aus der Zusammenarbeit eines evangelischen und eines römisch-katholischen ökumenischen Arbeitskreises" [Pneumatic Shaking? From the Collective Work of a Protestant and Roman-Catholic Ecumenical Working Group], *Kerygma und Dogma* 8 (1962), 221–37. An English translation appeared as "A Report on the Work of an Ecumenical Group of Protestant and Roman Catholic Theologians," *Dialog* 2 (1963), 320–8. Schlink served on the Board of the Graduate School of Ecumenical Studies in Bossey between 1954 and 1975.

67 John W. O'Malley, *What Happened at Vatican II* (Cambridge: Harvard University Press, 2008), 23.

68 O'Malley, *What Happened at Vatican II*, 33.

69 Douglas Horton, *Vatican Diary 1962: A Protestant Observes the First Session of Vatican Council II* (Philadelphia: United Church Press, 1964), 20.

70 Douglas Horton, *Vatican Diary 1963: A Protestant Observes the Second Session of Vatican Council II* (Philadelphia: United Church Press, 1964), 32. Horton, who had served as Dean of Harvard Divinity School, was at the time of the Second Vatican Council a member of the WCC's Faith and Order Commission. His role at the council was as an official observer for the WCC.

reception for the observers at the start of the first session, Schlink was the one who gave the official response on behalf of all the observers.[71] This was a natural role for Schlink, given his friendship with Bea, who himself certainly helped to set a positive, welcoming tone when he referred to the observers at their initial reception as "my dear brothers in Christ."[72] Their presence in the basilica during all of the council's sessions had a positive effect on the deliberations that took place there.[73] At Schlink's urging, the non-Catholic observers (who initially totaled 46 and then 182 by the end of the fourth period) met regularly as a group with members of the Secretariat for Christian Unity, typically once a week on Tuesdays.[74] It is not surprising that at the start of the other sessions, Schlink was re-elected to serve on the small leadership committee of observers, which now also included a fourth member, namely, a representative of the Eastern Church.[75]

Schlink became an important conversation partner for the cardinals, bishops, and the *periti* (Roman Catholic theological advisors) who attended the council. During its course, he wrote more than sixty reports on the proceedings. While he was generally favorable toward the *ressourcement* dimension of the council, he was on occasion critical of the council's apparent presumption that the Roman Catholic Church was the only true church of Christ and that non-Roman efforts toward church unity amounted to nothing other than a return to Rome.[76] According to Schlink, such a mistaken view, if maintained, would only serve to re-enact the Counter-Reformation and to alienate further both the Protestant and Eastern Orthodox churches.[77] If the Roman Church could not acknowledge that the Eastern Orthodox and Protestant churches also belonged to the one church of Christ, there could be little hope for fruitful ecumenical dialogue between Rome and the other churches.[78] For Schlink, the best Catholic theologians of that time stressed that the church is a mystery and that it therefore cannot be defined. Such an insight, he thought, would be a useful starting point for further ecumenical discussion

---

71 Horton, *Vatican Diary 1962*, 20; Giuseppe Albergio, ed., *History of Vatican II*, 5 vols. (Maryknoll, Orbis, 1995–2006), 2:182.

72 See O'Malley, *What Happened at Vatican II*, 96–97.

73 O'Malley, *What Happened at Vatican II*, 97.

74 At the first session there were fifty-four non-Catholics in the tribune, but only forty-six of them were official "observers" who had been sent by those non-Catholic churches who had been invited to send delegates. Cf. Albergio, *History of Vatican II*, 2:179. By the end of the council, however, the distinction between "observer" and "guest" was largely nominal (ibid., 180).

75 Horton, *Vatican Diary 1963*, 32.

76 Horton, *Vatican Diary 1962*, 151 (paraphrasing Schlink). Toward the end of 1963, Schlink gave a lecture in Rome in which he claimed the title of "church" for the Protestant churches. In this lecture he again criticized the notion that some Roman Catholics held, namely, that "ecumen-ism" means a "return" to Rome. Cf. Alberigo, *History of Vatican II*, 3:295.

77 Cf. Horst Schlitter, "Edmund Schlink in Rom," in *Die Vision des Papstes: Erzählung* [The Vision of the Pope: A Story], 2nd ed. (Karlsruhe: Hans Thoma Verlag, 1997), 158.

78 Horton, *Vatican Diary 1963*, 25 (paraphrasing Schlink).

about the nature of the church, but it was not being fully recognized at the council itself. He was therefore grateful for those steps at the council that led toward "a new point of view," one that looked with "surprising fairness toward other Christians" and that gave "a powerful impulse to the ecumenical spirit."[79] An example of this new attitude were the meetings in November 1964 that Schlink and Visser 't Hooft (representing the WCC) had with Willebrands and a few other Catholic officials to discuss a new kind of ecumenical collaboration between the Roman Church and the WCC and the basic principles for further dialogue between them.[80]

Schlink did not hesitate to criticize other positions and arguments presented by Catholics at the council. For example, he let it be known that he thought that *Gaudium et Spes*'s reading of the world was too optimistic and that it seems to put the church into a "peculiar sort of atemporality" (*eigentümlicher Zeitlosigkeit*) in which it stands above the world and tells it how to order itself socially and politically.[81] Not only had his experience with the Nazis and *Deutsche Christen* led him to conclude that the world is radically fallen, but he was fully convinced that the church's proper role in the world is always oriented toward the gospel. Accordingly, he was quite critical of the council's view that the Christian church is the divinely appointed agent of humanization in the world. Such a view does not properly distinguish between the divine law and the divine promise of the gospel and it tends to muddle the church's proper calling.

More fundamentally, Schlink repeatedly leveled pointed criticism against perceived roadblocks to unity that are inherent within Roman dogma itself, particularly with respect to papal primacy and infallibility and the modern Marian dogmas, including language about Mary's role as "mediatrix." He also was troubled by those who seemed to treat canon law as if it is divine law. He could not see, for example, how the Roman Church could continue to defend the practice of using indulgences, actions that he thought contradicted the gospel.

Despite these criticisms, however, he saw the council as a whole as having tremendous significance for the further progress of the ecumenical move-

---

79 Edmund Schlink, as quoted in *Documentation Catholique* 60 (1963), 392 (also cited in Alberigo, *History of Vatican II*, 2:522).

80 Albergio, *History of Vatican II*, 4:475. An outcome of these discussions was the formation of a working group of representatives of the WCC and the Roman Catholic Church that met for the first time at Bossey in May 1965. At that meeting Schlink was one of three theologians appointed to a small committee to develop a proposal for addressing the nature of true ecumenical dialogue. The other key members included Yves Congar (1904–95) and Nikos Nissiotis (1924–86). Their official report to the Joint Working Group of the Roman Catholic Church and the World Council of Churches was published in *Ecumenical Review* 19/4 (1967), 469 ff. See also Edmund Schlink, "Die Methode des ökumenischen Dialogs," *Kerygma und Dogma* 12/3 (1966), 205–11.

81 *Gaudium et Spes* is "the Pastoral Constitution on the Church in the World of Today," promulgated by Pope Paul VI on 7 December 1965. See NK 135 ff.

ment. His full analysis of the council was widely read in both Roman Catholic and Protestant circles.[82] In his view an outcome of the council was to make clear the need for a "Copernican Revolution" in the self-understanding of the churches, to see themselves as each revolving around Christ, their center:

Every church is in danger of understanding itself as the center around which the other churches orbit as planets. This lies so close at hand because all Christians are certain that the church whose message brought them to faith—in which church they were incorporated into Christ through baptism, and through word and sacrament they are again and again nourished anew—is the one, holy, catholic, and apostolic church. But the working of Christ is not restricted to this one church. He works in freedom without being bound by the borders of our churches. We cannot be content to measure other churches in respect to ourselves, but we have to take our starting point with Christ, by whom we are measured along with all churches. He is the sun around whom we, together with other churches, orbit as planets and from whom we receive light. A kind of Copernican revolution is necessary in ecclesiological thinking.[83]

Following Vatican II, Schlink became a member of the Joint Commission of the WCC and the Roman Catholic Delegates of the Secretary of Unity. "This working group was given the task of examining how the collaboration of the World Council and the Roman Catholic Church could be more closely aligned. During the first years there I encountered with great joy a real seeking for new possibilities on the part of the Catholic representatives."[84] As he became more well-known within Roman Catholic circles, it was not surprising that a

---

82 A revised translation of this work is included as the second part of the present volume. Schlink sent a copy of *After the Council* to his *Doktorvater*, Barth, who sent him an appreciative note on 21 October 1966: "Sincere thanks for sending me your book on the council, which I have read with great interest. Your account deserves high praise and will, I hope, be diligently consulted on our side" (Karl Barth, *Letters: 1961–1968*, trans. Geoffrey W. Bromiley [Grand Rapids: Eerdmans, 1981], 225). Barth then proceeded to indicate he did not agree with Schlink "on the danger of the traditional complex of dogmas which is still in force among the Romans. Naturally they cannot retract what was proclaimed by earlier popes and councils. Nevertheless, from what I know of them, and have just seen confirmed in various bodies in Rome, they have the wonderful ability either (1) to explain away these honorable relics, or (2) to push them on the margin of what they now really want to think and say, or (3) to commemorate them with deep bows, or (4) to keep solemn silence about them. So long as one does not disturb them at this game, but encourages them to seek help along these lines, it has been my experience that one can engage in good and fruitful discussion with them. As a separated brother one may then look a little more hopefully than you do to the future of what is now going on there, in a way that seems to me to be irresistible" (Barth, *Letters:1961–1968*, 225–26). In September 1966, over the course of six days, Barth had met with Catholic theologians, including Cardinal Bea (who had invited him to Rome), Karl Rahner, and Joseph Ratzinger. Barth's visit included a very friendly one-hour private meeting with Pope Paul VI. For Barth's own critical questions that he raised in Rome, see Karl Barth, *Ad Limina Apostolorum: An Appraisal of Vatican II* (Richmond: John Knox Press, 1968).

83 Schlink, NK, 240.

84 Edmund Schlink, *Zehn Jahre nach dem Konzil–Eine kritische Bilanz* [Ten Years after the Council: A Critical Assessment] (Zurich: Paulus-Akademie, 1975), 18.

theologian from that church body would write a dissertation on his ecclesiology.[85]

In addition to his reflections on Vatican II, which also contain prescient remarks on the vitality of the non-Christian religions and the loss of Christendom's "security" in the world, Schlink published two further works in this period that relate to his ecumenical engagements. One is his study of the doctrine of baptism that provides a solid historical-critical investigation of the New Testament writings as a way of uncovering the dogmatic basis for the doctrine.[86] Professor Skibbe is correct to suggest that this work was a major resource for the historic WCC document, *Baptism, Eucharist, and Ministry*, on whose development Schlink also offered significant input through his activities on the WCC's Commission on Faith and Order up to the year 1975. The other work from this period is a fictional story that he wrote pseudonymously twelve years after the close of the council.[87] It tells the story of a contemporary pope who in the midst of an illness receives three visions of Christ that lead him to make a transformative and controversial pilgrimage to Jerusalem and then to begin a new ecumenical initiative: the unification of the Christian Church. The book ends with the author's concluding word, whose final paragraph clearly states the intended goal of the work as a whole: "A vision is not a program, but an impulse. It sets in motion. At the same time this narrative intends to be a warning to the churches not to harden themselves again toward one another, and fail to do what they are entrusted to do in the midst of a constantly increasing human crisis."[88]

---

85 Gerhard Schwenzer, *Die großen Taten Gottes und die Kirche: Zur Ekklesiologie Edmund Schlinks* [The Mighty Deeds of God and the Church: On the Ecclesiology of Edmund Schlink], Konfessionskundliche und Kontroverstheologische Studien, Band XXII, ed. Johann-Adam-Möhler-Institut (Paderborn: Verlag Bonifacius, 1969).

86 Edmund Schlink, *Die Lehre von der Taufe* (Kassel: Johannes Stauda, 1969). This was originally translated as *The Doctrine of Baptism*, trans. Herbert J. A. Bouman (St. Louis: Concordia, 1972). The four chapters of the book address respectively: (1) the basis for baptism (including subsections on the command to baptize, the historical antecedents to Christian baptism, and the variety of New Testament statements about baptism); (2) the saving activity of God through baptism; (3) the administration and reception of baptism (including a lengthy section on infant baptism); and (4) the form of the baptismal act.

87 Sebastian Knecht, *Die Vision des Papstes* (Karlsruhe: Hans Thoma, 1975). That Schlink was the real author remained a secret, known only to family and friends, until his death. Following his death, a second edition was published in 1997 under Schlink's own name: *Die Vision des Papstes: Erzählung mit einem Vorwort von Franz Kardinal König und Landesbischof Klaus Engelhardt* (Karlsruhe: Hans Thoma, 1997). It has been translated into English as *The Vision of the Pope: A Narrative*, trans. Eugene M. Skibbe (Minneapolis: Kirk House Publishers, 2001). According to a letter that Schlink wrote to his publisher, Arnd Ruprecht, in October 1975, he hoped that the pseudonymous nature of the work would attract a wider audience, especially in Roman Catholic circles, than if he were identified as the author. He indicated in this letter that the perspective of the "narrative" was different from the dogmatic position he would take in his *Ecumenical Dogmatics*. For the citation of the letter, see Eber, *Einheit*, 49.

88 Schlink, *The Vision of the Pope*, 79.

Final Years

After his retirement from the university on 31 March 1971, he published shorter works on such ecumenical problems as apostolic succession and the papacy. He also was elected to serve on the academic senate of the Ecumenical Institute in Tantur/Jerusalem, which had been formed in the wake of Vatican II and whose academic focus was on "the mystery of salvation."[89] This appointment provided him with other opportunities to interact with other theologians on important ecumenical issues. He remained active in this group until 1980.[90]

Most of his energy in this post-retirement period was devoted to the dogmatics he had promised to write after the completion of his *Theology of the Lutheran Confessions.* Convinced that the goal of complete organic church unity in Christ could only be achieved *theologically,* he stressed the need for a truly "ecumenical dogmatics" as integral to overcoming the divisions within Christendom. His massive *Ecumenical Dogmatics* was published just one year before he died suddenly of an embolism (following surgery) on 20 May 1984. Five days later, his son-in-law, Bishop Dr. Klaus Engelhardt, preached the funeral sermon on the basis of the promise in John 10:27–30: "No one can snatch them out of the Father's hand."[91]

Friends and family remember Schlink and his wife as lovers of classical music (she especially of Mozart and he especially of Bach), as talented musicians, as warm and interesting conversationalists, as caring and friendly hosts. He was a creative scholar and critical thinker, who sought to serve Christ and the needs of the *una sancta* in all of its forms and expressions. He modeled the vision of ecumenical unity that he so often articulated in order to assist the strengthening of the bonds of human and ecclesial community. To be sure, as both Dr. Eber and Dr. Skibbe have noted, Schlink's was "only one voice in the choir of learned voices in the church," but still "his was a voice that echoes into the present."[92]

---

89 Edmund Schlink, "Das Ökumenische Institut in Jerusalem/Tantur und die Lage im vorderen Orient" [The Ecumenical Institute in Jerusalem/Tantur and the Situation in the Near East], *Im Lande der Bibel* 3 (1973), 8.

90 One of the more important lectures that Schlink gave at Tantur was on the notion of "the hierarchy of truths" that was taken up and discussed at the Second Vatican Council and which he thought opened a positive way for discussing ecumenically the "hierarchy of statements" and expressions in the *Oecumene* in relation to the fundamental truth that is the living God who has revealed himself in Jesus Christ. This October 1972 lecture was published as "Die 'Hierarchie der Wahrheiten' und die Einigung der Kirchen," [The 'Hierarchy of Truths' and the Unification of the Churches], *Kerygma und Dogma* 21 (1975), 1–12.

91 Skibbe, *A Quiet Reformer*, 105.

92 Eber, "Edmund Schlink," xxii.

It [this voice] can never replace this choir but can only sing in support of the choir and hope to be recognized as one of its voices. For no individual can fully portray the reign of God or his deeds. That is the task of the church as a whole, and indeed this happens not only in its life but also in its prayers, sermons, worship and confession, and in its love, service, and suffering.[93]

93 Edmund Schlink, ÖD 71, as cited by Eber, "Edmund Schlink," xxii.

Abbreviations

AB Edmund Schlink, *Ausgewählte Beiträge. Kirchenkampf—Theolo-gische Grundfragen—Ökumene*, in Edmund Schlink, *Schriften zu Ökumene und Bekenntnis*, vol. 5, ed. Ursula Schnell (Göttingen: Vandenhoeck & Ruprecht, 2010).

AC The Augsburg Confession

Althaus Paul Althaus, *The Theology of Martin Luther*, trans. Robert C. Schultz (Philadelphia: Fortress, 1966).

Apol. The Apology to the Augsburg Confession

Aquinas Thomas Aquinas, *The Summa Theologica*, trans. Fathers of the English Dominican Province (New York: Benziger Brothers, 1947). References are to the part, the question, and the article.

Barth Karl Barth, *Church Dogmatics*, 13 vols., trans. G. W. Bromiley (Edinburgh: T & T Clark, 1936–69). References will be to principal volume, I–IV, and their parts.

BC Robert Kolb and Timothy J. Wengert, eds., *The Book of Concord: The Confessions of the Evangelical Lutheran Church*, trans. Charles Arand et al. (Minneapolis: Fortress, 2000). References are to the page number.

BDAG Frederick William Danker, ed., *A Greek-English Lexicon of the New Testament and Other Early Christian Literature*, 3rd ed., based on Walter Bauer's *Greichischdeutsches Wörterbuch zu den Schriften des Neuen Testaments und der frühchristlichen Literaur*, 6th ed., trans. William F. Arndt, F. Wilbur Gingrich, and Frederick W. Danker (Chicago: University of Chicago Press, 2000).

CC Edmund Schlink, *The Coming Christ and the Coming Church*, trans. J. H. Neilson et al.(Edinburgh/London: Oliver & Boyd, 1967; Philadelphia: Fortress, 1968).

DC *Deutsche Christen* = Christians in Nazi Germany who introduced Nazi ideology into the Protestant churches

Denzinger Henrich Denzinger, ed., *Enchiridion symbolorum: definitionum et declarationum de rebus fidei et morum/Compendium of Creeds, Definitions, and Declarations on Matters of Faith and Morals*, 43rd ed., ed. Peter Hünermann, Robert Fastiggi, and Anne Englund Nash (San Francisco: Ignatius Press, 2012). References are to the paragraph numbers that appear in the outer margins of this bilingual (Latin-English) edition.

EKD *Evangelische Kirche in Deutschland* = The Protestant Church in

	Germany. This is the federation of Lutheran and Reformed churches in post-WWII Germany.
FC Ep	The Formula of Concord (Epitome)
FC SD	The Formula of Concord (Solid Declaration)
KC	Edmund Schlink, *Der kommende Christus und die kirchlichen Traditionen: Beiträge zum Gespräch zwischen den getrennten Kirchen* (Göttingen: Vandenhoeck & Ruprecht, 1961; reprinted in Edmund Schlink, *Schriften zu Ökumene und Bekenntnis*, vol. 1, ed. Klaus Engelhardt [Göttingen: Vandenhoeck & Ruprecht, 2004], I:3–276). References are to this latter volume.
LC	The Large Catechism of Martin Luther
LW	*Luther's Works* (American Edition), 55 vols., ed. Jaroslav Pelikan and Helmut T. Lehmann (St. Louis and Philadelphia: Concordia and Fortress, 1955--).
NK	Edmund Schlink, *Nach dem Konzil* (Göttingen: Vandenhoeck & Ruprecht, 1966).
NRSV	The Holy Bible, New Revised Standard Version (Washington, DC: Division of Education of the National Council of the Churches of Christ in the United States, 1989).
ÖD	Edmund Schlink, *Ökumenische Dogmatik: Grundzüge*, 3rd ed., in Edmund Schlink, *Schriften zu Ökumene und Bekenntnis*, vol. 2, ed. Michael Plathow (Göttingen: Vandenhoeck & Ruprecht, 2005).
PL	*Patrologiae Cursus Completus*, Series Latina, ed. J.-P. Migne (Paris: 1844 ff.)
RSV	The Holy Bible, Revised Standard Version (Washington, DC: Division of Education of the National Council of the Churches of Christ in the United States, 1977).
SC	The Small Catechism of Martin Luther
SÖB	Edmund Schlink, *Schriften zu Ökumene und Bekenntnis*, ed. Klaus Engelhardt et al., 5 vols. (Göttingen: Vandenhoeck & Ruprecht, 2004–2010)
Tanner	Norman P. Tanner, ed., *Decrees of the Ecumenical Councils*, 2 vols. (Georgetown: Georgetown University Press, 1990). References are to the volume and page number(s).
TDNT	Gerhard Kittel and Gerhard Friedrich, eds., *Theological Dictionary of the New Testament*, 10 vols. trans. Geoffrey W. Bromiley (Grand Rapids: Eerdmans, 1964).
TWNT	Gerhard Kittel and Gerhard Friedrich, eds., *Theologisches Wörterbuch zum Neue Testament*, 10 vols. (Stuttgart: W. Kohlhammer, 1957).
TLB	Edmund Schlink, *Theologie der lutherischen Bekenntnisschriften*, 4th ed. (München: Chr. Kaiser Verlag, 1954; reprinted in Edmund Schlink, *Schriften zu Ökumene und Bekenntnis*, vol. 4, ed. Günther

	Gassmann [Göttingen: Vandenhoeck & Ruprecht, 2008]). References are to this latter volume.
WA	*D. Martin Luthers Werke: kritische Gesamtausgabe* [Weimar Ausgabe], 65 vols. in 127 (Weimar : Hermann Böhlaus Nachfolger, 1883–1993).
WCC	World Council of Churches

Book One:
The Coming Christ and Church Traditions:
Essays for the Dialogue among the
Separated Churches

Introduction: The Task

Because Christendom has become increasingly divided in its historical development, a deep shame has emerged over this, its condition in our time. An elemental urge for unity has awakened in all churches. It manifests itself above all in the longing for fellowship in the Lord's Supper and for joint servant ministry[i] in witness to Christ in the world. This call to unity has been sounded most urgently through the voice of the younger churches that no longer want to see the message of Christ in the context of the heathen world refuted by the disunity of Christians. In Europe this call has found its greatest echo among the laity and Christian youth, who constantly experience that threat through nihilism.[ii]

Against this desire for unity stand the deeply entrenched traditions of the separated parts of Christendom: forms of the worship service that have developed in history, formulations of dogmas, and the determination of church order, especially regarding the ordering of ministerial offices.[iii] At important points these differences appear not only as a diversity but also as an opposition. These differences are furthermore burdened by non-theological—anthropological, cultural, and political—factors, which are not applicable to all realms of the whole church [Ökumene]. Corresponding to the differences among the traditions is also the fact that the conceptions of the desired unity are by no means in agreement with one another. Even in a common prayer for unity, people do not pray for the same thing. Given this hard evidence, many people conclude that nothing more can be attained than having the separated parts of Christendom draw closer toward one other, that is, toward a more or less loose cooperation in serving one another in mutual aid and in servant ministry to the world, whereby, in the absence of unity, charitable and social tasks could be taken up as a common cause.

But there can be no doubt that Christ wants nothing less than the unity of Christendom in faith and confession, in the reception of his meal, and in the fellowship of the churches' ministerial offices. In this respect, the enthusiasm of the youth, who long for full unity, is justified over against the resignation of many older people. Christ wants to manifest himself in the unity of Christendom to the world as the one Lord to whom all are subject and through whose victory on the cross the enmity between human beings has been overcome and peace has dawned. Indeed, he not only wants unity but he has created it. It is not only his goal but in him it is already a reality. As his work, the church is the one church in all places and at all times. While its unity can certainly be called into question and disfigured by human beings, it cannot be destroyed. Consequently, our task is not to create the unity of the church but to describe the unity that is given in Christ and to put aside everything that obscures it.

But how is this to happen? One has to recognize with cool-headed realism that the existing church traditions cannot simply be skipped over, for each Christian has come to know the message of salvation in the context of a given church tradition, and within that tradition each has become a member of the one church, the body of Christ, through baptism. This is unconditionally valid, whether one affirms the principle of tradition or not, regardless also of whether one reflects about the church tradition or understands oneself to be directly and immediately contemporaneous with the earliest Christian community. Whoever would skip over the reality of multiple traditions would not be able to overcome the existing separations but only increase them further. The task is not to ignore the separations among the church traditions but to open up those traditions to one another. One can only wish that the theologians of the separated churches would devote themselves to this scholarly task with the same longing and passion by which the enthusiasts for unity seek to skip over the tradition.

In the present situation in which Christendom is open to unity, we must thus distinguish between two stages of ecumenical dialogue. First, we have to see beyond the borders of the particular church in which we came to faith in Christ and in which, on the basis of baptism and in our reception of the body and blood of Christ, we know ourselves to be members of the one, holy, catholic, and apostolic church. We have to look in hope and love for the signs and reality of precisely the same one church in those parts of Christendom that are divided from us. Only when the one church is again clearly recognized there, is the way open for the second stage, namely, for the dialogue about unification. If one were to engage in the second stage before the first, it would fail, even if at first it might seem to succeed.

Viewed as a whole, Christendom today finds itself at the beginning of the first stage of ecumenical dialogue. The experience of unity, which breaks through the separations, demands theological clarification, if it is not to lead to confusion and disappointment. But how will the separated traditions open up to one another in this first stage of the dialogue?

It is not enough to compare other traditions with one's own and to find in them what is already in one's own. Rather, we must inquire into the historical, apostolic foundation upon which the Holy Spirit builds the church and to which all parts of Christendom appeal in one way or another. We must attempt to understand the other Christian traditions—taking into account their particular historical conditions as much as possible—as the transmission and development of the apostolic witness to Christ and, in addition, of the apostolic exhortations and directives. This entails at the same time the necessity to inquire critically into one's own tradition in order to discern to what extent the apostolic tradition has been preserved and unfolded in it or has also been obscured and distorted.

In looking back to the apostolic witness to Christ, we are at the same time being pointed forward to the Parousia of Jesus Christ proclaimed by the apostles.[iv] Jesus Christ is not only the historical basis of the church but also the present and coming Lord of the church. The nature of the church traditions and their relationship to one another would not be understood if one were content merely to look back to their historical development. Jesus Christ comes as the Judge of them all—that is, as Judge not only of the world but also of the church. The traditions will only be opened up to one another when their provisional nature is understood, indeed when the provisional nature of the church is understood. Within most traditions, however, ecclesiology is taught in strange isolation from eschatology.

This search for the church beyond the borders of one's own church tradition may not be limited to such parts of Christendom that are closely aligned to each other from the start, as for example the Evangelical-Lutheran and the Reformed Church or also the Orthodox and the Old Catholic Church. Rather, the *whole* of Christendom needs to face the question about the one church and to venture taking up dialogue, also with those churches that at first seem to be very far off. Only within the horizon of the whole of Christendom will the opening up of the particular traditions to one another take place in such a way that the opening up of the heart of the one impels the others toward unity. For the members of the Reformation churches[v] this means that they are only seriously engaging in ecumenical dialogue when they undertake it also with the Orthodox Church and the Roman Church.

If one looks at the present situation of Christendom realistically, despite the desire for unity that has emerged, it is clear how difficult, almost unending, the task of the first stage of ecumenical dialogue is. Everyone who participates in ecumenical dialogue is aware of the temptation to become skeptical and to draw back into one's own church body [*Konfessionskirche*][vi], or to give way to the fanatical enthusiasts [*Schwärmern*][vii] who think they can be content merely with the invisible unity of the church. But God's Spirit is already at work in opening up the separated parts of Christendom to one another, namely, by bringing to light what has been kept of the apostolic tradition in the different church traditions and brought about by the living Christ—and by making it a common gift for all of Christendom. Permeating through the walls that separate the churches, a sense of unity in that fullness is already beginning to be perceptible, even though we cannot yet grasp it conceptually and articulate it demonstrably. But these perceptions of emerging unity urgently desire visible embodiment.

All of the essays in this volume stem from dialogues among the separated churches in which I have participated over the past years, both in the World Council of Churches[viii] and in meetings with theologians of the Roman Church and the Russian Orthodox Church. Consequently, the selections are intentionally restricted to issues in the first stage of ecumenical dialogue, particularly those essays that focus on bringing clarity to issues of methodology in this dialogue. Most of the selections are essays that were delivered at ecumenical conferences. Since in each case the remarks are determined by the concrete particularity of the church whose representatives were engaged in the dialogue, the form of the presentation here has normally remained unchanged, although this has led in a few places to some overlapping and repetitions. Nevertheless, the form of the address and of the paper corresponds in a special way to the present stage of ecumenical dialogue.

Although the individual chapters arose from very different occasions and in meetings with representatives from very different churches, they nevertheless form a systematic unity. "The coming Christ and church traditions" [*Der kommende Christus und die kirchlichen Traditionen*] is the theme that increasingly came to the foreground in the course of these meetings. But this title should not be understood as implying a critical examination here of the *concepts* of tradition within the various churches and a systematic development of the concept of tradition as such. That would only be possible in the larger context of the treatment of the issues regarding the biblical canon, dogma, and biblical and theological hermeneutics, and thus only within ecclesiology as a whole. In this book the concept of tradition appears only in passing. Instead, the mutual elucidation of the *actual* traditions of the separated parts of Christendom for one another is the theme. The actual content of the traditions and the concepts of tradition do not largely coincide. Consequently, the issue of tradition has generally become the most complicated issue in polemical theology. Here the issue will be approached with all modesty in terms of the *actual* differences.

Editor's Notes

[i] The German noun *Dienst*, as it is used here and throughout Schlink's writings, implies more than "service" or "ministry" or "office." It will thus be rendered normally as "servant ministry," but also as "ministry" or "service," depending on the context. While *Dienst* is a near synonym to *Amt*, Schlink normally uses the latter to stress the "office" of the servant ministry. Cf. endnote 3 below.

[ii] By *nihilism*, Schlink was referring to the fundamental, pervasive questioning of life's meaning. He addresses the complex context of this concept, using slightly different terms, in *After the Council*. Cf. esp. the first sub-sections in chaps. 1, 8, and 13 of that book.

[iii] Within German Lutheran theology the word *Amt* translates the Latin terms *officium* and *ministerium*, which refer to the service, function, task, commission, authority, duty, office, or the responsibility connected with or derived from the office of a minister. Schlink typically uses *Amt* (plural: *Ämter*) to stress the *office* of ministerial service. Therefore, when the word occurs without an obvious modifier, it will be translated as "office," "ministerial office," or "ministry," depending on the context. When modified by an adjective, it will be translated as "office" or "offices."

[iv] As Schlink makes clear in his next sentence, the Greek term *Parousia* here refers, as in the New Testament in general, both to the *presence* of the risen Christ and to his future *coming again*.

[v] This is Schlink's preferred way of referring to the two main branches of German Protestantism, namely, the churches that subscribe to the Augsburg Confession (i.e., the Evangelical-Lutheran Church) and the Reformed Church.

[vi] In Schlink's German context the term *Konfessionskirche* implies more than merely a "denomination" (in the American sense of this term). Rather, it points to the *confessional* or *doctrinal* identity and nature of a particular church body or tradition, even of those church bodies and traditions that do not have explicit confessional statements or creeds. This term will normally be translated as "church body" or "confessional group" (i. e., one comprising multiple church bodies from the same confessional tradition).

[vii] The label *Schwärmer* (from the swarming of agitated bees) was first applied by Martin Luther to the so-called Zwickau prophets. A principal characteristic of the phenomenon of "enthusiastic" (literally, "filled with the Spirit") movements in the history of the Christian church is the claim to a direct operation of the Spirit, apart from the means of grace. Such movements have also tended to see the locus of salvation as being elsewhere than the external, historical acts of God in Jesus Christ. Moreover, such movements have disparaged the earthly, historical church as an institution, which they reject in favor of a "heavenly" or ideal spiritual community. Luther accused the *Schwärmer* of having "swallowed the Holy Spirit, feathers and all" (LW 40.83), and of confusing God's law and gospel. He also criticized them for rejecting the distinction between the two ways in which God works in the world (i. e., through law and gospel), for disparaging the physical means of grace, for divorcing the earthly from the spiritual (i. e., divorcing "flesh" and "Spirit"), and for essentially misunderstanding the nature of the incarnation and its implications for the church. Schlink is here thus aligning himself with a long-standing history of criticizing those who ignore or disparage the concrete, historical reality of God's salvific act in and through the incarnate Christ and his church, warts and all.

[viii] The German designation for the World Council of Churches is *Der Ökumenische Rat der Kirchen* ("The Ecumenical Council of Churches"), which Schlink uses, for example, in the title of the next chapter. Frequently he shortens this simply to *Der Ökumenische Rat* (The Ecumenical Council). On occasion he will also use the more familiar English title, *Der Weltrat der Kirchen* or *Der Weltkirchenrat* (The World Council of Churches), often shortened simply to *Der Weltrat* (The World Council). While the traditional German designation for the World Council of Churches appears to be theologically significant, it will always be translated here as "The World Council of Churches" (WCC) or "The World Council."

Part One: Methodological Considerations

Chapter One:
The Task and Danger of the World Council of Churches[1]

I.

The World Council of Churches has probably been the most paradoxical organization in the history of the church thus far. This becomes clear already in the report of the First Section of the World Council that met in Amsterdam in 1948,[2] but it becomes even more completely clear in the carefully considered and precisely formulated Statement[3] concerning the self-understanding of the World Council that was made in Toronto in 1950.[i]

The Constitution and "Basis" that was adopted at Amsterdam defines the World Council as "a fellowship of churches which recognize our Lord Jesus Christ as God and Savior."[ii] The Toronto Statement adds to this: "The Basis of the World Council is the acknowledgment of the central fact that 'no other

---

1 An address delivered on 13 October 1951 to an ecumenical study conference in Berlin-Spandau. [This address was initially published as "Aufgabe und Gefahr des Weltrates der Kirchen" (The Task and Danger of the World Council of Churches) in the inaugural issue of *Ökumenische Rundshau* (1952), 1–13. The same essay was published under a slightly different title ("Aufgabe und Gefahr des Ökumenischen Rates der Kirchen") in KC 1.13–23. An English translation by G. Overlach and D. B. Simmonds was published in CC (3–15) as "The Task and Danger of the World Council of Churches." Overlach and Simmonds incorrectly give the date of the address as 13 October 1954. –Ed.]

2 German Edition: *Die Unordnung der Welt und Gottes Heilsplan*, vol. 1, *Die Kirche in Gottes Heilsplan* (Tübingen: Furche, 1948). [English Edition: *Man's Disorder and God's Design: The Amsterdam Assembly Series*, four volumes in one book, vol. 1, *The Universal Church in God's Design* (New York: Harper and Brothers, 1947). –Ed.] See my critical report about the preparatory work of the First Section: Edmund Schlink, "Die Kirche in Gottes Heilsplan: Die Ergebnisse der ersten Sektion der Weltkirchenkonferenz in Amsterdam" [The Church in God's Plan of Salvation: The Results of the First Section of the World Conference in Amsterdam], *Theologische Literaturzeitung* 73 (1948), 641–52.

3 German Edition: "Die Kirche, die Kirchen und der Ökumenische Rat der Kirchen: Die ekklesiologische Bedeutung des Ökumenischen Rates der Kirchen,", *Ökumenische Dokumente. Quellenstücke über die Einheit der Kirche*, ed. Hans-Ludwig Althaus (Göttingen: Vandenhoeck & Ruprecht, 1962), 104–13. [English Edition: "The Church, the Churches, and the World Council of Churches: The Ecclesiological Significance of the World Council of Churches," *Ecumenical Review* 3, no. 1 (1950), 47–53. –Ed.] Cf. Peter Brunner, "Pneumatischer Realismus: Bemerkungen zur theologischen Bedeutung der 'Toronto-Eklärung'" [Pneumatic Realism: Remarks on the Theological Significance of the "Toronto Statement"], *Evangelisch-lutherische Kirchenzeitung* 5 (1951), 122–24.

foundation can be laid than that is laid: Jesus Christ.'"[4] And yet the Basis of the World Council is no common confession, since the interpretation of it is left to each church. Indeed, it remains an open possibility for each church to regard other churches in the World Council as not having the true confession, that is, as being heretical.

The churches of the World Council believe that the church is one. Indeed, they have expressed this explicitly: "Our unity in Christ is not only the theme of that toward which we are to be striving. It is an experienced fact" (Oxford, 1937[5]; see also the solemn Affirmation of Unity from Edinburgh, 1937[6]).[iii] Through "the powerful work of the Holy Spirit" we have been drawn together and "perceive that despite our separations we are one in Christ.... As we together seek this church (that is, the body of Christ), we discover our unity with one another in the relationship with him who is its Lord and Head" (Amsterdam).[7] And yet the World Council does not understand itself as the *una sancta* [of which the Nicene Creed speaks].[8] It is not a *koinonia* [fellowship] of churches in the New Testament sense of this word, nor a council of churches as in the ancient church, for what is missing is fellowship in the Lord's Supper and the mutual recognition of the represented churches as church.

"The member churches acknowledge that membership in the church of Christ is more inclusive than membership in their own church"; they "perceive in other churches elements of the true church" (Toronto Statement).[9] In the World Council, however, there is no consensus about what the elements of the true church are and how they are to be recognized.

The World Council issues messages to its member churches and, beyond them, to the whole of Christendom and to the world. These messages are a call to repentance and a witness to the Lordship of Jesus Christ, words of comforting assurance [*tröstlicher Zuspruch*] and exacting claim [*fordernder Anspruch*].[iv] The World Council thus, in effect, carries out the most important function of church government. At the same time, however, it holds that "it has no church governmental authority over its member churches and, in addition, may not act in their name" (Toronto Statement).[10] For example, no church

---

4 "The Church, the Churches, and the World Council of Churches" (sec. 4, par. 1), 50.

5 Cf. Max Huber et al., eds., *Kirche und Welt in ökumensicher Sicht: Bericht über die Welt-kirchenkonferenz in Oxford über Kirche, Volk und Staat* (Genf: Forschungsabteilung des Öku-menischen Rates für praktische Christentum, 1938), 261. [English Edition: J. H. Oldham, ed., *The Churches Survey Their Task: The Report of the Conference at Oxford, July 1937, on Church, Community, and State* (London: George Allen & Unwin, 1938), 58. –Ed.]

6 Leonard Hodgson, ed., *The Second World Conference on Faith and Order* (New York: Macmillan, 1937), 205–7.

7 *Die Unordnung der Welt und Gottes Heilsplan*, 227. ["Report of Section I: 'The Universal Church in God's Design,'" in *Man's Disorder and God's Design*, Book One, 204. –Ed.]

8 "The Church, the Churches, and the World Council of Churches" (sec. 3, par. 1), 48.

9 "The Church, the Churches, and the World Council of Churches" (sec. 4, pars. 3 and 5), 50–51.

10 "The Church, the Churches, and the World Council of Churches" (sec. 3, par. 1), 48. [The

government of the member churches is obligated to publicize to its own congregations a message adopted by the World Council (even if it has been adopted unanimously).

"From the common membership in the World Council there is a practical implication, namely, that member churches know themselves to be in solidarity with one another, to stand by one another in time of need, and to refrain from actions that would be contradictory to relationships among brothers and sisters" (Toronto Statement).[11] Yet what this means remains an open question. It does not necessarily mean, for example, the renunciation of the anathema against another member church.

One could cite other examples, but it is already clear that these paradoxes are so far reaching that they pose a constant threat to the existence of the World Council. The World Council can only live with these paradoxes as long as it does not become comfortable with them, but presses on as an eschatological movement, namely—in the level-headed and clear knowledge about the anomaly, indeed the shame and disgrace of the present divided state of Christendom—hastening to meet the coming Christ, who will gather his own into one flock and will hold us all to account. One could, to be sure, understand these paradoxes as an ecclesiological variant of the Reformers' dictum, "*simul peccator et justus*" [at the same time a sinner and righteous]. Just as this dictum does not articulate a static but an eschatological dialectic— that is, it does not want to normalize sin as simply a given but wants to expose the reality of sin ("*peccator in re*" [sinner in fact]) and to convey to the sinner the righteousness of Christ ("*iustus in spe*" [righteous in hope]), which means to come to the individual and to make that person whole—so these paradoxes of the World Council, referred to above, dare not mean that we can be content with the present state of affairs. In other words, the World Council can only live with these paradoxes as long as it remains in movement toward the re-unification of the churches, for it is as the one church, not as the divided church, that the churches are to be awaiting their Lord and Judge. If the World Council does not proceed forward on the way toward unity, but stands still, then it will die from these paradoxes. It will so lose credibility that it will be a laughing stock before the world, and the shame of divided Christendom will be greater in the sight of God and the world than if we had never started to set up a World Council in the first place.

German text is slightly different from the English wording in "The Church, the Churches, and the World Council of Churches." –Ed.]

11 "The Church, the Churches, and the World Council of Churches" (sec. 4, par. 7), 52 [The German text is slightly different from the English wording in "The Church, the Churches, and the World Council of Churches." –Ed.]

II.

Now the ecumenical movement, namely, the World Council, has undoubtedly shown significant and encouraging progress in its brief history:

1. The separated churches have been able to get to know one another anew and have drawn closer together. The feeling of being detached strangers has been largely overcome. The churches have become well acquainted with one another. Indeed, we have discovered sisters and brothers *in Christo* where we had not previously expected to find them.

2. The joint worship services of the representatives of the separated churches have had a profound influence on the ecumenical conferences. Here the mutual encouragement of the gospel has been heard. Here have we prayed with one another. Here some of the barriers in the practice of the Lord's Supper have been overcome, and where this was not possible we have learned to attend prayerfully the celebrations of the Lord's Supper of those churches that are separated from us and through meditation to join them spiritually in receiving the body of Christ.

3. From such discovery of the sisters and brothers has grown a comprehensive and devoted work of love, which represents perhaps the most extensive and certainly the most unusual relief work in the history of the church thus far, for here aid was not only brought to churches that are similar to the donor churches but also to confessions that are quite dissimilar. The criterion was solely the need, the name of Christ, and love.

4. Beyond the inter-church mercy in action, the discovery of a common social and political responsibility gave a strong impulse. Not only providing help for suffering Christians in need but also concern for the rights of oppressed people in general has become the content of the most significant negotiations, decisions, and actions of the World Council.

5. Beyond the practical issues and starting points of the movement for "practical Christianity" that began at Stockholm in 1925,[v] the World Council has become a place for central, fundamental theological reflection in a joint scholarly endeavor to address the whole range of issues concerning the church and the world.[12] Beyond the questions concerning such matters as the state,

12 Cf., e. g., *Der Weg von der Bibel zur Welt: Bericht von zwei ökumenischen Studienagungen über die Autorität der Bibel für die soziale und politische Botschaft der Kirche in der Gegenwart*, ed. Alan Richardson and Wolfgang Schweitzer (Zürich: Gotthelf, 1948) [English Edition: *Biblical Authority for Today; a World Council of Churches Symposium on "Biblical Authority for the Churches' Social and Political Message Today,"* Alan Richardson and W. Schweitzer, eds. (Philadelphia: Westminster, 1951). –Ed.]; *Die Treysa-Konferenz 1950 über das Thema: Gerechtigkeit in biblischer Sicht* (Genf: Die Studienabteilung des Ökumenischen Rates der Kirchen, 1950) [English Edition: *The Treysa Conference on "the Biblical Doctrine of Law and Justice": Report of a Conference Arranged by the Study Department of the World Council of Churches, Treysa, Ger-*

the theological basis of law, the responsibilities of society, the meaning of work, and so on, as well as evangelism, all of which have been addressed in a very fruitful manner, there are still further opportunities to address issues that find acknowledgment among the various churches and give them new impulses.

All this work is in full swing.

III.

By contrast, progress in the actual ecclesiological task is unmistakably minimal. Already at Lausanne in 1927[vi] it was declared: "God wants unity.... However we may justify the beginnings of the disunion, we lament its continuation and recognize our duty from now on, in repentance and faith, so to labor that the broken walls of Christendom will be rebuilt.... God's Spirit has been (during the Conference) in our midst.... We can never again be the same as we were before."[13] Beyond this, the conferences at Oxford and Edinburgh bore witness to the unity of the church in Christ as our shared experience. Amsterdam, however, did not bring about any essential progress in the perceptions and statements about the church. The progress there consisted solely in the legal establishment of the World Council of Churches, which replaced the preceding ecumenical *movement* and its living fellowship of ecumenically interested *individuals* with a *legally established* collaboration of the *churches*.

In light of this observation, we must not of course underestimate the fact that the churches in past years have come to know one another anew and have learned to see one another in a new perspective so that they have gained a clearer perception about their agreements and disagreements. And the recognition of this shared understanding has often become surprisingly, overwhelmingly, and unforgettably more important. This is the result of a methodical comparison of the churches' confessions, a method which was effectively refined at Amsterdam so that not only agreements and differences but also "the agreements in the differences" and even "the differences in the agreements"[vii] would be investigated and identified. This was also the principal method used in the preparations for the World Conference on Faith and Order at Lund in 1952.[14]

---

many, August 2d to 7th, 1950 (Geneva: The Study Department of the World Council of Churches, 1951). –Ed.].

13 *Die Weltkonferenz für Glauben und Kirchenverfassung in Lausanne 1927, deutscher amtlicher Bericht*, ed. Hermann Sasse (Berlin: Furche, 1929), 531. [The official German report by Sasse differs slightly from the official English report: *Faith and Order: Proceedings of the World Conference, Lausanne, 1927*, ed. H. N. Bate (New York: D. H. Doran, 1927), 460. –Ed.]

14 Cf. especially the three important volumes, *The Nature of the Church*, *Intercommunion*, and *Ways of Worship* (London: SCM Press, 1952). (Since 1952 the comparative method in the work of

This method is, however, purely formal. It can be applied basically to both Christianity and Judaism or even to Christianity and non-Christian religions. It is primarily a static method. Such a formal, analytic method requires none of the participants to change, forces none of the participating churches to sacrifice, but instead it presupposes a certain static situation, namely, a firm stand and settled structure of the churches that are then to be compared with one another. Indeed, each church has the chartered right, given in the Constitution of the World Council, to be and remain as it is. And if this method at first led to happily surprising results of far-reaching agreements, it also had to lead (because of the increasing exactness of its application) to new clarity about the profound differences that had been underestimated in the enthusiastic early days of the ecumenical movement. This is clearly evident in the exposition of the second section in the Report of Section I at Amsterdam, "Our Deepest Difference."[15] I am convinced that we have reached an entirely natural limit of the method hitherto used in the work concerning "faith and order" and that we can make no further progress in this way. Indeed, if we continue in this way, one that demands no sacrifices on the part of those involved, ever greater difficulties will arise.

The present condition of the movement toward unity within the World Council is analogous to this static method. To be sure, since the beginning of the ecumenical movement there have been some significant associations and unions by the separated churches: Above all, in the Far East, as in the Church of South India and the union of the Church of Christ in Japan; in Europe, for example, the agreements over reciprocal participation in the Lord's Supper between the Anglican Church and the Lutheran churches in Sweden and Finland, as well as between the Anglican Church and the Old Catholic Church; moreover, the association of the German Reformation churches in the federation of the EKD. Further such approaches and associations are under way.[16] But in all these cases, it is a matter only of agreements between closely related churches. The major church bodies, even aside from the Roman Church, remain on the whole unchanged next to one another.

Faith and Order has receded into the background and has been replaced by new starting points that are oriented toward biblical foundations.)

15 *Die Unordnung der Welt und Gottes Heilsplan*, 227–28 [*Man's Disorder and God's Design*, vol. 1, 204–5. –Ed.]

16 Cf. Oliver S. Tomkins, *Um die Einheit der Kirche* (München: Kaiser, 1951), 92 ff. [ET: Oliver S. Tomkins, *The Church in the Purpose of God* (New York: World Council of Churches, 1950), 67–78. –Ed.] (On the present state of the negotiations for union, which have increased considerably since 1951, cf. the "Survey of Church Union Negotiations 1957–59," *Ecumenical Review* 12, no. 2 [1960], 231.)

IV.

From this state of affairs there emerges for the World Council the danger of a false contentedness in relation to the ecclesiological task.

Is not our common *faith* in the unity of the church sufficient for unity? Indeed, this has been repeatedly affirmed by the separated churches at the world conferences. But being content with such a position would amount to confessing a docetic understanding of the church and a false spiritualism, for the body of Christ is always at the same time a visible fellowship of its members in word, sacrament, and ministerial office.[viii]

Similarly, is not the diversity of the churches the organically developed wealth of the body of Christ that corresponds to the Pauline multiplicity of charismata?[ix] This kind of organic thinking was already set forth before by Schleiermacher and others during the period of Romanticism.[17] But can we speak of a truly blessed multiplicity, while this multiplicity is not grounded in unity? The church is constituted as the one body of Christ through the reception of the body of Christ in the sacrament. Wherever fellowship in the Lord's Supper is lacking, there is no truly blessed multiplicity, but rather instead separation, disorder, disgrace, and shame.

Or is the solution to the ecclesiological problem found by retreating to the old assertion, "The church to which I belong is the *una sancta*, and I must simply lead the members of the other churches to join my church?" But such a retreat is no longer defensible for anyone, since all of the churches in the World Council recognize the existence of members of the body of Christ beyond the borders of their own church.

Or should we avoid all these dangers of appeasement, of false contentedness and inertia, by means of a radical *actualism* that simply bypasses and does away with the doctrinal disagreements between the churches instead of solving them? We know the slogans: Not creeds, but deeds! Not church confession, but only actual confessing! Not church dogma, but actual teaching! Not ministerial offices, but only actual serving! Not liturgical order, but only real witnessing! And so on. But such an enthusiastic attempt to bypass every separation would not only be contrary to the early catholic church but also contrary to the oldest witnesses in the earliest Christian community, as modern New Testament scholarship has shown. There can be no doubt that such an ecumenical actualism—the twin brother of existentialism—would not lead to the unification of the churches but only to yet another church body. Such an actualism does not help, since its result, even if it were able to tear down all the differences, would only be a de-individualized church, a kind of pureed church, similar to today's sociologically de-individualized peoples.

---

17 Cf. Ludwig Lambinet, *Das Wesen des katholisch-protestantischen Zwiespaltes* [The Nature of Catholic-Protestant Discord] (Einsiedeln-Köln: Benziger, 1946), 61 ff.

V.

So how should further progress be made in ecumenical work on ecclesiology?

1. Our work together has to focus more intensively and comprehensively than has been the case until now on the scholarly study of the Bible. Through joint exegetical research the churches will need to open up themselves through a new, more radically determined listening to the original biblical witness. The biblical-theological contributions for Amsterdam clearly still remained stuck in traditional ways of thinking that were oriented toward particular church bodies, so that at times it seemed as if the Bible was primarily used by the churches in the ecumenical movement to justify their own position. Meanwhile, however, modern exegetical scholarship has developed methods for investigating the history of religions and traditions and ideas, methods which have produced results that are still insufficiently noted in ecumenical dialogue, but which could be very fruitful. This also applies, for example, to the perceived differences in the witness of the various New Testament writings—differences which occurred as the one gospel was advancing into ever new historical spaces. In that the ancient church not only tolerated these differences but validated[18] them in the demarcation of the New Testament canon as differences within the unity of the church, they present ecumenical work with an extremely important and promising task. This task is made easier by the fortunate fact that the member churches of the World Council, despite their differences regarding the relationship between Scripture and tradition, *actually* acknowledge again and again in blessed agreement that the Bible is the supreme norm and rule of church doctrine and practice. This is in contrast to the Roman Church, whose interest in the historical apostolic tradition is not perceptible in its most recent Marian dogma.[19]

2. The presuppositions that each one of us brings to our joint ecumenical work must be made explicit in a much more comprehensive and radical way than they have been so far:

---

18 Unfortunately, Ernst Käsemann has overlooked this, when he answered "no" to the question, "Is the New Testament canon the foundation for the unity of the church?" Cf. Ernst Käsemann, "Begründet der neutestamentliche Kanon die Einheit der Kirche?," *Evangelische Theologie* 11 (1951), 13–21 (reprinted in *Exegetische Versuche und Besinnungen*, vol. 1 [Göttingen: Vandenhoeck & Ruprecht, 1960], 214–23). [ET: "The Canon of the New Testament and the Unity of the Church," in *Essays on New Testament Themes*, trans. W. J. Montague, Studies in Biblical Theology 41 (London: SCM, 1964), 95–107. –Ed.]

19 Cf., in addition, the *Evangelisches Gutachten zur Dogmatisierung der leiblichen Himmelfahrt Mariens* [Protestant Opinion on the Dogmatizing of the Bodily Ascension of Mary], 3rd ed., ed. Edmund Schlink (München: Chr. Kaiser, 1951) and the very instructive report by Friedrich Heiler that summarizes the critical responses of the various churches to the new dogma: Friedrich Heiler, *Das neuen Mariendogma: Im Lichte der Geschichte und im Urteil der Ökumene* [The New Marian Dogma in the Light of History and in the Judgment of the Christian Churches], Ökumenische Einheit 2 (München: Reinhardt, 1951).

a) This holds true, first of all, for dogmatic pre-understandings, which are often, as a matter of course, unacceptably understood to be identical to the biblical witness and which hinder our joint listening anew to the messages in the Bible.

b) This also holds true for philosophical presuppositions that are operative in the dogmatic formulations of the various churches. There are dogmatic differences that are in reality differences stemming from philosophical terminology but are not differences in the varying witnesses to the truth. Here a much more comprehensive work of scholarly translation must be provided than has generally been done so far.

c) We must also consider the anthropological presuppositions of the various forms of thinking, the particularities of the "*I*" that does the thinking, the basic forms of subject-object relationship, and so on. These anthropological structures which are *in concreto* very different will indeed be fractured by revelation, but at the same time they are used in service to the witness.[20] They will not be erased, but remain operative in the doctrinal expressions of the individual believers and churches. Here, too, a difficult task of translation needs to be done.

d) We must become more conscious of the political and social factors that have played a role in dividing the churches and which continue to bind us in ways about which we are quite unaware.

e) This holds true regarding unconscious presuppositions in the widest sense. "Forgotten factors" (Dodd)[21] fit in here as well, for example, matters that are taken for granted, such as loyalty to strong church personalities and key events in church history, obvious pride in one's own tradition, and so on.

3. The history of the churches, especially the origin of church separations, must be critically interpreted anew through joint research into all of the factors that have been mentioned above. The history of the churches has seldom been given sufficient consideration in ecumenical work. Some people have looked only at the present situation of the churches and sought to gain immediate unity by jumping over the historical differences (a tendency found not only in American thinking but also in pietistic and rationalistic thinking). Other people have looked to church history but solely in an eclectic manner so as to justify their own church body. Here again church history was not taken seriously. Meanwhile, every church separation continues to have its effects in the life of the subsequently separated churches, similar to a trauma in the inner life of a person. One can try to suppress this trauma from one's consciousness, but then its effect will be even more disturbing. The sickness of the disunity of the churches only gets worse when one avoids the real historical process of the

---

20 I treat this in more detail in my book, *Der Mensch in der Verkündigung der Kirche* [The Human Being in the Preaching of the Church] (München: Chr. Kaiser, 1936), 20 ff., 209 ff., 283 ff.

21 C. H. Dodd, "A Letter Concerning Unavowed Motives in the Ecumenical Discussion," *Ecumenical Review* 2, no. 1 (1949), 52 ff. See also Tomkins, *The Church in the Purpose of God*, 79–91.

separation instead of facing it unsparingly towards oneself. We must together seek in a new way to find the front in the various historical situations in which the gospel and the unrepentant, human urge to secure oneself were struggling with one another.

4. The most pressing issue in all of this is to focus on Christology, for it is the starting point for every particular doctrine and question of church order. This has occurred relatively infrequently in the ecumenical work up until now.[22] The Basis of the World Council is indeed Christological and it even establishes its limits.[23] Nevertheless, it is also open to various interpretations.[24] It asserts nothing about the way of Jesus Christ, namely, the way of his cross and resurrection, nor about the incarnation and exaltation as well as his second coming. Also the *pro nobis* [for us] of his person is undeveloped, even though the words "our God and Savior" exclude a false metaphysical understanding. In recent years ecumenical conferences have shown that the churches of the World Council are able to assert together much more than the Basis explicitly states. There are indeed many wide-open possibilities for unfolding our common faith in Christ in common words of witness and teaching. We must keep in mind that the great diversity of Christological expressions in the New Testament has up until now only been partly appreciated in the history of dogma.

VI.

The German participants in these tasks dare not overlook the important help that has been given in the fact that the Augsburg Confession is the doctrinal basis of most churches in the Protestant Church in Germany, far beyond the United Evangelical-Lutheran Church, even into some Reformed regions.

On the one hand, the articles of the *Confessio Augustana*[x] dealing with the church obligate us to point again and again in our ecumenical work to that which is most basic, namely, that the church's unity is by its very nature a unity of faith and thereby a consensus in the preaching of the gospel and in the administration of the sacraments. There were times at the beginning of the ecumenical movement when this consideration was found to be troubling.

---

22 Cf. the important Christological symposium, *Mysterium Christi: christologische Studien britischer und deutscher Theologen* [The Mystery of Christ: Studies in Christology], G. K. H. Bell and Adolf Deissmann, eds. (Berlin: Furche, 1931), which was the outcome of ecumenical work between British and German theologians.

23 This Basis is incompatible, e. g., with the older Liberal Protestantism (see the discussion in the *Schweizerischen Theologischen Umshau* 1951–52). Rudolf Bultmann has also pointed out that this "Basis" is hardly compatible with his theology of the New Testament. See Rudolf Bultmann, "Das christologische Bekenntnis des Ökumenischen Rates" [The Christological Confession of the World Council], *Evangelische Theologie* (1951/52), 1–13 (reprinted in *Glauben und Verstehen*, vol. 2 [Tübingen: J. C. B. Mohr, 1952], 246–61).

24 Even though the Basis is thought to be Trinitarian it could, for example, be understood to support patripassianism.

Posing the question of truth ever anew— non-negotiable for the participation of the Reformation churches—is today, however, acknowledged as a necessity in all churches throughout the world [*in der Ökumene*].

On the other hand, with its decisive commitment to the *doctrina evangelii* [doctrine of the gospel], the *Augustana* gives everyone freedom to search after sisters and brothers in the other churches, a freedom that hardly exists in any other dogmatically committed church. Because this church has been taught that the church is "the assembly of all believers among whom the gospel is preached purely and the holy sacraments are rightly administered in accord with the gospel,"[xi] everything focuses on the event of the present action of Jesus Christ through word and sacrament. Even if a church has the purest, most intact confessional position, the best ordering of worship and ministerial offices, all this cannot replace the actual preaching of the gospel and administration of the sacraments in accord with Christ's institution. In this respect, the concept of the church in the *Augustana* calls into question ever anew the existing churches of this confession. At the same time, this concept points to the fact that the unity of the church is not based on having the same ordering of ministerial offices or the same order of worship or the same form of church government, nor even the same confessional writings and the same demarcation of the biblical canon.[25] If only the one apostolic gospel were preached and the same sacraments instituted by Christ were administered! The Lutheran Confessions do not understand themselves to be *nota* [marks] of the *una sancta*, nor do they demarcate which writings belong to the biblical canon. The present, acting Jesus Christ is the one and all. His voice is to be heard, wherever it calls! But where the voice of the Good Shepherd is heard, there also is the church.

VII.

Despite all of this, we cannot, of course, overlook that even the careful setting of goals and the use of good methods cannot effect or establish the irreplaceable presupposition for a further convergence and ultimate union of the separated churches, namely, a change of heart. Neither the most careful scholarly work, nor clever diplomacy can bring about this change. It cannot be brought about by friendly persuasion, scolding, or threatening. Such a change is the work of the Holy Spirit alone. But the working of the Spirit is not a miracle for which we are to wait as if for an act of fate, for we know that God wants to give us the Holy Spirit. While all prayerful petitions are conditional petitions ("Not my will, but yours be done!"), the petition for the sending of the Spirit is unconditionally God's will. We also know that the Holy Spirit witnesses to Christ and comes by means of the witness to Christ. The

---

25 Cf. the second main section in chap. 5 ("The Expanse of the Church according to the Lutheran Confession") below.

inspiration of Scripture does not refer merely to the inspired nature of Scripture but also to the active inspiration by means of the word of Scripture. In this respect, the Holy Spirit is not an unknown; rather, we know that the Spirit wants to work, what he wants to work, and how he wants to work. So we are called to strive for the gifts of the Spirit. This insight, namely, that only God's Spirit can change hearts, does not imply we are to wait around lazily or maintain a comfortable attitude of theological self-righteousness, but rather it means intense, unceasing prayer and unremitting study of Scripture. If we withdraw from doing these things and merely flirt with the idea of the unity of the church, God will, in his judgment, smash us together and unite us in a way similar to what we have already experienced in various places during the Second World War.

In contrast to the World Conference at Lausanne, the World Council, constituted at Amsterdam, rightly proposed no ideal model of the united church nor even several ideal models, but forwent that in principle altogether and instead left the process of unification alone to the Lord of the church, who is himself working through the Spirit. Nevertheless, the following presuppositions are certainly indispensable:

1. The humble readiness to serve those churches that are separated from us with the best that God's grace has bestowed upon us in the past and the present. This is the presupposition of *agape* love, the readiness to give ourselves to our neighbors for the sake of Christ.

2. The recognition of our own misuse of the gifts God has given us—a misuse that we ourselves have perpetuated—the recognition of our guilt, ingratitude, want, and poverty. In our condition of being torn asunder, we lack fullness.[xii] This is the presupposition of repentance, the deep shame over the scandal of our own guilt in the separations. In this repentance every security is taken from Christians; the bulwarks of one's hardened, self-sufficient form of piety become transparent in the presence of God.

3. The heart-felt longing to seek after sisters and brothers in the other churches, the openness toward the discovery of the gifts that God has given them by his grace, and the desire to participate in them. This is the joy of hearing the voice of the Good Shepherd in the other churches—the joy of a heart that is completely opened, deeply longing, and expectantly attentive. And it is the uninhibited, confident readiness to surrender oneself to the working of the risen Christ, wherever he may be at work.

4. Where the unification of separated churches becomes a reality, no church can remain entirely just as it is. Unification always necessarily entails at the same time a sacrifice of one's own possession, a relinquishment of securities and habits that were previously taken for granted. Nevertheless, that type of relinquishment does not imply a loss, for such sacrifice is a joy, a being-gifted, a reception of a greater treasure. We have already received much from such treasure in ecumenical encounters. Much more still lies before us.

Editor's Notes

[i] This statement was received by the 1950 meeting of the WCC's Central Committee, which met in Toronto, hence "The Toronto Statement." Its basic purpose was to address the implications of membership in the WCC for the member churches' own self-understanding of the church in relation to church bodies that have very different understandings of ecclesiology. The Toronto Statement, which was largely written by Oliver Tomkins and W. A. Visser 't Hooft (and then revised after further theological feedback), attempted to define more clearly what the WCC was and what it was not. It begins with five important disclaimers: (1) the WCC is not and must not become a "superchurch"; (2) the WCC's purpose is not to negotiate unions between the member churches; (3) the WCC is not and must not be based on a particular understanding of the church; (4) membership in the WCC does not imply a relativizing of the ecclesiology of the particular member churches; and (5) membership in the WCC does not imply the acceptance of a particular understanding of the nature of church unity. The bulk of the document sets forth eight positive assumptions of the WCC member churches: (1) that "conversation, cooperation, and common witness" are based on "the common recognition that Christ is the divine head of the body"; (2) that the church of Christ is one; (3) that membership in the church of Christ is "more inclusive" than the membership of any one church body; (4) that the relationship of other churches to the one, holy, catholic church needs to be considered but that, nevertheless, membership in the WCC does not imply that "each church must regard the other member churches as churches in the true and full sense of the word"; (5) that elements of the true church are recognized in the member churches; (6) that member churches would consult together in order to seek the will of Christ with respect to the common witness he would have them make to the world; (7) that member churches recognize their solidarity with one another and seek to refrain from actions that are out of step with being brothers and sisters in Christ; and (8) that member churches enter "spiritual relationships" through which they learn from one another and help one another so that the body of Christ is edified and the churches renewed.

[ii] "The Constitution and Basis of the World Council of Churches," adopted at Amsterdam (1948), reprinted in *Documents of the Christian Church*, 3rd ed., ed. Henry Bettenson and Chris Maunder (New York: Oxford University Press, 1999), 426–27. The Basis is the shared point of reference for all WCC member churches. It was revised in 1961 (to make it a more Trinitarian confession) and in 1975 (to clarify the WCC's functions and purposes).

[iii] "Oxford" refers to the Second Conference of the "Life and Work" branch of the ecumenical movement, held at Oxford, 12–26 July 1937. The 425 members of the Conference included 300 official delegates from more than 120 different church bodies. "Edinburgh" refers to the Second Conference of the "Faith and Order" branch of the ecumenical movement, held at Edinburgh, 13–18 August 1937. More than 500 individuals from approximately 120 different church bodies were in attendance. An outcome of both of these conferences was their respective approvals to form the World Council of Churches. That outcome, however, did not happen until the constituting assembly of the WCC in Amsterdam in 1948. For the 1937 Affirmation of Unity, cf. *A History of the Ecumenical Movement, 1517–1948*, 2d. ed., ed. Ruth Rouse and Stephen Charles Neill (Philadelphia: Westminster, 1968), 434–35.

[iv] Schlink here echoes language that appears in the second thesis of the Theological Declaration of Barmen: "Just as Jesus Christ is God's assurance [*Zuspruch*] of the forgiveness of all our sins, so also, and with the same earnestness, he is God's powerful claim [*kräftiger Anspruch*] upon our entire life. Through him a joyous liberation from the godless conditions of this world occurs for us, a liberation for spontaneous, grateful service to his creatures." For the German original, see Martin Heimbucher and Rudolf Weth, eds., *Die Barmer Theologische Erklärung: Einführung und Kokumentation*, foreword by Wolfgang Huber (Neukirchen-Vluyn: Neukirchener Verlag, 2009), 33–43. For an English translation of the complete declaration, see "Pericope of the Week: The Theological Declaration of Barmen," trans. Matthew L. Becker,

matthewlbecker.blogspot.com/2012/10/pericope-of-week-theological.html, accessed on 20 October 2015.

[v] This was the First Conference of the "Life and Work" branch of the ecumenical movement. It met in Stockholm, 19–30 August 1925. More than 500 representatives from the major Christian church bodies (with the exception of the Roman Catholic Church) participated.

[vi] This was the First Conference of the "Faith and Order" branch of the ecumenical movement. It was held at Lausanne, 3–20 August 1927, under the leadership of Bishop Charles H. Brent (Protestant Episcopal Church in the United States). Its purpose was to promote doctrinal unity among the separated churches of Christendom. More than 400 representatives from approximately 110 different church bodies participated in this conference.

[vii] Schlink does not here provide the source for these phrases, but he elsewhere links them to Karl Barth, who had suggested this method to participants in the Faith and Order movement prior to the constituting assembly of the WCC. Barth's "dialectical" approach was then taken up by the leaders of the Faith and Order Commission. According to its secretary at the time, "The method is to examine our supposed agreements to discover what disagreements they conceal and also to examine our disagreements to see what agreements they contain" (Oliver S. Tomkins, *The Church in the Purpose of God* [New York: World Council of Churches, 1951], 26). The footnote on that same page gives additional information: "It is an open secret that the method was first suggested by Professor Karl Barth, but it was quickly welcomed by the Lutheran chairman and by the leading Orthodox and Anglican members of the group, so it can hardly be called a 'party-line.'" This pamphlet provided an introduction to the work of the Commission on Faith and Order in preparation for its Third World Conference that was held at Lund, Sweden, in August 1952. In his analysis of the Second Vatican Council, Schlink also refers to this same Barthian dialectical-ecumenical method. See NK 121. However, there he uses slightly different language to describe it: "*die Gemeinsamkeiten in den Unterschieden*" ("the commonalities in the differences") and "*die Unterschieden in den Gemeinsamkeiten*" ("the differences in the commonalities"). Cf. endnote 13 in chap. 6 ("The Council and the Non-Roman Churches") of *After the Council*.

[viii] Docetism (from the Greek word δοκέω = "I seem") was the tendency in the early church, especially among the so-called "Gnostics," to view the humanity of Jesus as apparent and not real. Jesus *seemed* human, but he really was not. In the context of Christology, docetic understandings of Jesus undermine his full humanity. In the context of ecclesiology, a docetic view of the church minimizes its human, earthly reality and considers the church mainly as a heavenly, spiritual ideal.

[ix] The Greek term χάρισμα (plural: χαρίσματα) means "gift of grace" or "freely bestowed divine favor." Cf. BDAG 1081. Schlink frequently transliterates the singular form of the word into German as *Charisma* and the plural form as *Charismen*. On occasion he also uses the German word *Geistesgabe(n)* ("spiritual gift[s]") to refer to the same gift(s). Some scholars render *charisma* and *charismata* into English as "chrism" (singular) and "chrisms" (plural), while others simply transliterate these Greek terms into English. Here and elsewhere in this edition, the second option will be taken. Likewise, the German word *Charismen* will be rendered as "charismata," while *Geistesgabe(n)* will be translated as "spiritual gift(s)." Schlink also uses a related term, *Charismatiker*, which will be rendered as "spiritually gifted individual," that is, a person who has received one or more of the charismata that are listed in the New Testament (e.g., in 1 Cor. 12 and 14).

[x] This is Schlink's preferred manner of referring to the Augsburg Confession of 1530 (often shortened simply to the *Augustana*).

[xi] AC VII (BC 42–43)

[xii] Cf. Eph. 4.13.

Chapter Two:
The Structure of the Dogmatic Statement as an Ecumenical Issue[i]

At ecumenical encounters one frequently observes that members of the separated churches are able to pray and bear witness together to a far greater extent than they can agree on common dogmatic statements. Put more precisely, the members of the one church are, to a much greater extent, able to make the prayers of another church their own heart-felt prayer, and to hear the proclamation of the others as pertinent, powerful, and strengthening proclamation for themselves, than they are able to accept the dogmatic statements of others as binding statements. This observation cannot be brushed aside with the comment that prayer and preaching are merely edifying and that here emotional moments, especially the experience of community, exclude the application of the strict theological standards by which we are accustomed to measure dogmatic statements. To be sure, we cannot deny that such enthusiastic moments play a role at ecumenical conferences. But the above observation is valid regardless. It has been and will be made time and again, indeed also by those Christians who give the same vigilance and accountability to each of the words in their prayers and their proclamation as they do for their dogmatic statements. Here, the striking thing is just this, namely, that in the form of prayer and the proclamation that largely accords with the same content—be it Christological or anthropological, soteriological or ecclesiological—it is possible to speak with one voice, while it is either impossible or only possible to a much lesser extent to come to agreed-upon dogmatic statements. This raises the question: What happens in the transmission of the theological content of the statement in prayer and proclamation into the form of dogmatic statement? What is the special quality of the structure of the dogmatic statement in contrast to the structures of prayer and proclamation, and how have these various structures affected the content of the statement?

I. The Dogmatic Statement in the Context of the Basic Forms of the Theological Statement

For the following train of thought we are assuming the gospel as the message of the death and resurrection of Jesus. The gospel is not only the report of the man Jesus and his historical destiny; nor is it merely the assurance that "for you he died and was raised," but it is at the same time the word through which the risen Christ himself acts redemptively as the present Lord. Moreover, the gospel is also not only the message about the action of God, who delivered Jesus into death and who raised him from the dead, nor is it only the assurance of the love of God, which is revealed in this action, but through the gospel God himself acts in his love for the sinner, uncovers that person to be the sinner that that person is, makes that person righteous, and creates that one anew. The gospel does what it promises. It is the power of God that not only calls for faith but also awakens faith.

The divine address that goes forth through the gospel cannot stand without the response of the one who believes. The gospel is that power of God that wants to continue working through the one who believes. Whoever were to refuse to give the response of faith would soon enough lose faith itself. What is the response that is asked of those who believe?

The word of faith with which those reply, whom God has first loved, is two-fold: The loving address to God and the loving address to the neighbor. The response to the call of the gospel is prayer to God and bearing witness to human beings. The two responses are not to be separated from one another, although they do not address the same *Thou*—indeed both are as different from one another as heaven and earth, indeed, as light and darkness.[ii] Love for God cannot exist without love for the neighbor, and love for the neighbor cannot exist without love for God. "Those who say, 'I love God,' and hate their brothers or sisters, are liars" (1 Jn. 4.20). Likewise, it is just as impossible to separate prayer to God and bearing witness to human beings. Although entirely different persons are being addressed here, the one address cannot exist without the other. That prayer and witness belong inseparably together is seen most clearly in the original act of responding faith, namely, in confession. Prayer and witness come together here in a single statement.

1. The Basic Forms of the Theological Statement

In order to examine the structure of the dogmatic statement, it is essential first of all to consider the different forms of the response of faith and to pay attention especially to their varying pronominal structure. In this connection we must focus on systematically identifying the most elementary, basic forms that underlie the plethora of the kinds of faith response in the Old and New Testaments.

a) Prayer is the response to the gospel in the address of the divine *Thou*. In this response [of prayer] the believer grasps the work of salvation that is proclaimed and occurring in the gospel—one grasps it as having happened for oneself and as empowering oneself, and one lays claim on it as one's own. Prayer begins with the action of God for the sinner and in turn bears witness to this action before God, and in fact as it is fitting to God: namely, that the believer confesses himself or herself to be an unworthy creature, that the believer thanks God for his act of salvation, and that in appealing to it the believer pleads for the action of God. As in the Old Testament Psalter, where God's constituting act of redemption for Israel is always praised anew, where

God is thanked for it, and where, in the appeal to that act—and thereby to God's revealed name—further acts on behalf of God's nation and its members are being requested, so similarly, the response of the New Testament community to God's act of salvation *in Christo* takes hold of this act in ever new thankfulness and petition, doing so with praise and prayer in the name of Jesus. The believer thus responds to God in such a way that he or she calls upon God as "the Father of our Lord Jesus Christ" (for example, 2 Cor. 1.3) and prays to God "in the name of Jesus" (compare John 14.13 ff. and 16.23 ff.), "through Jesus Christ our Lord" (Rom. 7.25), "in Christ Jesus" (Ignatius, Rom. 2.2), for "it is Christ Jesus who died, yes, was raised from the dead, who is at the right hand of God, who indeed intercedes for us" (Rom. 8.34). In such response, the act of salvation is recognized not merely as a one-time event but also as an event that has happened once for all and thus as both historically unique and present at the same time. Jesus has not only died and risen, but as the one who has died and has risen he is the present Lord, who intercedes for us. Those who pray take seriously the love that God has demonstrated on the cross, in that they entrust themselves, on the basis of this act of love, to the God who is love, and in that they count on the love of God that is new every morning and which also includes the future.

As address to the divine *Thou*, prayer is at the same time the expression of the human *I*. The *I* belongs to the very essence of the prayer of thanksgiving as well as of the prayer of petition. This *I*, to be sure, is not to be separated from the *We* of the congregation—in the Lord's Prayer the *I* only appears in the *We*—and yet the *I* in the fellowship of the praying congregation remains the irreplaceable, historically unique individual in that person's encounter with God, who has reached out to that one very personally. So one's gratitude is thanksgiving, not only for the saving act that has once occurred, nor is it only for the saving act that has occurred on behalf of the church, but in all of that, gratitude is for the act of salvation granted *me*, despite my sin. The same holds true for the prayer of petition: the *I* is inextricably bound up with the *We* of the congregation and beyond that to all who are in need of intercession. But in all of that the issue is *my* guilt, *my* spiritual struggle, *my* need. In the hearing of God's word and in the response of the prayer, a dialogue thus takes place between God and the person in which the person addressed by God becomes the *I*, who may praise, question, petition, and even besiege God as a *Thou*.

b) Among the various forms of prayer *doxology* assumes a special place in view of its pronominal structure.

In doxology believers do not ask God anything for themselves, nor do they ask God to act for other people, but they only worship God. While the first three petitions of the Lord's Prayer pray for the coming of the kingdom, the doxology of the congregation confesses "for thine is the kingdom and the power and the glory forever and ever." Doxology is all about the praise-filled recognition of the reality of God. God can thus be addressed in the second person—as, for example, in the doxology of the Lord's Prayer. But, as a rule, doxology speaks of God in the third person: God is not addressed as a *Thou* but praised as a *He*. When we translate the original Greek "Glory be to God on high..." (Lk. 2.14) or "to him be glory forever and ever" (Rom. 11.36), that does not imply that God is first granted "glory" or majesty through the doxology. Instead, the doxology "gives" God the "glory" that God already has. More precisely, it praises the majesty that God has and is, and indeed has and is even if a person does not give God the honor. Doxology is the reflection of the eternal divine majesty in the praise of human beings.[1]

Doxology is based on God's act of salvation. Because God has accomplished his action for human beings, in fact for the world, God is praised by the believer. This is quite clear in the praise psalms in the Old Testament: Because God, who is enthroned on high, has shown mercy in his act of salvation in history for those who are nobodies, he is praised without end as the Lord, who graciously stoops down from on high and who indeed *is* without end majestically sublime and merciful, gracious, kind, and lowly. Adoration arises from the acknowledgment of God's historical act. This praise is the unfolding—in the literal theo-logical sense—of gratitude for God's action in that the psalmist's gratitude breaks out into hymnic praise and adoration of the eternal God himself. "The fact that descriptive praise lives from narrative praise," does not however mean that God's act of salvation in history itself would also be reported in the "descriptive psalm of praise." Rather, despite the inseparable inner connection, it is a matter here of two different "genres" [*Gattungen*] of praise psalms (Westermann)[2] and of two different forms of praise—differentiated as gratitude for God's act of salvation and worship of the divine essence. Likewise, doxologies found in the New Testament live from God's act of salvation, from the act of salvation *in Christo* which, despite the Parousia yet to come, is already entirely fulfilled. The congregation on earth may now already thus participate in the songs of victory of the glorified, who

---

1 The doxological statement does not occur, as one might suppose, first with the advance of the gospel into Hellenistic areas, but is found already in the Old Testament and indeed not only in scattered individual statements but as a basic form of communal and personal life. Thus Claus Westermann, in continuing the form-critical analyses of the psalms by Gunkel, Begrich and others, has distinguished between two "basic types": "the narrative and the descriptive psalm of praise. They have the same essential characteristic, namely, that God is praised in them. In the one, God is praised for a definite, specific rescue, and in the other God is praised for the fullness of his being and action" (Claus Westermann, *Das Loben in den Psalmen* [Göttingen: Vandenhoeck & Ruprecht, 1953], 14 [ET: *The Praise of God in the Psalms* (Richmond: John Knox, 1965), 22]). The descriptive praise "is not a confession of the rescued, but it beholds 'the mighty God's great deeds' at all times and in all places and praises him for them all" (ibid., 22 [32]). Thus it is not confined to God's action in history, in which God has condescended from his majestic heights to bend down to his people and the individual person, but it praises the nature of the divine action to have mercy on sinners from on high. In short, it praises God's eternal, majestic power and his eternal grace. "In the structure of these psalms one senses the propensity to praise God's divine being in its fullness" (ibid., 97 [134]). This basic form of adoring praise has reached its richest unfolding in the New Testament in the prayers of the heavenly liturgy in the Book of Revelation.

2 Westermann, *Das Loben in den Psalmen*, 96 [133]. Cf. 20 ff. [30 ff.] and 83 ff. [102 ff.].

celebrate the defeat of all the powers hostile to God and the fulfillment of God's lordship, and who praise God and the Lamb. Because doxology is grounded in God's act of salvation, the latter is also referred to frequently and explicitly in the words of New Testament doxology. But their use is not essential to the wording of the doxology, and even when they are explicitly mentioned in a doxology they appear there more as the occasion and basis for the doxology than as constituting its actual content (compare, for example, Rev. 4.11; 19.1 ff.). Doxology is ultimately about God himself—about God on the basis of his mighty acts toward us and toward the world—yet about God who does not fully disclose himself in these acts but does them in the freedom of the almighty and loving Lord, who already existed before his acts and who will continue to be after them, who is the first and the last, the beginning and the end. Doxology is not merely about God's action in history, but about God himself, about his eternal reality. "Holy, holy, holy is the Lord of hosts; the whole earth is full of his glory" (Is. 6.3). This statement is valid regardless of whether or not the earth gives glory to the Lord. "Holy, holy, holy is God the Lord, the almighty, who was and is and is to come" (Rev. 4.8). "To the king of the ages, immortal, invisible, the only God, be honor and glory forever and ever" (1 Tim. 1.17). "Amen! Blessing and glory and wisdom and thanksgiving and honor and power and might be to our God forever and ever" (Rev. 7.12). The central concern in these and many similar statements is the acknowledgment of God as God, who forever and ever, who before his mighty acts of salvation and after them, is the same holy, almighty, glorious and wise one. Statements about God's being, essence, and attributes thus occur in the etymological unfolding of doxology that praises God's eternal all-history-encompassing aseity. The same holds true for the adoration of Jesus Christ, who is praised not only as the crucified and risen one but also as the eternal who encompasses time, and thereby also as the pre-existent one, who, like the Father, is the first and the last, the beginning and the end.

In doxology the *Thou* gives way to the divine *He*, and yet the *I* of the person who sings it disappears as well. While the *We* and the *Our* are not always absent (compare, for example, Rev. 19.1), neither is the *Thou*. But generally the *I* of the one praying recedes. In doxology one asks nothing for oneself, nor does one give thanks for God's action for oneself, nor does one pay attention to oneself as the one offering praise. Neither the *I* of the one praying nor finally one's act of offering praise is mentioned in the wording of the doxology. Not only does the concrete individual *I* recede but also the *We* of the congregation, yet it is surely persons who are singing the doxology. The basic form of doxology is not "God, I praise you," but "God be praised!" It is not "God, I glorify you," but "God is glorious." Although doxology is the response of an individual to God's action for that person, here one keeps silent about oneself. In doxology God himself is the one and only focus. Hence doxological statements are "objective" to the greatest degree. Still, the absence of the word *I* from many doxological statements does not imply being an uninvolved onlooker but the utmost involvement, since the *I* of the one offering praise, while absent in the wording, is not absent in the actual worshiping: In doxology the *I* is offered up in sacrifice. Doxology is thus always at the same time a sacrifice of praise.

c) Witness is the response to the gospel in addressing the fellow human *Thou*, both the individual *Thou* and the collective *Thou*. Bearing witness is also the response to the gospel, since here believers testify to their fellow human beings about the very work of salvation which in the gospel God has proclaimed to them and done for them. The witness to the gospel is thus a further instance of the good news of the gospel. The gospel that has been heard may never be the silent possession of the believer. The gospel is a busy word, storming into the world, a word through which the exalted Christ is taking possession of the world that God has handed over to him. Christ places each believer into the service of his victorious calling and his urgent redemption, and sends that believer forth as a witness. Like prayer, bearing witness takes various forms: be it in a carefully prepared and coherent address; be it in conversation; be it in the congregation or in missionary outreach into the world; be it more assuring or more demanding. Yet all these forms of bearing witness have one thing in common, namely, that they are grounded in God's act *in Christo*, that is, they occur in the name of Jesus Christ. If bearing witness occurs in the name of Jesus Christ, one can be certain that the exalted Christ owns this witness and manifests his presence through it; namely, he himself wants to speak and to act through human witness.

The *Thou* addressed in the witness is not God. Despite any and all recognition of his effectual impact on the world as a result of the witness, God is always spoken of in the third person. The *Thou* in the witness is one's fellow human being, moreover one's fellow human being in that person's unique historical reality. The very act of salvation that God has worked in the believer is in turn to be witnessed by the believer to his or her fellow human being in respect to the latter's concrete sins and needs, that individual's concrete enmeshment in political, ideological [*weltanschauliche*] and religious forces, in his or her concrete conceptual and linguistic world. The gospel must be unpacked in such a way that grasps and illumines the complete present historical situation, and it grasps that present world in that it seeks and finds the concrete historical present of every individual *Thou* and every particular people [*Volk*].

In addressing the concrete *Thou* in the witness, the *I* of the one bearing witness, as a rule, also expresses itself, and it does so, in fact, not only in the sense that the person is, after all, a believer who is bearing witness—in this sense the *I* also participates in the doxology, although its wording expresses nothing personal about the individual who voices it—but rather, in witnessing, in contrast to doxology, the self of the believer comes to voice, and often also *explicitly*; for it proclaims God's act of salvation not merely as a past happening but as the event that, having happened once and for all time, is decisive for the present and is at work as God's salvific activity in the present. When the *I* of faith comes to voice in the witness-bearing, it is the witness who is speaking here, who does not merely pass on what he or she has heard, but who stands up for the truth of what he or she has heard, who proclaims the act of salvation as something that person has experienced. The grace received by the witness and the calling issued to the witness belong as such to the witnessing itself.

d) Among the various forms of address that bear witness to fellow humans, *doctrinal teaching* [*Lehre*] assumes a special position in view of its pronominal structure.

The concept of teaching in the New Testament writings is not uniform. When the writers of the synoptic gospels refer to the words of Jesus in individual statements and in collective summaries as *teaching* [*Lehren*] and as *proclamation* [*Verkündigen*], both terms can often be used synonymously. This usage reflects Jesus' relationship to Moses and the law, which is both an interpretation of the law and an abrogation of it, and the establishment of something New.[3] *Teaching* and *preaching* appear as interchangeable terms also elsewhere in the New Testament writings, and occasionally their formulaic combination appears as a hendiadys. In Paul one finds a more detailed differentiation of the statements that believers use to address their fellow humans on the basis of the divine acts of salvation. So, for example, in Rom. 12.6 ff., he distinguishes "prophecy," "teaching," and "exhortation." In 1 Cor. 12.8 ff.: "word of wisdom," "word of knowledge," "prophecy," "speaking in tongues," and "interpretation of speaking in tongues." In 1 Cor. 14.26: "psalm," "teaching," "speaking in tongues," "revelation," and "interpretation of speaking in tongues." Here it is not only a matter of various statements of faith but of various spiritual gifts, that is, forms of servant ministries that are given to and carried out by the various members of the congregation. In part, these gifts are so directly apportioned to specific persons that Paul does not merely speak of these services as functional but also as personal, that is, of "prophets," "teachers," and so forth (1 Cor. 12.29; see also Acts 13.1, and Eph. 4.11). What does Paul mean here by "teaching"—particularly in contrast to prophecy as the relevant, here and now, revelatory, strengthening, and guiding word of the Spirit and of Christ who is present and active through the Spirit? Teaching does not only mean ethical *parenesis* [exhortation],[4] the communication of moral principles that are attached to the message of salvation. This is already contradicted by Galatians 1.12, where the gospel is said to be the content of teaching. Instructions for the obedient life are, for that

---

3 Concerning the emergence of Jesus' proclamation as doctrine against the background of Jewish doctrine, see Karl Heinrich Rengstorf, "διδάσκω," TWNT 2.141 ff. [TDNT 2.135–65 –Ed.].

4 See, for example, Martin Dibelius, *Die Formgeschichte des Evangeliums*, 2d. ed. (Tübingen: J. C. B. Mohr, 1933), 241: "The transmitters of this paranesis apparently became above all the teachers frequently mentioned in early Christian literature." [ET: *From Tradition to Gospel*, trans. Bertram Lee Woolf (London: Ivor Nicholson and Watson, 1934), 240 (trans. modified). –Ed.].

matter, also given through prophecy, which is distinct from teaching. And yet, at the same time, the Pauline concept of "teaching" cannot be interpreted as a subsequent statement based on gospel *kerygma* [proclamation] in the sense that the statement would explicate the act of salvation experienced by the believer through the proclamation, namely, as the new self-understanding opened up to the believer through this action: "God's revelation . . . is the basis for a knowledge and a teaching, insofar as it makes possible a new understanding of oneself" (R. Bultmann).[5] "For Paul, teaching" is theology "as the deliberate and methodical explication of the understanding of faith."[6] Against this, it is important to note the close connection between teaching and tradition that Paul held, as shown by H. Greeven.[7] Teaching is concerned above all with the transmission of tradition shaped in the faith community, including the traditions of the Lord's sayings, of reports about the acts and suffering of Jesus, as well as about the appearances of the risen Christ, together with the transmission of kerygmatic, confessional, hymnic, and other characteristic types of traditional material. That would, of course, also include the transmission of mutual responsibilities within the faith community.[8] Prophecy and teaching thus form "the vertical and the horizontal components" in the witness of the congregation and are thereby "strictly related to one another": "prophecy without teaching degenerates into fanatic enthusiasm [*Schwärmerei*]; teaching without prophecy petrifies into law."[9] This means that teaching is not merely the subsequent explication of the act of salvation that has occurred through the gospel message. Rather, Paul again and again supports and substantiates the message by drawing on the tradition of teaching. The result is that the message—in a decisive way as explication of the teaching—encounters, with its concrete assurance, the here-and-now person in his or her particular circumstances. Consequently, Paul understands both the concrete address of the prophetic word and the function of teaching as effects of the Spirit. The risen Lord works not only through the concrete address that calls for obedience but also through tradition and thus through teaching. In his enumeration of the charismata of the Spirit Paul never opposes kerygma to teaching. Rather, the one kerygma comes to voice in a variety of

---

5 Rudolf Bultmann, "Kirche und Lehre im Neuen Testament,"*Glauben und Verstehen*, vol. 1 (Tübingen: J. C. B. Mohr, 1933), 178 [ET: "Church and Teaching in the New Testament," *Faith and Understanding*, vol. 1, trans. Louise Pettibone Smith (New York: Harper and Row, 1969), 210, trans. modified. –Ed.].

6 Bultmann, "Kirche und Lehre im Neuen Testament," 186 [218–19, trans. modified. –Ed.].

7 Heinrich Greeven, "Propheten, Lehrer, Vorsteher bei Paulus" [Prophets, Teachers, and Leaders according to Paul], *Zeitschrift für die Neutestamentliche Wissenschaft* 44 (1952/53), 1–43. See his references on pp. 20 ff.

8 See Greeven, "Propheten, Lehrer, Vorsteher bei Paulus," 23 ff. Thus the "form of doctrine," to which the baptized were to be entrusted (Rom. 6.17), might be the teaching about the very facts of the Lord's crucifixion, death, burial, and resurrection into which the sinner has been incorporated through baptism. (Cf. ibid., 20 ff.)

9 Greeven, "Propheten, Lehrer, Vorsteher bei Paulus," 29.

statements. This variety bears witness to and makes present God's one final act of salvation *in Christo*. In this sense teaching should here be considered as one particular form *within* the various forms of witness. In this connection we should note that Christian teaching from the very beginning does not confine itself to the passing on of received tradition, but it also interprets the individual pieces of tradition, especially in their relationship to the Old Testament Scriptures. An interpretive engagement, for example, of the phrase "according to the Scriptures" that Paul uses to ground his citation of the citation of a piece of tradition in 1 Cor. 15.3 ff., has a different structure in the context of teaching from the explication of the salvific acts as transmitted in the concrete assurance of the word of preaching and pastoral care.

Statements of doctrine not only serve to protect the faith but also aim toward its renewal and spreading. But they do not focus in the same direct way on the particular *Thou* of one's fellow human beings in their concrete here-and-now situation as does preaching. Teaching does not address the contingent situation as the prophetic word does with its pointed word of judging, justifying, and exhorting, which is directed toward the specific individual person or the specific congregation or toward the world in its current state of turmoil and corruption. While teaching is also concerned with individuals, it addresses them less directly, insofar as it hands on and develops what God has done in history for and through human beings—for his people, to and through Jesus, to this and that individual whom Jesus encountered, and further to and through the apostles. But even though the particular *Thou* (both the individual *Thou* and the collective *Thou*) addressed by the teacher disappears in the words of teaching, and the historical facts that other people have experienced are transmitted and interpreted in relation to their salvation-history context (evident in the relationship between the Old and New Testaments), this transmission differs from historical reporting as we understand it today. It is a faith statement, and it always aims to awaken faith. As teaching about the mighty deeds of God, it provides the indispensable basis for the advance of the various forms of witness into the world. In this respect, teaching is not divorced from witnessing. Likewise, both the history of the synoptic tradition and that of the elements of the earliest Christian tradition recognizable in the New Testament letters make clear that also in the transmission of singular historical facts and sayings, an awareness—often a quite unconscious one—of the given socio-religious context is evident in emphases, omissions, and interpretations in the transmission. Nevertheless, teaching is distinguished from the concrete, direct call to repentance, the word of assurance, and the gospel claim. Its form of address to individuals remains uniquely indirect, awaiting its unfolding in the prophetic word and thus in preaching and pastoral care.

Just as the particular *Thou* of one's fellow human beings tends to disappear in the work of teaching, so also does the *I* tend to disappear more in teaching than in the concrete and direct address of missionary proclamation or conversation. Indeed, with respect to tradition, its origin is of course more important than its transmitter, who in most instances remains anonymous. When he or she is teaching, the believer speaks very little as witness to the act of salvation that is taking place for him or her and the congregation in the present. Rather the believer is passing on what he or she has received, preserving its identity precisely throughout the changing historical situations, and holding firmly to the received message of the historical witnesses. More precisely, teaching is directly interested in preserving the historic, once-for-all act of salvation by God *in Christo* as the ground for all the various responses of faith, even when this act of salvation is explicated in its relation to God's actions in creation and in the history of the Old Testament covenant people.

So not only do the statements of doxology appear characteristically "objective," but also, though differently, do those in teaching. Common to both is that the *I* of the person who is making these statements and the concrete then-and-there situation in which that person is making them remain in the background. They are not essential to either form of statement in the sense that they do not need to be stated. The same is true for the *Thou* of one's fellow human beings to whom the teaching is addressed and finally for those fellow human beings in whose presence the doxology is sung. Common to both doxology and teaching is that God is spoken about in the third person. Nevertheless, naturally the particular *I* is not absent in both forms of faith statement, since it is, of course, actual people who are making them. The existential character of these statements is precisely that the particular historical *I*—in the service to teaching and finally in the singing of the doxology—surrenders itself to God's historic act of salvation, indeed to God's eternal glory. In this way, the individual becomes an instrument for passing on the teaching and a sacrifice of praise.

Yet at the same time the difference between teaching and doxology should not be overlooked: Teaching is directed toward people, doxology toward God. Teaching speaks of acts that God has done in history and, beyond that, it speaks of the creation in the beginning and of the consummation at the end. Doxology, on the other hand, ultimately and actually praises God himself as the Lord in his eternal holiness, omnipotence, love, and wisdom. He is the God who does not first become Lord through his acts, but he is doing his mighty acts, has done them, and will do them in the glorious freedom of his love. Thereby doxology is based on the mighty deeds of God and thus on witness and teaching.

e) In *confession* all of the responses of faith are concentrated in a unique way.[iii]

Confession sets forth so clearly the gospel which has been received, that there can be no doubt that the very same act of salvation, the very same Lord, which the gospel proclaims, is here confessed in faith. This occurs in the briefest way when the human Jesus is called by one or more of his titles of honor, namely, as Christ, the Son of God, the Lord. In this briefest form, cross and resurrection are not explicitly mentioned, and yet they are also contained in these confessions of faith insofar as the resurrection of the crucified one is the presupposition for the recognition of his honor. However, even when the suffering of Jesus and his resurrection are explicitly mentioned in the confession, it is not content with these facts as such, but at the same time confesses by means of the titles of honor that the Lord, as the crucified and risen one, is present in the congregation and that in his presence the confession is made. The confession soon began to expand beyond this briefest form with statements about Jesus' Parousia and about the incarnation of the Son of God, and further with statements about God the Father and the Holy Spirit. And then from there, in the course of church history, the one confession—through multifarious alterations of its original basic structure—continued to broaden out more and more and to undergo further and further differentiation.

In confessing the faith, the believer becomes subject to Jesus Christ, the present Lord. But although the one confessing the faith is aware of this presence, as a general rule the person does not speak directly to Christ himself in the confession. The believer does not confess, "Thou are the Lord," but instead speaks about him in the third person: "Jesus Christ is Lord." The aforementioned disappearing of the *Thou* is consistent with the fact that in the confession, as a rule, Jesus is not called upon as "my Lord," as surely as my person is wholly subject to this Lord and my person is unconditionally accepted by him. But for all of that, Jesus Christ is acknowledged as my Lord exactly in that he is confessed simply as the Lord, the one to whom God has subjected all things. Precisely when—giving up any claims under the notions of a personal encounter between God and human beings (*Thou* and *Thine*, *I* and *my*)—the believer confesses the all-embracing action of God's salvation in Christ, he or she then at the same time is confessing the act of salvation that has taken place for him or her.

Confession is made in the presence of human beings; indeed the relation to one's fellow human beings is intrinsic to the very nature of such confessing, for in confession the individual believer joins the confession of the congregation. In the case of baptism, presupposed at the very least is the presence of the baptizer, who accepts the confession of faith and who thereupon carries out the reception of the person into the congregation by means of the baptism. Members of the congregation thus participate as witnesses to that confession. Moreover, confession is to be made before those who are not believers, yes, even before those who are enemies and persecutors. Since the confession is all about the subjection of all things under Jesus Christ, the Lord of the church, both the church and the world have their place in confession, insofar as it is made in their midst and acknowledged by the church. But despite this relation to the people of the world around us, they are not directly addressed by the confession. The *Thou* is missing. Indeed, as a rule, they are not at all mentioned in the actual words of the confession.

Confession is a statement of the believer. This is expressed with the opening words, "I believe...." However, in the original creedal formulations we do find no explicit statement *about* the act of believing, for here everything focuses on the one in whom one believes. The *I* is thus not essential to the wording of the confession. The *I* can be included in the *We* of the confessing church: "We believe." The *I* may even disappear altogether: "Christ is risen," "Christ is the Lord." To be sure, the confession is necessarily *my* confession, and it is all about *my* unconditional commitment to Christ the Lord. Otherwise it would be no confession. And yet this commitment in the confession is so complete, that there is no further mention of my act of whole-hearted dedication as such in the words of the creed. In the confession the one who is confessed is so absolutely the Lord, that the *I* of the person confessing is gone from the creedal statement. But at the same time that means the *I* may know itself to be safely sheltered in the *We* of the church and, with this *We*, in the Lord of the church's confession.

Every structural element intrinsic to the creed contains at the same time a delimitation: Subordination to Christ is at the same time renunciation of the powers that had ruled us beforehand; agreement with the confession of the community of faith is at the same time separation from the faith statements of other communities; and the self-surrender in faith includes the confession of one's own guilt and a turning away from one's own past. All these negations are in fact contained in every confession, but they are by no means always explicit in the text of the confession. In the original act of confession the negation is embedded in all that the "Yes" affirms, without being specially expressed.

Confession uniquely combines prayer and witness, doxology and teaching. Even if God is not addressed as *Thou* in the confession, it still is offered to God and is directed to God, as in prayer. Even if one's fellow human beings are not addressed as *Thou* in the confession, it is still spoken and as such is directed to them as witness. Without being simply teaching, confession participates in the way in which it speaks God's final act of salvation but without directly applying it to specific here-and-now individuals. Without being simply doxology, confession participates in the structure of doxology that praises God and his Christ in the glory of their Lordship over history. The different basic forms in which faith responds are united and concentrated in confession in an unparalleled "objectivity" [*Sachlichkeit*] in the creedal statement: apparently no encounter between *I* and *Thou*! And yet precisely thus, the response that befits God the Lord and Savior, who encounters the sinner through the gospel by free grace alone. This "objectivity" of the confession is that of a judicial action, namely, the "Yes" of the believer to the judicial act that God has carried out for the sake of the world—the "Yes" to the covenant that God has established in the death of Christ.

f) These different basic forms of responding to the gospel belong together in the spoken words of the congregation and of each individual believer. That these forms belong together is not merely factually evident in the New

Testament writings, but it is also a fundamental principle. Even if the gift of prophecy is given to one Christian, to another the gift of teaching, to another the word of wisdom, still to another a psalm, and so on, this extensive differentiation of responses does not exclude but rather presupposes that the response of faith in confession, prayer, and bearing witness are due God from every Christian. Only through all of the basic forms together can the whole response to the gospel be expressed. Only in this complete way can a response to God be made that is truly fitting, since God is not an object of perception and statements like other objects, which we can perceive, investigate, comprehend, and define. On the contrary, God encounters us in the gospel as the Lord who claims us and is gracious to us and who wants to be honored by us as this Lord in the abundance of his glory, to be honored by the whole person and thus by the person in all of his or her personal relationships: in the total turning of the person to God, in renunciation of the world, and in the person's turning toward the world in the mission of God. For that reason, the clarification of the basic forms of theological statement is not only of phenomenological interest, but it is of *normative* significance. And since the whole response to the gospel cannot be expressed in each individual basic form but only through all of them together, this clarification has great consequence for the *content* of this response.

If the response of faith were restricted only to one of the basic forms, this would not only mean a morphological impoverishment but also a curtailment of the content. Beyond that, it would imply disobedience to God, since it would mean a refusal to acknowledge fully his act of salvation and the abundance of his eternal glory revealed in it. The resulting isolation and absolutizing of any one basic form would also soon distort the content of other basic forms within the totality of the responses of faith that could quite legitimately be expressed in this particular basic form. Doxology without petitionary prayer is no longer true doxology. Teaching without concrete assurance is no longer true teaching. Witness without prayer would no longer be undertaken in the power of the name of Christ, just as confession without prayer and bearing witness would soon waste away. Where God is acknowledged only as *He* and no longer entreated as *Thou*, God is no longer honored as Father. Where only the historical act of salvation is being taught but is no longer being assured to the neighbor as the here-and-now act of salvation for him or her, witness is no longer being borne to God's acting as an eschatological, redemptive act.

In all these basic forms of faith response, the fundamental issue is God, that is, the explicit appeal to God, whether one prays to him, or he is proclaimed or worshipped, or his deeds are taught, or whether—all these in one—he is confessed. For that reason, statements of the believer in all these basic forms can be designated as theological statements. The term *theological statement* will, then, be understood not simply as a reflective scholarly statement in contrast to the basic faith statement but as referring already to this basic faith statement itself, and it is decisively important to keep front and center the fact that the starting point for all true theological statements is found in the elementary statements of faith themselves. But then it becomes at once clear that the theological statement as such cannot simply be talk *about* God; it is above all addressing God, it is preaching in the name of God, confessing commitment to God, worshiping God—and only with all of these statements together is it "doctrine of God."

g) Finally, we must still consider that each of the above cited five basic forms of pronominal theological statement can undergo morphological alteration, depending on whether these statements are made in *personal, informal* language or in *formulaic, prescribed* language. Traditional formula come to be crystallized above all in the actions of teaching and confessing and of offering praise. Verbal conventions of this kind may then also be used in preaching and then identified as *kerygmatic formulas*. Consequently, as that occurs, individual kerygmatic, confessional and liturgical formulas, as well as formulaic phrases used in teaching, are not often easily distinguished in detail from one another, since they are all responses to God's act of salvation witnessed to by the gospel. So kerygmatic formulas can be brought into confession or used in hymns, just as conversely formulas from confession or liturgy can be used in preaching. In turn, all such formulaic statements are the subject matter of the doctrinal tradition, that is, of what is being taught. But petitionary prayer and the sermon, especially the missionary sermon, being what they are, use fewer such formulas than do doctrine, confession, and doxology, for each petitionary prayer lays out the concrete here-and-now situation before God, and in a sermon the witness aims directly at this same situation. In the pronominal structure of the theological statements there emerge important differences, depending on which of the basic responses of faith have been formulaically worded (for example, whether confession or preaching, whether petitionary prayer or doxology) and depending on the extent to which formulaically worded statements are displacing or have even altogether eliminated informal expression. Of consequential importance, furthermore, is the spatial area for which such a formula claims validity. Does a given formulaic statement (that is, a statement with the exact same wording) claim validity for the parish area of an individual congregation or for the regional conference or synod of congregations or for the whole of global Christendom? These structural shifts, too, are not merely of phenomeno-logical interest, but are of great, fundamental significance, insofar as thereby the concrete instances of the particular here-and-now responses of faith, and at the same time thereby the here-and-now personal surrender to God's act of salvation, are precisely in these actions being eclipsed. Despite these significant differences, the formulaic and informal modes of faith response nonetheless belong together, just as it is only within the fellowship of believers—but in this fellowship precisely as an inimitably unique individual, revealed and loved by God—that the believer says "Yes" to the gospel. Only in the right interplay of formulaic statements and vital informal expression does the church demonstrate itself to be the unchanged, one church through all ages, a church that is precisely the same in that it penetrates with its vital and relevant witness into ever new realms of the world. Yet it is important to note, that despite the impressive agreement in the witness of the New Testament writings to the unique act of salvation of God *in Christo*, and despite the multifarious formulaic elements that continue to be discovered, not once has one definite formula appeared with which the death and resurrection of Jesus would have been confessed and proclaimed by all of the earliest Christian witnesses *with the same wording.*

2. Structural Problems of the Dogmatic Statement

If we inquire further about the place of dogmatic statements within the various basic forms of theological statements, we should first note that the term *dogmatic statement* can have two meanings, namely: (a) a statement of dogma itself, that is, one formulated as dogma by a church or received as such by it and recognized as binding for the church's speaking and activity; and (b) a statement of dogmatics that grounds and interprets current dogma or that, beyond this, in some circumstances, makes statements that are received and used by the church as a preparation for defining further dogmas (see the genesis of some of the confessional writings of the Reformation). This latter understanding of dogmatic statement is significantly broader than the first, just as the history of theology is significantly richer than the history of dogma. Naturally, both meanings are closely connected and overlap to a considerable extent. What follows is mostly about dogmatic statements in the broader sense. We shall thus only briefly point out a few important structural changes in dogma and then deal more extensively with structural shifts in the statements of dogmatics.

The root of dogma is the confession of Christ. The question aside, namely, about when and in what sense the term *dogma* entered into the church,[10] it is still clear that the history of dogma, what it has been and is about, begins in the earliest Christian confessional formulas. Considering the singular concentration of all responses of faith in confession—when inquiring into the origins—one should of course not strictly separate confession-like, hymnic-doxological, and kerygmatic-dogmatic formulas, and in no way exclude the latter. In the Apostles' and Nicene (Niceno-Constantinopolitan) creeds dogma is still articulated in the structural form of confession. Both of these symbols from the ancient church combine doxology and doctrine, prayer and witness into one, and it is in this singular concentration of all the responses of faith that they are confessed—whether by the baptismal candidate or by the whole

---

10 See August Deneffe, "Dogma, Wort und Begriff" [Dogma, Word, and Concept] *Scholastik* 6 (1931), 381 ff. and 505 ff.

worship assembly. This basic creedal form has not been kept intact in the history of dogma. On the contrary, individual structural elements, which are contained in the confession as the originating act of faith, began to become self-existent and to distinguish themselves in various different forms of dogma.

A structural shift is already evident in the initial words of the Chalcedonian Definition. No longer does one hear "we believe" (as in the Nicene Creed), but "we unanimously teach what is to be confessed."[iv] To be sure, the content of the Christological statements in the Chalcedonian Definition are unmistakably marked by a doxological structure, but its opening words make clear that the issue is no longer the creedal confession to be used in the worship service itself but doctrine about correct confession. The shift in the structure of dogma from creedal confession to doctrinal teaching prevailed at once in the West, indeed so thoroughly that the doxological force disappeared not only in the opening words but also in the statements contained in the body of the confession.

A further structural shift is evident in the Athanasian Creed. While the statements in the body of the creed, especially those regarding the attributes of the divine Trinity, still have a distinctly hymnic ring to them, the formulaic words that open the creed show that the creed has moved away from the action of confessing the faith within the context of the worship service: "Whoever will be saved must above all things hold to the catholic faith, without which, if each one does not keep it whole and inviolable, one will without doubt be lost eternally. This is the catholic faith, that we worship...."[v] Not only does a shift take place in this dogma from the liturgical act of confessing to doctrine about the correct confession, but what is more, the momentum *implicit* in every confession, namely, to separate correct from erroneous belief, begins to become *explicit* here, even if at first only in the creed's opening and closing formulaic statements. As a result of the increasing articulation of this momentum toward separation, it is then but a step to develop the negative theses, whereby the rejected erroneous statements are explicitly formulated in dogmatic terms, and whereby finally even such dogmatic theses are defined that consist only of negative statements, namely, anathemas against other doctrinal statements. With this shift, however, not only did the doxological character of confession recede into the background but so too does the positive character of its witness: In place of witness before the world there is now separation from the world. The Athanasian Creed has rarely been used as a confession in the worship service. If it is, however—as anathemas were made a definite part of the liturgy in the Eastern Churches' Festival of Orthodoxy—then these dogmatic statements are structurally far removed from the original action of confessing.

Dogma encounters a further structural shift in the *Confessio Augustana*. That confession was initially addressed to the emperor and served as the summary of faith before him and the Holy Roman Empire.[vi] The author and signatories of that confession were especially concerned about the proclamation of the pure gospel, and thus there is in this confession a focus on preaching. In the Augsburg Confession "teaching" and "preaching" are interchangeable concepts. Consequently, entire sections of Article IV of the Apology of the Augsburg Confession are effective at providing the comforting assurance of justification. They do not merely set forth a doctrine about this assurance. Likewise, one can still clearly recognize a similar structure of pastoral comfort in the doctrine of predestination set forth in the Formula of Concord. At the same time, one cannot overlook the fact that the confession which is set forth in these confessional writings is no longer the concentration of all the forms of faith response. To be sure, the Augsburg Confession was spoken in the presence of God, but when that happened it was not directed to God but to the emperor, that is to say, to fellow human beings. So the elements of worship of God and doxology, which are contained in the original act of confessing, are not expressed here. This structural modification makes understandable why the confessional writings from the Reformation period were not used as confessions in the worship service but became effective only as "confessional writings." However in the course of the history of their interpretation (as is seen already in the "repetition and clarification"[vii] of the Augsburg Confession by the Formula of Concord), the normative function of doctrine by means of preaching was not maintained. Rather, the content of the preaching became increasingly understood as doctrinal instruction.

In addition to such structural changes in dogma, as the preceding examples have shown, we must note a further very significant fact, namely, that since the emergence of the imperial church in the fourth century, dogmatic agreement was more and more seen in the enforcement of one and the same formula, whereas the general practice in the first centuries was to give mutual acknowledgment to the various confessional formulas used by the different congregations or territorial churches.

Just as the morphological starting point for dogma is the confession, so the morphological starting point for dogmatics is doctrine. Here too we leave out of consideration the historical question about how certain terms were discovered and used in church doctrine, for example, when teaching was first called "dogmatics." Evidently, this did not occur until the seventeenth century. Also here we will confine ourselves to its structural aspects.

The unfolding of teaching, that is, of doctrine, took place in the life of the church, to begin with, in the instruction of catechumens and their preparation for making their profession of faith, for their baptism and admission to the Lord's Supper. In this form, teaching occurred in closest connection to assurance and exhortation, to the call to repentance, to confession, to baptism, and still further it modulated again and again into the structure of witnessing (see, for example, the edifying character of the catechetical instruction of Cyril of Jerusalem).[viii] The unfolding development of doctrine, however, necessarily went beyond instruction for baptism. Conflict with philosophy and heresy demanded its further development—also for those who were already baptized, in order to warn, enlighten, and strengthen them (so, for example, the catechetical school at Alexandria did not confine itself to preparing catechumens for baptism). In particular, the instructional preparation for those assuming ministerial offices went far beyond instruction for baptism. Here doctrine is no longer being articulated in direct connection with actual witness nor with the concrete call to repentance and faith or the invitation to baptism and the Lord's Supper. Rather, all of this becomes now the subject of teaching; it is no longer teaching about the act of salvation, which is preached in the here-and-now witness to particular individuals, but it becomes the doctrine about this preaching, the doctrine about the act of repentance and of faith, and so forth. Teaching is thus no longer the tradition and the interpretation of its statements, but it becomes the doctrine about the tradition.

With such a continuing development of doctrine in the course of history there has been a tremendous expansion of its contents and hence of the material that has to be studied. Indeed, this has become increasingly the case the more separated we are from the age of the apostles:

The teacher cannot restrict himself or herself to passing on what he or she has heard directly. Rather, he or she must go back to the original apostolic teaching and message as the valid basis for all later teaching. Against this basis what the teacher has heard is to be critically tested. The teaching also cannot be limited to one particular stream of tradition in the message of earliest Christianity (for example, only to the Pauline tradition or the Johannine), but it must be based on the whole of the earliest Christian teaching and proclamation, and work through this totality. Because God's act of salvation in Jesus Christ occurred in the midst of history, it follows that the witness of the historical eyewitnesses who were called by Jesus and who witnessed his deeds, his death, and his resurrection will always remain of decisive significance for church doctrine.

Furthermore, doctrine cannot be restricted to statements which were made by a particular teacher in his or her unique historical setting and in his or her specific confrontation with unbelief, heresy, and worldly powers. Rather, doctrine must rather work through all the dogmatic decisions that the church in the course of its history has reached over against different false doctrines and principalities, for it is only when we fully understand the ever-changing forms of assault by false doctrine against the gospel throughout history that we gain clarity about the nature of false doctrine. And only when we understand the dogmatic decisions in the history of the church, are we able to gain clarity about the task of making dogmatic decisions today. Only then will we gain clarity about the abiding identity of the doctrine of the church that transcends time and space. That task will include the need to work through the acknowledged and disputed statements, the concurrent and contradictory ones, the Christian, pseudo-Christian, and anti-Christian ones that in fact are accompanying the journey of the church.

Doctrinal teaching also cannot restrict itself simply to statements from the Bible and church dogma and to statements from the world that contradict the Bible and dogma. Rather, it has to interpret the dogmatic decisions in relation to the totality of theological work that has been done. Dogmatics thus has to work through in great detail not only the history of dogma but also the history of theology. If we keep before us the fact that the confession of faith brings together and concentrates all of the responses of faith and that dogma is rooted in the confession, then, beyond that, dogmatic scholarship will not only need to work through theological *teaching*—be it biblical-exegetical, theological-historical, or dogmatic in nature—but also to take into consideration the full range of faith responses which have come to voice in the life of the church. Dogmatics must thus do its work in relation to the various other responses of faith: in preaching, pastoral words of demand and assurance, as well as in prayer, thanksgiving, and doxology. In other words, it must also take into account the history of preaching and of the liturgy and deal with the issues that arise in the present with regard to prayer and bearing witness.

In the course of its history the material content of doctrine has thus greatly expanded. Yet the concern in this expansion is not with a disconnected multiplicity but with a totality, indeed, with one and the same thing. And this expansion is also not merely the factual result of church history, but it occurred out of an inner necessity, since dogmatic teaching is concerned with God's act of salvation that has occurred once-and-for-all, the very same reality that is valid and present in the course of time and the variety of place. In the midst of all of the various assaults and temptations in this world, the issue is abiding in the crucified one, whom God has established as the Lord of the believers, indeed, as Lord of all. Dogmatics is centered on this one who encompasses at the same time both God's acts of creation in the beginning and of the new creation at the end. Then, too, given the manifold variety of materials that dogmatics needs to work through, it is also about the totality and fullness of the church, which in the manifold variety of its prayers, witnessing, and confessions—in the course of time and in the variety of places—is and remains the one church. But just as every creedal statement implicitly or even explicitly contains a rejection of other statements, so the dogmatic quest for the unity of the church in the historical multiplicity of its responses to God's act of salvation is at the same time the quest to perceive the borders of the church. Seeking to perceive the borders of the church inherently means at the same time seeking to avoid drawing the wrong borders and thus to avoid distorting and failing to appreciate the fullness of the body of Christ. The question of the basis for church unity in view of the multiplicity, variety, and contradictoriness of the faith responses belongs inherently to the task of dogmatics: In what way and to what extent can this multiplicity be understood as a unity? In other words, dogmatics is to teach not only about the faith response given to God by the individual believer, but also about the response of faith directed to God by the whole fellowship of believers; yet, on the other hand, the issue in dogmatics is not only the response that one congregation in one place at one time is to give, but the response that congregations of all times and all places are to bring forth to God.

The expansion of doctrinal teaching into what we today call *dogmatics* has carried with it structural changes, which are significant for its content. These changes do not as yet emerge through the point of view of the unity and totality that is basically present in Christian teaching from the very beginning. Nor do they yet emerge through the assimilation of the vast and steadily expanding material from the history of biblical exegesis, the history of dogmas, and the history of the church. Of far-reaching significance, however, are the changes that have occurred in the relationship between the statements of doctrine and the other basic forms of theological statement.

a) In the course of its development, doctrine has not only focused its special activity on explicating the mighty deeds of God and the other forms of response given by faith, but it has also incorporated them into the specific structure of teaching. Teaching is then no longer similar to instruction for baptism, which leads to other acts, namely, repentance, faith, prayer, and bearing witness, but it becomes doctrine about faith, repentance, prayer, and witnessing, and is thus in danger of reducing these other forms of theological statement merely to the function of teaching (which, to be sure, is of basic importance for all of the other responses of faith, but which remains nevertheless subservient to them all). With the same concern for "objectivity" [*Sachlichkeit*] that teaching has in its examination and systematic explanations of the traditions of Jesus' words and deeds (for example, the institution of the Lord's Supper), his death and resurrection, as well as the confessional, kerygmatic, and other formulas, the apostolic mandates, and the other elements in earliest Christian tradition in their relationship to the Old Testament Scriptures and their continuing significance in the history of the church, so teaching now speaks about that which is expressed and has occurred in the act of prayer, of bearing witness, and of doxology. But these statements undergo change when they are separated from their original form and function, which is structured quite differently from teaching, and are thus objectified into the form of doctrine. The address to God in prayer is changed into talk about God and about the person who prays. The address to one's fellow human being in the name of God is changed into talk about God and about people who speak and listen. The event of personal encounter becomes objectified in doctrine. The concrete historical nature of this encounter is replaced by universal or general statements. Kergymatic words of assurance and the New Testament exhortations, prayers, thanksgiving, confessions, and hymns—all are turned into the raw material of doctrinal teaching for the sake of deriving from them statements of doctrine that are theoretical and preferably timeless.

The teacher of doctrine thus runs into the danger of removing himself or herself from the situation of being addressed by the assuring and demanding words of the gospel—that is, from the situation of being encountered by the God who addresses the teacher in the word—and of trying to think and teach in a neutral position from which this encounter between God and human beings can be observed, described, and brought into dogmatic formulas. But if one tries to maintain such a neutral position in one's theological thinking from which one thinks one can look down upon the revealing God and human existence as if they were two opposing entities that can be compared, then considerable changes have entered into the problematic issues of theology. The focus shifts from the redemption that the believer experiences in the gospel to an interest in theoretically defining the relationship between what God has contributed to redemption and what human beings have contributed. It raises the theoretical problem of clarifying the relationship between divine grace and the human will, of divine and human causality in the event of redemption. The focus also shifts from the demand and the threat of judgment that each individual encounters in God's word to an interest in the theoretical problem regarding the possibility that human beings can fulfill this demand. And the focus shifts from what we have done in our rebellion against God and from what we have received in the obedience of faith—so much so that the believer also acknowledges his or her faith as a gift of the Holy Spirit—to an interest in the capabilities of human beings in general. Faith in the gospel that is brought about through struggle, sighing, and clinging solely to the gospel is not the same thing as faith that is taught, as doctrinal teaching that the sinner is redeemed by the gospel *and* by clinging solely to the gospel, struggling, and so forth. Likewise, it is one thing if the believer confesses that he or she is redeemed solely by the gospel and it is quite another matter if it is taught that God's grace works so effectively that people are unable to resist it. Similarly, it is one thing to preach, "You shall love God," but quite another thing to teach, "Human beings are able to love God." The summons, "Believe!" is something other than a doctrinal teaching about an ability of human beings to believe. The Pauline statement, "Work out your redemption with fear and trembling, since God is the one who works in you, both to will and to fulfill it" (Phil. 2.12 ff.) makes complete sense as *paraclesis*, that is, as assuring exhortation to the believer, but as a statement of theoretical doctrine it contains an irreconcilable contradiction. Without doubt significant dogmatic problems, most far-reaching especially for Western Christendom, actually arose only as a result of changes in the structure of theological statements.

Statements of doxology also undergo similar changes when they are brought into doctrinal teaching and then used as statements of doctrine (something that appears especially self-evident, given their uniquely "objective" character). Doxological statements about God's being, essence, and attributes, which are used to worship God, now become metaphysical statements of doctrine about God. But then the special quality of doxological statements is no longer in view. Doxological statements are ultimate statements, beyond which nothing further can be said by human beings. They are statements in which believers offer themselves, their words, and the coherence of their thoughts as a sacrifice of praise to God's glory. But when used as statements of doctrine, these ultimate statements are turned into initial statements, that is, they are turned into theoretical premises for logical deductions and thus parts of a theoretical system. While statements of doctrine and of doxology seem to have the same objectivity, in that they speak of God in the third person and refrain from focusing on the person who is speaking them, we cannot ignore the fact that both forms of statement have not only a different life-setting [*Sitz im Leben*] in the church but also a different task that stems from their content. The structure of each statement cannot be projected onto the other or reduced to the other without bringing about changes of meaning as well. The most radical consequence of such structural shifts is evident in the history of the doctrine of predestination. The doxological recognition of God's immeasurable grace that alone saves and of his eternal decision to love becomes, in the structure of a theoretical teaching, the issue of determinism, in the face of whose terribly consistent logic doxological jubilation is silenced.

By extending the basic form of doctrine to the specific acts and content of the other basic forms of theological statement there is a danger that the one doing the teaching will forget or leave the life-setting where he or she hears, believes, confesses, prays, worships, and bears witness, from which position alone statements of faith in the form of doctrine can be made as part of the choir that is comprised of the multitude of basic forms of faith statements. The one who teaches doctrine is tempted to choose a position above, from which he or she seeks to observe, think, and speak, from which God's two-fold address in the words of judgment and grace, in the demanding and bestowing word, in law and gospel, becomes clearly seen and perceived as a rational unity. But as long as we are in this world, God's word encounters us as a two-fold address, and we do not have the unity of this two-fold address as our possession. We cannot dispose of it as a perceptible content. Rather, we may only seize it again and again in the act of believing, namely, in acknowledging the divine judgment against us and in hastening to the Christ who was judged for our sake—hastening to hear the gospel and to receive the Lord's Supper, while at the same time hastening back to God's saving act received in baptism. The one who teaches doctrine is thereby at the same time in danger of stepping aside from those who are hastening toward the coming revelation of Christ and the consummation of faith in the vision glorious. Such a teacher is in danger of stepping aside in order rather to teach from a location that corresponds to that of the glorified in heaven, who have been delivered from their dialectical existence. And beyond that, by means of the misuse of doxological statements, the teaching of dogmatics falls into the temptation of abandoning the position of those in this world who are known by God and of soaring above them in such a way that the teaching has the audacity, on the basis of divine revelation, to adopt the position of God himself—of God's own considering, perceiving and teaching—and speculatively to derive the actions of God logically from the nature of God.

b) These structural changes in teaching as such do not imply that the other responses of faith go silent. Rather they can still be heard in the life of the church as beforehand, alongside of the all-embracing reach of doctrine. But unavoidable tensions will develop between such teaching, which has appropriated and indeed variously absorbed and reused the other basic forms of theological statement, and the actual living out of these responses in the life of the church and in the piety of individual believers, for the actual response and the theological statement about this response are two different things. As a supplement to scholastic theology there thus erupted a mystical-ascetic literature; as a supplement to seventeenth-century Protestant Orthodoxy, Pietism; and Kierkegaard's form of existentialist philosophy broke forth in opposition to the mildly speculative Danish dogmatics of that period. But beyond that, the basic form of doctrine can exert such dominance over the other basic forms of theological statement that the way they function is changed or almost completely displaced in the life of the church and in theological thought. Preaching in the church then becomes instruction and a doctrinal lecture, the witness of the Christian to other human beings becomes a theological discussion, and the songs of the church become doctrinal poems. Such phases can be discerned in the history of most churches. The more one-sided these phases are, the greater the reaction will be on the part of the other basic forms of faith response. This can lead as far as deep alienation between teaching and preaching, as well as between teaching and prayer, and even between teaching and the life of the church in general.

c) Conversely, however, one of the other basic forms of faith response may likewise succeed in dominating the others. This then would have immense consequences for the basic form of teaching:

If the informal expression of personal prayer, the experience of answered prayer, and the leading of the Spirit dominate the thinking of the believer, then teaching is in danger of becoming merely the description of religious experience.

If doxological statements dominate the thinking of the believer, then teaching is transformed into metaphysical ontology whereby the historical nature of God's activity fades away; for then no statement can be made about the human being, since the human being is silent about his or her individual self in doxology, or the ontological structure of the theological statement is also transferred to human beings and the world.

If the liturgical-sacramental events dominate the thinking of the believer, then under this domination doctrine becomes *mystagogy*, that is, meditative interpretations of the mysteries of these activities and of the traditional formulaic words used in them.[11] Here liturgical formulas take the place of dogmatic decisions.

But also the basic form of witness-bearing, namely, the form of the historical and concrete word that reveals and strikes the particularity of the *I* and the *Thou* can assert itself in such a way that it displaces the other basic forms of theological statement from the theological thought-world and inhibits their functioning. If this basic form of personal encounter is thus isolated and given total dominance, then the statements about God himself— about God's being, essence, and attributes—that transcend the respective revelatory event, must seem suspect, in fact, impossible. The more the radical particularity of the witness is stressed—in the one-sided interest in what God is saying personally now—the less and less important the acts of God in history become, and salvation history is dissolved into the present moment of one's "historicality" [*Geschichtlichkeit*]. As a consequence, the possibility of making dogmatic statements that remain valid through the centuries is basically denied.

All of the previously cited structural problems relating to teaching that we have identified are not merely formal in nature; they also have a bearing on the content of dogmatic statements. These also need to be considered, even where apparently the same thing is being said in a different basic form. When, however, a basic form is isolated and as such is made into the dominant response of faith, then it functions similar to an alien philosophical pattern— be it a metaphysical-ontological one or an historical-existential one—and leads to a rigid system that suppresses the full range of the responses of faith that are commanded by God. Such a rigid system destroys church doctrine. It is thus no accident that some of the most consistent and one-sided forms of theological systematics have become detached from faith in God's act of salvation and yet could continue to function as a philosophical system. One sees this in the relationship between scholasticism and the Enlightenment as well as between Kierkegaard and modern Existentialism. Now dogmatics has, to be sure, expressly pointed to the limits of doctrine, even during times when dogmatics was most fully developed. The seventeenth-century Protestant dogmaticians were not the first to do this, since the medieval scholastics had also emphasized that church doctrine is practical, in contrast to being purely theoretical. Doctrine is, moreover, the theology of those who are still under way, who have not yet reached the goal (a *theologia viatorum* in contrast to a *theologia comprehensorum*),[ix] a perception of faith, not of sight. The medieval scholastics also stressed that church doctrine is concerned only with the

---

11 Concerning the changes in the understanding of "mystagogical theology," see Friedrich Kattenbusch, "Mystagogische Theologie," in the *Realencyklopädie für protestantische Theologie und Kirche*, 3rd ed., ed. J. J. Herzog and A. Hauck, 21 vols. (Leipzig: 1896–1913), 13. 612–22 [ET: "Mystagogical Theology," in the *New Schaff-Herzog Encyclopedia of Religious Knowledge*, ed. and trans. Philip Schaff et al., 12 vols. (Grand Rapids; Baker [reprint], 1949–57), 8.66–68. –Ed.]

knowledge that God has communicated by grace, not with the knowledge that God has about himself (*theologia ektypos* in contrast to *theologia arche-typos*).[x] Each of these classical distinctions is still important. Today, however, one will need to consider more precisely where the limits of doctrine are being transgressed, and this includes considering the structure of dogmatic statements within the whole range of the responses of faith.

II. The Dogmatic Statement in Relation to the Basic Forms of Human Perceiving

We began by considering the "basic forms of theological statements," by which we meant the elementary forms in which God expects each individual believer and the fellowship of believers to respond to his gospel. Thus far we have spoken only about the structural problems in the dogmatic statement that result from the relationship of these basic forms to one another. Beyond that, there are structural problems in theological teaching that have an entirely different origin, one that is not the result of the divine address itself and the full range of responses for which it calls, but the result of natural differences among the individuals that the gospel impacts. There are various religious, philosophical, and ideological presuppositions, which refer to the pre-understandings that people have about God, the world, and themselves, which precede their encounter with the gospel. There are differing experiences in one's world, various historical presuppositions, and social-economic con-ditions—and these too influence one's initial understandings of God, the world, and so forth. The languages in which these pre-understandings are expressed are also different. Nevertheless, we cannot stay focused on the differences in human *understanding*, but we must consider humankind as *a whole*. The differences in our pre-understanding are not merely the result of varying experiences in one's world, of different traditions, of different languages and historical decisions but are also the result of different basic forms of perceiving that are given in the different ways that individuals are constituted psychically and physiologically. All people have a perception of themselves and of the reality surrounding themselves, which they hold in basic forms of perceiving that are distinctly different from one another, which cannot be learned or also then be forgotten as is other knowledge content, but which forms are given concretely in their being human and through which all of their cognition takes place. It is in this sense that we are speaking of basic anthropological forms of perceiving. Yet it would be wrong to try to derive the multiplicity of religious, philosophical, and ideological conceptions from them. They are rather the result of the interaction of individual decisions, personal experience, unquestioned assumptions that have been handed down, and so forth. But in all of this, the different basic anthropological forms of perceiving are operative so that in our consideration of the dogmatic statement we cannot avoid looking at them as well.

1. The Basic Anthropological Forms of Perceiving

What is at stake with these forms is not the outcome of a conscious decision. They are not chosen as one might choose the application of a method. These basic forms are rather—and this is the issue here—modes of perception, of which a person is generally quite unaware. They are intrinsic to one's perceiving and operative in one's thinking in a way that is similar to the way the peculiarities of one's psychical and physical constitution generally affect one's life. The concept of the form of perception thus may not be limited to forms of conceptualizing, making judgments, and drawing conclusions. It is rather about the most basic forms of human relationship in general, namely, one's fundamental approach or attitude to one's world and to oneself. These forms of perceiving cannot be separated from the basic forms of the self-object awareness and the awareness of existence. These forms, too, are not chosen. It is not a matter of deciding to get in the right frame of mind or to behave in a certain way toward some situation, but it is rather a matter of a form of being, of being situated in a situation wherein the decisions are being made. These forms of perceiving, moreover, may not be confused with grammatical, syntactical, and stylistic forms of the different languages or with the regional differences that come about when different people use the same language. As surely as the basic forms of perception can only be investigated on the basis of linguistic expressions, so surely are they of course anthropologically more fundamental than the expressions are, since language can be appropriated and handled on a far wider scale as an extraneous form.[12] Precisely because of the

---

12 In recent times these problems about the morphology of perceiving have been investigated and presented from the most disparate perspectives. Above all, one should note the works by Ernst Cassirer, *Philosophie der symbolischen Formen*, 3 vols. and Index (Berlin: Bruno Cassirer, 1923–31) [ET: *The Philosophy of Symbolic Forms*, 3 vols., trans. Ralph Manheim (New Haven: Yale University Press, 1953–57) –Ed.]; Karl Jaspers, *Psychologie der Weltanschauungen* [Psychology of Worldviews] 3rd ed. (Berlin: Springer, 1925); *Philosophische Logik* [Philosophical Logic], vol. 1 (München: R. Piper, 1947), esp. 302 ff.; Hans Leisegang, *Denkformen* [Forms of Thinking] (Berlin: Walter de Gruyter, 1928); and Jean Gebser, *Ursprung und Gegenwart*, 2 vols. (Stuttgart: Deutsche Verlags-Anstalt, 1949–53) [ET: *The Ever-Present Origin*, trans. Noel Barstad and Algis Mickunas (Athens: Ohio University Press, 1985, 1991). –Ed.] In addition, the basic forms of perceiving have been investigated not only on the basis of historical texts but also by means of methods used in experimental psychology. In that connection, the works by the discoverer of the Eidetic Phenomena, Erich Jaensch (*Über den Aufbau der Wahrnehmungswelt und die Grundlagen der menschlichen Erkenntnis* [Concerning the Structure for the Perceived World and the Foundations for Human Perception], 2d ed., 2 vols. [Leipzig: Barth, 1927–31]), and of his students (see especially Hermann Weber, *Experimentell-struckturpsychologische Untersuchungen über das Denken und die Denktypen* [Experimental-Structural-Psychological Investigations into Thinking and Types of Thinking] [Leipzig: Barth, 1930]) have especially

self-evident way in which every person thinks in his or her own concrete basic forms, these basic forms of perceiving are of considerable significance in the structural problems of the theological statement.

a) Basic Forms of the Self-Object Awareness
At this point it remains an open question whether the object in relation to the self is a person or a thing, whether it is a community, a whole, or a single entity. Important in this context rather is the question, in what form does all this that is differentiated from the self, become aware to the self as "object" [*Gegenstand*]? With that question in mind, the comparative investigation of the self-object awareness shows that objects are by no means experienced by each person as a vis-à-vis *other*, strictly speaking, but that here far-reaching structural differences exist.

i) The world with its plethora of objects can so thoroughly penetrate the self's awareness, that the self is not experienced as separated from the world, but in a way as "fused" [*eingeschmolzen*] into it—that is, it is not distinct from the world, but it is utterly absorbed into it. The issue here is about such a close participation of the self in the object-entity—namely, about such a living of the self in the happenings of the world—that this can virtually be expressed as an identification of the self and that object. Lévy-Bruhl[13] has called this form of the self-object awareness "participation mystique," and Ernst Cassirer has termed it "coalescence and coincidence" [*Konkrescenz und Koinzidenz*].[14] This surrender of the self to the object and the self's participation in it— indeed its living in the object—is not the result of a decision or of a consciously chosen attitude. Nor does it entail the consciousness of a relationship, in the sense that the self, separated from the object, would first have to establish a relational basis for community with it. Rather, here the perceiving takes place precisely in the basic form of the self's being open and committed to the object.

ii) The self-object awareness can, on the other hand, be determined by the

---

demonstrated that thought forms are anchored in the concrete psychological-physiological unity of a human being. The fact that there are different basic forms of perceiving by human beings has been proven by empirical research, even though the typological classification and systematic coordination of these various structures are still debated in some points. As a supplement to the following overview, I refer to my book, *Der Mensch in der Verkündigung der Kirche*, 20–111, where I examine the forms of thinking in a different context, along with more precise argumentation and further citation from the relevant literature. I am again taking up the most important results from that earlier investigation here in relation to the different question being examined in this investigation.

13 Lucien Lévy-Bruhl, *Das Denken der Naturvölker*, trans. Paul Friedländer, 2d. ed. (Vienna: Wilhelm Braumüller, 1926) [Original French Edition: *Les fonctions mentales dans les sociétés inférieures* (Paris: F. Alcan, 1910); ET: *How Natives Think*, trans. Lilian A. Clare (London: George Allen and Unwin, 1926) –Ed.].

14 This is, however, not merely about a form of knowledge among primitive peoples. It is also found in civilized nations and indeed not merely among children but also among adults.

self that perceptively comprehends the world, shapes it, and in a way makes it its own. Here one does not perceive by surrendering oneself to the object, but the self reaches out in a way to the object and incorporates it into the domain of its own individual experience. Thus, for example, synesthesia and metaphors not only provide interpretations of the world, but they also inform it with qualities and relationships that perceiving within the framework of subject-object thinking is unable to establish. This shaping of the world is also not a conscious act of transforming it; rather, it is in the basic form of the self-object awareness that the perceiving takes place so that the world is quite naturally animated by the self. Now, to be sure, a transformation of the object also takes place in "mystical participation." And both transformations are equally strange, suspicious, and flawed for the perceiving that takes place within the framework of subject-object thinking. But the basic form of the fusion of the self into the world, and of the fusion of the world into the self—of the surrender of the self to the object, and of the incorporation of the object into and by the self—are profoundly different for the self's object awareness and are connected with entirely different forms of the self's awareness.

iii) The perceiving that occurs in the basic form of a sharp separation between the self and the world, that is, in the awareness of a particular "object" that stands opposite the self and that is distinctly and objectively different from the perceiving subject, is not at all so self-evident, as has been generally assumed in modern Western thought. The basic form of the subject-object split is only one among several others. In these forms, observing and establishing, on the one hand, and participating and shaping, on the other, are separated. It is here that the problem of the relationship between the self and the object actually first arises. Here arises the problem of eliminating individual subjectivity in one's perceiving, as does the related problem of eliminating the sources of error that threaten one's objectivity. At the same time there arises here the problem, one which is distinct from that of our objective perception, namely, the problem of the interpretation of the object by the subject and the significance of the object for the subject.

b) Basic Forms of Existence Awareness
The various basic forms of self-object awareness include different kinds of consciousness of the self-experience. When the self is fused with the world, it is less aware of itself than when it is face-to-face with the world. Furthermore, the self can be experienced as a complete unity and as divided (without at once having to call this self-experience schizophrenic). The self can be experienced in steady stability or also as undergoing change, or even as being estranged from itself. What is meant by the basic forms of existence-awareness here are not different kinds of consciousness but differences in the "situation" of the self's experience in the totality of its inner life. The self, after all, is not experienced in isolation from its ascertaining, feeling, thinking, willing, and so forth. And the self certainly does not experience itself as an abstract

transcendental *I* that is presupposed in a similar way by all human beings, as in Kant's *Critique of Pure Reason*. Instead, the self becomes conscious of itself *in* the other functions of its inner life. Also here we find important differences that are deeply grounded in the psycho-physical unity of the person, according to which some people in this function of the inner life and other people in that function, exist as themselves and become conscious of their existence— differences which in turn have further consequences for the existential character of thinking as such. What is at stake also here are basic anthropological forms that are not consciously chosen.

i) There are people whose existing takes place above all in their commitment to the reality of the world and in their participation in what occurs around them. It therefore makes sense to speak here of an existing in the function of apprehending and thus in "viewing" [*Schauen*] in its broadest sense (not merely visual). Of course with this statement we would have already gone beyond the existence-awareness at issue here since it would objectify it by external psychological observation and subsume it under various psycho-physiological functions. Decisive, however, is that here one does not experience oneself as face-to-face with the object and thus also not in an act focused on the object or in a relationship that is to be produced between the self and the object. Instead, one experiences oneself in what is happening in the world around oneself. Here the self is "like an empty space in which objects encounter one another and unfold their meanings" (H. Weber).[15] Here one does not only exist in apprehending things but one exists in the things that have been apprehended. This corresponds to the fact that in this basic form of existing there is no deliberate, progressive, and regulative way of thinking that predominates, and above all the self does not actually exist through such thinking. To a certain extent, thinking accompanies that which is being viewed—it serves as a means and continuation of the viewing rather than having arrived at an intentional development of its own by means of an existential decision.

ii) If by *feelings* one means not only feelings of sensation or feelings of the lived body, and not only feelings of pleasure and aversion, but also, in the sense of Max Scheler's "strata of feeling,"[16] purely psychological and spiritual feelings (as pure feelings of the self and feelings of the personality), then one is to speak of another basic form of existing, in feeling. Here feeling is not merely an incidental effect of apprehensions, thought processes, decisions of the will, and so forth, but the underlying "state or condition of the self" [*Ichzuständ-*

---

15 Weber, *Experimentell-strucktur-psychologische Untersuchungen über das Denken und die Denktypen*, 68.

16 Max Scheler, *Der Formalismus in der Ethik und die material Wertethik: Neuer Versuch der Grundlegung eines ethischen Personalismus*, 2d ed. (Halle: Max von Niemeyer, 1921), 340 ff. [ET: *Formalism in Ethics and Non-Formal Ethics of Values: A New Attempt toward the Foundation of an Ethical Personalism*, trans. Manfred S. Frings and Roger L. Funk (Evanston: Northwestern University Press, 1973), 332 ff. –Ed.]

lichkeit], the existential basis from which apprehending is valued, developed, heeded, and even acted upon (and, conversely, overlooked, devalued, left undeveloped). Here one is not existing in one's apprehending or one's thinking or acting as such, but these functions are the outcomes of a deeper existence-awareness within the complexity of the life of feeling which is in part pressing its way into awareness and in part already expressed in the consciousness as clear thoughts, value judgments, and impulses. Thus also in this basic form, thinking as such is not existential, that is, it is not the psychological function in which one actually is or in which one experiences oneself as an actual self. Also the intuitive thinking that emerges from the depths of feeling is not deliberate thinking in the sense of deciding, setting a goal, and being conscious of a norm. Naturally, deliberate thinking is no less present within this basic structure than within the others, but it is secondary. Here [in this basic form of existing] a thinking that is clear in content, definite, purposefully progressive, and decisive only comes to unpack and assemble itself from complexly related and as yet unclarified intuitions, which then in retrospective reflection are being analyzed, arranged, developed, and whose significance is thus brought to awareness.

iii) Still other human beings exist primarily in their decisions to act and in their activities, hence in the decisions and actions of their will as well as in the feelings that propel them. In this way these people experience themselves as themselves. The other mental functions, such as thinking, are adjoined to these feelings and subordinated to them. No decision of the will and no action takes place without thinking, of course, but here thinking is the means to the end and the end is activity. Also, in this basic form of existing, the thinking does not actually constitute existence, but rather serves it. Even if thinking deliberately aims at and produces practical results, the person is still not actually existing in the knowledge that results from thinking but in the action which follows from it.

iv) Where human beings are existing in a state of thinking, this holds true regardless of the extent to which this thinking is related to empirical apprehension, the unfolding of emotional intuitions or to activity. Also, abstract thinking has in this case the character of an elemental reality. Likewise, a dialectical progression from abstract antitheses to further abstract theses and antitheses is here an elemental fulfillment of life in which a human being exists as a whole. Here thinking is not added on to existing in the self's basic state of feeling. Nor is thinking simply the means for the fulfillment of existence in action. Rather the world and even the feelings are the occasion and material for the fulfillment of existence in thinking, and the action is but the implementation of the existential decision made in the act of thinking. Also this kind of existence-awareness is such a basic form. An understanding of these basic forms of existence-awareness cannot generally be presupposed and thus also cannot be generally readily awakened, as has been widely assumed in the realm of systematic theology.

c) Basic Forms of Perceptibility [*Anschaulichkeit*] and Imperceptibility [*Unanschaulichkeit*]

In the thinking of every human being there are both perceptible and imperceptible elements. This is true despite the fact that, as the psychology of thinking has shown, basically every object can be thought without having actually been seen and thus can be represented in "pure thoughts" in the consciousness.[xi] Now it is an important, proven fact of empirical psychology that the proportion of perceptible and imperceptible elements varies considerably from person to person, that in turn different forms within these perceptible and imperceptible elements predominate among various individuals, and that these different forms then condition the content of the individual perception. Moreover, the concept of "perceptibility" [*Anschaulichkeit*] may not be restricted to visual functions; rather, it encompasses the representational and imaginative range of all the sense organs (after all, we also speak, for example, of a sound image [*Klangbild*]). These differences should not be overlooked, even if within a thinking that is definitely perceptual, the imperceptible realm of thought plays a fundamental role. Here too we are concerned with basic forms of particular individuals in their entirety. They are not only forms of thinking but also forms that construct a person's apprehension of the world, forms which are grounded in the person's physiological structure. It is no more possible to separate the basic forms of perceiving in terms of perceptible or imperceptible thinking from what constitutes the entirety of a person than to separate the psychology of the senses from the physiology of the senses.

i) The basic form of perceptible thinking is characterized above all by the fact that representations play an essential role in thinking, and indeed not merely as occasional elements (as such they are probably never completely absent from any kind of thinking) but as a basic form for grasping an object. Here one reflects more deeply as one moves in a special way toward representations and away from them. Rarely, but then more forcefully and definitely than with representations does the perceptible impetus in thinking become more effective in the so-called eidetic phenomena, which one frequently finds in children but also in certain adults. They are to be distinguished from sensory images in that, although they convey no actual apprehensions, they do convey the impression of the physical presence of the object they are portraying. These perceptual images not only affect the perceivers through the impression of physicality, but they permit them retroactively to decipher from the eidetic phenomena specific details of the apprehended object that were not clearly grasped in the act of apprehension. In that way they can function in a special manner as sources of perception. In contrast to these visual phenomena, representations are perceptually less vivid but are also more flexible, even if they are imperceptible thoughts. Within the basic form of perceptibility, given the diversity of differences in the human constitution, a prevalence of the kind of mental and perceptual images can be observed, whereby in each case a certain sense has priority. So, for example, we can distinguish between the visual, the acoustic, and the motor types of representation.

ii) By contrast, what is decisive for the basic form of imperceptive thinking are pure thoughts. In fact, here are also represented in the form of pure thought the concrete perceptual objects from previous apprehensions and with them earlier apprehensions from the person's consciousness. This imperceptibility of representation provides greater possibilities for abstraction and thereby at the same time greater ease for deliberate thinking as such. Within this basic form the thinking of some people will be more aware of the imperceptible objects, while that of others will be more aware of the relationships between the objects. Indeed, in extremely formal non-perceptual thinking, the objects will become mere occasions for relationships or examples of them, which for this form of thinking are more real than the objects themselves.

iii) In addition to this we must reckon with basic forms of awareness that in various ways stand between being definitely perceptible and definitely imperceptible. Transitions from perceptible representations to imperceptible ones are present, for example, in the determination of thinking by means of verbal images or by means of concepts of feelings, which are derived to be sure from what is perceptible, but in which, however, the perceptible surfaces only as a parable that points to what is the imperceptible. In this respect, the thinking that unfolds here is only indirectly perceptible. It is especially important also to note the possibility that thinking may be determined by figures that indeed have their origin in the perceptible realm, that here however have become altogether schemata for thinking. Such figures, such as the triangle or the circle, can be of great systematic consequence in controlling as schemata the progression of thought and putting in order the objects that are being imagined.

d) The Basic Forms of the Movement of Thought

There are forms of thinking in the movement of thought which are determined by the particularity of the object of perception—for example, matters of mathematics, physics, biology, or those of a more personal nature. Here, however, the focus is on such thought movements that—through their dominance in certain persons and through the persistence with which these persons apply them to the greatest diversity of objects of perception—show themselves to be basic forms of human perception. These forms of thought movement are not shaped by the particularity of the objects, even if they do not of course emerge without being perceived as objects. On the contrary, they affect the selection of objects of perception. As experiments in the psychology of thinking have shown, the process of thinking generally corresponds much less to the rules of logic or even to inferences and conclusions that consciously follow these rules, than to a moving current in which deliberate, progressive thinking and sudden associations, intuitions, and so forth, are variously intertwined with one another. The movement of thought takes place itself differently from when it is retrospectively summarized conceptually with inductive and deductive reasoning and is represented verbally. The flow of thinking proceeds only in part in conscious linearity, but rather proceeds often with thoughts, ideas, concepts of feeling, that burst in intuitively, that start off illogically, or also that appear associatively—and that at the same time thus interrupt the flow. We will restrict ourselves here to the movement of thought in the strict sense, namely, to the process of deliberate thinking, which as such wants to persuade by means of the sequence of thought or by furnishing proofs. Karl Jaspers has referred to such structural differences in terms of the "technique of thinking" [*Denktechnik*], a concept that is open to misunderstanding insofar as what is decisive here is precisely not a learnable technique and one that, once learned, can then be applied by everyone.[17] Leisegang has spoken of these structural differences as "forms of thinking" [*Denkformen*], but one must bear in mind that the issue of the thought form is not confined only to the form of the conscious, deliberate movement of thought. If and where Leisegang has in this connection spoken pointedly of different kinds of logic, there might here be a mixing of logic and the psychology of thinking.[18] We will rather need to interpret the differences that appear in the forms of the movement of thought as variations within one and the same problematic of the identity of the single discipline of logic.

i) In the circular form of thinking the movement of thought takes place in the linking of concept A with concept B; the latter is newly established and then tied together again with A so that by tracing its way along these concepts, the thought returns to its starting point: from A to B and then from B to A. This basic form can be expanded by means of any number of linked terms in the following order: A to B, B to C, C to D, D to E, and so forth until N, then N to A.[19]

In this movement of thought, beginning and end, basic premise and conclusion, cause and effect cannot be clearly kept apart, even though the train of thought begins at a certain point and proceeds by logical and substantiated reasoning. But the train of thought returns again in a characteristic way to its origin. Concepts are tied together with one another in such an interdependent way that what is concluded from a premise is itself being used as a premise for conclusions, whose results are in agreement with the original premise. So the thinking here proceeds not only from cause to effect but from effect again back to cause. This kind of thinking is not characterized by uninterrupted progress towards a goal, but by a comprehensive, mutual interdependence of concepts and conclusions in a circular movement. This circular thinking corresponds to thinking that contemplates an object of perception from differing angles— either perceptively or imperceptibly—whereby the mutual linking of the

---

17 Jaspers, *Psychologie der Weltanschauungen*, 76 et passim.
18 Leisegang, *Denkformen*, 4 et passim.
19 Leisegang, *Denkformen*, 61 ff.

object's features constitutes the truth about the perception of the object. Even what appears to be contrary is embraced in this circular form of thinking and is drawn into its purview. In this basic form of thinking the reversibility of the relationship between the ideational content of certain concepts is experienced as convincing and conclusive.

ii) In the teleological form of thinking, by contrast, the movement of thought does not turn back to its starting point but keeps going forward in an irreversible direction. Here contradictions are not resolved by a common arrangement in a circle but by a common alignment toward a goal, not by tying them together in a return to the starting point but by progressing forward in time. As in the circular form of thinking, so also here what is defining is not linear thinking that exhibits sequential causality; however, in contrast to circular thinking, determinative here is the linear force of progressing forward.

iii) To be distinguished from both of the preceding basic forms is the movement of thought that takes place by ascent and descent within a conceptual and syllogistic system that is hierarchically arranged. "The relationships of concepts to one another are thought of in the form of a pyramid. The concepts are situated within a continuous row of genres and species in a relationship of subordination."[20] The milieu and multiplicity of concepts are here managed into order by a thinking that unmistakably ascends through species and genre classifications to ever fewer general concepts, a thinking that in turn, from this vantage point, deductively grasps the single instance. Conclusions are persuasive when they assign objects their rightful place within this system. This basic form of thinking is specifically analytical and takes place especially through causal reasoning. Contradictions are excluded insofar as they cannot be fit into the system. This form of thinking is familiar to us through the classical development of Western logic.

We here forgo coordinating with one another the sets of forms of thinking that have been respectively discussed above under the four aspects of each of the basic forms of human perceiving—that of the self-world awareness, of existence-awareness, of perceptibility and imperceptibility, of the movement of thought; and we forgo drawing up a typology of the entirety of human perceiving by means of a summary of each set of forms of thinking of the four respective basic forms of perceiving.[21] Rather, the four sets of the basic forms are deliberately to remain as open sets, for we are concerned here with the particular individual, not with the construction of a further typology that joins the crowd of existing, competing typologies and theories about how human beings are constituted. We also forgo here coordinating the various

---

20 Jaspers, *Psychologie der Weltanschauungen*, 77.

21 Obviously, such connections exist, for example, between the forms of thinking discussed in each of the four initial sub-sections above, that is, those addressed under sub-section "i" in each of the four basic forms.

basic forms with the various stages in the history of human development or that of different peoples. These forms can be found both in historical succession and in peoples and individuals who exist in the same time period. The discussion of those four aspects and the distinctions under each does thus not intend to be a comprehensive systematization of the basic anthropological forms of perceiving. Here we have elaborated only enough to make clear the reality of such basic forms.

Nevertheless, precisely in such a forgoing of a comprehensive system of the basic anthropological forms, it will become all the more clear that these various basic forms are themselves eminently significant presuppositions for the various developments of systematic thinking. Each of the basic forms mentioned provides the starting point for a distinct system of the perception of one's self and of one's world. None of these forms is to be understood as a mere form, as if its content were to remain unaffected by the form. Rather, these forms of perception are much like the sense organs, of greatest importance for what the perceiving person selects from out of the plethora of living reality that surrounds him or her and is that person's very self. It is clear that the above exhibited basic forms of perceiving, if consistently applied and developed, lead to quite distinct religious, philosophical, and ideological theses and systems. Thereby one will, of course, have to understand by "a system," not merely the conceptual housing [*Gehäuse*] for a definite kind of content but also a particular systematics or method of thinking (as, for example, in the transcendental method of Karl Jaspers, although here "housings for thinking" [*Denkgehäuse*] are rejected).

2. Structural Problems in Theological Perceiving

We must now ask further: What happens to these basic anthropological forms of perceiving when a human being is confronted by the gospel, through which God acts in his love to judge and redeem a given individual? What happens when one surrenders oneself in faith to Christ as one's Lord?

a) The gospel strikes a human being not merely as an abstract individual of humanity, but it strikes the particular human being in his or her historical uniqueness and irreplaceability and thus at the same time in his or her special psycho-physical entirety. To be sure, through the gospel God tears one out of the isolation in which one secludes oneself from God and from one's fellow human beings, God exposes one as a member of a sinful human race, and God transfers the believer into the fellowship of God's people, the new humanity. But God exposes each individual in his or her own sin and redeems that person from his or her own bondages and gives to each person the special gifts of grace. The gospel thus also strikes each individual in the concrete structure of that person's basic forms of perceiving and in that individual's resulting relationship to the surrounding world. The gospel strikes a person in the concrete "situation" [*Ort*] of his or her existing, in order to open up for that person, this specific human being, a new existence. The gospel strikes each human being at the center of his or her life; it strikes that person in his or her heart.

b) When the gospel strikes a person, it shakes that one to the very core of his or her foundations and it disrupts the basic forms in which he or she had thought to secure his or her life in the midst of the surrounding world. The things one takes for granted—the concrete awareness of one's existence and the "housing" of one's understanding and control of one's world—become shattered. The religious and ideological constructs which have taken shape in the basic forms of one's perceiving are refuted.

Consequently, in regard to the basic forms of the self-object awareness, one cannot grasp God's dealing with oneself either in the form of merging with the other or in the form of transforming the other, or in the form of the subject-object dichotomy. A direct merging into God is made impossible by the gospel as the message of the historical human being, Jesus Christ; only by faith in him as the historical mediator do we have fellowship with God. The forms of God's image shaped on the basis of one's own are shattered when through the gospel God encounters us quite simply as Lord God. But likewise, persisting in the subject-object dichotomy is ruled out for the believer because God has become a human being in Jesus Christ, one of us, and has put his Spirit into our hearts. So the believer is in Christ, and yet Christ never ceases to be vis-à-vis the believer. And so Christ encounters us in the witness and in the poverty of our fellow human beings without ceasing to be their Lord. So God's Spirit is in our hearts, crying in our groaning: "Abba, Father," while at the same time, he is the Lord God, the Creator, to whom we pray, "Come, Holy Spirit." Here neither transcendence nor immanence may be kept in systematic isolation from one another. Neither can be simply excluded from God's dealings with human beings.

In a similar way, the basic forms of awareness of one's existence are incapable of grasping the human self-understanding that opens itself up for the believer by means of the gospel. Every pre-understanding that one has of oneself is called into question and broken in two by means of the gospel. Our transgressions against God will be revealed, both those we commit today as well as those we committed long ago. Forgotten and repressed guilt will become conscious, and what has grown cold will burn again. We are being held to account by God's address to us in our very identity as a person, and so we are being exposed as those who not only committed sins but who are sinners and who have forfeited their lives. It is precisely to these sinners that God says through the gospel: "You are my beloved, you are my child." Through faith in the gospel the sinner knows himself or herself to be one who has been justified by Christ before God—one who is declared righteous and has been made righteous. In the light of this faith one knows oneself at the same time to be one who has been preserved and led by God the Creator, out of pure goodness, through acts of judgment and kindness, even when one did not yet believe in God. The gospel thus calls a person to deepest awareness. But even that is not the decisive factor, since there are various degrees of awareness of one's existence, even apart from this faith. The special character of Christian self-understanding consists rather in this, to put it bluntly, that it is not a self-understanding at all. To be sure, the believer knows himself or herself to be a sinner. Sin is, in the actual and exclusive sense, that person's deed. One's knowledge of oneself as a creation and as altogether righteous is, however, the knowledge of the mighty deeds of God the Creator and Redeemer, who has created and who sustains one, and who, through the gospel, justifies one anew each day and gives one that new life. We do not recognize our righteousness in ourselves, even though it is a gift to us, but we know it only in Christ, who was made to become for us the righteousness of God and who gives himself to us through the gospel. As we observe ourselves, however, our righteousness is hidden under imperfections, indeed under sins. Nor do we recognize our new life in ourselves, even if we have been transferred into it, but we know it only in Jesus Christ. He is the new human being, the in-breaking of the new creation. He is our life. By faith in him, in him alone, is our life to be sought and found, not in our own experience. "Set your minds on things that are above, not on things that are on earth, for you have died, and your life is hidden with Christ in God" (Col. 3.2 f.). So believers "have" life, and yet this life is not their life, but the life of Christ. "I have been crucified with Christ; I live, yet not I myself, but Christ lives in me" (Gal. 2.[19–]20). By knowing themselves as righteous and alive, believers do not actually recognize themselves to be such, but do recognize God's act of salvation in Christ for them. It is in this sense that one steps outside of oneself through the act of faith. Consequently, Paul separates faith comprehensively from all the forms through which one imagines to have and secure one's existence, whether it be one's willing and doing or one's experience of the world and one's knowledge of wisdom.

Even the basic forms of perceptibility and imperceptibility are made powerless by the gospel. God's act of salvation in Christ, which the gospel proclaims and which occurs through the gospel, is perceptible and imperceptible at the same time and in such a special way that the perception of this act of salvation can be designated neither as perceptible nor as imperceptible. Nor, moreover, is the concept of perceptibility here to be restricted to the visual sphere, but it must include whatever can be apprehended and imagined. As an historical human being, Jesus could be seen, heard, and touched, and yet he could not be known as Christ, as God's Son and the Lord, by means of seeing, hearing, or touching. This knowledge is the perception of faith, which recognizes the historical human being Jesus as Christ and God's Son, despite his insignificance and perceived lowliness, despite the disconnection between his claim to absolute authority and his failure on the cross. Although he appeared as the risen one to his disciples, the saying remains valid: "Blessed are those who have not seen and yet believe"

(John 20.29). We hear the gospel, yet do not receive the grace that it proclaims simply by the hearing but by faith. We taste bread and wine in the Lord's Supper, yet we do not receive forgiveness and life in Christ's body and blood merely by the tasting, but by faith. The recognition of God's act of salvation is thus an imperceptible knowing. And yet this recognition of faith does not stand in contradiction to seeing, hearing, tasting, and thus to perceptibility and imagination in the broadest sense. The reason for this is that faith clings precisely to the word that it hears and to the food that it tastes. It recognizes as God's word the human word that proclaims the good news of the gospel, and it recognizes the bread and wine in the Lord's Supper as Christ's life-giving body and his blood. Faith clings fully to the Jesus of history and recognizes his majesty precisely in his human lowliness and his victory in his defeat on the cross. Precisely when we see in faith the one who has become *flesh*, the following holds true: "and we have seen his *glory*" (John 1.14). This glory can be grasped through none of the basic forms of perceptibility and imperceptibility.

Each of the adduced basic forms of perceptible images, imaginative ideas, diagrams, imperceptible concepts, and so forth, is opened up in its own particular way by the gospel. Thus in none of the basic forms can *one* concept or *one* relationship or *one* imaginative idea or *one* image alone grasp God's act of salvation in Christ. In the Gospel of John there thus pile up in the "I am" passages the images in which Christ bears witness to all people that he is the bringer of salvation. These images do not fully coincide with one another nor do they simply complement one another, but they mutually strip from one another their quotidian perceptual meaning.[22] Of similar central importance as the above images in the Gospel of John are the schemata taken from a legal setting and used in the Pauline letters to bear witness to God's act of salvation *in Christo*—whether they have an origin in private, contractual, penal, or cultic law. The concern here, right from the start, is not in the specific particularity of the persons and objects of the legal proceedings, but in the actual relationships coming to pass between them. For that reason, these schemata are to a large degree imperceptibly conceptual in nature. In the Pauline letters there pile up such relationship-schemata as redemption, atonement, justification, cultic expiation, and so forth. These schemata, too, do not coincide with one another nor do they simply complement one another, but they mutually call one another into question with respect to their juridical stringency. At the same time, each of these schemata of relationship is undone in a particular way in the witness to the act of salvation: Neither the debtors nor their guarantor pays for the redemption, but the creditor, namely, God himself. Here it is not the warring parties that are reconciling themselves, but God reconciles to himself those warring against him; here not the innocent is

---

22 See, for example, John 10.7 ff. and 12 ff., where Christ is described as the door and the shepherd at the same time. If taken literally, these descriptions would be mutually exclusive.

acquitted but the guilty one, and in fact, on the basis of the condemnation of the innocent one, and so forth. Perceptible and imperceptible thought, when struck by the gospel, reaches the point where what is self-evident about its ways and means of thinking is exploded. God's act of salvation in Christ cannot be grasped by them. If one holds fast to the integrity of these ways of thinking, this salvific act appears as nonsense. In the hearing of the gospel, however, it is not only in all these images and schemata together but also in each one of them individually that the whole Christ encounters the believer.

Ruptured also are the basic forms of the movement of thought and their particular ways of confirming and concluding. Teleological thinking is opened up because God breaks into the teleologies of this world through his free grace *in Christo* and crosses them out. The coming of Christ is the goal of God's plan of salvation and at the same time the smashing of the goals of human thinking, planning, and doing. The expectation that the believer has is not only an expectation of the fulfillment of God's plan but at the same time an expectation of God's judgment. Believers think teleologically in that they hand over their teleological thinking to the Lord, about whose coming they know neither the day nor the hour. Circular thinking is opened up since the gospel breaks open the contradictions between light and darkness, sin and grace, life and death, God and world, this present age and the one that is coming, and demonstrates that they are not polarities within a larger circular system nor permanent complementary entities. Rather, their relationship is one of an eschatological struggle in which the victory, though already won, will however only become visible in the end. Likewise, the hierarchical form of thinking (an ordering of superior to subordinate, of above to below) does not succeed in comprehending the relationship between God and the world, since God *in Christo* encounters the world as the Lord who is wholly other—wholly other not only in his power but in that he, the Most High, has come down to us *in Christo*, the most humble.

c) The basic forms of perceiving, when struck by the gospel, are opened up and are disrupted in their systematic consequences, and yet the believer's perceiving does not become formless. The believer continues to perceive in his or her concrete form of perception, although as in a form now opened up and disrupted, since as a disruption of a concrete form of perception, the disruption itself has a concrete structure, namely, that of a disrupted form. Theological thinking, too, does not cease to be the thinking of particular individuals. The gospel not only strikes the very heart of people in judging and rescuing them in what constitutes their concrete psycho-physical reality and thus in the concrete structure of the basic form of their perceiving, but it also places them into service and summons from them the response of faith in confession, prayer, and bearing witness. As a particular, historical, unique, and irreplaceable individual, such a one should now, in the wholeness of his or her psycho-physical existence and on the basis of God's act of salvation for that person, become a witness before other people to this act of salvation. The creaturely existence of the individual is not extinguished thereby, but is used by God for servant ministry and is offered up as a sacrifice to God in the response of faith. Just as one confesses one's sins, in that one, and precisely that one, has committed in the concrete situation of one's existing—and repents in that one turns away from those specific sins—so one also is a witness, in that he or she, and precisely he or she, gives witness in the concrete conditions of his or her creaturely existence and thus also through his or her basic forms of perceiving. This does not imply of course that one is now secured and self-sufficient in one's basic forms of perceiving, though they have indeed been opened up and disrupted; nor can one shield oneself with them against the in-breaking God, nor dream of God's act of salvation by means of them. So one testifies further to God's act of salvation in the concrete forms of one's perceiving and recognizing. Although expanded, opened up, and disrupted, these basic forms of human knowing exhibit a singular staying power.[23] God's act of salvation is witnessed to in the disrupted basic forms of self-object awareness. Faith is distinguished from the self's former self-understanding in the disrupted forms of the existence-awareness. The incarnation of God in the flesh and the history of his eschatological activity are proclaimed in the disrupted forms of perceptibility and imperceptibility and in the movement of thought. Thus also the differences between the writings collected in the New Testament are not only differences that relate to their terminology and historical contexts but are also differences in the authors' forms of thinking.[24] These differences must be kept in mind when one compares statements from the different texts. In the different basic forms of perceiving, different statements can mean the same thing and statements that sound the same can mean something different.

d) The basic forms of human perceiving can, of course, also assert themselves in theological knowledge and statement and ossify in those forms by resisting their being opened up and disrupted. This being opened up is, to be sure, never completely finished. That will only happen once our faith has been replaced by sight in eternal glory. "For now we see in a mirror, dimly, but then we will see face to face. Now I know only in part; then I will know fully, even as I have been fully known" [1 Cor. 13.12]. Where, however, believers weary in eschatological hastening toward the future opening up of their knowledge, where they stop moving forward, and consolidate their personal possession of the Christian faith, there the basic anthropological forms begin

---

23 This fact can be assumed not only in the Christian instruction of children—where one presupposes until the teen years the perceptual form of their thinking and the still fully undisrupted awareness of the subject-object dichotomy—and not only in missionary preaching—where one aims at the awakening of faith and bearing witness precisely in the context of concrete structures of the foreign thinking—but this persistence of the basic forms of knowing can also be demonstrated in the empirical-psychological investigations of accounts of conversion.

24 This point is especially clear when one compares the Pauline and Johannine texts. See Edmund Schlink, *Der Mensch in der Verkündigung der Kirche*, 40 ff., 59 ff., 75 ff., and 100.

anew to limit and falsify the knowledge of God's act of salvation, and theological systems arise that call one another into question or even mutually exclude one another. Depending on the selected variations of the self-object awareness, God's act of salvation *in Christo* is distorted in either a mystical or an idealistic way, or in the perceptual form of the subject-object split Christ becomes objectified as mediator between the opposites of God and the world. Likewise, depending on the basic form of awareness of one's existence, the concept of faith becomes anthropologically formulated, and then by transferring the human form of being aware of existence to God the nature of God becomes defined accordingly as either entirely knowing or willing or doing. The fullness of grace is no longer recognized if believers elevate absolutely their experience—as perceived in the basic form in which they are aware of their existence—as a universal norm for the reality of grace: one person in the feeling of God's presence, another in the prevailing success of ethical action, and still another in new knowledge. Likewise the forms of perceptibility and imperceptibility with their particular images, ideas, concepts of feeling, schemata or diagrams (for example, that of unity within a dialectic duality) can elevate an absolute claim in theological thinking and speaking so that they subordinate other basic forms or dismissively reject them. Also when the basic forms of the movement of thought assert themselves, that has far-reaching consequences for the whole of theological knowledge and teaching, as well as for its systematic arrangement, and especially for the relationship between salvation history and eschatology.

Here we have already been dealing no longer only with theological knowing but also with theological statements. Naturally, basic anthropological forms of perceiving have an impact not only on theological knowledge but also on theological and dogmatic statements. Nevertheless, we need to continue distinguishing between knowledge and statement and to bear in mind that the relationship between knowing and speaking, despite their dependence upon one another, is not only one of correspondence. Even if thinking seeks verbal expression and finds clarification and formulation in it, there still is wordless thought, that is, thought which cannot be adequately expressed in words. Language is always, after all, already a given reality for the thinking and speaking of individual persons which, depending on its particular plentitude, still offers limited possibilities of expression in the adoption and also the modification of the traditional language. As surely as the basic form of perceiving comes to expression in speech, so the existing linguistic structure can in turn also lead to a faulty expression of the perception. The possible variations here in the relationship between thinking and speaking dare not be disregarded.

III. The Complexity of the Problem of the Theological Statement

Before we turn to the question of how the two types of basic forms relate to one another, we shall try to give an account of the place that these forms hold within the whole range of issues raised by the theological statement. Obviously this set of issues is much too complex to be fully encompassed by those we have already examined under the two preceding perspectives, namely, those within the pronomial structure of the theological statement and those included in the basic anthropological forms of perceiving. In the attempt to reorient ourselves we run of course into an irksome gap, namely, the fact that contemporary theological scholarship lacks a comprehensive study of the theological statement as such. This is indeed true for both Protestant as well as Roman Catholic theology: A "logic of theological statements" is missing (G. Söhngen).[25] This gap is all the more striking in that the issues raised by the theological statement, regardless of what form it takes, is of fundamental significance for all churches—not merely for the "church of the word."

If we begin with the issue of human statements in general, it is clearly not a concern of only *one* scholarly discipline. Without claiming completeness and without being able to enter here into a discussion about a more precise definition of the following, one can say that each and every statement raises issues about: (a) epistemology, (b) logic, (c) linguistics and philology, (d) history, (e) psychology and anthropology, (f) sociology, and (g) ontology. Each and every statement is a subject for *all* of these disciplines. Placing epistemology at the beginning and ontology at the end of this list means to embrace all of the individual disciplines with the truth question about the content of the given statement.

This differentiation of the disciplines is of relatively recent origin, and it continues apace. Since the time of Aristotle and Stoic philosophy, in the intellectual history of the West up to the dawn of the modern age, the scholarly treatment of the issues raised by human statements was dominated by logic, and because of this linguistics remained essentially confined to Latin grammar. One sought to reconcile language with logic and to reduce or eliminate linguistic anomalies that came to light through the philosophical logic of language. Although in the period of the Enlightenment a great number of newly discovered languages needed then to be learned and understood, Rationalism proved itself to be a secularized heir of the scholastics also in its treatment of the problematic of the human statement. It did this insofar as it subjected language to the criterion of human reason, followed a process of criticism and logical reasoning, and adhered to the principle that there is

---

25 Gottlieb Söhngen, *Philosophische Einübung in die Theologie: Erkennen, Wissen, Glauben* [Philosophical Training in Theology: Perceiving, Knowing, Believing] (Freiburg: Alber, 1955), 129.

finally only *one* reasonable grammar. Under this rule of logic, a human statement *qua* statement was understood one-sidedly as a statement about a given subject matter, but not in its various forms, as address, question, command, and so forth.

The special character of language could only be recognized once it had broken free of the dominating grip of logic and ontology. As is generally known, this breakthrough took place above all through the work of Herder and the study of the humanities [*Geisteswissenschaften*] in the Romantic period.[xii] The diversity of languages now came to be understood as the organic expression of the wholeness of humanity and of entire peoples, as the treasure house of their historical knowledge, as the unity of trans-individual and individual achievement, of the people's awareness and of their becoming aware. And the possibilities of having entirely different grammars began to appear. But there was still a long way to go—through one-sided and overreaching investigations in ethnology, physiology, psychology, the natural sciences, and so forth—until language as an objective means for forming a community and language as the act of speaking were clearly distinguished and until a systematization of statements was developed in light of their basic function in *conversation*.[26] Foundational here were the works by Ferdinand de Saussure,[27] who systematically distinguished between *le langage* [the general human ability to communicate], *la parole* [human speech], and *la langue* [the specific languages of human beings], and by Karl Bühler,[28] who developed a systematic conception of the three-fold execution of language as "proclamation, evocation, and representation" [*Kundgabe, Auslösung, und Darstellung*]. That then led to the identification of the "original phenomenon" [*Urphänomene*] in the construction of language: "If we take a sentence not only as the representation of a set of facts but also as a part of living conversation," then such a sentence must necessarily "fulfill three conditions in order to be meaningful: it must have the intended effect upon the hearer, it must truly represent the case as it is, and it must express what the speaker thought (B. Snell)."[29] These different and very important attempts at developing a morphology of language have a common, systematic starting point in the speech-act.

The speech-act is always concrete. It happens at a particular time in a particular place. It presupposes a specific speaker (a transmitter), a specific audience (a

---

26 See Hans Arens, *Sprachwissenschaft* [Linguistics] (Freiburg: Alber, 1955), 204 ff.

27 Ferdinand de Saussure, *Grundfragen der allgemeinen Sprachwissenschaft* (Berlin: de Gruyter, 1931). [Original: *Cours de linguistique générale*, ed. C. Bally and A. Sechehaye, with the collaboration of A. Riedlinger (Lausanne/Paris: Payot, 1916); ET: *Course in General Linguistics*, trans. W. Baskin (Glasgow: Fontana/Collins, 1977). –Ed.]

28 Karl Bühler, *Sprachtheorie* (Jena/Stuttgart: Gustav Fischer, 1934). [ET: *Theory of Language*, trans. Donald Fraser Goodwin (Amsterdam/Philadelphia: John Benjamins, 1990). –Ed.]

29 Bruno Snell, *Der Aufbau der Sprache* [The Construction of Language] (Hamburg: Claassen, 1952), 15.

receiver), and a specific set of facts to which it refers. All three of these elements—sender, receiver, and set of facts—change from one speech-act to another. The speech-act, however, also presupposes something else: in order that the one addressed understands the speaker both must speak the same language. What is more, the availability of a living language present in the consciousness of the members of a linguistic community is the precondition for every speech-act. In contrast to a given speech-act, which is always uniquely located in space and time, a language or linguistic system is something general and constant.[xiii]

The linguistic system has "no other justification for its existence than that it makes possible the speech-acts and it subsists only insofar as concrete speech-acts are related to it" (Fürst Trubetzkoy).[30] Here linguistics develops its own systematic method, which is clearly different from that of logic. Regarding the difference between the meaning of a word and a logical concept and regarding the similarities between linguistic and logical judgments, there are the important studies by Hans Lipps.[31] "*Attributing* [*Zuerkennen*] a characteristic in *judgment* [*Urteil*] is something different from *stating* something *predicatively* [*prädikativ aussagen*] as a characteristic."[xiv] "That on the basis of which something is *recognized* [*erkannt*] is different from that on the basis of which it is *named* [*angesprochen*] and recognized 'as something' [*als etwas*], namely, with regard to what it is 'uniquely' [*eigentlich*] 'in itself' [*an sich*], for example."[32] "With Kant a 'judgment' [*Urteil*] regarding a concrete *constitution* [*Konstitution*] of an object is either analytic or synthetic, but it is not a 'statement' [*Aussage*]."[33] Concepts and judgments in logic are not equivalent to concepts and judgments in language. To be sure, the concepts and judgments used in logic are operative in language, and yet making judgments in language and defining the meaning of words takes place in such actions whose distinctive features have not been understood by logic, and for which but little space has been allotted in the teaching about the modality of judgments.

Just as in linguistics, the psychology of thinking also had first to free itself from the domination of logic, for the psychological question about the process of thinking is different from the question about the inherently logical correctness of a thought. The psychological investigation of thinking thus results by and large in no advance by means of the well-known forms of logical syllogism, even if the results of the thought process are consistent with these

---

30 Nikolai Trubetzkoy, *Grundzüge der Phonologie* (Göttingen: Vandenhoeck & Ruprecht, 1939) [ET: *Principles of Phonology* (Berkeley: University of California Press, 1969) –Ed.], as quoted by Arens, *Sprachwissenschaft*, 488.

31 Hans Lipps, *Untersuchungen zu einer hermeneutischen Logik* [Investigations of Hermeneutical Logic] (Frankfurt a. Main: Klostermann, 1938); idem, *Die Verbindlichkeit der Sprache: Arbeiten zur Sprachphilosophie und Logik* [The Forthcoming Nature of Language: Studies in Linguistics and Logic] (Frankfurt a. Main: Klostermann, 1944).

32 Lipps, *Die Verbindlichkeit der Sprache*, 15.

33 Lipps, *Die Verbindlichkeit der Sprache*, 20 (footnote 16).

rules of logic. In fact, it happens that certain matters break into one's consciousness (for example, through intuitions that skip over the intermediate steps of logic), but whose logical correctness, though at once experienced as self-evident, is then explicated only subsequently by means of logical conclusions. The issue of the statement, moreover, is also different in psychology from what it is in linguistics. As surely as the statement is almost always at the same time an act of thinking, so surely does the thinking, which then expresses itself in a statement, neither necessarily nor exclusively occurs with concepts of words or by rules of sentence construction. As important as verbal ideas are, for instance, for thinking that is not expressing itself, and as indispensable as the statement is for the precise formulation of concepts that are thought and for the clarification of thinking in general, yet the problematic in the psychology of thinking still needs to be kept distinct from that of linguistics. The relationship between thinking and the subjective act of speaking and between thinking in general and an objective language is very complex and varies from person to person. In this connection, it is important that the way of framing the question in neither the psychology of thinking nor the psychology of language be limited to events in human consciousness. In addition to the psychology of consciousness, we must take into account the psychology of thinking and physiological interrelationships, and thereby the concrete psychosomatic totality of the person, which impacts his thinking and speaking.

After linguistics and the psychology of thinking had freed themselves from the clutches of logic, there followed in the second half of the nineteenth century the reverse attempt, namely, to derive empirically a system of logic from the laws of language and above all from psychologically established, regular patterns of thinking. Psychology's dethroning of logic from a normative social science to an empirical social science that deals with the rules of thinking was the reaction of Positivism against the dominate intellectual powers in the preceding history of Western thought. Over against this development it was the decisive achievement of Edmund Husserl[34] and his student Alexander Pfänder[35] to demonstrate most rigorously the unique distinctiveness of the issues in logic, psychology, and linguistics. The separation of these disciplines from one another led at the same time to a purification of traditional logic from its historical conditioning by the classical languages and to the possibility of a more systematic focus.[36]

Less dramatic and foundational than the conflict between the normative

---

34 Edmund Husserl, *Logische Untersuchungen*, vol. 1, 2d. ed. (Halle: Niemeyer, 1913). [ET: *Logical Investigations*, vol. 1, trans. J. N. Findlay (London/New York: Routledge, 1970). –Ed.]

35 Alexander Pfänder, "Logik," *Jahrbuch für Philosophie und phaenomenologische Forschung* 4 (1921), 139 ff.

36 For that, see Bruno von Freytag-Löringhoff, *Logik* (Stuttgart: Kohlhammer, 1955) and Joseph M. Bochenski, *Formale Logik* (Freiburg: Alber, 1956), 311 ff. [ET: *A History of Formal Logic*, trans. Ivo Thomas (South Bend: University of Notre Dame Press, 1961), 286 ff. –Ed.]

sciences (logic, epistemology, ontology, and aesthetics) and the natural and social sciences in how they treated the issue raised by the statement was the way in which the natural and social sciences differed in how they each framed the linguistic, philological, historical, ethnological, and sociological issues. And these issues are in part closely connected and overlapping. If we note that every statement is the subject of all these scholarly disciplines, it will of course become obvious that there is today not only no comprehensive theology of language but also no comprehensive philosophy of language, which summarizes and systematically sets forth the results and issues in the individual disciplines, which are specializing more and more and growing further and further apart from one another. To an even greater degree than philosophical anthropology, the philosophy of the statement presents itself today as a multiplicity of starting points that are rooted in the various perspectives of the natural and social sciences as well as in the individual disciplines of the normative sciences.

Under which of these perspectives has the problem of the statement been discussed in theological scholarship and especially within systematic theology? We must content ourselves here with a brief overview that will orient us.

a) Although the term *epistemology* [*Erkenntnistheorie*] gained acceptance only in the nineteenth century, the issue that it denotes is much older. In this respect it may be said that *the epistemological aspect* of theological statements has always been most thoroughly discussed in systematic theology. The whole history of dogmatics is full of discussions about revelation and reason, faith and knowing, faith and experience, word and Spirit, and so forth, and, as is generally known, the determination of these relationships has been most multifariously defined. For example, some have taught that faith contradicts knowledge, while others have held that faith makes knowing possible. As a result, in the problem area of epistemology the *special character* of the theological statement here, in contrast to other such statements elsewhere, has been most intensely studied.

b) In this connection *the logical aspect* of the theological statement has also been discussed in systematic theology, especially by medieval scholastics and Protestant theologians in the period of Protestant Orthodoxy. This applies above all to theological *concepts*, namely, the semantic issue of the relation between idea [*Vorstellung*], word, and thing. The ever changing history of the concept of analogy shows that in it the problem of the special character of the theological statement is thoroughly realized, especially regarding the possible application of human ideas and terms to God. Moreover, in the discussion of this issue more attention was given to nouns and adjectives than to verbs. On the other hand, the systematic discussion of theological *conclusions* played a far lesser role. The direct applicability of the basic syllogistic forms of logic to the theological statement was more convincing than the direct applicability of given concepts, which was being called into question by the problem of analogy. In recent Protestant theology the systematic discussion of the logical aspect of theological statements has stepped noticeably into the background, and in fact not only where one avoided this issue altogether by asserting that theological thinking is irrational. Thus, for example, the theological concept of paradox has never undergone an exact, logical clarification—neither by Kierkegaard nor by Heim, Tillich, or Barth.

    c) Since theology has always had to deal with texts written in foreign languages, it has always been confronted with *the linguistic aspect* of the theological statement. The systematic-theological discussion of this aspect, however, was hindered for centuries by the fact that theology, too, did not sufficiently distinguish between the problem of logic and the problem of linguistics in the theological statement, and thus the specifically linguistic problems in the theological statement remained concealed by the logical and epistemological discussion. So, for example, Thomas Aquinas understood "the names of God" quite generally to be the words by which God is designated.[37] Even in his discussion of his favorite name for God, "The One Who Is" [*der Seiende*],[38] Thomas ignores the divine self-declaration of the name of Yahweh through God's historical revelation, disregards God's will that people call upon God by means of this name, and the promise that God has given to those who call upon him by means of this revealed name. And Thomas can, conversely, use the Latin term *donum* [gift] in basically the same manner as the proper name of the Holy Spirit,[39] even though the Holy Spirit is not called "gift" [*Gabe*] as such, neither according to the biblical texts nor in the liturgy of the church, though he is certainly asked for as a gift. Just as the different linguistic functions of words in the statement (as description, address, and so forth) were concealed by the logical discussion of concepts, so too the different functions of sentences (as assurance, confession, petition, and so forth) were concealed by the discussion about judgments and syllogistic conclusions. When linguistics had freed itself from these con-straints in more recent times, the linguistic discussion of the theological statement generally understood itself as part of the general task of universal linguistics, just as after Schleiermacher theology was understood to be part of the humanities. Therefore justice was widely not done to the special character of the theological statement. But then, in the 1920s, when Ferdinand Ebner, Karl Heim, and Martin Buber[xv] and others discovered the special character of the *I-Thou* relationship and its significance for the theological statement, this important basic form of personal encounter was soon wrongly absolutized and placed in opposition to ontological statements. Otherwise, it is striking how limited a role the linguistic problems of the dogmatic statement play in

---

37 Thomas Aquinas, *Summa theologica* 1, question 13.
38 Aquinas, *Summa theologica* 1, question 13, article 11, *corpus and ad primum bis ad tertium* [the first answer through the third answer in the body of the article].
39 Aquinas, *Summa theologica* 1, question 38, article 2.

the dogmatic principles of all churches bodies in comparison to the problems of epistemology.

d) There has also, of course, always been *the historical aspect* of the theological statement, but it was obscured through the systematization of history, whether in an historical-philosophical or historical-theological way, and through the understanding of dogma as timelessly valid truth. The development of modern historical scholarship, however, broke open the tight grip that dogmatic theology had had until recently on the historical issue. Thus, in this polemical turn from the hegemony of dogmatic theology, the historical character of the theological statement (in respect to its presuppositions, the occasion for its development, its fronts, the conceptuality that it used, and so forth) was investigated, to begin with, in the framework of historical research. Yet given the usual methods used there, specifically, the historical principle of analogy,[40] the special character of the theological statement as response to God's revelation was in general not taken seriously enough. On the other hand, dogmatics at this time—insofar as it did not surrender its task altogether and give up developing and setting forth the doctrine that remains the same for the church throughout all time—did not give sufficient attention to the historical character of the dogmatic statement. In its quest for timelessly valid statements, dogmatics has in general made the problem of identity and validity in the multiplicity of historically time-bound statements—and in the changing of the historical fronts—too easy for itself.

e) The psychological and *anthropological aspect* stepped even further into the background, not only in systematic theology but also in historical theology. Of course the relationship between religious experience and theological statement had always been discussed time and again and the theological statement had been understood in part as a direct expression of experience. But then in the middle of the nineteenth century, there arose a specifically psychological research which, after initially focusing on a psychology of the senses, developed quickly as a psychology of thinking and feeling and then later beyond that as typological and psychosomatic research. But systematic theology either overlooked the significance of this development for the problem of the theological statement or noted it only insofar as it dealt with the psychology of the processes of *human consciousness* [*Bewußtsein*].[41] The psychological problem of the statement is, however, far

---

40 On the principle of analogy, see Ernst Troeltsch, "Historische und dogmatische Methode in der Theologie" (1898), *Gesammelte Schriften*, vol. 2 (Tübingen: J. C. B. Mohr [Paul Siebeck], 1913), 729 ff. [ET: "Historical and Dogmatic Method in Theology," *Religion in History*, trans. James Luther Adams and Walter F. Bense (Minneapolis: Fortress, 1991), 13 ff. –Ed.] [This footnote is identified as "39a" in the original text. The next one is identified as "39b." The final four footnotes here are thus numbered differently from the original numbering in the German edition. –Ed.]

41 See, for example, Karl Girgensohn, *Der seelische Aufbau des religiösen Erlebens* [The Psycho-

more comprehensive, since it is rooted in the psychosomatic wholeness of the person, that is, in the very multifarious concrete conditions of human knowing and speaking in the basic forms of the self-object relationship, of the fulfillment of existence, and so forth. In theology's restriction solely to human self-*understanding* in relation to the psychosomatic wholeness of the person and in theology's misguided aim to formulate an *unchanging* image of the human being through all the changes of history in relation to all the multifarious ways in which the human being is constituted, theology has almost completely overlooked their significance for the problem raised by the theological statement and its interpretation.

f) Also the important results of research into the history of literary genres and the history of traditions and into the sociological perspectives that are implied in the question about the *life setting* [*Sitz im Leben*] of these forms and traditions, still need to be developed systematically in terms of their *sociological aspect*. This systematic exposition should aim for a comprehensive definition of the different sociological functions which precisely dogmatic statements exercise within the different churches.

g) All these aspects are significant for clarifying the questions which are raised by the dangerous wavering of Christendom between ontological and up-to-date-existentialistic statements. What are the statements that the self-revealing God calls us to make in response?

In any case, this brief, critical overview has confirmed the following: Just as there is today no comprehensive philosophy of language, so we lack a comprehensive theological treatment of the issue of understanding the statement that would systematically bring together the fruitful results and investigations of this issue by the various disciplines and critically examine them. But when the theological statement was being discussed in the context of theological research under only individual aspects—for example, the linguistic, psychological, or sociological aspects—it is striking how this was commonly undertaken as a matter of course on the basis of presuppositions of the aforementioned non-theological disciplines: the theological statement was treated within the general phenomenon of language and speaking, of feeling, willing, and thinking, of social relationships, and so forth. Now the theological statement occurs, to be sure, within all of these phenomena, but its basis is different from that of all other statements in that it is a response to God's revelation. Because the theological statement occurs in response to God's revelation, the latter has transforming effects on thinking, on speaking, on historical decision, on social relationships—in short, it transforms all these contexts and aspects in which each and every statement is to be investigated. The special character of the theological statement consists not only in the special way in which it is grounded in revelation but also in its special

---

logical Structure of Religious Experience], 2d. ed. (Gütersloh: Bertelsmann, 1930). [This is footnote "39b" in the original text. –Ed.]

structure as a response to this revelation. The theological statement thus raises a *special* problem not only in the framework of epistemological and ontological issues but also in the framework of logic and the natural and social sciences. In the course of history-of-religion research on biblical texts the far-reaching transformation of concepts has indeed become increasingly evident, which the message of revelation brought about with the use of non-biblical language. And the same holds true for the use of non-biblical concepts in the history of dogma. Basically, however, the same problem exists with all the individual scholarly disciplines in which the theological statement is to be discussed. And in this respect those historical and philological findings concerning the theological conceptualization have not been fully and systematically examined. In other words, they have not been made fruitful for dealing with the issue of the theological statement in the perspectives of the other disciplines.

Still less do we find a comprehensive attempt that undertakes to go beyond a systematic discussion of the issue of the theological statement in relation to the issue of the statement in general (that is, not only that of the theological statement) in the light of revelation. The initial approaches toward a systematic-theological treatment of the linguistic statement in general were available in Luther's statements on grammar and logic as well as in Hamann's and in turn in Ferdinand Ebner's use of the philosophy of language to understand the person being addressed by means of God's word. Hamann thus developed a *"philologia crucis"* [philology of the cross] on the basis of a *theologia crucis* [theology of the cross].[42] But these initial attempts have found no further development in the vast issue of understanding the statement in our time. As a rule, the issue of understanding the statement in general is not treated in light of the gospel; rather, the gospel is treated as one specific issue within the general issue of understanding the statement, similar to how the contemporary encyclopedic ordering of the sciences in general is not developed on the basis of the knowledge of revelation but instead theology is located in the humanities within the overall academic structure of all the scholarly disciplines, the arts and the sciences.

This critical overview is intended to place both of the basic structures which we have examined in sections I and II above within the larger context of the issue of understanding the theological statement. It should now be clear that not only the whole issue of the dogmatic statement but also the special issue of its formal *structure* is more complex than can be comprehended completely, on the one hand by the basic pronominal form of the theological statement or, on the other hand, by the basic form of anthropological perceiving. In addition, there is a plethora of other issues relating to the structure which are

---

42 See Walter Leibrecht, "Philologia crucis: Johann Georg Hamanns Gedanken über die Sprache Gottes" [Philology of the Cross: Johann Georg Hamanns Thoughts about the Language of God], *Kerygma und Dogma* 1 (1955), 226–42. [This is footnote "40" in the original text. –Ed.]

conditioned by differences in language, experience, inherited worldviews, social and ethical factors in one's world, and so forth. Thorleif Boman, for instance, in his comparison of Greek and Hebrew thinking, has identified differing structures, not only of thinking but also in the function of the word, the type of description, the use of numbers, as also in conceptions of space and time. He then connected these differences to fundamental differences between the Greek and Hebrew modes of existence in terms of hearing and seeing.[43] The structures of religious, philosophical, and ideological [weltanschaulichen] ideas, as well as those of time and space are the result of numerous historical, psychological, linguistic, and other factors that overlap one another. By contrast, the two types of basic forms that have been discussed above in sections I and II are *fundamental*. Although they are hardly ever addressed in discussions of the general issue of the dogmatic statement, they are especially important since they embrace the linguistic, historical, and other issues in a particular way: the basic anthropological forms of perceiving provide the concrete, natural presupposition of the decision that is implied in every statement—and the basic forms of theological statement provide the valid form in which all speaking of God is placed into obedient service.

IV. The Dogmatic Statement in the Mutual Interaction of the Theological and Anthropological Basic Forms

If we abbreviate the pronominal basic forms of the theological statement as theological basic forms and the anthropological basic forms of perceiving as anthropological basic forms, then we must ask how both of these basic forms relate to one another? How do they affect one another?

The structural problems of doctrine, which, on the one hand, arise from the basic forms of the theological statement and, on the other, from the basic anthropological forms of experiencing reality, are of a very different order. The latter forms are givens before the gospel encounters individuals, while the former are awakened and called for by this encounter. The latter exist case by case in the concrete structural constitution of the *various* human beings; no individual human being lives in all these basic anthropological forms at the same time. By contrast, the basic forms of the theological statement belong essentially together in the response of *each* individual human being. But despite all the differences of the spiritual gifts it is certain that every believer owes God the response of confession, prayer, and bearing witness and thus participates also in the worship and the teaching. While both of the basic

---

43 Thorleif Boman, *Das hebräische Denken im Vergleich mit dem griechischen* (Göttingen: Vandenhoeck & Ruprecht, 1952). [ET of the 2d. German edition (1954): *Hebrew Thought Compared with Greek*, trans. Jules L. Moreau (London: SCM, 1960). –Ed.] [This is footnote "41" in the original German text. –Ed.]

forms—the theological and the anthropological—contain the starting points for constructing systems, behind which individuals barricade and secure themselves against the fullness of God's act of salvation, the anthropological basic forms do this by nature. In each instance, they must first be broken open by the power of the gospel, which awakens faith. The theological basic forms, however, presuppose the gospel and faith; here distortions of a system develop only when one of the individual basic forms of response is overemphasized or even isolated, claiming a priority or domination over the others. The response of the believer is thus endangered in various ways by the theological and anthropological basic forms: by theological one-sidedness, on the one hand, and by anthropological self-assertion, on the other. The reciprocal influence of each of the basic forms on the other can now be outlined as follows:

a) When a given basic form of theological statement is singled out from the other basic forms, assimilates the other basic forms into itself, and controls the full expression of the others, there is the possibility that the corresponding basic anthropological forms might assert themselves over against the revelation and dominate the theological statements. Every basic form of theological statement, if isolated and allowed to dominate the others, is transformed into a rigid scheme, which ultimately can be managed as well without faith. Both the objectivism of a theological thinking and speaking that derives primarily from the structure of doxology and the subjectivism of a theological thinking that derives primarily from the structure of God's assurance are facing opposite one another similar to philosophical systems in which corresponding anthropological basic forms have found their self-justification; for, after all, each of the basic anthropological forms contains the starting point for very distinct religious, ideological, and philosophical patterns or even systems. The differences among the anthropological basic forms intensify cases of one-sidedness which arise in the structural shifts of doctrine.

b) Where the response of faith, however, is heard in its substantive abundance—and that at the same time always means in mutual interaction with all of the basic forms of the theological statement—there the anthropological differences and even the different basic forms of perceiving will be specifically opened up to one another in characteristic ways. Where God is simultaneously addressed as *Thou* and proclaimed as *He*, where God's deeds are simultaneously taught and God himself is worshipped, where human beings are simultaneously addressed as *Thou* and yet pray as *I* and *We*, where they bear witness and offer up their worship as a sacrifice of praise—there the rigid schemata of an objectivism or a subjectivism, of an actuality [*Aktualismus*] or an ontology, but also the sacrosanct schema of the *I-Thou* relationship and all other corresponding systems are broken through. The overcoming of the hardening of one's heart by means of the gospel finds its confirmation and its continuation in the mutual interaction of the basic forms of the response of faith. In this action of the theological statement, completely unfolded in all of its forms, the people will be opened up to one another and, without ceasing to exist in their particular historical uniqueness, they will be opened up for existence in the fellowship of knowing and confessing, of praying and witnessing, of worshiping and teaching.[xvi] What takes place when the full range of faith responses thus becomes heard, is the Pentecost break-through of the barriers of languages, of the modes of thinking, and of historical traditions—the deliverance from the prison that the concrete creaturely shape of human existence has become through the self-crippling power of sin.

c) The basic forms of the theological statement are thus of deeper and more consequential significance for the problems raised by dogmatic statements than the basic anthropological forms of perceiving.

V. The Issue of the Unity of Dogmatic Statements

We began with the experience that in ecumenical meetings of separated Christians common statements in prayer and witness are widely able to be made, while common dogmatic statements about the corresponding content appear impossible. We have refrained from discussing other similar experiences, for example, that in ecumenical meetings it is easier to undertake joint biblical exegesis than it is to formulate common principles of scriptural interpretation. Instead we have restricted ourselves to this question: What happens when statements of prayer and witness are transposed into the form of the dogmatic statement? The investigation of the basic forms of the theological statement in their relationship to one another has shown that each of the basic forms is connected with particular substantive tasks. The transpositions of a statement from one basic form into another, and expansions of a basic form by inclusion of another, thus have substantive consequences. As a result not only formal changes but also substantive ones take place, which through the basic anthropological forms of perceiving are still further reinforced. It thus became clear that the investigation of the basic forms of the theological statement is not merely of phenomenological interest. The concern here is not merely for an accurate description of the ways in which faith responds, but rather for the theological recognition of the full range of the response of faith that God *commands*. This also applies in another way to the investigation of the basic forms of human perceiving. Here too the concern is not merely a descriptive one but involves the acknowledgment of the will of God, who expects every individual to give a complete response of faith and to do so from within one's concrete, creaturely conditions. We thus came to the conclusion that the issue relating to the structure of the dogmatic statement is at the same time an eminently substantive issue in dogmatics.

In view of the special difficulties that the separated churches face in their struggle for unity as a result of their distinct and mutually opposing dogmatic statements, some think it advisable that we should first of all try to reach agreement in matters of common ethical action (life and work) in Christendom and, while doing so, eliminate dogmatic questions or even declare that agreement about dogmatic statements is basically unnecessary for unity *in Christo*. From this point of view, dogma is the chief troublemaker for unity, while unity in prayer, witness, and responsible action seems easy to achieve. We must not overlook that this type of attitude in the ecumenical movement— despite serious work on the questions of doctrine, worship, and ministerial office (faith and order)—has repeatedly threatened to gain dominance, especially in North America, as well as in the "younger churches." Nevertheless, this conception is based on a fundamental error. The root of dogma is confession. But where the unity of the church is, there this unity, by its very nature, will also necessarily be voiced in the unity of confession. If the church were to offer the response of faith only in prayer and witness, without confession, its response would be incomplete. The downplaying of dogmatic statements in ecumenical work is thus basically impossible. Moreover, such an undogmatic and anti-dogmatic union of the church would break down, not only in the opposition of those churches that are bound to dogmas but also in that, upon closer inspection, even those Christian fellowships that are hostile to dogma in fact have quasi-dogmatic principles, which—though not formulated as dogma—nevertheless operate in effect divisively among the churches. Similarly, those who reject tradition in principle cannot escape the fact that they exist within the tradition of their own Christian fellowship and speak and act on the basis of their being bound to it.

Instead of downplaying dogmatic differences we must take these differences seriously and strive for unity in dogmatic statements, which is essential for the unity of the church, and to do so through new ways of framing the issues and new methods for addressing them. But what does this mean, namely, "unity in dogmatic statements"? It is widely taken as self-evident that this unity consists in the unity of the same formulation which has been accepted by all believers. Nevertheless, the premise of uniformity in dogmatic statements and for the enforcement of the same creedal formulas within the worldwide church is rather relatively late in origin. During the first centuries a variety of local creeds existed next to one another, and their unity consisted in the reciprocal acknowledgment by one local church of the creedal statement of another—but not in the expulsion of the others' creeds and the replacement of one's own. The fact that the unity of dogma does not necessarily consist in the unity of the dogmatic formula is not entirely forgotten—even after the enforcement of the same dogmatic formulas by the Roman Empire in all of the regions of the church. The medieval Roman Church in its ecumenical negotiations with the Eastern Church thus required that it acknowledge the *filioque*[xvii] without, however, requiring the reception of that formula into the Eastern Church's text of the Niceno-Constantinopolitan Creed. In basically the same way, in our time, the churches of the Augsburg Confession that are united in the Lutheran World Federation required that the Church of Batak in Sumatra acknowledge the Lutheran Confessions as a condition for church fellowship without, however, requiring their complete reception, and in turn the churches in the Lutheran World Federation acknowledged the confessional statements of the Batak Church.[xviii] We need not here explain the merits of uniform dogmatic statements nor the dangers—which, it needs to be said, consist above all in the fact that unity in formula pushes aside the confessions which the local churches are to develop in their unique historical situation, and thus the reception of uniform dogma weakens the existential, substantive decisions of the local churches and replaces them with a formal act of submission. We are concerned here only with this basic assertion: Unity in dogmatic statements need not consist in the common acceptance of one and the same formula, but can also consist in the fellowship that gives mutual acknowledgment to different dogmatic formulas. Even the unity of the New Testament canon encompasses different witnesses to Jesus Christ, and the one gospel in it is transmitted in the form of four "Gospels."

With this understanding of unity as a fellowship of reciprocal acknowledgment, the problem of ascertaining and expressing dogmatic unity becomes of course much more complicated than when unity is understood as uniformity. Uniform formulas are relatively easy to deal with, but unity that is based on reciprocal acknowledgment is something that must to a greater degree be sought, researched, and discovered. Uniformity in dogmatic statements requires only a "Yes" or a "No." But unity through reciprocal acknowledgment raises the question: In which of the various dogmatic statements can unity in dogma be recognized and acknowledged? Answering this question can only be undertaken through a comprehensive ecumenical dogmatics.[xix] Here we can offer only a few brief remarks on method.

a) In order to recognize unity in the various dogmatic statements it is indispensable to undertake a careful philological investigation, particularly a careful analysis of the concepts which are used, both in connection with their previous non-theological use and with regard to their substantive and linguistic definition by the biblical witness. Unity in dogmatic statements can be hidden by differences in terminology, as may be seen, for example, in the historical development of trinitarian dogma in the ancient church. In that historical development, the Greek term ὑπόστασις [*hypostasis*], when translated as *substantia*, must have given the appearance of tritheism, and, on the other hand, the Latin term *persona*, when translated as πρόσωπον [*prosopon*], must have given the appearance of modalism.

b) It is further indispensable to undertake a careful historical investigation, particularly with respect to the historical presuppositions and historical fronts in which the dogmatic statements were made on the basis of the biblical witness over against specific errors and other threats at that time. Unity in dogmatic statements can be hidden by differing or even seemingly contradictory statements, which had been formulated over against mutually opposite fronts, as may be seen, for example, in the emphasis placed by the Eastern Church on human freedom in view of the threat posed by a Gnostic-naturalistic understanding of human beings, on the one hand, and in statements by the Western Church about the *servum arbitrium* [the enslaved human will] in view of the threat posed by a Christian understanding of human beings that emphasizes an ethic of voluntarist activism.

c) But we cannot just stop with philological and historical analysis, two methodological perspectives that have become self-evident today. It is also necessary to consider the anthropological presuppositions which existed in the respective region and which have influenced dogmatic statements. So, for example, some people apprehend and process their world primarily by *seeing* and others by *hearing*, and this difference also affects dogmatic statements and can have far-reaching consequences for Christology and anthropology, for doctrine about worship, and for determining the relationship between word and sacrament. Here, too, the unity of dogmatic statements can be hidden under various dogmatic statements which confess the mighty deeds of God through the various basic structures of human knowing and being.

d) Beyond that, we must consider the place which the different dogmatic statements, in view of their structure, assume within the basic forms of the theological statement. The root of dogma is, to be sure, confession, in which all of the basic forms of faith response are concentrated. But in the course of history dogmatic statements have in many ways departed from this root and have undergone significant structural changes in adjusting to other basic forms. Not all of these structural changes necessarily needs to be rejected, but one must clearly see that these changes have substantive effects and that some of the issues in dogmatics have only first come about through such changes. The unity of dogmatic statements can thus be hidden among various dogmatic formulations insofar as they are made in the different basic forms of the theological statement. Thus, for example, the statement *simul peccator iustus* [at the same time sinner and righteous] is actually found throughout the whole of Christendom, also within the Roman Church, as a statement of existential confession of sin and faith. But this same statement must appear as a denial of re-creating grace, particularly of the re-birth in baptism, to the person who misunderstands it as an ontological-metaphysical definition of Christian existence.

e) Indispensable, finally, is the investigation of the *actual* validity which the differing dogmatic statements have had and currently have in the respective regions of the church and among the confessional churches. The unity of the church can be hidden under differing dogmatic statements whose validity is variously understood in the respective churches. For example, they could be understood as the present norm for every pronouncement of the church, or as an exemplary sign of the church's past, or even simply as a banner of the fellowship, whose significance is sociological but is no longer substantively defined. Depending on the type of validity, there can be unity in the actual confessing and teaching of the separated churches, despite differing dogmatic statements, but the reverse can also be true: unity can also be lacking among churches which otherwise agree on the same dogmatic statements.

In view of these remarks it is clear that the answer to the question about the unity of dogmatic statements requires a more comprehensive scholarly effort than has been spent in ecumenical dialogues up to the present time. Here it is that all the issues in biblical hermeneutics break open since dogmatic statements must be interpreted in light of each of the given perspectives of the apostolic message and be evaluated by it. It is the permanent basis of every church pronouncement, indeed both as the permanently foundational and substantive statement and as the permanently exemplary and mandatory act of proclamation in the church's advance into the world. But added to the problems of biblical hermeneutics are the special problems of dogmatic hermeneutics. In both cases it is insufficient to take into consideration the self-understanding with which we approach the statements that are to be interpreted; still less is it legitimate to make a generalization out of a specific self-understanding and apply it as a critical norm in the interpretation of texts. To be sure, given that all understanding occurs within a hermeneutical circle that includes the word that is encountered and the person who hears it, the effort to recognize and understand the unity in statements must proceed with knowing about the differences in human self-understanding—yet not only their differences in *understanding*, but also their differences in the human beings as concrete *entities* [*Ganzheiten*]; and thus that effort must also proceed in knowing about differences in the concrete basic forms in which human beings perceive and make statements, without their being aware of these forms. The problems of biblical and dogmatic hermeneutics are still today viewed too simply.

Nevertheless, the question about discerning unity in the different dogmatic statements is not only more difficult but also more promising than it is commonly adjudged. So let us begin our investigation of the dogmatic statements of the separated churches not merely by using philological and historical methods, but also through morphological methods, which means, above all, by investigating these statements in relation to the whole cosmos of faith statements found within these churches. Then we will discover a greater level of agreement than might be expected from consideration of individual dogmatic statements themselves in isolation. But we will make the same discoveries in completely different places in the life of the church and in completely different basic forms of theological statement from those in our own church and from there from what we expected to find in other churches. Consequently, it will become clear that some dogmatic statements were not originally and essentially statements of doctrine, but are statements of prayer and proclamation that were transposed into statements of doctrine and, as such, must be interpreted anew. Likewise, it will become clear which dogmatic statements in the original sense correspond to the form and task of teaching.

But if thus, by means of the various dogmatic statements throughout the separated churches, the riches of the statements begin to become transparent—the fullness which God has disclosed to believers through his revelation in Christ—then the vision of the unity and fullness of the church will be opened up, and dogma, in its original form of confession, in which all the statements are concentrated, begins to shine anew.

Editor's Notes

[i] This essay was initially published as "Die Struktur der dogmatischen Aussage als ökumenisches Problem," *Kerygma und Dogma* 3, no. 4 (1957), 251–306. The essay appears in KC 1.24–79. An English translation by G. Overlach and D. B. Simmonds appears in CC (16–84) as "The Structure of Dogmatic Statements as an Ecumenical Problem."

[ii] Schlink's use of the informal second person pronoun (*Du* and *Ihr*) will be translated throughout this essay as "Thou," since he is using the term in a way that explicitly links to Martin Buber's understanding of the *I-Thou* relationship. Cf. Martin Buber, *Ich und Du* (Leipzig: Insel Verlag, 1923); ET: *I and Thou*, trans. Ronald Gregor Smith (Edinburgh: T&T Clark, 1937).

[iii] The German term translated here as *confession* or *confession of faith* is *Bekenntnis*. It will normally be translated as *confession*, unless it is clear that Schlink meant it in the sense of *profession*, *creed*, or *statement of faith*.

[iv] "The Definition" from the Chalcedonian Creed (22 October 451), Denzinger 301 (cf. Tanner 1.86).

[v] The Pseudo-Athanasian Profession *Quicumque* (ca. 5th c.), Denzinger 75–76.

[vi] This confession, authored principally by Philip Melanchthon (1497–1560), was read aloud to the emperor on 25 June 1530. The Apology to the Augsburg Confession (1531) was prepared by Melanchthon as a defense of those articles that had been criticized in the Roman Catholic Confutation (of the AC), which had been read before the emperor on 3 August 1530.

[vii] Cf. FC SD title: "A General, Clear, Correct, and Definitive Repetition and Explanation of Certain Articles of the Augsburg Confession" (BC 524).

[viii] In 347 Cyril of Jerusalem (c. 315–386) delivered twenty-four catechetical lectures to catechumens preparing for baptism. His instructions provide a detailed description of the preparation for baptism in fourth-century Palestine.

[ix] That is, "a theology of sojourners," in contrast to "a theology of know-it-alls."

[x] That is, "a theology that is a copy of the original," in contrast to "a theology of the original itself."

[xi] With his use of the technical term *Denkpsychologie* ["psychology of thinking"], Schlink is here referring to the ground-breaking work of Oswald Külpe (1862–1915) and the so-called Würzburger School of structuralist psychology, which did experimental work on the mental processes involved in thinking.

[xii] Cf., e.g., Johann Herder [1744–1803], *Philosophical Writings*, ed. Desmond M. Clarke and Michael N. Forster (Cambridge University Press, 2007).

[xiii] Schlink provided the source and bibliographic information for this quote in his next footnote. The quote is from Nikolai Trubetzkoy, *Grundzüge der Phonologie* (Göttingen: Vandenhoeck & Ruprecht, 1939), 5.

[xiv] Schlink provided the source and bibliographic information for this sentence in his next footnote.

[xv] The Austrian philosopher Ferdinand Ebner (1882–1931), the German Lutheran theologian Karl Heim (1874–1958), and the Jewish philosopher Martin Buber (1878–1965) made

significant use of the *I-Thou* relationship, both in terms of the relationship between God and human beings and between human beings themselves.

[xvi]   Schlink's phrase here is *Erkennens und Bekennens, Betens und Bezeugens, Anbetens und Lehrens*. It may be no accident that the first term in each pairing is oriented toward God, while the second term refers to actions in relation to the world and the church.

[xvii]   The Latin word *filioque* ("and the Son") was added by the Western Catholic Church (at the Third Council of Toledo in 589) to the Niceno-Constantinopolitan Creed to express the double procession of the Spirit "from the Father and the Son." The addition of this dogmatic formula to the original creed was one of the major factors in the schism between the Eastern Church and the Western Church.

[xviii]   The Protestant Christian Batak Church in Indonesia (mainly northern Sumatra), which was formed in 1930, joined the Lutheran World Federation in 1952. A year earlier this church body had adopted a statement of faith, which drew upon Scripture, Luther's Small Catechism, and the Augsburg Confession. This statement, the first to be drawn up by an autonomous church that originated in the modern missionary movement, was accepted by the LWF in lieu of the Augsburg Confession.

[xix]   Schlink himself undertook this task, the outcome of which is his 800-page *Ökumenische Dogmatik*, published in 1983 (the year before his death). The translation of this work is the second volume in the American Edition of Schlink's writings.

Part Two: Aspects of the Dogmatic Foundation

Chapter Three:
The Christology of Chalcedon in Ecumenical Dialogue[1]

When in 1054 Pope Leo IX excommunicated the patriarch of Constantinople, Michael Caerularius,[i] and the separation between Eastern and Western Christendom thus became permanent—despite all further attempts at union—not in dispute was the common recognition of the Christological decision of Chalcedon. The same holds true for the separation between the Roman Church and the Reformation churches in the sixteenth century. When the pope excommunicated Luther and his adherents and the latter took steps to re-order the evangelical-Lutheran churches, not in dispute was the acknowledgment of the Christology of Chalcedon. Despite the well-known differences about Christology among Luther, Calvin, Zwingli, and Brenz, their common determination to uphold the Christology of Chalcedon, together with Rome and Byzantium, cannot be disregarded. This determination has found clear expression in the confessional writings of the Reformation. In this respect, not only the three so-called ecumenical creeds (the Apostles' Creed, the Niceno-Constantinopolitan Creed, and the Athanasian Creed) but also the Chalcedonian Definition deserve to be regarded as an ecumenical symbol— indeed, it has more justification to be so regarded than the Apostles' and Athanasian Creeds, which are not authoritative for the Eastern Church.

It is thus all the more serious that it was not possible for the World Council of Churches officially to accept the Christological statements of the Chalcedonian Definition, together with the Nicene or Niceno-Constantino-politan Creed, as a common basis for the assembled churches. The reasons lie in part with those younger member churches of the World Council of Churches, for whom the dogmatic decisions of the ancient church are

---

1 This paper was presented to the task force on "Christ and the Church" in the context of the World Council of Church's Commission on Faith and Order (Oxford, 1956). [The paper was first published in French as "La Christologie de Chalcedoine dans le dialogue oecuménique," *Verbum Caro* 12, no. 45 (1958), 23–30. The German version, "Die Christologie von Chalcedon im öku-menischen Gespräch" was published in *Bekenntnis zur Kirche: Festschrift für Ernst Sommerlath zum 70. Geburtstag* (Confession of the Church: Commemorative Book for Ernst Sommerlath on the Occasion of His 70th Birthday), ed. H. Amberg (Berlin: Evangelische Verlagsanstalt, 1959), 213–19. This same essay appears in KC 1.80–87. An English translation by Roy Harrisville was published as "The Christology of Chalcedon in Ecumenical Discussion," *Dialog* 2 (1963), 134–38. Another English translation, by G. Overlach and D. B. Simmonds, appears in CC (87–95) as "The Christology of Chalcedon in Ecumenical Discussion." –Ed.]

unknown because—skipping over church traditions—they want to let themselves be guided by the direct encounter with the word of Scripture and by the present working of the Holy Spirit. But also in such churches as the Lutheran and the Reformed, in which the decisions of the ancient church were expressly affirmed, these decisions did not remain undisputed. Ever since the Age of the Enlightenment, opposition arose, for one thing, against the interpretations of the Chalcedonian Definition that came up after 451, particularly against the doctrine of the *anhypostasis* of the human nature of Jesus, against the doctrine of the two wills of Jesus Christ, and against the *communicatio idiomatum* [communication of attributes], which implied that the human nature of Jesus Christ was in possession of divine attributes.[ii] In this further development of the Chalcedonian Definition, some feared that Jesus Christ, the human being, would be lost. But going beyond that, modern neo-Protestantism directed its opposition against statements of the Chalcedonian Definition itself, particularly against the concept of nature used there, which seemed to call into question the historical Jesus—all the more so, when some tried to clarify Jesus' historical activity by means of a theoretical application of the doctrine of the two natures, for example, when his miracles were explained as actions of his divine nature and his hungering, thirsting, suffering, and dying were explained as actions of his human nature. The unity of the historical Christ seemed to disintegrate here. So, among other objections, which will not be considered here, the relationship between the ontological (Harnack: "physical" [*physikalischen*]) and the historical statements in Christology moved into the center of the discussions about the Chalcedonian Definition. They thereby display the characteristic nineteenth- and twentieth-century tendency altogether to eliminate the ontological statements and to restrict themselves to the historical ones. But this tendency, if carried out to its conclusion, would mean the complete abandonment of the Chalcedonian Definition.

For ecumenical work to progress, it is of decisive importance that the churches do not split up into those that adhere to the Chalcedonian Definition and those that can find no use for it, but that together they seek a new interpretation and appropriation of the Christology of the ancient church in the changed intellectual situation of our time. This is necessary not only because large and important churches adhere to the Chalcedonian Christology as the *condition sine qua non* for any unification of the church but also because a rejection of the Chalcedonian Definition, upon closer inspection, inevitably implies a rejection of essential biblical statements or, at the very least, an abridgment of the response of faith to the biblical witness. Hence in what follows, we identify a few considerations that are important for a fresh interpretation and appropriation of the ancient church's Christology, particularly for the clarification of the relationship between historical and ontological statements in Christology.

I. Over against the objection that the so-called Chalcedonian doctrine of the two natures presents the historical Christ in ontological, metaphysical, "physical" concepts, we should not overlook the fact that, among the various responses that faith gives to the message of God's act of salvation, a specific response also comes to voice in the New Testament writings and even in the Old, a response that has a clear affinity to ontological statements. It is the doxology, as it necessarily comes to voice from time immemorial in the worship assembly, along with petitionary prayer, proclamation, and teaching. But in turn, all these responses of faith, including doxology, are remarkably centered in the confession. Doxology is grounded in God's historical act of salvation, but it is not content with merely praising this act of salvation. Rather, it praises God himself as the one who is the same from and to all eternity. God is not engrossed wholly and solely in his act of salvation for us, for his church, for the world, but it is in the freedom of the one who is the same forever and ever that he has accomplished the act of salvation; and he wants not merely his act to be praised but he himself to be praised. Like petitionary prayer, doxology is not directed to people, but to God. But in contrast to prayer, doxology does not address God as *Thou* but rather acknowledges him as *He*, who is the same from and to all eternity. Nor is God entreated in doxology for what he should do but is rather praised for who he is in his eternal glory, holiness, might, power, and wisdom. So one repeatedly finds statements about God's being and essence in biblical doxologies (see, for example, Rom. 9.5; Rev. 4.8 and 7.12).

Dogmatic statements from the ancient church are to a particularly high degree determined by the structure of doxology, for they are determined by the structure of *homologia* [confession][iii] in the liturgy, in which the doxological element is unmistakable. The *homologia* is not directed primarily to the world, but to God. It is offered up to God as the sacrifice of praise by the church. The dogmatic decisions at the councils of Nicaea and Constantinople are thus intentionally liturgical statements of confession. Although the Christological decision of Chalcedon was itself not formulated as a liturgical confession nor was it used in that way, it is nevertheless most closely related to the liturgical *homologia*. It wants to serve this *homologia*, and it still bears the unmistakable traces of hymnic-doxological language.

II. But once the nature of doxology has been recognized, it is not surprising that the ancient church appropriated ontological concepts of Greek metaphysics for the formulation, unfolding, and interpretation of doxology. For one thing, the doxological statements about God's being, essence, and attributes were, by the very nature of the case, a point of connection. Furthermore, doxology had to find its voice in the historical setting of Hellenism, in its language, and in its conceptuality, and it had to be interpreted for this Hellenistic world. But this need in no way imply a domination by alien factors or syncretism. On the contrary, it can be precisely shown that concepts from Greek philosophy employed in the dogmas of the ancient church underwent profound correction, disruption, and transformation, and that here the paramount concepts of pagan thought were eloquently employed in service to the witness of faith—that therefore the missionary advance of the Apostle Paul into the Greek world continued in the ancient church's history of dogma.

III. The development of Christology in the ancient church, which occurred in the controversy with Adoptionism and Arianism, led first to dogmatic statements about the divinity of Jesus Christ in distinction from all created things. The Christological statements of the Nicene Creed—particularly "God from God, Light from Light, true God from true God, begotten, not made"— clearly have a hymnic-doxological character, and it is in relation to this structural framework that the ontological-conceptual formulation "who is from the being (substance) of the Father" and "*homoousios*" [of the same being], should be understood.[iv]

IV. The Christological dogma of Chalcedon appropriated these statements of the Nicene Creed and for the concept of *ousia* (*substantia*) used at the same time that of *physis* (*natura*).[v] This concept is also to be understood in the framework of the ontological structure of doxology. Beyond the dogmatic decision of Nicaea and Constantinople, dogmatic statements about the humanity of Jesus were now added in the controversies with Monophysitism and Nestorianism, and in fact these statements employed the very same terms *perfect* [*vollkommen*], *true* [*wahrhaftig*], *equal in essence* [*wesensgleich*], and *nature* [*Natur*] that praise the divinity of Jesus Christ. The humanity of Jesus Christ is thus included in our praise and worship. This is indeed most appropriate, since the dogmatic statements of Chalcedon aim after all to teach how the *homologia* should be offered up to Jesus Christ in the fellowship of the church. The Lord to whom it is offered is the exalted Christ, who in his resurrection has not ceased to be truly human and thus our brother. As the exalted Christ he remains true God and truly human to all eternity.

V. Doxological statements are grounded on God's historical act of salvation. They have history as their presupposition, though as a rule not as their content. The prayers of thanksgiving have as their content the mighty deeds of God, but the content of the prayers of adoration is God himself in his divinity and lordship over history and in his unchanging selfhood. In a characteristic way, then, doxological statements are ultimate statements, in that while they proceed from God's act of salvation in history and are impossible apart from this presupposition, they do not however necessarily refer to it. So it cannot be surprising that the history of Jesus Christ—his preaching and his miracles, right up to his death on the cross, and then in turn his resurrection, ascension, and Parousia—are not mentioned in the Chalcedonian Definition, with of course the exception of the incarnation, and thus the origin of the God-*man*, who is confessed by the church.

VI. Although the Christological statements of Chalcedon do not mention the history of Jesus Christ (with the exception of his birth), they do not stand unrelated next to the historical tradition of Jesus' preaching and miracles and his way through suffering to glory. Rather, they give a response that is appropriate to it. The Chalcedonian Definition is the adequate response to the mystery of the vicarious representative action [*Stellvertretung*] which God has accomplished for our salvation in the totality of the historical action and passion of Jesus Christ. God's Son became a human being so that we human beings could become God's children. The righteous one took upon himself our sins so that we who are sinners could become righteous. He who is the divine life died on the cross so that we who are dead could become alive, and so on. The Chalcedonian Definition is the doxological response to God's act of redemption which was accomplished in the course of the historical life of Jesus Christ as the vicarious mission of the Son of God. Were Jesus Christ not praised as truly God and truly human, he would also not be acknowledged as our vicarious representative, and our redemption would not be accomplished. The presupposition of the Chalcedonian Definition is the doctrine of redemption, which was advocated by Irenaeus against those who speculated about the *Logos* and which was advocated by Athanasius against Arius. This doctrine of redemption cannot be dismissed as "physical" since it has picked up the basic idea of vicarious representative action found in the New Testament, particularly in Paul's writings (even if partly in other terminology), and found its continuation in the Reformation doctrine of the happy exchange between the righteous one and sinners.[vi] The Chalcedonian Definition thus corresponds to the history of Jesus Christ which—from his birth, baptism, temptation and Messianic self-concealment to his abandonment by God and death on the cross—was a vicarious representative action in our stead. The Chalcedonian Definition is not about the two natures as such, but about the complete integrity of Jesus' divine and human nature, apart from which his vicarious representative action would be illusory.

VII. If the Chalcedonian Definition is to be interpreted as a dogma—which Definition, although not itself a liturgical *homologia*, still aims to teach how proper *homologia* is to be offered in worship and is in this sense related to dogma and serves it—then it must not be confused with a theoretical clarification. It wants to serve the adoration of the mystery of the person of Jesus Christ, the Lord of the church. This connection with the life of the church has not always been maintained in the history of the interpretation of Chalcedonian Christology. Although the *anhypostasis* of the human nature and the doctrine of the two wills can be a compelling, logical conclusion of the Chalcedonian Definition, yet these inferences are not already being actualized in the act of worshiping the Redeemer. Rather, they are the results of an academic consideration of the Chalcedonian statements and an ongoing analysis and clarification of the terms used therein. Because the later scholastic development of dogmatic statements about the person of Jesus Christ abandoned the structure of doxological statements—despite all the emphasis on the unfathomableness of the mystery of his person—and because it appropriated the structure of academic consideration and expository instruction, it was inevitable that one tried to explain the historical actions of Jesus Christ by means of Chalcedonian Christology, namely, in distinguishing between the actions of the human nature and those of the divine nature. It was just as inevitable that some tried to explain the real presence of the body of Christ in the Lord's Supper by means of the doctrine of the *communicatio idiomatum*. But such attempts involved reading too much into the Chalcedonian Definition. The criticism against Luther thus remains justified, namely, that, in spite of his adherence to the Chalcedonian Definition, his doctrine of the communication of attributes actually went beyond its statements.

VIII. Since doxological statements are ultimate statements in which God's eternal deity is praised and worshipped on the basis of the historical act of salvation, these ultimate statements cannot be used as logical premises from which God's historical activity could be conclusively derived. To be sure, doxology is grounded in the message of the historical acts of God and thus corresponds to these acts, but it praises God in his eternal selfhood and freedom, in which he is from eternity to eternity. Because God has accomplished the acts of creation and redemption and will fulfill the new creation all from the freedom of his love and not from any necessity, these acts cannot be deduced from the statements of doxology regarding God's being, even though such statements correspond with God's acts. Just as the acts of God the Creator, Redeemer, and New Creator cannot be deduced from the praise of the eternal, holy Trinity, so also the particular details of the historical course of Jesus Christ cannot be deduced from the praise of the God-man. Not even the important distinction between the earthly reality of the humiliated Son of God and the transfigured heavenly embodiment of the risen and exalted Lord ensues from the praise of Jesus Christ as truly God and truly human. At this point, the statements of Chalcedon have their incalculable limit, which is given with the essence of doxology. From the confession "truly God and truly human" the historical course of the humiliation and exaltation of Jesus Christ can neither be deduced nor theoretically explained. The Christological statements of Chalcedon can thus in no way replace the tradition of the history of Jesus, but they are rather the further response of the church to the history of Jesus Christ. Similarly, in the worship service, doxology is the further response of the congregation to the public reading of Holy Scripture and to the preaching of the humiliation of God's Son and the exaltation of the man Jesus.

IX. The Chalcedonian Definition confesses Jesus Christ as truly God and truly human by appropriating the basic terms from Greek philosophy, namely, *nature* and *person*. This appropriation involved a profound alteration of the pre-understanding of these concepts at that time. Beyond that, we must not overlook the profound change that the concepts of person and nature have undergone since then.

a) The concept of person in the ancient church must not be confused with "person" and "personality" in the sense that these concepts have today in the humanities and psychology. If one understands person as the center of individual consciousness, as the self-awareness of an individual, and if one understands personality as the individual structure of character, as the particular stamp of a person's predisposition and experience, then this has nothing to do with the concept of person in the ancient church. It is rather equivalent to the concept of nature in the ancient church. The concept of person, as it is used in the Chalcedonian Definition, remains psychologically non-observable.

b) Likewise, the concept of nature in the ancient church cannot be confused with what is commonly understood today as nature in contrast to spirit. Rather, the Chalcedonian concept of nature also includes spirit, and indeed both the human spirit, on the one hand, and the divine Spirit, on the other. In that way, nature conveys the quintessence of Jesus Christ's total, essential consubstantiality with God and with us human beings.

c) At the same time, however, we must not overlook the fact that in statements about Jesus' human nature and about Jesus' divine nature the term *nature* does not mean the same thing. This becomes clear as soon as the statements of the Chalcedonian Definition are developed into statements about the attributes of both natures. The omnipotence, eternity, omnipresence, infinity, immutability, and so forth, of the divine nature are not opposite to the impotence, temporality, limitation, finitude, mutability, and so forth, of the human nature in the rigidity of logical opposites. The total superiority of the divine over the human nature excludes any complementary dependence of the statements about the divine nature upon statements about the human nature. God the Almighty is so much Lord of all power that he is also Lord when he becomes the impotent one. Precisely in his powerlessness he demonstrates the glory of his power. God the eternal and the omnipresent one is so much Lord of all time and space, that he is also Lord by entering time- and space-bound creaturely existence. But by so acting, he does not cease to be the eternal and omnipresent God. Rather, precisely in this finitude he demonstrates himself to be the infinite, whose eternity and omnipresence surpass all possibilities of human imagination. God's immutability is exactly the freedom of his love, in which he inclines himself to the sinner by becoming flesh and suffering the cursed death of the sinner.

X. Statements about history and statements about ontology do not take the form of "either-or" in Christology, but rather they belong together. How they belong together is to be explained by paying attention to the various basic structures of the theological statements. The response of faith to the kerygma takes place in various structures of statement. The history of Jesus is the kerygmatic content of its transmission in the form of doctrine and of its proclamation in the form of witness. Jesus Christ, truly God and truly human, is the content of the doxology that responds to this proclaimed and believed history of Jesus Christ. The Christological dogma, presupposing the tradition of the New Testament teachings, began to be set down especially in doxological statements.

When these statements came to be interpreted more and more as the doctrine of the person of Jesus Christ, it became necessary to develop along with it also the doctrine of the work of Jesus Christ and finally that of his two states.[vii] In that development, statements about the person of Jesus Christ (which are structurally ultimate statements) became primary ones, which were regarded as premises for the doctrine of the work of Christ and his two states, and were made the criterion for the history of Jesus. Against this doctrinal development arose the protest of nineteenth-century scholars engaged in research on the historical Jesus and the twentieth-century existentialist-kerygma theologians. Both, however, have failed to recognize the place of the Chalcedonian Definition in the life of the church, namely, its aim of serving the doxological *homologia*, something that had been thoroughly forgotten in the scholastic development of the doctrine of the two natures. The statements of Chalcedon have to be interpreted and appropriated anew, not in opposition to the history of Jesus, but understood rather as a guide for the praise and worship of the historical Christ, who as exalted Lord is present in the church.

Editor's Notes

[i] Tensions between the patriarch of Constantinople and the bishop of Rome had been periodically strained since the early middle ages, but the excommunication of Patriarch Michael Cerularius (c. 1000–1059, patriarch after 1043) by Pope Leo IX (1002–1054, pope after 1048), in July 1054, is generally regarded as the final step in the separation of Eastern (Greek) and Western (Latin) Christianity.

[ii] In the Christological disputes of the sixth century, Leontius of Byzantium (485–543) established the distinction between the *enhypostasis* (personal union) and the *anhypostasis* (impersonal union). The unity of the man Jesus with the second person of the Trinity was expressed in post-Chalcedonian Christology with the *enhypostasis* of Jesus in the *Logos*. Human nature is enhypostasized by the *Logos* because it is possessed, used, and manifested by the *Logos*. *Anhypostasis* refers to the notion that Jesus, the man, is distinct from the *Logos* or that the *Logos* recedes into the background (*anhypostasis* = "lacking the hypostasis of the *Logos*").

[iii] *Homologia* (ὁμολογία = "saying the same thing") is the Greek word for "confession" or "profession."

[iv] Cf. Denzinger 125.

[v] Cf. Denzinger 301.

[vi] Cf. Luther's 1520 treatise, "The Freedom of a Christian": "The third incomparable benefit of faith is that it unites the soul with Christ as a bride is united with her bridegroom. By this mystery, as the Apostle teaches, Christ and the soul become one flesh…. Accordingly, the believing soul can boast of and glory in whatever Christ has as though it were its own, and whatever the soul has Christ claims as his own…. Christ is full of grace, life, and salvation. The soul is full of sins, death, and damnation. Now let faith come between them and sins, death, and damnation will be Christ's, while grace, life and salvation will be the soul's" (LW 31.351).

[vii] Christ's humiliation and exaltation

Chapter Four:
Christ and the Church

Twelve Theses for an Ecumenical Dialogue between Theologians of the Protestant Church in Germany and the Roman Church[1]

In his investigations of the concept of the church in the New Testament Karl Ludwig Schmidt set forth this thesis: ecclesiology is Christology—a thesis that was certainly not new but which is in no way self-evident in the context of Protestant theology. At the outset I want to say that I am not able to understand my topic in terms of this equation, and specifically for the following reasons:

1. Ecclesiological concepts in the New Testament are very diverse and in no way merely Christological. Alongside Christological designations of the church, such as σῶμα τοῦ χριστοῦ [body of Christ], νύμφη [bride], γυνή [wife], there are also pneumatological ones, such as the temple of the Holy Spirit, and theological ones, such as ἐκκλησία τοῦ θεοῦ [church of God], λαὸς τοῦ θεοῦ [people of God]. Thus ecclesiology must be developed as a whole in a Trinitarian way, whereby it cannot be overlooked that in the confessional writings of the ancient church the statements about the church are directly related to the statements about the Holy Spirit. From here it is but a step to teach within a Trinitarian exposition that the church is the *opus proprium* [the proper work] of the Holy Spirit.

2. The multiplicity of ecclesiological concepts in the New Testament corresponds to the multiplicity of answers that tend to be given to the question concerning the origin of the church: Is it grounded in the outpouring of the Holy Spirit, that is, in the event of Pentecost? Is it grounded in the death and resurrection of Christ and thus at the same time in the sending of the apostles as the called eyewitnesses of his resurrection? Is it grounded in the election of the covenantal people of the Old Testament? Or in the creation of the first human beings, or in the eternal decree of creation that preceded the creation (the essential truth in the post-apostolic statements about the pre-existence of the church)? All of these questions, each in its definite coordination (not to be further discussed here), are to be answered affirmatively. Also the question of

---

1 These theses were initially presented and discussed at a joint conference of a working group of Protestant and Roman Catholic theologians on 25 March 1953 at the Protestant Academy in Tutzing, Germany. [This document was published as "Christus und die Kirche: 12 Thesen für ein ökumenisches Gespräch zwischen Theologen der evangelischen und der römischen Kirche," *Kerygma und Dogma* 1, no. 3 (1955), 208–25. It appears in KC 1.88–105. These theses were translated by Mary Lusk and published as "Christ and the Church: 12 Theses for a Discussion between Protestant and Roman Churches," *Scottish Journal of Theology* 10 (1957), 1–23. This same translation appears in CC (96–118) under the title, "Christ and the Church: Twelve Theses for an Ecumenical Discussion between Theologians of the Evangelical and the Roman Churches." –Ed.]

the origin of the church requires a Trinitarian answer. When the church, above all, celebrates Pentecost as the day of its birth, then in this way it has understood itself as the *opus proprium* of the Holy Spirit.

3. But even in view of the specifically Christological designations of the church, the equation "ecclesiology = Christology" is not advisable since it expresses only *one* of the various relations between Christ and the church and isolates it in a dangerous way. Equating ecclesiology and Christology is suggested by the New Testament statements about the church as σῶμα χριστοῦ, in which, of course, the irreversible ordering of head and body cannot be overlooked: only Christ is both head and body, while the church is only his body. Furthermore, there are the statements about the church as the bride of Christ, which express even more strongly a pairing of Christ and the church toward their unity. Then, too, however, one must take into consideration all of the New Testament statements in which Christ confronts the church as the Lord, indeed, as the Judge of the church. Ecclesiology must also consider such warnings of the exalted Christ as those directed to the church at Sardis: "Repent! If you will not awake, I will come upon you like a thief...." (Rev. 3.3). These statements are opposed to a thorough-going equating of ecclesiology and Christology in a way similar to how it is impossible to equate the doctrine about what is created with the doctrine about God the Creator.

Under the theme of "Christ and the Church" we will not treat ecclesiology as a whole nor ecclesiology in the full scope of its Trinitarian context, but simply with respect to the special aspect of its Christological reference. The scope of this theme is defined in the following twelve theses, the first ten of which begin with the words, "The church is..." Most of these theses will be only briefly explained. But the statements concerning the attributes and marks of the church must be developed at greater length since these are of special significance for the theological discussion that is controversial. Then, in conclusion, we must ask the questions: What does "*is*" mean here? What does it mean to say that the church "*has*" attributes?

I. The church is the people of God called by Christ from the world.

Jesus Christ died on the cross for the world, and in his resurrection he is exalted as Lord over the world. The world's self-glorification and arbitrary self-rule are placed under Jesus' judgment. At the same time, the redemption from this judgment is opened up in him for everyone who believes in him. We are called out from the world by the gospel of Jesus' death and resurrection. This call is not only a report about Jesus, nor is it only the announcement of the redemption of those who believe in him. The gospel is at the same time also the word by which the risen Christ is himself active in the present. By the gospel Jesus Christ accomplishes the redemption of the believers, and by the gospel he shows himself in power as the exalted Lord. Through baptism we have not only received the sign of Jesus' death and resurrection, but our "ownership" has been transferred to Christ, we have been delivered into his death, crucified with him, have died and been buried, in order that we live with him (Rom. 6.3 ff.).

We are thus gathered out of the world by Christ and are united in him. We are added to the New Testament people of God—both Jews and Gentiles—in which the earthly differences between nations, classes, and sexes are eschatologically annulled. In the people of God all the various different ones in the world are "one in Christ Jesus" (Gal. 3.28).

As members of the New Testament people of God we are placed under the kingship of Christ. We no longer belong to ourselves but to Christ our Lord. From him we daily receive forgiveness, life, and fellowship anew. Together, we are subject to his command.

II. The church is the prophetic, priestly, royal people sent by Christ into the world.

Christ has called us out of the world in order to send us as his messengers into the world. He has given us a new origin from outside the world so that we proceed from this origin into the world. As those who have been freed by Christ we must proclaim to the world its end, and to those who are enslaved, freedom in Christ. Both movements—being called out from the world and being sent back into it—belong essentially together in the concept of the church.

The church is sent into the world by the Lord, who as the crucified and risen one rules the world and intercedes for it in the threefold office of prophet, priest, and king. By his sending, the church receives a share in this office that corresponds in image to his. The church is the prophetic people—by whom the mighty deeds of God are being praised before the whole world (Acts 2)—and "the royal priesthood" (1 Pet. 2.9). If in the old covenant *individual* people were called to be prophets or priests or kings, and if these individuals stood over against one another and the people, so now the church as a *whole* is one people of prophets, priests, and kings. Everything that is to be said about the different spiritual gifts in the New Testament (also about the special nature of a charisma of prophecy) and about the church's ministerial offices fits within this reality of the prophetic, priestly, and royal office of Christ, which embraces the whole church and places it into service—the same Christ who makes every member of the church a prophetic witness and a royal priest. In the servant ministry of the church, sent into the world, the threefold office of Jesus Christ becomes real before the world.

Sent into the world, the church is the vanguard and instrument of the reign of Christ breaking into the world. Only if this sending of the church into the world is included in the concept of the church will the relationship between the church and the kingdom of Christ be properly recognized. The church is the kingdom of Christ in that its members are subject to Christ as Lord of the world and in that the church calls the world to acknowledge this Lord. The church is the impact and the instrument [*Wirkung und Werkzeug*] of the Lordship of the *Kyrios*.

III. The church is the worshiping assembly, in which Christ is actively present.[2]

This two-fold movement of being called out from the world and then sent back into it has its center in the worshiping assembly, in which God's act of salvation is proclaimed and praised and the Lord's Supper is celebrated. Christ called us into it by the gospel, he added us to it in baptism, and from it he sends us out in servant ministry to the world. The worshiping assembly is so very much the heart and center of the life of the church that *assembly*, in the concept of ἐκκλησία, has become the principal term for the church in the New Testament. The designation of the church as the body of Christ (which relates to the Lord's Supper) and its designation as the temple and house of God also point to this heart and center. The worshiping assembly stands also at the center of the Reformation concept of the church (Art. 7 of the *Confessio Augustana*).

The life of the church is concentrated with particular intensity in the worshiping assembly. In the worship event several dimensions need to be distinguished, to the first three of which we shall call attention now (and to two others in two subsequent theses): (1) the active self-realization of the crucified and risen Lord through word and sacrament; (2) our self-commitment to the Lord in the hearing of his word, in the reception of his body and blood, in confession, in prayers, acclamations, doxologies; and (3) our mutual service to one another, both to believers and non-believers, in witness and intercession.

In accordance with statements from the New Testament, through the present Christ each local worshiping assembly is, in the full sense, ἐκκλησία, σῶμα τοῦ χριστοῦ, ναὸς τοῦ θεοῦ. The worshiping assembly is this, not in view of all believers—since these are scattered throughout the world and belong to assemblies that are separated geographically—but in view of Christ, who is wholly present in every local assembly of believers. So the church that consists of all believers in the world should not be understood as the sum total of all local churches, but rather it is a κοινωνία [communion; fellowship] in the sense of a common participation in the one Christ, who is present, whole and undivided, in each local assembly.

---

2 Regarding theses 3 and 4, cf. chap.6, "The *Cultus* in the Perspective of Evangelical-Lutheran Theology."

IV. The church is the bride waiting for Christ, who already now, in the
worshiping assembly, takes part in the coming wedding feast.

We are underway to meet the coming Lord, whose appearance in glory we
await. In that way the church is like the bride who awaits the coming of the
groom to the wedding.

In the worshiping assembly we do not, however, merely *pray, μαραν θα*
["Our Lord, come!"], but the Lord, whom we summon, *comes* into our midst.
In the Lord's Supper it is not only the crucified and risen one who makes
himself present but also the Christ who is coming again. In him we already
share now in the great meal in the Kingdom of God, the eternal marriage feast
of the Lamb. The church is not only the bride but the wife of Christ. Although
we on earth are still journeying toward the goal, we here at the same time are
already at the goal. Although we do not yet see the promised glory, yet we have
a share in it already now by faith in the Lord, who gives himself to us in his
Supper.

The worshiping assembly is thus at the same time the present fellowship of
the believers on earth, together with the glorified believers of all times, whom
Christ will one day assemble in heavenly radiance. In the presence of the
coming Christ, the invisible unity of the militant church and the triumphant
church is a reality.

This is the fourth dimension of the worship event.

V. The church is the body of Christ, which in the worshiping assembly
is being built up for the new universe.

Through the reception of the body of Christ in the Lord's Supper we who are
baptized and believe in Christ are being built up as the body of Christ. Christ is
the head of his body. As head he rules the church, his body, which he faces as its
Lord. But at the same time, Christ is not only the head but the head and the
body. The church does not only live under him as its Lord, but it lives in Christ,
it is a part of Christ, it is the body of him who is himself the head and the body.
The unity of the church and Christ is not one of identity since Christ alone—
and never the church—is the head of the body, but that unity is the unity of the
body of Christ.

The body of Christ is growing—growing "*unto him*[i] in every way, he who is
the head, namely, Christ" (Eph. 4.15), and growing *from the head*, "from
whom the whole body, nourished and knit together through its joints and
ligaments, grows with a growth from God" (Col. 2.19). This growth takes place
through the knowledge of faith, in the fruit of good works, as well as in the
suffering of those who bear witness, who "complete what is lacking in the
afflictions of Christ for the sake of his body, which is the church" (Col. 1.24).

But above all, the growth of the body occurs through the addition of further members, who are the fruit of the gospel that is proclaimed in the world. So the body of Christ grows in the growth of the believers and in the size of their company, inwardly and outwardly, upwards and in the breadth of space and time in the struggle with the spiritual attacks and trials in the world. As "the firstborn from the dead," Christ is thus "the head of the body," "the beginning" (Col. 1.18), and the goal of the growth. But at the same time, however, Christ is "the perfect human being" (Eph. 4.13), in whom the body and all the members are fitted together under the head.

As the body of Christ, the church has a significance beyond just reaching out to human beings, namely, a significance that pervades the entire universe. The church is "the fullness of him who fills all in all" (Eph. 1.23). The power of Christ that fulfills the universe is present in the church; the church is the fullness of Christ which he extends into the universe. Indeed, the church is "the universe in its eschatological form" (Ernst Käsemann).[ii] In the church the creation comes to its goal—not as the world, but as the realm under Christ's Lordship. Thus it is that in the church the voices of all creatures who praise God as their Lord come together in harmonious sound. The worshiping assembly joins in the angels' song of praise, who offer the *Sanctus* to God. Of course the praise offered by the church in this world will not come to voice without supplications, petitions and loud sighing, and yet the new creation is already now a reality in Jesus Christ and the people who praise him.

This is the fifth dimension of the worship event.

VI. The church is the fellowship of the gifts of grace in whose multiplicity the one grace of Christ actively manifests itself.[3]

All of the New Testament writings bear witness to the fact that each member of the New Testament people of God is given the Holy Spirit. That the outpouring of the Spirit brings about a *multiplicity* of spiritual gifts is especially the testimony of Paul (but see also 1 Pet. 4.10 ff.). To each believer a special charisma is imparted: "All these are activated by one and the same Spirit, who allots to each one individually just as the Spirit chooses" (1 Cor. 12.11). Paul's teaching about the multiplicity of spiritual gifts is so fundamental that his statements may in no way be restricted to the congregations in Corinth (1 Cor. 12–14) and Rome (Rom. 12.6 ff.), not even to the Pauline congregations or to the earliest Christian community. Instead, the multiplicity of spiritual gifts belongs to the very nature of the church at all times and in all places. As the body of Christ, the church is also an organism of diverse gifts in which a concrete spiritual gift is freely imparted to each believer by the Spirit.

Each spiritual gift is διακωνία [service], given for the building up of the

---

3 Regarding theses 6 and 7, cf. sec. 1 in chap. 8 ("Apostolic Succession") below.

congregation. No one receives the spiritual gift for oneself. Therefore, in the midst of all the charismata, love is "the more excellent way" (1 Cor. 12.31), the surpassing "more precious way" [*köstlichere Weg*] (Luther).[iii]

In the multiplicity of God's gifts the fullness of the one Christ is made present in the congregation and through the congregation in the world. The multiplicity of charismata may appear in different forms in different congregations (see already 1 Cor. 12 and Rom. 12) and at different times, but it is always the appearance of the one χάρις[iv] of Jesus Christ. As head of the body he is the bearer and source of all charismata, and they in turn are all ordered in their service toward him. The fellowship of the gifts thus consists in their common participation in the one χάρις of Jesus Christ.

VII. The church is the congregation led by Christ himself through the pastoral office.[v]

The calling of all into membership in the prophetic-priestly people of God and thus into servant ministry has to be distinguished from the calling that commissions and authorizes particular members for a specific servant ministry.[vi] The servant ministry that is exercised on the basis of a concrete commissioning and authorizing in the church (as already in the foundational ministry of the apostles) has to be distinguished from the multiplicity of the freely emerging charismata and ministries of all believers. Now it is true that everyone who exercises a spiritually gifted ministry is identified with a concrete word of the congregation insofar as he or she is subject to the testing and judging of the congregation. This applies, for example, to the "Amen!" by which the Pauline congregation acknowledged the freely given witness in its midst as the witness of the Spirit. This applies in a different way also, for example, to the Pauline exhortation to acknowledge in willing obedience the ministry of Stephanas for the sake of his active engagement with the congregation (1 Cor. 16.15). But we must distinguish between the words that are *subsequently* assigned to those who exercise a spiritually gifted ministry and the calling that *precedes* the ministry, which sends specific individuals into a specific ministry and authorizes them thereto with prayer.

In this case we are speaking of the church's ministerial office: it is one such spiritually gifted ministry in the church which—in the midst of the multiplicity of spiritually gifted ministries in the church—is grounded in a special calling, commissioning, and sending. At the same time, all of the church's ministerial offices are distinguished from the historic apostolate in that it alone is accorded the unique and incomparable authority of the eyewitnesses to the Lord's resurrection, those who were themselves called directly by the Lord. This authority is foundational and normative for the church of all times. All of the other ministerial offices in the church have authority only in obedient subordination to the apostolic authority. Those church ministries that are based on a special calling that precedes them are especially the functions of founding and leading the church. We group these ministries together in the concept of the pastoral office, to whose various forms other offices of service [Diakonie] in the narrower sense are then added.

When the apostolic message is proclaimed in the pastoral office, the same promise which Jesus once gave to the apostles holds true for the pastors [Hirten = "shepherds"]: "Whoever hears you, hears me" (Lk. 10.16). When the pastor cries: "Be reconciled to God," then the pastor is like the apostle, "an ambassador for Christ," an instrument by which God himself exhorts the church and the world (2 Cor. 5.20). The consoling, exhorting, judging voice of the pastoral office is not only a human voice, but the voice of Christ, who uses human words as his voice. The same mission and the same promise that were given to the apostles are valid for the pastoral office in all times: "Sins you forgive, they are forgiven, and sins you retain, they are retained" (Jn. 20.22 ff. Compare with Mt. 16.19 and 18.18). In everything that the pastor does in obedience to the commission, the pastor encounters the congregation as the vicarious representative of Christ, the one good Shepherd. As the pastor thus leads the worshiping assembly, Christ himself leads the church through this ministerial office, and consoles, exhorts, strengthens, and judges it.

Because Christ is himself actively present in the charismata and ministries of the whole congregation, the leadership of the congregation therefore cannot be a lordship of the pastoral office over the congregation. Not only the pastoral office but also the freely voiced spiritual witness stands vis-à-vis the congregation, for Christ encounters the congregation also through that witness. Christ acts upon the congregation through the pastoral office, and he acts upon both the congregation and the pastor through the various spiritually gifted ministries. The pastoral office thus stands in the midst of the reciprocal ministries of all the members toward one another. The pastor stands in the midst of the manifold workings of the one grace of Christ through the manifold ministries of each to the other. Therefore also the spiritually gifted witnesses in the congregation are not to be examined by the pastoral office alone, but likewise the congregation has the responsibility and the task to examine, evaluate, and judge every freely rendered ministry, just as also the ministry of the pastor.

VIII. The church is "one, holy, catholic, and apostolic" (The Nicene Creed).

These four attributes of the church are interwoven with one another in a special way. The first three have the same Christological structure, while the fourth occupies a special position.

1. The unity of the church

We not only see a large number of locally separate assemblies, but already in the New Testament letters we read about various tensions, oppositions, and the forming of groups within the local congregations, for example, the oppositions in Corinth, even about the celebration of the Lord's Supper, and also tensions and oppositions between the apostles (Gal. 2.11 ff.). These tensions and even the forming of cliques did not hinder Paul from bearing witness to the unity of precisely these congregations and their members, nor from addressing those who were disunited among themselves about this their unity, nor from exhorting them to unity by appeal to that unity.

The unity of the church is not primarily the unity of its members but the unity of Christ who is acting upon them all and indeed at all times and in all places. It is one and the same Christ who has called them all through word and sacrament and has incorporated them into himself—one and the same Christ who is actively present in the multiplicity of spiritual gifts. Since all members of the church have been chosen by the one God, called by the one Christ, and renewed and gifted by the one Holy Spirit, the unity of those who believe in Christ, who have been baptized into Christ, and who receive the body of Christ in the Lord's Supper is a matter of faith—over against all their visible tensions, oppositions, cliques, and separate natures. Indeed, this unity is a reality created by God in Christ through the Holy Spirit.

Because those who believe in Christ, who have been baptized into him, and have received his body are one, they should strive for unity; because they are one, they should be one. On the basis of the unity gifted in Christ, the apostle exhorts them to make space for this unity in an orderly joint celebration of the Lord's Supper and in a mutual, loving inclusion of the spiritually gifted individuals, as well as in the reciprocal recognition of ministerial offices and in the mutual intercession and aid effort beyond the local congregation. Thus the exhortations of the apostle to the Corinthian congregation that refer to this subject generally take the structure of New Testament *paraclesis* [exhortation]. The imperative is spoken on the basis of the indicative of the act of salvation that has taken place and which is acknowledged in faith. The unity of the church is not a task and work of human beings, but rather it is on the basis of the unity effected by Christ that believers are to be one.

2. The holiness of the church

We do not see this holiness, when we gaze upon all those who consider themselves members of the church. Nor do we see it when we visualize the picture which the New Testament letters give us of the earliest Christian congregations. There we read of manifold sins; and even when the incestuous and some of the grossest sinners were excluded from the congregation, there was still enough to be admonished—presumptuousness, greed, legalism, little faith, misuse of Christian freedom, and lovelessness of every kind. Added to that were the hidden sins, then just as now. In fact, from the very beginning, the church was an "infirmary and care facility for the sick and those in need of healing" (Martin Luther, *Lectures on Romans* (1515/16), WA 56:276. [LW 25:263. –Ed.]).

The holiness of the church is not primarily the holiness of its members but the holiness of Christ imputed to this assembly and the holiness of the Spirit, who sanctifies these people in Christ and dwells in them. Only in this way can we understand the unabashed freedom with which the writers of the New Testament letters address as saints those same members of the congregation whose sins they have clearly brought to light. The holiness of the church is not the sum of the holiness of its members, but rather the holiness of Christ, who gives himself to the church and dwells at its center—in the power of the Holy Spirit, who sanctifies sinners. If we look at the members of the church, then we see that all are sinners and the church is a fellowship of sinners and not of saints. If, however, we believe in Christ, who is actively present in the church through the Spirit, we know that through the gospel and the sacraments this horde of sinners is justified and will be justified anew each day. In this sense the church is simultaneously a house of the sick and the palace of the healed—to the senses it appears as a house of the sick but with the eyes of faith it is a palace of the healed.

Because the church is holy through God's sanctifying work, therefore its members should set sin aside and strive after holiness. The exhortation to holiness presupposes the salvific act of holiness. Because the members are sanctified, they should lay hold of holiness. Because they are holy, they should live as holy. Thereby we should note that these New Testament imperatives are not directed only to particular members of the church but to entire churches. For that reason, this also applies to the church as a whole: Because it is sanctified, it should then be holy.

3. The catholicity of the church

If by catholicity we understand that the church encompasses the world geographically, we see very little of that in the New Testament writings, for what significance has even the route from Jerusalem to Rome in comparison with the whole world? Nevertheless, the meaning of the Nicene Creed is that the church was already catholic at the time of Pentecost.

The church is catholic because Christ, the exalted Lord, the *Pantokrator*, acts in it—he to whom is given all power in heaven and on earth. The word *catholic* does not occur in the New Testament writings. It is first found in Ignatius and indeed in a Christological context: "where Christ is, there is also the catholic church" (Ignatius of Antioch, *Letter to Smyrna*, 8.2).[vii] In the further development of the concept, the geographical extension of the church on earth became more prominent, and later a distinction was made between the factual and virtual geographical extension. In contrast, the Reformers liked to translate the word *catholic* as "Christian," in accord with the original formulation. We may connect with this an understanding of catholicity which one comes across repeatedly in the ecclesiology of the Eastern Church, according to which the catholicity of the church consists in the comprehensive multiplicity of the charismata, of theologies, and of believers. The catholicity of the church is the catholicity of Jesus Christ, Lord of all lords, Lord of the universe. As this Lord, he is presently active in the church; he incorporates believers into his body, which is the πλήρωμα [fullness] that fulfills the universe; through the variety of spiritual gifts he allows them to participate in the all-embracing richness of his grace; and he sends them into the world in order to proclaim to it the end of its own autonomy and to proclaim him as the Lord of the world. Because Christ is the *Pantokrator* in the midst of the church, because he empowers and sends it, the church is catholic. It is catholic on the basis of the catholicity of its Lord, which is imputed to it.

Because the church in Christ is catholic, it ought to be catholic. It does not first have to achieve its catholicity through its self-extension, but it has to believe in its Lord, who encompasses the universe and to obey him. Because it is catholic by faith, it is to make space for the abundance of his gifts of grace in the manifoldness of knowledge, of witness, and of servant ministry in the widest sense, by which the Lord makes himself present in his richness. Because it is catholic, it is to advance into all areas of the world in order to proclaim to all people him who is already their Lord, whether they know it or not, whether they acknowledge him or deny him. Since we do not first need to make Christ the *Pantokrator* by our own effort and need not first make the church catholic, our servant ministry, despite all spiritual attacks and trials, is in the end an untroubled and joyful one.

4. The Apostolicity of the Church

Apostolicity occupies a special position among the four attributes of the church. To be sure, it is true of each one of these attributes that it is realized only in conjunction with the other three. They are inseparably interwoven with one another as are the attributes of God. Even their enumeration is incomplete in a way that is similar to that of the attributes in the doctrine of God. Yet in this intimate interrelationship and unity of the four attributes, apostolicity has a special place insofar as Christ—the one, holy Christ who is exalted over the universe—encounters the church in fact only in the apostolic witness. Without the apostolic witness he would be absolutely hidden, and only on the basis of this witness is he in fact known. So the significance of apostolicity is that it is the attribute on which the other attributes of the church rest in a special way because without the ministry of the apostles Christ does not rule the church nor does he make himself present in it.

If we understand the apostles to be the called and enlightened eyewitnesses of the resurrection of Jesus Christ, then they are the foundation of the church, and not merely in the historical sense, namely, that the church was once founded through their ministry and thus on them. Beyond that, as the called eyewitnesses of the victory of Christ, they have an abiding, incomparable, unrepeatable, normatively unique position as authoritative vis-à-vis the church in all subsequent ages. There is no access to Christ by bypassing the apostolic witness to Christ. Only in the faith in the apostolic gospel is the church therefore the one, holy, catholic church in Christ. If the church is the apostolic church in its obedience to the apostolic message, then it is thereby the one, holy, catholic church.

Because this is so, the church for all time must heed the exhortation to abide by the apostolic gospel and, where it has departed from it or gone beyond it, to return to the apostolic message. This is the meaning of the call: *ecclesia semper reformanda est* [the church ought always to be reformed].

IX. The church is indestructible.

The structure of the attributes of the church becomes even plainer here, for of the relevant New Testament passages none speaks strictly of any attribute of the church, of *its own* capability to abide on the earth or of its incapability to be destroyed. Rather, they speak of *the promise of God in Christ.*

The world resists the message of the church. The message of the end of the world and the summons to submit to Christ the Lord is a disturbance to the world. The world wants its own eternity. It wants to remain the world. So it struggles against the church and does so in a two-fold manner: on the one hand, in open attack, oppression, persecution, and, on the other, by adapting itself to the church, in bringing the church into its service, and in secularizing it. This second way is the more dangerous. In one way or another, this struggle takes place under ever new camouflage and on constantly changing historical fronts.

To the church is given the promise that it will endure in the midst of all spiritual attacks and trials. "The gates of hell shall not prevail against it" (Matt. 16.18). The woman (the church) remains on the earth, even when her seed (the individual members) are killed (Rev. 12.6, 13 ff.). Even if it is almost choked by the weeds that the enemy has sowed secretly, it will abide until the time of harvest (Matt. 13.24 ff.).

This promise does not mean that the church will always remain in the same place, with the same increase in the number of its members, with the same order, with the same clarity of knowledge and love, with the same multiplicity of spiritual gifts. But never will the earth be without those to whom is given the promise that they will "inherit the earth" (Matt. 5.5). Never will the earth be without those for whose sake and for the completion of whose number God preserves the world in spite of sin and death. There will always be the one, holy, catholic, and apostolic church.

Because the church is given this promise, it receives the imperative to struggle against the powers of the world. Christ does not only promise "neither shall anyone pluck them out of my hand" (John 10.28), but he also commands, "Abide in me!" The struggle which the church is ordained to wage is an extremely strange one, and it is waged on both sides with very different weapons. The church struggles as it gathers around word and sacrament, as it thanks God, also for its spiritual attacks and trials, and intercedes for its enemies, as it confesses Christ before the world and takes upon itself suffering for its confession. It struggles as it proceeds in its λειτουργεῖν [service, worship] in the broadest sense, and as it remains that which it is from its very origin—as it abides in Christ. It struggles for the victor's crown by abiding in him who already is victor over the world.

In order to abide in Christ, the church in its history has delimited the New Testament canon and defined dogmas and ordered the church. These decisions have their common origin in service to the worshiping assembly, and historically they have been made in the struggle against threats to this assembly.

In the canon the church has collected the original documents of the apostolic message. The canon is the norm of the church's speaking and acting, yet not because the church would have created it but because the apostolic message is the normative foundation of the church for all time. With the canon the church has acknowledged the norm of the apostolic witness to Christ.

In dogma the church has confessed Christ. Dogma is authoritative for the church's speaking and acting, not because it would have been formulated by the church but because the Christ to whom the apostles have born witness is here confessed—he who is the same yesterday, today, and forever and who has ever to be confessed anew by the church on its historically changing fronts.

In its order, the church has defined the way in which the servant ministry of preaching and the administration of the sacraments is to occur. Also order has its binding validity, not because it was instituted by the church but because of the mission of the Lord to preach the gospel and because of his institution of the sacraments. In whatever its respective historical situation, the church has to acknowledge with its orders the ordinance of Christ.

Here we should not overlook the increasing range of possibilities within which the church has made these three decisions. By delimiting the canon it was bound to the historical, original documents that had been handed down (notwithstanding the whole problematic of the "antilegomena")[viii] and to their exact text. In dogma, the church has always borne witness to use its own words, in the choice between various concepts and in controversy with ever-changing heresies and worldviews. The ordering of the church is in its details conditioned to an even greater degree by the external presuppositions of the respective situation in which the church obeys the commission of its Lord. From here arises the issue of the historical variability of these church decisions and the various ways in which they have binding force in the church.

X. The church is visible in this world.

The church is hidden from the eyes of the world, as are the earthly Christ and the work of the Holy Spirit. To be sure, everyone can see the worshiping assemblies, hear their witness, and recognize the historical duration and spatial expansion of Christendom. But without faith the church cannot be recognized as the people of God. In the eyes of the world it is hidden in the abundance of religio-historical and religio-sociological analogies. It appears as only one religion among many. Neither its unity nor holiness nor catholicity is recognizable without faith in its Lord.

The church, however, is also hidden from the eyes of the believers. It is, to be sure, clear that those who have separated themselves from the worship assembly do not belong to the people of God. But beyond that, the people who are the children of God are hidden among the many who, though they may take part in the worship service, nevertheless do not lead a new life—whether it be that they deny to confess Christ before the world or that they persist in adultery, covetousness, lust for power, and so forth, or self-righteously boast before God and others of their irreproachable conduct and of their confession. Often enough the number of hypocrites seems greater than that of the true believers. One must, however, not stop here with such judging of others and one must in no way pre-empt the separating between the living and the dead members of the church, which is reserved for Christ as the coming Judge. Rather, it is precisely the believer who recognizes himself or herself again and again as the sinner, the hypocrite, the denier! Who could ever boast of his or her obedience before God? Who must not cry daily, "Forgive me my sins"? The one holy church is not merely hidden under the disunity and unholiness of others, but also underneath my own sins.

In the midst of the assemblies of this world the church is recognizable in no other way than in which sinners recognize themselves as justified and holy, namely, by faith in the gospel. The church is not the gospel but the assembly of sinners in which the gospel is preached. But the gospel is God's powerful, active word by which he effects faith and justifies and sanctifies believing sinners. The gospel persists in awakening faith and having a salvific effect, despite every contradiction leveled against it by human beings. Where it is preached and where those who hear it give their confession as a response to it, one may surely reckon that God is gathering his people, however questionable the assembly is in which this occurs. Where people are baptized, there is an implanting into the body of Christ, and where the Lord's Supper is received, there is the building up of the body of Christ, even when unbelief is judged in this event and the believers are hidden among the hypocrites. So the preaching of the gospel and the administration of baptism and the Lord's Supper are the marks by which the church can be recognized with complete certainty in this world.

Of course, where the gospel is proclaimed, there, along with faith, arise also new obedience, prayer, and witness, as well as spiritual attacks, trials, and suffering. There gifts of the Spirit emerge, by which one serves the other and in which the love of Christ is manifested in the midst of the world. In a broader sense all these effects can be designated as signs of the church. But they remain in the twilight of all human action. Often enough prayer is hidden underneath inexpressible sighing, and often enough the self-boasting of the "haves" is hidden underneath the witness to the world. The church is also visible in a larger sense in its order, its liturgy, and its service. But in the midst of all such visibility, the gospel and the sacraments remain purely and simply the *notae ecclesiae* [marks of the church]. They are related to all these others as the message of Jesus is related to his signs. Without faith in the message, Jesus' miracles were not recognized as signs of the lordship of God. Even other miracle-workers did miracles. Only on the basis of the *notae ecclesiae* does all the rest become signs of the church, and only thus is the church recognizable in the religio-historical and religio-sociological construct of Christendom. Gospel, baptism, and the Lord's Supper are the only distinguishing signs by which the reality of the church in the world can *unerringly* be recognized. The issue of the one, holy, catholic church is thus contingent upon the apostolicity of its message.

The gospel now is an "outward" word, which everyone can hear; and baptism and the Lord's Supper are as water, bread, and wine "outward" signs, which everyone can see and consider. The world acknowledges them only as human words and earthly occurrences. But faith recognizes in them God's word and deed. God's own word is encountered as an external, audible, human word; and Christ, the crucified and risen one himself, is imparted to the believer in an external, visible, earthly occurrence. So, for faith, the church is *visible* in this world. Although hidden beneath the sins of its members, it is nevertheless palpable in the gospel, which justifies believing sinners. If, with Augustine, Luther, and Calvin, one distinguishes between the visible and the invisible church, that is, between the assembly of all the baptized and that of the true believers, so one must add this: in the visible church of sinners, in which the gospel is preached, the invisible church is *visible*. In conformity with the usage in the New Testament letters we may now also in this church with the judgment of faith, love, and hope regard and address *all* those gathered as the saints of God because the gospel is at work here as God's active, justifying, sanctifying word. So the church is *visible to faith*, although it is hidden precisely in its worldly visibility, and it is invisible to unbelief, although unbelief sees it. Similarly, Jesus became visible to faith as the Christ, although in his self-humiliation he pointed away from himself to the coming Son of Man, and the Christ remained invisible to unbelief, although it saw and heard Jesus.

Consequently, the church belongs in the creed: "I believe in the Holy Spirit, one, holy, catholic, apostolic church." It has often been remarked that there is a difference here: "I believe *in* the Holy Spirit," but "I believe *the* church." The Holy Spirit is the Lord, but the church is his creation. The church does not have its place in the creed in the same way as God the Father and the Son and the Holy Spirit. I believe in God as my *Thou*, who has created and redeemed and sanctified me, and who daily acts anew as Creator, Redeemer, and New Creator of me and all people. The statement of faith about the church is, however, a statement about human beings upon whom God is acting. I cannot believe in the church any more than I can believe in myself as a Christian. But I believe in God—Father, Son, and Holy Spirit—who in his faithfulness has created the church and preserves it. Because I believe in the triune God, I also believe the church. God's new-creating work through the gospel brings about the church and makes the church recognizable, visible.

The attributes of the church and the *notae ecclesiae* are not identical. The attributes are the effects of the *notae*, for the distinguishing signs of the church—the word and sacrament—are the means through which Christ acts upon the church and gives himself to the church. Through word and sacrament he gives the church its unity, holiness, catholicity, and apostolicity, as well as its indestructible permanence.

XI. The threat of judgment applies to the church.

Christ will come in glory. He will overthrow all opposition. He will redeem the poor, those who hunger for righteousness, those who are waiting for him. Yet he does not come only as the Judge of the world but also as Judge of the church. It is in this sense that the earliest Christian community understood the parables about the wheat and the weeds and of the net with the good and the bad fish (Mt. 13.37 ff. and 47 ff.). In this sense we find again and again in the New Testament the call to repentance addressed to the churches—not only to individual members, but to entire churches (see especially the letters in Revelation). Indeed, the call to repentance applies to the whole of Christendom.

This call to repentance extends not only to false doctrine and vice, to little faith and disobedience of every kind. Beyond that, the call must unfold also in respect to the special dangers that only arise from such decisions by which the church wants to abide with its Lord in its conflict with the world. It is not the church that keeps God's word steadfast, but God through his word keeps the church steadfast. The church does not defend itself against all assaults, but

God defends it, and thus it persists. If the church has in this faith delimited the canon and defined dogma and ordered the church, this does not exclude the possibility that its preservation by Christ may be perverted into a self-preservation of the church, nor the possibility that the church may misuse the canon, dogma, and order as a means of self-preservation. So even in the church we know the danger of the scribes, who in their appeal to Scripture ignore the summons of the living Christ. We know the danger of such an orthodoxy which by its sticking to dogma overlooks the riches of Scripture and fails to make the confession that the church has to make in new here-and-now situations over against entirely different threats and false teachings. We also know the danger of an ecclesiastical legalism which stands in the way of the abundance of the gifts of the Spirit and the here-and-now leading of the church by its living Lord. There is a self-confidence in the church which makes it deaf to the call of the living Christ and to the sisters and brothers scattered throughout the world, and which makes the church blind to the constantly changing camouflages under cover of which the world seeks to devour the church. Canon, dogma, and church order have to *serve* the church's abiding in Christ. But Christ remains the living *Lord* of the canon, of dogma, and of church law.

XII. The promise of glorification by the Christ, who is coming again, applies to the church.

Out of the judgments Christ will redeem, perfect, and glorify the church. His Parousia will be the end of the believing, waiting, hastening, struggling and suffering church, but also of the church which is sinning, which is bound together with the world, and which seeks its own security. The church will then stop being a *corpus mixtum* in which the true believers are hidden among the hypocrites. The coming Christ will present the church in its purity. If now the church militant and the church triumphant are separated, at that time this distinction will come to an end. Then will be the end of the hiddenness of Christ in the human word of the gospel message and under the water, the bread, and the wine of the sacraments. Then we will see him, and the reality of having died with Christ and having arisen with him and the fellowship of the body of Christ will become visible. The coming Christ will encounter the church not only as the one who makes it perfect but also as its Judge. Above all, however, he encounters the church as the one who makes it perfect—as the bridegroom who goes out to meet his bride in order to celebrate with her the eternal marriage feast.

The first theses began with the words, "The church is…" We must now inquire, by way of conclusion, about the meaning of this word *is*.

The church is, because Jesus Christ, the crucified and risen one, acts ever anew upon it. Looking back on the theses, we may now say: The church is, in that Christ calls his people out from the world (I), Christ sends them into the world (II), Christ makes himself present in the worshiping assembly (III), Christ prepares the marriage feast (IV), Christ builds up his body (V), Christ unfolds his grace in the abundance of the gifts of the Spirit (VI), Christ leads the church through the pastoral office (VII). The explanatory remarks about the other theses were also derived from the working of Christ. But Christ does not merely work here and there, much less in an occasional and arbitrary manner, but continuously in the faithfulness of God. What he has begun he will also complete. The church is, in that Christ is continuously active upon it. The church was not before this action; and it is not for a moment without this action. Christ's working upon the church is at the same time the life of Christ in the church. For through baptism he takes the sinner into his death and his resurrection, and in the Lord's Supper he gives himself bodily as food to sinners. He is present in his church as the living one. In Christ's living presence the church has its being.

Christ acts on the church through the gospel (through preaching as the *sacramentum audibile* and through the sacraments as the *verbum visibile*). The word of the gospel encounters the church as a two-fold address: as assurance and claim, as gift and demand, as Christ's act of grace for the church and as Christ's command to the church, to live as befits the grace that has been received.

In the assurance of the gospel Christ grants to believers his righteousness, his holiness, his life. Through the gospel he shows himself as the Lord who grants to the believers everything that is his. By faith in the gospel the church is the one, holy, catholic, and indestructible church.

In the claim of the gospel exhortation Christ bids us to live from his strength. Because we are declared righteous, we ought to take hold of righteousness. Because we are made holy, we should strive for holiness. Because we have been transferred into his life, we ought so to live. On the basis of the life of Christ in the church, this exhortation holds true: Be one, be holy, be catholic, abide in him—be those who you are in Christ.

From the above, there emerges the answer to the further question: In what sense does the church "have" the attributes of unity, holiness, and so forth? These attributes come to the church in Christ's efficacious assurance and claim, more precisely, in an ever new assurance and an ever new claim—in his giving, which is new every day, and in his commands, which are new every day. The church "has" these attributes in a daily new reception and a daily new taking hold. In other words, the church has its attributes only in the double movement of being called out from the world by Christ and being sent forth into the world by Christ.

The church is one in being gathered by the one Christ, and in seeking for unity on the strength of being united with him. The church is holy in the reception of the holiness of Christ and in sanctifying itself on the strength of having been sanctified. The church is catholic as the possession of Christ, the

Pantokrator, and as his instrument for proclaiming his lordship to the world. The church is one, as it repents for its disunity and believes in the one Christ. The church is holy as it repents of its sins and believes in the holy Christ. As the church acknowledges its errors through self-examination in the light of the apostolic message, it is apostolic. As the church surrenders itself to die with Christ, it lives and abides. But should a church desire to hold fast as its own possession both its being and its attributes, divorced from Christ's assurance and claim that are new each day, then such an understanding of unity would lead to schism, such an understanding of holiness would lead to a denial of repentance, such an understanding of catholicity would lead to a claim of world domination, such an understanding of apostolicity would lead to a separation from the historic apostolate and thus to self-assertion over against Jesus Christ. The attributes of the church are to be acknowledged with fear and trembling as the ever new gracious acts of God's faithfulness in Christ. In this faithfulness the church has its being.

Statements about the being and attributes of the church thus take part in the structure of statements about the being of believers in Christ and about the attributes of believers: their righteousness, their holiness, and so forth. This instruction, to be sure, has an intrinsic limitation: my being in Christ, my being as justified and sanctified stands or falls with my ever new reception in faith of the righteousness and holiness of Christ, which he grants us through word and sacrament. But the church does not stand or fall with my faith. The church was before the individual came to faith, and it will abide even if the individual falls from faith. Statements about the church thus can never expand into personal generalizations. On the other hand, however, one cannot overlook the fact that the church is the fellowship of believers and that we can make true statements about the church only in faith. But in that respect, while the statements about the church cannot be separated from the personal existence of believers, one should watch out not to hypostasize the church.[ix]

Editor's Notes

[i] Schlink is here quoting Luther's translation of the Greek phrase, αὐξήσωμεν εἰς αὐτὸν τὰ πάντα (*Lasst uns... wachsen in allen Stücken zu dem hin...* ["Let us grow *unto* him in all ways," emphasis added]), which is a more accurate rendering than is found in many English versions, e.g., the King James Version ("grow up into him in all things..."), the Revised Standard Version ("We are to grow up in every way into him..."), the New Revised Standard Version ("we must grow up in every way into him..."), and the New International Version ("we will in all things grow up into him..."). Schlink's use of Luther's translation stresses we are to grow *unto* Christ or *toward* Christ, i. e., to become like him.

[ii] The source for this phrase by Ernst Käsemann is unknown, but the idea is expressed in his doctoral dissertation. See Ernst Käsemann, *Leib und Leib Christi: Eine Untersuchung zur paulinischen Begrifflichkeit* [Body and Body of Christ: An Investigation of the Pauline Conceptuality] (Tübingen: J. C. B. Mohr [Paul Siebeck], 1933), 184–6.

[iii] *Und ich will euch noch einen köstlichere Weg zeigen* [And I want to show you a still more precious way], 1 Cor. 12.31 in Luther's translation of the Bible.

[iv] In the New Testament the Greek word χάρις refers to God's grace, favor, or goodwill. Cf. BDAG 1079–1081.

[v] Literally, "the shepherd office" (*Das Hirtenamt*). This is Schlink's preferred way of referring to the ministerial office of the pastor.

[vi] Schlink here uses the verb *auftragen*, which can mean both "commission" (as in "order" or "instruction"), as well as "mission" or "task." One noun form is *Beauftragung* and another is *Auftrag*. The former will normally be translated as "commissioning," while the latter as "mission" or "commission," depending on the context. Elsewhere Schlink designates this "commissioning" or "missioning" as a "special sending" (*besondere Sendung*). That later combination of words will normally be translated as "commissioning" in order to distinguish it from a more general "sending." Cf. the second sec. ("Sending into Servant Ministry") of chap. 8 ("Apostolic Succession").

[vii] Ignatius of Antioch [c. 35 – c. 107], "Letter to the Smyrnaeans," 8.2, in *Early Christian Fathers*, ed. Cyril C. Richardson (New York: Collier, 1970), 115.

[viii] Included here are the so-called Old Testament Apocrypha as well as additional writings whose canonical authority was disputed and "spoken against" within the early Christian community, e. g., Hebrews, James, 2 Peter, 2 John, 3 John, Jude, Revelation, the Shepherd of Hermas, the Epistle of Barnabas, and so on.

[ix] Schlink's use of *hypostasieren* here refers to the application of divine and human attributes to the church, of thinking and speaking of the church in the same way that Christians think of Christ as two natures—divine and human—in one person (*hypostasis*).

Chapter Five:
The Expanse of the Church according to the Lutheran Confession[1]

I.

In Article VII of the *Confessio Augustana* the church is defined as the assembly of believers; and this assembly of believers is further defined by what occurs in it: The church "is the assembly of all believers in which the gospel is preached purely and the holy sacraments are administered in accord with the gospel."[i]

First of all, it should be observed here that the word of God is not named in a general sense, nor is the law, but the gospel is. The gospel is the joyful message of the justification of the sinner by God for the sake of Jesus Christ out of pure grace. This justification is not received on account of works by human beings, but solely by faith in the work that Jesus Christ has accomplished on the cross. The law is indeed not thereby excluded, but only in the proper distinction between the law and the gospel is the gospel preached purely. The gospel is God's proper word, while the law is God's alien word. What is more, the gospel

---

1 A paper written in 1949 in the context of preparatory work for the Third World Conference on Faith and Order at Lund, Sweden, in 1952. This essay sets forth implications for ecumenical work that are drawn from my book, *Theology of the Lutheran Confessions*, 3rd ed. (München: Kaiser, 1948). [This essay was originally published as "Die Weite der Kirche Augsburger Konfession," *Lutherische Rundschau* 1, no. 3 (1949), 1–13. It was translated into English as "The Breadth of the Church of the Augsburg Confession," *The Lutheran World Review* 1, no. 3 (January 1949), 1–14. In the original essay (also in its earlier translation), Schlink added the following introductory sentences: "The Lutheran Church today faces a two-fold danger. On the one hand, in its contact with other church bodies, it is threatened with the danger of ceasing to take seriously the issue of pure doctrine and of dissolving into a kind of fuzzy enthusiasm for church unity. On the other hand, there is the threat that the Lutheran Church will harden itself in a doctrinaire manner, anxiously withdraw into itself, and close itself off from rediscovering brothers and sisters in Christ in the other churches. If the Lutheran Church has succumbed or would succumb to either of these two dangers in this or that country, in both cases it would be equally unfaithful to its confession and would fail at the ecumenical task that the Augsburg Confession embodies. What consequences for ecumenical work can we draw from the concept of the church in the Augsburg Confession?" This original version of the essay that appeared in the first issue of *Lutherische Rundschau* (and translated in *The Lutheran World Review*) was further expanded and translated as "The Lutheran Churches (a) Germany," in *The Nature of the Church: Papers Presented to the Theological Commission Appointed by the Continuation Committee of the World Conference on Faith and Order*, ed. R. Newton Flew (New York: Harper & Brothers, 1952), 54–70. The first four and a half pages of this version, which provide a brief introduction to the nature of "confessing" in light of the so-called "church struggle" (*Kirchenkampf*) in Germany in the 1930s and the challenges to the Lutheran Church in the reorganization of the German Protestant churches after the Second World War, were added to the original article. The version that is printed in KC 1.106–15 and translated here lacks both the introductory sentences from the version published in *Lutherische Rundschau* and the additional introductory pages from the version edited by Flew. A truncated form of Flew's version appears in CC (119–31) as "The Marks of the Church according to the Augsburg Confession." –Ed.]

is linked directly to "preaching" [*predigen*], for it is after all the oral assurance of Christ *pro nobis*, the oral pronouncement of forgiveness. In the German and Latin texts "preaching" and "teaching" correspond to one another. What is meant is not the mute possession of a doctrine but the act of teaching doctrine orally; and again, not teaching that is divorced from giving assurance and comfort but teaching that is proclaimed.

In the same way, the emphasis is not on knowledge about the sacraments but on the actual administering of the sacraments. This must occur "in accord with the gospel" [*lauts des Evangelii*]. This means first of all that each sacrament must use its words of institution. A celebration of the Lord's Supper without the words of institution would not be a celebration of the Lord's Supper. However this rule must not be restricted to the liturgical order of sacramental administration, since the phrase "in accord with the gospel" extends to the right teaching about the sacraments. And again, the church is not essentially constituted by the mute possession of a gospel-oriented doctrine of the sacraments but by the "administration of the sacraments," that is, by the event of their being administered and their being received in relation to the right preaching about the sacraments.

If gospel and sacraments thus belong to the concept of the church, so do the sole "means" belong to the very nature of the church, by which God gives the Holy Spirit (Article V [BC 40–41]) and by which the Holy Spirit works.

In Article VII "the assembly of all believers" and the event of the preaching of the gospel and the administration of the sacraments are linked with the disputed words, *by which, in qua*. A corresponding "in" is found in a similar relationship in the Small Catechism of Martin Luther: "The Holy Spirit has called me by the gospel, enlightened me with his gifts…, just as he calls the whole Christian church on earth, gathers, enlightens…, in which Christian church he daily and richly forgives me and all believers of all sins…" (SC, the Creed, 6 [BC 356]; see also LC, the Creed, 54 ff. [BC 438 ff.]). The Holy Spirit calls the Christian church by the gospel and preaches the gospel in the Christian church. These statements already demonstrate that in the total context of the Lutheran Confessions the above "in" and "by" must be set forth in several relationships:

a) Gospel and sacraments are *in* the assembly of believers as the means by which the Holy Spirit awakens faith and brings about the assembly of believers.

b) Gospel and sacraments are *in* the assembly of believers as the service which is entrusted to this assembly and discharged by it. The church is "the mother who conceives and bears individual Christians through the word of God…" (LC, the Creed, 42 [BC 436]).

From this it follows that in the definition of Article VII of the Augsburg Confession the designation "assembly of all believers" and the assertion of the relative clause belong inseparably together. The relative clause adds nothing to the designation "assembly of all believers," but clarifies it. Hence it is possible—without mentioning gospel and sacrament—to define the church as "the assembly of all believers and saints" (Article VIII [BC 42–43]). Thereby nothing other is being said than what is expressed in Article VII. For the assembly of believers cannot exist at all without gospel and sacraments. Without preaching and sacraments it would crumble into nothing and would never have arisen.

In this definition of the church in Article VII of the Augsburg Confession there is no mention of the church's ministerial office. This occurs in Articles V, XIV, and XXVIII, for which reason there can be no thought in Article VII of preaching and the administration of the sacraments apart from the ministerial office. For no one should preach "*nisi rite vocatus*" [without a proper call] (Article XIV [BC 47]), that is, without a call into the ministerial office that Christ has instituted. Since Article VII only implies the ministerial office and does not explicitly refer to it, attention is focused on God's action through the gospel, and it becomes clear that the office is not an independently existing institution but only a service to the gospel.

Furthermore, it is striking that the confessions are also not mentioned in the definition of Article VII, although they at once emerge with the question of the meaning of *pure* and *recte*, of *rein* [pure] and *lauts des Evangelii*. But the confessions are a response to the preaching of the gospel and a fruit of the Holy Spirit, not his means, as are word and sacrament.

Finally, one should observe that the Bible is not mentioned in this definition of the church. This is all the more striking, since the Reformation stressed most emphatically that Holy Scripture is the sole norm of every doctrine of the church. That Holy Scripture is not mentioned in Article VII of the Augsburg Confession cannot therefore mean that the purity of the preaching of the gospel and the administration of the sacraments in accord with the gospel consisted in anything other than conformity to Scripture. But something is expressed here that is characteristic of the Augsburg Confession as a whole, which contains no article on Holy Scripture, and, beyond this, that also appears even in the Formula of Concord, namely, that it does not set forth in its "Summary Formulation" an enumeration of the canonical writings. Scripture is the sole norm of all church doctrine on the basis of the prophetic and apostolic gospel that is testified to in Scripture, that is, on the basis of the center to which the Old and New Testament bear witness: Jesus Christ.

The church is consequently defined by the event of the preaching of the gospel and the administration of the sacraments and thus by the Christ who is present, acting through the gospel and sacraments. The church is not yet present where the Bible, confession, and ministerial office are there, in silence, but rather where—on the basis of Scripture and in consensus with the ancestors of the faith, and with the brothers and the sisters—the gospel is preached and the sacraments are administered, the voice of Christ is heard, and Christ gives himself.

Consequently, in a similar way, the concept of church is distinguished from a false ontology as well as from its dissolution into individual, isolated events that lack all continuity. The continuity of the church consists in the identity of the gospel that is preached ever anew, and, for that reason, the church is visible. In that this gospel, by its very nature, accords with the apostolic gospel, the sermon takes place in apostolic succession. Because the public sermon occurs through the church's ministerial office (*"nemo debet in ecclesia publice docere aut sacramenta administrare nisi rite vocatus"* [no one may publicly teach in the church or administer sacraments without a proper call], Article XIV [BC 47]), one could also speak of an apostolic succession of the ministerial office. But this succession does not rest on the succession of ordinations (the call into the ministerial office can occur through officeholders as well as through the congregation), but rests rather on the identity of the gospel and the sacraments that Jesus Christ instituted and commissioned the apostles to pass on. If the series of ordinations in the Lutheran Church is unbroken from the ancient church up to the present day, this must be viewed as an external sign of the continuity of the church. The true apostolic succession does not depend on the laying on of hands, nor is it guaranteed by it. In all times the church preaches faith in the gospel. And when it does this, it is apostolic and it will remain "forever" to the end of the world (Article VII [BC 43]). This continuity is expressed in that the Lutheran Church has held fast to the confessions of the ancient church, it cites the church fathers as *testes veritatis* [witnesses to the truth], and it has retained the structure of the ancient church's liturgy.

II.

In Article VII of the Augsburg Confession the church is confessed as *"una sancta,"* as "one holy Christian church." It is by its very nature the one church, just as it is the holy, Christian, for example, as "the holy, catholic, and apostolic" church (Nicene Creed). It is one as the holy church because the one Holy Spirit works in it. It is one as the catholic church because the one Christ, the Lord of heaven and earth, rules it (*catholic* is translated as "Christian" in the Book of Concord). It is one as the apostolic church because its irremovable basis is the office of the apostles.

These statements about the unity of the church require demarcation at various points, in agreement with Eph. 4.5:

When it is taught in Article VII "that one holy Christian church must be and remain for all time," this cannot be understood to mean that the unity of the church is a future goal or a given task. Rather, unity belongs to the nature of the church. Either the church is the one church, or it is not the church.

But the *una sancta* is also not an otherworldly, transcendent possibility. Rather, it is a reality here on the earth. "We are not dreaming of a Platonic state ('of an imaginary church which is nowhere to be found') …, but we declare that this church exists ('is truly on the earth')" (Apol. VII.20 [BC 177]).

The unity of the church on this earth also does not consist, however, only as it were in the vertical dimension, namely, in the ever new acts of the one Christ and the one Holy Spirit through gospel and sacrament, but the unity of the church is always at the same time the fellowship of people with one another, upon whom God acts through word and sacrament. This is indicated already in the definition of the church as "the assembly of all believers." As surely as the gospel is being proclaimed respectively in the local fellowship of believers, Article VII looks nevertheless beyond the greatness or smallness of the local assembly, out to the whole of Christendom on earth. The Augsburg Confession indeed speaks not only of *the church*, but also of *the churches* ("*ecclesiae apud nos docent*" [the churches among us teach], AC I.1, II.1, III.1 [BC 36–39], and so forth]). Like Christendom on earth, the Christian congregation at a given place is also the church of Jesus Christ in the most proper sense. The definition of Article VII does not reject the latter but from the outset locks the door against a concept of the church which isolates individual congregations as independent entities. The word *harmonious* [*einträchtiglich*] in the next sentence of Article VII points further in the same direction. The *una sancta* consists not only in the reception of the one grace by isolated individuals, but it consists rather in the consensus of hearing and proclaiming the gospel and receiving and administering the sacraments. And this consensus, according to the Lutheran Confessions, is always two-fold, namely, a consensus with contemporary, living brothers and sisters in Christ and a consensus with the ancestors in the faith who went before us. Thereby the unity of the church by its very nature means fellowship in the Lord's Supper of all believers on earth.

In contrast, the unity of the church does not mean "that similar ceremonies instituted by human beings have to be observed everywhere." In this context "rites," "traditions," and "ceremonies" should not be too narrowly construed. Under these categories fall not only particular festivals and seasons but basically everything that is taken over from the past or set up currently within the ordering of the church by believers in the freedom of faith, whether it is the order of the liturgical service or the ordering of the ministerial offices. The concept of the church in the Augsburg Confession contains no definite determinations regarding the questions about a national church, a free church and the like, or about the form of church leadership. The Augsburg Confession also does not contain any definite positions on episcopal or synodical church leadership or about the particular development of the ministerial office in the local congregation through expanding the preaching office with diaconal, presbyterial, and other ministerial offices. Thus the Lutheran churches in Germany—most of which have gone over to an episcopal order since the end of the state church in 1918—stand in complete agreement with other Lutheran churches that have a synodical ordering (as in the United States) or those (as in Sweden) that have retained the office of bishop without interruption since the Middle Ages and thus can point to an unbroken succession of ordinations. The constitutive factor for church unity is not the form of the church's ministerial office, but rather it is solely the function of that office, namely, the preaching of the gospel and the proper administration of the sacraments.

For the Lutheran Church vis-à-vis the other church bodies, this teaching about the unity of the church means a great, constantly disturbing fact. This would not be the case if the Augsburg Confession taught only an otherworldly, eschatological unity or if the Lutheran Church were certain that beyond its borders the gospel was nowhere proclaimed. But at this point the Augsburg Confession is extremely cautious. While the congregations confessing their faith in Augsburg were one in their consensus about preaching the gospel purely and about administering the sacraments in accord with the gospel— and thus understood themselves as the *una sancta*—they also regularly took into account sisters and brothers in other, even heretical, churches with which the church of the purely preached gospel was in conflict. Even if in the Roman Church, bishops, teachers, and monks teach justification by human works and thus obscure the work of Christ, "yet there always remains a recognition of Christ among some pious people" (Apol. IV.392).[ii] Even if, in the doctrinally false Roman Church of the late Middle Ages and pre-Reformation days, preaching and the Lord's Supper were distorted, even at this time, as in all times, there still was a church on earth. And even if the gospel were confessed in a heretical church, if only in its liturgical prayers (Apol. IV.385)[iii] and were effective only in proper baptism, so even here one has to take account of believers in the diaspora on the basis of the overwhelming grace of God. This knowledge was taken seriously as an obligation to unite with these sisters and brothers. This "cautiousness" (*Leisetreterei* [lit., "stepping lightly" –Ed.]) in the Augsburg Confession is not to be judged merely negatively but rather also as an expression of a concerned effort toward unity, as cautious as it was untiring.

The concept of the church in the Augsburg Confession, when it is taken seriously, therefore regularly and necessarily gives rise to the strongest impulses toward the union of believers, for the *una sancta* is confessed to be a reality on this earth. Separations between believers are distortions of the one, holy, catholic, and apostolic church, a dishonoring of Christ, and a grave sin, which should let no congregation rest in peace.

III.

The unification of the separated churches has to begin with their mutual discovery of the others as church. How is the church to be recognized?

Here we need to distinguish between the problem of recognizing the *members* of the church and the task of recognizing the *church*, even if the church is never without its members.

Article VIII observes that "in this life many false Christians and hypocrites and even open sinners remain among the pious." "The church is hidden under the multitude of the wicked" (Apol. VII.19 [BC 176–77]); these constitute "the cross by which the kingdom of Christ is covered" (Apol. VII.18 [BC 176]). At the same time the Lutheran Confessions prohibit the church from cutting itself off from all nominal Christians, for this would be to pre-empt the Last Judgment, which the Lord of the church himself will accomplish. The Lutheran Confessions do indeed teach the exclusion from the church by excommunication of gross sinners, heretics, and those who despise the sacraments, and this excommunication is just as much an eschatological judgment as is God's absolution. But the church cannot and should not exclude the multitude of those nominal Christians. The *ecclesia proprie dicta* [the church, properly speaking] remains hidden in the *ecclesia large dicta* [the church, broadly speaking].

Nevertheless, the church is to be recognized with complete certainty, and indeed not only the church as an external religious fellowship but as "the assembly of believers,"—recognized, of course, not on the basis of its believing members, who are hidden among the nominal Christians, but once again on the basis of the gospel and the sacraments as its unmistakable signs. These are fundamental for the church, both in a causative and a cognitive respect. Where the gospel is preached purely and the sacraments are administered in accord with the gospel, there we reckon most certainly with the reality of the *ecclesia proprie dicta*, the fellowship of true believers, even if we cannot distinguish them in detail from the *ecclesia large dicta*, the merely external fellowship, for the gospel is the power of God which does not fail to awaken and renew faith. In this sense the true church, hidden under the variety of hypocrites, is visible on earth for faith.

These *notae ecclesiae* are taught as exclusive in the strict sense of the term [that is, as excluding the following –Ed.]:

The marks of the church are, for example, not the good works that believers do in love for God and others. These works, of course, are not rejected. They occur in the church "as thanksgivings to God" and are the weapons of Jesus Christ against the devil (Apol. IV.189 ff. [BC 150]). But hypocrites can also exhibit works, and it is precisely to believers themselves that their good works are hidden.

Likewise, a particular form of order is not a mark of the church, whether it is an order of the liturgical service or the ordering of ministerial offices or the ordering of the relations between church and state. The significance of order will thereby in no way be belittled; however, no particular form of order is constitutive for the church.

Finally, church discipline is also not a mark of the church, even if the power of excommunication is committed to the church by its Lord himself (see FC Ep XII.26 [BC 522]). The mark of the church is exclusively the preaching of the gospel, not the word that damns but the one that saves.

More striking is the fact that, in distinction from some statements in the confessional theology of revival [*Erweckungstheologie*][iv] from the nineteenth century, even the Lutheran Confessions were not named as marks of the church. In this connection, the Apology indeed speaks occasionally of confession (Apol. VII.3 [BC174]). This corresponds with a statement appealing to Nicolaus of Lyra that the church is there where "a right confession and declaration of faith and truth" are (Apol. VII.22 [BC 177]).[v] Since confession is always by its very nature a public word, it would make sense to identify it as a mark of the church, alongside the word and sacrament. Confession is, after all, bound most closely to word and sacrament as to content since it makes statements about what is pure proclamation of the word and what is right administration of the sacrament. It would thus make sense to designate the confessional writings, even if not a third *nota ecclesiae*, as a mark of the church in a derived sense since they teach and confess the two true marks of the church, namely, the gospel and sacraments. Nevertheless, we must be very cautious at this point, for in the passages above from the Apology the idea is clearly less about particular confessional documents than about the act of confessing. Just as the norm of the church is the biblical gospel and as the church is defined through the preaching of the gospel and the administration of the sacraments, so the Lutheran Confessions are not marks of the church as such, namely, as writings. Rather, they are marks in the events of *preaching* and *sacramental administration* that occur in accord with the confessional writings, namely, in accord with the gospel. The church is not to be recognized where the right confessional writings are valid constitutionally but the preaching is not in accord with them. On the other hand, however, the church can also be recognized where no definite confessional writings are in force, but where preaching and the administration of the sacraments are in accord with the gospel. As important as confessional writings are for the preaching of the church and as carelessly as the church acts if it dispenses with confessional documents, yet even then the confessional writings, if one holds fast to the Augsburg Confession, are marks of the church only in the actual event of proclamation that accords with the confessional writings. Without thereby letting the confessional writings disintegrate into ever new personal acts of confession, what has been said has significance for the marks of the church: confession is a mark of the church *within* the limits of the two sole marks, namely, the preaching the gospel and the administration of the sacraments. Since the confessional writings are by their very nature meant to serve the maintenance of gospel preaching and the right administration of the sacraments in the church, they are *nota ecclesiae in* this, their service. Thus the confessional writings are to that extent not a distinguishing sign of the church except as this *nota* coincides with the first two *notae ecclesiae* and only in the latter can these writings be recognized as a mark of the church.

IV.

This doctrine of the Augsburg Confession concerning the church implies an inescapable and lasting bond for the Lutheran Church in the ecumenical endeavors of our time. Neither the common threat of secularization and of anti-Christian powers against everything Christian nor the general disorder in the world that affects all Christians, neither church struggles nor war-time needs can as such be the basis for the union of the churches. Neither joint scholarly research nor liturgical movements, nor common social and political demands or obligations, can as such effect and bring about the unity of the church. Even the mutual assistance which the churches render one another in time of need does not as such create church unity. The Lutheran Church, to be sure, is open to cooperation with other churches in all such cases, and amid the shocks of our time is aware of its place within the fellowship of seeking and helping. Yet it can recognize the unity of the church only where *consensus de doctrina evangelii* [consensus in the doctrine of the gospel] exists. Here the Lutheran Church is bound by its confession.

What does "bound by its confession" mean? For the speaking and acting of the church the Augsburg Confession is obligatory as a consensus of the ancestors in the faith, of the sisters and the brothers, in the interpretation of Holy Scripture. As strongly as the factor of consensus is emphasized (see, for example, Article I of the AC [BC 37]: "*ecclesiae magno consensus apud nos docent*" [Our churches with great consensus thus teach] and the great number of citations from the church fathers, as well as the reference to dogmas of the ancient church), the consensus nevertheless has no weight of its own. The confessional writings are not obligatory as simply a consensus but only as a consensus in the right understanding of Holy Scripture. It is not the consensus that is judge over church doctrine and practice, but Holy Scripture. To be bound by the confession is the binding of the church to Holy Scripture as the sole norm. This binding is taught by the Augsburg Confession—not as a formal principle and not in a special article about the normative significance of Scripture—but rather in the witness to the center of Holy Scripture, namely, the gospel. The confessional writings are thus obligatory for the speaking and practice of the church since they jointly witness to the gospel on the basis of Holy Scripture. But the obligatory power of the confession does not simply manifest itself in the claim to conformity with the Scripture, but rather in the actual agreement with Scripture which again and again must be proved anew in the outcome of exegetical work.

To be bound by the confession includes the possibility, indeed under certain circumstances the obligation, for the church—over against new fronts of heresy—to unfold its confession through the interpretation of Holy Scripture, to supplement it, to guard it against misunderstandings, and to establish further confessional writings. In fact, as a general principle, being bound by the confession includes even the possibility of correcting hitherto valid statements in the confessional writings through a biblical-exegetical review on the basis of a better understanding of Holy Scripture. To be sure, neither an individual member of the church nor a theological school but only the church as a whole can authoritatively undertake such a correction. Being bound by the confession, however, precludes churches from proclaiming unity where *consensus de doctrina evangelii* is lacking, or where the confessional documents of the other churches reject the teaching of the Augsburg Confession regarding the gospel and the sacraments.

V.

This "being bound" of the Church of the Augsburg Confession means, on the other hand, at the same time the greatest liberation for union with other churches.

a) The Augsburg Confession faces the Lutheran Church with a constant and radical challenge, for, according to its teaching, the church is not yet present where one "has" the Augsburg Confession and where it is juridically guaranteed as "inviolable" by the church's constitution, but it is present where the gospel is preached purely and the sacraments are administered according to the gospel. The "church" is not yet present merely because it calls itself "Lutheran." Rather, the reality of the church is determined by the speaking and self-giving of the Christ who is present in word and sacrament. The Augsburg Confession in effect faces the Lutheran Church ever anew with the question, whether it really is "church" in its speaking and acting? Any and all self-glorification, all resting upon the laurels of the Protestant Reformers, all security in its possession of the Confessions, all comfortable self-sufficiency within the framework of its historically developed form—all these are shattered by the Augsburg Confession, for by it the church is asked about what is happening *hic et nunc* within itself. This questioning is the liberation of the church for Christ, who is constantly at work anew upon it, who was and is one and the same and will be forever.

b) The Augsburg Confession opens up, in a radical way, a view toward the brothers and sisters in Christ and thus for the one holy church beyond the borders of the Lutheran Church. The borders of the one church are thus not established by differences in the delimitation of the biblical canon. Those who disagree with one another about that delimiting of the canon (for example, regarding the value placed on the Old Testament Apocrypha) can still acknowledge one another as members of the one body of Christ, for the norm of all church speaking is the Bible, not in a formal or quantitative sense, but in its content, as the prophetic and apostolic witness to the gospel. The borders of the one church are also not as yet defined by differences between the local churches about the content of the confessional writings, provided they agree on the content of the doctrine of the gospel and the sacraments! In fact, basically the unity of the church can be a reality even without confessional writings—if only the pure gospel is preached and the sacraments administered in accord with it! Even the variety of orders of the liturgical service and of ministerial offices do not stand in the way of the unity of the church. The Augsburg Confession does not merely allow but requires that we penetrate through all these differences and barriers, and penetrate to the fullest extent of all Christendom and here to seek and find our brothers and sisters.

c) Being bound to the Augsburg Confession is an ever new liberation of the Lutheran Church since it is a matter of being bound by the gospel. Being bound by the gospel, however, is not an enslavement of doctrine and of life— enslavement would be the result of the law—but rather liberation for public praise of the mighty deeds of God. The Augsburg Confession sets no barrier of the law to the service of the church, but opens up to the church the great joy of servant ministry to all the world, which Jesus Christ has made his own possession through his death and resurrection. The Augsburg Confession erects no law of pure doctrine to correspond to the work-righteousness of a so-called orthodoxy, but calls us to the *kerygma*. The Augsburg Confession thus frees the church from the danger of doctrinairism, and from angst of the world, and from a posture of self-defense and self-preservation. The Augsburg Confession time and again reminds the Lutheran Church of the overwhelming richness of the gifts with which Christ endows it ever anew through word and sacrament so that it may thus serve the brothers and sisters in all the church bodies and unite with their offering of praise.

Editor's Notes

[i]   BC 32–33

[ii] This quote from the quarto edition of the Apology of the Augsburg Confession is omitted in the Kolb/Wengert edition of the Book of Concord. It is included in *The Book of Concord*, ed. Theodore Tappert (Philadelphia: Fortress, 1959), 167.

[iii] Schlink alludes to a section from the quarto edition of the Apology of the Augsburg Confession that is omitted in the Kolb/Wengert edition of the Book of Concord. It is included in Tappert's edition, 166.

[iv] The *Erweckungsbewegung* was a broad spiritual revival movement in German territories that occurred in the first half of the nineteenth century. While this movement had close ties to German Pietism, among Lutheran theologians there was a concern to relate the personal experience of spiritual rebirth to the Lutheran confessional teachings about repentance, the sacraments, faith, and good works. Cf. Matthew Becker, *The Self-Giving God and Salvation History: The Trinitarian Theology of Johannes von Hofmann* (New York: T & T Clark, 2004), 3–15.

[v]   Nicolaus of Lyra (c. 1270–1340), was a Franciscan who devoted himself to interpreting the Bible at the University of Paris. He is generally regarded as the most capable biblical scholar in the medieval period.

Chapter Six:
The *Cultus* in the Perspective of Evangelical-Lutheran Theology[1]

We all come from the historical event of the death of Jesus Christ for the world, and we are all moving toward the coming event of the end of history when Jesus Christ, who judges and saves, will reveal his glory to the world for which he died. The whole of humanity is encompassed by these two events, whether it knows it or not—whether it wants to admit it or not.

But we are not only encompassed by Jesus Christ as an event of a past which is ever receding and as an event of an indefinitely distant or near future, but we are all subject to Jesus Christ as the present Lord. The crucified one is the present Lord. In his exaltation God has already conferred upon him all the power and the glory which he will reveal in his Parousia. At the same time, however, as the exalted one he does not cease to be the man who bears the scars of his crucifixion on his transfigured body. As the one who sacrificed his life on the cross, the risen Lord is the eternal high priest who intercedes for his sisters and brothers on the basis of his unique historical self-sacrifice before God. Here too it must be said: the whole of humanity is subject to this Lord— whether it recognizes him as Lord or not.

In the midst of the world, however, the church is the fellowship of those who have submitted themselves to this Lord in faith, who praise him as Lord and who proclaim him to the world as the one-and-only salvation.

The church lives in this world in a two-fold movement: It lives as the people of God who have been called out of the world, who have received a new beginning through baptism into Jesus Christ, and who have been redeemed from the bonds and the judgment under which this world has fallen. At the same time, the church lives as the people of prophets, priests, and kings sent into the world, sent to proclaim salvation to the world and to intercede for it in prayer. In that way the church is the call-up and corps of God's kingly rule that is breaking into the world.

This two-fold movement in which the church lives in the world has its heart and center in the worshiping [*Gottesdienstliche*] assembly. What occurs in this assembly?

When I seek to answer this question, I have to begin by saying that in the

---

1 A lecture delivered on 1 August 1960 at the Roman Catholic International Scholarly Conference on "Worship and the Person of Today," which was held in Munich on the occasion of the Eucharistic World Congress. The formulation of this theme was set by the Congress. [This lecture was originally published as "Der Kult in der Sicht evangelischer Theologie," in *Der Kult und der heutige Mensch* [Worship and the Contemporary Person], ed. M. Schmaus and K. Forster (München: Hueber, 1961), 173–83. It was then published under the same title in KC 1.116–25. This lecture was translated as "Worship in the Light of Protestant Theology," *The Ecumenical Review* 13, no. 2 (January 1961), 141–52. A further translation by I. H. Neilson appears in CC (132–43) as "Worship from the Viewpoint of Evangelical Theology." –Ed.]

realm of Protestant theology there is a continual distinct reluctance to describe the Christian worship service [*Gottesdienst*][i] as *cultus* [*Kultus* = "an honoring of God"; "religious-sacrificial worship" –Ed.]. We talk about the pagan cultus [*Kult*], also about the Old Testament cultus, but only very seldom about the Christian cultus.

For on the cross Jesus Christ has offered up to God once and for all the atoning sacrifice for the sins of the world. Indeed, God himself has done this in giving up the Son to the cross. The death of Christ is thus the end of sacrificial worship [*Opferkultus*] by which human beings seek to appease God. But even the exalted Christ does not offer himself up again as a sacrifice to God. Rather, as the one sacrificed on the cross once and for all, he is the eternal high priest who never ceases to intercede with God for his own.

On the basis of this act of salvation on the cross, the Christian worship service is at its crux not a service of human beings to God, but God's service [*Dienst Gottes*] to human beings. Here God gives to the congregation the allotment of what Christ has accomplished for it. In the worship service Christ the Lord gifts himself to the congregation which he has purchased by his blood on the cross.

In this way Christian worship is different from Old Testament worship, just as the gospel is different from the law. Through the law God has demanded the obedience of human beings and made the attainment of life dependent on obedience to his demand. Through the gospel, however, God bestows life and exhorts people to walk in a new life on the basis of this new creation.

Just as Jesus Christ is the end of the law, so he is also the end of the *cultus*. That Christ is the end of the law, however, does not mean that he is the end of the divine command. But God's commandment encounters those who believe in the gospel no longer as law but as *paraclesis*, that is, as comforting, parental admonition. Accordingly, the authors of the letters in the New Testament—not only Paul—avoid describing the imperative of the gospel as law. That Christ is the end of the *cultus* means just as little as that he is the end of the worship service. But something so entirely new occurs in him that the old terminology is no longer adequate.

What occurs in the worship assembly of the Christian congregation? This question was answered by Luther in his famous sermon at the consecration of the Castle Church in Torgau in 1544: "…that nothing else is happening herein except that our dear Lord [Jesus Christ] himself speaks with us through his holy word and we in turn respond to him through prayer and the singing of praises" (WA 49.588.15 ff. [LW 51.333]). The Christian worship service is thus the action of God upon the congregation and the response of the congregation to God's action. We can also put it this way: The worship service is the service of God to the congregation, and it is the service of the congregation in the presence of God. This two-fold answer of Reformation theology to our question constantly recurs in the history of Protestant theology regarding the worship service, as also in the most important more recent study, *On the*

Doctrine of the Worship Service of the Congregation Gathered in the Name of Jesus, by Peter Brunner.[ii] In what follows I will endeavor briefly to comment on both of these statements about the action of the worship service in order later to develop them ecclesiologically and cosmologically.

I. God's Service to the Congregation

In the Christian worship service there takes place the remembering of God's mighty deeds and of the promises that God has given. This remembering refers to all of God's deeds: to the creation and preservation of the world, to the election and guidance of Israel and the church, but above all to his act of salvation in the death and resurrection of Christ. It likewise refers to all of the promises of God, above all to the promise of the Parousia of Jesus Christ.

This remembering takes place on the basis of Holy Scripture: as the reading of Scripture, as doctrine, and as proclamation. In this remembering, expression is given to the claim and the assurance, the demand and the gift that are contained in the deeds and promises of God for the gathered congregation. But above all it takes place in the assurance of the gospel: Christ was given into death for you! He was raised for you!

In this remembering of the act of God's salvation, God himself is present and is saving. Through the proclamation of his act of salvation he gives salvation. The New Testament expression *"Evangelium Christi"* says not only that the gospel proclaims Christ but that it proceeds from him; and again, not only that it proceeded from him historically but that he is working as the present Lord through the gospel—that through the gospel he lets us participate in his death and in his life. The gospel is God's active word, God's power. Thus it is not merely the message of God's act of reconciliation on the cross; rather, through the gospel, God makes us the reconciled ones. Nor is the gospel merely the doctrine that God justifies the sinner for the sake of Christ; rather, through the gospel God declares the sinner justified. And indeed this judgment, as God's gracious judgment, is at the same time God's re-creating word, which is simultaneously declarative and effective. In conferring upon us through the gospel the righteousness which he revealed in Christ on the cross, God removes us from the coming judgment of wrath and even now gives us the life which will become visible in the resurrection from the dead. Through the gospel he not only lets us take part in Jesus the crucified one but also in Jesus the exalted one, who will come as the Judge of the world.

In the remembering of Jesus Christ, bread and cup are then taken, blessed, and offered to the congregation to eat and to drink. In the remembering of Jesus' Last Supper, the same words are hereby spoken, which have been handed down as Jesus' words of institution: "This is my body for you." "This is the new covenant in my blood." In this action the death of Christ is also proclaimed. At the same time the future feast is anticipated which Jesus promised, which he will celebrate with his people in the kingdom of God.

What is more, in this feast of remembering, Jesus Christ is himself present and active. He himself, the exalted Lord, invites the congregation to the meal. He himself gives what his words of institution say: his body and the new covenant in his blood. He himself, the Lord, is here both the giver and the gift at the same time, for the forgiveness of sins and for union with him. In that in his giving he distinguishes between his body and his blood, the Lord gives himself to the congregation as the one who has sacrificed his life on the cross for it. As the eternal high priest he lets them take part in the atoning sacrifice which he made to God on the cross. In giving himself he brings the congregation into the new covenant, which God has established in his blood. In addition, the remembering of the coming meal in the kingdom of God promised by Jesus does not remain merely a memory or expectation. In that the Lord offers himself to the congregation as the one who has been sacrificed, he at the same time lets them take part in his victory and in his coming in glory. The prayer "*maran atha*" [our Lord, come!] is at the same time the confession "the Lord is coming!" He comes in the Lord's Supper on earth and even now lets people take part in the future wedding feast of the Lamb with the congregation.

God thus serves the congregation through word and sacrament. Through both he makes it possible for us to participate now in Christ's victory on the cross and in his Parousia, and he takes us into his salvific activity. Through both word and sacrament he acts to justify the congregation, to sanctify it, to make it alive, and to unite it with Christ. Neither is the proclamation of the word only directed to the life-giving meal, nor is the Lord's Supper only the confirmation of the life-giving word. Rather, in both together, God gives us life. For, after all, it is one and the same incarnate *Logos* who gives himself to us through word and sacrament. Determining the relationship between word and sacrament is in the last analysis such an exceedingly difficult theological problem only because the gift of God's grace is so immeasurable.

II. The Congregation's Service in the Presence of God

How does the congregation serve God who has stooped so low to it in Jesus Christ?

The service of the congregation consists above all else in that it lets this service by God happen to it and that it receives his inexhaustible gift in a way that corresponds to the majesty of the divine giver. How does it receive the Lord "truly, rightly, and worthily" [*wahrhaft würdig und recht*]?[iii] In no other way than in the complete surrender of the individual, of the heart and every limb, to the one who gave himself for us and who gives himself to us again and again. This surrender occurs in our turning away from ourselves, repenting of our past sins, in the renunciation of self-chosen plans and ways and, at the same time, in the surrender to him, in clinging to his word, and partaking in the meal of the new covenant. For both of these—the turning away from ourselves and turning to him—we can also say: the service of the congregation in the presence of God is above all faith. For faith is not without repentance and it entails taking hold of grace. At the same time, faith is certain of salvation, however not because of our repentance and our taking hold of grace but entirely because of God's act of grace to take hold of us.

This reception of grace in faith cannot remain silent. God has after all created humankind in his image so that human beings may give God the response of faith that corresponds to his address.

The congregation thus serves God by *confessing its sins*. It confesses itself unworthy to receive the Lord in its midst.

The congregation serves God further with the *praise of his grace*. It thanks him for all his mighty deeds and promises, above all for the act of salvation on the cross, for his acts in the past, and for the act that he himself now accomplishes in the worship service, for his act of salvation for us and for the whole world.

The congregation serves God still further with *intercessions* in the name of Jesus for the church and for the world. Praying to God in the name of Jesus means that while we pray we hold up to God the sacrifice that Jesus offered to him on Golgotha for the sins of all human beings.

In its service, however, the congregation does not restrict itself to thanking God for the historical act of salvation and praying for further acts which God has promised, but rather on the basis of these acts the congregation glorifies God through Jesus Christ as the one who he *is* from eternity unto eternity. In *doxology* the congregation glorifies the eternal sameness of the divine being and essence in which the truth of the promise is grounded.

All of these responses to God, however, are concentrated in the *confession of faith*. In the creed—as in baptism, so also in the worship service—the confession of sins, praise, adoration, and public witness are concentrated in a special way. In the multiplicity of these responses and in the spontaneity of their expression, the church confesses to be living daily anew solely by the grace of God.

In this commitment of oneself in the creedal faith and confession, the congregation offers itself as a sacrifice to God through Jesus Christ. The service of the congregation in the presence of God is the sacrifice of thanksgiving and praise that glorifies the sacrifice offered to God by Christ on the cross for the sins of the world and he lets the congregation take part in this sacrifice by means of word and sacrament. This service is the sacrifice of the Eucharist, which the church offers to God in its service. This is a total sacrifice. It cannot be limited to the heart and mouth of the person. It demands also the sacrifice of the body and of everything that belongs to the person. Thus the earthly gifts that are brought to God for the work and servant ministry of the church by its members are also described as sacrifices.

Here I will pause for a moment and ask: How are God's service to the congregation and the service of the congregation in the presence of God related to one another now in the worship service? Is it possible to distinguish between them at all?

God's service to the congregation occurs through the service of human beings. God speaks to and acts upon the congregation by means of human speaking and acting. Not merely the response of praise and prayer but also the assurance of the proclamation and the thanksgiving over the bread and cup occur in the spontaneity of the believing church and its members. Here again the congregation's service in the presence of God—with all of the spontaneity of the believing congregation—is at the same time God's action. This service is not only a response to God's action but is effected by God's action. It is the sacrifice of praise that God prepares for himself through the Holy Spirit. Thus God's service to the congregation and the service of the congregation in the presence of God not only belong together but they interpenetrate one another in a *single* spiritual event.

Thus the sequence of God's service and the congregation's service cannot be understood as the sequence of words and actions in the arrangement of the order of worship. Nor does this distinction mean that God's service and the congregation's service can be neatly assigned to different parts of the worship service. But certainly this distinction and this sequence of God's service and the congregation's service mark an irreversible inner order in Christian worship, an inner order which corresponds at the same time to the order of salvation history on which Christian worship is based and in which it exists.

Prior to the service of God by the church there occurred God's act of salvation in Christ: the sending of the Son into the flesh, the sacrifice of Jesus on the cross, and the proclamation of the victory of Jesus' cross in his resurrection from the grave. Prior to the service of God by the church there was the commission of Jesus Christ to remember him and to proclaim him to the world. Prior to the service of God by the church there was the promise that he will always remain with his own and will do his actions through them. Prior to the service of the church there were the apostles, the called eyewitnesses of the resurrection of Jesus Christ and the executors and servants of his mission and his promise. And prior to the service of the Church there occurred the outpouring of the Holy Spirit—not only, however, as a unique occurrence, like Christ's death and resurrection, but as an initial act of salvation which has been followed by more and more new outpourings on more and more new people.

This order in salvation history, on which the worship service is based, is at the same time the inner order which needs to occur in the Christian worship service. All human action through which God wants here to serve the congregation is once and for all determined by God's historical act of salvation and the mission and promise of the Lord that are connected to it. The spiritual spontaneity of the witnesses and pastors, through whom God acts upon the congregation, has only to serve the realization of the historical mission that Christ has given to the church and which has been handed down to us by the apostles. It is, after all, the nature of the Holy Spirit that he "does not speak of himself" (John 16.13), but "reminds" us of all that Jesus Christ has said (John 14.26). All that the Spirit makes present, every unfolding and concretizing of the Lord's words by the Spirit, confirms the finality of what Jesus Christ has said and done once and for all. The human speaking and doing by which God serves the congregation are thus completely enclosed within God's doing and brought into the one great movement of God's condescension into the depths of humanity, brought into his self-abasement, from his incarnation to the distribution of Christ's body and blood to the congregation in the Lord's Supper. This one continuous movement of God's condescension cannot at any point be broken by human beings or abbreviated by them, either in the action of those who serve in the worship service or in the thinking that occurs in theological reflection. For the movement of God's mercy aims at the assurance, "given for you." This movement reaches its fulfillment in the reception of his gifts by the congregation.

The person through whom God serves his congregation is thus merely the instrument through which God turns to human beings. That person does not reconcile God to human beings. God has already reconciled the world to himself in Christ (2 Cor. 5.18). The person has only to proclaim this act of reconciliation and to admonish, "Be reconciled to God!"—and in so doing those doing the proclaiming may be certain that God is admonishing through them (v. 20). The one so serving does not need to bring any atoning sacrifice for sin. After all, Christ has already made that sacrifice on the cross. That person has only to proclaim God's covenant in Christ's blood, has only to take bread and cup, to bless and administer them. And thereby that person can be certain that Christ himself administers his body and his blood in this meal to the congregation and thereby lets them take part in his sacrificial death on the cross.

Protestant theology is extremely restrained over against all of the obvious history-of-religion and syllogistic possibilities of a symbolic or even a realistically intentioned interpretation of the human act of blessing and bestowing by which God serves the congregation. The New Testament writings are famously most reticent in their statements exactly on this point. In the worship service we do not sacrifice Christ nor does Christ sacrifice himself afresh through our action. Christian worship is not an atoning sacrifice for sin offered by human beings to God; rather, it is Christ's once-for-all accomplished sacrifice for sin bestowed upon human beings by God, which the congregation receives by faith with adoring praise. The action of the church in the worship service is not a *sacrificium propitiatorium* but a *sacrificium eucharistikon* on the basis of the propitiatory sacrifice of Christ on the cross, in which God lets us take part through word and sacrament (see AC XXIV and Apol. XXIV, here especially §16 ff. [BC 260 ff.]).

III. The Ecclesiological Development of God's Service to the Assembled Congregation

In the Christian worship service God serves the people assembled there, he unites them with himself and with one another. In their reception of Christ's body, they are one body, his body. But God unites those assembled locally not only with one another but with all believers on earth, for it is the one Lord who bestows himself to his own here and in all places. Accordingly, the same word *ekklesia* is used in the New Testament to denote the local congregation as well as the whole people of God on earth. In the local congregation the fellowship of all believers is manifested.

This fellowship is not only fellowship with brothers and sisters who live contemporaneously with us but also fellowship with the ancestors who have preceded us in the faith, for, in every age, there is the one Lord by whose grace the believers live, the same Lord who acted upon them in the past and who acts upon us today. All of them, also the devout who lived during the old covenant, live by means of the sacrifice of Christ. The Old Testament cult of sacrifice already foreshadowed the reality of what was to come. So we serve God in fellowship with the apostles and the Old Testament prophets and with the known and the unknown members of the Old and New Testament people of God. The church of all times and places is manifesting itself in the Christian worship service. And indeed this fellowship consists not only in remembering historically those who have gone before us and on whose service we are building today, and it does not consist only in our preservation of their teaching in the worship service and in our praising God with their prayers. In the worship service we have fellowship with them as with those who are living even though they have died. In that in the Lord's Supper we already now take part in the coming wedding feast of the Lamb, we have—across the gulf of time and also across the problematic of our transitional state—fellowship with all whom the Lord will one day in his Parousia gather from every land and every age into eternal joy. It is in the adoration of the one Lord that the sojourning people of God on earth and those who have reached the goal are one.

IV. The Cosmological Development of God's Service to the Assembled Congregation

Through his service God also opens up for us at the same time the cosmic dimension of praise which he has prepared for himself in the non-human creation—that praise which has not been silenced by the fall of humankind. In the Christian worship service God is present as the Lord whom the angelic hosts praise without ceasing. By singing the *Gloria in Excelsis* and the *Sanctus*, the congregation joins this heavenly liturgy.

At the same time, God opens up to the congregation the praise for which he created the non-human visible creation. Despite all the deformation and the groaning of the earthly creation, faith recognizes that it also serves the glorification of God. Thus with the Psalter comes forth from the congregation the call to heaven and earth: "Praise the Lord *in heaven*…, praise him, sun and moon, praise him, all you stars of light…!" and "Praise the Lord *on the earth*, you sea monsters and all deeps, fire, hail, snow… mountains, trees, animals…!" (Ps. 148). Let each creature praise the Lord in his or her own way!

So arises in the Christian worship service the unanimous hymn of praise for which God created the universe. Heaven and earth are to adore the Lord and in their midst the human being as the image of God. Yet now the congregation's hymn of praise on earth comes to voice only in the form of prayers, pleadings, sighs, laments. Only in faith do we now take part in the adoration of the glorified saints and of the heavenly angelic hosts. The service of the congregation is still now surrounded by the groaning of the whole creation. And yet the church is already now the human voice of the hymn of praise, which the whole new creation will one day offer up to God.

The whole history of salvation is thus concentrated in a particular way in the event of the worship service, namely, the deeds that God has done and will do for humanity and the cosmos as Creator, Redeemer, and New Creator, and the appropriate response of human beings in the midst of all creation to these deeds. God's action and human action are unified in the worship service in that God condescends in Christ as servant and the congregation gives the glory to the crucified Christ as Lord and God. The liturgical event as a whole, as also the administration of Christ's body and blood "in, with, and under" bread and wine, thus participates in the structure of the incarnation.

In conclusion I come back again to what I said in my introductory remarks:

The worship assembly—the concentration of God's saving action—is the life-giving center of the vital activities of the church in the midst of the world, for again and again the Lord gathers here from the world those people scattered throughout the world, cleanses them from their sins, strengthens them in their temptations, unites them anew with himself. Again and again the Lord also sends his own into the world. In serving them he commands their servant ministry in the world, and in strengthening them he gives them authority for this service, the service of saving those who with the world fall under judgment unless they come to faith. Thus the sacrifice of self-surrender cannot therefore be confined to the assembly. If it is true surrender, then the sacrifice of praise by the congregation reaches from here into the world, and the whole life of the members of the congregation becomes the sacrifice of praise which extolls Christ. "And whatever you do in word or deed, do it all in the name of the Lord Jesus, giving thanks to God and the Father through him"

(Col. 3.17). The service to God offered by Christians is thus the daily sacrifice of the whole person in the obedience of acting and suffering. According to the teaching of the Reformers, the faith that receives God's gift cannot remain devoid of good works, although the believer does not receive grace because of the works. But faith in Christ makes us slaves of our Lord, and as his slaves we are set free for the joy of his service.

In this two-fold movement of the church—out of the world and into the world—the church is built up by God and it is the growing body of Christ, growing in talents and growing in members. It grows from Christ the head, who shares his sacrificed body in the worship assembly.

Of course, both the gathering from the world and the being sent into the world would be misconstrued if we were to think here only of the locally assembled congregation, for just as the one church of all times and places manifests itself in the local worship service through the self-giving of the one Lord, so the worship service by its very nature releases the urge to let the fellowship of all believers in Christ become visible beyond the local limits, in mutual comforting and admonishing, in helping and giving, and in the mutual sharing of talents and sufferings with which Christ distinguishes those who belong to him. This urge cannot stop at the boundary lines of the divisions that separate the various parts of Christendom from one another. This urge is rather the longing and loving search for fellowship with all who bear the name of Christ, in order to join with them in proclaiming to the world the Lord to whom it already belongs, even if it has not yet recognized it.

Editor's Notes

[i] The term *Gottesdienst* literally means "the service of God" (*Gottes* = "of God"; *Dienst* = "service"). Normally this German compound is translated into English as *worship* or *worship service*, as it will be here. The literal meaning of the word is crucial to Schlink's argument, however, since he plays with the two parts of it throughout the essay. *Gottesdienst* is first and foremost the *Dienst Gottes*, *God's service* to us in and through Christ and his sacrifice on the cross. This same Christ is now present and active through the word and sacraments in the Christian congregation. Faithful response to this divine service is the *Dienst der Gemeinde*, the service of the congregation, in hearing, repenting, praying, singing, confessing, bearing witness, doing works of mercy, etc. *Gottesdienst* thus encompasses both God's service to the congregation and the congregation's service to God.

[ii] Peter Brunner, "Zur Lehre vom Gottesdienst der im Namen Jesu versammelten Gemeinde," in *Leiturgia: Handbuch des Evangelischen Gottesdienstes* [Leiturgia: Handbook of the Evangelical Worship Service], vol. 1, ed. Karl Ferdinand Müller and Walter Blankenburg (Kassel: Stauda, 1954), 1.82–361. ET: *Worship in the Name of Jesus* (St. Louis: Concordia, 1968).

[iii] This phrase comes from the Preface to the Lord's Supper at the beginning of the Service of Holy Communion.

Chapter Seven:
Law and Gospel as a Controversial Issue in Theology[1]

Without question we are here concerned with one of the most difficult topics in general that arises in controversial theological dialogue. This is the case for a variety of reasons, not only because in the various parts of Christendom the two concepts "law" and "gospel" are by no means always and everywhere understood in the same way, and not only because the "and" that links both concepts together contains many possibilities for correlating them (for example, between connection and antithesis, between unity and disunity), which are by no means everywhere viewed and stressed in the same way. Beyond these reasons, the difficulty here consists in the fact that precisely in the treatment of this topic special problems—problems involving the ability to formulate and articulate dogmatic statements—arise in ways we do not encounter in the Christological and Trinitarian dogmatic decisions of the ancient church. This difficulty is especially the case in this topic the more one is aware not only of the salvation-historical sequence of law and gospel but also of their simultaneous interaction in which both words of God address each person anew again and again. This has, however, already taken place above and beyond the New Testament conceptuality in all churches in that they speak, even if in very different ways, of a lasting validity of the law for Christians. The ever new and overwhelming encounter of God with every human being in the word thus creates difficulties of a particular kind for the dogmatic statement. The issue of comprehending this event in dogmatic terms requires special clarification.

In what follows the subject matter will, to begin with, be developed systematically in six sections. We will not take up our point of departure with Luther or the Lutheran Confessions but rather with the New Testament, above all, namely, with several fundamental conceptual distinctions in Pauline theology. The point of departure is thus made with biblical presuppositions that all churches have in common. The seventh section then has as its subject the ecumenical significance of the distinction between law and gospel. The primary aim here is not to present and discuss the well-known points of controversy between statements of the Protestant Reformers and those of the Council of Trent, but it is rather an attempt to clarify the methodological

---

1 The basic ideas in this paper were shared at the joint conference of a Protestant and Roman Catholic ecumenical study group on 6 April 1960 in Heidelberg. In this connection, cf. also the paper which was given by Gottlieb Söhngen at the same conference and published under the title, "Gesetz und Evangelium" [Law and Gospel], in the quarterly journal for disputed issues in theology, *Catholica* 14 (1960), 81–105. [Schlink's lecture was published as "Gesetz und Evangelium als kontroverstheologisches Problem," *Kerygma und Dogma* 7, no. 1 (1961), 1–35. It appears in KC 1.126–59. An English translation by I. H. Neilson appears in CC (144–85) as "Law and Gospel as a Controversial Theological Problem." -Ed.]

presuppositions and perspectives under which the controversial theological dialogue about these distinctions would have to proceed in the midst of the scholarly issues of our time. Perhaps some new approaches for the dialogue will be achieved in this way.

I. The Issue of Distinguishing between Law and Gospel

In God's address to the sinner the following are to be distinguished:[2]

a) The word of the Old Testament law and the word of the New Testament gospel.

After the broken old covenant God made the new covenant. After Moses came Jesus Christ. Νόμος [law] is, according to Paul, the quintessence of the commands revealed by God to Moses and through Moses to the Old Testament people of the covenant. Εὐαγγέλιον [gospel] is the message of Jesus Christ, decisively the word of the cross, which is, however, always at the same time the word of the risen crucified one. The difference between God's Old Testament and New Testament word consists not only in the sequence of the divine message in time but also in what God has said and is saying through both of these messages, indeed in what he has done and is doing through them. The well-known and most important antitheses in which Paul juxtaposes law and gospel are as follows: through the law God requires the works of human beings, through the gospel God calls people to faith. The law proclaims the principle: whoever does the works that are required will live (Gal. 3.12), but through the gospel life is imparted to the believer apart from works of the law. Through the law God reveals sin (Rom. 7.7), he makes it alive (7.9), and increases it (5.20); through the gospel, however, God justifies the sinner. The law works death (Rom. 7.10), but the gospel brings life. The law is powerless; it cannot make alive (Gal. 3.21; Rom. 8.2), but the gospel is "the power of God for the salvation of everyone who believes" (Rom. 1.16). The law is the letter vis-à-vis stone tablets, but through the gospel the Spirit of the living God works in hearts (2 Cor. 3.2 ff.). The antitheses in the Letter to the Hebrews are perhaps even sharper. The law of the old covenant is here described as "weak and useless, for the law made nothing perfect," but Christ has "set aside" the law and introduced "a better hope, through which we draw near to God" (Heb. 7.18 f.). Close to the Pauline antitheses stands also the sharp Johannine juxtaposition

---

2 In the five-fold distinction set forth in this first part I link up with my essay, "Gesetz und Paraklese" [Law and Paraclesis (Encouragement)], in *Antwort: Festschrift zum 70. Geburtstag Karl Barths am 10. Mai 1956* [Answer: Commemorative Book on the Occasion of Karl Barth's 70th Birthday on 10 May 1956] (Zollikon-Zürich: Evangelischer Verlag, 1956), 323–35, and I refer the reader to the more detailed New Testament references given there (324 ff.). [This essay was reprinted in *Gesetz und Evangelium: Beiträge zur gegenwärtigen theologischen Diskussion* (Law and Gospel: Contributions to the Present Theological Discussion), 2d ed., Ernst Kinder and Klaus Haendler (eds.) (Darmstadt: Wissenschaftliche Buchgesellschaft, 1986), 239–59. –Ed.]

of Moses and Christ, law and grace (Jn. 1.17). In short, the law commands, the gospel gives. The law uncovers sin, the gospel covers it up. The law judges, the gospel justifies. The law kills, the gospel makes alive. In fact, all this is valid not only of the Old Testament ceremonial and judicial law, as one might expect, but precisely also of the moral law.

b) On the other hand, in God's Old Testament law one must make a two-fold distinction: between God's assurance [*Zuspruch*] and God's claim [*Anspruch*], between God's electing call and God's commanding call, that is, between the Old Testament promise and the Old Testament demand of the law. By *nomos* Paul denotes not only the Old Testament demand of the law, particularly therefore the Pentateuch, but in a broader sense all of the Old Testament Scriptures, also the prophetic books. Within this broader concept of *nomos* he again distinguishes law and promise and thereby uses a special concept of the law besides the broader one. More correctly, the sequence reads: promise and law, for the law "entered in" after the promise (Rom. 5.20). This distinction between νόμος and ἐπαγγελία [promise] is no less sharp than that between νόμος and εὐαγγέλιον. In the old covenant God has already promised as a gift of grace: righteousness (Rom. 4; Gal. 3.21), life (Gal. 3.21 ff.), the Holy Spirit (Gal. 3.14), sonship (Gal. 4.22 ff.), and so on. The faithful in the old covenant already had a share in these promised gifts, although all these promises pointed toward their fulfillment in Jesus Christ. But they share in the promise independently of the law and independently of the works of the law. If the promise were tied to the law and dependent on the fulfillment of the law, it would be null and void. "The promise that was granted to Abraham and his seed, that he should inherit the world as an inheritance, did not come through the law, but through the righteousness of faith" (Rom. 4.13). Even sharper is the antithesis of Gal. 3.18: "If the inheritance would have come from the law, then it would not have come from the promise; but God proved himself gracious to Abraham through the promise."

c) In the New Testament gospel we must also distinguish between assurance and claim, between God's gift and God's command, that is, between the gospel and exhortation. The gospel encounters the congregation as the assurance of righteousness and as the calling to serve righteousness (Rom. 6.19), as the assurance of salvation and as the directive "to work out your salvation with fear and trembling" (Phil. 2.12), as the power which creates new life, and as the command to walk in a new life. The apostolic proclamation makes itself heard as an indicative, indeed, as the reminder of the eschatological act of salvation that has occurred in the perfect tense for the believer, and as an imperative. The imperative is thus grounded in the indicative, namely, on the act of salvation which God has completed through the gospel for the believer, particularly in baptism. This grounding of the imperative in the act of salvation that has occurred for the believer is characteristic for the exhortations in the New Testament letters beyond Paul. For the sake of this grounding the appropriate sequence in which the two-fold address is to be distinguished within the gospel is: assurance—claim, gospel—command. Unlike the contrasting relationship of law and gospel, as well as of law and promise, here assurance and claim are closely bound together in a distinctive way, for God requires nothing of the believer that he has not already given him or her though the gospel. He requires of the believer only that the believer live as the one he or she has been made through the gospel: as the one justified, delivered, made alive, as a member of the body of Christ. For the distinctive character of this New Testament admonishing Paul uses the words παρακαλεῖν [to comfort] and παράκλησις [encouragement], which can only be rendered imperfectly as "to exhort" [*Mahnen*] and "exhortation" [*Mahnung*], for exhorting and comforting are closely bound together in a distinctive way in *paraclesis* [encouragement]. After all, this admonishing of the gospel is the unfolding of the assurance of God's act of salvation in Jesus Christ.

These three fundamental distinctions contain two further ones: Although God's word encounters people as a two-fold address in both the old and new covenants, namely, as assurance and claim, it is still necessary to distinguish between the assurance found in the Old Testament and that of the New, and also between the claim found in the Old Testament and that of the New.

d) The Old Testament promise must be distinguished from the assurance of the New Testament gospel, for the gospel proclaims the one who is promised in the old covenant as the one who has come in Jesus Christ. It proclaims the dawn of the promised time of salvation in him and the completely new thing that God has done and is constantly doing through the Holy Spirit for his people in the midst of this decaying world—the new thing that is now hidden but will one day be brought to light and fulfilled through the Parousia of Jesus Christ. The difference between the Old Testament promise and the gospel is thus not merely a temporal difference of the sequence in the divine assurance before and after the coming of Jesus nor a temporal difference of the sequence in human knowing, of first expecting and then recognizing, also of first knowing dimly and then clearly—before and after the coming of Jesus. On the contrary, the difference is indicated by the fact that in the death and resurrection of Jesus and through the outpouring of the Holy Spirit, God has accomplished the act of salvation, which changes everything as of now.

e) The Old Testament demand of the law must be distinguished from the command of the new covenant, the *paraclesis*, and indeed with the same precision the Old Testament promise must be distinguished from the assurance of the New Testament gospel, for the *paraclesis* does not command the new walk in true righteousness so that the person will be justified by these works; on the contrary, it is because the person is made righteous by the gospel that the *paraclesis* exhorts righteousness. Here the following does not apply as it once did under the law: Whoever does these works will live. Rather, because a new life has been given to you, walk in the new life. At no point does Paul designate *paraclesis* as law, although he occasionally includes commands of the law in it (Rom. 13.9). At no point does he designate obedience vis-à-vis *paraclesis* as a work of the law, although love is the fulfillment of the law (Rom. 13.10). Just as law and gospel are distinguished, so also are law and *paraclesis*. The law is powerless, but *paraclesis* participates in the sin-destroying and renewing power of God, which works through the gospel. The reluctance to designate exhortation of the gospel as law is characteristic also of the other New Testament letters. The household codes are thus nowhere designated as law. The same is true for the exhortations to love that are expressed anew again and again in the First Letter of John on the basis of the love of God that has appeared in Christ. Here the discussion is about the ἐντολή [command], which is both old and new (Rom. 2.7 ff.), but not about the νόμος. Only at the margins of the New Testament canon does this begin to change. But even the Letter of James shows a reticence in that it does not designate its imperatives with the same word νόμος (in an absolute sense!), as was the case with respect to the Old Testament law. The ancient church did, of course, soon begin to designate the New Testament imperative and even the gospel as *nova lex* [new law] or, even without the addition of distinctive attributes, to designate it as pure law (in an absolute sense!). In doing so, it cannot refer to Paul, nor to his occasional statements about "νόμος τοῦ χρι-στοῦ" [law of Christ] (Gal. 6.2) and the "νόμος τοῦ πνεύματος τῆς ζωῆς" [law of the Spirit of life] (Rom. 8.2), for the concept of *nomos* is taken up polemically here in order to express most sharply the very opposite of the *nomos:* the law of the Spirit is not the counterpart of the demanding law but rather the living working of the Spirit in the believer. The law of Christ is not the counterpart of the law's demand to love but rather the present reality of the love of Christ, which is given free reign in faith. But if the concept of law is to be used over and above such occasional paradoxical flash points to designate New Testament *paraclesis* in systematic breadth, then that will depend decisively upon its not being used in an absolute sense; and it will depend furthermore upon the newness of this law being worked out very clearly in contrast to the Old Testament law.[3] The same is true if *paraclesis* is designated as the *tertius usus legis* [third use of the law], as occurred most emphatically through Calvin. Here, too, it will depend decisively on whether this *tertius usus* is distinguished with complete clarity from the other truly proper ways of proclaiming the law and its effective working (its *usus politicus* [political use]) and its *usus elenchticus* [accusing use]).[i] If these distinctions are maintained, the concepts of *nova lex* and *tertius usus legis* need not necessarily obscure the distinctiveness of *paraclesis*. Looking back on the history of the church, one must of course acknowledge that there the concept of law has a proclivity of its own, which has in fact again and again led to a legalistic misunderstanding of

---

3 Cf. this with statements by Gottlieb Söhngen regarding the doctrine of the new law [*nova lex*] in the *Summa Theologica* of Thomas Aquinas (II.1.q. 106). See Gottlieb Söhngen, *Gesetz und Evangelium: Ihre Analoge Einheit* [Law and Gospel: Their Analogical Unity] (Freiburg; München: K. Alber, 1957), 51 ff.

the imperatives in the New Testament. For that reason, Luther did not designate *paraclesis* as such as *nova lex* or as *tertius usus legis*, but rather understood it, depending on the case, as the *usus practicus evangelii* [the practical use of the gospel].[4]

The theological issue of distinguishing between law and gospel within the one word of God emerges clearly only in the intersection of three fundamental differences, namely, between the Old Testament law and the New Testament gospel, between the Old Testament promise and the Old Testament demand of the law, and between the New Testament gospel and the New Testament exhortation, and the two further differences contained therein between the Old Testament promise and the New Testament gospel, as well as between the Old Testament and the New Testament command. And in fact these five distinctions intersect literally and factually in the cross of Jesus Christ. Jesus Christ, the incarnate Word, died to the law so that the gospel would be proclaimed as the message of the end of the law. His death transformed the Old Testament promise into the message of its fulfillment. At the same time, his death transformed the Old Testament demand of the law into the comforting exhortation of the gospel. Christ is the end of the law, pure and simple, both of the Old Testament promise and of the Old Testament demand of the law, for he has fulfilled both. He also fulfilled the law whose demand God has written into the hearts of all people (Rom. 2.15) and by which God makes all people accountable before his judgment seat. As the fulfiller of the law, Christ is the gospel. In his death God has put into effect his new covenant with sinners.

As is the case with the whole issue of properly distinguishing between law and gospel, the issue of the sequencing of "law and gospel" or "gospel and law" is also a multi-dimensional question. The sequence "gospel and law" is intellectually valid, since the gospel is the presupposition for the true recognition of the definition of the law. The sequence "law and gospel" is historically valid, for God sent his son after Moses and put into effect the new covenant after the old one. Within the doctrinal elements of the Old Testament law and the New Testament gospel the reverse sequence is, on the other hand, also valid, namely, "promise and law" as well as "gospel and exhortation"; for God's commanding is grounded both in the old and the new covenant on the basis of his act of salvation, which he accomplished out of his free love for ancient Israel and the church, and through which he at the same time has promised, as this very Redeemer, also to lead his own into the future. But both these sequences, "promise and law" and "gospel and exhortation," remain enclosed by the irreversible actual succession of the old and new covenant. For this reason, the set phrase that summarizes the many dimensions of this issue

---

4 Cf. this with Wilfried Joest, *Gesetz und Freiheit* [Law and Freedom] (Göttingen: Vandenhoeck & Ruprecht, 1951; 2d. ed., 1956), especially 82 ff.; Paul Althaus, *Gebot und Gesetz* [Command and Law] Gütersloh: Bertelsmann, 1952) [ET: *The Divine Command* (Philadelphia: Fortress, 1966), –Ed.]; and Lauri Haikola, *Usus legis* [Use of the Law] (Wiesbaden, Otto Harrassowitz, 1958).

of the sequence of law and gospel has always been termed "law and gospel," not "gospel and law." Moreover, the actual sequence of "law and gospel" then also recurs again in the believer hastening again and again from the word of judgment to God's word of grace, from acknowledging the divine "No!" to singing the praise of the divine "Yes!" in Jesus Christ.

Now we have to distinguish law and gospel, of course, not only in the historical consideration of the actual succession of the old and new covenant, and certainly not only from a theoretical position apart from the old and new covenant—such a position of an observing bystander does not exist—but we have to distinguish law and gospel through faith in the gospel, that is, as a member of the New Testament people of the covenant, as those who by baptism have been plunged into Jesus' death, and as those who, in the midst of the spiritual attacks and trials of this world, are heading toward the coming Judge of the world. But then we will recognize not only the distinction between the Old Testament law and the New Testament gospel but also, at the same time, the gospel in the Old Testament law and the law in the New Testament gospel. Thereby our topic becomes a most existential issue, one that again and again is a new concern about life and death for Christians.

II. The Gospel in the Old Testament Law

As members of the church we can no longer read the Old Testament Scriptures as the Jews do, for through faith in Jesus Christ we recognize the Old Testament law as fulfilled. Because the Old Testament *promise* is fulfilled in Jesus Christ, we no longer perceive it as promise but as gospel, as the good news of the salvation that has come. Because the Old Testament *demand of the law* is fulfilled by Jesus and we have died to the law by faith in Jesus Christ, we no longer perceive the Old Testament demand of God as the law which puts to death but as comforting exhortation of the gospel.

That the veil of the Old Testament is done away with for the one who believes in Jesus Christ (2 Cor. 3.12) means, to be sure, for the time being, the recognition that the ministry of the old covenant is condemned, judged, put to death; that it was a ministry of the letter, not of the Spirit, and that it was a ministry of only a lesser glory, indeed—in comparison to the ministry of the new covenant—it was of no glory (2 Cor. 3.6ff.). The unveiling of the Old Testament thus signifies the challenging and refuting of the understanding of the Mosaic Covenant—widespread in Israel and voiced especially in the Psalter—that the Mosaic Covenant has already given the sinner righteousness and life abundantly. It is now also clear that the historical transformation of the Old Testament demand from the free, commanding word of God into the law of God engraved in the letter of the law, which finally encompassed life inescapably, was no accident. In any case, Paul has declared the function of the law—to make sin abound—as the divine task that was given to him from the very start. Through Christ, life under the Old Testament law is unveiled as provisional, as waiting, questioning, failing, as the not-yet that God intended, which is now past and has been dismissed. Thus in Christ the Mosaic Covenant is unveiled as the "old" covenant.

But precisely this unveiling allows one to recognize that the Old Testament bears witness to Jesus Christ. Not only do individual passages bear witness to the coming one, but the Old Testament as a whole gives an outline of the coming Redeemer. Not only the Old Testament promises, which explicitly point to a coming one, who will establish righteousness and peace, but also the particular contradictions that exist between divine authority and the human reality of the Old Testament prophets, priests, and kings; and beyond that, the existence of the Old Testament people of the covenant and its devout ones will now be recognized as witnesses to the coming redemption. We now hear the witnesses to the Old Testament expectation in their relation to the Old Testament contradictions and questions as witness to the final answer that God has given to sinners in Jesus Christ. In faith in Christ we may live from the fulfilled Old Testament promise as from the gospel, and we may perceive the command of God in the old covenant as divine fatherly instruction.

In this two-fold unveiling, the Old Testament Scriptures are the Bible of the congregation of Jesus Christ. In the light of the glory of the gospel it becomes clear that the glory of the law can hardly be described as glory (2 Cor. 3.10). But precisely through this unveiling of the law, the surpassing glory of the gospel comes to light. The Old Testament law, as at once the glorious and not-glorious (2 Cor. 3.7–11), bears witness simultaneously to the inexhaustible treasures of the gospel for the one who believes in Jesus Christ.

III. The Law in the New Testament Gospel

The gospel proclaims God's act of salvation in Jesus Christ: God placed Jesus under judgment on the cross, a judgment which befits the sinner, and God revealed him in the resurrection as the one who knew no sin and who by suffering and dying took the sins of the world upon himself. Thus the gospel is by its very nature at the same time the proclamation of the judgment which the sinner deserves. It proclaims this judgment as the judgment borne by Jesus and thus as the acquittal and redemption for everyone who believes in Jesus Christ. But thereby the gospel does not cease to require the acknowledgment of the judgment that we deserve. The call to faith is always at the same time a call to repentance. But thus the redeeming gospel can become God's word of judgment. The gospel brings about life for the one who believes in the coming of God's Son, and it brings death to the one who rejects the obedience of faith. "Those who believe in him will not be judged. Those who do not believe are already judged, because they have not come to faith in the name of the one Son of God" (Jn. 3.18 [modified—Ed.]). Thus Paul, the preacher of the gospel, understood himself to be "a sweet fragrance of Christ among those who are being saved and among those who are perishing: to these a fragrance of death to death, to the other a fragrance of life to life" (2 Cor. 2.15). Just because God, who justifies and makes alive, acts through the gospel, no one can hear the gospel and remain the same person who he or she was. Either one yields to this divine saving activity, or one falls under the verdict of God's wrathful judgment. Indeed, through the gospel God is doing the work of the law with the most pointed intensification and conclusive radicalness, for Jesus Christ is the last message of God, after he had previously spoken through Moses and the prophets—the final address, which is followed by no other. As this last and definitive address, Jesus Christ is to be proclaimed and believed. After all he suffered definitively the judgment of God upon human beings. There is no other acquittal for the sinner in all eternity than by faith in this Lord who has been judged for us.

What is true of the assurance of God's act of salvation in Jesus Christ is true also of the imperative of the gospel, which is grounded in the indicative of the act of salvation. The exhortations of the New Testament letters call for the believer not only to believe in the redemption by Christ but also to await the coming Day of Judgment. The same people who receive justification by faith alone in Christ, apart from works, are now exhorted to do such works so that they can stand on that Day. Again and again Paul pointed to the coming Day of the revelation of the righteous judgment of God, who will recompense each one according to his works. This verdict of judgment will be two-fold depending on the work: for some it will be acquittal to life, for others the sentence to perdition. Paul announced this judgment not only to the world but also to the congregation, and in so doing expressly included himself (see, for example, 2 Cor. 5.10), that is, he announces the judgment to the same ones to whom by the gospel he announced the verdict of justification and thereby the eschatological acquittal. So within Paul's proclamation there are two opposing verdicts being announced: the eschatological verdict of justification that is received by faith independently of the works, and the judgment according to the works. This antithesis Paul did not resolve logically, and it cannot be resolved logically. It can neither be removed from the Pauline message as a Jewish remainder, nor can the preaching of judgment be limited to non-believers. Instead, the announcement of the judgment belongs inseparably to the gospel of Paul. In this sense he can say: "According to my gospel, God will judge the secrets of everyone by Jesus Christ" (Rom. 2.16). Accordingly, within a broad definition of the gospel that designates the entire New Testament message, we need to distinguish not only between gospel and *paraclesis* but also between the gospel as the message of salvation and the announcement of the judgment according to works.

In the expectation of the coming judgment, the exhortations of the apostle with respect to the sins in the congregation can become not only imploring and warning but also threatening, judging, and punishing. Then they are not only the comforting, entreating unfolding of the gospel and of the new life effected by the gospel, but they become the demonstration of sins, the threatening announcement of the divine judgment and a chiding wrestling for the sake of the members of the congregation who are in danger. This warning finds its most pointed concentration in the anathema against such members of the congregation who do not live by grace. With the anathema the apostle has not only announced the coming divine judgment, but through the anathema the handing over of the sinner to the punishing judgment of God is carried out.

God thus acts through the New Testament gospel, not merely to justify but also to judge, not merely to save but also to condemn, not merely to make alive, but also to put to death. So long as we are journeying through the world we have to take seriously this two-fold working of God through his word. Precisely through faith in Jesus Christ we have to acknowledge our sins daily and to pray, "Forgive us our debts." We hear the gospel not only as the message of the one who died for us but also as the message of the Son of God who was brought to the cross by us. We hear the exhortation of the gospel not only as the assuring imperative by which God develops our faith but also as the threatening warning and the judging verdict by which God uncovers the disobedience of believers. Thus Jesus Christ is every day anew the Savior and Judge of believers. The believer is free from the law only in that the believer at the same time in repentance acknowledges the claim of the law that is proclaimed by the good news of the gospel as the claim fulfilled by Christ.

Even though this function of the gospel to announce and carry out the judgment corresponds to the judging function of the law, at no point did Paul designate his exhortations as law—even when they became threatening, indeed judging—and still less did he designate his gospel as such, even when it judges the unbeliever. Even where Paul recognizes himself as "the aroma of death unto death" (2 Cor. 2.16), he knows himself as the servant of the gospel, not of the law, for the law had only a temporary validity, until the revelation of the gospel (Gal. 3.19). Christ is the end of the law (Rom. 10.4). Despite this unambiguous salvation-historical understanding, which is also prevalent throughout the other New Testament letters, it is legitimate (by virtue of its content) to describe the gospel's function of announcing and declaring judgment as law. As questionable as it is to describe New Testament *paraclesis* as such as law, it is appropriate in view of the special threatening and judging function which it fulfills toward the sinful member of the congregation. In this sense, Luther also taught the abiding validity of the law for the Christian. As Paul had defined the concepts of law and gospel in terms of their salvation-historical sequence, Luther, like the ancient and medieval church, understood the law no longer as the past but as a threatening present. Of course, in contrast to the customary church usage of terms, he acknowledged, to be sure, the function of the law for the Christian in the exposing of sins, judging and putting to death, but in contrast to that, he avoided using the concept of law to designate *paraclesis*—the comforting, fatherly instruction of God that is grounded in the renewing power of the gospel.

IV. The Unity of Law and Gospel

Thus in the Old Testament law we at the same time encounter the gospel, and in the New Testament gospel we at the same time encounter the law. The distinction between law and gospel is thus not merely a distinction between the Old and New Testament, but rather it goes right through the Old Testament word of God and right through the New Testament word of God. It is a distinction not only in the historical sequence of God's dealings with humanity but also in their being simultaneously together in God's dealings with every human being—ourselves included.

But in view of such simultaneity and intertwining, how are law and gospel still to be distinguished? In fact, they will be properly distinguished only by the person who knows about their belonging together, indeed, about their unity, for the fact that law and gospel belong together is itself grounded in the unity of their origin in the triune God, who speaks and acts through both words.

Law and gospel are the address from the one God. This unity is by no means only that of an imperceptible moment of origin in time, but it consists in that the Redeemer speaks and acts through law and gospel. God's commanding and bestowing, God's judging and redeeming address, God's old and new covenant—all are free acts of one and the same divine love, acts of his merciful condescension to sinners. In fact, the same God speaks and acts through law and gospel, the same God who in the beginning created humankind in God's image and has placed human beings under the promise and command of God's image. The Creator, who bears witness to himself as Lord to all people through the works of his creation, deals with those who have fallen into judgment by means of law and gospel as the Redeemer. Law and gospel are the revelation of one and the same righteousness of God. The same righteousness that God requires of the sinner through the law, he assures the sinner of, through the gospel. The same love that he commands through the law, he works—through the good news of the act of love on the cross—as the fruit of the Holy Spirit in those who believe in Christ. The same sanctification that the law demands is produced by the gospel. We can continue: law and gospel are the revelation of one and the same divine love and righteousness, faithfulness and wisdom, lovingkindness and holiness of God in Jesus Christ.

Law and gospel have their unity in Jesus Christ, in whom God has come to us sinners. Law and gospel together bear witness to Jesus Christ: as a promise of the one who is coming and as a message of the one who has come, as an exhortation to obedience and as a message of the one who was obedient, as an announcement of judgment and as a message of the one upon whom judgment was carried out. Through the law that kills, God drives the sinner to the same

Christ, into whose life he transfers the sinner through the gospel. Jesus Christ is thus the one *Logos* of God, whom God proclaims through the Old Testament law and through the New Testament gospel, through the prophets and through the apostles.

Law and gospel are the work of the one Holy Spirit. Even if God does not bestow the Spirit—who renews the heart—through the law but only through the gospel first, the law is nevertheless still "spiritual" (Rom. 7.14), for God shows through the law the same spiritual human being whom he creates through the gospel. Thus, even though God does not create the new person through the law, he nevertheless drives the sinner through the law to the beckoning pleas of the renewing work of the Spirit. On the other hand, the Holy Spirit produces in the believers the fruit which the law had previously demanded in vain, that is, had demanded but had not produced. The effect of the Holy Spirit is the same love which the law demanded but which did not bestow because of its impotence. Where the fruit of the Holy Spirit—love, joy, peace, and so on—is present, there the saying is valid: "Against such there is no law" (Gal. 5.23), for the fruit of the Spirit corresponds to the demands of the law. Yet this fruit is not produced by the law, but by the gospel.

That the law and gospel belong together is thus grounded in the unity of their origin in the triune God, in the unity of his divine will that manifests itself through both addresses. The same love in which God created human beings in the beginning so that they would love him in return, encounters the sinner as demand in the law and as gift in the gospel. The same image of God in which God created human beings in the beginning encounters the sinner as command in the law ("You shall be holy, for I am holy") and as assurance in the gospel, the assurance of the work of Jesus Christ, who sanctified himself for the world. The gospel brings about the transformation into the image of God that appeared in Jesus Christ—the transferring into the sonship, which is revealed in the "only begotten Son." In the different forms of the law and the gospel and the different ways of encountering them, one and the same divine will of love manifests itself, which from the beginning of creation is directed to the people of God, the fellowship of the sisters and brothers of the eternal Son of God.

The revelation and accomplishment of this one intention of love takes place in an historical sequence. That the law and gospel belong together should not be understood as a timeless unity. It appears rather in the course of God's activity in history. It is no static unity but rather the decisive turning-point that has occurred in the humiliation and exaltation of the Son of God and in the outpouring of the Spirit, an historical turning-point which takes place anew whenever the gospel is preached to those who come to faith in Jesus Christ. Law and gospel thus belong together in an irreversible coordination of their ministry. The law is the task-master unto Christ (Gal. 3.24) so that we become righteous by faith and freed from the law. But to be freed from the law means to live in the power of the Holy Spirit whose fruit corresponds to the command of the law. The unity of law and gospel consists thus in the event of the transition from the existence of the sinner under the law into the life of the believer under the gospel. For that reason, the unity of law and gospel is then properly taught only when law and gospel are distinguished.

V. Distinguishing between Law and Gospel

But how are law and gospel to be distinguished, if in the Old Testament law we at the same time encounter the gospel, and in the New Testament gospel we encounter at the same time the law? How are they to be distinguished if they are one in Jesus Christ?

Does the distinction between law and gospel consist solely in distinguishing between unbelief and believing, so that the same word saves the believer and judges the non-believer? As surely as the gospel can be distinguished from the law only in faith, the distinction between law and gospel is not to be found in the acts of not-believing and believing. Neither faith nor unbelief creates the distinction between law and gospel. Rather, it precedes faith and unbelief as a distinction in God's word. Only by means of the distinction in God's word is faith and thus the certainty of salvation possible.

Is the distinction between law and gospel only the distinction between the two-fold effect of God's working, so that through one and the same word he rescues the one and damns the other, makes the one alive and puts the other to death? As surely as God is free to put the ones to death and make the others alive through one and the same word, so the distinction between law and gospel is nevertheless not only a distinction in the effect of God's working, but is also the distinction in a two-fold address by which God proclaims two different things.

The distinction between law and gospel also does not consist merely in that through his one word God deals in a two-fold manner with each human being: uncovering and covering, tearing down and building up, judging and acquitting, being wrathful and loving. As surely as God works also in the Christian in a two-fold way, so surely is the effect of this two-fold working not a miracle hidden behind the one word, but rather the effect of this two-fold working takes place through the two-fold *address* [Anrede] of God and is manifest in the two-fold address of God:

Through the law God requires everything of us; through the gospel he grants us everything. Through the law God commands what we are to offer to him; through the gospel God offers himself in Christ for us. Through the law God announces judgment upon sinners; through the gospel he proclaims to them that the judgment suffered by Christ means acquittal. Through the law God uncovers the reality of the sinner; through the gospel he covers the sinner with the righteousness of Christ. These are not only different effects of the one word of God but are also different words through which God does the acts of judging and acquitting, of putting to death and making alive, which are proclaimed by them. Despite the unity of the speaking and working of God, both words cannot be identified with each other. Despite the historical ordering of the law toward the gospel in the unity of God's will, we are again and again being called into question and astonished by the two-fold address of God in such a way that it is impossible to derive the law logically from the gospel or the gospel from the law and to resolve their basic difference from each other.

Law and gospel are to be distinguished as long as we are on our journey in this world, for the whole human race—whether it knows about it or not, whether it recognizes this or denies it—is journeying toward the Day when Christ will come in his glory and will judge all the living and the dead. Then he who is the one Word of God will speak two different words: to the ones, "Come, you who are blessed of my Father," and to the others, "Go away from me, you who are cursed" (Mt. 25.34, 41). The church is hastening toward this coming Day. For now, both words are still to be proclaimed to every human being. But some day both words will stand separately so that only one of the two will be addressed to each and every human being. Through the proclamation of the differing words of gospel and law, the church is to serve this final subjection of the world to Jesus Christ, the Judge of the world. In the expectation of its Lord the church proclaims the acquittal of believers in the judgment and the judgment according to works, and it thus calls everyone to repentance and faith.

Beyond that, however, the distinction between binding and loosing is a most concrete one: in God's mission the sins of human beings will *either* be forgiven *or* retained. As surely as the message of God's judgment and grace goes forth to each human being, there are just as surely decisions against God's grace by which unrepentant sinners now place themselves once and for all under God's "No." If the church no longer dares "to bind sins" of the unrepentant sinner and thinks all it can do is to forgive sins—whether the sinners desire it or not—then it fails to recognize the mission that has been given to it, and indeed then it fails to recognize not only the seriousness of the divine law but also the glory of the gospel, the heavenly joy over the sinner who repents.

VI. The Gospel as God's Proper Word

Now it is of course absolutely crucial not to stop with the observation about the succession and intertwining of law and gospel, of their unity and difference. Law and gospel are, after all, not timeless ideals but rather the ever new, most concrete, historical event of God's commanding and bestowing, judging and saving, putting to death and making alive. Is it not in fact here all about the very existential question: Is God gracious to me, *or* is he angry with me? Is it not in fact here about a still further question: Am I to speak God's acquittal *or* God's judgment to my fellow human beings? Is it not finally about a decisive either/or and not only about a both/and. Distinguishing law and gospel means answering *in concreto* these questions that come daily anew. Were we faced here only with an indecisive both/and, we would face only despair.

But how can a person carry out this distinguishing? How can one grasp this distinction completely in a dogmatic formula? Is this distinguishing not precisely altogether concrete and thus to be carried out again and again anew? In fact one may not ignore for a moment that this concerns the speaking and acting *of God* in two different ways: Got himself is the Lord, who has distinguished between law and gospel and does so ever anew. The dogmatic statement has to point to God's own actual activity of distinguishing, but it cannot replace it. Dogmatic thinking here changes into a hastening, a pleading, a grasping, and a stooping down, for the concrete distinguishing between law and gospel takes place through God's working in the power of the Holy Spirit. The gift of the Holy Spirit and the two-fold commission—to remit and to retain sins—belong together by their very nature (Jn. 20.22 ff.). Neither through a dogmatic formula nor through ethical casuistry can the concrete distinguishing between God's two words be pre-empted. Distinguishing between law and gospel is to be sought in prayer from God himself. In that he himself distinguishes between both words, he leads us toward the coming Day.

There is, of course, one thing that dogmatics has to teach most steadfastly above and beyond the sequence and intertwining of law and gospel, and their unity and difference. What is more, absolutely everything depends on dogmatics teaching this clearly: *God's proper word* is the gospel, not the law. God's *proper judgment* is the acquittal, not the sentence of condemnation. God's *proper work* is making alive, not the putting to death. "God did not send his Son into the world in order to judge the world, but that the world might be saved by him" (Jn. 3.17). Jesus Christ died on the cross, not in order to perpetuate the guilt of human beings, but in order to blot it out. As long as the age of grace lasts, as long as humanity still is waiting for the arrival of the Judge of the world, the last decisive word has not been spoken, but God works on—through all of his commanding, judging, and putting to death—toward salvation by faith in the gospel. The Judge of the world is still the Christ who died *for us*. In this sense the law is God's *alien* work and the gospel God's *proper* work. This holds true even of the word by which God binds and retains sins. Even this most extreme word of the law stands in service to the gospel, for it is the most paradoxical, most extreme preaching of divine love, even if it relinquishes every assurance of love and leaves the unrepentant person expressly to the judging activity of God; for this most extreme word of the law is the last summons to the unrepentant person: Turn around, so long as there is still time!

Distinguishing between law and gospel is thus by no means the acknowledgment and proclamation of a timeless dialectic of two equally weighted contradictory statements, but rather the urgent proclamation of the glory of the gospel—so superior to the law—which presses forth ever anew into the most varied of historical situations, hastening to the sinner. Distinguishing between the law and the gospel thus takes place when, under the announcement and proclamation of the law that puts to death, the Christ who was put to death is preached and praised above all. He is the revelation of the divine will of love that disarms sin, death, and law. No magnitude of sin, no abyss of forsakenness, no hopelessness of despair may keep the preacher of the gospel from distinguishing between law and gospel in this way and not otherwise.

Distinguishing between law and gospel is thus learned in *Anfechtung*. What does *Anfechtung* mean?

It is called an *Anfechtung* when people attack the congregation of Jesus Christ and persecute the believers, take them prisoner, and even kill them. Such sufferings, which people bring upon the congregation, is by no means to be underrated, and yet they are, as such, not really *Anfechtung*, for in this suffering Christians can know themselves to be completely secure in the hand of their Lord.

It is similarly called an *Anfechtung* when unseen powers of destruction surround and attack the congregation, elicit desires and anxieties to tempt it to fall away and to awaken enmity against it. The attacks of devilish powers are likewise not to be underrated, and yet they too are not the real *Anfechtung* of the congregation. The promise has surely been given to it: "The gates of hell shall not prevail against it" (Mt. 16.18).

The real *Anfechtung* begins where we recognize that neither people nor powers can attack, tempt, or torment the congregation if God had not given them the power to do so. Real *Anfechtung* arises for the congregation not through antagonistic people and powers but through God's word, namely, when the congregation in its needs sees itself measured against God's holy commands and recognizes itself as delivered up to God's righteous judgment. That is the true *Anfechtung*, when the same God who has given his promise to the congregation reveals its sins, when through his exacting claim he strikes from its hands the promises behind which it hides its vices, and when he leaves no doubt that he is the deadly enemy of sin. If the decline of the congregation is revealed, then Moses and the prophets, Jesus' Sermon on the Mount and cross and even the comforting, exhorting apostles become enormous, threatening figures who take one's breath away. Then only sin instead of grace, only wrath instead of love is shown by God. Then sins are glaringly apparent, and not one deed remains of which we could boast or which we could even excuse.

In the *Anfechtung* Christians may not deny God's judgment that is rendered against them, but they must acknowledge it as righteous judgment, they must humble themselves under God's mighty hand: "Indeed, we have deserved God's judgment." But at the same time, they may and should faithfully plead God's promise over against God's judging word. If God says to you, "I am angry with you," then you plead to him: "But you were angry with your Son." If God says to you, "I hate your sins," then you say to him: "Yes, but you made your Son to be sin." If God says to you, "I forsake you," then you implore him:

"That is not true; for you have forsaken Jesus Christ. Indeed, you yourself have taken our God-forsakenness upon yourself in your Son. His righteousness is now mine. I am secure in his steadfastness, in his steadfast suffering unto death." Christ was not merely attacked [*angefochten*][ii] by the Devil and by human beings, but by God himself, who forsook him on the cross. He called that God "mine" who had become the distant God. He still named him his God, who appeared impotent in view of the agony of his dying. The congregation undergoing *Anfechtung*—as it therein acknowledges the divine wrath—has, through faith in Christ, to praise the divine love.

In bowing in repentance beneath the word of the judging God and clinging in faith to the word from the cross, the Christian is distinguishing between law and gospel. This is the distinguishing: in knowing God's righteous law, to hasten to the gospel; in acknowledging God's deserved judgment, to grasp the righteousness of Christ in faith. But it is not as if through this distinguishing law and gospel it were so distinguished for the first time. God distinguished them once and for all time in his act of salvation on the cross. Here the juridical claim of the law was taken with complete seriousness and at the same time brought to an end. We need only to grasp this distinction again and again.

In this daily hastening of the believing sinner from God's deserved wrath to God's undeserved love, in this daily fleeing away from God's "No" to God's "Yes" in the daily petition, "Forgive us our sins," the sequence returns in which God has first revealed in history the Old Testament law and then the New Testament gospel. The succession of the two-fold divine address in world history is at the same time the direction in which the congregation is going toward its returning Lord and Redeemer.

The church's teaching may not isolate the gospel: The good news of the gospel would no longer be proclaimed if the demand and judgment of the law were denied. The church's teaching may also not isolate the law: God's exacting claim would not be taken seriously if God's mercy in Christ's death were concealed. Law and gospel, however, may not also be taken as equal: Even this can only end in hubris and despair. The church must distinguish law and gospel in that it proclaims the gospel as God's proper word—by keeping open and pointing salvation's way of rescue from the law's judgment of condemnation to the gospel's judgment of justification. Dogmatics serves the distinguishing between law and gospel by leaving a place open for the distinguishing that God himself accomplishes: "For as high as heaven is above the earth, so great is his grace for those who fear him. As far as the east is from the west, so far does he remove our transgressions from us" (Ps. 103.11 ff.).

VII. The Ecumenical Significance of the Distinction between Law and Gospel

The distinction between law and gospel is of the greatest significance actually for the whole of Christendom, for God always encounters us as the exacting and giving one, and again as the giving and exacting one. Again and again God calls to repentance and faith and new obedience. Again and again the human being seeks to withdraw from this call of God, whether through libertinism or through legalism or through despair or through self-security. Thus this security in which human beings barricade themselves from the living God can refer to their reliance on their own works, but also to their use of the means of grace. In the midst of such different temptations and hardenings, which vary both locally and temporally, the church has to proclaim both God's demand and also his grace in order to destroy the self-security of human beings and raise up those who are downcast. Properly distinguishing between law and gospel is thus an ever new task of the sermon and pastoral care. The orders of the liturgy, catechetical instruction, confession of sin, and church discipline—all have to serve this distinguishing.

It is all the more striking that this central theme of "law and gospel," which is relevant for every moment of the church's speaking and acting, plays only a negligible role in the *dogmas* of the different parts of Christendom viewed as a whole. It becomes readily clear if one compares the few dogmatic decisions on this topic with those which in one way or another have been set forth and made binding by all churches in the Christological and Trinitarian questions.

The Church of the Augsburg Confession occupies an exceptional position here. Again and again Luther referred to the distinction between law and gospel as the decisive issue in theology as a whole. If he also called the doctrine of justification the *articulus stantis et cadentis ecclesiae* [the article on which the church stands and falls], that is not a contradiction, for justification is the acquittal that the one judged by the law receives by faith in the gospel—apart from works demanded by the law. The justification of the sinner thus cannot be taught without distinguishing between law and gospel. This distinction in turn embraces the entirety of the issues: judgment and justification, God's wrath and God's grace, obligation and freedom, faith and works, and so on. We encounter the distinction between law and gospel, however, not only in the theology of the Reformers but also in the statements of church dogma that have been formulated and subscribed to by the Reformation churches in the confessional writings with the claim to binding authority. Admittedly, the formula "the distinction between law and gospel" is missing in the Augsburg Confession. This distinction, however, is substantively addressed in two different articles, "On Justification" (Article IV) and "On the New Obedience" (Article VI). And between both of these articles stands—and not accidentally—"On the Preaching Office," and thereby the gospel and sacrament as "means" of the Holy Spirit (Article V). Then in the Formula of Concord, the Fifth Article explicitly addresses "On the Law and Gospel," and the Sixth Article turns to "The Third Use of the Law" against Antinomianism, yet without identifying "*paraclesis*" as such with the concept of law.[5]

---

5 In this connection, see Ragnar Bring, "Gesetz und Evangelium und der dritte Brauch des Gesetzes

In view of the differences between the Lutheran distinction between law and gospel and Karl Barth's teaching of the unity of both,[6] it should be pointed out that in the sixteenth century no conflict was perceived between the Lutheran and the Reformed doctrine on this point that would have become the subject of theological controversies similar to those over the Lord's Supper or the doctrine of predestination. Although Calvin emphasized more strongly than Luther the unity of the old and new covenants[7] and also in his teaching of the *tertius usus legis* went beyond Luther's concept of the law, one must note that within the whole of Christendom the old Reformed doctrine of law and gospel is closer to the Lutheran one than the corresponding statements of doctrine in the other church confessions. On this point Karl Barth's doctrine is essentially a new teaching, also in relation to Calvin.

The fact that in the Eastern Church a dogma on law and gospel is missing is not surprising since in general it did not go essentially beyond the Trinitarian and Christological dogmas. In its dogma it remained with what can be expressed in the structure of doxology. Admittedly, in the letters (from the years 1574–81) of the Ecumenical Patriarch Jeremias II to the Tübingen Lutherans[8] in which he took a position regarding the Augsburg Confession that had been sent to him, there exist statements which touch on our topic, and on occasion these letters have even been accorded the rank of confessional writings.[9] But these texts have never acquired the same significance in the

---

in der lutherischen Theologie" [Law and Gospel and the Third Use of the Law in Lutheran Theology], *Zur Theologie Luthers: Aus der Arbeit der Luther-Agricola Gesellschaft in Finland* 4 [On the Theology of Luther: From the Work of the Luther-Agricola Society in Finland] (Helsinki: Komissionsverlag Akateeminen Kirjakauppa, 1943), 43–97.

6 Cf. Karl Barth, *Evangelium and Gesetz*, Theologische Existenz Heute 32 (München: Chr. Kaiser Verlag, 1935) [ET: "Gospel and Law," in Karl Barth, *Community, State, and Church: Three Essays*, ed. and with an introduction by David Haddorff (Eugene, Ore.: Wipf and Stock, 2004), 71–100. –Ed.]

7 H. H. Wolf, *Die Einheit des Bundes, das Verhältnis von Altem und Neuem Testament bei Calvin* [The Unity of the Covenant: The Relationship between the Old and the New Testament according to Calvin], Beiträge zur Geschichte und Lehre der Reformierten Kirche 10 (Neukirchen: Verlag der Buchhandlung des Erziehungsvereins, 1958).

8 A German edition of this correspondence appeared under the title, *Wort und Mysterium* (Witten: Luther-Verlag, 1958). [For an English translation, see: George Mastranotonis, *Augsburg and Constantinople: The Correspondence between the Tübingen Theologians and Patriarch Jeremias II of Constantinople on the Augsburg Confession* (Brookline: Holy Cross Orthodox Press, 2006). When in 1573 Baron David Ungnad von Sonnegk (ca. 1538–1600) was appointed ambassador of the Holy Roman Empire to Constantinople, he took with him as his chaplain, Stephen Gerlach (1546–1612), who was a graduate of Tübingen University. Gerlach brought letters to the ecumenical patriarch from Jakob Andreae (1528–1590), who was then the chancellor of Tübingen University, and Martin Crusius (1526–1607), who taught Latin and Greek there. In 1574 Andreae and Crusius sent another letter to Patriarch Jeremias II (1530–1595), along with a 1559 Greek translation of the Augsburg Confession. The patriarch replied briefly in 1574, and then two years later there began a series of theological exchanges—three letters from the patriarch and two replies from the Tübingen professors—which lasted until 1581. –Ed.]

9 Thus in the collection of Johannes M. Karmiris, *ΤΑ ΔΟΓΜΑΤΙΚΑ ΚΑΙ ΣΥΒΟΛΙΚΑ ΜΝΗΜΕΙΑ*

Eastern Church as the dogmas of the ancient church, and their content makes clear—in their more exhortatory treatment of the issues of justification and obedience—that there exists in the Eastern Church no firm dogmatic tradition on this topic and no set conceptuality for treating it.

It is all the more surprising that the Council of Trent did not take up the topic of law and gospel—surprising, too, because this topic had played an important role for Augustine and also, as Gottlieb Söhngen has recently shown, for Thomas Aquinas, and because the Reformers explicitly appealed to Augustine.[iii] The concept of the gospel in the Pauline sense as the power of God, as message of Jesus Christ by which Jesus Christ is presently active—thus the gospel as *verbum efficax* [efficacious word], as *sacramentum audibile*, as the action-word [*Tat-Wort*] of God—is lacking. To be sure, the gospel is occasionally mentioned in the statements concerning the pre-condition of justification (Session VI, chap. 4),[iv] but only baptism (chap. 7, compare 4) is mentioned as *causa instrumentalis*, which then enters later in the sacrament of penance (chap. 14). The justification of the sinner does not occur through the gospel but through baptism. The significance of the gospel is in this respect reduced to the call to baptism and thus at the same time to the call to repentance, faith, hope, love as acts of preparation for receiving baptism (chap. 6). But if the Pauline concept of the gospel is missing, so also is the distinction between law and gospel, which is neither explicitly *verbotenus* [mentioned] nor present in the structuring of the statements from the Council of Trent, for everything that is said here about the new obedience and the necessity of works stands under the one heading of "*de iustificatione.*" Justification and obedience are not distinguished here in terms of topic, as they are in the Augsburg Confession, but they interpenetrate each other. One cannot of course overlook the fact that the formula "law and gospel" is to be understood as the concentration of the topics of "judgment and justification," "faith and works," and so on. These topics, however, were also dealt with thoroughly by the Council of Trent, even if in contrast to the theology of the Reformers. To that extent the decree on justification by the Council of Trent and the canons belonging to it are to be taken seriously as an indirect contribution to the doctrine of law and gospel.

In the dogmatic treatment of the distinction between law and gospel considerable differences thus exist within Christendom. Moreover, the particular answers have not yet even been mentioned here that are being given to our question, for example, by Methodism and the other holiness movements, as they have arisen in manifold ways from the various churches. The differences exist not only between the dogmatic decisions themselves but also in whether this topic has been dealt with generally in a dogmatic decision at all.

ΤΗΣ ΟΡΘΟΔΟΞΥ ΚΑΘΟΛΙΚΗΣ ΕΚΚΛΗΣΙΑΣ [The Dogmatic and Symbolic Monuments of the Orthodox, Catholic Church], 2 vols. (Athens: by the author, 1952–3).

Now when engaging in dialogue about controversial theological topics, one cannot be content to note the absence or also the presence of dogmatic statements and to compare these statements with one another in order then to establish and defend them according to the standpoint of the participants. Instead, some basic methodological considerations must be taken into account and corresponding steps must be taken in order to work through to determine the real differences and to make a true comparison between the dogmatic statements.

a) We cannot disregard the fact that the dogmatic statement—despite the central place of the confession in the life of the church—is only *one* among many other statements of faith. Faith responds to God for his act of salvation also in prayer, worship, witness, doctrine, and so on. Also, the dogmatic statement is not the only statement in which the *consensus* of the faith comes to be formulated. Statements in the liturgy, catechesis, traditions from the ancestors of the faith, religious tracts, and so on, also mean more in the life of the church than merely the statements of the individual believers who formulated them, but they function as statements that form and demarcate the church fellowship. All of this is especially to be considered in relation to our topic, for the dogmatic statements about law and gospel are indeed not an end in themselves but rather are appointed to serve the other statements of faith, namely, in the *proclamation* of law and gospel. The basic statement is the proclamation itself. The dogmatic statement about proclamation wants to serve the proper application of the proclamation, but it cannot replace proclamation itself. Since by no means all statements of faith and all functions of the church's activities have become the subject of dogma—and this cannot at all be expected—we must always bear in mind the other statements of faith if we want to understand the doctrine of a church it its entirety. On account of the peculiar complexity of our topic we will moreover have to reckon with the possibility that only one side of this issue emerges in dogmatic statements but the other emerges in proclamation or in the liturgy or in other places in the life of the church. In the living encounter with the other churches, all sorts of surprises are possible. Even where the Reformation formula *simul justus et peccator* is unknown as a *dogmatic* statement, it can still emerge *in fact* as an existential statement in the confession of sins of just such people as are acknowledged as saints in their church. Even where the necessity of works for salvation is emphasized most strongly, it can *in fact* be self-evident that *in articulo mortis* [in the moment of death], and not only here, saving grace is assured without any condition. Likewise, the situation of spiritual attack and trial is, after all, familiar in every church. Even if it has not been raised into *dogmatic* consciousness and not been made the starting point for dogmatic statements, terrified consciences have again and again lived *in fact* by faith alone. On the other hand, however, it can also follow that a doctrine of justification, holding fast with strict exclusivity to *sola gratia* and *sola fide* has in a way become a possession so that knowing the doctrine plays *in fact* the role of a work.

b) So then we must bear in mind the different historical fronts in which the statements of dogma were formulated. This is especially important with respect to our topic since at stake here is a matter of proclamation that must be directed at very different possible dangers to the Christian life. Already at the time of Paul he proclaimed God's assurance and claim differently against Judaistic legalists than he did against Gnostic libertines. Then in the course of church history other fronts arose. The dogmas did not grow uniformly in all directions out of the confession of Christ, and their formulation was not determined by the principle of systematic completeness. Rather, they were provoked by particular false doctrines and dangers threatening the church, and were each formulated in this concrete defense. Dogma grew more in recoil than by even, organic growth. So it is not unimportant from which presuppositions the dogmatic statements about law and gospel are being made: from despair under the law that one strives to fulfill or from fright concerning the hubris that scorns God's law. Without question the Lutheran Confessions and the Council of Trent are not making their statements on the same front. The Lutheran Confessions, like Luther, battle primarily against works righteousness, which obscures the gospel, and then no less intensively against antinomianism, which isolates the gospel from the law and wants it to be the solely valid word of God for the Christian. The Council of Trent, on the other hand, turns itself primarily against the danger of a libertine scorn of the law and of the works of obedience, whereby it turns at the same time against Pelagianism, with which it does not want to be and cannot be confused. The dissimilarity between these two fronts was further radicalized in that the fathers at Trent apparently did not heed the Reformation's struggle against antinomianism but in their canons treated the Reformers as antinomians. Also, Jeremias II in his answer to the Tübingen Lutherans—no doubt under the influence of information from Rome—turned his attention above all against the antinomian danger.

c) We must further bear in mind the concepts that the dogmatic statements use, namely, both the biblical and the later ones, in which the response of faith was given in the respective historical front. With each dogmatic statement there takes place an act of selecting individual concepts from the many which occur in the Bible along with the same topic and, in addition, a selecting from the many possibilities that the conceptualities of the then-and-there world suggest. From the many, individual concepts are lifted up, expanded, and clarified in order then to be used as dogmatic concepts to tie together that multiplicity of concepts. Thus in the New Testament writings the two-fold divine address is by no means always designated by the concepts of law and gospel. *Gospel* is not the only term for the divine activity of salvation through the word. *Law* is hardly the term for the Christian's being fundamentally called to account by God's command. And the formula *law and gospel* is not even found in Paul. The dogmatic formation of concepts is always an act of systematic concentration that goes beyond biblical exegesis, even though it must always justify itself in relation to exegesis. For that reason, the New Testament statements about the act of salvation that God does through the gospel for the believer are also very diverse: justification, sanctification, the making alive, transformation into the image of God, and so on, without every one of these concepts appearing in every New Testament writer. The dogmatic formation of concepts in the Eastern Church has taken up above all sanctification and the transformation into the image of God (divinization); the formation of concepts in the Western Church, above all justification and sanctification. To this should be added that in the New Testament writings righteousness, holiness, life are conveyed as gift and as what is required of the believer and is promised as the reward for obedience. As those declared righteous, the believers should grasp righteousness. As the sanctified, they should become sanctified. As those who have awakened to life they should fight the good fight in order to receive the crown of life. In their conceptuality, however, dogmatic statements have to a great extent not retained this two-fold use of the same concept for God's assurance and claim. Thus in the Eastern Church, and in a certain respect also in the Roman Church, God's act of grace is taught above all as sanctification, his demand however as command of righteousness, while in the Protestant Church the act of grace is described as justification and God's demand is often described as sanctification. The dogmatic statement arises, however, not only in the choice of concepts, but, beyond that, differences result from the fact that in the New Testament writings God's gift and demand are not everywhere related to each other in the same way. Jesus' message and demand is handed down differently in the Jewish-Christian circle in which the Gospel of Matthew emerged (Jesus is attested here in the Sermon on the Mount, despite his violation of the Mosaic law, as the bringer of a new *Torah*), differently in the Gospel of Luke. Paul taught the New Testament imperative differently from James. Thus differences result in dogmatic statements if one proceeds from Paul and then takes up the imperatives in James or if one would attempt to take the opposite way, which of course from the outset does not suggest itself in view of the one-sidedness of the letter of James and his lack of explicit statements about God's act of salvation in Jesus Christ.

d) Deserving of special attention with respect to the distinction between law and gospel is the structure of dogmatic statements,[10] for it is a matter here of dogmatic statements about other statements, namely, about the proclamation of God's assurance and claim and thus a matter of the assurance and claim of God himself, who encounters the sinner in the human word of the

---

10 Cf. Edmund Schlink, "Die Struktur der dogmatischen Aussage als ökumenisches Problem," *Kerygma und Dogma* 3 (1957), 251–306 [See chap. 2 ("The Structure of the Dogmatic Statement as an Ecumenical Issue") above. –Ed.].

proclamation and the administration of the Sacrament. If one investigates the structure of statements by the Reformers and those from the Council of Trent concerning the event of justification, one will find particular differences.

The structure of Luther's statements is defined by the act of hearing God's address. It is not as if this act were only the presupposition of this statement and then were made into the subject matter of doctrine. On the contrary, it is characteristic for Luther that in his doctrinal statements he remains as close as possible to the structure of the actual hearing. Stated bluntly, he makes them in the act of hearing, in the act of sacramental reception.

Naturally he does not stop there; he also makes statements about proclamation and the proper administration of the sacraments. But even here it is characteristic that they remain very close to the act of proclamation and administration. It is not accidental in Reformation theology that *docere* and *praedicare* are used synonymously. Luther does not make the event of the divine address, the personal encounter of God with human beings—that is, being called into account by God's law and the promise of salvation by the gospel—into the object of consideration, but he makes the statements in the act of the occurrence, in the event of the encounter, in being personally struck, whether it is that the person truly hears the address of God or whether it is that he serves it when he preaches the word and administers the sacraments. This structural starting point must also be kept in view when scholastic-ontological concepts are used in Reformation theology. They now stand in another context and no longer mean the same thing.

In the event of the divine address I recognize myself as a lost sinner, as the one who has not fulfilled God's law, who cannot eradicate the captive power of my guilt and has come under God's deserved judgment of wrath. That is, I recognize not only individual sins but my being a sinner. Each of the above statements holds totally true in one's being struck by God's word. At the same time, however, I am called by the gospel to receive justification, sanctification, life—all by faith in Christ, entirely for nothing. In the act of faith, I do not look upon myself—everything I see about myself conflicts with what the gospel conveys to me—but I look upon Christ. Nor do I look upon my act of faith, but only upon Christ, in whom God is gracious to me. In the act of faith, it is not my act of faith, my obedient acceptance of the gospel, my turning from sins, my turning to the grace content of my faith, but the gospel to which I cling, the promise of God who is gracious to me for the sake of Christ and who separates me from my sins. In the act of faith, justification by faith alone and justification by Christ alone are thus identical.

If dogmatic statements remain in the structure of this occurrence, anthropological statements experience a characteristic limitation.[11] They are

---

11 On the question of the position from which the anthropological statements of the Lutheran Confessions are formulated, see Edmund Schlink, "Der Mensch als Sünder" [The Human Being

essentially statements about the human being as sinner. But the statements about the righteous, the sanctified, the one made alive—all these are made as statements about the act of salvation by which God justifies and sanctifies the sinner and makes that one alive. As certainly as God justifies and sanctifies the *human being* and transfers him or her into a new life, just as certainly is the human being a righteous person, a sanctified person, and a living person only because God acts upon that one in Christ, lets that individual participate in the righteousness, the holiness, and the life of Jesus Christ. In the structure of personal encounter dogmatic statements about abiding in the new life, which had its beginning in baptism, are not interested in statements about an inherent quality or *habitus* [disposition] which the human being now has. On the contrary, they remain thrown upon the promise of the faithfulness of God, who will complete the work he has begun. As emphatically as Reformation theology has spoken of the comforted conscience, of new impulses of the heart, of the new delight in God's commands, of the urge to new obedience, and so on, yet in these dogmatic statements it is not a matter of a new quality in the human being, but of the living working of the Holy Spirit, who, as the one poured into hearts, remains at the same time the Lord of hearts, and who, as the gift, remains also the free, divine giver. The human being cannot boast of the workings of the Spirit. He or she also cannot make them count before God as the basis for justification. God bestows them solely by grace.

The dogmatic statement which is made in the structure of the personal encounter consequently remains bound to the word by which God addresses the human being. It is no accident that the Reformation formula is not *law and grace* but *law and gospel*, for the *means* by which God acts toward the human being are above all in view here. Thereby the dogmatic statement remains focused on the distinction between law and gospel that takes place ever anew in the act of acknowledging sin and of faith. Reformation theology is so compelled by the event of the divine address that it is incapable of going beyond the distinction encountered in it between God's commanding and bestowing, God's judging and saving act and is incapable of seeking any theoretical resolution between law and gospel. Rather, all interest is directed to the fact that both addresses remain acknowledged side by side un-balanced and unmingled. After all, sinners, whom the law condemns, can believe that they are saved by the gospel, apart from the works of the law.

By contrast, the decree on justification from the Council of Trent makes its statements in the structure of description (*descriptio*, chap. 4), that is, of the description of the human course of life from its beginning in original sin (chap. 1) through the Last Judgment and to the attainment of eternal life as a reward for the good works completed on the basis of grace (chap. 16). This course is described by dealing sequentially with the preparation for

as Sinner], lecture at a Protestant-Orthodox ecumenical conference, *Evangelische Theologie* 11 (1951), 324–331.

justification (chaps. 5 and 6), with justification in the event of baptism (chap. 7 ff.), with the growth of justification in the obedience to the commands (chap. 10 ff.), with the renewed justification by the sacrament of penance (chap. 14) and with the possibility of the loss of the grace of justification through mortal sin (chap. 15). Not only the organization, but the structural basis of the dogmatic statements is different here from the Lutheran Confessions. To be sure, one must not misunderstand this structural shift as if in the description of the human course of life the theological statements had been replaced by anthropological ones. Throughout, there is more than enough talk, not only about the works that the commands of God require but also about God's grace. But the statements about God's talk and action do not occur in the structure of hearing by the one struck by God's two-fold address, do not occur as a statement of the *I* uncovered and called by the addressing divine *Thou*. Rather, the encounter between God and humankind is here made into an object of consideration and description, and thereby in reflecting and asserting one is stepping out of the immediacy of being struck in the encounter with God. In that the dogmatic statements about God's judging and justifying action are being made in the framework of the human course of life, they participate in the distinctive objectivizing nature of consideration and description.

It is self-evident that in this structural starting point human action becomes more strongly the subject matter of dogmatic statements. In the event of being addressed by God I recognize myself as a lost sinner; as one justified, however, I recognize myself not in looking at myself, but solely by faith in Christ, whose righteousness the gospel conveys to me. In the consideration and description of this event there occur with increasing importance statements not only about humankind as sinner but also about the process of recognizing sins, and statements not only about the righteousness of Christ conveyed to faith but also about the process of faith. There now arises the interest in describing this process as completely as possible in its connection with love, hope, turning away from sins, new resolutions, and so on, and by means of such a description as exists in the Tridentine statements about the *modus praeparationis* [mode of preparation] (chap. 6) to guard against a depravation which is caught sight of in the Reformation's slogan *sola fide* [by faith alone]. But the Reformation statement did not serve a description; on the contrary, it served the invitation that proceeds from the gospel to receive righteousness as a sinner without meeting any and all prior requirements of one's own. Moreover, the consideration and description in the reflection on the process that prepares for justification does not stop with the process itself, but it inquires deeper into it for the possibilities which human beings have to be able to prepare themselves for justification. Contrary to the Reformers, the freedom of the fallen human being is taught here, without which that preparation appears to be impossible. The Reformation's doctrine about the *servum arbitrium* [the enslaved will] was, however, not primarily a statement of theological reflection but the confession of the sinner, namely, that one cannot, by any action of one's own, break free from the captive power of guilt and one's being forsaken.

From the structural starting point of description a further result is that the effects of grace in the human being become more readily the subject matter of dogmatic statements than is the case in the act of hearing and believing itself. If in this act it is decisive that through the gospel the *iustitia aliena* [alien righteousness] of Jesus Christ is conveyed to me a sinner, then an increasing interest now arises that God's righteousness is being infused into the human being and inheres in individual as that one's righteousness (Denzinger 1546 [Tanner 2.678]). If in the actual present encounter with God it is a question of his turning gracefully to me for Christ's sake, in the structure of description and reflection it is increasingly a question of grace as a *habitus* of the human being which makes good works possible for her or him. The statements about the personal working of the Holy Spirit are widely replaced by statements about the grace-filled new nature of the human being. Thus "a certain anthropocentricity" of the Tridentine decree on justification is clearly evident.[12] It is not to be confused with the structurally defined *pro me* of Reformation theology, which is entirely different.

These shifts bring with them a shift in the framing of the issue in general. If in the Reformation confession it is a matter of the distinction in God's address that encounters us and cannot be removed by any theological reflection, namely, the distinction between God's claim and comfort, demand and gift, judgment and justification, then in the structure of the Tridentine examination and reflection the basic issue turns out to be the relationship between God's grace and human obedience in view of the salvation goal to be attained and, beyond that, the relationship between the possibilities of human freedom and what is rendered possible by God's grace. It is now not a matter of the ever new discovery of the distinction between law and gospel, but of determining the relationship between divine and human action that is as free as possible from contradictions.

Important differences in content correspond to the different structure of the dogmatic statement. This is to be briefly explained in the following pairs of concepts.

i) The judgment of the law and the judgment of the gospel: Through the judgment of the law God establishes what human beings have done and judges them according to their deeds. Through the judgment of the gospel God declares the godless to be righteous, conveys to the sinner precisely what does not accord with his or her deeds. Moreover, this judgment is not merely the setting of a valuation, namely, that the godless is accounted righteous; but it is

---

12 Hans Küng, *Rechtfertigung: Die Lehre Karl Barths und eine katholische Besinnung* (Einsiedeln: Johannes-Verlag, 1957), 112 [ET: *Justification: The Doctrine of Karl Barth and a Catholic Reflection* (New York: Nelson, 1964), 106.]

also a creative word-deed of God: God makes the godless righteous. Accordingly the Apology of the Augsburg Confession, in agreement with Luther, understands justification to be at the same time the renewal of the sinner. This profound difference between the analytic judgment of the law and the synthetic judgment of the gospel has been maintained throughout the confessional writings of the Reformation, which dispense with a theoretical resolution. The Tridentine doctrine, however, has formally adjusted the justifying judgment to fit the judgment of the law: justification follows as an analytical judgment on the basis of the grace that has been infused, namely: "according to the measure which the Holy Spirit allocates to the individual" (chap. 7). In the act of justification the working of grace and the judgment are so ordered to each other that the working of grace makes possible the analytical judgment of the declaration of justification.[13]

ii) The human being under the judgment of the law and under the assurance of the gospel: Under the law human beings recognize that they have not only committed sins but that they are sinners, that is, as entire individuals, with all their thoughts, words, and deeds. In no way can they stand in the sight of God, and they must agree with God's judgment of damnation. Through the gospel, however, the sinner is rescued from the divine judgment of wrath and is acquitted from the coming Last Judgment. By faith in the gospel sinners know themselves to be entirely justified and accepted by God. Their entire further life is embraced by this eschatological acquittal, even though they daily pray anew for the forgiveness of sins. The confessional writings of the Reformation have maintained both the totality of statements about the confession of sins and the totality of statements about faith in justification. Also here the Tridentine doctrine has resolved this tension, that is, by introducing quantitative concepts: Human beings are righteous according to the "measure" of the Spirit given to them (chap. 7); they "grow and become more righteous" according to the cooperation of faith and good works (chap. 10). Corresponding to this is the fact that the Reformation formula *simul justus et peccator*, when it has been treated sympathetically by Roman Catholic theologians, undergoes a re-interpretation in the sense of *partim peccator—partim iustus* [partly sinner—partly righteous].[14]

iii) Faith and works: The justification of sinners occurs apart from their works, by faith[15] in the gospel. The one justified is expected to do works of righteousness in obedience to God's commandment. The Reformers spoke of faith also in thoroughly active expressions: Faith seizes the divine promise, it

---

13 See Aquinas, *Summa theologica* II.1, question 113, art. 8.

14 Hans Urs von Balthasar, *Karl Barth: Darstellung und Deutung seiner Theologie* (Köln: Jakob Hegner, 1951), 378 ff. [ET: *The Theology of Karl Barth*, trans. John Drury (New York: Holt, Rinehart and Winston, 1971), 277 ff. –Ed.]
   –Ed.], and Hans Küng, *Justification*, 231 ff. [ET: 236 ff. –Ed.]

15 The formula *by faith alone*, as is generally known, is first found not in the Reformers, but already earlier, for example, in Basil, Chrysostom, Cyril of Alexandria, Augustine, and others.

counts on it, it dares to venture with it; faith is an intention, a turning of oneself away from sin, a turning of oneself toward Christ, an "active thing." But however emphatically they called for decision and the act of faith, in the event of justification faith is *mere passive* [merely passive], the reception of the act of salvation that God does in Christ for the sinner through the gospel. All active-verb statements here are only statements of neediness and longing. The distinction between trusting-receiving faith in the gospel and the new obedience called for by faith vis-à-vis God's commandments is thoroughly maintained in all its rigor by the confessional writings of the Reformation. The Tridentine doctrine, however, also resolves this difference. Already in the statements about the preparation for justification (chap. 6), but fully in the chapters on the growth in justification (10) and on the final justification in the Last Judgment (16), it adds human action to faith; indeed, it expressly rejects the understanding of faith as merely trusting in the lovingkindness of God who forgives sinners for the sake of Christ (canons 12–14).

iv) The certainty of salvation and the fear of judgment: Without being theoretically resolved, the proclamation of eschatological acquittal and the announcement of judgment according to works stand side by side in Pauline proclamation. The certainty of the believers is grounded on the justifying verdict of the gospel so that no one can accuse them, and nothing can separate them from the love of God—a certainty that skips over the distance between now and the Last Judgment that is still not yet and at the same time encompasses the election that precedes the call (Rom. 8.29 ff.). And the announcement of judgment according to works has validity for those same believers: Even if they are conscious of no disobedience they are not therein justified (1 Cor. 4.4). They are called to work out the eschatological deliverance with fear and trembling (Phil. 2.12). Reformation theology maintains both the certainty of faith *and* the uncertainty on the basis of works, and it denies every *securitas* for the Christian. The Protestant confessional writings teach the *certitudo salutis* [certainty of salvation] by faith in the gospel and in the acknowledgment of the deserved judgment. The Tridentine doctrine of justification, however, has systematically brought both opposing statements into resolution,[16] in that, for the sake of the judgment according to works, it not

---

16 The limits of the special structure of the Tridentine doctrine of justification were clearly visible in the speech of Seripando on 8 October 1546 regarding the question of the final justification in the Last Judgment. "One may not speak about it from the standpoint of speculation, but practically, not as a mere systematic theologian but as a pious Christian! And with all seriousness he considers each of the fathers individually in view of the decision of conscience, on which everything depends: 'Will you, if you come before the judgment seat of God, be judged strictly according to law and justice on the basis of the works which you believe to have done in the grace of God?' If he considers his situation accurately, then that person must—Seripando thinks—recognize the truth of the word of Augustine: 'Woe also to the most pious human being, if God examines him without lovingkindness!'" (Hanns Rückert, *Die Rechtfertigungslehre auf dem Tridentinischen Konzil* [The Doctrine of Justification from the Council of Trent] [Bonn: Marcus und &Weber, 1925], 230). Throughout Seripando's speech, "there trembled the subdued

only rejected *securitas* but also *certitudo* (chap. 9) and restricted the certainty of election to the questionable exception of private revelation (canon 16).

In determining the relationship of each one of the four pairs of concepts named above the Reformers taught the distinction and refrained from a theoretical solution of the contradictions.[17] If in spite of this the respective pairs of statements do not disconnect, it is not on account of a theoretical resolution, nor only because in both it is a question of the same God and the same human being, but because God's *proper* address encounters us in the *gospel*, through which—in view of the law—he allows us to flee to the crucified one. This theoretical unsettledness in the dogmatic statements is determined by the hearing of this two-fold address of God—an address that is, however, at the same time abundant in its assurance—an address of God, for whose freedom space is left open to judge and to save. Also in the Tridentine statements there is concern for the prevenient nature of grace and its prevalence. Grace begins to work on human beings through the call, without any merits existing on their behalf; only through grace can one turn oneself to the righteousness that counts before God (chap. 5). In other parts of the decree on justification the knowledge of grace, which is imparted despite the demands of the law, is also not lacking. But in that the Council of Trent in the structure of its statements moves away from the event of God's speaking and acting, makes it the object of examination, description, and clarification, and, above and beyond acknowledging the distinction in God's speaking and acting, aims for a systematically unified determination of the relationship, this Tridentine shift away from God's speaking/acting occurs with each of the four pairs of concepts cited above in the horizon of the law, namely, by weakening the statements about the verdict of justification, the justified human being, faith, and the certainty of salvation in conformity to the verdict and demand of the law and its declaration of judgment. Not only does the Council of Trent hereby persist in continuing that old weakening of the Pauline distinction between law and gospel,[18] which began already with the apostolic fathers, but beyond that, it is basically true that the law by nature offers a logically more

---

passion of a man fighting for his religious life" (Hubert Jedin, *Die Geschichte des Konzils von Trient*, 4 vols. [Freiburg: 1949–1975], 2.209 [ET: *A History of the Council of Trent*, 2 vols. (St. Louis: B. Herder, 1957–), 2.248. –Ed.] But "as strong as the defense which the Christian consciousness appears to be for the adherents of the two-fold righteousness, that defense is weak if it is placed under the magnifying glass of intense theological consideration" (ibid., 2.215). [ET: 2.255. –Ed.]

17 On the special character of theological paradox in relation to the logical concepts of antinomy, aporia, absurdity, ineffability, etc., as well as the theological concept of annoyance, see Henning Schröer, *Die Denkform der Paradoxalität als theologisches Problem* [The Way of Thinking Paradoxically as a Theological Problem] (Göttingen: Vandenhoeck & Ruprecht, 1960).

18 Cf. Thomas F. Torrance, *The Doctrine of Grace in the Apostolic Fathers* (Edinburgh: Oliver & Boyd, 1948) and Victor E. Hasler, *Gesetz und Evangelium in der Alten Kirche bis Origenes* [Law and Gospel in the Ancient Church Up to Origen] (Frankfurt: Gotthelf, 1958).

consistent framework for a systematically unified way of thinking than the gospel, in which God's incomprehensible, free grace breaks into the world which stands under the law.

One may, however, add to this comparison a reference to the fact that seventeenth-century Protestant Orthodoxy unfortunately did not leave off at making their dogmatic statements in the act of hearing the two-fold address of God. Instead, it proceeded to separate the doctrine of the appropriation of salvation (*de gratia spiritus sancti applicatrice* [the applicative grace of the Holy Spirit])[v] from the article on law and gospel (*de mediis salutis* [on the means of salvation]) and to develop it descriptively in the construction of an *ordo salutis* [order of salvation], whereby—in a way different from the Council of Trent—the law here also secured the system of dogmatic statements. From this transition to description it was a ready move when Pietism then made statements about grace—in an emphatic manner and one often detached from the means of grace—as statements about *experiences* of grace, something which was far removed from both the Reformers[19] and the Council of Trent. The more, however, the statements about God's encounter with human beings are made into statements about human experiences, the more particular differences of the religious experience of individual persons or groups or even epochs take the place of dogma, and further separations always result.

e) Dogmatic statements cannot be compared with one another as timeless and isolated statements. We must instead keep in mind (i) their place in the midst of other statements of the church, (ii) their historical front, (iii) their conceptuality, and (iv) their structure. Consequently, to the comparison of different dogmatic statements belongs a questioning and seeking that breaks through the mere wording, namely, the effort to translate them from one historical front to the other, from one conceptuality to the other, from the one way of thinking and structure of statement to the other, and so on. This task of translation is valid for every controversial issue in theology. But hardly anywhere is it so difficult as with the topic of "law and gospel," for here fundamental difficulties of dogmatic formulation break open, which were alien to the Christological and Trinitarian dogmas of the ancient church.

The root of church dogma is the confession of Christ and thus doxology. In doxology it is possible to speak "objectively." Its content is Jesus Christ himself, with no mention in it of the historically changing human being who makes the confession. The doxological confession of Christ was further developed through statements about the history of Jesus (birth, death, resurrection), in other words, through statements of historical tradition. Here,

---

19 Lutheran theology in the nineteenth and twentieth centuries thus had to pursue anew the distinction between law and gospel not only in critical engagement with the Enlightenment but also with the old Protestant Orthodoxy and Pietism. For the history of this engagement, cf. Robert C. Schultz, *Gesetz und Evangelium* [Law and Gospel] (Berlin: Lutherisches Verlagshaus, 1958).

too, the speaking can be "objective," for these acts have been accomplished once and for all and they are being confessed without that thereby explicit statements are being made about the historically changing human beings who make the confession. Also, the later Christological and Trinitarian dogma, by its very nature, contains only statements which praise the triune God in his eternal aseity and Jesus Christ as truly God and truly human, as the Son of God who became a human being once for all for the sake of our redemption. In dogmatic statements about law and gospel, however, the issue is not about doxological statements of being, nor about statements of doctrine concerning God's once-for-all accomplished acts in history, but of God's ever new activity toward human beings in their historical situation at any given time, namely, of God's ever new two-fold calling and working in the historical diversity of the restricting conditions of the individual and that person's attempts to evade God's calling, whether by libertinism or by legalism. Here the issue is about dogmatic statements concerning the ever new encounter in which God speaks to human beings, commanding and giving, and in which the human being—in that individual's particular historical location at any given time—has to respond to both words of God's address.

In view of the difficulties which this issue presents for dogmatic formulation, it cannot be surprising that dogmas about it originated only late, even though the church actually dealt with this issue from the beginning in sermons, pastoral care, and church order. It is not surprising that some churches have to this day not come to any formal dogmatic decision here and that on the other hand the dogmas that have been formulated precisely about this issue diverge in an especially delicate manner so that more separations in Christendom have arisen precisely over these questions than over others. Correspondingly, controversial theological dialogue on these differences is, in a special way, in danger of the differences becoming hardened or drifting off into relativism.

How is one to begin carrying out the task of translation? It must be kept firmly in sight that dogmatic statements about law and gospel are not basic statements in the same way as the confession of Christ and also the confession of the Trinity, which has its place in the worship life of the church and is repeated in the liturgy. This is rather a matter of dogmatic statements that make basic statements (or assertions) of the church, namely, about the proclamation of law and gospel. Thus the different dogmatic statements about law and gospel may not be compared directly with one another, but they must be translated back *into the basic statements of proclamation itself*, which they are intended to serve.

In this sense questions are to be put to the Tridentine doctrine of justification, for example: In proclamation, what is the meaning of the outpouring of grace as the basis for the verdict of justification? In the act of proclamation, does not the context of that basis dissolve and vanish in the unity of God's justifying action? In the hearing of God's word, what do the statements about the quantitative more or less of being justified mean? In the action of hearing, does not each Christian confess himself or herself to be entirely a sinner, and does the Christian not believe that he or she is accepted by God as a whole human being, as a person? In hearing the proclamation, what do *habitus, qualitas, iustitia inhaerens* [inherent righteousness] mean? Is the believer not here directed to the faithfulness of the gracious God, who will complete what he has begun in the believer? In the proclamation, what does the rejection of *certitudo* mean? Should not perhaps only *securitas* be rejected here? In the proclamation, what does the description of faith in its relation to love, hope, and so on, mean? Is not the gospel invitation being proclaimed here no less than God's exacting claim?

Only in the effort to re-translate in this way do the basic statements emerge which actually determine the life of the church and which must be compared between the churches. Doubtless some dogmatic contradictions will lose their sharpness and perhaps even be completely resolved in such a re-translation of the statements *about* the proclamation back into statements *of* proclamation. The fact, of course, remains that the Council of Trent is silent[20] about the gospel as the justifying word-act of God and that it made its dogmatic statements one-sidedly in the front against antinomianism, but not with regard to consciences terrified under the law.

f) In addition to this, we must finally ask whether all the structures of the statement are equally suited for making dogmatic statements about God's speaking and acting by means of law and gospel. This question is basically to be negated from the start, for the multiplicity of the structures of theological statement forms a cosmos in which each one has particular functions and possibilities of statement and in which not one can replace the other. The structure of prayer is different from that of witness; that of doxology is different from that of doctrine. To be sure, they are all concentrated in the structure of confession, and yet confession does not make the other statements superfluous. Law and gospel, however, are to be heard and proclaimed, baptism and the Lord's Supper are to be received and administered. Thus those dogmatic statements about the appropriation and acquisition of salvation are the most adequate when they remain as close as possible to the structure of hearing and receiving the word and sacrament. The more theological thinking and statement-making move away however from this structure, the greater is the danger that the difference between law and gospel, on which our salvation depends—whether at the expense of the gospel or the expense of the law, but most often at the expense of the gospel—is weakened or

---

20 This deficiency is today beginning to be seen even by Roman Catholic theologians. See Johannes Betz, "Wort und Sakrament" [Word and Sacrament], in *Verkündigung und Glaube: Festschrift für Franz X. Arnold* [Preaching and Faith], ed. Theodor Filthaut and J. A. Jungmann (Freiburg: Herder, 1958), 76–99., and Karl Rahner, "Wort und Eucharistie" [Word and Eucharist], in *Aktuelle Fragen zur Eucharistie* [Relevant Questions on the Eucharist] (1960), 7 ff.

even lost in a theoretical determination of their relationship so that the human being arrives at a meaning about the believer's confession of sins which competes with the operation of God's grace or even so that the statements about God's demanding and bestowing act of salvation will be largely replaced by a description of the human being's pious frame of mind, as occurred in Pietism and Schleiermacher. It remains to observe that in the New Testament writings the statements about justification, rebirth, new obedience and the fruit of the Spirit are only seldom made in general assertions about God and human beings, but as a rule in the form of witness, assurance, exhortation, and warning, and that here a theoretical resolution of the contradictions contained in them is forgone. The New Testament dialectic between indicative and imperative, unresolved by logic, is also the adequate form for the dogmatic treatment of our problem. In this dialectical structure one can at the same time express what needs to be said over against legalism and against antinomianism. That in the Tridentine structure of the description, the problem of determining this relationship nevertheless cannot finally be solved is shown through the history of the conflict between Molinism and Thomism at the turn of the sixteenth and seventeenth century—a conflict which to this day could not be ended by dogmatic decision but solely by the papal prohibition against the continuation of this conflict.[vi]

The ecumenical significance of the Lutheran distinction between law and gospel consists in the fact that here this topic, which is actually central for the church, has been made the content of dogmatic statements, and these statements have been formulated in such an immediate and direct relationship to God's two-fold speaking and acting that room is left open for the freedom of God's saving action. The structure of the personal encounter in the word is obviously not the only one in which the dogma of the church is to be formulated. However, for the dogmatic statements regarding God's address in law and gospel, it is the appropriate structure.

Editor's Notes

[i] The *usus politicus* is the political or civil use of the law to serve public life as a force for restraining manifest sin. The *usus elenchticus* is the elenctical use of the law to manifest and refute sin. In Lutheran Orthodoxy this is often called the *second* use of the law, the law "as mirror."

[ii] *Angefochten* is a verbal form of *Anfechtung*.

[iii] Schlink did not provide a footnote here, but he most likely was referring to Gottlieb Söhngen, *Gesetz und Evangelium. Ihre analoge Einheit theologisch, philosophisch, staatsbürgerlich* [Law and Gospel: Their Analogous Unity, Theological, Philosophical, Civic] (Freiburg: Alber, 1957).

[iv] The chapters that Schlink refers to parenthetically are from the "Decree on Justification" [*Decretum de iustificatione*] from the Sixth Session of the Council of Trent, 13 January 1547. Cf. Denzinger 1520–1583 and Tanner, 2.671–81.

[v] In the order of salvation, this is the grace that is applied by the Holy Spirit, which works salvation in the regenerated, converted, and sanctified believer.

[vi] Molinism refers to the view of grace that was taught by Luis de Molina (1535–1600) and his defenders. They held that the efficacy of grace is ultimately dependent upon God's foreknowledge of those who freely cooperate with this divine grace. Its efficacy is not grounded in the divine grace itself, which is what Thomas Aquinas taught, but in God's foreknowledge of free human actions. Molina's position was widely supported by the Jesuits, but attacked by Dominicans and other traditionalists, who defended Aquinas' teaching. This controversy between the Molinists and the Thomists was addressed at a special congregation in Rome (1598–1607), but the points at issue were left undecided. Since the sixteenth century both positions have been defended by Roman Catholic theologians.

Chapter Eight:
Apostolic Succession[i]

"Apostolic succession" is commonly understood to refer to the succession and authority of the church's ministerial office for all later time, which is grounded in the historically unique apostolic office. This succession, however, can be defined very differently with respect to details:

a) As the unbroken succession of the laying on of hands by bishops, starting with the apostles. This is understood to some extent as entirely formal, largely without regard for a *consensus de doctrina*, at least by some Anglicans, though by not all.

b) As the unbroken succession of the laying on of hands by bishops and of the tradition of apostolic doctrine and ordering. This complex understanding is that of the Orthodox Church, the Roman Church, and to some extent also the Anglican Church.

c) As the unbroken succession of presbyterial (going from pastor [*Pfarrer*] to pastor) laying on of hands together with the tradition of apostolic doctrine and ordering. This understanding of apostolic succession is held today by some Scottish theologians.

d) As the transfer of apostolic doctrine from officeholder to officeholder, whereby the succession of laying on of hands of bishops belongs to this succession not as a necessary sign but still as a significant sign. This is roughly how one can briefly describe a widely held understanding in the Lutheran Church of Sweden. This understanding of apostolic succession or "the historic episcopate" is also found in part in the Church of South India.

e) Going still further, one could understand "apostolic succession" without regard for the unbroken series of laying on of hands and refer to it as the transfer of apostolic doctrine from one ministerial officeholder to the next. But this use of the term is no longer common today. In general the succession of the laying on of hands, however carried out and interpreted, belongs to the concept of apostolic succession.

Now one cannot, of course, overlook the fact that the dogmatics of all churches deal not only with the church's ministerial office that is grounded on the apostles but also with the apostolic church itself. Moreover, "apostolic church" means not only the church in the apostolic age but also the church of all times. After all, is not the church as a whole grounded on the foundation of the apostles? But if the church of all times and places is to be confessed with the Nicene Creed as apostolic, that raises not only the issue of the apostolic succession of the ministerial office but also that of the apostolic succession of the church. The issue of succession cannot be reduced to the issue of the apostolic succession of the ministerial office. Rather, it is to the entire congregation, to each of its members, that Paul's exhortation applies: "Be my imitators" (Luther translates it: *disciples* [*Nachfolger*][ii], 1 Cor. 4.16; compare 1 Thess. 1.6). The apostolicity of the church cannot be restricted neither to the historical foundation of the apostles nor to the apostolic discipleship of the ministerial officeholders. The concern here is rather about the apostolic succession of the church *and* of the ministerial offices, about the ministerial offices *and* the *church.* Both belong inseparably together. Thus, to that end, our topic is here more sharply defined as the apostolic succession of the church and of the church's ministerial office. Only when both of these topics are treated together, will it become clear what ecclesiological significance is to be conferred to the special issue of apostolic succession in the sense of the unbroken series of the laying on of hands by bishops.

In what follows, sections 1–4 examine charisma and ministerial office, sections 5–8 the apostolate and church, and section 9 church and ministerial office. In section 10 conclusions will be drawn up from the preceding for the issue of apostolic succession.

I. The Church as the Fellowship of Charismata

The church is grounded on the foundation of the apostles through the outpouring of the Holy Spirit, who has made all of its members witnesses to the mighty deeds of God in Christ. This witness of the prophetic, priestly, royal people of God is not like a choir that sings in unison, but like a mixed chorus of many voices. That *all* of the members of the New Testament people of God have been given the Spirit is the testimony of all the New Testament writings. That the outpouring of the Spirit brings about the public *witness* in all members of the church is the Acts of the Apostles. But that the outpouring of the Spirit itself takes place in a *multiplicity* of spiritual gifts[1] is above all especially the testimony of Paul. Each believer has received a particular spiritual gift. One and the same Spirit "allots to each one individually as the Spirit wills" (1 Cor. 12.11; compare v. 7). In this connection it is important to note First Peter (4.10 ff.), where it is likewise presupposed that each member of the congregation has received a special charisma. Paul's teaching about the multiplicity of spiritual gifts was so fundamental for him that his statements can in no way be restricted to the congregations in Corinth and Rome or even

---

1 Eduard Schweizer, *Das Leben des Herrn in der Gemeinde und ihren Diensten* [The Life of the Lord in the Congregation and Its Ministries] (Zurich: Zwingli, 1946); Hans von Campenhausen, *Kirchliches Amt und geistliche Vollmacht in der ersten drei Jahrhunderten* (Tübingen: J. C. B. Mohr, 1953), esp. 59 ff. [ET: *Ecclesiastical Authority and Spiritual Power in the Church of the First Three Centuries*, trans. J. A. Baker (Stanford: Stanford University Press, 1969), esp. 55 ff. –Ed.]; and Ernst Käsemann, "Amt und Gemeinde im Neuen Testament," in *Exegetische Versuche und Besinnungen*, vol. 1 (Göttingen: Vandenhoeck & Ruprecht, 1960), 109–34. [ET: "Ministry and Community in the New Testament," in *Essays on New Testament Themes* (Philadelphia: Fortress, 1982), 63–94. –Ed.]

only to the Pauline congregations in the era of the church's founding. Rather, the multiplicity of spiritual gifts, according to the statements of Paul, belongs to the very nature of the church at all times and in all places, for as the body of Christ, the church is an organism of many gifts and servant ministries. Paul has made these statements so universal and fundamental that they cannot be relativized historically but must be incorporated into the doctrine of the church and ministerial office, even though there was no reflection on this multiplicity of gifts in most of the other New Testament writings.

The concrete spiritual gift is allotted to each believer out of the freedom of the Spirit. No defined order has been handed down by which the individual members receive the concrete spiritual gifts. Indeed, all have received the Spirit as they came to faith and were baptized, and the Spirit again and again works in and through those who participate in the worship assembly. One can come to baptism and to the Lord's Supper, but which concrete spiritual gift the individual receives, that is dependent upon the freedom of the Spirit itself. There is no mention of a definite way by which an individual could come to have a particular spiritual gift. Here we have to keep open the various possibilities: Charismata can be received already in the reception of the gospel in faith or through baptism or through the laying on of hands in connection with baptism or through a later hearing of the gospel and in the reception of the Lord's Supper, but also apart from any special action, as an answer to prayer and pleading. The gifts of the Spirit also appear spontaneously when a congregation faces emergencies and special needs, on which God has mercy by bestowing spiritual gifts. The believer should pray to receive the spiritual gifts, and in fact to receive the most important of these (compare 1 Cor. 12.31 and 14.1).

The multiplicity of spiritual gifts is set forth in the concrete details that are given in the lists of charismata in 1 Cor. 12.4–10; 12.28–30, and Rom. 12.6–8, as well as Eph. 4.11. These gifts have to be distinguished from the list of the fruit of the Spirit, which is given in Gal. 5.22, for the charismata are imparted to different members of the congregation, while the spiritual fruit of love, joy, peace, and so forth, are expected of all Christians. But strict boundary lines should not be drawn here (compare, for example, the transition from 1 Cor. 12 to 13 and also the verses following Rom. 12.9, in which love is again mentioned).

In what follows those observations are briefly highlighted about the lists of charismata that are especially significant for the issue of apostolic succession:

a) It is clear that there is no firmly established catalog of spiritual gifts that is valid for congregations in all places and—we may add—at all times. By comparing Rom. 12.6 ff. with 1 Cor. 12.4 ff., one can immediately notice that, over and above the list in Corinthians, Romans adds *diakonia* [service] (in the narrow sense of the term), *didaskalia* [teaching], *paraclesis* [exhortation], lovingkindness, understanding, and that, on the other hand, speaking in tongues, healing, "wonders," discernment of the spirits, and also the *logos sophias* [utterance of wisdom] and the *logos gnoseos* [utterance of knowledge] are missing in Romans but are in the list in First Corinthians. It is not that at all times the same spiritual gifts will be present in every congregation, but that at all times spiritual gifts will be present for every member of the congregation.

b) In all of the lists of charismata, however, there emerges a certain hierarchical ordering of gifts. Coming first are the specifically kerygmatic spiritual gifts: 1 Cor. 12.8, the word of wisdom and the word of knowledge; 1 Cor. 12.28, apostles, prophets, and teachers; Rom. 12, prophecy; and Eph. 4.11, apostles, prophets, and evangelists. By contrast—and this is most significant—the spiritual gifts of leader (1 Cor. 12.28), of administrator (Rom. 12.8), of pastor[iii] (Eph. 4.11) are first mentioned at a later spot, after the specifically kerygmatic gifts and even sometimes after the gifts of healing and other gifts of helping. To be sure, in Eph. 4.11 teachers follow after pastors, but also here prophets and evangelists come first.

c) Apostles are named in the first position in the ordering of the charismata in 1 Cor. 12.28 and Eph. 4. The apostles are cited here not only because of the otherwise prominent aspect of their special calling but because of their spiritual empowerment, as the church-founding spiritually gifted ones. In fact, the manifold charismata are concentrated in Paul himself in a unique way. He is prophet, teacher, wonder-worker. He can also speak in tongues, has the gift of leadership, and so on.

d) It already here becomes clear that a sharp distinction cannot always be made between the charismata. A prophet can be at the same time a teacher. How closely prophets and teachers work together is shown, for example, in the Acts of the Apostles 13.1 ff.: Prophets and teachers send Paul and Barnabas.

e) In the list of charismata we find some statements that designate only the gifts and their activity and other statements that designate the person. Thus 1 Cor. 12.28 begins with the latter, such as apostle, prophet, and teacher, and then goes on to list wondrous powers, gifts of healing, and so forth. This alternation between the designations of the person and the statements about the spiritually gifted activity is found also in Romans 12. From the designations of the person is inferred that the gifts of the Spirit, even if they are given freely by the Spirit, do not come and go arbitrarily, nor do they arbitrarily jump from one person to the other. Rather, a certain constancy of the same concrete spiritual gifts is presupposed, which makes the designations of the person possible.

f) Even if in all of the lists of the charismata the specifically kerygmatic charismata are prominent, and the servant ministries of the other powers and gifts of helping are ordered after them, we cannot overlook the fact that *all* of the charismata serve the word, namely, the witness to God's act of salvation in Christ. Even the charismata which are not specifically kerygmatic are related to the word, display the image of Jesus, and may be designated as the radiance of the *Logos*, for all the charismata are the results of the power of Christ, occur in the power of his name, and are a concrete unfolding of the confession, "Jesus is Lord." In the multiplicity of the spiritual gifts is realized the fullness of the one Christ in the congregation and, through the congregation, also in the world. The multiplicity of charismata can appear in various forms in different congregations and at different times, but it is always the appearance of the one *charis* of Jesus Christ. As head of the body he is the bearer and the origin of all charismata, and they in turn are all ordered in service to him and are the unfolding of the power of his name, to which they bear witness one way or another. So the fellowship of the charismata consists in their common participation in the one grace of Jesus Christ. Christ himself is the actual, true, and original bearer of all the charismata. He is the one apostle, the one teacher and evangelist, pastor and deacon of the new covenant. He is, as head of his body, the leader of his church and, as revealer of the power of God, the origin of all powers, wonders and signs in Christendom. In this sense of the common participation in the one grace of Jesus Christ, the church is the fellowship of the spiritual gifts. *Koinonia*, after all, means the participation of the believers in the gift of God. *Koinonia* is thus not directly *community* [*Gemeinschaft*], but is rather common participation, and in this participation then also, to be sure, fellowship of the participants with one another.

g) Because each charisma is a participation in the one *charis* of Christ, the multiplicity of charismata is at the same time the multiplicity of the mutual service of the members of the church to one another. Not merely service to God but at the same time service to the brothers and the sisters: "Serve one another with whatever gift each of you has received" (1 Pet. 4.10). In the worshiping assembly this mutual service of everyone to everyone else appears in a concentrated form. The value of each charisma is measured according to its significance for the gathered congregation and its edification. The more one charisma serves the others, the more highly it is to be respected. Consequently, in the midst of all the spiritual gifts love is the "more precious way," as Luther translated 1 Cor. 12.31. Spiritual arbitrariness and disorder are forbidden by the Apostle, that is, by Christ himself. The legitimacy of the spiritual gifts proves itself in that they persevere in an abiding, free, and whole-hearted relationship to the Body of Christ and are understood as functions of *agape* love. As appropriate to the nature of the church, this servant ministry takes place in respect to the brothers and the sisters and then, in fellowship with the brothers and sisters, in respect to the world. Each charisma is a servant ministry in the church and as such, at the same time, is a servant ministry at the point where church and world meet.

h) For this reason, space is to be made for the spiritual gifts in the congregation. To be sure, they have to be tested. Certainly one has to form an opinion about them and to judge them. They are to be evaluated according to their usefulness for the edification of the church, and yes, under certain circumstances, as in speaking in tongues, to keep them in check. False spirits are to be completely excluded. But the deep concern in the Pauline statements comes explicitly to voice in his appeal not to dampen the Spirit and to strive after the spiritual gifts.

II. The Sending into Servant Ministry

The presupposition of each one of the servant ministries in the church is the calling and sending that has come through the gospel. The gospel calls persons from the world into the new people of God and sends them as the prophetic, priestly, royal people into the world. Through the gospel and baptism all the members of the new people of God are placed under the lordship of the Spirit, who in freedom grants each one a charisma meant for him or her and thus takes each one into service. Baptism is, however, always one and the same thing, whereas the spiritual gifts received in baptism or also at a later time is a different one for each Christian. The Spirit, whose coming is pleaded for, is always one and the same, but it pleases him in his freedom to bestow himself in various spiritual gifts to each one in a differing way. In the action of the one gospel and the one baptism, manifold spiritual gifts just break forth anew again and again in the church; and although each member of the church has been called by the same word and through the same baptism, as have the others, yet each receives a special gift. Thus, in general, the concrete charisma is not preceded by a concrete word of calling that corresponds to it. Rather, the concretizing of the gift of Christ breaks through in the congregation and in its individual members in the freedom of the Spirit, without a concrete word of calling, and is retrospectively to be acknowledged as a gift that has been bestowed.

We now have to distinguish this calling of all into membership in the people of God and with it into servant ministry from the calling which individuals receive to a *special* ministry, one for which they are commissioned and authorized. The multiplicity of the freely emerging charismata and ministries carried out by all the believers is to be distinguished from the servant ministry that is exercised through a *concrete* calling and authorization in the church, as existing in the foundational ministry of the apostles. Here a concrete word of sending comes to believers and encounters them. In this case it is not only an inner compulsion that urges them to a concrete servant ministry, but a concrete command that comes upon the individuals and places them into ministry and installs them concretely. Now, to be sure, all of the charismata come not from human beings but from God, yet they function and appear as an inner compulsion for a concrete servant ministry. The mission of the sending, however, is the concrete external word that the individuals encounter as an external word, which remains upon them and again and again urges obedience from them in the servant ministry in which it has put them. Every believer receives a charisma, but not every believer receives such a concrete mission. These concrete callings, installations, and authorizations can be summarized in the concept of *commissioning* [*besonderen Sendung*]. There is frequent mention made about such a special sending or commissioning in the Acts of the Apostles[iv] and in the Pastoral Letters, but there is seldom any mention in the undisputed letters of Paul (2 Cor. 8.19 is here an exception).

The commissioning of specific members of the church for a specific ministry is, according to the New Testament, often reported as taking place with the laying on of hands. As is well known, we are here dealing with the adoption of a custom of installation into an office—a custom already documented in the Old Testament—whose continuation is then found in the ordination of Jewish scholars.[2] We can thus surmise that callings with the laying on of hands took place in the earliest Christian community in Palestine from the very beginning and that the laying on of hands took place in connection with such callings, even where it was not explicitly mentioned (as, for example, in Acts 14.23). To be sure, we cannot thus surmise that every calling in earliest Christianity occurred with the laying on of hands, just as we must in general be careful to avoid applying statements in the New Testament regarding the ordering in a given congregation or in a given area of mission to all congregations.

For which concrete servant ministry is the special sending or commissioning done, according to the New Testament texts? Not for healing nor for works of miracles, not for individual forms of witnessing, such as the "word of wisdom" or the "word of knowledge" (1 Cor. 12.8). Nor in the New Testament do we hear about a special laying on of hands for the gift of speaking in tongues as Paul understood that gift. Rather, the New Testament reports which deal with the commissioning focus on the ministry of missionary church-founding and of church leadership, as well as on ministries assisting in the founding and leading of churches. The tasks of missionary church-founding and church-leading correspond to the servant ministry into which the apostles had been called. They, too, were not freely operating spiritually gifted individuals who then later received the "Yes!" and "Amen!" from the congregation; rather, the concrete sending preceded their spiritually gifted ministry. Admittedly, they had been called by the risen Lord; all subsequent callings occurred through human beings. In this way, all these later callings are different from the calling of the apostles. All these callings are in that respect distinguished from the callings of the apostles, but they do indeed entail the mission of following in the train of the apostles and continuing their ministry.

About this special sending or commissioning the following key points need to be highlighted:

a) The sending is not left to the arbitrary will of human beings, even though it occurs through human beings. This becomes very emphatically evident in the election that precedes the laying on of hands. The particulars in the New

---

2 Eduard Lohse, *Die Ordination im Spätjudentum und im Neuen Testament* [Ordination in Late Judaism and in the New Testament] (Göttingen: Vandenhoeck & Ruprecht, 1951).

Testament make clear that the mission, sending, and imparting of the Spirit are by no means at the disposal of human beings, but rather that those doing the sending fast, pray for the Spirit, and not only for the one who is to be called but also for those who have to do the calling, for the discernment of the spiritual gifts in those who are to be called already itself presupposes the Spirit who alone is able to recognize the spiritual gifts and to distinguish among them. The presupposition of the Spirit in the ones calling is especially important where the relevant, concrete spiritual gift is initially to be prayerfully implored, with the laying on of hands, upon the one who is to be called—and not only as a gift that has already been discerned. The leading of the Spirit is attested as of decisive importance—the Spirit who calls, installs, and presents before the congregation the one whom he wants to be sent. This is how the pertinent witness of the prophets is to be understood in this context (Acts 13.1 ff., also 1 Tim. 1.18 and 4.14). That is to say, the Spirit gives instruction through the spiritually gifted individuals about whom he wants to have sent and, beyond that, also where he wants the person sent.

b) In the sending, human words and human hands serve as the instrument of the sending God. God calls through the mouth and hand of the church, as through his instrument. This is already the sense of the pericope about the calling of Matthias (Acts 1.24 ff.): Lots were cast precisely because the Lord is the one to choose and not human beings. Compare also Acts 13.2: In a time of worship and fasting, the Holy Spirit, and thus the Lord, summons them for a calling and makes known whom he has called. The prophets and teachers send them with the laying on of hands, but then it states again: Saul and Barnabas are sent out by the Spirit. Human beings are merely organs. Also Acts 20.28 speaks of the installing through the Spirit.

c) God authorizes through the call, but two things need to be distinguished within the authorization:

i) Commissioning as the explicit placing into service of an already existing charisma. Thus Acts 6.3: "Pick out from among you seven men of good standing, full of the Spirit and of wisdom, whom we may appoint to this task." See also the evidence in the Pastoral Letters regarding the prerequisites for those who can be installed as bishops. In these passages an already existing charisma, or according to the Pastoral Letters at least an aptitude to teach, is already acknowledged with the commissioning and is taken up into the ministry.[3]

ii) In addition, through the commissioning God bestows the charisma that qualifies one for the ministry of the pastor. The commissioning to the concrete

---

3 This significance of the laying on of hands, however, may not be generalized, and understanding it as the imparting of the Spirit cannot be fundamentally excluded. Rudolph Sohm did this when he wrote: The laying on of hands has as its presupposition that for the one who receives it, "the charisma, which enables the receiver to be a teacher is already dwelling within him. The laying on of hands is thus not the root cause of the charisma, but its presupposition" (Rudolph Sohm, *Kirchenrecht* [Canon Law], vol. 1 [Leipzig: Dunker & Humblot, 1892], 63).

servant ministry grants to believers, who as such are urged by God's Spirit, also the concrete charisma for the concrete servant ministry to which God has called them. The call is not a command of the law, but of the gospel. The gospel, however, is the power of God, the act-word of God. So the commissioning is also the power of God. It is in general a part of the nature of the New Testament imperative that is grounded in the indicative mood and at the same time includes the grace that is necessary for the fulfillment of what has been commanded. Consequently, the laying on of hands is not an empty sign, but rather with it what is commanded by God and requested of God is effectively appropriated. The laying on of hands at the commissioning is, to be sure, different from other kinds of laying on of hands that are described in the New Testament, such as for healing or for blessing or for the imparting of the Spirit after baptism.[4] However, as in all of these other special-ministry actions— according to the New Testament witness—what is prayed for with the laying on of hands is received, which is also true with respect to the charisma received for the concrete servant ministry into which a member of the congregation is sent with prayer and the laying on of hands. "Ordination was not considered a mere form or symbolic action, but an action that imparted the Spirit" (J. Jeremias).[5] On this basis, confidence in one's ordination is possible, in fact, also in the case of looking back on the ordination once received. On that same basis, this comforting certainty is possible: I have been called, I have been sent, sent, in fact, precisely by the external word; for I can know that this external word is not a word of the law, neither is it simply an empty word of promise, but a spiritually efficacious word. The one ordained can know that the charisma of the office will give him the strength to proclaim the gospel rightly, and he should in this certainty "rekindle God's gift of grace which was given to you through the laying on of hands" (2 Tim. 1.6).[6]

---

4 Johannes Behm, *Die Handauflegung im Urchristentum* [The Laying on of Hands in Earliest Christianity] (Leipzig: A. Deichert, 1911); H. D. Wendland, "Handauflegung, II. biblisch" [Laying on of Hands, biblical], RGG 3.54.

5 Joachim Jeremias, *Die Briefe an Timotheus und Titus* [The Letters to Timothy and Titus], in *Das Neue Testament Deutsch*, ed. Paul Althaus and Gerhard Friedrich, vol. 9 (Göttingen: Vanden-hoeck & Ruprecht, 1934), 30–31 (excursus on 1 Tim. 4.14).

6 This point receded in the Reformers' understanding of ordination that had to be developed in the course of their disputation about the Roman Catholic ordination of priests, and it has often been overlooked in scholarly research (see Paul Drews, "Die Ordination," *Deutsche Zeitschrift für Kirchenrecht* 15 [1905], 66–90; Georg Rietschel, *Luther und die Ordination*, 2d ed. [Wittenberg: Herrosé, 1889]). But that point is not missing, as is clear from the ordination prayers. See, for example, Peter Brunner's analysis of the act of ordination which Luther carried out when he installed Nikolaus von Amsdorf as bishop of Naumberg: With the laying on of hands accompanied by prayer, "the moment of the Paraclete's assurance appears in concentrated form, for here assurance becomes a blessing. The hands that are laid in the ordination on the one ordained are hands 'that bless.' For the one ordained this blessing is the visible assurance of power, courage, and comfort for the leadership of the office of ministry that is now laid upon him" (Peter Brunner, *Nikolaus von Amsdorf als Bischof von Naumburg*, Schriften des Vereins für Reforma-tionsgeschichte 179 [Gütersloh: G. Mohn, 1961], 73 f.; see also Peter Brunner, *Das Amt des Bischofs*

d) Just as the calling of individuals into the people of God occurs through the words of human beings, so also does the sending/commissioning of specific members of God's people into a specific servant ministry. Which people do the calling? Obviously, only members of the church, but which members? Here two lines have to be distinguished:

i) The New Testament writings report, on the one hand, about the implementation of a special sending or commissioning by those who themselves have been sent into ministry through a commissioning. Thus in Acts 14.23 Paul and Barnabas install elders[v] in Asia Minor; and in Titus 1.5, Titus, who was himself called to be a fellow-worker of Paul (2 Cor. 8.19), is given the task of installing elders. In 1 Tim. 2.5, it is said that Timothy, who was himself first called, should install others through the laying on of hands. It is not completely clear in Acts 6.6 who laid hands on the seven. According to language and syntax, the best answer to that question is: the same ones who chose the seven and then presented them to the apostles (there is no explicit mention of a change in the subject of the sentence). But Luke here would have meant that the laying on of hands occurred by the apostles.

ii) The New Testament writings report, on the other hand, also about a commissioning given by those who themselves have not received a commissioning. Thus, in Acts 13.1 ff. there is the commissioning of Paul and Barnabas by the prophets and teachers in Antioch, for nowhere in the New Testament is there mention of an installation of prophets through the laying on of hands. Neither is an installation of the teachers involved here likely. According to 2 Cor. 8.19, Titus was called by the congregations to be the fellow-worker of Paul, without any mention here of called officeholders. According to 1 Tim. 4.14, Timothy was sent into his special ministry through the laying on of hands by the elders, and according to 2 Tim. 1.6, through the

---

[The Office of Bishop] Schriften d. Theol. Konvents Augsburger Bekenntnisse 9 [Berlin: Lutherisches Verlagshaus, 1955], 15 ff.). Beyond this particular act of ordination it can be generally observed that, according to Luther, ordination is "the confirmation—happening in the presence of the gathered church—of the calling [*Vokation*], efficacious commissioning, and blessing into the ministerial office; by it, a person has been placed (by God!) definitely into the ministerial office. Thereby the laying on of hands has not only an official significance but also a benedictional one, which it gains from its connection with the ordination prayers." "Melanchthon teaches that the meaning of the ordination is the public confirmation of the rightful calling [*Vokation*] by other *ministri verbi* [ministers of the word] through whom Christ himself calls into the ministerial office, commissions, and blesses for the ministerial office through the mediation of the Holy Spirit," whereby the laying on of hands comes to have not only a *significative* [symbolic] meaning but also a benedictional one" (Hellmut Lieberg, *Amt und Ordination bei Luther und Melanchthon* [Office and Ordination according to Luther and Melanchthon], Ph.D. diss. [Erlangen, 1960], as self-reported by Lieberg in *Theologische Literaturzeitung* (1960), columns 704–5. Less confident in this respect is Wilhelm Brunotte, *Das geistliche Amt bei Luther* [The Spiritual Ministerial Office according to Luther] (Berlin: Lutherisches Verlagshaus, 1959), 187 ff. Significant for ecumenical dialogue is Heubach's systematic exposition of Reformation and neo-Lutheran starting points (Joachim Heubach, *Die Ordination zum Amt der Kirche* [The Ordination to the Ministerial Office of the Church] [Berlin: Lutherisches Verlagshaus, 1956]).

laying on of hands by Paul; and we cannot easily presuppose about the elders that they themselves had first been ordained into their ministry through the laying on of hands. There is some evidence that the elders mentioned in the Pastoral Letters were those members of the congregation who belonged to the congregation for already a long time or possibly as the first members of the congregation, who had demonstrated their Christian faith through purity and a blameless life, through works of love, and so forth, and were therefore held in high esteem in the congregation, but who would not have thereby received a special installation into an office of elder. The installation of elders, which is mentioned in the Pastoral Letters, would then instead be the installation of elders as bishops.[7]

It has been attempted to coordinate these different statements in the New Testament, grouped under (i) and (ii) above, so that the election was made by the congregation but the laying on of hands was always by ministerial officeholders. But such a clear-cut arrangement of this kind is historically far from certain. It can indeed, however, be assumed that the commissioning by the ministerial officeholders would be done with the involvement or at least the approval of the congregation and, on the other hand, the commissioning by the congregation or members of the congregation would be done with the participation or at least the acknowledgement of the ministerial officeholders, insofar as they were present. From what has been said, it follows that the New Testament writings show no interest in the successive series of laying on of hands from the apostles through their co-workers and disciples and then from them to subsequent pastors of the local congregation. Even then, where such a series is presupposed as an existing fact, the interest clearly does not rest on the succession of the laying on of hands but on the tradition of pure doctrine (see, for example, 2 Tim. 2.2). The notion of a succession in the charisma of the ministerial office, efficacious and guaranteed through the series of the laying on of hands by bishops, belongs to a much later time, in the third century.[8]

---

7 This interpretation is, however, controversial and the place of the *presbyter* [elder] in the early Gentile-Christian congregations, at least according to the Pastoral Letters, is far from clear in both the German and the English theological literature. The reasons for this are the following: "The special problem regarding the use of the term πρεσβύτερος [elder] in Judaism and Christianity arises from the two-fold meaning of the word. It is either a sign of age or the title for one who bears a ministerial office. Both meanings are often not clearly distinguished from one another" (Günther Bornkamm, "πρεσβύτερος," TWNT 6.634 [TDNT 6.651–83. –Ed.]. Moreover, one should consider the possibility that the term *elder* within the context of Jewish-Christian congregations did not mean the same thing as "elder" within Gentile-Christian congregations.

8 Von Campenhausen, *Kirchliches Amt und geistliche Vollmacht*, 163 ff. [*Ecclesiastical Authority and Spiritual Power*, 149 ff.]; E. Molland, "Le développement de l'idée de succession apostolique" [The Development of the Concept of Apostolic Succession], *Revue d'Histoire et de Philosophie Religieuse* 34 (1954), 1 ff.

III. The Concept of the Church's Ministerial Office

The dogmatic problem of the church's ministerial office is for one thing created by the fact that the New Testament uses very different terms to describe the given ministries that are grounded in a commissioning but more by the additional fact that the ministry of founding and leading a congregation in earliest Christianity was in no way carried out on the basis of a commissioning.

The dogmatic teaching about the ministerial office cannot overlook the fact that on the one hand the undisputed letters of Paul, in which the congregation is presupposed and addressed as the fellowship of manifold spiritually gifted ministries, do not speak of a special calling into these ministries (apart from the apostle himself and the passage we cited above about the calling of Titus). On the other hand, however, in the Acts of the Apostles and especially in the Pastoral Letters, in which the commissioning plays an emphatic role, the multiplicity of spiritual gifts and servant ministries that are given to each member of the congregation does not appear. To be sure, it is also presupposed in these writings that the Spirit is given to every Christian, and over and above this the book of Acts emphases that the spiritual gift has its effect in every Christian's witness in the world, but missing here is the specifically Pauline understanding of the congregation as a cosmos of diverse spiritual gifts and servant ministries. This distinction between the authentic letters of Paul and these other New Testament writings is magnified in the observation that in the letters of Paul the ministry of leadership (1 Cor. 12.28) and of oversight (Rom. 12.8) are also mentioned as gifts that occur in the midst of the congregation in the freedom of the Spirit without commissioning. Here the actually occurring servant ministry—not the commissioning into the ministry—is the basis for the obedience that the congregation owes them, the congregation within which they are working. Paul thus exhorts the Corinthians to be subject to the house of Stephanas for the following reason: "Because they were the first fruit from Achaia and because they have been ordained for the ministry to the saints" (1 Cor. 16.15). The fact that here the very first believers began to work, gathered a congregation, and served it, is the reason for the exhortation of the apostle to be obedient to this house. In addition, one has to reckon with the fact that the earliest Christian community expanded through such spontaneous mission work.

These important differences in the founding and carrying out of the ministry of church-planting and leading have long been overlooked. After they were recognized, however, they were frequently exaggerated[9] so that the

---

9 This tendency, which is present in the work of some of today's German New Testament scholars, has received its radical expression in the ecclesiology of Emil Brunner. See Emil Brunner, *Das Misverständnis der Kirche* (Zürich: Theologischer Verlag Zürich, 1951 [ET: *The Misunder-*

charisma and the ministerial office were set against each other, and it remained unclear to what extent these two very different foundations and forms of servant ministry did not exclude fellowship within earliest Christianity.[10] For this reason, it is important to keep in mind what these two complementary understandings of servant ministry have in common.

a) Foundational for each servant ministry in the church is the apostolic office and along with it the direct and immediate calling and authorization of the eyewitnesses of the risen one. This is fundamental, whether the ministry takes place on the basis of a commissioning or as a consequence of the charismata that have blossomed without a commissioning, for the presupposition of each ministry in the church is faith in the gospel proclaimed by the apostles. Over and above this there are also the New Testament writings— where a commissioning into the servant ministry through the apostles is not presupposed—a source for the fact that the apostolic word is a word of assessing, admonishing, and comforting, and also a word that sometimes pushes back against the sundry spiritually gifted ministries that have freely blossomed. See, for example, Paul's clear devaluation of speaking in tongues (1 Cor. 14).

b) The presupposition for each servant ministry in the church, whether that ministry is based on a commissioning or occurs as a consequence of a freely given charisma, is one's own self-giving to Christ, the Lord, by faith in the gospel and through one's reception of baptism. Every ministry in the church has its foundation in baptism, by which the believer is received into the prophetic and royal priesthood of the church, which is called out from the world and sent into the world to minister.

c) Not only the charismata blossoming in the church apart from a commissioning but also the servant ministry that is the result of a commissioning in the church has its origin in the freedom of the Holy Spirit, for the commissioning is after all precisely not left up to the disposal of human beings. Rather those to be called, who are identified by the Holy Spirit in a preceding period of testing, are those whom the Spirit wants to have called. In

standing of the Church, trans. Olive Wyon (Philadelphia: Westminster, 1953). –Ed.]); idem, *Dogmatik*, vol. 3, *Die Lehre von der Kirche, vom Glauben und von der Vollendung* (Zürich: Zwingli-Verlag, 1960). [ET: *Dogmatics*, vol. 3, *The Christian Doctrine of the Church, Faith, and the Consummation*, trans. David Cairns and T. H. L. Parker (Philadelphia: Westminster, 1962). –Ed.] In this connection, the anti-institutional spiritualism of Brunner goes beyond even that of Rudolf Sohm, when, in distinction to Sohm, Brunner does not recognize the central significance of the worship service for the nature, form, and ordering of the church (see Brunner, *Dogmatik*, 3.48 ff. [*Dogmatics*, 3.58 ff. –Ed.].

10 Jean-Louis Leuba, *Institution und Ereignis, Gemeinsamkeiten und Unterschiede der beiden Arten von Gottes Wirken nach dem Neuen Testament* [Institution and Event: Similarities and Differences between the Two Ways God Works according to the New Testament] (Göttingen: Vandenhoeck & Ruprecht, 1957), especially 99 ff. [ET: *New Testament Pattern: An Exegetical Enquiry into the "Catholic" and "Protestant" Dualism*, trans. Harold Knight (London: Lutterworth Press, 1953), especially 93 ff. –Ed.]

the commissioning God himself is acting in the freedom of his grace. The human beings who are doing the commissioning are only his instruments.

d) It is inappropriate to set the New Testament statements about the ministry of spiritual gifts over against the servant ministry that occurs on the basis of a commissioning, that is, to set charisma over against ministerial office, for the commissioning occurs through the exalted Christ, who reigns through the Spirit. The commissioning is the imperative of the gospel, which is the power of God. Through the commissioning, the task and power to fulfil the task are imparted at the same time. The commissioning produces spiritual empowerment. The ministry which occurs on the basis of a commissioning is thus at the same time a spiritually gifted ministry.

e) The freely emerging charismata cannot be set over against a servant ministry that is established on the basis of a commissioning, that is, they cannot be understood as the manifestation of a hubbub of enthusiasm in opposition to order or as an impulsive interaction between people in opposition to a personal stability. There is a widespread misunderstanding that spiritual gifts merely have an ecstatic and more or less chaotic character; spiritual gifts do not wander about or vacillate senselessly. One should rather reckon much more with a stability that works itself out in a correspondingly stable ministry in the congregation. Thereby one can hardly distinguish the external effects of the gifts from the deliberately transmitted ministerial offices.

f) Not only the ministry of the freely emerging charismata but also the action of the called ministers as it is implemented remains under the examination and judgment of the congregation. Also the authority that has been given through a commissioning does not preclude the possibility that the called minister will commit an error or be guilty of a moral failure. The New Testament letters warn not only against false prophets or other spiritual outcomes that are not from God but also against false and self-enriching officeholders. Because God's Spirit is living in all members of the church, each spiritually gifted individual stands under the judgment of the others but especially under the judgment of those who have received the gift of spiritual discernment (1 Cor. 12.10; compare 14.29 ff.).

g) To be sure, not every spiritually gifted ministry is grounded in a concrete word of a commissioning, and yet a concrete word is imparted to all spiritually gifted people, even if their ministry is not grounded in a commissioning, insofar as their ministry remains under the examination and judgment of the congregation. This judgment comes to expression in the "Amen!" with which the congregation acknowledges the witness as a witness of the Spirit in its midst and thus makes that witness its own. The congregation expresses a judgment in its "Amen!" The "Amen!" does not merely mean, "Yes, yes, so be it!," nor is it merely a human word, but rather it is the discernment of the Spirit who is working in the congregation and making it capable of distinguishing between true and false spirits. Also a concrete word is coordinated to the actually occurring spiritual ministry in the exhortations through which the apostle or another called minister exhorts the congregation to acknowledge and submit itself to the ministry that is occurring in its midst (see again 1 Cor. 16.15–16). In this case, the concrete word comes retrospectively as an acknowledging word and one that urges acknowledgment to a spiritually gifted ministry that is already occurring. Also the spiritually gifted ministry that occurs without a commissioning is affirmed by God's word, by the commissioning to witness to the world, a commissioning which actually applies to every member of the New Testament people of God, and by the concrete word of the judgment of the congregation and the called ministers through which this ministry is acknowledged by the Holy Spirit. This "Amen!" of the Spirit is a word of confirmation and also at the same time a word that strengthens and inspires trust for further ministry.

Nevertheless, the diversities that remain within all of these commonalities need to be taken seriously, differences which exist side by side in the founding and form of the ministry in the earliest Christian community, especially in the Pauline congregations, on the one hand, and the congregations established by Jerusalem, on the other. There is no indication that an ordering of elders and bishops, based on a special calling, existed in the congregations in Corinth or Rome at that time, when Paul wrote to them. The generalizing of commissioning as a principle begins with First Clement, which then continues its development in the doctrine of ministerial offices in the ancient church, both Western and Eastern, and also by the Reformers, particularly by Calvin. It is equally impossible, however, to generalize about the Pauline notion of the church's servant ministry as the multiplicity of freely emerging charismata and then to reinterpret the commissioning as merely the confirmation of the previously occurring spiritual gifts or as an indication of the beginning of Catholicism. Instead, one has to reckon with these various foundings and forms of ministry existing alongside each other and with each other in the early church from the start. The servant ministry of church-planting and church-leading was carried out partly on the basis of a commissioning by the apostles or by others who were called to the ministry of church-planting and church-leading, partly on the basis of the commissioning by the congregation or by prominent members within the congregation (but not by a commissioning), and finally, the ministry of church-planting and church-leading was also carried out in a spiritually gifted manner without a commissioning.[11]

11 Already for these reasons it is not possible to presuppose historically that episcopal functions were performed in the earliest Christian congregations solely on the basis of an installation by an apostle and that in general a series of laying on of hands connected later bishops with the apostles. This has also been clearly acknowledged by a group of Anglican theologians and among the Orthodox by Sergei Bulgakoff ("The Hierarchy and the Sacraments," in *The Ministry and the Sacraments*, Report of the Theological Commission Appointed by the Continuation Committee of the Faith and Order Movement , ed. Roderic Dunkerley (London: Student Christian Movement Press, 1937), 96.

The dogmatic teaching about the ministerial office cannot, therefore, be determined by generalizing on the basis of just *one* of the notions in earliest Christianity. Rather, dogmatics has the task of taking seriously the different possibilities in its dogmatic reflections and to make space for them. By contrast, either a one-sided generalizing or an unhistorical harmonizing always brings the danger of suppressing spiritual life and with it the danger of dividing the church. One must simply be clear that the dogmatic concept of the church's ministerial office is not already there in the New Testament statements themselves, but can only be the result of systematic reflection on those statements.

That the concept of the church's ministerial office is not already there in the New Testament, but has to be developed through dogmatic reflection, is also evident from the fact that the earliest Christian writings, as is well known, do not contain a consistent term that corresponds to the developed concept of the ministerial office. For one thing, there is reference to elders, which in some places means people who have been specially ordained to be an elder, but in other places the term simply means people who are honored as the oldest or as the first believers without special installation. The ordering of elders is of Jewish or Jewish-Christian origin. Beyond that, there is reference to bishops and deacons, who carry out their ministry on the basis of a special installation (see Acts 20.28 and the Pastoral Letters; in addition Paul names them in Phil. 1.1 without any further details). Bishops and deacons have their origin in Gentile-Christian congregations. One can add that in Acts, the Pastoral Letters, First Peter, and Second and Third John, elders are to be sure presupposed, but that in the undisputed letters of Paul there is no reference to elders. Paul does then speak of the gift of "leadership" (*kybernesis*, 1 Cor. 12.28) and of the gift of grace, which is working in those who take care of the congregation as "administrator" [*Vorsteher*] (Rom. 12.8; see also 1 Thess. 5.12). He speaks further about those who "toil" [*sich abmühen*] and about the "zeal" [*Eifer*] with which some commit themselves to the congregation. Paul thus emphasizes that the administrator and the gift of leadership are subordinate to the prophets and teachers. The Pauline term *service* [*diakonia*] has often been translated as *ministerial office* [*Amt*] or *ministerium*, also by Luther, but with this same word Paul describes each spiritually gifted ministry, whether of those who preach or of those who help, just as he also gives to the term *diakonos* a wide range of meanings and does not restrict it only to the one installed to be an assistant to the bishop. The Pauline term of the steward (*oikonomos*) of the mysteries of God, which is used in 1 Cor. 4.1 to describe the apostolic ministry, is used again in Titus 1.7 in reference to the bishop, and in 1 Pet. 4.10 it is used to refer to every member of the congregation. So also this term cannot be made to serve as a specifically New Testament concept of ministerial office. Hebrews 13 refers to "leaders" [ʹηγουμένων, *Führenden*] and of their responsibility for the souls entrusted to them without it being clear of how they came to their position of leadership.

Finally, in Eph. 4.11, in the list of the gifts of grace (after the apostles, prophets, and evangelists but before the teachers), there is the reference to pastors [*Hirten* = "shepherds"], the use of which has a Christological designation. Also Acts 20.28 says of bishops and 1 Pet. 5.2 of elders that they are "to tend" [*weiden*] the congregation. In light of all of this, it is noteworthy that missing within this great multiplicity of New Testament designations for ministry is one that points to a uniquely sacred origin, such as belongs to a priest but also to a king.

If we keep all of this in view, it is again clear that the concept of the ministerial office constitutes a task that requires systematic reflection and decisions, for the multiplicity of New Testament designations for the ministry of church leadership also includes various possibilities for the execution and form of this ministry and creates the obligation for dogmatics to define the concept of ministerial office in such a way that none of the approaches set forth in the earliest Christian community will be fundamentally excluded. Thus, in the absence of a term that is used consistently in the New Testament, the concept of ministerial office, even more than the concept of the apostolate, is a dogmatic concept. To be sure, such a concept includes the clear substantive contents of the New Testament—otherwise it would not be a normative dogmatic concept—but it includes them in a systematic, concentrated way, for it has to highlight systematically the heart of these very diverse contents from the New Testament and must then, in a manner similar to the dogmatic concept of the apostolate, to allow room for the distinctive scattering and multiplicity of ministries.

For the dogmatic concept of the church's ministerial office we choose as our starting point now not the freely emerging, spiritually gifted ministries but the commissioning into the ministry.

The basis for this starting point cannot be the fact from church history that the carrying out of the church's servant ministry was increasingly made dependent on a special calling that preceded it and that the church's words and actions were in this sense increasingly *clericalized* [*verbeamtet*] (just compare, for example, the picture that Paul gives of the worship assembly at Corinth with the picture of the form of the worship service as reported by Justin around 150 and by Hippolytus around 200); for this increasing suppression of the free, spiritually gifted expressions could also be a constriction and ossification of the church's servant ministry. But also the reference to the early deterioration of the free, spiritually gifted expressions—as became evident in the heresies of Gnosticism and Montanism,[vi] as well as in the variety of medieval movements and in the spiritual enthusiasts [*Schwarmgeistern*][vii] at the time of the Reformation—cannot serve as a sufficient basis for the starting point of the dogmatic understanding of ministerial office through a sending, for basically it is equally possible that called officeholders could succumb to teaching false doctrine, lusting after power, and so forth, and that conversely at the same time by means of the freely emerging charismata these watchmen will be granted to the church, which the church needs. But indeed the sending has to take on more and more significance basically and necessarily given the increasing temporal distance from the church-founding ministry of the apostles. The church can only live by abiding with the historical Christ, the crucified and risen one, as its present Lord. This means, then, that it must abide with the witness of the apostles, the called eyewitnesses of this Lord. Because of this growing temporal distance, the tradition of the apostolic message, doctrine, and ordering had to gain in significance and, along with it, the sending into ministry, which is serving this tradition, for everything depends absolutely upon the apostolic word continuing to be heard in the church without falsification and upon all the other voices that are heard in the church agreeing to be subject to it. Given the significance of the apostolic tradition, one can understand that the ordering of the church reflected in the Pastoral Letters was placed under the authority of Paul. Indeed, in view of the significance that Paul gave to the tradition in his undisputed letters, the possibility cannot be excluded that in his old age, in view of the further expansion of the church, he backed and promoted an order of ordination and an ordering of ministerial office through his authority (in the sense of the Pastoral Letters). The relationship between word and Spirit, between the historical singularity of God's act of salvation and the ongoing working of salvation by the Spirit, which is foundational for the life of the church, finds its appropriate expression in the emphasis on the commissioning, for the work of the Spirit is to bring to remembrance, that is, to refer back to the singular historical act of salvation in Jesus Christ and to the apostolic word, and in this way to make the act of salvation present. Spirit and tradition, then, are not in opposition to each other but belong together.[12] Yet at the same time, it cannot be forgotten that the multiplicity of freely emerging, spiritually gifted manifestations and ministries in the Pauline congregations were in fact not left without the leadership of someone who had the authority of a commissioning, that is, without the leadership of the apostle. The Pauline reports are after all documents that show how the apostle worked specifically in the congregations, comforting and exhorting, recognizing but also warning them, and at all times directing them on the basis of his special authority. With the disappearance of this very concrete leading and directing of the apostle (which was still presently effective, even when it was exercised from a distance), the ministry that was based on a special calling had to gain in significance—namely, the ministry of the spiritually gifted person who on the basis of this calling encountered the congregation with a given authority and

---

12 Daniel Jenkins, *Tradition and Spirit* (London: Faber and Faber, 1951); Hans von Campenhausen, "Tradition und Geist im Urchristentum," in *Tradition und Leben: Kräfte der Kirchengeschichte*, ed. Hans von Campenhausen (Tübingen : J.C.B. Mohr [Paul Siebeck], 1960), 1–16. [ET: "Tradition and Spirit in Early Christianity," in *Tradition and Life in the Church* (London: Collins, 1969), 7–18. –Ed.]

who was not only in the same category as the other spiritually gifted individuals who were dependent on a subsequent acknowledgment by the congregation.

Consequently, we understand that the church's ministerial office is a kind of spiritually gifted servant ministry which, in the midst of the multiplicity of the charismata and servant ministries that are given to the church, is based on a commissioning. This commissioning has been handed down to us from earliest Christianity as a calling and sending into the servant ministry of church-planting and church-leading as well as into the associate ministries. We thus unite the missionary ministry of church-planting with the ministry of church-leading in the concept of the pastoral office, for the missionary ministry already implicitly contains the ministry of leading nascent congregations, and likewise the servant ministry of leading an existing congregation contains within it the task of further missionary ministry to the world. Thus, from the multiplicity of New Testament designations for the ministry of leading we are choosing that of *pastor* [*Hirt*] because it is more positively established than that of bishop and elder in the broader history of the church in terms of church law, and also because it has not changed or been narrowed down as much with respect to its New Testament meaning. The concept of the pastoral office is thus more suitable to make space for the New Testament multiplicity of starting points in the doctrine of the ministerial office.

At the same time, however, the concept of the pastoral office must remain open to the Pauline understanding of the church as the fellowship of charismata and ought not to be closed in principle to the possibility that the charismata of church-planting and church-leading might freely emerge. When Paul acknowledged the spiritual gifts of leading, administrating, and the self-installation of the first believers without a special calling and admonished the congregation to be obedient to such a ministry, this occurred in a missionary situation. The doctrine of the pastoral office must therefore remain open to this ever-present missionary situation on the edge of the ordered church. Christians who have been forced by circumstances into a purely heathen society, who through their witness to Christ bring heathens to faith, baptize them, and celebrate the Lord's Supper with them, act in the pastoral office if they have done all this in keeping with apostolic doctrine and ordering, even if before they are carried off into the heathen terrain they had not been given prior authorization by means of a special assignment to carry out this ministry. In the isolation of the prison camp or forced labor camp they are in fact acting in fellowship with the church and its pastors, and when these latter encounter the former and their congregations they cannot fail to acknowledge their pastoral ministry and congregation. The spiritually gifted ministry of the Christian is not only based on a commissioning but indeed in every case it is based on the apostolic gospel, which the Lord wants proclaimed to the world. The dogmatic teaching about the ministerial office cannot exclude any possibility of the growth of the church that was a missionary actuality in the expansion of the earliest Christian community. In doing that, such freely emerging ministries remain dependent on the "Amen" of the church and thus at the same time on the recognition of the called pastors.

IV. The Task and Forms of the Pastoral Office

Just as the New Testament writings do not produce any definite concept of the ministerial office that would correspond to the dogmatic concept of the office, so they also do not contain any unified and exact statements regarding the functions of "elders," "bishops," "administrators," "leaders," and so on, which have been summarized here under the concept of the pastoral office. In part, the statements about what the elders, bishops, and so forth do remain colorless and indefinite, and they do not permit us to form any more concrete ideas about the execution of the ministry of church leadership. In part, substantial differences become apparent in the statements. Thus, for example, the ministry of the administrator and of leadership—which is listed in Rom. 12.8 and 1 Cor. 12.28 at a relatively later spot, after the prophets and teachers—was publicly carried out differently from the ministry of the bishop described in the Pastoral Letters, who is so crucially the servant of the word that alongside that ministry there appears to be no longer much room for the special ministry of the prophets and teachers. A more precise dogmatic definition of the functions of the pastoral office cannot therefore simply be achieved by adding up the statements scattered throughout the New Testament but must also here be achieved through dogmatic reflection, that is, through the systematic reflection on the nature of the church that needs to be led. Moreover, in view of the diversity of New Testament statements, one cannot postulate that these functions, arrived at systematically, appear everywhere and altogether in the same way wherever the pastoral office was acknowledged. Rather, from the start one must reckon with the diversity of forms of the pastoral office and the various emphases and personal distribution of its functions.

As we seek to define more clearly the *functions of the pastoral office* on the basis of the nature of the church, we must keep in mind that if the New Testament speaks of the "*ecclesia*" or of the "people of God" or of the "body of Christ" or of the "temple of the Holy Spirit," the heart of all these terms for the church is the worshiping assembly. Hence, the function of the pastoral office is

a) leading the worship assembly. This means

i) especially proclaiming the word and offering the Eucharistic prayer in this assembly;

ii) making space for the manifold witness of the spiritually gifted individuals in the worshiping assembly;

iii) excluding the voices of the spirits that are not from God, but at the same time also excluding the gross sinners, and thus exercising church discipline;

iv) administering the congregation's gifts—insofar as they are not necessary for the celebration of the Lord's Supper—for the poor and for special needs, both within and beyond the local congregation;

v) installing deacons.

b) leading the missionary expansion into the world, which has to proceed from every worshiping assembly. This means, namely

i) calling those who are far off, baptizing them, and gathering them;

ii) sending the members of the congregation into mission.

These tasks can of course be further unfolded with respect to their individual details. Important here is the observation that, in view of all these identified functions, the pastoral office is primarily the *ministerium verbi divini* but that it is surrounded by the manifold gifts of the Spirit in the congregation, all of which ultimately serve the word, either directly or indirectly.

Also the more precise definition of the possible *forms of the pastoral office* does not as yet result from an adding up of the diverse statements scattered throughout the New Testament, which are in part quite indefinite. For one thing, there is talk of a local congregation, in some cases of one, in other cases of more than one, and furthermore about pastors who, like Timothy and Titus, are responsible for leading more than one church and who thus can be designated as overseers of pastors. Then we hear of pastors, who have no recognizable pastoral connection to a local congregation, who bear a missionary responsibility for an area in which congregations are still to be planted. Finally, we hear in the New Testament of pastors and of their assigned helpers (deacons in the narrower sense), as well as of such fellow-workers, who received a temporally limited task, thus "apostles" in the broader sense of the term ["sent ones" –Ed.]—members of the congregation who, for example, were given the task of transporting a collection, a task, that is, that ends once the offering is transported.[13] Also here we cannot be satisfied with mere

13 On the basis of the New Testament texts, the threefold form of the church's ministerial offices (bishops, elders [presbyters], and deacons) that came to establish itself in the ancient church cannot be presupposed to have been a general institution in the earliest Christian congregations. Here there is one of the greatest historical difficulties for the Anglo-Catholic doctrine of ministry (see especially K. E. Kirk, ed., *The Apostolic Ministry* [London: Houghton and Stoughton, 1946]), but not only for it. Within the Orthodox Church Sergei Bulgakoff has recognized this clearly: "The origin of the three degrees of Holy Orders as the basis of Church organization is one of the most difficult problems of modern ecclesiastical history. The sources at our command render its solution more or less hypothetical. The most probable conclusion, suggested by historical data, is that the threefold ministry in its present form was not known in the Apostolic and post-Apostolic Church of the first century. We find evidence of it at the beginning of the second century (at the time of the first epistle of Clement, of the epistles of St. Ignatius, and later" ("The Hierarchy and the Sacraments," 95). Bulgakoff draws some very important and, in the

observations, but must systematically derive the most important possible forms of the pastoral office from the nature of the church:

a) Every local congregation is thoroughly and completely "*ecclesia*," "body of Christ," "temple of the Holy Spirit." The local congregation is not just a part of the church, is not just a member of the body of Christ, is not just a stone in the temple of the Holy Spirit. Correspondingly, the pastoral office in every local church is thoroughly and completely a pastoral office. It lacks nothing with respect to authority.

b) This understanding of every local church as "*ecclesia*," "body of Christ," and "temple of the Holy Spirit" does not lead to any individualistic isolationism but rather precisely to the fellowship of the local churches with one another, for the same Christ is after all present in each local congregation. Correspondingly, no pastor can persist in isolation but has to rely on the acknowledgment and the fellowship of the other pastors.

c) The term *ecclesia* in the New Testament refers not only to the local congregation but also to the entire church on earth and to the fellowship of local congregations in a particular area. Correspondingly, the pastoral office bears responsibility not only for local congregations but also for the fellowship of regional churches in a country and, further still, for the fellowship of all churches on earth. Thus within the common responsibility of all pastors for the church, the nature of this church results in various forms of the pastoral office with varying areas of responsibility. These forms also arise for the following reason:

d) The church is the growing body of Christ that is advancing into the world, and thus it is always planting additional local congregations and entire church regions. Both the church as a whole and the church as a local congregation take part in this growth. Corresponding to the relationship of mother and daughter congregations is the relationship of fathers and sons in the pastoral office. A structure of the pastoral office thus results in a coordination of pastors and overseer pastors.

e) The relationship between the whole church and the local congregations is not one between the sum and its parts; rather, it is a relationship of fellowship as common participation in the whole Christ. The relationship between the whole church and a local congregation is not one of addition but rather one of being intertwined, for the whole Christ is present in each local congregation and thus at the same time the whole church is really present in each local congregation. The relationship of pastoral ministries to each other in local

context of Orthodox ecclesiology, in no way self-evident consequences for understanding apostolic succession. Just as little as the threefold form, the well-known Calvinist four-fold division of the church's ministerial office cannot be demonstrated as the basic ordering of the earliest congregations. More important than the attempt to establish an *historical* basis of a definite ordering of offices in the church in the apostolic era is the *systematic* unfolding of the possibilities contained in the wealth of New Testament statements, whereby the starting point is readily available in the concept of the church.

congregation, regional churches, and in the whole church must correspond to this. This relationship is not only defined as an ordering of over and under, but at the same time as fellowship, as for one another and with one another. In other words, the directives about the overseer pastor and the obedience with respect to the overseer pastor are enclosed within the command that each should be subject to the others in the Lord.

f) In a unique way the church is simultaneously a unity and a plurality. Correspondingly, the pastoral office occurs in the form of both unity and plurality. It is quite likely that originally, in the earliest Christian congregations everywhere, there was a plurality of pastors in ministry and that only after some time a monarchical episcopate developed. (It is disputed if this form is already set forth in the Pastoral Letters.) But one cannot find a single starting point in the New Testament for the authority of a single person over the entire church. With regard to the special place of Peter within the circle of the apostles, there can be no doubt that it was not one of being set above the other apostles. Rather, he is described as the speaker within the circle of the apostles, and this also holds true only during the initial period of church-founding.

g) In addition then come further differentiations within the church's ministerial office:

i) Specific functions can be distributed among the pastoral ministries so that one pastor hands over specific functions of leadership to another and thus obeys him as the overseer pastor; so, for example, the local pastor can relinquish the practice of church discipline and hand it over to the overseer pastor;

ii) Differentiations through the setting up of diaconal ministries, that is, through the transfer of individual functions of the pastoral office to other members of the congregation who do not themselves hold the pastoral office; and

iii) Differentiations through tasks for a stipulated period, such as congregational visitations or missionary endeavors or also the transport of the offerings.

To this overview of the most important perspectives for the organization of the forms of the pastoral office one should still add that in the theological reflection on the office, as is well known, significant differences developed very soon, depending on which of these functions and forms were especially noted and given theological validity. For example, the Pastoral Letters emphasize the function of keeping doctrine pure, the letters of Ignatius emphasize the representation of the one Christ through the office of the bishop, First Clement emphasizes the function of order. These differences found their continuation in church history and the history of church confessions. In the ancient church these differing conceptions were not perceived as contradictory, church-dividing positions.

It is decisively important that the dogmatic teaching about the ministerial office keep open the extent of the possible starting points found in the New Testament and that it consider that there is a difference between the dogmatic formulation and its formulation in church law, for in the historical decision about the directives in church law one must choose a definite form of order, and one must often do this in the midst of specific frontal assaults from several sides, whether from the degeneration of the freely emerging charismata or from the degeneration of the ministerial office itself. But these decisions of church law must not be put on the same level with the dogmatic concept of the ministerial office, which is substantially wider than that which is realized in each specific situation of church law. The abundance of New Testament starting points for the ordering of the church is larger than what can be realized only in *one* ordering of a church as it is set forth in its church law.

V. The Concept of the Apostolate

In order to clarify the relationship between the apostolic succession in the church and the pastoral office it is first necessary to deal with the apostolic office.[14] In the course of this, however, I have to restrict myself in the next four sections to highlighting only what is of significance for our particular topic. In order to define the concept of apostolic office it is essential to distinguish between two constitutive elements:

The sending out of the twelve by the earthly Jesus had been of limited duration in time. After they carried out their mission, they returned to Jesus. But then the fellowship of the disciples was broken in a way that was similar to how the old covenant was broken through the disobedience of Israel; the disciples broke it through their arrogance and lack of faith in view of the passion of their Lord. The foundation for the apostolic office is thus the appearances of the risen one. In fact, ultimately being an eyewitness of Jesus' earthly life is not an absolute precondition for the apostolate. In any case, Paul thought of himself as an apostle of Jesus Christ solely on the basis of the appearance of the risen one without having been a disciple of the earthly Jesus. The first element in the concept of apostle is thus being an eyewitness to the resurrection of Jesus Christ.

Nevertheless, being an eyewitness as such did not make one into an apostle. This becomes quite clear through 1 Cor. 15.5 ff. If the appearance of the risen one had been in itself the sufficient foundation for the apostolate, then the more than 500 brothers and sisters would have all been apostles. While they

---

14 K. H. Rengstorf, ἀπόστολος, TWNT 1.408 ff. [TDNT 1.407 ff.]; Gerhard Sass, *Apostelamt und Kirche: eine theologisch-exegetische Untersuchung des paulinischen Apostelbegriffs* [The Apostolic Office and the Church: A theological-exegetical Investigation of the Pauline Concept of Apostle] (Munich: Kaiser, 1939); Hans v. Campenhausen, *Kirchliches Amt und geistliche Vollmacht* [*Ecclesiastical Authority and Spiritual Power in the Church of the First Three Centuries*], chaps. 2 and 3.

were indeed witnesses, they did not become apostles. Rather, foundational for the apostle is the sending by the risen one, which is added to being an eyewitness. This sending was at the same time an authorization. The mission given by the risen one was no unfulfillable demand, but at the same time a promise of a divine fulfillment, the promise of the present Christ and of the efficacy of the Holy Spirit.

These two elements—being an eyewitness and the sending by the risen one—are constitutive for the dogmatic concept of the apostle; for the fulfillment of their task, the apostles were then equipped through the outpouring of the Holy Spirit, whom they received in the midst of the other believers and watchers.

On what basis now does the carrying out of their mission, and along with it their function in and for the growing church, consist?

a) The apostles proclaimed the act of salvation, whose eyewitnesses they were, the resurrection of the Christ who died on the cross, and this proclamation is, to be sure, not only the communication of the fact, but its development as a divine act of salvation in the assurance to Jews and Gentiles, in the kerygmatic advance into ever new conceptualizations and worldviews. The unfolding of this "for you" is at the same time the proclamation of the claim of Jesus Christ as the Lord and the announcement of his judgment.

b) Thereby, because the apostles proclaimed the gospel, faith and the fellowship of believers came into being; congregations came into being. The apostolic ministry was that of the builder, of the planter. They did not restrict themselves to the relevant assurance and claim of the gospel, but they also gave instructions for ordering the life of congregations, for the order of the worship service, for the common ministry of the spiritually gifted individuals, for the fellowship of Jewish-Christians and Gentile-Christians with each other, for marriage, for collecting the offerings, and so forth. They also undertook installations into the ministry of congregational leadership and they strengthened the authority of those who presided in the congregations.

c) The apostles were the bond of unity for the earliest congregations. The unity of the congregations in the exalted Christ and in the Spirit became an historical reality through the ministry of the apostles, through the witness of the same to the Lord who appeared to them, through missionary journeys to the congregations, through the sending of messengers and letters, through mutual petitionary prayers, through the organization of the offering collection for Jerusalem, and so forth. If the apostles were effective as the bond of unity for the congregations, then this presupposes that the apostles themselves represented a unity with one another. Against an idealization of this unity—an idealization that already clearly began in the Acts of the Apostles and soon was completed in the ancient church—the letter of Galatians especially offers warning. There we experience tensions and real conflicts among the apostles. But neither can we overlook the obligation to unity that was acknowledged by all of them, their commitment to this unity, and the unity that is factually existing in the one Christ, a unity which does not consist in a pyramid of hierarchical ordering of over and under but in the fellowship of service, that is, it is brought about at the same time in the mutual recognition of being sent by the Lord, whereby the special role of Peter is not to be overlooked in the earliest time of the founding of the church.[15]

It is now essential to make clear that the concept of apostle, which we have been using here—we spoke above about the apostolic *office* [*Amt*] because it has to do with a ministry based on a commissioning—is a dogmatic concept, to which no New Testament concept of *apostolos* consistently corresponds in similar meaning. The factual situation in the New Testament does not need to be set forth here in detail. It is well known that the Gospel of John avoids the title of apostle for the Twelve, that Matthew uses the word only once—and perhaps not even once in the original manuscript—and that Mark uses it only once. To be sure, Luke speaks frequently of the apostles, but he refers in this way only to the Twelve, not to Paul (with the exception of Acts 14.14, where Barnabas is also referred to as an apostle). On the other hand, Paul did not restrict the concept of apostle, neither to the Twelve nor to the Twelve and himself: Gal. 1.19 refers to James as an apostle, as well as others; Rom. 16.7 refers to Andronicus and Junia as apostles, and so forth. The New Testament has no uniform concept of apostle. To be sure, we need to distinguish between the apostles of Jesus Christ and the apostles of the congregations, but even then the New Testament conceptuality is not uniform, and we must see clearly that the concept of apostle, which soon became common in the ancient church, is already a dogmatic concept. Although the concept of the apostolic office points to the essence of clear New Testament contents—otherwise it would not be a legitimate dogmatic concept—it is not drawn directly from New Testament statements but is rather the result of its systematic-theological processing.

Just because this concept points to the heart of the New Testament it cannot be used in an exclusive sense but must retain a certain openness and diffuseness since the differences in the New Testament use of the term *apostle* means at the same time an openness regarding the borders of the apostolic circle. Thus the concept of apostle was broad, according to Paul, or narrow, according to Luke. The diffuseness in the concept of apostle corresponds to the fact that the apostles were surrounded by prophets, evangelists, and teachers, in each case without any clear-cut distinction being made between their ministries. The dogmatic concept of the apostle thus grasps the constituting

---

15 Hermann Strathmann, "Die Stellung des Petrus in der Urkirche," [The Place of Peter in the Early Church] *Zeitschrift für Systematische Theologie* 20 (1943), 223 ff.; Oskar Cullmann, *Petrus, Jünger Apostel Märtyrer* Zürich: Zwingli Verlag, 1952) [ET: *Peter: Disciple, Apostle, Martyr* (Philadelphia: Westminster, 1953)]; Otto Karrer, *Um die Einheit der Christen–Die Petrusfrage–Ein Gespräch mit Emil Brunner, Oskar Cullmann, Hans von Campenhausen* (Frankfurt a. M.: Knecht, 1953); Nikolaj Afanassieff et al., *La Primaute de Pierre* (Paris: Delachaux & Niestle, 1960) [ET: *The Primacy of Peter* (London: The Faith Press, 1963)].

center of the New Testament conceptuality of this term, but it cannot ignore the diffuseness that radiates from this center. Otherwise dogmatics would lose its historical basis and no longer be in a position to see correctly the early Christian relationship between charisma and ministerial office, and it would no longer be in a position to provide a persuasive argument for the authority of the New Testament canon, which indeed, as we noted above, does not consist solely of writings produced by apostolic hands.

VI. The Apostles as Foundation of the Church

Through the ministry of his called and authorized eyewitnesses Christ himself has acted to judge and save the world and to build up the church. In their words and deeds Christ has demonstrated himself as the one speaking and acting in the present. In Christ's stead they were ambassadors through whom God exhorted the people. The apostle therefore stands in the place where earlier Christ stood. This holds true also about the suffering of the apostle: In that he took part in the suffering of Jesus Christ, he was the representation of the suffering Christ in the midst of the congregation and before the world, and as representation of the suffering Christ he was the agent of the power of the exalted Lord. The apostles therefore appear before the world as the vicarious representatives of Jesus Christ. So the witness of the apostles was the word of God, binding and loosing, and the power of their message was the power of God, the working of the Spirit. So the apostolic office is an act of salvation of God, which is added to the act of salvation in Christ. That salvific act is certainly not added as an independent act separable from Christ; rather, it is added as the salvific act of the ministry of Jesus Christ, as an "office of reconciliation." This ministry is, however, still a special act of salvation of God insofar as apart from the apostolate the salvific act of Christ would have remained hidden from the world. The ministry of the apostles is an eschatological act of salvation, which is added to God's act of salvation in Christ insofar as the salvific act on the cross is breaking into the world through the called witnesses of the resurrection.

The apostles were not only the builders and planters of the *earliest Christian* community, but they are the builders and planters of the church *in all times and places*. Their ministerial office is and remains utterly unique. Only the apostles have proclaimed Christ as the called eyewitnesses of the risen Lord. To be sure, every calling into the church's ministerial offices occurs through the exalted Lord, but it usually occurs in all times and places through means, namely, through the mouth and hands of human beings. On the basis of the historical uniqueness of their direct and immediate calling by the risen one, the apostles are the foundation of the church, not merely of individual congregations but of the church of all times and places (compare Matt. 16.18; Eph. 2.20 and Rev. 21.14). This statement does not imply any competition with those passages that refer to Christ as the foundation of the church, for in the ministry of the apostles Christ is the foundation-stone, the cornerstone, and the keystone.

To what extent are the apostles foundational for all further servant ministry and all further life of the church? Here the same three points must be mentioned again, which were discussed earlier.

a) The apostolic gospel is the authoritative message of Christ for the church of all times. It corresponds entirely to the starting point found in the undisputed letters of Paul and also in a concentrated way in the Pastoral Letters, where one is exhorted to remain true to the doctrine of the apostle, for Paul had spoken of the gospel in such a way as to speak of *his* gospel so that the apostle and the gospel cannot be separated from each other. Of course it is not only the *content* of the apostolic witness that has authoritative significance, but also the apostolic *act* of servant witnessing. Acknowledging the apostle does not consist simply in reciting apostolic words, but rather it is continuing in what the apostles have done to advance the proclamation of God's act of salvation into the world.

b) Furthermore, foundational is the apostolic ministry of church leadership. Here, too—in fact, here even more so—it is not only the *factual* directives of the apostles which have been handed down that are obligatory for all later times but also the *act* of the apostolic directing. The church has to follow this example in that it must endeavor ever anew in each case to order its ministry aright.

c) The apostles are the abiding authoritative bond of unity of the church of all times and places, a bond of unity through their message about Christ, but also through the differences that are evident among them in the theological unfolding of the message of Christ and in the understanding of the church and its order in the New Testament writings, for precisely in these differences, the apostles are the paradigm for the extent and limits of church unity. The ancient church acknowledged the differences within the New Testament writings— their traditions of the gospel, their theologies, their starting points for the ordering of the church—as existing within this unity, in that they received them in a canon of Scripture.

This three-fold foundational and unrepeatable function of the apostolate is affirmed by the Eastern Church, the Reformation churches, and also the Roman Church. In this fundamental affirmation there is no contradiction. The differences first appeared at a later time, namely, with the question regarding the sources of apostolic tradition: Where is the apostolic witness to be found? In the New Testament writings? In the oral tradition? Or in the current teaching office, even aside from Scripture and a historically demonstrable tradition? In view of all of this, profound differences arise in the concrete determination of the content of what is apostolically obligatory. But despite these differences, the fundamental acknowledgment of the apostles as foundation of the church is of greatest significance. This alone makes possible the ecumenical dialogue.

VII. The Apostles as Members of the Church

How the apostles understood themselves in relation to the congregations is most clearly and reliably set forth by Paul. To be sure, one cannot generalize about the Pauline understanding without further ado, since one must reckon with the differences in the relationship between apostle and congregation when one compares the Jerusalem basic conception with the Pauline. Nevertheless, the following general statements can be made.

Together with all members of the church the apostles stand under the Lord; they were justified sinners among the others. What they are, they are solely by grace. Indeed, the apostles sinned in a special way, like Peter as the denier and Paul did as the persecutor of Jesus Christ. Together with all members the apostle must also appear before the judgment seat of God and be revealed along with his deeds. The person of the apostle is nothing; his witness is everything. Thus, according to his own self-judgment, the apostle appears to be the greatest sinner, one untimely born, an aberration, a doormat, unworthy, tormented by demons.[viii] Decisive is this: "It is not I who live, but Christ who lives in me" (Gal. 2.20).

The apostle stands as a witness vis-à-vis the congregation and brings it everything, and yet at the same time the apostle stands as a justified sinner under the Lord and before him is nothing. The apostles thus live as every Christian does, namely, from the congregation's comforting witness. They live from the intercessions of the congregations, and again and again we read how Paul asks that they should pray for him so that his work could progress, that his sorrow be taken from him, and so forth. In that way, the apostles live from the ministry of the congregation. As recipients they are dependent not only on material gifts and payments for services rendered but also on the spiritual gifts of strength and comfort that the congregations bestow upon them.

VIII. The Servant Ministry of the Apostles in the Fellowship of the Church

Since the findings in both of the previous sections ("The Apostles as Foundation of the Church" and "The Apostles as Members of the Church") belong together, this cannot remain without consequences for the execution of the apostolic ministry. The apostles act in fellowship with the other members of the church. This becomes clear both in the Acts of the Apostles (for example, Acts 15) and in the letters of Paul (for example, 1 Cor. 5.4). In other respects, it is also characteristic for Paul to strive constantly for the "Amen" and cooperation of the congregation, for it also had received the Spirit. In that the congregation submits itself to the word of the apostle, it also shares in Christ and in his Spirit and is equipped and called to test and judge everything. But its cooperation is not restricted to testing and judging. The apostle did his ministry surrounded by the manifold ministries of the Spirit, who is actively working through the treasure of his gifts. Even where the multiplicity of spiritual gifts is not explicitly mentioned in the New Testament it is clear that the apostle—whether surrounded by spiritual ministries [*pneumatischen Diensten*] or by elders [*Ältesten*]—does not represent an isolated authority. Once more it is important here to stress the diffuseness in the concept of apostle, about which we spoke above. The apostles do their ministry surrounded by prophets, teachers, evangelists, who at times are working across several congregations, as the apostles do, too, and surrounded by manifold other spiritual persons [*Pneumatikern*], elders [*Presbytern*], and initial believers in the local congregations. Thus, alongside the apostles, prophets are also mentioned as a foundation on which the church is built (Eph. 2.20). Since the prophets are here mentioned after the apostles, the author was probably thinking of New Testament prophets. This aspect of the fellowship of the apostolic ministry with the other ministries was then also acknowledged in the compilation of writings in the New Testament canon, only some of which, of course, originated directly from the apostles.

The office of the apostle will only then be correctly understood if we keep in mind this two-fold and ultimately three-fold set of circumstances. The apostles were called prior to the outpouring of the Spirit, they received the Spirit together with the other members of the church, and they worked in fellowship with them. This set of circumstances can also be expressed in this way: Through the calling of the risen one the apostles are brought into prominence in relation to all other members of the church, but they live as members of the church surrounded by the assurance of all who receive the Spirit, and they work in the congregations and in the world surrounded by the witness of all who receive the Spirit. Here it can also be stated that the apostles are called in order to build up and plant the church. Indeed in order to be the foundation of the church, they are at the same time themselves members of the church, which is built through the Spirit on the one foundation, Jesus Christ, and they work together with the other members of the church and are, together with them, the church. Only the person who sees these three aspects together, namely those described in sections VI–VIII, can rightly recognize what it means to say that the apostles are the foundation of the church. Only on the basis of all of this, does a complete understanding of apostolic succession emerge.

IX. Pastoral Office and the Church

The whole church, together with the pastoral ministries and all charismata, is grounded on the apostles, that is, on Jesus Christ, who, as the risen one, has authorized the apostles and who, as the exalted one, rules the church through the Holy Spirit. Each and every one of the offices of servant ministry and of the other charismata must prove itself as a true service when measured according to the fundamental norm of the apostles, as servant ministry that takes place in the power of the Spirit. Everything that was said above (sec. 5) about the apostles as foundation of the church is now otherwise to be reiterated for the church with all its installed pastors and all who are spiritually gifted.

Within the multiplicity of spiritual gifts that are given to all the members of the church, the commissioning into the pastoral ministry is to be understood as a continuation of the commissioning of the apostles—a continuation, not in the sense of further installation as apostle, but rather in the sense of a continuation of the servant ministry that the apostles have foundationally begun. Since the apostles are historically unique—because of the appearances of the risen one granted them and because of his direct sending—the apostolate, as the company of eyewitnesses to the resurrection, ones who were directly elected by Christ, can have no continuation, but is extinguished with the death of the apostles. But the mission that was given to the apostles has not expired, for it embraces the missionizing of all peoples to the end of the world. And with that, the sending of the apostles extends beyond the persons of the apostles, for it concerns the "All" over which Jesus has been set as Lord—all peoples of all countries and all times until the Parousia. In this respect, from the very nature of the commissioning of the apostles, there follow every other special commissioning; thus the pastoral ministry in its various forms is necessarily derived from the apostolic office so that the mission given to the apostles will be carried out to the end of the world. Every other later sending occurs through the exalted Lord, not directly and not foundationally, but through human beings. In this way the pastoral office of all later times is profoundly distinguished from the apostolic office. Nevertheless, insofar as the pastoral office continues that of the apostles—on the basis of the mission that was imparted to the apostles and that was still not fulfilled at the time of their death and thus had not yet expired—it can be described as apostolic with the same meaning, just as the church of all times is confessed in the Nicene Creed to be the apostolic church. In this way, the pastoral office remains distinct from the apostolic office itself in a way analogous to the distinction between the Christian and Jesus Christ.

Because the church of all times, along with its pastoral ministries and charismata, is founded on the apostles, in determining the relationship between the pastoral office and the church, the same three elements that were highlighted in the last three sections about the apostolic office have to be revisited:

a) The pastors in relation to the church. The pastoral office faces the church, for Christ speaks through this office to the church as its Lord. In everything that pastors do in obedience to their mission, they encounter the congregation as vicarious representatives of Christ, the one good shepherd. When they proclaim the apostolic message, "Be reconciled to God!," then, like the apostle, they are an ambassador in the stead of Christ, an instrument through which God himself exhorts the church and the world (2 Cor. 5.20). In that pastors proclaim the apostolic message, the same promise that was given to the apostles holds true for them: "Whoever hears you, hears me" (Lk. 10.16). The comforting and exhorting voice of the pastoral office, although a human voice, is not human comfort and exhortation but God's voice, which "rings down from heaven" (AC 25.3 f.). In that the pastoral office carries out the apostolic message, God himself is active in his power, just as through the apostolic office. The pastor, as also the congregation, in all human doubt and uncertainty, can and should be most surely comforted about God's act through the pastoral office. The same thing applies to the pastor's actions in the administration of baptism and the Lord's Supper. It also applies to the action of the pastor in binding and loosing and sending. Through the leadership of the pastoral office Christ himself leads the church. The good shepherd feeds his flock through the pastors called and gifted by him and taken into his service. The pastoral office thus faces the congregation since Christ himself speaks through this office to the congregation, strengthens it, and leads it. To be sure, every spiritually gifted witness and every spiritually gifted ministry has authority in the church, for this is the way the Spirit acts, the one who is the Lord. But the spiritually gifted ministry of the pastoral office has an authority that is given ahead of time, in contrast to independent spiritually gifted ministries, since in this respect it is grounded in the commissioning that authorizes it. In contrast to the independent spiritually gifted ministries, the pastoral office has an authority that authenticates itself not merely in the execution of that office, which then is acknowledged later by the congregation; rather, its authority is actually given in advance, insofar as it is already presupposed in a commissioning. On the basis of such a commissioning, the believers can be sure that this person is authorized by God for this ministry. For this reason, from the very outset pastors can count on being met with the expectation that God is acting through them to lead the congregation. The authority of this pastoral office does not of course merely consist in the special calling but also in ever new obedience over against this calling. When the spiritual gift is received, which authorizes one for the ministry, then the same can be said here about what is generally true of the outpouring of the Holy Spirit. The Spirit is the gift that has been granted to us in that he is and remains at the same time the Lord who wants ever to be summoned anew and who wants to bestow himself. To be in the Spirit is not a characteristic of the person but the ever-new working of the Spirit in the faithfulness of God, the one who is creating anew. Thus the authority of the pastoral office does not consist in the bare historical fact of the commissioning, but rather in the ever-new apprehension of this commissioning, in the ever-new stoking and enflaming of the charisma that is given through the commissioning (2 Tim. 1.6). But the daily necessity for this obedient apprehension of the authority does not cancel the authority that was previously given in the commissioning, but rather is grounded in it.

b) The pastors as members of the church. The pastors stand under the Lord, along with all members of the church. The officeholder stands in the midst of the congregation under the judging and saving activity of God. Like the others, the pastor is dependent on grace and intercessory prayer. Pastors, too, must appear before the judgment seat of God, and in fact not in spite of their commission but because of it, which as such brings with it special dangers. The very idea of a personal superiority over against the other Christians would be a delusion. In fact, the pastoral office means precisely the opposite, for nothing is more humbling than this office, nothing reduces one to nothing more than the knowledge about being installed as the vicarious representative of Christ. Ordination is the end of one's own plans, ways, means and words, for the pastoral office means that *Christ* wants to feed his flock through this called person.

   c) The servant ministry of the pastors in the fellowship of the church. What was said above about the fellowship of the ministry of the apostles and the other church members cannot now be watered down in the statements about the pastors coming after them. Pastors lead the congregation in fellowship with the other spiritually gifted ministries. This is true for the pastoral office in the local congregation as well as in the larger regional church and in the church as a whole. Moreover, it cannot be only a matter of the fellowship of pastors with each other but also about the fellowship of pastors with the members of the church who have not received a commissioning but who are awakened to servant ministry by the same Spirit. Here we need to observe once more that the office is not separated from the other charismata by a special designation in the New Testament; there is no verbal parallel in the New Testament for our dogmatic concept of the ministerial office. Correspondingly, it is not demonstrable from the New Testament that the servant ministry of the pastor, of the pastoral administrator, and so forth came about only after a prior commissioning. Here there are transitions and diffusions that do not permit themselves to be grasped in the schema of over and under, but rather are shown to be effective in the completely different structure of fellowship and mutual acknowledgment in the course of life and service in the church. Besides, one cannot forget that Paul speaks of "administrators" and the gift of "leadership" and also "pastors" in the Letter to the Ephesians after he has spoken of the actual kerygmatic ministries, and that still in the Didache, which presupposes the office of bishop (15.1 ff.), one finds the instruction to leave the Eucharistic prayer of thanksgiving up to the prophets, if any should be present (10.6).[ix] In the statements of the New Testament we find pastors surrounded by spiritually gifted individuals and elders, in the course of which, at least in the Gentile-Christian congregations during the first century, there was truly no elected college of elders with definite ministerial functions, but only an informal group of elderly, honored, and esteemed individuals, the initial believers, and so forth. The commissioning of elders—and with it the office of elder—likely belonged to a later period within the domain of Gentile Christianity. But as the case may be, it is in the nature of the pastoral office to be surrounded by functioning ministries of the congregation and precisely, indeed, also by its witness.

d) Not only does the pastoral office face the congregation but the independent spiritually gifted witness in the congregation also faces the pastoral office. Christ deals with the congregation through pastors, but he also deals with both the congregation and the pastors through manifold charismata. The pastoral office exists in the midst of the mutual service of all members to one another. The pastor exists in the midst of the manifold workings of the one grace of Christ through this service of the one to the other. The spiritually gifted witnesses in the congregation are not to be tested and judged one-sidedly by the pastoral office, but likewise, conversely, the congregation has the task and the authority—like every spiritually gifted ministry—also to test and judge the ministry of the pastor.

At this point the provocative question arises regarding the final authority in the church: Is this authority the ministerial office or the congregation? This question is also contained in the often-discussed problem, namely, what was indeed earlier, the office or the congregation? It is decisive that the New Testament gives no answer to this "either-or." Even the pastoral office is penultimate. Christ alone is the final authority, who is presently working in the congregation through the Holy Spirit. Thereby, as the called witnesses to the risen one, the apostles are at the same time the fore-ordained authority for the ministerial office and the church. The office of the apostles is, after all, the grounding for the church's ministerial office and the church as a whole. Neither the church's ministerial office nor the church is the final authority but both must be answerable to the final authority that was proclaimed as foundational by the apostles, namely, the Lord. Corresponding to this is the fact that the ancient church did not know of a legal solution regarding final authority, and its synodical decisions remained dependent on the agreement of the churches. It is amazing that the Eastern Church, even today, in contrast to Rome, gives up trying to secure an ultimate solution to the question about final authority. Furthermore, according to the understanding of the Eastern Church, councils and bishops and even congregations can err. Only the church as a whole cannot err. But if one asks Eastern theologians about the means by which this infallibility of the whole church expresses itself, this question is left ultimately and characteristically open.[16]

---

16 Thus, e. g., S. Zankow: Ecumenical is "not the ecumenical council in and for itself but only that which the whole church in the entire course of church history has recognized and acknowledged to have been really a true ecumenical council. The whole church is that which alone gives a council the aura of ecumenicity and thus seals its decisions as infallible. For this reason, synods or their decisions are infallible only insofar as their witness about the faith of the church was infallible. And that is something that in the final analysis only the church itself, the whole church and it alone, decides or bears witness to" (*Procés-verbaux du premier congrés de théologie orthodoxe à Athènes* [Proceedings of the First Conference on Orthodox Theology at Athens], ed. Hamilcar S. Alivisatos [Athens: Pyrsos, 1939], 281). A presupposition here is the conviction

X. Apostolic Succession

Apostolic succession cannot mean a continuing further calling to be an apostle, but only a following in obedience with respect to the apostles, the called eyewitnesses to the resurrection of Jesus Christ—whether this following is based on the general calling of all the baptized, or whether it occurs on the basis of the special calling into the pastoral ministry.

a) The apostolic succession of the church and of every one of its members consists above all:

i) in the faith in the apostolic message and in obedience to the apostolic instructions and exhortations;

ii) in the witness of the apostolic gospel entrusted to each Christian, that is, in the multiplicity of the charismata given to every one of them;

iii) in the witnessing and successful advance of the gospel into the world and in the building up of the congregation, for every charisma is a ministry of building up the congregation and occurs at the same time in the front between church and world. In this sense every Christian disciple follows in the church-building activity of the apostles and has a shared responsibility in the ministry of the pastor;

iv) in the nurturing of the fellowship with the Christians, with the churches in the entire world. This impetus belongs intrinsically to the apostolic succession of the church and also of every member of the church, for apostolic succession is only there where the apostles are taken seriously as the bond of the unity of the church of all times and places.

b) The apostolic succession of the pastoral office demonstrates itself in that:

i) every pastor is placed under the apostolic example[x]—in his preaching, teaching, leading and administering;

ii) the pastor, like the apostles, exists in relation to the church as the mouth and vicarious representative of Christ;

iii) the pastor, like every member of the congregation, is dependent daily anew on God's grace;

iv) the pastor feeds the church not merely in fellowship with other pastors but also in fellowship with the spiritually gifted ministries that surround the pastoral office in the church.

"that the general consciousness of the *pleroma* [fullness] of the church in questions of faith is infallible. Meant here is the consciousness of the clergy and laity as a totality, for the spiritual and laity, directors and listeners, lords and servants, men and women are members of the Body of Christ and together form the *pleroma* [fullness], the whole, the body of the church, which in Orthodoxy is thought of alone as infallible" (J. N. Karmiris, "Abriβ der dogmatischen Lehre der orthodoxen katholischen Kirche," [Outline of the Dogmatic Teaching of the Orthodox Catholic Church] in *Die Orthodoxe Kirche in griechischer Sicht* [The Orthodox Church in Greek Perspective], ed. Hans Heinrich Harms, et al., 2 vols. [Stuttgart: Evangelisches Verlagwerk, 1959–60], 1.93).

c) Neither the apostolic succession of the church nor that of the ministerial office could be taken seriously if the relationship between the apostles and the church would not also be followed in the fellowship of mutual serving and of the common servant ministry to the world, for not only the apostolic message and directive but also the structure of the apostles' working for and with the church are foundational for the church of all times, and are to be maintained in obedient discipleship by all pastors and churches.

d) From this basic assertion it follows that there are basically three ways into the pastoral office that can be acknowledged to be in obedience to the effective working of the apostles:

i) The sending into the pastoral ministry by those who have previously been sent as pastors themselves—following the acknowledgment of the pastors or, beyond that, the cooperation of the church, that is, by such church members who have not themselves received ordination;

ii) The sending into the pastoral ministry by the church, that is, by such members of the church who have not themselves been sent as pastors—following the acknowledgment by the called pastors or, beyond that, their cooperation;

iii) The acknowledgment by the church and called pastors of an actually existing pastoral ministry that that has emerged in spiritual freedom.

It is obvious that of these three ways the first has earned priority today and is valid as a rule, for as the temporal distance from the apostles has increased, the pastoral office and also a special education for the office had to gain more and more importance if the church was to guard apostolic tradition. Ordination by means of the ordained has rightly become the established practice in the church. Nevertheless, the other two ways cannot be excluded in principle since they too correspond to the relationship of apostle and church, and also in these ways the apostolic church grew. This openness is of great ecumenical significance.[17] Without it certain spiritual breakthroughs in church history— whether missionary advances in heathen lands or movements of spiritual renewal inside a tired and self-righteous church—remain incomprehensible; and without this openness the divisions that have thus arisen within Christendom remain incurable.

e) How are we now to evaluate apostolic succession in the narrower sense of

17 Although the freely emerging charismata play an entirely subordinate role in the abundance of Anglican literature on the issue of the church's ministerial office, this openness is still found in the fact that God can act in the church today as in the earliest period and directly call individuals by the Spirit into a ministry and authorize them to this ministry and to its being carried out without the cooperation of the calling church. The church then has the task of acknowledging by the normally ordered [*ordentliche*] office these freely emerging, spiritually gifted ministries ("non-regularized ministers") and fit them into the normal order [*geordneten*] of life in the church. Cf. Arnold Ehrhardt, *The Apostolic Succession in the First Two Centuries of the Church* (London: Lutterworth, 1953); idem, *The Apostolic Ministry* (Edinburgh: Oliver & Boyd, 1958).

the sequence of the laying on of hands by ordained bishops? The laying on of hands is not the condition without which there can be no apostolic succession of the pastoral office nor the existence of the church. It does not produce an apostolic succession and authority that the other ordinations lack. Already during the Christological controversies in the ancient church it did not prove to be the unfailing means by which the apostolicity of doctrine and of the church was secured, and the similar thing also became clearer again and again in the later history of the church. Nevertheless, the sequence of laying on of hands through ordinations by bishops is to be considered a *sign* for the apostolic succession of ministries and of the church. It is a sign through which is expressed the fact that the church is only the church of Christ when it knows itself to be grounded on the apostles. The sequence of episcopal laying on of hands is thus a sign at the same time for the unity and catholicity of the church,[18] for only the *ecclesia apostolica* is the *una sancta catholica*. As a *sign* of apostolic succession, ordination in the sequence of episcopal laying on of hands that has been established through the course of church history is to be welcomed, and where it is lacking, we should strive to introduce it.[19] But this *signum* [sign] must never be detached from the *res* [thing itself], namely, from the tradition of apostolic teaching itself. The sign of apostolic succession can neither replace the necessity of submitting ever anew to the historic teaching of the apostles, nor devalue the pastoral ministry that exists without this apostolic sign.

f) Whether one goes beyond these statements or lags behind them, it is crucially important for every ecumenical dialogue that the succession of pastoral ministries and that of the church not be torn apart but treated

18 This understanding of apostolic succession is in several respects close to that which was set forth by a group of Anglican theologians in the anthology, *The Historic Episcopate*, ed. Kenneth Carey (London: Dacre, 1954). These theologians sought to overcome the alternatives that have defined the disagreement between the Anglo-Catholic and Evangelical wings in the Anglican Church during the last decade, a conflict in which, on the one side, apostolic succession through the episcopate is taught as belonging to the *esse* [essence] of the church, while on the other side it is taught as belonging to the *bene esse* [well-being] of the church. This anthology has rightly shown that the Anglo-Catholic conception is historically untenable and the Evangelical theory of "well-being" is theologically inadequate. Over and against these two positions, the historic episcopate is here given a new interpretation within the totality of life in the church and as a sign of the unity and fullness of the church that encompasses both space and time (a theory of the historic episcopate as belonging to the *full-being* [*plene esse*] of the church). Cf. in the above anthology the contributions by Robinson and Montefiore.

19 The more cautious "Erklärung des Ökumenischen Ausschusses der Vereinigten Evangelisch-Lutherischen Kirche Deutschlands zur Frage der apostolischen Sukzession vom 26. Nov. 1957" [Declaration of the Ecumenical Commission of the United Evangelical-Lutheran Church in Germany on the Issue of Apostolic Succession, 26 November 1957] in view of the ecumenical development as a whole is likely to have no final significance. Cf. Hugh Montefiore, "Kommentar zur Erklärung des Ökumenischen Ausschusses der Vereinigten Evangelisch-Lutherischen Kirche Deutschlands zur Frage der apostolischen Sukzession vom 26. Nov. 1957," in *Ökumenische Rundschau* 7 (1958), 140 ff.

together. But beyond the special issue of succession, it is absolutely decisive for the future of ecumenical dialogue that the early Christian category of fellowship be recovered for the sake of understanding the unity of the church. This holds true not only for the issues relating to church order but also for the issues relating to dogma, for in both of these areas the earliest Christian community shows a much greater multiplicity of starting points than what materialized in the later history of dogma and church law, a diversity that—amid the divisions of the church—was held to be compatible with the unity of the church. Only through the retrieval of the category of fellowship can the unity of the ancient church be understood, and that which has fallen apart into entrenched positions in the course of church history be unlocked and opened up for one another.

Editor's Notes

[i] A paper delivered in 1957 at the spring meeting of the Ecumenical Committee of the United Evangelical-Lutheran Church in Germany. (The footnotes were added later when the paper was prepared for publication.) This essay was published as "Die apostolische Sukzession," *Kerygma und Dogma* 7, no. 2 (1961), 79–114. It appears in KC 1.160–195. A version of this essay (missing many of the footnotes) was translated as "Apostolic Succession: A Fellowship of Mutual Service" in *Encounter* 25 (1964), 50–83. That translation, likewise lacking many of the footnotes, also appears in CC (186–233).

[ii] Literally, "one who follows."

[iii] The typical German word for *pastor* is *Pfarrer*. In this essay, however, Schlink rarely used this term. Instead, he preferred the literal terms *Hirte* (shepherd), as in this sentence, and *Hirtenamt* (shepherd office). These terms will be rendered here by their English equivalents, "pastor" and "pastoral office."

[iv] Cf., e. g., Acts 8.14; 11.22; 13.3–4; 15.22, 25, 30, 34.

[v] Schlink here uses the word *Älteste*, literally, "the oldest ones." He will also use the original Greek term that is used in the New Testament, namely, *presbyteroi*. Both of these terms will be translated here as "elders."

[vi] Gnosticism took many diverse forms in early Christianity but all stressed the importance of special *gnosis* ("knowledge") of God and the world, which was secretly revealed by Jesus to his closest disciples. Characteristic of most forms of Gnosticism is a disparagement of the material world, which was held to be evil and something from which to escape. Montanism was an apocalyptic movement in the late second century that was tied to Montanus, who lived in Phrygia. He and his followers expected the imminent outpouring of the Holy Spirit on the church. Montanus himself evidently claimed to be the Paraclete promised in John. Montanus and his fellow prophets and prophetesses engaged in ecstatic prophetic activity. Their asceticism attracted large numbers of Christians in Asia Minor and North Africa.

[vii] Cf. endnote 7 in the introduction ("The Task") above.

[viii] Cf. 1 Cor. 15.8, 9; 2 Cor. 11.23–12.10; 1 Tim. 1.15.

[ix] Cf. Kurt Niederwimmer, *The Didache: A Commentary*, trans. Linda M. Maloney, ed. Harold W. Attridge (Minneapolis: Fortress, 1998), 203 ff., 161 f.

[x] Cf. 1 Pet. 2.21.

Chapter Nine:
On the Issue of Tradition

Theses for an Ecumenical Dialogue between Theologians of the German
Protestant Church and the Russian Orthodox Church[1]

I.

Jesus Christ, the crucified and risen one, is the foundation of the church. As the
called eyewitnesses to Jesus Christ, the apostles are, with him, the foundation
of the church.

II.

At all times and in all places the church must remain on the foundation of the
apostles. Only as the apostolic church is it the one, holy, catholic church. The
church is thus given the task of maintaining apostolic tradition.

III.

Apostolic tradition is what is to be taking place in *all* of the speaking and
acting of the church. In its advance into ever new areas of the world and in its
disputing with ever new religions and philosophies, the church has to
proclaim the apostolic message in ever new languages and statements, to
unfold the apostolic confession of Christ, and to continue in apostolic prayer,
baptism, and the breaking of bread. In these historical developments in word
and deed, the church may trust that Jesus Christ is not only remembered
historically, but also, as the exalted Lord, he is acting *presently* in the church
through the Holy Spirit and, through the church, in the world. This is the
special character of apostolic tradition in contrast to other traditions of
historical deeds and words. Apostolic tradition is thus living tradition which
by its very nature takes place in a multiplicity of historical developments.

1 Delivered and elucidated on 27 October 1959 in the Protestant Academy in Arnoldshain at an
ecumenical conference of representatives of the Russian Orthodox Church (Moscow patriarchy)
and the Protestant Church in Germany. [This essay was published as "Thesen für ein Gespräch
zwischen orthodoxen und evangelischen Theologen über das Problem der Tradition" in *Tradition und Glaubensgerechtigkeit* [Tradition and the Righteousness of Faith] (Witten: Luther, 1961),
27–35. It appears in KC 1.196–201 as "Zum Problem der Tradition: Thesen für ein ökumenisches
Theologen der evangelischen und der orthodoxen Kirche." An English translation by I. H.
Neilson appears in CC (234–41) as "On the Problem of Tradition: Twelve Theses for an Ecumenical Discussion between Theologians of the Evangelical and Orthodox Churches." –Ed.]

IV.

In the unceasing conflict between church and world the apostolic tradition, as living tradition, is directly endangered in a special way: the world attacks the church by means of false teachings and power, not only from the outside but also by members of the church and groups within it who—acting in the name of Christ and referring to the apostles—strive to tear the church from its historical, apostolic foundation. In the diversity of the traditions that cite as their authority the apostles and their disciples, true and false traditions thus need to be distinguished with constant watchfulness.

V.

In the midst of the stream of the church's life, the church has thus established the apostolic tradition in a special way in the canon of the Bible, in dogmas, and in the ordering of the church so that, as constants, they determine authoritatively the multiplicity of the church's activities, make known the borders of the church, and secure the unity of the church. Hereby the authority of the canon, dogma, and church order is based not on the decision of the church itself, but rather in the given authority of the apostles, which is acknowledged by the church through its decisions. The New Testament canon is thus the church's collection of the historical original documents of the apostolic message, while dogma is the church's unfolding of the apostolic confession of Christ, and the ordering of the church thus serves to carry on the servant ministry that the Lord had bestowed upon the apostles and, through them, upon the church.

The New Testament canon is distinguished from dogma and the ordering of the church in that the apostolic message is not formulated by the later church but has only been received, while in dogma and church order the church acknowledges the authority of the apostles in its *own* words and obligates its members to obedience to this authority. Within all other apostolic tradition the biblical canon is thus given prominence because we receive in it the *authentic* tradition of the apostolic message (whether in the words of the apostles themselves or in the words of the earliest Christian community) and therein the *authentic* tradition of Jesus' words and deeds.

VI.

Jesus did not command his disciples to write but to proclaim, and Paul wrote his letters not for the purpose of producing a New Testament Bible but solely as a substitute for his bodily presence and for his oral proclamation. This fundamental importance of the *viva vox* [living voice] is for earliest Christianity appropriately characterized by a living freedom and a great diversity of witnesses, prayers, theologians, and orderings of the church—a multiplicity which is also reflected in the differing traditions of the synoptic Gospels and the Gospel according to John.

At the same time, already in the earliest Christian community there were definite traditions in set wording, not only of the words and deeds of Jesus but also of doctrinal ("*kerygmatic*"), confessional, hymnic, and other liturgical formulas, which then in church history became the starting point for the rapid establishing of set forms of the liturgy, of dogma, and of church order in general. The more comprehensively this process proceeded, the more the informal witnessing and prayers of the spiritually gifted individuals declined in the worship service and gave way to the ministerial office, and the sermon itself and the informal prayer of the officeholder receded in relation to liturgical worship in set forms. The more uniformly—fully since the start of the imperial church—one and the same set liturgy, confession, and ordering of the ministerial office was sought and implemented, the more the multiplicity of the living tradition became marginalized.

The apostolic tradition is not only threatened by the fact that it is being torn from its historical foundation (the Gnostic-Enthusiastic danger),[i] but also by the fact that its living enactment in ever new and relevant words of witness, confession, and prayer, and in ever new deeds of servant ministry, and thereby also its necessary and essential historical multiplicity, is being marginalized (the ritualistic-legalistic danger).

VII.

Ecumenical dialogue concerning the dogmatic meaning of tradition suffers from the fact that (1) people have not sufficiently distinguished between the historical process of handing down apostolic tradition and the dogmatic concept of tradition in which there has been reflection about this process; and (2) the term *tradition* does not designate the same thing in the various churches:

1. In the process of handing down apostolic tradition in church history, the following most important steps need to be highlighted:

   a) The oral tradition of the words and deeds of Jesus and the oral proclamation about Christ by the apostles, complemented by their letters.

   b) The writing-down of Jesus' words and deeds, their collection in various "sources" [*Quellen*] and their being reworked in various gospels, while at the same time the oral tradition of Jesus' words and deeds that were not set in written form continued to be transmitted. At the same time the continuation of the apostles' oral proclamation about Christ was furthered by succeeding generations, in the course of which the apostolic letters were also read in such congregations to which the letters had not originally been sent.

c) The collection of gospels and letters, among which was the Acts of the Apostles, in the course of which the limits of the New Testament canon were still not set. But whereas Papias of Hierapolis was still seeking after the oral tradition of the Lord's words, already with Tertullian, Irenaeus, and the other anti-Gnostic fathers there is virtually no further reference to *concrete* historical traditions of the words and deeds of Jesus that are not recorded in the Gospels.[ii] The oral tradition of the Lord's words and deeds, which at first continued alongside the Gospels, was evidently by about the year 200 so deeply absorbed into the life of the church or so distorted by the Gnostics, that its wording could no longer be reliably ascertained. At the same time the continuation of the oral proclamation about Christ by the apostles ensued, in the course of which the New Testament writings were accorded an authority just as foundational as the Old Testament writings.

d) The demarcation of the New Testament canon as source of the apostolic tradition—in the context of the growing formulation of set forms of liturgy, dogma, and the ordering of ministerial offices (all occurring at the same time as the growth of the canon), which are likewise to serve the apostolic tradition.

e) After the completion of the canon, the further growing of the liturgy, dogma, and the ordering of the church—in the context of a growing tradition of scriptural interpretation in exegesis, of preaching, and of dogmatic teaching, whereby individual theologians from the time before and after the demarcation of the canon were granted a prominent authority by being identified as church fathers and church teachers—in the context moreover of manifold notions and customs of piety.

f) Every church actually exists in a tradition, whether it reflects upon it and develops a dogmatic concept of tradition or does not.

2. In view of this multilayered set of facts, it is necessary to clarify precisely:

a) What is to be designated by the concept of apostolic tradition:

i) the entire stream of the life of the church, including the notions and customs of the peoples' piety?

ii) the stream of the church's speaking insofar as it appears in the life and activity of the church's ministerial offices?

iii) the biblical canon, dogmas, the ordering of the church, liturgy, church fathers and church teachers?

iv) the biblical canon and dogmas?

v) or only the biblical canon?

b) But if one speaks about "Scripture and Tradition," it must be clarified whether one understands by tradition only the dogmas, or dogmas and the ordering of the church and liturgies, or in addition the teachings of the church fathers and church teachers, or besides this the statements of the church's ministerial officeholders or, beyond that, also the statements within the peoples' piety.

c) It must then be clarified what authoritative rank is to be granted to these different components of the tradition in relation to each other.

VIII.

The position of the Reformation toward tradition is not yet discerned if one only pays attention to its *concept* of tradition. Rather, one must examine what use has been made of tradition *in actuality*. With the word *tradition* the Lutheran Confessions—in their rejection of medieval corruptions—referred almost exclusively to "human opinions" of a ceremonial or jurisdictional nature, which had been wrongly disseminated as "having been handed down by the apostles" (for example, Apol. VII.38 [BC 181]).

IX.

The Lutheran Confessions ground their dogmatic statements by scriptural statements, by referring to the dogmatic decisions of the ancient church, which they explicitly adopt, and by citing Latin and Greek church fathers. With the dogmatic decisions of the ancient church their anathemas were also explicitly taken over (compare Jan Koopmans, *Das altkirchliche Dogma in der Reformation* [Ancient Church Dogma in the Reformation] [München: Kaiser, 1955]). The most impressive evidence of the importance that was conferred upon the church fathers is the *catalogus testimoniorum*, the "list of interpreters of Holy Scripture and orthodox teachers in the ancient church," contained within the Book of Concord. This collection of quotations of mostly Greek fathers should serve to prove that the Book of Concord has not "deviated" from the teaching "of the orthodox teachers in the ancient church" and did not introduce "new, strange, self-conceived, unusual and unheard ways of speaking."[iii] In the Lutheran Confessions the tradition of the conciliar decisions of the ancient church and the church fathers thus *in actuality* plays an important role alongside the apostolic tradition contained in Holy Scripture.

X.

In the *Confessio Augustana* (1530) there are no fundamental statements about the hierarchical ranking of the authority of Holy Scripture, dogma from the ancient church, and the comments of church fathers. But in the preface to the Formula of Concord (1580) it is then explicitly declared "that the one rule and norm, according to which all teachings and teachers are to be evaluated and judged, are solely the prophetic and apostolic writings of the Old and New Testaments."[iv] "But other writings, of older or newer teachers... are not to be considered as equal to Holy Scripture," but only to be acknowledged as interpretation of Scripture, "as witnesses who indicate how and where this teaching of the prophets and apostles has been preserved since the time of the apostles" (from the FC Ep, 1 f.)[v] The authority of the church fathers is thus a derived authority. It does not exist alongside the authority of the prophets and apostles, but rather it consists in the fact that it serves the preservation, and that means at the same time that it serves the actual historical unfolding of the *authentic* prophetic and apostolic message contained in Holy Scripture.

This determination of the relationship of the authorities by the Protestant Reformers was nothing fundamentally new vis-à-vis the theology of the ancient and medieval church. Since the demarcation of the New Testament canon, tradition had been given weight alongside Scripture, above all as the church's understanding of Scripture, but not as an independent authority existing next to Scripture. Thus, according to Irenaeus and also Vincent of Lerin, Holy Scripture contains the whole teaching of the apostles in its entirety (compare Josef Geiselmann in the Roman Catholic anthology, *Die mündliche Überlieferung* [Oral Tradition] [München: M. Hueber, 1957]). Also Thomas Aquinas, who reworked tradition in large measure, in the fundamental *quaestio* 1 in part one of his *Summa theologiae* held that Scripture alone is the source of theological scholarship. "Holy Scripture enjoyed throughout the whole of antiquity and the middle ages such a high esteem that traditions, vis-à-vis Scripture, appear no more than an annex" (Geiselmann, *Die mündliche Überlieferung*, 166).[vi] The *fundamental* assessment of Holy Scripture by the Protestant Reformers was not new, but rather the *critical use* which the Reformers made of Holy Scripture vis-à-vis corrupt medieval traditions. In contrast to medieval theology they no longer artificially harmonized Scripture and tradition but subjected church traditions to the standard of Holy Scripture and purified them by applying this evaluative standard. The authority of the Reformers themselves and that of church ministerial officeholders, as well as all piety and the orders of the worship service, and so forth, remained subject to the same standard in the Reformation churches.

XI.

The purification of Western church traditions by the Lutheran Reformation cannot be confused with a biblicistic purity. Only what obviously contradicted Holy Scripture was to be set aside. On the other hand, much of what had developed in the course of church history that did not contradict Holy Scripture was maintained. In this respect the Lutheran Reformation differs from that of Calvin. The knowledge that the apostolic message by its very nature is not primarily a book to be read but is to be transmitted in the act of oral proclamation prevented Luther from overlooking the liveliness of the apostolic tradition in ever new historical words and deeds of the church and from scorning what had grown up in church history. Beyond Luther, Melanchthon then considered the tradition of the ancient church, in contrast to medieval tradition, fundamentally valid as a true interpretation of Scripture and with the Scripture represented the consensus of the ancient church—also because of its age—as the foundation of church unity (compare Otto Ritschl, *Dogmengeschichte des Protestantismus* [The History of Dogma in Protestantism], 4 vols. [Leipzig: Hinrichs, 1908], 1.193 ff.).

XII.

From these presuppositions one needs to understand that the Tübingen theologians in their correspondence with the Ecumenical Patriarch Jeremias II proceeded from the conviction that the Church of the Lutheran Reformation has the same faith and is just as apostolic a church as the Orthodox Church of the East,[vii] for they recognized the dogmatic decisions of the ancient church as a proper interpretation of Scripture over against the errors of that time and held fast to those decisions and were at the same time certain over against the Western false doctrines of their time to have taken a position that was just as much in accord with Scripture as the fathers of the ancient church were in their different historical front. This new starting point with Holy Scripture as the "one rule and norm," in knowing that the apostolic tradition happens primarily through the *viva vox evangelii*, permits one to understand anew the differences in church traditions that have arisen in history and to recognize again in the midst of the different historical developments the one apostolic basis.

Editor's Notes

[i]   Cf. endnote 7 in the introduction ("The Task"), endnote 8 in chap. 1 ("The Task and Danger of the World Council of Churches"), and endnote 6 in chap. 8 ("Apostolic Succession") above.

[ii] Papias of Hierapolois (c. 60–130), Irenaeus (c. 130-c.200), and Tertullian (c. 160-c.220).

[iii] The Catalogue of Testimonies (*Catalogus Testimoniorum*), written by Jakob Andreae (1528–90) and Martin Chemnitz (1522–86), is a listing of Scripture passages and quotations from early-church fathers on the person of Christ, especially regarding the *genus maiestaticum*. In 1580 this document was added as an appendix to the Book of Concord to forestall charges that the Formula of Concord had introduced "*novas, peregrinas, proprio arbitrio excogitates, inusitatas et inauditas loquendi formulas*" (*Concordia Triglotta*, ed. F. Bente [St. Louis: Concordia, 1921], 1107).

[iv] Preface to the Formula of Concord (Epitome), 1 (BC 486).

[v]   Preface to the Formula of Concord (Epitome), 2 (BC 486).

[vi] Cf. endnote 3 in chap. 9 ("Scripture, Tradition, Teaching Office") of *After the Council*.

[vii] Cf. footnote 8 in chap. 7 ("Law and Gospel as a Controversial Issue in Theology") above.

Part Three: Conciliar Encounter

Chapter Ten:
The Sojourning People of God[1]

I.

The church finds itself on the way between the first and the second advent of Jesus Christ. It finds itself sojourning toward its Lord, who is coming again. It does not know what all will yet happen to it on this way through the world. But it knows for certain that at the end of this way the Lord stands as the victor over the world and all contradiction. Then he will gather his own from all lands and peoples and times and celebrate the great Lord's Supper with them. Then, after all conflict and strife, there will be *one* flock and *one* shepherd. When the Apostle Paul writes, "Our salvation is nearer to us than when we first believed" (Rom. 13.11), this word is all the more valid today, for the second coming of Christ is closer than ever before. Christ will come to redeem his people.

Let us not forget: The Lord will come not only as the Redeemer but also as the Judge, that is, not only as the Judge of the world but also as the Judge of Christendom. "We all must appear before the judgment seat of Christ" (2 Cor. 5.10). Then he will say to the one, "Come, you who are blessed of my Father," and to the others, "Depart from me, you who are cursed" (Mt. 25.34, 41). Then will he carry out a separation that will cut deeper than all other separations which we people on earth undertake. In contrast to this separation at the Last Judgment, the church separations are also only provisional, and despite all of their seriousness lack eschatological finality, for the separation that Christ will undertake at the end of the world goes right through *all* churches. None of the churches gathered here can count on remaining

---

1 A lecture delivered in Lund, Sweden, on 17 August 1952 at the opening session of the Third World Conference for Faith and Order. [This lecture was published as "Das wandernde Gottesvolk" in *Theologische Literaturzeitung* 77 (1952), 577–84. It was later published under the same title in *Lund. Dritte Weltkonferenz der Kirchen für Glauben und Kirchenverfassung: Der Konferenzbericht mit den wichtigsten Reden und Dokumenten samt einer Einführung von Bischof i. I. D. Dr. Wilhelm Stählin* (Lund: The Third World Conference on Faith and Order: The Conference Report together with the Most Important Addresses and Documents and an Introduction by Bishop Dr. Wilhelm Stählin), ed. Wilhelm Menn (Tübingen: Furth, 1954), 102–9. The same lecture appears in KC 1.202–10. An English translation of it by I. H. Neilson was published as "The Pilgrim People of God" in *The Third World Conference on Faith and Order*, ed. O. S. Tomkins (London: SCM, 1953), 151–61. That same translation was published in *The Ecumenical Review* 5, no. 1 (1952), 27–36, and in CC (245–55). –Ed.]

undivided then. Even to those who have eaten and drunk before him and have heard his word (Lk. 13.26 f.), even to those who have prophesied in his name and have done great deeds, the Lord will then say, "I never knew you; all of you depart from me" (Mt. 7.22 f.).

But who then will be saved? The poor in spirit, the hungry and the thirsty (Mt. 5.3, 6); those who are ardently waiting and watching (Mt. 25.1 ff.); the restless who in this world know that they are entirely in an alien land and that here they have no continuing city; those who long for and expect the solution of all problems solely from the coming Lord alone. But above the rich, the satiated, the laughing, the ones who are comfortable and beloved in this world stands Christ's word, "Woe!" (Lk. 6.24 ff.)

We are here gathered as separated churches. But before us all stands the Lord who is coming again, whether we are mindful of this or not. We all find ourselves already in the net that he has cast out, even if this net has not yet been drawn out of the sea, and yet we imagine we are swimming around in the water freely and cheerfully. But the net will surely be drawn up from the water and the good fish and the rotting fish will be separated (Mt. 13.47 ff.). As disunited as we may still be, we are in fact united as those inextricably enclosed in *one* net and as those delivered into the hands of the *one* Lord and fisherman.

II.

This judgment is not only a future one but it is already taking place now over large parts of the world and broad regions of Christendom. I am thinking here of the terrible historical catastrophes and persecutions that God has allowed to fall upon many of our brothers and sisters. For them—with the rise of anti-Christian ideological powers and their demand for an obedience that claims the whole person—God has already allowed the eschatological time of testing and sifting to begin. In these perils and in the temptation that accompanies them, namely, to save one's own life by denying Christ's claim of lordship and by handing over the brothers and sisters, the most serious and ultimate of separations are already now taking place. Here the Lord has already taken the winnowing-fork into his hand and has begun to winnow the churches in order to separate the wheat from the chaff (Mt. 3.12).

The outcome of this separation that takes place in catastrophes and times of spiritual attacks and trials can be foreseen just as little by a person as the outcome of the separation on the Last Day. It can then happen that large and proud churches, which seemed to stand firmly, fall apart like a house of cards, and only a small segment of them stand firm in the temptation. Congregations, which have the reputation of being alive, show themselves then all of a sudden to be dead (Rev. 3.1) Leading church figures, upon whom Christians were accustomed to gaze, all of a sudden have no liberating word of comfort and instruction for their flocks. Then separations and reversals of a wholly unforeseen kind take place. The first will be last, and the last will be first.

At the same time, however, the dividing walls that stand between the church bodies then become singularly transparent. There occurs in the time of spiritual attack and trial a revaluation and transformation of the norms by which the separated Christian communities have been judging one another up until now. The great comes forth from the small, the essential from the non-essential, the *one* from the many. But much of what was traditionally held to be great and essential and church dividing appears now as small and non-essential; for the viewpoint of those who withstand the temptation and in the time of spiritual attack and trial remain with Christ, the sole Lord of the church and the world, is radically wrenched forward. The past sinks in the upheaval; there remains only the gaze upon the coming Redeemer and the longing cry for the coming of his kingdom. Thus, in prison cells and forced-labor camps and on the way to executions, the fellowship of the separated sisters and brothers becomes a reality today, as Vladimir Solovyov saw in his vision of the antichrist.[i] In this way Christ gathers his one people already now in the midst of the separations of this time.

This unity of God's people that comes into view in the great perils is experienced as a reality given by God, that is, as the reality of the present Christ. Whoever experiences that reality cannot see in it only, say, a desperate escape or an emotional excitement which has been caused by the unusualness of the situation, but it is for the person an undeniable, God-given reality.

III.

It is all the more astonishing how little this event, in which the traditional church-dividing walls have become transparent, is affecting the rest of Christendom. To be sure, the rest of Christendom remembers with sympathy the persecuted churches, but the particular topics and issues are as a rule totally different here from over there. Also the treatment of the issue of church traditions is different, namely, it is much more determined by historical tradition here than over there. With all sympathy one can only in a very restricted way place oneself in the situation of those sisters and brothers, let alone draw consequences for one's own situation.

But it is even more astonishing how quickly that experience of the unity of the sojourning people of God fades then for many, when the time of persecution has ended. After the ordering of the church had been very widely disturbed in the catastrophe, they often only too naturally return to the earlier ordering, seek guiding rules in their own past for the reconstruction, and thus at the same time restore the old differentiation of the church bodies between one another.

But can that experience of unity be so lightly passed over? Can it be dismissed with the remark that it was only the case of an exceptional situation, of emergency measures, and of very unusual experiences? Why then is the same not valid in the *normal* situations as it is valid in those extreme situations? Have we forgotten that being alienated, being misunderstood, and lacking peace is precisely the normal situation of the church in the world, and that being acknowledged by the world and having peace with the world is the anomaly? The church finds itself in this world always in an extreme situation, and often enough periods of persecution were less dangerous to it than the pact of peace with the world, which respects and guarantees the state of the church that has historically developed. "Beloved, do not let yourselves be astonished by the fiery ordeal which is testing you, as though something strange were happening to you, but rather rejoice insofar as you share in the sufferings of Christ" (1 Pet. 4.12 f.). Precisely in tribulations there will be genuine experiences, and hope is strengthened, which will not come to nothing (Rom. 5.3 ff.).

In its efforts at unification, Christendom will have to learn from these poorest and yet richest brothers and sisters, from these their most despised and persecuted members, who are nevertheless most honored by God. Even if their mouth is mostly shut, their way still speaks strongly. Even if this way is often hidden to us, and yet before God they are revealed as his true people. We need to learn from them how to be torn away from our focus on the past and to shift our eyes firmly forward, toward the coming Lord. This is the sole direction in which the focus of those who are undergoing spiritual attacks and trials is still meaningful. The movement forward, however, is also the direction toward which the entire earliest Christian witness is aimed. Hastening forward in this direction, we ought to be looking at one another with new eyes.

IV.

In recent years one often heard talk of a crisis, which has made the work of the Commission on Faith and Order difficult. Is this assertion correct?

If there is a crisis here, it does not in any case consist in a lack of *interest* in the subject of "faith and order." This interest has grown considerably in the course of the twenty-five years since the Lausanne Conference. One can think, for example, of the inter-church liturgical movement and of the widespread interest that has awakened among church bodies regarding the sacrament, ministerial office, and the issue of tradition.

Nor is it possible to speak of a lack of *results* in the work so far. In the course of the work, the separated churches have learned to know each other anew and to see each other with new eyes. They have reached a clear understanding of where they agree and differ, whereby what they have in common has often been recognized as surprising, overpowering, and unforgettably great. The distant alienation between the churches is today largely overcome.

Also, there is by no means a lack of additional *tasks*. Decisively important topics, such as Christology and eschatology, are still awaiting a thoroughgoing treatment. The same holds true of many matters in pneumatology, especially about the issue of the unity and multiplicity of charismata in the body of Christ. In addition, important perspectives, which are suited to the further clarification of the issues that have already been treated, are still urgently awaiting systematic application. One can think, for example, about the significance of the anthropological and philosophical presuppositions of the ways of thinking in which the different churches make their statements of faith. Of course, the more the churches have drawn closer to each other, the more comprehensive the task becomes, which they see set before them.

If there is talk about a crisis in the work of "Faith and Order," this cannot be based on the fact that this work has been combined since 1948 with that of the other conferences of Stockholm and Oxford in the World Council of Churches; for the work of the study-section in Geneva, which has grown out of the "Life and Work" movement, has become to such a pleasing extent a truly theological piece of work, thoroughly grounded in Scripture, so that it and the Commission on Faith and Order complement each other in the best possible way.

Despite all of this, however, there might be something correct suggested in this, when some today speak of a crisis. In any case, the work of "Faith and Order," it seems to me, finds itself in a crisis about the method that has been used up until now. This method was above all that of a systematic and comprehensive comparing of all the church bodies, a method that concerned itself with arriving at the maximum of what is held in common. After this method had initially led to surprising results in far-reaching agreements, the increasing precision in its application allowed the existing differences and disagreements to be more forcefully recognized than was the case in the enthusiasm of the first awakening of the ecumenical movement. And that cannot be otherwise, for this method of comparing is a statistical method. It assumes a certain finality about the distinctive shape of the different churches that can be compared to one another, and it considers the churches as static structures. It does not reckon with transformations and it demands no sacrifice on the side of the participating Christian communities. For this reason, this method as such does not ultimately lead any further on the way to unification, even if one will never be able to do without it.

Moreover, ecumenical work is placed in crisis by that which God today is doing to the separated churches in many countries. This goes far beyond the result of even such a careful statistical comparison. God himself has placed the work of "Faith and Order" in crisis, namely, for one thing, through the new fellowship that has originated among our most oppressed and persecuted brothers and sisters, and for another, through the awakening of the young churches, who are determined to "forget what is behind" and "to press on toward what is ahead" (Phil. 3.13) and who are leaving behind the historical traditions to strive for the unity that corresponds to the one Lord who is coming to meet us. Here transformations are actually taking place. Here traditional particularities are being sacrificed. And behold: these sacrifices prove themselves to be the reception of a treasure, they prove themselves to be such a blessing that they can no longer be described as a sacrifice.

The crisis in the work of "Faith and Order" might consist in the fact that the vanguard of the sojourning people of God seems today to be already further ahead than the condition of our own present deliberations. Over against what is actually taking place today in some countries in the form of a turbulent grasping of the goal commanded by God, our work up until now appears to some to be theoretical and slow and far too backward-looking.

V.

With this criticism one cannot, of course, disregard the fact that the churches assembled for ecumenical world conferences have already taken an unprecedented, revolutionary step forward. In fact, this has taken place in the oft repeated, solemn declaration of their unity in Christ. After Lausanne, Oxford, and Edinburgh, they in Amsterdam have again confessed: "We praise God and thank him for the mighty deed of his Holy Spirit, through whom we were led together and through whom we recognize that we—despite our separations—are one in Jesus Christ" (Report of the First Section).[ii] This attestation of the unity of the churches in Christ was an advance of the greatest importance. What has taken place here?

Is this proclamation of unity merely a rhetorical statement that is to cover over the disgrace and shame of a fractured Christendom? No.

Is this proclamation merely the expression of a hope, and does it only identify a goal to be reached? No. Already in Oxford the answer to this question has been given: "Unity in Christ is for us not only a goal which we set for ourselves. It is a reality which we know from experience" (Message to the Christian Churches).[iii] It is a present reality. But in what sense is the unity a present reality?

Is it merely present in the church body to which the individual delegates in each case belong? No, for it is, of course, attested by all together as "our unity."

Is this unity visible to everyone? Is it an empirical reality in the strict sense? No, not that either, for the Christians who have here attested to their unity in Christ belong to separated churches and by and large have no fellowship in the Lord's Supper with one another.

So a rhetorical statement, after all? No. Rather, the attestation to unity is the witness of faith, which leaps over what it sees and clings to Jesus Christ, who is the one Lord over all of our separations and over and beyond all our comprehension, who rules his people and presently deals with them.

The confession of our unity in Christ, despite our visible division, is a statement of faith that is similar to the attestation of the death of our sinful body in baptism. "Do you not know that all of us who have been baptized in Jesus Christ have been baptized into his death?" Do you not know, "that our old man has been crucified with him, that the body of sin might be destroyed, that henceforth we are not to serve sin?" "Consider yourselves to be indeed dead to sin and alive to God in Christ Jesus our Lord" (Rom. 6.3, 6, 11). All this is true, even if we do not see it. As the baptized, we are dead to sins, even if we recognize ourselves daily to be sinners and have every reason to pray daily to our Father in heaven: "Forgive us our sin." Just as the faith that trusts we are dead to sin with Christ in baptism leaps over our visible sins—just as we are certain by faith in the crucified one that we sinners are justified before God—so we are certain that despite all divisions we are one in Christ. And as the certainty of having died to sin is grounded in the baptism we have experienced, so the certainty of unity has its basis in the experience that we have had in our encounters, namely, in that we have heard the voice of the one Good Shepherd out of the mouth of those gathered with us, comforting and admonishing over and above all separations. This mutual witness to Christ expresses the fact that we are baptized into the same Christ.

VI.

Also this recognition of unity can lead to a crisis in ecumenical work because God's invisible act of grace always wants to take shape in the lives of those so graced. The indicative of God's act of salvation always brings with it the imperative that calls for obedience in response to the act of salvation. Because we have died with Christ in baptism, we should "walk in a new life" (Rom. 6.4). "Shall we persist in sin in order that grace may abound? By no means! How should we, who are dead to sin, want to live in sin?" (Rom. 6.1 f.) For the baptized to want to remain in sin would not only be an anachronism but a grave sin. But the same thing that is valid for the individual baptized person is also valid for the fellowship of the baptized: Shall we persist in our division in order that the unity may abound? By no means! How should we, who recognize our unity in Christ and have confessed it, want to live in division? It has already been rightly declared at Lausanne: "We can never again be the same as we were before" (The Call to Unity).[iv]

Have we really become different from what we were before?

One cannot declare unity ever anew and at the same time persist in division. The indicative of the recognized unity contains at the same time the imperative to carry out the unification. It is not permissible to want to find the unity of the churches only in the common *faith* in unity. Such a contentment would be a docetic concept of the church and a forbidden spiritualization, for the body of Christ is always at the same time a visible fellowship of its members in word, sacrament, and ministerial office.

One cannot, however, take comfort from the fact that the great number of our churches, the organically unfolded riches of the body of Christ, fits with the Pauline statements about the multiplicity of spiritual gifts. We are not permitted to equate this multiplicity with the separated churches today, for the church is constituted as the body of Christ through the fellowship of the body of Christ in the Lord's Supper. But where fellowship in the Lord's Supper is lacking, not organic multiplicity is present, but disorder and shame.

But we also cannot any longer withdraw into our own church body, for we cannot forget that we have encountered sisters and brothers from the other churches whom we have recognized as members of the *one* church.

And in the ecumenical movement itself we all are placed in crisis precisely by the recognized unity. Without actual progress toward union the repeated declarations of unity, made in the presence of Christendom and the world, will be unbelievable. Without realization of the unity granted us, this act of grace by God becomes an accusation. The blessed recognition of unity itself places us then under God's judgment.

These statements above do not dispute the fact that there are also separations among those who call themselves Christian that *must* be carried out in obedience to God. Then it is a matter of eschatological separation between church and pseudo-church, between the lordship of Christ and the lordship of the powers of corruption that are camouflaged as Christian; then it is a matter of eternal life and eternal death. But surely we must dispute the claim that in all the existing divisions within Christendom today it is a matter of this last unavoidable separation.

VII.

Allow me to break off here and return to the starting point of the lecture.

The church is the sojourning people of God. It finds itself in this world on the way toward its returning Lord. It does not know everything it will experience on this way. What is certain, however, is the fact that the Lord is coming toward it in order to gather his own who are scattered in the world so that they may live united with him in eternal glory.

Let us hasten forward on this way and *not stand still*. Let us look forward and not be stuck focusing on the present. Let us tear our focus from the visible divisions that we have still not overcome and look firmly to the one Lord whom we are going to meet. In looking forward in expectation of the coming world Judge and Redeemer, we will recognize the provisional character—the lack of finality—of the kinds of things that divide us.

Let us hasten on the way forward, not stand still and also *not* look *backwards*. Let us live in expectation, instead of firmly clinging to the past. Let us tear our focus away from the one-sidedness, which has often become so rigid, the one-sidedness in considering those historical events in which the church division once took place. Let us direct our focus toward the much deeper and more profound separation that the Lord who is coming again will carry out upon all churches, and toward the unity in the eternal glory which he will then accomplish. In looking forward the past comes forth in a new light and the kinds of issues, which appeared to us in the past as unsolvable, are solvable.

Let us hasten forward. Only in the expectation of the Second Advent do we rightly understand the biblical witness of the first advent of our Lord, for the entire New Testament message directs us forward, and only in hastening forward do we kneel in the proper way before it. Only in hastening forward are we able to understand it rightly. Only in the expectation of the Lord who is coming again do we have fellowship with the Lord who came in the flesh, for the crucified one, as the one who is coming again, knocks on the house we ourselves have built, in which we have hidden ourselves from God and the brothers and sisters, and barricaded ourselves against them, in that he says: "See, I stand before the door and knock; if anyone hears my voice and opens the door, I will come in to him and eat my meal with him, and he with me" (Rev. 3.20).

Editor's Notes

[i] Vladimir Solovyov (1853–1900), a Russian philosopher, wrote "A Short Story of Antichrist," which sets forth a vision of how genuine twenty-first-century believers in Christ reunite during the reign of the antichrist.

[ii] "Report of Section I," "The Universal Church in God's Design," *Man's Disorder and God's Design*, Book One, 204. Cf. footnote 2 in chap. 1 ("The Task and Danger of the World Council of Churches") above.

[iii] *The Churches Survey Their Task*, 57. Cf. footnote 5 and endnote 3 in chap. 1 ("The Task and Danger of the World Council of Churches") above.

[iv] "Final Report of the First World Conference on Faith and Order at Lausanne (August 3–21, 1927)," in *A Documentary History of the Faith & Order Movement, 1927–1963*, ed. Lukas Vischer (St. Louis: Bethany, 1963), 28.

Chapter Eleven:
Christ—The Hope for the World[1]

I.

If we inquire about the future of the world, we cannot help but run into the New Testament's announcement of the end of the world. "The form of this world is passing away" (1 Cor. 7.31). "The world with its lust is passing away" (1 John 2.17). The New Testament at the same time announces to us a great tribulation that will come upon the world before it passes away: war and famine, a disintegration of community, massive numbers of deaths, and natural disasters. We are commanded to pay attention, when such things take place. Where there is talk of the coming Christ as the hope, such talk is always also about the end of the world.

Against the announcement of its end, the world defends itself with its own hopes. Even many Christians have grown deaf to this announcement. They set it aside as Jewish apocalyptic thinking. But at the same time it is an unavoidable fact that anxiety about the end holds sway over humanity today. The hopes of the world have become particularly desperate. Everywhere thoughts and dreams are filled with visions of horrors. One fears that the massive destruction of people that took place in the two world wars will return in a gigantic escalation. One sees before one's very eyes the collapse of skyscrapers and the destruction of metropolises. The further development of the atomic bomb has most vividly and concretely opened before us the prospect of the end of humanity and the destruction of the planet. Precisely with its progressive developments humanity seems to have run into its limits.

There is, of course, an essential difference between the anxiety of contemporary humanity and the New Testament announcement of the end. We are afraid of people who could misuse their power to unleash horrific catastrophes. We are afraid of the atomic powers of nature over which human beings could lose their dominion. But according to statements in the New Testament, the catastrophes of the end times are not merely human misdeeds or the consequence of human failures but *God's* action. *God* will prepare the end of this world. From *God's* throne go forth the commands that send the apocalyptic riders throughout the earth (Rev. 6.1, 3, 5, 7). They are "the bowls

---

1 An address delivered on 15 August 1954 at the opening plenary session of the Second Assembly of the World Council of Churches in Evanston, Illinois. [This address was published as "Christus— die Hoffnung für die Welt" in *Evanston Dokumente*, ed. F. Lüpsen (Witten: Luther, 1954), 135–44, and in *Theologische Literaturzeitung* 79 (1954), 705–14. It appears in KC 1.211–20. It was translated into English as "Christ—the Hope of the World" and was published in *The Ecumenical Review* 7, no. 2 (1955), 127–39, and in *The Christian Century* 71 (1954), 1002–5, 1010–11. That same English translation was published in CC (256–68). –Ed.]

of the wrath of God," which will be poured out on the earth (Rev. 16.1 ff.). God has "given people up to a debased mind, to do what is of no good" (Rom. 1.28). The end of the world is the Day of God's judgment.

And we further hear, this judgment over every human presumption God has given over to Jesus Christ. Christ will come as the Judge of the world. He will break into the world "like a thief in the night" (1 Thess. 5.2). He will pounce on the world like a vulture on a cadaver (Mt. 24.28). The appearance of Christ will be the end of the world. "Then all the families on the earth will wail" (Rev. 1.7).

What then has happened to "Christ—the hope of the world"?

If with this theme we only focus on the continued existence of this threatened world, then we will miss the point of our conference theme. If we expect from Christ only the securing of this world so that humanity can pursue undisturbed its freedom, its businesses endeavors, and the improvement of its standard of living, then Christ is not the hope of the world, but rather the end of this world's hopes, for Christ is the world's end. The name of Christ does not permit itself to be misused as a slogan in the struggle for the self-preservation of this world.

The decisive question is not, "How do we get through these wars and catastrophes?" The real question is, "How can we stand in the presence of *God?*" Our real threat does not come from people, powers, or forces in nature, but rather from God, whose judgment no one can escape. The hidden root of our anxiety is our anxiety before God, who will bring to nothing the pride of this world. This is the question, "Is there a rescue in the face of God's judgment?"

II.

We will then only speak rightly of Christ as the hope of the world if we humble ourselves under God and rightly acknowledge God as the Judge of the world. Yes, we have deserved God's judgment. We have not given God the honor that is due to him. We were only thinking of ourselves when we should have been serving our fellow human beings. We have often enough been silent when we should have loudly raised our voices. We have too often been afraid when we should have loved, and judged when we should have forgiven. The unrighteousness, the oppression, the bloodshed of this world cries to heaven, and the history of the church itself is not only a praise of God but is again and again a scandal. "We have sinned, done what is not right, acted wickedly and rebelled. We have turned from your commands and ordinances" (Dan. 9.5). "If you, Lord, kept a record of sins, O Lord, who could stand?" (Ps. 130.3).

Only if we repent and confess that we have forfeited our lives before God, will we recognize Christ as hope of the world.

Christ is the hope as *the crucified one.* Look on this man, crowned with thorns on Golgotha, despised and rejected, who hangs on the cross! Look on this man with the disfigured body and the bloody countenance, the very essence of every human woe and shame! Hear from his mouth the cries, "I thirst," "My God, my God, why have you forsaken me?" The pious brought charges against him. The authorities condemned him. His friends deserted him. But the deepest depth of his agony was his being forsaken by God, his suffering of God's judgment. But this man Jesus Christ did not die for his own sins. "Surely he has borne *our* sickness and carried our sorrows" (Is. 53.4a). "He was wounded for our transgressions and bruised for our sins" (v. 5a) God "has made him who knew no sin to be sin for us so that in him we might become the righteousness which is valid before God" (2 Cor. 5.21).

The one who was judged for the world will appear as Judge of the world. As the one who has borne the sins of the world, Christ is coming to the world. As the one who died for the world, he acts on behalf of those who cry to him in God's sight. We must cling to the crucified one. Upon the crucified one we must place our hope. Only by faith in him will we find rescue on the Day of Judgment, will we be declared "not guilty," despite our sins, for the crucified one is given to us by God for our righteousness.

Christ is our hope as *the risen one*. God has raised the crucified one from the dead. Through this action God himself has affirmed of Jesus, "This man alone died without sin, this one is my son." God has torn him from the bands of death and set him into that life which is free of all the limitations of this world. He is the new human being. God made Jesus the victor over all his enemies, has lifted him up, and has given to him "all authority in heaven and on earth" (Mt. 28.18). Christ is the Lord of the world. But Christ has not kept this victory to himself. Just as he died for the world, so he also arose for the world. He was victorious over the powers of sin and transience in order that those who believe in him will likewise become victors. He thrust his way through to that life, as the first fruits, in order that many might participate in it as well. Hardly having escaped from death, the risen one turned to his own who had forsaken him or even had denied him, presented himself to them, and offered them his greeting, "Peace be with you!"

On the crucified one who is risen, let us place our hope! He is our victorious brother, who will appear as Judge of the world. He is the first fruits of the new creation, who is preparing this world for its end. The conqueror of every need is coming. He will appear in order to awaken his own, just as he has been awakened, in order to make them victors, just as he is a victor. He will gather together the new humanity whose head he is. Then there will be a new creation.

Christ is thus the hope of the world, not as a guarantor for the continued existence of this world, but rather as Redeemer from all the bonds of this world. Christ is the hope of the world in that he calls out people from the world, in that he gathers together his people from the whole world, the people who are strangers in this world and whose citizenship is in heaven. Christ is the hope of the world only insofar as the world does not remain the world, but rather allows itself to be transformed through repentance and faith. Christ is the end of the world, with its joy and sorrow, and thus, precisely in this way, is he the hope for the world, for in the passing away of this world, he will bring forth the new creation.

III.

Christ is thus coming to the world as its Redeemer and Judge. We do not in truth hope for him as Savior of the world if we do not at the same time await him as Judge of the world. Just as little, however, do we fear him in truth as Judge, if we do not await him as Savior. Then he will receive some and the others he will reject. He will raise up the ones to life and the others to death. To some he will say, "Come to me, you who are blessed by my Father," and to the others, "Go away from me, you who are cursed!" (Mt. 25.34, 41). He will shatter to pieces the rule of the mighty, of the rich, of the self-secure with their unrighteousness, and he will destroy the complacency of the satisfied, of those who are laughing and dancing, and those who are at home in this world. But the spiritually poor, those who suffer, those who hunger and thirst for righteousness, the peacemakers (Mt. 5.3 ff.), those who look longingly for his coming (Mt. 25.1 ff.)—all these he will save.

This future separation is taking place already now. Through the word of the cross God is already now putting to shame the wisdom, the virtue, and the power of this world, and he is saving the foolish, the unworthy, and the powerless. "God chose what is low and despised in this world, even things that are not, in order to bring to nothing what is something" (1 Cor. 1.28 f.)

Already now the coming redemption is taking place. Already in the midst of this world, the gospel announces the acquittal of believers in the coming judgment. Through baptism and the Lord's Supper, the believer takes part, already now, in the power of the resurrection to come. Whoever is reborn to a living hope through the Holy Spirit is already a new creature. Christ thus gathers his people through the gospel, already now in the midst of this world, to walk with him in a new life. In the church the coming new creation [Schöpfung] is already a present reality: "If anyone is in Christ, that one is a new creature [Kreatur]. The old is past. Behold, everything has become new" (2 Cor. 5.17).

For this reason, the time in which we live is the end time:

In his resurrection Christ broke through the spell of this world and was exalted to be Lord over the world. All people and powers are subject to Christ, whether they know it or not, whether they acknowledge him or revolt against him.

In his coming again he will make his victory visible to all and bring to an end every tumult of this world.

The time of this world is thus solidly circumscribed by the victory of Christ. To break out of this encirclement is absolutely impossible. In this situation of hopelessness, the call of the gospel sounds forth, by which the world is summoned to acknowledge its Lord. It is the end time. That means, "Today, when you hear his voice, do not harden your hearts!" (Heb. 3.7 f.).

That this is the end time seems to many people to be disproved by the nearly 2000 years that have elapsed since the coming of Jesus. Many have become perplexed about the promise of his future appearance. But the long stretch of time is no refutation of the promise. It is not a sign of God's weakness, as if he were unable to fulfill what he proclaimed through Jesus and the apostles. It is the time of God's patience, God wills that many be saved. It is the time of the church, of the growing body of Christ. But when the body of Christ shall have grown to full stature, when the number of the elect shall have been completed, then the world will pass away and then shall the new creation step forth from its hiddenness.

IV.

What does it mean to hope in Christ?

To hope means not to sleep, but to be awake and on highest alert. To hope means not to dream, but to be awake in radical soberness. Being sober does not mean the calculations of this world, but the expectation of Jesus Christ. To hope does not mean to grow tired, but to be active with the greatest exertion. Not paralysis but activity is characteristic of those in the apostolic age in whom Christian hope is alive, for we do not know at which hour the Lord will come.

What are the actions of hope?

The first action of hope is to proclaim the gospel to the whole world. The Assembly of the World Council has rightly made evangelization the theme of its Second Section. Because God redeems through the gospel, and only through the gospel, therefore there is emblazoned above the one who hopes the command of the redeemer to proclaim the gospel. If God has called us out of the bondages of this world, then he sends us into the world so that we call the others.

This command holds true for everyone who hopes in Christ. No one can keep this hope silently to himself or herself without losing it.

This command makes us *debtors* to all people. God does not want anyone to be lost.

This command demands that we *repudiate* the unquestioned assumptions of our nationality and cultural heritage. Even more, as has often enough been the case in the history of missions, we must become a Jew to the Jews, a Gentile to the Gentiles, weak to the weak—in order to win them. Only in self-denial will we be a servant of Christ (compare 1 Cor. 9.19 ff.).

The command of God the Redeemer requires the greatest *haste*, for we do not know how much time is still left.

Absolutely decisive, however, is that we proclaim the gospel purely and rightly.[i] The preliminary work of the Second Section has concerned itself above all with the *methods* of evangelization. The Assembly itself must deal to a greater extent with the *content* of evangelization. That is all about the message of God's judgment over against the world and the sole salvation that comes by faith in Christ.

Delivering this message appears difficult, for the world does not want to hear anything about its end, and the word of the cross is foolishness to it. And yet the proclamation of the gospel is basically easy and full of unspeakable joy, for we do not have to subject the world to Christ, but rather long ago God has already placed it under Christ. We have only to proclaim to the world the one who is already its Lord. It is not we who have to save people, but rather Christ wants to speak through our witness himself and to do his saving actions. It is not we who bring about faith, but rather God's Spirit.

V.

The second action of hope is to work for the just ordering of this world. This is rightly the theme of the Third through Sixth Sections.

The ones waiting for the coming Christ know about God's patience and long-suffering, by which he still continually preserves this world despite its arrogance and the fact that it has fallen into judgment. He allows his sun to shine on the good and the evil. He allows both believers and unbelievers to live. He preserves not only the Christians but also the heathen and the anti-Christians. To all of them God the Preserver gives days of grace in which to decide for Jesus Christ.

For this reason, the command of God the Preserver is at the same time emblazoned above those who hope. He commands us to work for the preservation of every human life, regardless of whether or not these people believe in Christ, and also regardless of their nationality or race or social status. He thus also commands us to be concerned for their freedom, for God preserves people in order that they may make responsible decisions in his presence. But working for life and freedom means being concerned for earthly justice and earthly peace—among individuals, social classes, races, nations, and states—and active participation in the ordering of human society in the broadest sense, not only in assisting individuals personally but also, for example, in law-making.

Like the command of God the Redeemer, so also the command of God the Preserver applies to *every person* who hopes in Christ. Such a person cannot leave this expectation solely to political leaders.

Likewise, this command makes us *debtors to all* people. Those who hope are not permitted to restrict their assistance to the circle of those who think like themselves.

Furthermore, this command demands that we *repudiate* the customary and unquestioned assumptions, and urges us to great *haste*, since for the first time in their history the nations face the task of ordering humankind on a global scale, and since at the same time the former orderings show themselves to be both inadequate and broken.

The Christian cannot withdraw from the struggle among political programs and secular hopes, for the world wants immortality for itself and considers its programs as salvation. Because Christians are freed from utopianism by their expectation of the Lord, they owe the world a sober witness. They have to expose the real situation of humankind and cut through the fog of propaganda. Because Christians are set free by faith from legalistic thinking, they can never be satisfied with general programs. They have to lift up their voice when doctrine is turned into an anathema and existing law is used to support injustice, and to call for those actions that are required in the concrete historical situation. Because Christians are saved by the sacrifice of Christ, in the struggle for a just ordering they will be selfless in defense of their own interests, but demanding and adamant in their concern for the enslaved, the hungry, and the forgotten. Because Christians have the patience of God in mind, they will oppose with all their strength the use of weapons for mass destruction and they will also seek peace and understanding where this appears hopeless. Because Christians hope in Christ, they will be fearless in the midst of all the menacing threats of this world.

With all this in mind, we cannot forget that peace on earth is not in itself peace with God. Justice [*Gerechtigkeit*] in this world is not itself righteousness [*Gerechtigkeit*] before God. Earthly freedom is still not true freedom, and life in this world is not eternal life. Striving for the just ordering of this world is not the realization of Christ's kingdom on earth; it is not the new creation. Christ's kingdom breaks into the world by the gospel. The fellowship of believers is the new creation.

But God the Preserver commands us to work for the preservation of the world up to the last Day. The world is, after all, still his creation, despite its arrogance. Christ, after all, still died for this world. In the course of the world's passing away, it is still God's will to bring his creation [*Schöpfung*] to its goal in the new creature [*Kreatur*].

The command of God the Redeemer and the command of God the Preserver are not to be separated from each other. Not only the evangelization of the world but also working for the just ordering of the world is the action of hope and love and thus the service of God. But both actions are related to each other in an irreversible manner. We are not to proclaim the gospel in order thereby to preserve the world, but we need to work to preserve the world so that many will be saved from the world through the gospel. For God preserves the world in order to bring salvation through the gospel; he does not save in order to preserve this world. Evangelization does not exist in service to the just ordering of this world, but indeed the just ordering of this world exists in service to evangelization. To fail to recognize this has again and again been the temptation of the church. It is also a temptation for the World Council. So thus says the Lord: "Heaven and earth will pass away, but my words will not pass away" (Mt. 24.35).

VI.

Will we have success with our actions of hope?

The front is today different from what it was in the apostolic period. Heathenism is in decline. We face the post-Christian person. Such individuals have heard of the gospel. They have experienced the liberation from the bonds [*Bindung*] of this world and from the lordship of gods and demons. They have heard of the passage, "Everything is yours,… world, life, death, present, future" (1 Cor. 3.21 f.). But they have torn this freedom away from submission to Christ. They have usurped the lordship over nature. They have themselves undertaken to create the eternal kingdom of peace and no longer wait for Christ's coming. This freedom that is gifted by Christ and yet torn away from Christ hangs heavy today upon the nations, destroys their religions, and creates the final cleavage in the opposition between East and West on both sides. This freedom is a menacing threat to life, for freedom without any commitment [*Bindung*] leads to the use of violence, and the struggle for the rule of the world by these free people leads to horrific annihilation. When looking back on both world wars and focusing on the post-Christian and anti-Christian powers surrounding them, and given the prospect of a third world war with atomic weapons, many people are filled with fear and paralysis, and they allow themselves to think that their actions appear pointless.

It is said to us, "When this begins to occur, look up and raise your heads, because your redemption draws near" (Lk. 21.28). "When you hear of wars and rumors of wars, do not be alarmed. This must take place" (Mk. 13.7). The tumult of this world is for the ones who hope the sure sign of Christ's coming. The world would not bluster so, if he were not the victor. The autumn storms of this world are the signs of the coming spring. The shocking devastations of this time are the labor pains of the new creation.

We ask once again: Will our work have success?

The gospel travels through the nations of the world. But at the same time our generation is witnessing oppressions and persecutions of the churches to such an extent that the persecutions of Christians in the ancient church could appear almost trivial by comparison. For the sake of the gospel, many have been deprived, been taken prisoner, and were killed. In order to preserve their lives many have denied the gospel and have fallen away from the faith. Mission outposts have vanished and entire regions of the church no longer have churches. Churches that were once mighty have collapsed and now live in the catacombs of our time.

It is also true that "this must take place" (Mk. 13.7; Rev. 1.1). The way of the church can be no other than the way of its Lord: through suffering to glory! The judgment begins in the house of God (1 Pet. 4.17). God shakes and sifts his church in persecution in order to test and purify it, in order to separate the wheat from the chaff. But those who humble themselves under the mighty hand of God and take up their own cross soon realize that it has already long been borne by Christ. In their suffering, believers participate in Christ. In their disparagement, imprisonment, and death, the crucified Christ becomes visible and he demonstrates the power of his resurrection. They are his most beloved children who are honored by God to be witnesses of Christ, not merely through the songs of praise that come from their lips but also in the sacrifice of their body. Their defeat is in truth their victory. It is not the powerful, privileged church, the one acknowledged by the world, but rather the powerless, suffering church that is the revelation of the glory of Christ. The church that is dying with Christ is the triumphant church.

Will we see success from our actions? This is the question of hopelessness.

We do not know what success we will see in this world from our evangelization and our working for a just world order, but we do know most definitely that our work "in the Lord is not in vain" (1 Cor. 15.58). Christian hope is independent of what our eyes can see before us, whether it be successes or failures. It is not accidental that in the New Testament, talk of hope is directly related to spiritual attacks and trials (Rom. 5.3 ff.; Rom. 8.18 ff.; 1 Pet. 1.3 ff.). Christian hope is grounded solely on Christ. For this reason, it can never be put to shame. Therefore, Christian hope expects always the best from God and is unceasingly active in the struggle against the powers of darkness: "If God is for us, who then can be against us? He did not spare his own Son.... Will he not also bestow upon us all things with him?" (Rom. 8.31 ff.).

This is not the hope of the world, but the hope of the church. To this hope the church has to summon the world.

VII.

Is this really the hope of all of us? Is our faith really "the victory that has overcome the world" (1 Jn. 5.4)?

We are gathered here as separated churches. To be sure, the historical divisions are only to a very small extent due to disputes over eschatology. This observation, however, does not mean that the separated churches really live in Christian hope, for where hope is alive, there the existing differences and separations will be seen with new eyes and a deep shame will result from the fact that we, through our disunity, contradict the unity of the body of Christ and thus make it easy for the world to reject the message about Christ as its sole hope. "Our being one in Christ and our disunity as churches" is therefore rightly the theme of the First Section of the Assembly and is at the same time basically the theme of all sections of this Assembly.

If hope were really alive in all of us, then we would have less fear in the presence of people than fear in the presence of God; then we would have less concern for preserving the particularities of our church bodies and more concern for how we stand in the presence of God. "For we must all appear before the judgment seat of Christ" (2 Cor. 5.10). A separation will then take place that will be much deeper than all the divisions within Christendom, a separation which is final. Then the verdict can be handed down against entire church bodies: "Because you are lukewarm and neither cold nor hot, I will spit you out of my mouth" (Rev. 3.16).

If this hope were really alive in all of us, then we would know that not only the world but also the form of the church is passing away. We would more clearly understand the provisional nature of our church activities, of our orderings of the church, and even of our dogmatic formulations. The church too will be transformed. In the new creation there will be "no temple," "for the Lord, the almighty God, and the Lamb are its temple (Rev. 21.22). Then we will not only believe the word but we will see God.

If this hope were really alive in us, then we would rejoice less in the untroubled existence of our church bodies, less in their security and preservation, and rejoice more because the gospel is extended and people are being saved through faith from the bonds of this world. "Only that Christ is proclaimed! ... In that I rejoice" (Phil. 1.18). And our greatest renown would be the chains and sufferings of the brothers and sisters from all the church bodies throughout the world.

If this hope were really alive in us, then we would not constantly gaze backwards, but rather we would hasten forwards toward the Lord. We would not be so much in love with the history of our own church body, but rather would be open to the working of Christ in the whole world. By focusing on what lies ahead, the walls between the church bodies become transparent.

If this hope were really alive, then we would also be able to understand more clearly the non-theological factors that divide the church bodies; for those factors gained their importance only because the church made a pact with the world and expected from it the security that only Christ can give.

Let us consider: We all come from Christ, from his death and his resurrection. We all are going towards Christ, the one who will come as Judge and Savior of the world. We all are encompassed by him. He is present in our midst as the one who has come and the one who is coming.

Let us give him all the honor and put aside everything by which we darken his glory in the presence of the world.

Editor's Notes

[i] Cf. AC VII

Chapter Twelve:
Transformations in the Protestant Understanding
of the Eastern Church[1]

When, in his *History of Dogma* (especially the second volume) and in his book, *The Essence of Christianity*, Adolf von Harnack published his extremely critical and disparaging judgments about the intellectual and theological condition of the Eastern Church, he directed his attention not only against the Eastern Church of recent times but also against the doctrinal decisions of the ancient church that the Reformers had explicitly retained and by which the Reformation churches had consciously bound themselves to the Eastern Church (above all, the dogmatic decrees of the councils of Nicaea, Constantinople, and Chalcedon).[i] Harnack's opinion is, to be sure, not representative of the Reformation churches as a whole, but merely of the liberal group of the so-called *neo-Protestantism*.[ii] Alongside neo-Protestantism, which knew itself to be fundamentally at variance with the doctrine of the Reformers and with that of seventeenth-century Protestant Orthodoxy that followed it, there was never a lack of voices in the Protestant Church—not even during Harnack's time—which did not energetically speak against this separation of the church's self-understanding from its foundations in the ancient church. Nevertheless, Harnack's theses significantly influenced thinking about the intellectual formation of the Western world, and perhaps at no other time has the Eastern Church been so critically investigated and found to be so alien as in the first two decades of the twentieth century. This is all the more true, when voices from the Roman Church, such as those of Bonomelli and Konrad Lübeck,[iii] seem to correspond to the judgments of Harnack regarding the rigidity, ignorance, and general low quality of the Eastern Church (compare Fr. Heiler, *Urkirche und Ostkirche* [1937], 555 f.).[iv]

This situation has changed profoundly during the past thirty years.

First, the world was all ears when the persecution of Christians in Bolshevik Russia began to be known. A church that produced thousands of martyrs cannot be so rigid and moribund as it had been reputed to be by some.

Then there came various encounters with Eastern Orthodox immigrants—both theologians and laity—and with the Eastern Orthodox congregations,

---

1 The basic thoughts of this paper were delivered in a guest-lecture to the Theological Academy in the Holy Trinity-St. Sergius Monastery in Zagorsk near Moscow on 31 March 1958. [This address was published as "Wandlungen im protestantischen Verständnis der Ostkirche," *Ökumenische Rundschau* 6, no. 4 (1957), 153–64. It was included under the same title in *Eucharisterion: Timetikòs tòmos – Festschrift* for Hamilkar Alivisatos, ed. Gerassimos I. Konidaris (Athens: Typographeion tēs Apostolikēs Diakonias tēs Ekklēsias tēs Hellados, 1958), 385 ff. This version appears in KC 1.221–31. An English translation of a modified version of this lecture was published as "Changes in Protestant Thinking about the Eastern Church" in *The Ecumenical Review* 10, no. 4 (1958), 386–400. That same translation was published in CC (269–84). –Ed.]

filled with refugees, who often gathered together with a heartfelt loyalty that was as great as their hardship. The liturgy and piety of the Eastern Church began to emit an illuminating power in the Western world that had not been known before and also had not been expected.

But this impression remained at first only sensational and aesthetic; it did not yet signify a breakthrough to an actual understanding with respect to the alien character of the Eastern Church (earlier notable exceptions in Protestant theology were Karl Holl and Friedrich Heiler).[v] But this breakthrough only began to occur widely when the German Protestant Church itself became an oppressed and persecuted church, whereby liberal, cultural Protestantism disintegrated and the church was forced to undergo a new self-examination. In the struggle against the ideology of National Socialism, confession (Dogma) became important in a new way, as did the church's ministerial office in the struggle against the encroachment of totalitarian power. In the midst of hostile attempts to crush the confessing congregations,[vi] the worship service, which gathered the congregation together, assumed a new significance; and the more arrests increased and congregations, pastors, and many individual Christians were cut off from each other, the more the unity of the church became the central focus of thinking, hoping, and living, a unity that in all times and in all places is one and the same, in Jesus Christ. People began to hear the comforting voice of Jesus Christ, the one Good Shepherd, even in such church bodies where up until that point they had not been accustomed to hearing it. At the same time, however, the confession and the liturgy of the ancient church gained new vitality in the worshiping assembly, and, in the awakening liturgical movement, the unity of the church was experienced through the appropriation of the same words by which the church, from the earliest times onward, confesses God, praises him, and calls upon him with one voice. The close relationship between dogma and liturgy in the ancient church became evident again.

All of this also led to a new perspective on the Eastern Church, and precisely those elements against which liberal neo-Protestantism had leveled its criticism appeared in a new light. This could be articulated in various ways. Here I will restrict myself to a few remarks on the topic of dogma in its relation to the liturgy, that is, I will seek to shed light upon the transformation in the modern Protestant understanding of the Eastern Church by referring to a certain very important structural element that has frequently been insufficiently considered in the evaluation of Eastern dogmatic decisions. There is, after all, generally the perception that the operative *basic structure* [*Grundstruktur*] in doctrine, the ordering of the church, and its life is often more illuminating and significant for understanding another church than the examination of the *details* of its doctrines, church order, and life.

I.

One of the chief indictments that were raised against the historical development of dogma in the Eastern Church is that of Hellenization, in the sense of an alien influence on the gospel, of a syncretism between Christian faith and pagan philosophy. With that was meant especially the appropriation of the ontological, metaphysical, *physical* [*physikalischen*] conceptuality of Greek philosophy in the formulation of the Trinitarian and Christological doctrines. As a matter of fact, between this conceptuality and the Hebrew way of thinking in the Old Testament and in Jesus there is a difference that cannot be overlooked, and the Hellenization in the ancient church goes far beyond the statements of the Apostle Paul that had already moved into the Hellenistic realm. Moreover, the Eastern Church of course made no secret of its Greek heritage, nor was it ashamed of it.

In light of the Neo-Protestant criticism of this given state of affairs, it has of course been overlooked that among the various responses that faith needs to give to the message of God's act of salvation there is one definite response—attested by the New Testament writings and, indeed, already present in the Old Testament community—which bears a clear affinity to ontological statements and invites the use of ontological concepts. This is the doxology, as it is always and necessarily expressed, both in the worship assembly and in the prayers of the individual. Doxology is directed to God, and yet, as a rule, God is here addressed not as a *Thou*, as in other prayers, but rather as a *He*, who is the same from everlasting to everlasting. In doxology God is also not implored to do something or told what he should do, but rather he is praised for who he is in his eternal glory, holiness, might, power, and wisdom. Accordingly, the biblical doxologies contain statements about God's being, essence, and attributes.

Now it is crucial for our understanding of dogma in the ancient church that we keep in mind its setting in the life of the church. Dogma originated as confession in the context of the worship service, the confession which is offered to God by the church as a faithful sacrifice of praise. This is readily apparent in the original Nicene Creed and in its further developed form, the Niceno-Constantinopolitan Creed. These are homologies [confessions] in the worship service.[vii] Even the Christological formula of Chalcedon, although it is not a confession that is directly used in the worship service, is still related to creedal confessing within the worship service, that is, also in the same manner that was used in the decisive statements of homology [confession] in the Nicene Creed.[2] Now the confession can be unfolded in various directions, since in it are united many different kinds of faith response. Without question, however, the aspect of doxology stands front and center in the mind of the

---

2 Cf. secs. 4 ff. in chap. 3 ("The Christology of Chalcedon in Ecumenical Dialogue") above.

Eastern Church. Dogma is above all the adoration of God. But since doxology contains statements about God's essence, being, and attributes, by which God's eternal aseity is praised, it was entirely theologically legitimate that the ancient church also utilized the ontological concepts from Greek metaphysics (that were then current in the church's environment) in carrying out its praise of God and thus to offer to God as its sacrifice of praise the best that Greek thinking had recognized and expressed. In this way philosophy was taken into the service of confessing Christ. The metaphysical concepts that were thus used were in no way left intact in theology, but rather they underwent significant changes in their service to the homology in the worship service.

II.

The Eastern Church is also reproached for not having firmly established any dogmas about human beings in their relation to grace, as did occur in Western Christendom in connection with the struggle of Augustine against Pelagius and his followers, and then again at the time of the Reformation, and also afterwards, namely, the dogmatic decision regarding the problems of original sin, of the free will, and so forth. The friendship and justification that Pelagius received in Palestine and which Julian and even Caelestius experienced for a time in Constantinople, and the weak response in the East to the Ephesian condemnation of Pelagianism, were an early cause of Western mistrust of the East on this point.[viii] Besides, of course, one meets—even today—some Orthodox theologians who, to be sure, acknowledge Augustine as a gifted literary figure in the church but not as a church father.

One certainly cannot overlook the fact that the Eastern Church had no real interest in articulating a dogmatic definition of sin and in determining what capacities sinners still have for their relation to grace. If one, however, recognizes the basic doxological structure of dogma in the Eastern Church, then the reticence of this church regarding anthropological dogmas is not surprising, since it belongs to the very nature of doxology that the human being withdraws entirely into the background. Even if the homology begins with the words πιστεύομεν [we believe] or *credo* [I believe], as a rule the words *I* or *mine*, *we* or *our* do not occur again in it. Rather, it is *God's* actions in the world and in the church that are confessed. Indeed, in pure doxology, the words *I* or *we* simply do not occur, not even in an introductory formula. Rather, the talk is only about God: "Holy, holy, holy is the Lord God of Sabbaoth. All the earth is full of his glory!" (Isa. 6.3). Certainly, in earthly worship it is the human being who initiates the doxology. Certainly, it is God's act of salvation on the individual person that is the basis for his praise and adoration. But in the act of adoration the gaze of believers is directed completely away from themselves to God; one makes no side-glances back to oneself or to the relationship between God's activity and one's own. Rather, in doxology God is the sole and total focus. It has no other content than God himself. In this respect, the lack of anthropological dogmas in the Eastern Church is a consequence of its dogmatic starting point, namely, the structural determination of its dogma by means of the homology in the worship service.

Now of course theology cannot get along without statements about human beings. Such statements are indeed also abundant in the Old and New Testament writings. In fact, there is an abundance of anthropological *theologoumena* [theological assertions] in the Eastern church fathers, wherein one notes their fervor regarding the freedom that the sinner still possesses (a fervor that is entirely alien to Augustine and the Protestant Reformers) and their extensive appropriation of Greco-philosophical anthropology with but little modification of it by biblical anthropology (compare, for example, John of Damascus, Ἔκδοσις II.12–24).[ix] Nevertheless, the anthropological statements in Eastern theology were not elevated into an explicit dogma about human beings, and this should not be regarded only as a negative, for the Christological and Trinitarian statements are fundamentally distinct from anthropological statements insofar as God's act of salvation in Christ has been brought to fulfillment once and for all and the Triune God is the same from everlasting to everlasting. But human beings, however, live in history, subject to change and transience. Their self-understanding is constantly changing. People are tossed back and forth, lured first this way and then that way toward wrong understandings of themselves—between libertinism and determinism, between individualism and collectivism, as well as many other misunderstandings of themselves—and in this situation they are called to believe in God's decisive act of salvation *in Christo* and to praise God. In that regard, anthropological dogmas are necessarily subject to the historical change of fronts to a greater degree than the Christological ones; and it is clear that not only numerous profound crises but also church divisions in Western Christendom emerged precisely in the course of the effort to dogmatize such statements about the relationship between sin and grace—doing so in the context of changes to human self-understanding—statements which encounter the given anthropological self-understanding really as a call to repentance and to faith in the person's relevant life-experience. But do such firmly formulated anthropological statements also resonate with all the people who become members of the same church body a century or two later?

III.

The Eastern Church has been reproached of the fact that in its dogmatic development it has been at a standstill for over a thousand years, although during the past millennium a great number of new issues have arisen in the intellectual world and within Christendom itself, to which the church has had to respond in further dogmatic decisions. Already at the Synod of Chalcedon there was, of course, a strong aversion to formulating a new dogma, and without the emperor's insistence it would hardly have come to be. This aversion later became even stronger. "It was not only the inborn traditionalism of all religions that was opposed to change; it was also that concern for the ritualistic treatment of dogma which resisted change and suffered hurt with each new dogmatic formulation" (Harnack, *Dogmengeschichte*, 4th ed. [1909], 2.443 [4.274]). "It is only when one observes how the dogmatic controversies were—of necessity—always controversies about words which clamored for inclusion in the liturgy that one realizes they were bound to awaken mistrust.... The dogmatic controversies of the seventh century were in reality only an insignificant epilogue which merely gave dogma the deceptive appearance of being possessed of independent existence" (ibid., 2.444 [4.274–75]). According to Harnack, μυσταγωγία [mystagogia], that is, seeking to go deeper into the mysteries of the faith, "gradually led to the withering away" of μάθησις [doctrine] (2.443 [4.274]). Mystagogical theology stifled dogmatics and replaced it (compare also ibid., 2.511 [4.351–52].

The reasons for the early atrophy of the development of dogma in the Eastern Church are certainly many and various. Partly they resulted from the profound shock that persisted, especially in the Eastern Church, after the Arian controversies in the decades after 325 and the monophysite, monergistic, and monothelite controversies in the centuries after 451.[x] Partly they resulted from the fact that the Eastern Church was deprived of the freedom to make further dogmatic decisions by the emperors, whose chief concern was the unity of the empire; then, at a later time, even to assemble an ecumenical synod that represented all the regions of the Orthodox churches was a practical impossibility. But there was also an undeniable atrophying of the original strength of Greek systematic theology in the transition to a traditionalistic-scholastic form of thinking. In the midst of the various historical reasons there is a most important one, namely, the connection to the liturgy that dogmatic statements have, which had an inhibiting effect on the further formation of dogmas. But one will surely not do justice to this content if one only draws attention to a *terminological* liturgical formalism and to a mistrust over against every *terminological* change or enlargement. Rather, the fact that the Eastern Church ceased dogmatizing shows that it wanted to retain—and did retain—precisely the same *structure* of dogmatic statements in which the dogmatic development of the ancient church had begun, that is, in the structure of the doxological homology that is sung and offered to God in the worshiping assembly. The Eastern Church was concerned not only about retaining the *wording* of that which has been historically formulated and is now customarily used in the church, but it wants to remain faithful to the *structure* of the dogmatic starting point in the ancient church, namely, the structure of confessing, which at the same time is praise offered in the worship service and binding doctrine. For this reason, one cannot simply assert that the dogmatic work of the Eastern Church was stifled and replaced by mystagogy; rather, the dogma of the ancient church was from the beginning a constituent part of the worship service. But if the basic doxological structure of dogma is kept in mind, then it will become clear that it is quite impossible to make statements about the sacraments, about church and state, about the issue of natural law, and so forth, in the same structure that is used in doxological homology; for the very nature of doxology is such that it—certainly in the reception of the sacraments, certainly in the church, and thus at the same time in the world, and in the relationship between church and state—still cannot have as its content the sacraments as such, or the church as such, or the world as such, but rather only the Triune God who is acting through them. If dogma is understood from the start as doxological confession, and if this starting point is maintained, then within this structure no dogmas arise about the sacraments as such, about the church as such, about the state as such, and so forth, but rather the interest is directed to the actual administration of the sacraments, to the actual present life of the church in the world, and thus to the establishment of an ordering of liturgy and church law in which this administration takes place and in which God will be offered the true homology.

This persistence of the Eastern Church, in the historical development of its dogma, to adhere to its starting point cannot be regarded simply as a weakness; rather, thereby two basic, important advantages abide in this church which can gain ever greater ecumenical significance:

1. If the Eastern Church lacks a line of dogmatic decisions, which in one way or another were adopted in Western Christendom, this does not mean that the Eastern Church has been simply silent about these topics. For example, regarding its statements on the sacraments, the Eastern Church has hardly stated anything in the form of *dogmatic statements about* the sacraments, but it has in fact drawn up *liturgical directives and directives in church law for the administration* of the sacraments. It has thus in no way relinquished the sacraments to human arbitrariness. The same applies to ecclesiology. The concentration of the statements about the sacraments and the church on the directives for the proper *administration* of the sacraments and of the life of the church, and the great reticence with respect to the formulation of *dogmas* about these subjects, means that a very definite danger could not have had so strong an impact in the Eastern history of dogma as it did in Western Christendom, namely, the danger that dogmatic thinking might separate itself from the salvific *event* and might imagine that through thinking it could assume a vantage point from which it could theoretically look down upon and, to a certain extent, calculate and balance off against one another the cooperation between God and human beings, divine grace and the human will, God's sacramental gifts and the earthly elements (water, bread and wine), the invisible and the visible church. That dogmatic thinking and piety in the Eastern Church did not diverge as much as they did in parts of the West, is an advantage. Without doubt, in *the history of theology*, in both the East and the

West, some problems have first arisen because of this separation of theological thinking from the carrying out of God's activity—problems which may be described to some extent as matters that seem to be problems since they are no longer concerned with the reception of salvation and the witness to it, but rather with the theological explanation of this salvation. But in contrast to the Eastern Church, in Western Christendom some theological problems of that sort were also resolved *dogmatically*, and since these dogmas address questions that are no longer *immediately* defined by the reception of and the witness to the salvation occurring in the worship assembly, it is little wonder that the dogmatic formulas, which address these questions diverge from one another, both from one period of history to another and from one church body to another. Despite its theological reflection about such problems, the Eastern Church has in large measure refrained from that kind of *dogmatizing* and thus it has had more respect for the mysterious character of salvation than has the West.

2. The cessation of dogmatic development *can* be a weakness. It would indeed be so if a church in such a condition would be content merely to recite its settled dogmas repeatedly and would neglect to interpret them and to apply them in relation to new historical problems. It would also be a weakness, for example, if such a church attempted—merely by means of analogies based on existing dogmas—to clarify those issues where no decisions on dogma had been taken, as this has been done by some Eastern theologians, for example, to clarify the issue of the Lord's Supper by means of analogies based on the doctrine of the incarnation and to clarify the issue of church and state by means of analogies based on the doctrine of the two natures. Neither the uniqueness of the Lord's Supper nor that of the relationship between church and state become important in this approach. But a reticence to formulate dogma need not, in and of itself, signify a weakness any more than a steady, sanguine advance toward new and ever more detailed dogmas is a sign of intellectual and theological strength. It could very well be just the opposite, for a dogmatizing that develops more and more details, as the history of dogma in the Roman Church indicates, becomes such an immense scaffolding that the movement of theological thinking in it becomes more and more hindered and its catholic breadth is lost. A dogmatizing that concentrates on the Christological-Trinitarian center of dogma, however, makes space for the free unfolding of the abundance contained in Holy Scripture, which needs to be unfolded in the actual missionary advance in the concrete intellectual-historical situation of that particular environment. There is a type of progress toward a "treasure" [*Reichtum*] of more and more specialized dogmatic formulations, which deny the full range of the biblical witness and thus are in truth a poverty. On the other hand, there are settled dogmatic formulations that seem to show a poverty, which in truth yield a treasure here because the abundance of the biblical witness is disclosed through the Christological-Trinitarian center of

dogma, and thus the way is opened for the free unfolding of catholicity in theological thinking and in the witness of the church.

If one attempts to appraise the history of dogma in the Eastern Church from these two perspectives, then it becomes evident that the Eastern Church, precisely because of its characteristic dogmatic reticence, possesses very great and, in many respects, unique ecumenical possibilities; for it has been repeatedly shown in past ecumenical dialogues on the issues of "faith and order" that the dogmas which are dividing the churches have to be understood in a new and basic way in their setting in the life of the church, that is, especially in their function in the liturgy and in the proclamation of the church. The further dogmatic assertions become separated from this center of the worship service, the more difficult it is to come to an agreement about them among the separated churches. Conversely, there has been the often astonishing experience at ecumenical conferences that these same churches, despite their being divided from one another, were able to pray with one another and to receive from one another the living proclamation of God's acts of salvation. In that the Eastern Church, in its dogmatic statements, has stopped very closely to what takes place in the worship service, it has also retained the possibility of opening up dogma in a very special way by means of the worship service. It thus assumes a middle position between those churches, such as the Roman Church, which cause church divisions through their hyper-dogmatizing, and the extreme wing of Protestantism, which (in contrast to the Roman hyper-dogmatizing) rejects every dogmatic commitment and through its principle of dogmatic freedom distinguishes itself also from the Reformers. In saying this, of course, everything depends on whether contemporary Orthodoxy can muster the intellectual and theological strength and versatility to make use of the fundamental mediating position it received so that it can interpret what it has inherited from Athanasius and Cyril—who utilized conceptuality from the first centuries of the church—and apply that inheritance to today's concrete issues and to do so in the conceptuality of the twentieth century.[xi] This same issue holds true for every church that seeks to make use of a dogmatic heritage from the past, therefore, also the Church of the Lutheran Reformation.

IV.

This train of thought would be incomplete if it did not now also point to the fact that there are various basic structures of faith response, not merely the liturgical-doxological, by which people respond to God's act of salvation in Jesus Christ. Besides the address to God in prayer, there is the address of one's fellow human beings in preaching. Besides the adoration of God in the doxology, there is the tradition about God's acts that is passed on through doctrine. But all of the responses of faith are concentrated in the confession.

Dogma is rooted in the confession. But because the various structures of faith response are concentrated in the confession, it became possible that in the history of dogma first one of these forms and then another was determinative, whether it be, for example, the doxological or the kerygmatic. Further structural changes resulted, whereby dogma was no longer formulated as confession in the context of the worship service or as the word of adoration or as the word of witness, but rather as doctrine concerning the right way to confess, to worship, and to preach. A further structural change followed, whereby dogma was no longer affirmatively taught as doctrine—what to believe, to confess, to praise, and to attest to—but rather it was restricted to defining in the anathema only that which cannot be believed. The element of separation from the world, which is always implicit in the original act of confessing, became the explicit and, not infrequently, the sole content of dogmatic statements. These structural shifts, which as such cannot in any way be deemed negative from the start, must be kept in mind when one is comparing the dogmas of various periods in the history of the church and also when one is comparing the dogmas of the different churches.

On this basis, a difference arises in the structure of the dogmatic statements of the Eastern Church and the Church of the Reformation. To be sure, *all* of the structures of faith response are alive in the *worship services* of both churches: prayer and doxology, witness and doctrine, and all of these are concentrated in the confession of faith; but in the historical development that occurred in the Eastern Church, *dogma* was determined especially by the element of doxology contained in the confession of faith, whereas in the Church of the Reformation it was determined by the element of preaching. The Church of the Lutheran Reformation did, of course, hold with conviction the confessions of the ancient church, both as dogma and as the constituent part of the liturgy, but then it did not formulate its own further dogmatic statements in the form of doxological homologies, but rather in confessional writings, such as the *Confessio Augustana*, that were addressed publicly in the presence of God to the emperor and the empire. In addition, in the *Augustana*, *docere* [to teach] means, as a rule, "to preach," to proclaim," "to witness." As a result, none of the confessional writings from the Reformation was formulated for use in the liturgy of the worship service or incorporated into it. This structural shift continued to have an impact in the further development that led to seventeenth-century Protestant Orthodoxy, in that *doctrina*—even when, as a concept, it no longer signified preaching itself but rather the doctrine about that which was to be preached—still remained primarily aimed at the sermon and not did not become mystagogical theology.

In these structural differences one does not yet see any irreconcilable oppositions, but some can well develop from them. On the one side, this would be true if the ontological structure of the doxological statements were made into the predominating structure of theological thinking in general, and also of the statements about human beings; for then not only would the historical character of human beings be called into question but so too would the contingency of God's actions of salvation. Correspondingly, on the other side, it would be true if the structure of witness, of assurance, of being encountered by God's address, and thus the *I-Thou* correlation of the encounter, would be absolutized to the exclusion of all other statements; for then the divinity of God would be called into question, since God is not after all entirely contained in the act of revelation through the historical encounter, but rather reveals himself in this act as the one who is the same from everlasting to everlasting. But if either of these structures of theological statement is given special emphasis and is even radicalized and made to dominate all of the other structures of theological thinking, then false alternatives and church-separating oppositions arise. But then it is no longer only separated churches that confront one another but also ontological and personalistic philosophical systems, where Christians entangled in the one are not able to understand the dogma of the other as a confession of Christ.

In the ecumenical encounter of the churches, we are today confronted with the task of not only comparing the existing dogmatic differences with each other but giving them a fresh interpretation in view of the root of dogma in the original act of confessing the faith and to recognize the functions of the various dogmatic statements within the full range of the faith responses enjoined upon us by God.

Editor's Notes

[i] Adolf von Harnack, *Lehrbuch der Dogmengeschichte*, 4th ed., 3 vols. (Freiburg i. B: Mohr, 1909–10; ET: *History of Dogma*, 7 vols., trans. Neil Buchanan [Boston: Little, Brown & Co., 1901]); idem, *Das Wesen des Christentums* (Leipzig: Hinrichs, 1900; ET: *What is Christianity?*, trans. T. Bailey Saunders [New York: G.P. Putnam's Sons, 1901]). Harnack (1851–1930) was the principal historian of the early church at the University of Berlin (after 1888).

[ii] *Neuprotestantismus* or Liberal Protestantism emerged in the early nineteenth century in the wake of the Enlightenment, and it eventually became the dominant form of theological reflection in German universities between the Franco-Prussian War (1870–71) and the end of the First World War (1918). Broadly speaking, it was an outgrowth of eighteenth-century German Rationalism that furthered the critical spirit of the German Enlightenment in relation to Protestantism. Influenced by the anti-metaphysical philosophy of Immanuel Kant (1724–1804) and (less so) by the idealist philosophy of Georg Hegel (1770–1831), this form of Protestantism was also shaped by forces emanating from cultural Romanticism and Prussian nationalism, especially after the defeat of Napoleon (1815). The principal theologian in this tradition was Friedrich D. E. Schleiermacher (1768–1834), co-founder of the University of Berlin. This stream of Protestantism has also been labeled *Kulturprotestantismus*, since it reinterprets Christian-Protestant teaching to coincide with a cultured/educated outlook, one that takes into account modern scientific knowledge, technology, and secular political and economic structures and theories. After Schleiermacher, the most important figures include Albrecht Ritschl (1822–89), Wilhelm Herrmann (1846–1922), Ernst Troeltsch (1865–1923), and Harnack, who represents its zenith.

[iii] Jeremias Bonomelli, *Die Kirche* [The Church] (Freiburg i. B.: Herder, 1902); and Konrad Lübeck, *Die christlichen Kirchen des Orients* [The Christian Churches of the East] (Kempten : J. Kösel, 1911).

[iv] Friedrich Heiler, *Urkirche und Ostkirche* [The Early Church and the Eastern Church] (München, E. Reinhardt, 1937).

[v] Karl Holl (1866–1926) was professor of church history at the University of Berlin. He wrote several essays on Byzantine Christianity. Cf. Epiphanios of Salamis, *Panarion*, ed. Karl Holl, 3 vols. (Leipzig: J.C. Heinrich, 1915–33); idem, *Amphilochius of Ikonium in seinem Verhältnis zu den grossen Kappadoziern* (Tübingen: J. C. B. Mohr [Paul Siebeck], 1904). Friedrich Heiler (1892–1967) was a professor at the University of Marburg and then later at the University of Munich. His academic focus was on the history of religion. In addition to the work cited in endnote 4 above, cf. Friedrich Heiler, *Im Ringen um die Kirche* [The Struggle for the Church] (München: Reinhart, 1931).

[vi] That is, those congregations that confessed the Theological Declaration of the Synod at Barmen, the so-called "Barmen Declaration," and who collectively came to be called "the Confessing Church."

[vii] Cf. endnote 3 in chap. 3 ("The Christology of Chalcedon in Ecumenical Dialogue") above.

[viii] British-born Pelagius (fl. c. 400) and his fellow ascetic, Caelestius (fl. c. 400), taught a doctrine of freewill that left no room for divine grace. After the fall of Rome, Pelagius and Caelestius traveled to North Africa, where Augustine became their fiercest critic. Between 412 and 418 Pelagius and his teachings were condemned by several North African councils. He eventually settled in Palestine, where he and his ideas were warmly received by monks there. Pelagius remained in the East, although the date and place of his death are unknown. Caelestius left Africa for Ephesus, where he was ordained, and then a few years later settled in Constantinople, although he was eventually expelled from there, too. Julian of Eclanum (c. 386–454), a disciple of Pelagius, refused to accept the latter's condemnation, which was officially announced by Pope Zosimus (d. 418) in 417, and also left for the East. There he was initially given some support by Nestorius (d. 451), the patriarch of Constantinople, who intervened on Julian's behalf in a letter to Pope Celestine (d. 432), and, for a time, by the emperor Theodosius II (401–50). Eventually, however, Julian was condemned in an imperial edict (429) and, along with Pelagius, at the Council of Ephesus (431), which also condemned Nestorianism.

[ix] John of Damascus [c. 675–c.749], *Exposition of the Orthodox Faith*, trans. S. D. F. Salmond, in the *Select Library of Nicene and Post-Nicene Fathers*. 2nd Series, ed. Philip Schaff and Henry Wace, vol. 9 (Oxford: Parker, 1899; reprint: Grand Rapids: Eerdmans, 1963).

[x] Monophysitism teaches that in the incarnate Christ there is only a single divine nature, not two natures (divine and human), as confessed at the Council of Chalcedon (451). Monothelitism was a seventh-century movement that understood the incarnate Christ to have only a single will, not two wills (divine and human), as confessed at the Council of Constantinople (680) and the Council of Rome (679). A slight variation on Monothelitism is "monergism," which holds that Christ had a single force of will or activity, not two wills. Cf. endnote 5 in chap. 14 ("Ecumenical Councils Then and Now") below.

[xi] Athanasius (c. 296–373) became bishop of Alexandria in 328 (although he was thereafter frequently forced into exile), and Cyril (d. 444) in 412.

Chapter Thirteen:
The Significance of the Eastern and Western Traditions for Christendom[1]

Whether a Christian fellowship affirms or rejects the principle of tradition, nothing changes the fact that every Christian actually stands within a concrete historical tradition. A multiplicity of traditions has resulted from an inner necessity. Already in the New Testament writings we find different transmissions of the words and deeds of Jesus and different forms of the apostolic message, for the message of the one Christ had to be unfolded in the Jewish, Greek, and Gnostic world of that time. Moreover, various traditions had to be developed as the gospel was brought to further nations, and beyond that, at the same time, additional decisions had to be adopted about matters of doctrine and order.

The multiplicity of traditions signifies a treasure, provided fellowship is firmly maintained among the various traditions. Then there are the manifestations of the catholicity of the church, for catholicity consists not only in the spatial expansion of the church but also in the multiplicity of the witnesses, the prayers, the theologies, the ministerial offices, and the charismata. Where, however, fellowship in the Lord's Supper and in the mutual acknowledgment of the ministerial offices is broken off, there the variety of traditions becomes an offense: The traditions begin to lock themselves off from one another, to harden themselves against one another, and to cripple the missionary service of Christendom to the world.

Already early on in Christendom, Eastern and Western traditions began to differentiate themselves from one another, both in the liturgy and in the theology and understanding of the ministerial office. Ignatius of Antioch argued differently from Clement of Rome, just as Irenaeus did in comparison to Tertullian. Moreover, Eastern and Western traditions faced one another, not as fixed entities, but rather they were both differentiated in various ways, they interpenetrated one another geographically and substantively, and they each cross-pollinated the other. Their differences signified a treasure from which we are all still drawing today.

These differences, however, were not firmly maintained as treasure. The

---

1 A lecture delivered on 20 August 1959 to the Central Committee of the WCC in Rhodes, Greece. [This address was published as "Die Bedeutung der östlichen und westlichen Traditionen für die Christenheit," in *Ökumenische Rundschau* 8, no. 4 (1959), 165–73. It was also published under the same title in *Informationsblatt für die Gemeinden in den niederdeutschen lutherischen Landeskirchen* 9, no. 14 (1960), 223–27, and in *Evangelische Welt* 13 (1959), 497–501. It appears in KC 1.232–40. An English translation of this address, "The Significance of the Eastern and Western Traditions for the Christian Church," was published in *The Ecumenical Review* 12, no. 2 (1960), 133–42 (reprinted in CC [285–95]), and in *The Journal of the Moscow Patriarch* 2 (1974), 43–48. It has also been published in French and Greek. –Ed.]

more people began to insist, under the influence of the legal form of the Roman Empire, that the unity of the church is uniformity in worship, in dogmatic formulas, and in the ordering of ministerial offices, the more people felt the multiplicity of the traditions to be a shortcoming. The more the geographical ordering of the church coincided with the arrangement of provinces in the Roman Empire, the more the church districts, with their different local church traditions, were drawn into the political conflicts between the Eastern and the Western divisions of the empire and of those belonging to the imperial provinces, and thus the different church traditions were also felt to be in conflict with one another. When the schism finally occurred between Eastern and Western Christendom, the primary occasion was not the difference in liturgical and theological traditions but rather how the ordering of the church had been inextricably bound to political powers and their governmental-legal order. Only now differences in liturgical and theological tradition were felt to be church dividing. Indeed, some on the one side began to feel that those on the other side were not only schismatic but also heretical, and they began to treat them accordingly. This found its most horrific expression in the Fourth Crusade of Western Christendom against Constantinople, and in the crusades undertaken by the German Order of Knights in the Baltic region, not only against the heathen Slavs but also against Orthodox Christians.[i] These events, by which the Eastern Church was weakened in the struggle against the Turks and Mongols with very grave consequences, have for centuries burrowed themselves into the consciousness of the church people, and have appeared to make nearly every difference church dividing, even with regard to the question about using leavened or unleavened bread in the Lord's Supper.

In spite of all this, during the last four hundred years it has become increasingly difficult to speak of a strict opposition between the Eastern and Western traditions, and indeed for various reasons. At the time of the Reformation, large regions of the Western church broke away from specifically Western traditions, namely, the papacy, and were founded afresh upon apostolic doctrine and the dogmatic decisions of the ancient church. Although the Reformation churches are not united with the Eastern Church, yet they have never separated themselves from it. They were only heirs of that old division between East and West. Both Luther and then later the Tübingen professors (who began corresponding in 1573 with Jeremias II, Patriarch of Constantinople) spoke about the Eastern Church in the confidence that they were one with it in the faith.[ii] Even if one then had to acknowledge that the Eastern Church had more in common with the Roman Church than one had formerly assumed in Germany, nevertheless, since then, the severity of the opposition between East and West has been overcome, especially in the consciousness of the Church of the Lutheran Confession and of the Church of England. But also today the separation between Eastern and Western traditions no longer holds geographically in the strict sense. There are today Orthodox churches in the West and Western churches in the East. In addition, many Western and Eastern traditions have changed in the tumult of the events of world history. If today, for example, the Parisian church historian Kartashev tries to transfer the conception of the Eastern symphony between church and state to modern democracy, or the Moscow patriarch acknowledges the Communist state as an authority, that symphony is no longer the tradition of the Eastern Church.[iii] And if the pope concludes concordats with sovereign states, that is no longer the administration [*Handhabung*] of the two swords in the sense of Boniface VIII, although this claim has not been retracted in principle.[iv] If one speaks today of an opposition between East and West, one means something different from the opposition between the Eastern and Western church traditions.

Above all, however, the severity of the opposition between Eastern and Western tradition has been diminished today, for God's Spirit has given to many people on both sides a sense of shame about the divided condition of Christendom and has poured into their hearts the longing for unity. By working through the divisions, we are again beginning to have an inkling about the treasure that lies hidden in the differences between the Eastern and Western traditions. From that perspective, when inquiring into the significance of church traditions, it is no longer sufficient for us today to describe first and foremost the significance of *one's own* tradition for the other church bodies, as was done for centuries. Rather, the task has become newly important for us to recognize the positive significance of the *other* tradition.

For that reason, I want to speak above all about the significance of the Eastern tradition for Western Christendom. Since the basic structures of Christian traditions are often more essential than liturgical and dogmatic details, as well as those in church law, I will—in the necessarily brief space here—refer to three basic structures of the Eastern Church which, in my opinion, are especially significant for Western Christendom.

1. In the worship services of all churches, God's mighty deeds in history and the promise of the coming redemption are expressed verbally in the Scripture readings and the sermon, the Lord's Supper and the prayers. But in no church is the worship service so strongly determined by the structure of the hymn and the adoration as in the Eastern Church. In its canons, *stichera*, and *troparia* the Gospel of the day is unfolded in ever-new forms of praise.[v] Praise is offered, however, not only for the act of salvation which is reported in the biblical text but to God himself, who is the same for ever and ever in the one glory of the Father and of the Son and of the Holy Spirit. As the message about the historical act of salvation is taken up into the adoration of the eternal God and his Christ, this act of salvation is experienced in the liturgy as occurring in the midst of the congregation. In the doxological turn toward God the temporal interval between then and now disappears in a characteristic way. The same holds true for the interval that divides our *now* from the consummation still to come. In the praise of the victory of Christ on the cross and in the resurrection and in the adoration of the eternal triune God, the future glory is experienced

in the worship service as present. The believers are translated into that glory, and the threatening visible reality of this world fades away. In the liturgy of no other church is the victory of Jesus Christ in its import for the whole cosmos unfolded so triumphantly and the presence of the future new creation praised in such a rapturous way as here. Here the eschatological jubilation rings on and on, in which the earliest Christian community celebrated the Lord's Supper.

2. In this connection the characteristic structure of dogma of the Eastern Church must be seen. All churches have dogmas; even those Christian fellowships that as a general principle reject dogmas are actually marked throughout by faith convictions that are held in common. Dogmas can be expressed in very different forms. But it is characteristic of the Eastern Church that dogma and liturgy have not been separated from one another and that dogma is primarily formulated as a liturgical statement. The dogma of the Eastern Church comes to voice in the worship service as a statement of confession and doxology. Arising necessarily from the structure of doxology are also the ontological statements that are characteristic of the Greek doctrine of God and that cannot be confused with an alien domination of the gospel by metaphysics. The formulations of the Trinitarian and Christological dogmas of the ancient church were liturgical statements or, at any rate, statements intended directly to serve the praise of God in the worship service. From time immemorial the Eastern Church, unlike the Western, has maintained an aversion to abandoning this liturgical setting of the dogmatic statement and to elevating such confessional statements into binding dogmas that no longer permit themselves to be expressed in the structure of doxology. The confessional writings that were thus produced during the disputes with the West in the seventeenth century—for example, the *Confessio Orthodoxa* of Peter Mogila and the *Confessio Dosithei*—never received the same authority in the whole of the Eastern Church as did the dogma of the ancient church.[vi] With strictest adherence to the dogma of the ancient church, the Eastern Church thus remained open in principle to the possibility of creative theological thinking, something that had been widely closed off in the West due to many far-reaching efforts at formulating and establishing dogmas.

3. Something else to be noted is the particular structure of the relationship between church and ministerial office. Despite the emphasis on hierarchy, this relationship is, however, not only determined by ordering of superior to subordinate. Rather, all ordering of above and below, of superior and subordinate, is enclosed within the fellowship. The relationship between ministerial office and congregation is at the same time a togetherness. This is apparent both in the worship service and in the fact that the supreme authority in the Eastern Church is not a single officeholder but the ecumenical synod, and that the decisions of the synod in turn are not valid unless they receive the confirmation of the church members. By foregoing any supreme authority, secured in church law, that would have complete jurisdiction over the whole

church, more space is respectfully made in the Eastern Church for the working of the Holy Spirit than in the Roman Church, a working which cannot be hampered by any ordering of ministerial offices. In that Jesus Christ is honored as the sole Lord of the church, there thus remains space also for the multiplicity of autocephalous churches, for the incarnate Son of God, as the exalted Lord, wants to enter the concrete historical situation of all nations and languages through the Holy Spirit.[vii] The unity of the church is the fellowship of churches that rightly believe the faith. That the Eastern Church understands its relationship to civic authority, above all, as a spiritual service—but that it has itself not grasped for possession of civic authority—corresponds to the doxological structure of the worship service and of dogma and to the fellowship-structure of church order. In the conception of the symphony of ecclesial and civic office, the church has affirmed its spiritual power as a worldly powerlessness.

One could, of course, inquire about whether or not it was only external factors that have hindered the Eastern Church from developing in a similar way as did Western Christendom. One could say that the reason the Eastern Church did not progress with further dogmatizing, as the West did, was the fact that it was not in a position to hold further ecumenical councils, due to political upheavals. That it is a fellowship of autocephalous churches is due to the fact that the patriarch of Constantinople, despite all his efforts, was unable to hinder the formation of national churches. And the reason the patriarch did not become a secular potentate like the pope was due to the fact that in the East there never arose such a political vacuum as there was in the West between the fifth and eighth centuries. However, there can be no doubt that it was not only these external political constellations but strong internal inhibitions in the Eastern Church itself that opposed such dogmatic developments. They would have contradicted the very nature of the Eastern Church.

The basic structures of Western Christendom are different.

To be sure, while here, too, the hymn is not missing, the concrete assurance of the act of salvation is in the foreground, not its portrayal in the form of a hymn. Likewise, the adoration of God's eternal glory is not missing in the Western Church, but the statements about God's eternal being recede in relationship to the acknowledgement of his present, powerful action through word and sacrament. Also not missing is the certainty of the presence of the glory to come: In the Lord's Supper we already now participate in that great future Lord's Supper in God's kingdom. At the same time, however, the *not-yet* character of the transfiguration of the world and the interval that separates us from the future glory is at the same time felt more strongly. In the Western worship service the individual experiences not so much a "being-snatched-from-the-world" in the mystical experience of "heaven on earth," as being placed into servant ministry to the world. As in the Western Church the voluntaristic characteristics in the representation of God have again and again come to the forefront in a more pronounced way than in the Eastern Church, so also in the worship service of the Reformation the historical nature of the ever-new address of God plays a decisive role, as does the historical nature of the obedience of faith in the concrete situation.

Correspondingly, Western Christendom did not stop with the dogmas of the ancient church but proceeded to make further dogmatic decisions as new problems and dangers arose. In doing so, these decisions also did not remain within the structure of doxology but set down a large number of firmly formulated statements in the form of theological doctrine about human beings, about grace, about the relationship between human action and God's action in salvation, and so forth. Also the Reformation churches did not set down their dogmatic statements as confessions for use in worship, but instead formulated them in the form of confessional writings, whose purpose, to be sure, in contrast to scholastic theology, was not to serve the clarification of theoretical dogma but to serve the task of proclamation. Therefore, the structure of their dogmatic statements was determined not by ontological relations but by the personal encounter between the God who speaks and gives and the individual who hears and receives.

Moreover, already early on, the interest of Western Christendom was directed more towards the practical and legal issues in the activities of the church, while the speculative theological achievement of the Latin Fathers before Augustine lagged behind that of the Eastern Fathers. From this basic position of Roman thinking there then developed in the West, as is commonly known, an increasingly legalized understanding of dogma, of repentance and grace, and of church order, up to papal centralization and the struggle for world domination. In contrast, the Reformation taught the justification of the sinner by grace, the distinction between the two kingdoms, and the understanding of church unity as a fellowship of churches.

On the basis of these Western presuppositions, there was often talk of a weakness in the Eastern Church. For this WCC meeting I need not speak of the criticism that is being leveled against the fellowship-structure of the Eastern Church in light of papal centralization, for on this point the Reformation churches stand with the Eastern Church. No doubt, however, some in the West see a shortcoming in that the Eastern Church stopped with the dogmas of the ancient church and refrained from making further dogmatic formulations of an equal authoritative claim with respect to theological and ideological matters that arose later on. Above all, however, one sees in the Eastern Church's concentration on the Divine Liturgy a widespread retreat of the church from its real responsibility in the world, and one sees in the emphasis of all Eastern hymnody on the eschatological presence the surrendering of this world to its own autonomy and the abandoning of its need for social and legal transformation. Is the Eastern Church still really taking seriously the fact that God commands the Christian to be obedient in the midst of this world, that is, not only to witness to Christ and to participate in the church's worship life but also to be obediently committed to justice and freedom in human society?

After all, does not God command our obedience, not only as Redeemer but also as the Preserver of the world? Similar questions have also been asked by members of the Eastern Church itself, and not only by Vladimir Solovyov.[viii]

When discussing these issues one must in all fairness take due account of the fact that for centuries the Eastern Church was oppressed by Arabs, Mongols, and Turks, which hindered it from having an impact on its environment. In addition, however, one has to distinguish between the question about the dangers which accompany those fundamental structures of the Eastern Church and the question about whether the Eastern Church must *necessarily* succumb to these dangers. This latter question, in my opinion, has to be answered in the negative.

All dimensions of the Eastern Church's life are concentrated in its liturgy in such a way that Eastern Christendom has not only been sheltered in it during times of oppression and has remained steadfast by means of it, but from this center it can also again and again advance into the world with authority. The history of the Eastern Church's mission is proof of it. The jubilation in the Eastern Church's hymns need not mean the abandonment of the world, just as the eschatological jubilation of the earliest church's Eucharistic fellowship did not stay locked in the hearts of the believers. Rather, it is out of this jubilation that the good news of the gospel broke forth into a hostile world. The experience of the presence in worship of the expected eschaton has always had the strongest transformative effects upon people. To be sure, the Eastern Church has viewed its ethical task in the world more in terms of the sanctifying transformation of people than in the implementing of new social and legal orderings. But where there is a genuine renewal of people to faith, love and hope, this cannot remain without having an effect on the social order.

Nor is it true that the commitment of the Eastern Church to the doxological structure of dogmas from the ancient church necessarily entailed a shortcoming in its coming to terms with current issues from later periods. Also, the Eastern Church had discussed issues in anthropology, the doctrine of grace, and so forth that went beyond the dogmas of the ancient church, and the Augustinian theme of "God and the soul" has indeed not remained unknown to it. The speeches of Symeon, the new theologian (ca. 1000), are not the only proof for this.[ix] In contrast to Western Christendom, however, the insights that arose from such discussions and that had a great influence on the Eastern Church were not raised to the status of additional binding dogmas. Rather, they found their expression and recording in liturgical texts, in instructions for sanctification, in forms of piety, and of course naturally in didactic writings. In that the Eastern Church, in contrast to the West, did not establish much of its insights as binding dogmas in canon law, and with all of its strict commitment to the Trinitarian and Christological dogma of the ancient church, it has remained basically freer than some elements of Western tradition. There is, therefore, no reason why it should necessarily become ossified in traditionalism. Rather, we should expect it, on the basis of the spiritual power rooted in its liturgy, to take up the great issues of our time aggressively and to make a vibrant, independent contribution toward their solution.

Conversely, however, Western Christendom must bear in mind that precisely on such points where it has gone much further than the Eastern Church there arose far-reaching divisions. The more people abandoned the structure of fellowship and centralized the ordering of the church, the more the priesthood of all believers rose up against it, even so far as calling into question the ministerial offices altogether. The more the worship-life setting of dogmas in the life of the church was given up in order to dogmatize in coherent, theoretical propositions in a binding way in canon law the doctrines of human beings, the relationship between nature and grace, and other doctrinal teachings, the more—with the historical change of human self-understanding and with the experiences of grace—other statements also made the claim for binding dogma in canon law. And the more, in the West, the presence of the eschaton in the worship service was supplemented by the actuality of political preaching or even replaced by it, the more the church was dragged into the divisions of the world. The more people in the West strove for uniformity in the decisions about all these issues and sought to make them binding in canon law, and sought the unity of the church in the unity of the formulations, the more it led to divisions.

Each of the church's traditions is exposed to its special dangers, and all the more so as it makes an exclusive claim over against the other traditions. But the basic structures of proclamation and doxology, and of the historical, personal, and the ontological statement belong together, as also the expectation of the coming Christ and the certainty that his future is present now. For that reason, I am convinced that on essential points the Eastern and Western traditions complement one another and can mutually warn and defend one another against the specific dangers in their respective positions. Along with this, the importance of the Eastern tradition for Western Christendom must not be underestimated. It can also help us to think through from fresh perspectives the Western conflicts between the Roman Church and the Reformation churches, up to and including the free Protestant fellowships. By contrast, it seems to me absurd if one in the West would want to push for proselytizing within the Eastern Church. Such proselytizing should be stopped out of respect for the fact that the Eastern Church not only thoroughly suffered centuries-long oppression by Arabs, Mongols, and Turks, but also by the fact that in our twentieth century it has suffered with exemplary faithfulness the bloodiest persecution of Christians in the whole of church history, and thereby it has demonstrated a spiritual power that is significant for the strengthening of the whole of Christendom.

I have above all been speaking about the significance of the Eastern tradition for Western Christendom. Since I myself stand in a tradition that has been shaped by Augustine and Luther, this may appear paradoxical. I could have in fact spoken to a much greater degree about the insights and impulses of the Reformation, which, I am convinced, are of great significance for the Eastern Church, for I have no doubt that a number of important statements in the apostolic message that cannot be relinquished have been less developed in the Eastern Church than in the West. Through the centuries, however, the different traditions of Christendom have become so alien to one another, and this estrangement is still so undiminished, that the *first* step must be for each of us to seek to understand the significance of the *other* traditions. We must *first* seek to inquire into what we are able to recognize as spiritual fruit in the *other* traditions, which grow from the soil that all churches have in common, namely, the ground of the apostolic message. We today in the East and the West face the task of doing better than the medieval union councils did, which were essentially concerned with the enforcement of a dogmatic uniformity and a centralized ordering in canon law.[x] We can also do better than the sixteenth-century letter writers in Tübingen and Constantinople, whose exchange almost immediately came to a standstill over the principle of tradition. Above all, we have to inquire about the treasure that is hidden in the various traditions and to seek the unity of the church, not in uniformity but in the fellowship of traditions.

Editor's Notes

[i] In 1201 a group of Western European crusaders and Venetian investors planned to re-take Jerusalem after first conquering Muslim Cairo, but that plan failed for logistical reasons. The Venetians thus set their sights on Constantinople, the capital of the Byzantine Empire and center of the Eastern Church. The crusaders brutally attacked the city in 1203 and 1204. In July 1204, the city was sacked, art was destroyed or stolen, the library and numerous churches demolished, and many of the city's inhabitants looted, raped, and murdered. Schlink is here also referring to the so-called Northern Crusades, which took place throughout the thirteenth century. A key participant in these battles was the German Order of Knights, otherwise known as the Teutonic Order, which had been formed as a military-religious order at the end of the twelfth century. Some of its battles were against Eastern Orthodox Christians, e.g., the so-called Battle on Ice between the Livonian branch of the Teutonic Order and the Republic of Novgorod, which occurred in April 1242.

[ii] Cf. footnote 8 in chap. 7 ("Law and Gospel as a Controversial Issue in Theology") above.

[iii] Anton Kartashev (1875–1960) initially taught Russian church history in St. Petersburg. After the Russian Revolution he was arrested by the Communists. In 1919 he fled to Finland and eventually settled in Paris. There he helped to cofound St. Sergius Orthodox Theological Institute, where he taught church history until his death. Dr. Schlink is likely referring to Kartashev's essay, "The Church and National Life," which appeared in *The Church of God: An Anglo-Russian Symposium*, ed. Eric L. Mascall (London: SPCK, 1934).

[iv] In his bull, *Unam sanctam* (18 November 1302), Pope Boniface VIII (ca. 1230–1303) set forth the teaching that both temporal and spiritual authority are under the pope's jurisdiction. Cf. Denzinger 870–875.

[v] In the Eastern Church a *sticheron* (plural: *stichera*) is a brief liturgical hymn which is attached to a verse (στίχος) of a psalm or other scriptural passage. A *troparion* is a short hymn that celebrates the event or saint that is commemorated in the office for the day.

[vi] Peter Mogila (1597–1646) was an Eastern Orthodox theologian who studied at Paris and later became the abbot of a monastery in Kiev. He eventually became the Metropolitan of that city.

His *Confession* was widely approved as an authoritative summary of the Orthodox faith. Dositheos (1641–1707), Patriarch of Jerusalem, composed his Confession for the 1672 Synod of Jerusalem. He did so primarily to define and defend Orthodox doctrine over against Calvinism and the theology of Cyril of Lucaris (1570–1638), patriarch of Constantinople, who had expressed sympathy for certain Calvinist teachings.

[vii] The autocephalous (= "self-headed") churches are united in doctrine and worship, they recognize each other as canonical, they are in full communion, and together they constitute "the Orthodox Church." There are either thirteen or fourteen such regional churches (e. g., Ecumenical Patriarchate of Constantinople, Patriarchate of Jerusalem, Patriarchate of Moscow, Patriarchate of Romania, Church of Greece, Church of Poland, etc.).

[viii] Cf. endnote 1 in chap. 10 ("The Sojourning People of God") above.

[ix] Symeon the New Theologian (949–1022) was a Byzantine monk. He is the last of the three saints canonized by the Eastern Orthodox Church. Cf. Symeon the New Theologian, *Discourses*, ed. and trans. C. J. de Catanzaro (Mahwah, NJ: Paulist, 1980.)

[x] Two major attempts at achieving reunion between the Western and Eastern churches took place at the Second Council of Lyons in 1274 and at the Council of Florence in 1438–39. While the Council of Lyons was able to promulgate union, it came to an end in 1289. The Council of Florence also was able to promulgate a union ("The Decree of Union"), but the Orthodox synods that met in its wake were unable to ratify it, and this union, too, proved ephemeral. Sticking points remained the primacy of the bishop of Rome and the *filioque*.

Chapter Fourteen:
Ecumenical Councils Then and Now[i]

Provided no unforeseen events intervene, in these coming years two ecumenical assemblies of churches will take place in close proximity to one another, namely, the third assembly of the World Council of Churches in New Delhi and the second Vatican council of the Roman Catholic Church.[ii] The same churches will not participate in both of these assemblies. At best, *observers* from the Roman Church will participate in the assembly of the World Council, while, at best, *observers* from the churches that belong to the World Council will be authorized to witness the Vatican Council. Even a reciprocal *advisory* cooperation is unlikely to occur. At the second Vatican council only members of the Roman Church will have an official "seat and vote," which at the third assembly of the World Council only member churches of the Council will have. To be sure, also some parts of the Orthodox, Lutheran, and Reformed churches and of other Christian fellowships (for example, the Baptists) will not be present in New Delhi; but nevertheless these church bodies, and in fact all the church bodies of the world, other than the Roman Church, will be represented.

In these side-by-side meetings of two ecumenical synods or councils the world will behold a manifestation of the divided condition of Christendom, and indeed all the more so since both want to generate worldwide public interest through all of the means of modern reporting (press, radio, television). Even if some in Europe and America have become accustomed to Rome's positioning apart from the rest of Christendom, we cannot underestimate the consequences of such side-by-side meetings for the Asiatic and African world, for in its divided condition Christendom presents itself to these peoples in upheaval as being just like Islam and Buddhism in their various divisions and like the separated peoples of the world. The message of the one Lord Jesus Christ appears refuted by those who proclaim it. It appears to those who believe in Christ that that message has not brought peace. Indeed, despite its faith in the one Lord, Christendom itself appears not to have achieved even as much as the United Nations has, despite all of its weaknesses.

If we understand an ecumenical council to be an assembly of representatives from the whole of Christendom on earth, then the side-by-side meetings of two ecumenical councils appear as a *contradictio in adjecto* [a contradiction in terms], for only one of them—or neither of them—can be deemed an ecumenical council.

If one concludes this way, then one of course sees the problem posed here only from an external point of view, for to begin with, the synonyms *synod* and *council* have here only a very general and superficial meaning, as the etymological origin of each demonstrates, and on the basis of its basic literal meaning, we could of course easily embrace both the assembly of the World Council and the second Vatican council under the sociological term of *assembly* [*Versammlung*] (synod, council). But that still says nothing about what is expressed if, for example, the World Council of Churches would itself designate its assemblies as ecumenical councils. Above all, however, we cannot overlook the fact that neither the theological term *council* nor the word *ecumenical* is unambiguous. Both terms can have very different meanings, since both have a history behind them in which substantial changes to the meanings of the terms have occurred.

One must thus differentiate[1], on the one hand, the papal understanding of *council*—as it developed in the Middle Ages, gained acceptance in modern times, and was set down in sections 222–229 of the *Codex Iuris Canonici*[iii]— from, on the other hand, the understanding of *conciliarism*, which determined many councils in the later Middle Ages and which likewise had a further influence.[iv] Both of these two conceptions must in turn be distinguished from, on the one hand, the earlier imperial synods of the ancient church, which were convened by the Roman emperor and largely determined by him to be ecumenical, and, on the other hand, from those synods of the ancient church that preceded these others, which were free of state interference and which probably first took place in Asia in the conflict with Montanism. The distinctive character of these latter synods is (for our historical knowledge) most clearly evident in the area of the African church. But these basic forms are only the four most important ones in church history, and each of them expresses a particular understanding of the church. Added to them is an abundance of variations: Already in ante-Nicene Christendom the synods that met to address the life of the church in Rome and Alexandria never had the same significance as those in Asia, Greece, and Africa. Then, after Nicaea, the provincial synods need to be differentiated from the patriarchal synods and the other individual synods within the organization of the empire that had an ecclesiological structure that was different from those synods in the ante-Nicene period and from those later on (after the disintegration of the Roman Empire), for example, the synods in Spain and the imperial synods in Germany, which again had a distinctive character. In turn, the understanding of the term *council* by the Reformation churches is not to be equated with conciliarism; rather, new impulses from the ancient church's thinking about synods became active here. Over against these very different councils the so-called Apostolic Council (Acts 15) has a special place insofar as the office of apostle is unique and unrepeatable.

---

1 Cf. the overview of the history of the councils that has been given by Georg Kretschmar ("Konzilien," *Evangelisches Kirchenlexicon*, 3 vols. [Göttingen: Vandenhoeck & Ruprecht, 1959]), 2.935 f.; and Hubert Jedin (*Kleine Konzilsgeschichte* [Freiburg: Herder, 1959; ET: *Ecumenical Councils of the Catholic Church: An Outline*, trans. Ernest Graf (Freiburg: Herder, 1960)]), in addition to the multi-volume work, *Die ökumenischen Konzile der Christenheit*, ed. Henry Beck, Georg Kretschmar, and Hans J. Margull (Stuttgart: Evangelisches Verlagswerk, 1959).

In the course of history the term *ecumenical* has also undergone profound changes.[2] Within our particular way of framing the issue we must here above all keep in mind the two following distinctions. As the ancient church began to speak of ecumenical councils, the term *ecumenical* was initially used in reference to its prior meaning as a geographical term. It thus referred to the councils of all churches in the inhabited world, and since the borders of Christendom essentially coincided with the borders of the Roman Empire, that meant the term referred to the councils of all churches in the Roman Empire. But then the ecclesiological significance of the term became increasingly prominent over against the geographical. The term *ecumenical* was then used to refer to the whole church on earth; beyond the geographical universality of the church, it came to refer also to the church's catholicity. From here onward, the use of the term *ecumenical* that began at the time of the Reformation, namely, to designate what the separated churches had in common[3], has to be distinguished from how it is commonly used today, a meaning which first gained widespread acceptance in the nineteenth century, namely, to refer to the efforts of the separated churches to work toward unity. Because of this change in meaning it must here be stated that the announcement of an ecumenical council by Pope John XXIII has been widely understood by the public to have the sense of an impending council to unite the whole of Christendom. Both of these two most important definitions are here also surrounded by a wealth of various other definitions, just as the neighboring term *catholic* has also been more precisely defined very differently. Further possible meanings of the term *ecumenical* still have to be brought to light in the course of this examination.

Because the concept of the ecumenical council can be defined very differently, two ecumenical councils [occurring at the same time] need not necessarily mean an opposition to one another. Everything depends rather on how both of the approaching assemblies understand themselves and what takes place in them. When one speaks of the church assemblies at New Delhi and the Vatican as ecumenical synods or councils, one must not be content with considering them merely from an external point of view but must move forward to capture the theological significance of both assemblies. It is therefore imperative at the start to raise the question, whether and in what sense both of these worldwide church assemblies are to be designated as ecumenical councils, not only sociologically but also ecclesiologically. At the same time, of course, comparing them with the ecumenical councils of the ancient church is of special interest, while, to be sure, the unrepeatable historical conditionality of the latter has to be taken into account, which then

---

2 W. A. Visser't Hooft, *Der Sinn des Wortes "ökumenisch"* (Stuttgart: Evangelisches Verlagshaus, 1954). [ET: *The Meaning of Ecumenical* (London: SCM Press, 1953). –Ed.]

3 Ernst Kinder, "Der Gebrauch des Begriffs 'ökumenisch' im ältern Luthertum" [The Use of the Term "Ecumenical" in Early Lutheranism], *Kerygma und Dogma* 1, no. 3 (1955), 180–207.

makes it impossible to apply them as a norm in *every* respect. This question about the distinctive nature of both councils does not yet address the issues that will be deliberated by them nor the resolutions that will be adopted by them, but does address the councils' fundamental ecclesiological significance, their form, possibility, and authority. So in the following it must first be asked, in what sense (I) the assembly of the World Council of Churches in New Delhi and (II) the second Vatican council of the Roman Church can each be designated as an ecumenical council. On the basis of the answers to both of these questions, what both of these councils could mean for the unity of Christendom (III) is then to be discussed. These questions require a series of distinctions.

I.

In what sense can the assemblies of the World Council of Churches be designated as councils, that is, as ecumenical councils? Which factors are constitutive for these assemblies?

1. In the first place, we stress those factors that correspond to the tradition of councils of the ancient church, whereby we are thinking not only, to be sure, of the councils of the imperial church since 325 but also the synods that preceded them.

a) The synods of the ancient church grew historically out of the assembly of the local congregations, that is, out of the worship assembly. Just as the worship assembly and the service occurring in it were the central starting point for the development of the ordering of ministerial offices, so they were also the starting point for the development of the synod. The latter originated when leading members of other congregations joined in the deliberations of a local congregation. But also with the growth in the numbers of participating members from the various other local churches, *the worship character* of the assembly was maintained. All of the deliberations were embedded in the worship service, arose from it, and were applied to it. The prayer for the Holy Spirit and the certainty of his leadership determined the synodical deliberation and the resolutions in the same way as were the prayers, testimonies, and doxologies of the other worship activities. So also for the assemblies of the World Council of Churches, which on each occasion are the guest of a specific local church, the worship services not only provide an external framework but they determine and permeate in a most decisive way the entirety of their joint deliberations and resolutions. The multiplicity of the testimonies and prayers that will here be voiced by all churches, and heard and prayed by all, reveals an overwhelming richness and often lets the unity *in Christo* to be expressed more clearly than is the case in the more theoretical statements of the resolutions. The same is true of the prayerful participation in the celebration of the Lord's Supper by the various churches, even if here intercommunion is until now only in part possible.

b) If the synods of the ancient church grew out of the assembly of the local congregation, that means that originally *all members of the congregation* participated in the deliberations and the adoption of resolutions. Surely the church is the fellowship of all those who have received the Holy Spirit and in whom the prophetic promise has come to fulfillment: "And no one will teach and say to the others or to his brother or sister, 'Know the Lord!'; rather, they will all know me, both great and small, says the Lord" (Jer. 31.34). Accordingly, in the Lucan report about the so-called Apostolic Council, at the decisive moment we read: "Then, *together with the whole congregation*, the apostles and the elders resolved" (Acts 15.22).[4] The same holds true for the early synods of the ancient church, as is entirely clear, for example, from the letters of Cyprian.[5] The element of responsible collaboration on the part of the universal priesthood of all believers was also preserved here, even when the number of bishops coming from other locales increased. In the imperial ecumenical councils the collaboration of the laity was reduced essentially to that of the emperor and his commissioners, while that of the clerics was not limited only to the participation of bishops but included various elders and deacons as well. At the imperial councils under Charles the Great, and in the general councils of the Roman Church in the Middle Ages, the participation of princes and secular estates was on occasion a very large one. The assemblies of the World Council stand in an old synodical tradition in that here not only the leaders of the member churches meet together but *the laity* are *also* represented in great variety. Stated more precisely theologically, not only the church's ministerial officeholders but also the freely emerging charismata and servant ministries come here to engage in deliberation and the making of resolutions. This means a great richness in that here the spiritual experiences and impulses—not only from the most different of churches and countries but also from the most different areas of responsibility for evangelization, education, social work, political action, and so forth—come together for exchange, for clarification, and for the common mission of bearing witness to Christ before the world. So these assemblies are a representation of the fellowship of ministerial offices and freely emerging charismata by which Christ manifests himself to the world.

c) The ante-Nicene synods were, as a rule, convened and presided over by

---

4 This resolution referred to both the sending of Paul, Barnabas, et al. to Antioch and to the decree that they brought with them. One cannot draw the conclusion from this text that for the time being "the doctrinal issue was decided by the apostles and bishops" and then the congregation only participated in the election and sending of the messengers (so Thomas Sartory, "Das Konzil—eine innerkatholische Angelegenheit?" [The Council—an Inter-Catholic Matter?], *Ökumenische Rundschau* 9 [1960], 65). On the issue of the congregation's participation, see Ernst Haenchen, *Die Apostelgeschichte* (Göttingen: Vandenhoeck & Ruprecht, 1956), 389, 393 [footnote 1], 397. [ET: *The Acts of the Apostles: A Commentary*, trans. B. Noble et al. (Philadelphia: Westminster, 1971), 444, 451 (Footnote 1), 453 –Ed.].

5 Cf. Rudolf Sohm, *Kirchenrecht* [Canon Law], vol. 1 (Leipzig: Dunker & Humblot, 1892), 258 ff.

the bishop of the respective local church, in any case, not by a governmental authority. In this respect, the ecumenical synods of the ancient church were a *novum*, for thereafter the convening and directing of the synods, as well as the ratification of synodical resolutions, were done by the emperor or his commissioners. We know, for example, from the Council of Chalcedon in 451 to what extent the emperor intervened and compelled the council delegates, despite their well-founded aversion to formulate a new confession of faith. In contrast to this, the assemblies of the World Council of Churches meet, deliberate, and adopt resolutions independently of any kind of political power, and thus on this point they are closer to the pre-Nicene synods than to the imperial ecumenical synods since 325. To be added to this is the fact that in the World Council of Churches no given ministerial office is acknowledged to have a power by which the free course of the council's proceedings and resolutions would in any way be limited. The assemblies of the World Council are, on the contrary, *free synods*. They are free in the election of their presidents and the members of their committees, free in the selection of their topics, in the setting up of the agenda, and in carrying out the deliberations. The resolutions come about through the free consensus of the synod participants, wherein all votes have an equal weight.

d) If we compare *the topics* that have been dealt with in the councils of the ancient church with those in the assemblies of the World Council, a considerable expansion and transformation can be ascertained. In the ancient church the concern was to articulate the confession of Christ in view of the issues that arose in the Mediterranean region, when the gospel encountered Greek philosophy and oriental-Hellenistic Gnosis. Today the concern is to articulate the witness to Christ in view of the great multiplicity of religious and philosophical ideas, anthropological presuppositions, and forms of thinking that the church encounters in the various peoples and cultures throughout the whole world. The issues involved in delivering the message of Christ have increased enormously and create challenges for Christendom in new ways. There is still something else that must be considered: The ecumenical synods of the ancient church took place within the given and acknowledged political order of the Roman Empire, whereas today Christians from all of the various peoples, races, and nations on earth convene at ecumenical assemblies, and some of those nations are rejecting and threatening each other most sharply and, yes, some are even fighting. It is thus inescapable that the ecumenical assemblies today also consider what responsibility God's will of love places upon Christians in the midst of the social, racial, and political disorder of this world. However, even in view of the expansion of issues that obviously arose with the spread of Christianity, the basic topics then and now remain the same. As in the synods of the ancient church, so also today, the primary concern are questions of church doctrine (above all the message of Christ in the contemporary world) and church order (for example, the constitution of the World Council of Churches and the organization of its agencies). In addition there is also the task of filling ministerial offices—of course, not the election and consecration of bishops, as in the synodical proceedings of the early church, but rather the election of the presidents and the members of the various working bodies of the World Council.

e) What is *the norm* under which the synodical deliberations take place then and now? For both the ecumenical councils of the ancient church and the World Council of Churches the common principle is that the church must bear witness to Christ in new ways and unfold that witness anew in relation to changed historical fronts, but that it dare not and cannot teach anything new, things the church had not taught from the beginning. Consequently, the apostolic message applies to all participants as foundational and normative. Today the apostolic message is mediated to everyone through the tradition of his church, and these church traditions have, in the course of almost two thousand years of church history, naturally become much more varied than could have been the case in the year 325. As in the councils of the ancient church, so also today, all synod delegates are free to argue in the deliberations from the understanding of the apostolic foundation that has been set down in the tradition of their church. In doing this, the differences between the church traditions that are represented in the assemblies of the World Council lie open for all to see, as are the differences in determining the relationship between Scripture and tradition. In the course of the deliberations as a whole, those arguments from church traditions that are adopted are the ones that stem from Holy Scripture. In this way, Holy Scripture again and again proves its ecumenical force, not as if there were an agreement on a common scriptural principle, but because Holy Scripture itself is the prophetic and apostolic authority acknowledged by all the churches. The diversity of church traditions thus is actually shown to be valid in the multiplicity of scriptural interpretations.

f) One of the most difficult issues in the history of the councils is that of acknowledging the binding character of the conciliar decisions and thus at the same time that of acknowledging the binding character of the council itself for the whole church, in other words, the issue of *reception*. Hubert Jedin has pointed out that the process of reception, which has led the contemporary Roman Church to enumerate twenty ecumenical councils up to and including the First Vatican Council, has still not been clarified in a scholarly manner with respect to its details.[6] Beyond that, the issue of reception is one of the most difficult issues in general, in historical and systematic theology and in the study of church law. If one views the whole history of the councils, it is clear that the process of reception has undergone as many changes as the council, for the concept of reception is a correlate to that of conciliar authority. It is surely the case that with respect to the ecumenical councils of the ancient church the concept of the imperial-legal reception and the actual carrying out

6 Jedin, *Kleine Konzilsgeschichte*, 10 [*Ecumenical Councils*, 4 –Ed.].

of the reception by the church did not coincide, and that in practice the latter resulted in profound corrections to the imperial-legal decisions that the emperors made through the ratification and publication of the synodical resolutions. The resolutions of the council were legally valid for all churches in the empire on the basis of this imperial act. In practice, however, some of these resolutions were not established in the life of the church and had to be changed and replaced by subsequent council resolutions. Indeed, whole councils that had been convened as ecumenical, that had understood themselves to be ecumenical, and whose resolutions had been publicized as valid for the whole church, later had to be stricken from the lists of ecumenical councils and are today no longer valid in any church as such. This is in no way true only for the so-called "Robber Synod" of Ephesus in 449.[v] That councils can err is not a revolutionary proposition of the Reformation but already a fact in the history of councils of the ancient church. If at the time of the imperial ecumenical synods the reception of synodical resolutions by the church and thus also by the church's laity came to have such great significance, this was the heritage of the ante-Nicene understanding of the church and of the synods as the fellowship of the Holy Spirit. Because the local synod was certain of the assistance of the Holy Spirit when it made resolutions that affected the whole church, it knew itself to be dependent upon the consent of the other local churches on earth that are directed by exactly the same Holy Spirit. What would not correspond to this understanding of the synod as a fellowship of the Holy Spirit that encompasses all Christians, would be for some to designate an ecumenical synod as an infallible authority of the church merely because of its having been legally, incontestably convened, carried out, and concluded. This particular concern about reception has remained alive in the Eastern Church[7] up to today and has validity also in the Reformation churches. This understanding of reception in the ancient church is apparent when the resolutions of the assembly of the World Council require reception by its member churches and not only the consent of their synodical representatives alone.

   g) In what sense then are the assemblies of the World Council of Churches to be designated as *ecumenical?*

   They are not ecumenical if one would want to call such a gathering *ecumenical* only when the gathering actually consists of the representatives of all churches on earth. But this was also hardly the case with any of the councils of the ancient church. Of course they are virtually ecumenical insofar as all churches of the world that confess Jesus Christ as God and Savior have been

---

7 See Emilianos von Meloa, "Wesen und Möglichkeit eines ökumenischen Konzils seitens der orthodoxen Kirchen" [The Nature and Possibility of an Ecumenical Council on the Part of the Orthodox Churches], *Die ökumenischen Konzile der Christenheit* [The Ecumenical Councils of Christendom], ed. Hans Jochen Margull (Stuttgart: Evangelisches Verlagswerk, 1961), 285–312. [Cf. footnote 16 in chap. 8 ("Apostolic Succession") above. –Ed.]

invited to become a member of the World Council and there is no obligation connected with this invitation that would in addition require any of these churches to deny at any point its own traditions. Every church is invited to come and take part with "seat and vote" in the deliberations of the World Council, and to do so as it is. This invitation obviously holds true also for the Roman Church.

The assemblies of the World Council of Churches are, however, also ecumenical in the other sense, which was emphasized in the introduction, for they are concerned about the common witness to Christ by a divided Christendom and about the unification of the separated churches. This ecumenical aspect determines all of the topics of the common deliberations in their wider scope, be it about issues of faith or of order or about the social and political responsibility of Christendom in the contemporary world.

Finally, one can still point to the fact that because the concept of *ecumenical* is in many respects so similar to that of *catholic*, both terms are often used indiscriminately. It is insufficient to understand catholicity primarily quantitatively and geographically, as the Roman Church tends to do, whereby it distinguishes between the actual and virtual or between the factual and the legal universality of the church. Instead, the term is to be defined primarily Christologically and pneumatologically, as is done especially in the tradition of the Eastern Church, for *catholicity* designates at the same time the all-encompassing richness of the various spiritual gifts, ministerial offices, and estates through which the one all-encompassing *Kyrios* manifests himself in the church and through the church in the world. Also in this sense we may designate the assemblies of the World Council of Churches as *ecumenical*, for in them one encounters the richness of the manifold knowledge, testimonies, and servant ministries that developed in the various church traditions under God's historical guidance.

2. At the same time, however, entirely unavoidable are the profound differences that exist between the assemblies of the World Council of Churches and the ante-Nicene and post-Nicene synods of the ancient church. Indeed, one has to note that the assemblies of the World Council differ from almost all other synods in Christendom, that is, not only from those of the Roman Church but also from those of the Reformation churches. These differences reach deeply into the commonalities indicated above.

a) What takes place in the worshiping fellowship in the assemblies of the World Council cannot be underestimated. But they are not a *communio* of all who are assembled there in the Lord's Supper. When, for example, at the end of the Orthodox liturgy the non-Orthodox who are present also are offered consecrated bread as a beautiful sign of Christian love, that is still not the fellowship in the sacramental body and blood of Jesus Christ. But other churches also are not yet able to admit to the Lord's Supper Christians who do not belong to them, or do so only with certain limitations.

b) With this lack of altar fellowship it is already clear that the World Council of Churches is not a fellowship of churches in the New Testament sense, for the church as the body of Christ is built up through the common reception of the sacramental body of Christ. In the assemblies of the World Council separated churches pray together, deliberate, and pass resolutions, churches which in part do not mutually acknowledge each other as churches in the true sense of the word. This includes the fact that they in part also do not mutually acknowledge one another's ministerial offices. To be sure, we cannot underestimate the fellowship *in Christo* that is there and is constantly growing, but nevertheless the separations have not been overcome and this means that in each instance the participants and their common activity are called into question.

c) Since very different church traditions encounter each other in the assemblies and some of them even contain explicit anathemas against statements of the other traditions represented there, the common foundation is in some respects undefined and slim, despite Holy Scripture being shared by all. Of course the various traditions are being opened up more and more for one another in the ecumenical work, and the common reflection on the New Testament witness allows much of what separates the churches to appear in a new light. But still, the bondages have not been overcome and these—whether they are of a traditional nature or of a modern one—hinder the common hearing of the apostolic message. The pallor of many theological pronouncements of the World Council results from the large number of traditions that have still not yet been entirely opened up to one another, for they endeavor to express what *all* of the member churches there present can express in common, despite their still unresolved divisions.

d) Corresponding to this is the fact that the authority of the resolutions of the assemblies of the World Council of Churches is relatively weak. Every church is free either to accept the resolutions or not. Of course the authority of the ecumenical synods of the ancient church also demonstrated itself first in the process of their reception by the church. It was through this process that the synodical resolutions had to establish themselves. And yet their authority was greater than that of the World Council of Churches insofar as the synods of the ancient church were supported by a given, if also at times threatened, visible unity of the church, and for that reason from the beginning elicited a greater level of trust. The weakness of the World Council's authority, however, follows necessarily from the fact that the disunity of the churches assembled in it has not yet been overcome. Corresponding to this is the fact that the rejection of the resolutions of an ecumenical assembly by a member church in no way signifies the end of its membership in the World Council of Churches. Rather, the right of such rejection is explicitly secured by the constitution of the World Council. The authority of the World Council of Churches is thus not only weaker than that of the synods of the ancient church but also weaker than that of the council that Luther had called for and was ready to recognize, for he was prepared, for the sake of the unity of the church, to bow to the authority of a free council that was based upon Holy Scripture.[vi] Given this weak authority and the almost total lack of any legal securities for the establishing of their resolutions, the assemblies of the World Council of Churches depend solely on the working of the Holy Spirit, who convinces hearts, opens them up to one another, and binds them anew in Christ—that is, not only the hearts of the individual Christians but also the separated churches themselves.

3. In looking back on the preceding analysis we need to note the following:

In the assemblies of the World Council of Churches there reappear, on the one hand, essential impulses from the synods of the ancient church, whereby of course not only the imperial synods of the ancient church are taken into account but also the structure of the ante-Nicene synod. On the other hand, however, the differences are so profound that the assemblies of the World Council of Churches cannot be designated as a continuation of the councils of the ancient church. To be sure, nothing prohibits them from being called councils. This has also occasionally happened.[8] Moreover, one can designate them as ecumenical councils for good reasons. But whenever this happens, they must be clearly and definitely distinguished from the ecumenical councils of the ancient church. They are not councils in this historical sense. This misunderstanding was rightly and explicitly rejected already in 1916 during the preparatory negotiations for the first World Conference on Faith and Order.[9] Also later, at no point in the documents of the World Council of Churches does there arise any equating of its assemblies with the ecumenical councils of the ancient church.

One might, however, now ask whether they ought not to be considered as continuations of union councils, such as occurred at Lyons in 1274 and in Ferrara-Florence in 1438–39.[vii] At that time, too, representatives of separated churches deliberated and made decisions together. But at that time it was a matter of only two separated churches, the Roman and the Eastern, and their respective dogmatic presuppositions and those concerning canon law were not nearly as different as are the many church bodies and their confessions

---

8 Thus, e. g., Werner Elert at the first plenary session of the World Conference on Faith and Order at Lausanne in 1927: "For this reason, we wish for this council that it will find the unity of Christians in the truth and that it will speak the truth through clear decisions, without compromising with falsehood." "…Therefore, our second wish for this council is that the great unity for which it strives will not destroy the unities that already exist, but as a mother will receive her mature and independent children into her house" (Werner Elert, "Address at the First Plenary Session," reprinted in *Die Weltkonferenz für Glauben und Kirchenverfassung zu Lausanne*, ed. Hermann Sasse [Berlin: Im-Furche-Verlag, 1929], 102, 103–4.). [Elert emphasized these sentences through the use of italics. –Ed.]

9 Cf. the "Plan for the World Conference": "There is one thing we have in mind that essentially distinguishes the conference from all ecumenical assemblies of the past… It possesses no legislative power… This conference distinguishes itself still in other respects from the councils of the past, but this is an especially noteworthy difference." "The task… is not to imitate one of the councils of the undivided church" ("Plan for the World Conference," as quoted by Sasse, *Die Weltkonferenz für Glauben und Kirchenverfassung*, 33 [Footnote 71]).

represented in the World Council or even as different as the Eastern Church and the Roman Church are today. This would, of course, be only a quantitative difference between those historical union councils and many ecumenical assemblies today. Beyond that, however, one needs to ask basically whether these assemblies may be at all designated as union councils in the full sense. Even though these assemblies are concerned with the unity of the church, nevertheless, according to its constitution, the World Council itself still does not have the task of leading negotiations for union. This is left rather to the free initiative of the individual member churches. For this reason, its assemblies are in many respects to be distinguished from the historical union councils.

The assemblies of the World Council of Churches are thus a *novum* in the history of the church. In what does their newness consist? The synods of the ancient church proceeded from the presupposition of the unity of the church, and they sought to defend and strengthen this unity against threats in matters of doctrine and church order. The assemblies of the World Council, however, presuppose a divided Christendom. To be sure, they also proceed from a unity, namely, from the acknowledgement of the one Christ as God and Savior. But this being-one in Christ is still hidden under the disunity of the churches. The assemblies seek the unity in which this being-one comes to be visibly presented and expressed in full church fellowship. So they are a wager of faith, of love, and of hope—of the faith that Christ demonstrates himself as powerful beyond the borders of one's own church body; of the love that seeks and finds the brothers and sisters beyond these borders; and of the hope that the fire of the Holy Spirit will consume the borders that still now divide us from them. In this way the assemblies of the World Council do not claim to have already anticipated and manifested the hoped-for unity. They do not understand themselves to be the executive organ of a super-church.[10] They want only to serve and help the growing unity that God is bringing about through his Holy Spirit, when and how it pleases him.[viii]

II.

It is self-evident that the assemblies of the World Council of Churches do not replace the synods of the individual churches or even devalue them. These assemblies do not want to do that and they also cannot do that. The same was true already of the ecumenical synods of the ancient church. Alongside them additional provincial and metropolitan synods occurred, as well as other particular synods, and the Council of Nicaea had explicitly arranged in its canons for further regularized meetings of particular synods. That ecumenical

---

10 Visser't Hooft, "Überkirche und ökumenische Bewegung," *Ökumenische Rundschau* 7 (1958), 157 ff. [ET: "The Super-Church and the Ecumenical Movement," *The Ecumenical Review* 10, no. 4 (1958), 365–85].

synods do not replace the particular synods, however, was even more rightly the case of the assemblies of the World Council of Churches, for in them after all (in contrast to the synods of the ancient church) the more or less separated church bodies assemble, over which the World Council has no jurisdictional power. In this respect the relationship between its world conferences and the particular synods today is directly reversed from what it was in the ancient church. Every particular synod today has greater power to obtain authority for its decisions than the assemblies of the World Council of Churches.

We cannot here treat the multiplicity of forms of the various particular synods in Christendom, their ecclesiological significance, nor the scope of their jurisdiction. I will restrict myself to highlighting a distinction that recurs in every church body, namely, the distinction between the synods of a definite region—defined by geographical, national or linguistic boundaries—and the general councils of the church body as a whole. With the term *general council* [*Generalkonzil*] I take up a word that Western Christendom, after its separation from the Eastern Church, had used to designate its councils in the Middle Ages, which then in the further course of the history of the councils were received in part by Rome as ecumenical councils and were as such numbered in the sequence of the ecumenical councils of the ancient church. Designated as a general council is here the assembly of all churches that adhere to one and the same confession on earth. In this sense general councils would be, for example, the assemblies of the Lutheran World Federation, the hoped-for pan-Orthodox council of the Eastern churches, the Lambeth Conference, the General Assembly of the Alliance of the Reformed Churches, and so on.

Among these general councils those of the Roman Church have a special place insofar as a greater part of Christendom belongs to it than to approximately all of the other churches combined, and then also, above all, because the Roman Church is the only one that designates its individual general councils as ecumenical councils (it numbers the second Vatican Council as the twenty-first ecumenical council). By contrast, since the Great Schism of 1054 the Orthodox Church has refrained from enumerating further ecumenical councils, although it has convened additional synods, and a considerable number of Orthodox theologians fundamentally hold the opinion that as long as the division of Christendom continues the Orthodox Church cannot convene any ecumenical councils but only pan-Orthodox ones.[11] The general synods of the Reformation churches also do not understand themselves to be a continuation of the ecumenical councils of the ancient church, even if in each case here the representatives of the same confession come together from all parts of the world and in addition representatives from other church bodies participate as guests and convey

---

11 Cf. the very illuminating discussion of this matter by the Congress of Orthodox Theologians, which met in Athens in 1936 (*Procès-verbaux du premier congrès de théologie orthodoxe*, ed. Amilkas S. Alivizatos [Athens: Pyrsos, 1939], 256–300).

greetings in order to foster the unity of faith and love. If occasionally, for example, the assembly of the Lutheran World Federation is designated an ecumenical synod by some individuals, this is an erroneous use of the term since only *one* confessional group is truly represented here with "seat and vote."

We now have to ask in what sense the general councils of the Roman Church are to be designated as ecumenical councils.

1. Here, too, for the time being, we will highlight the most important impulses that they have in common with councils of the ancient church.

a) Much of what was established in the above analysis of the assemblies of the World Council would now have to be repeated here. This holds true, for example, regarding the significance of the worship context in which the conciliar deliberations are embedded (also for the Roman Church), the prayer for the coming of the Holy Spirit, the certainty of the Spirit's help, the basic openness for newly identified issues in Christendom at each given time, the desire to say nothing new but only to unfold the basic apostolic principles within new situations. Since these impulses have already been addressed in the previous section, they do not need to be elucidated again here.

b) At the same time it is clear that the councils of the Roman Church, precisely in view of those points that we had determined to be a weakness of the World Council of Churches, are incomparably more consistent and robust and also closer to the synods of the ancient church. Here in the Roman Church the fullness of fellowship in worship—something toward which the World Council of Churches is still striving—is a self-evident presupposition. Here, in the Roman Church, the sacramental *communio* and *concelebratio* are not a problem but a reality.[ix] No member of these synods is excluded from it. Since the worshiping assembly is the heart of the church's activity and also of what the church is as a concept, this unity in worship, as it is realized in the council of the Roman Church and also, in this respect, in the other general councils of Christendom, comes to have a very crucial importance.

c) Accordingly, the plural word *churches*, as it is used within the Roman councils, means something different from what it means in the assemblies of the World Council of Churches. Also, the Roman councils understand themselves to be an assembly of churches, but these are churches that mutually acknowledge themselves to be churches in an unrestricted, completely dogmatic sense, in that they all acknowledge the bishop of Rome as their common head, to whom they are subject to, both dogmatically and in terms of canon law. These are not separated churches that stand more or less closer to each other, as is the case in the World Council of Churches.

d) Since all of the participants in a Roman council proceed on the basis of the same presuppositions regarding canon law and the same dogmatic presuppositions that have been stipulated as binding in a very far-reaching way, from the outset a greater level of definitiveness and clarity is possible in those conciliar decisions than is the case in the World Council of Churches.

Their joint statements do not have to be sought after and formulated within as large of an expanse as is presented by the differing traditions represented today in the World Council of Churches.

e) The jurisdictional power of the Roman council and the authority of its decisions for the churches represented here are incomparably greater than that of the assemblies of the World Council for the churches represented in it. This is true even though the authority of a Roman general council today is less than that of the pope.

2. If we compare the councils of the Roman Church to the ecumenical synods of the ancient church, here too, of course, profound differences cannot be overlooked. These differences did not arise initially from the declaration about the pope's infallibility at the First Vatican Council, but since then they have become especially clear and totally unavoidable.

a) The differences are already evident within what has just been highlighted as an agreement. The problem does not yet begin with the enormous expansion of conciliar topics, which for the Roman councils as well as for the general councils of all of the other churches and for the synods of the World Council of Churches resulted from the spread of Christianity around the world, for this expansion in topics was essentially and necessarily a consequence of the growth of the church. The pressure, however, for a comprehensive and advancing perfection in establishing firm formulations of dogma and canon law, to the point of casuistry, is characteristic of the Roman way of thinking, which remained foreign to the Eastern Church and the Reformation churches, even though they too spread all over the world. To be sure, the ecumenical councils of the ancient church also presupposed a greater uniformity in dogma and canon law among the churches represented in those councils than the assemblies of the World Council of Churches. But a Roman council is different from the synods of the ancient church in that it deems— not only quantitatively but also as a general principle—a matchless uniformity in liturgy, doctrine, and the ordering of the church (a uniformity that is further detailed in canon law) as necessary for church unity than was the case in the ancient church, but it is also different today from what is the case in some other churches.

b) Also, the independence that the Roman councils gained in relation to the convening, conducting, and ratifying authority of the emperor was not only a natural consequence of the growth of the church beyond the borders of the Roman Empire; rather, it happened in a basic decision against the determination of the relationship between church and emperor that the ecumenical councils of the ancient church held to be self-evident and that remained self-evident in the Eastern Church even after the beginning of the Great Schism. One will come to understand this gaining of independence not as a return to the independence from governmental authority that the ante-Nicene synods had; but it happened rather in the course of long, difficult struggles in which the popes denied the emperors not only their Constantinian function in relation to the church but also their possession of a secular power that had been conferred upon them directly by God, something the popes themselves claimed to confer. Neither the Great Schism between East and West nor the division that occurred in the sixteenth century is understandable historically if one overlooks this claim of the popes to possess secular power.

c) A further point is related to the above. To be sure, in the ecumenical councils of the ancient church the Christian emperor had a quasi-episcopal function—the Byzantine emperors even had certain rights in the Holy of Holies[x]—but at the same time the emperors were actually functioning among only clergy as the remnant of the universal priesthood of all the church's laity, whose vote was a part of the decision-making, as once in Jerusalem at the so-called Apostolic Council and then also in the ante-Nicene synods. In the course of the history of Roman councils a profound change took place in the composition of synods. While large numbers of laity were still involved in many medieval councils, since then a complete clericalization of the Roman councils has occurred. At the present time, those who participate with "seat and vote" are only bishops or, more precisely, only cardinals, patriarchs, primates, archbishops, bishops, certain abbots and other representatives of the high clergy.[12] The church's laity are completely excluded. Their voice can be expressed only indirectly, namely, through the mouth of their bishops. This is a very important difference not only in contrast with the synods of the Reformation churches and some of the synods of the Eastern Church but also in contrast with the ancient church. So, too, the direct involvement of the lower clergy is also excluded from the decision making.   ·

d) The most profound difference between a Roman council today and the ecumenical councils of the ancient church, however, consists in the changed status of the pope. The presence and participation of the Roman bishop or his legates were not constitutive for the idea and validity of a council in the ancient church. It is thus well known that the Second Ecumenical Council of Constantinople in 381—which ended the Arian controversy and adopted the very important additions to the wording of the Nicene Creed, whose validity extends throughout Christendom today—took place without the presence or representation of the Roman bishop. Only the Eastern churches were represented. Moreover, the validity of the conciliar resolutions of the ecumenical councils of the ancient church—both for the empire and for the church as a whole—did not depend on the Roman bishop's ratification. Well-known, too, is the fact that his objection to Canon 28 of the Fourth Ecumenical Council of Chalcedon—which, to be sure, positioned the see of Constantinople behind that of Rome yet also granted it the same prerogatives as the see of Rome in relation to the other patriarchs—did not result in the repeal of this conciliar decision but only that this canon would be regarded as invalid for that part of Western Christendom subject to the Roman see.[xi] In the following

---

12 Canon 223, *Codex Iuris Canonici*, issued and promulgated by Pope Pius X (Rome: Vatican, 1917).

period the relationship between the Roman bishop and the council changed quite dramatically. This is then most clearly evident in the changed ecclesiological status of the Roman bishop that emerged in the declaration from the First Vatican Council regarding papal infallibility, wherein the definitions stated by the pope *ex cathedra* are "*ex sese, non autem ex consensus ecclesiae*" [of themselves, and not by the consent of the church] infallible and irreformable.[13] Corresponding to this is Canon 218 of the *Codex Juris Canonici:* The Roman Pontiff "has not only a primacy of honor but the full and supreme power of jurisdiction over the whole church, both in matters of faith and morals and in those things that affect the discipline and government of the church spread throughout the whole world."[xii] Consequently, the council has become *fundamentally* superfluous and, when it is convened, completely dependent on the pope's readiness (to a greater or lesser degree) to pay heed to the voices of the gathered bishops, just as the church's laity are completely dependent on the readiness of the bishops (to a greater or lesser degree) to voice their concerns at the council. Since ultimately only the pope decides to convene a council, to select its topics, to constitute its preparatory commissions, to determine its agenda, and in this respect also to determine its resolutions—since only with his approval do the resolutions of the gathered bishops become resolutions of the council—it cannot be a surprise that today a council of the Roman Church is widely held to be only a representative advisory body of the pope, and that there is a growing concern that it is now primarily the representative framework for supplying the clarification of the will of the pope and the presentation of his power.

e) The process in the ancient church of receiving conciliar resolutions by the church has become null and void through the declaration of the pope's infallibility. There remains only the possibility of submission or excommunication. The validity of the councils and their resolutions is now no longer dependent on the process of their being established in the churches or of their being rejected by the church's laity, but only of their confirmation and proclamation by the pope.

3. Once one acknowledges the similarities between the councils of the ancient church and those of the contemporary Roman Church one will thus have to recognize that also the latter represent a *novum* over against the councils of the ancient church. One cannot lose sight of the key fact that since the beginning of the Great Schism between East and West the Roman councils have undergone a process of gradual transformation for nearly 1000 years to become what they are today—nor can one lose sight of the fact that some have repeatedly tried to maintain a strict identity between the councils of the ancient church and those of the modern Roman Church by making use of the development of ideas from the philosophy of German Idealism. This idealistic claim of "identity" is contradicted already by the considerable conciliar zig-

13　Denzinger 3074 [Tanner 2.816. –Ed.].

zagging in the medieval development, but it is completely contradicted by the very different historical facts of what actually took place in the councils of the ancient church. That the councils of the Roman Church today represent a *novum* is irrefutably clear if one keeps in mind the definitions of an ecumenical council that are typically used in the Roman Church today. Whether defined by Forget as "the solemn assembly of the bishops from around the world, convened by the pope and subject to his authority and guidance, for the purpose of discussing together the affairs of the church and setting down laws"[14] or by Archbishop Dr. Lorenz Jaeger as "the solemn assembly of Catholic bishops from around the world who are convened by the authority of the pope and who, under the presidency of the pope, deliberate and make decisions concerning the affairs of the whole of Christendom"[15]—it is evident that according to these definitions the ecumenical councils of the ancient church were not ecumenical councils.

Of course the councils of the Roman Church are a *novum* in the history of the council in a very different sense, indeed actually in the opposite sense, compared to the assemblies of the World Council of Churches. While the latter proceed from the situation of a divided Christendom, the Roman councils, by disregarding all the Christians who are not subject to the pope, proceed then from the internal, visible unity of the Roman Church. If the councils of the World Council are seeking to encompass the whole of Christendom and, presupposing all who share the name of Christ, in order to advance toward common statements in matters of faith and church order and, beyond that, to work together and to strive for visible unity, the course of the Roman councils, by contrast, is determined by the desire to safeguard and consolidate the Roman Church's own existing visible unity more and more dogmatically and through canon law, over against all movements and powers that could weaken this unity. If the danger of the World Council of Churches is that its member churches are satisfied with the bustle of a parliamentary-level cooperation rather than reaching visible unity, the danger of the Roman Church is that, instead of recognizing the catholic fullness of the Christ who is at work in the world, it would seal itself off in a centralized solipsism.

We now ask in what sense the second Vatican council can be designated as *ecumenical.*

If one wanted to understand an ecumenical council as the assembly of the representatives of all churches on earth, then the second Vatican council would be just as little an ecumenical council as the assembly of churches in New Delhi, for not only are some of the invited bishops of the Roman Church

---

14 Jacques Forget, as quoted in Jedin, *Kleine Konzilsgeschichte,* 14 [*Ecumenical Councils,* 12. –Ed.].

15 Lorenz Jaeger, *Das ökumenische Konzil, die Kirche und die Christenheit: Erbe und Auftrag,* Konfessionskundliche Schriften des Johann-Adam-Möhler-Institus Nr. 4 (1960), 87 [*The Ecumenical Council, the Church and Christendom* (New York: P. J. Kenedy & Sons, 1961), 79 (trans. altered –Ed.)].

hindered from attending, as has been the case at all previous Roman councils, but especially because all non-Roman churches will be absent. Nevertheless, one could also here speak of a virtual ecumenicity of this council. The word *virtual*, however, then comes to mean something different from what it means at the assemblies of the World Council of Churches, for when other churches had been invited to the First Vatican Council this invitation also contained the demand to submit to the pope and to accept all of the dogmatic decisions of the Roman Church. This submission was considered the condition for the right to vote as a participating delegate in the council. For this reason, it is well known that none of the non-Roman churches that had been invited accepted this invitation. In contrast to the World Council, the Roman Church prompted no other church to attend than those that were already Roman and, being the Church that it is, to deliberate and make decisions jointly with the Roman Church.

Now one could designate the second Vatican council as *ecumenical* under the second meaning of the term, which we set forth in the introduction, namely, in the sense of the aspirations for the unification of the church in the modern age. To be sure, no joint deliberations or decisions between the Roman Church and the non-Roman churches are planned for this council (in contrast to those of the World Council), but nevertheless this council, according to the will of the pope, should serve the inner deliberations and orientation of the Roman Church toward the unification of Christendom. In this sense the other churches certainly cannot and will not dispute the ecumenism of the announced second Vatican council. In this connection, however, one cannot overlook the fact that, according to the self-understanding of the Roman Church, its councils do not become ecumenical councils only when they are specifically aimed at reunion. Rather, according to this self-understanding, they are ecumenical *eo ipso* [for this very reason], completely independent of whether or not they explicitly address the topic of reunion; for the Roman Church designates its general councils as ecumenical because it fundamentally acknowledges no other church as *church*, in the true and full sense of this word. In an exclusive way it maintains that it is the one, holy, catholic, apostolic church on earth. It is self-evident that no other church can acknowledge the general councils of the Roman Church as ecumenical in this sense.

Finally, if one still considers that ecumenicity consists in the catholic abundance of spiritual gifts, ministerial offices, and servant ministries through which the Lord manifests himself in Christendom, to limit to bishops the right to be voting representatives of the churches in the Roman councils amounts to a considerable restriction, as do the set statements of progressively unfolding dogma and canon law in the Roman Church—more than in any other church—so as to leave relatively little room for the freely emerging, spiritually gifted witness and servant ministry. Given this perspective many will be inclined to recognize at the assemblies of the World Council an incomparably greater level of catholicity and ecumenicity.

III.

If one designates the upcoming church assemblies at New Delhi and the Vatican as ecumenical councils, then the concept of *the ecumenical council* signifies something very different in each setting, indeed, something essentially contradictory.

Now the question arises: Within the history of church councils, which is more of a *novum* than the other, the assembly of the World Council of Churches or the council of the Roman Church? This question cannot easily be answered because the divergences of each over against the councils of the ancient church lie in entirely different domains. In some respects the Roman idea of the council is undoubtedly much closer to that of the ancient church. In other respects, however, elementary structures of conciliar interaction and activity that have been lost in the Roman Church occur again in the World Council of Churches, and this point is so significant that there is no fundamental obstacle to hinder one from also designating the assemblies of the World Council as ecumenical councils, even if they are as such a new and special kind of this. Moreover, however, to compare these two ecumenical synods of our time with those of the ancient church is not ultimately decisive. As significant as it also is—in order to identify more accurately the distinctive character of what occurs in contemporary councils—yet the Council of Nicaea still cannot in every respect supply the norm by which subsequent councils are to be evaluated dogmatically and in terms of canon law, for the ecumenical councils of the ancient church were the constitutional form of conciliar activity in the Roman Empire, shaped by the theological, philosophical, and political issues of that environment. However, given that for both the Roman Church and the World Council of Churches the council is in fact fundamentally set free from a civic authority that convenes and leads it, and given that it is oriented toward issues far removed from those that confronted the ancient church, both have acknowledged the fact that the ecumenical councils of the ancient church are, in the strict sense, unrepeatable, even though the church is one and the same at all times. Therefore, to designate a council as a *novum* need not entail a criticism; rather, such a designation takes seriously the historical character of the church.

If it is already difficult to make a judgment about which of the two ecumenical synods in our day is to a greater degree a *novum* in the history of the church, it is entirely impossible to make a judgment about which of them is stronger and which is weaker. Also these terms can be applied in very different domains. In the context of spiritual events worldly weakness can truly be a strength and worldly strength can truly be a weakness. Here we only need to be reminded of Paul's word: "If I am weak, then I am strong" (2 Cor. 12.10). So, for example, the obvious strength of the Roman council could prove to be a weakness, inasmuch as its tenacious hardening and securing of dogma and canon law, as these have developed historically, could make it more difficult for it to recognize and follow the concrete divine instruction that is issued to Christendom in the changed situation of the world in our time. Conversely, the dogmatic and jurisdictional weakness of the World Council of Churches could prove to be a strength, inasmuch as in this weakness, from the outset, it is dependent on reaching out in radical openness to what the Holy Spirit is today saying to the congregations and to what he is wanting to do in his power through them. It *could* be so! But who would dare to claim that it *is* so? Reserving judgment on this point is all the more necessary, given that the legal order and the actual spiritual life of the church hardly ever coincide completely. It could also be entirely different, namely, that in a legally centralized and legally constituted church the spirit of fellowship is actually alive, but that in a federated-synodical organization one parliamentary group of churches suppresses the others—just as it could also be that a church that designates Scripture *and* tradition as the source of its life could actually be holding to the truth of Scripture more strongly than a church that emphasizes the scriptural principle in an exclusive way yet in its doctrine has actually been affected by ideological currents of the time. Here one can only say: "Whoever thinks he is standing ought to watch out that he does not fall" (1 Cor. 10.12). The unveiling of the church's strength and weakness is ultimately an eschatological event. God will execute this in his courtroom. This judgment cannot and must not be preempted by anyone.

But how are both of these very different ecumenical councils, that of the World Council of Churches and that of the Roman Church, to be related to each other in view of the unity of Christendom?

The answer to this question could be given most easily if we would now apply to both councils a concept of ecumenicity that has still not yet been mentioned in our exposition but that is suggested by the development of synods in the early church. This concept of the council would not be determined by the idea of actually or virtually *representing* the whole of Christendom on earth. That idea of representation, which has widely established itself in the understanding of a council in both the Roman Church and the World Council of Churches under the influence of ideas from natural law, actually develops, after all, only relatively late in ecclesiology and is an alien intrusion into the original understanding of the unity of the church and of the synods.[16] Instead, here one should proceed from the hard evidence in the New Testament, that the same word *ecclesia* refers to the local congregation as well as to the whole church on earth, as well as also to the fellowship of local congregations in a geographical region. Consequently, the whole church is not to be understood as the sum total of all local congregations but as present in

---

16 Wilhelm Maurer, "Typen und Formen aus der Geschichte der Synode" [Types and Forms from the History of the Synods], in *Schriften des Theologischen Konvents Augsburgischen Bekenntnisses* 9 (1955), 78–99.

each local congregation. After all, Paul also referred to both the whole church and the local congregation as the body of Christ. This use of the concept of church is therefore possible because the whole Christ is present in every local worshiping assembly, and the gathered are built up as his body through the sacramental gift of his body. The understanding of synods that corresponds to this understanding of the church originates from the presence of the Lord in every worshiping assembly and thus also in each particular synod, not from the view that synods are representatives of congregations. In the context of this early church conception of the unity of the church a particular synod can also be described as ecumenical since in it the whole Christ, the Lord of all the churches on earth, is presently acting through his Spirit. Not the attendance of representatives of all churches would here be constitutive for the ecumenicity of a council, but the actual attendance of the Lord and the aid of his Spirit. This ecumenicity would then have to demonstrate itself in the "Yes!" that the other churches—in whom the same Lord is also at work through his Spirit—speaks to the resolutions of such a synod, to the extent that they are of significance for the whole church. With this understanding of a council it would be possible and entirely legitimate ecclesiologically to designate as *ecumenical synods* two synods that are meeting in different places at the same time and that are composed of representatives from differing churches. Their ecumenicity would then be grounded in the ecumenical Christ, the Lord, to whom the whole world is subject, and it would demonstrate itself through the present working of the Holy Spirit in the mutual acknowledgment of their resolutions.

Can this understanding, however, be applied to the relationship between a Roman council and an assembly of the World Council of Churches? Obviously not at the present time, for the councils of the Roman Church do not understand themselves as particular synods but as representing the whole church on earth. Nevertheless, one cannot exclude the possibility that a convergence could actually arise in the direction of a mutual "Yes!" of the one assembly to the resolutions of the other and thus change the manner in which divided Christendom has presented itself to the world until now.

We now ask what significance these two councils—despite their dissimilarity—could have for the unity of Christendom by means of the synodical work they accomplish. To what extent could they move toward each other for the sake of a future unity of Christendom and thereby help to mitigate the offense that their being side-by-side presents to the eyes of the world?

1. When we consider both of their church structures there emerges the deepest contrast between the centrality of the pope in the Roman Church and, in many respects, the non-binding conciliar cooperation of the World Council of Churches. Both conceptions are far removed from the earliest-Christian and ancient-Christian structure of fellowship. Both would have to move from their present opposing starting points toward the structure of *koinonia*. For the Roman Church this would mean the necessity of a de-centralizing development toward the fullness of the church; for the churches of the World Council

this would mean the injunction not to remain content with the current loose form of cooperation among the separated churches but to move forward on the way to unity in the multiplicity that has historically developed. In the Roman Church it is a matter of moving from a centralized uniformity toward fellowship in unity, whereas in the World Council it is a matter of moving from a loosely bound togetherness toward unity in fellowship.

a) Usually one thinks here primarily about the ordering of the church's ministerial offices in relation to each other and about the responsibility of the laity in the church. For the Roman Church—after the First Vatican Council had only defined the position of the papacy in a very one-sided way—this would mean above all that it would have to determine anew, to unfold, and to mutually coordinate the mission of the bishops in their relationship to the pope and the mission of the universal priesthood of all believers (that is, the function of the "lay-apostolate") within the totality of the church as the fellowship of manifold spiritual gifts. In turn, the World Council would have to move forward from the incomplete and loose cooperation of the church's ministerial offices of the different member churches to the mutual acknowledgment and coordination of the same, whereby the relationship of ministerial offices to the mission of the laity would likewise also have to be determined more precisely, which task, by comparison, in the Roman Church is already much better known and consequential in its far-reaching effects.

b) If the Roman Church would emphasize the supervisory pastoral office more strongly as the fellowship of bishops, then this would not be without consequence for understanding the unity of the church. Such unity would be seen less in a centralized uniformity determined by Rome than in the fellowship of churches, and it would thereby make space for the multiplicity of languages and forms in which the one worship service is celebrated by the congregation gathered in the name of Jesus. There would then open up free space for meeting the manifold pastoral-care and liturgical needs that within the Roman Church have been seeking to be met for a long time but which have been hampered by a centralized uniformity. Conversely, in the context of the manifold differences that exist in their worship life, the churches of the World Council have the task of setting forth clearly what in each case is indispensably necessary for the implementation of a Christian worship service.

c) If we take seriously the *koinonia*-structure of the church, then this too would not be without consequence for understanding the unity of dogmatic statements. Today most churches understand "dogmatic unity" to mean the acknowledgment of one and the same dogmatic formula by all church members, and thus the uniformity of binding dogmatic propositions. But this was certainly not the understanding in the first centuries. For example, from this time we know of a great multiplicity of baptismal confessions, which were used in various geographical regions of the church, whose differences in part allow us to make inferences about the concrete historical situation in which they emerged. Yet their dissimilarity, as such, did not call into question the unity of faith and doctrine. On the contrary, everything depended on the content of the various formulas in the confessions. The unity of faith, of doctrine, and of the church did not depend on having the same formula, but rather such unity manifested itself through the mutual acknowledgment of the various confessional formulas by the various churches. The desire for uniformity in confessional statements only gradually gained acceptance after the first imperial-ecclesial synod at Nicaea, although in the Eastern Church until now it restricted itself to the basic Christological and Trinitarian statements. The structure of dogmatic unity as a fellowship of dogmatic statements—that is, a fellowship of mutually acknowledging the identity of what is being confessed in the various statements—will today have to be taken seriously in view of the global spreading of the Christian faith, for the same confession of Christ needs to be made today, after all, in geographical, cultural and religious domains and various historical fronts that are far more different from those in the ancient Mediterranean world. For example, is it necessary for natives of India to learn Aristotelian philosophy first in order to understand Christian dogma, and will they, if they take this route, then be in a position to make their confession of Christ so that it will be understood in the historical situation of their life-world? Reclaiming the *koinonia*-structure of dogmatic unity is of the greatest importance, both for the mission of the church and for the unification of a divided Christendom. The Roman Church needs to make greater use of its own basic principle, namely, that not the form but the content—so also not the temporally conditioned philosophical terminology but the truth of the dogma—is obligatory, and it will need to do so more than is generally being done. In turn, the World Council of Churches will have to make relevant in an updated way the fact that its member churches are able to say together incomparably more than what it has succeeded in expressing in its Basis and in its previous messages and declarations.

2. If one would, however, restrict oneself to the perspective of the *koinonia*-structure of the church, then the way that the Roman Church and the World Council of Churches need to take in opposing directions in order to arrive at an encounter with each other would still be seen as too pragmatic, and as a result—even if nothing else would be taken into account—church fellowship in the sense it had in earliest Christianity and the ancient church would hardly take place; instead, the danger of an amorphous puree of churches would probably arise, which none of the participants can want. Only then will a movement of the separated churches toward each other not undermine the way of fellowship in Christ, provided that movement does not restrict itself to a morphological trade-off and that both sides jointly pledge themselves to be normed by the apostolic message. The apostles, after all, as the called eyewitnesses of Jesus Christ's resurrection, are the foundation of the church at all times and in all places. A legitimate approaching of the separated churches to one another can only begin to occur when, on both sides, one resolves to

refer back to this apostolic foundation and on this basis mutually seek to understand one another anew.

a) This means clearly elaborating the diversity of Christological and pneumatological statements in the New Testament, as well as the diversity regarding the formulas for confessing, organizing congregations, and the ordering of ministerial offices, and to inquire about what these differences mean for the unity of the church. Moreover, one must take into consideration that not only the personal character of the authors is reflected in these differences but also the different traditions from the local congregations of those authors and also the traditions from different regions of the church. These differences within earliest Christendom were apparently not perceived to be destructive of the unity of the church, and the ancient church explicitly confirmed this when it incorporated these writings into the New Testament canon. If one investigates these different witnesses by means of historical criticism, the abundance of starting points and possibilities for an unfolding of dogma and church order into set forms becomes evident; that is, there are apparently more possibilities than were realized in the transition of the message of Christ that soon occurred into Hellenistic areas, and in the transition of that message that occurred into an increasingly legal unification of imperial law, and later in the transition of that message into the particular history of dogma and church law of the individual church bodies. The understanding of church unity has to be obtained anew from this earliest-Christian multiplicity of statements and church ordering, in that not only these statements and church orderings as such but also the starting points contained in them and the possibilities opened up in them as normative basis of the church of all times and places are to be elaborated and made aware of in clear historical distinction from the later realization of them.

b) The reality of the separated church traditions needs to be interpreted as far as possible from this foundational abundance of possibilities, for however the relationship between Scripture and tradition is determined by the individual churches, in every case Holy Scripture is the form of the historical-apostolic tradition held in common by the separated churches, and furthermore, all churches at least agree that their statements cannot contradict this foundation that has been handed down in Scripture. Endeavoring to interpret the traditions of the separated churches on the basis of the earliest-Christian abundance of possibilities will have its limitations. Some traditions are to be understood only as a very one-sided realization, some only as a one-sided corrective of another one-sided realization, and still others as a complete distortion. But some traditions, which we had previously held as distortions, will now become evident as the development of a tradition that was not previously seen by us and that was not a possibility from that earliest-Christian abundance realized in our own tradition. Some traditions that had been considered as errant developments in church history will now be recognizable as the realization of overlooked possibilities or as a new breakthrough of repressed possibilities.

c) Theological knowledge thus penetrates through the walls that separate the churches to something that is a reality in the other churches, a reality we lack, but also to that which is to be our service to the other churches. Through the separations emerges the knowledge of an original commonality that reaches far deeper than the divisions and that directs the separated churches to one another again and again so that even in their being separated they cannot get away from each other—for no church lives only by returning to the historical-apostolic well-spring and drawing from it but also by engaging that which is realized in the other churches from this same source and which it now encounters there—be it only in the form of a corrective or even of a distortion.

3. But even this endeavor to gain theological knowledge as such, even if it produces positive results, would still not lead to a unification of the churches. Again and again one makes the observation in ecumenical dialogues: One can be completely agreed biblically and exegetically, over and above the borders of the church, but this still does mean a consensus in dogma. We can also, moreover, be in complete agreement about understanding the historical genesis of given dogmatic statements and about discovering that they were only a one-sided unfolding of biblical statements that were thoroughly conditioned by given historical situations—and yet this does not entail the canceling of the anathemas that are bound to these dogmatic statements. One can also have jointly recognized which dogmatic statements unfold the abiding center of the apostolic confession of Christ and those which contain time-bound, peripheral statements that emerged in conflicts long past—and yet these statements, too, which have lost all relevance, persist as walls that separate the churches. Undoubtedly, the endeavor to gain knowledge through theological research, which we have outlined in the previous section, is insufficient when it comes to drawing the churches closer together and to the unification of the church. Rather, the churches must open themselves up to one another. But here we encounter limitations that are extremely difficult to overcome.

a) Every individual church lives within its given tradition, regardless of whether or not it defends a principle of tradition. Even in those churches that reject the principle of tradition, this tradition can be actually more determinative than it is in those churches that explicitly teach such a principle, for the former nevertheless reflects on its tradition, while the latter unreflectively accepts its own as self-evident. On the other hand, however, the traditions of the separated churches stand in the way of ecumenical openness the more their form [*Gestalt*], in the strict sense of that term, is formulated and established dogmatically and in church law and has been made in principle the norm of church unity. This has most comprehensively taken place in the Roman Church, whereby the historical evidence for the content of this tradition in Scripture and the tradition of the ancient church is no longer regarded as constitutive of what today is considered apostolic tradition,[17] and whereby, moreover, all dogmatic statements, together with the anathemas that are expressed in them, are held to be binding in the same way and unalterable for all time. Also, the Eastern Church teaches that alongside Scripture there is a normative, binding, sacred Tradition, but its content with respect to dogma is restricted essentially to the foundational Christological and Trinitarian confessional statements that are adhered to by most segments of the divided Christendom. Thus, according to the judgment of many Orthodox theologians, the Eastern Church holds that the formation of dogmas has come to an end. But in any case, what is constitutive is the return to the tradition of the ancient church, a return that is authenticated historically. In contrast, the position of the Roman Church, which goes fundamentally and factually far beyond that of the Eastern Church, presents an enormous difficulty for its ecumenical relations with other churches. Given its understanding of tradition, it can proclaim, in an almost positivistic manner, its current understanding of the faith as the apostolic norm, and so its summons to unity comes across above all as the imperative, "Become as I am!"

b) Every individual church believes itself to be the one, holy, catholic, and apostolic church. Without this faith its speaking and acting would be absolutely pointless. But this faith does not necessarily include identical statements about the borders of the one, holy, catholic and apostolic church and its members. From the beginning, each of the Reformation churches has reckoned on there being members of the body of Christ in other churches, indeed also in the "pope's church," since also in it baptism, the creed of the ancient church, and so on, have been maintained. The *una sancta* is, to be sure, visible in one's own church body, but it is greater than this, and thus it is also to be sought for within other churches. Moreover, the Lutheran Reformation acknowledged the Eastern Church as a whole as church, as the correspondence of the Tübingen Lutherans with Patriarch Jeremias II demonstrates. To be sure, the Eastern Church identifies itself more strictly as the church of God on earth, but its relationship to the other churches is not dogmatically settled in its details,[18] and the canonical decrees allow some leeway,[19] something stated explicitly by many Orthodox theologians, according to which the body of

---

17 Cf. the Heidelberger "Evangelische Gutachten zur Dogmatisierung der leiblichen Himmelfahrt Mariens" [Protestant Opinion concerning the Dogmatizing of the Bodily Assumption of Mary], 3rd ed. (München: Kaiser, 1951). [Schlink was the principal author of this opinion by the Protestant theology faculty at Heidelberg. –Ed.]

18 *Procès-verbaux du premier congrès de théologie orthodoxe*, 260 ff.

19 Cf. the investigations of canon law by Hieronymus J. Kotsonis, ΠΡΟΒΛΗΜΑΤΑ ΤΗΣ "ΕΚΚΛΗΣΙΑΣΤΙΚΗΣ ΟΙΚΟΝΟΜΙΑΣ" [Problems of "Church Management"] (Athens: Ekdoseis "He Damaskos," 1957), and idem, Η ΚΑΝΟΝΙΚΗ ΑΠΟΨΙΣ ΠΕΡΙ ΤΗΣ ΕΠΙΚΟΙΝΩΝΙΑΣ ΜΕΤΑ ΤΩΝ ΕΤΕΡΟΔΟΞΩΝ [The Normative View concerning Intercommunion with the Heterodox] (Athens: Ekdoseis "He Damaskos," 1957).

Christ is wider than the borders of the Eastern Church itself.[20] Of all the churches, the Roman one has identified its own reality most exclusively with the *una sancta*. The *Codex Juris Canonici* thus designates all other Christian fellowships as *sectae acatholicae* [non-catholic sects][xiii] and does not even clearly differentiate them from non-Christian groups. Given its very sharp judgments about "pan-Christians," the encyclical of Pius XI, *Mortalium animos* (1928), could, in effect, be understood to mean that for Rome non-Christians are considered to be less incriminated than non-Roman Christians. Finally, the encyclical of Pius XII, *Mystici corporis Christi* (1943), so strictly identifies the borders of the body of Christ with those of the Roman Church that it goes far beyond important statements contained in Roman Catholic tradition regarding the mystical body of Christ and his soul.[21] Although within the Roman Church the discussion of the issue of church membership of *individuals* is still in process and the complexity of this issue is coming more and more to the forefront, yet the judgments about the non-Roman *churches as a whole* appear to be so unequivocally dogmatic and a matter of canon law that the Roman Church can hardly establish a union, in the proper sense of this word, with another church, but can only demand the submission of that other church and bring about its absorption.[22] Here, too, only the imperative appears possible: "Become as I am."

c) These are the barriers for whose surmounting no signs are yet visible today,[23] even though they cannot have any eternal permanence. In any case,

---

20 Reinhard Slenczka, "Die Einheit der Kirche als dogmatisches Problem in der neueren ost-kirchlichen Theologie" [The Unity of the Church as a Dogmatic Issue in Modern Eastern Orthodox Theology] (Th.D. diss., University of Heidelberg, 1960). [This was later published as *Ostkirche und Ökumene. Die Einheit der Kirche als dogmatisches Problem in der neueren ost-kirchlichen Theologie* (Göttingen: Vandenhoeck & Ruprecht, 1962). –Ed.]

21 Sebastian Tromp, *Corpus Christi quod est ecclesia* [The Body of Christ, That Is The Church] (Rome: Gregorian, 1937), 114 ff.

22 This also follows, for example, from the Roman judgments regarding the celebrations of the Lord's Supper by other churches. It is well-known that the Roman Church denies that the Reformation churches, including the Anglican Church, receive the body and blood of Christ in their celebrations of the Lord's Supper. The Roman Church denies this also regarding the Church of the Lutheran Confession, even though this church explicitly confesses the real presence of the body and blood of Christ in the Lord's Supper—in, with, and under the bread and wine. Since the Church of the Lutheran Confession lives from the sacramental gifts of the body and blood of Christ, an anti-Christian decision (in the truest sense) would be demanded of it, if it wanted to attain unity with the Roman Church, for it would have to deny—for the sake of consensus with the valid dogmatic presuppositions of the Roman Church—that Christ has for centuries administered his body and his blood to the Lutheran Church all over the world, wherever and whenever the Lord's Supper has been celebrated. Such a denial, however, is obviously impossible.

23 Such a sign could indeed perhaps be seen in the voice of the Roman Catholic layman Gerhard Kroll ("Thesen eines katholischen Laien zum Konzil" [Theses of a Catholic Layman for the Council], *Materialdienst des Konfessionskundlichen Instituts* 11, no. 2 [1960], 29–31): "1. The council should consider whether a more comprehensive faith is necessary today for the salvation of people than during the time of the apostles, or whether the Catholic Church proposes

they have not yet been surmounted when one refers to schismatics and heretics as brothers and sisters and when one does not speak of the reunion of the separated churches as a submission and return to the Roman Church, and also when Roman theology today speaks of its own complicity in originating the divisions, for this complicity cannot be restricted to the moral failures of former popes and other participants but extends to dogmatic anathemas and articles and judgments of canon law. The repentance of Christendom must be much deeper than most people today think. That this is widely overlooked is undoubtedly connected to the fact that the problematic of the divided Christendom is generally treated one-sidedly by *looking back* historically on the origin of the divisions and the particular church traditions, but too infrequently by *looking forward* to the coming Lord, who will judge all churches and make his final separation among the members of every one of them. For all Christian fellowships the Parousia of Jesus Christ is immanent. The apostolic message proclaims not only the Christ who has come but also the Christ who is coming. The Lord will come not only as the redeemer but also as the Judge, that is, not only as the Judge of the world but also of Christendom. Is Christendom aware of the one who is coming? Is it awaiting its coming Lord? The church has become much older than the apostles expected. Christendom, to be sure, has not ceased referring to the second coming of the Lord in its confession of faith, but in many places the spirit of expectation, of hastening and running toward its Lord, has diminished. Is it not the case that Christendom has widely clung tightly to this earth? To what extent does it still understand itself as the sojourning people of God in a world that is coming to an end? Or has the church—with the heavy baggage of its long history and the armored tanks of its traditions—become once more merely a part of this world?

4. In conclusion, we will inquire into what is to be expected of both forthcoming ecumenical councils for the unity of Christendom. Undoubtedly, every attempt to answer such a question calls for maximum restraint, for one would misjudge the spiritual reality of a council if one thinks one can determine its results in advance. The Holy Spirit works in his freedom. It is

also truths to be believed that are not unconditionally necessary for salvation. –2. The council should, in the affirmative case with respect to content, distinguish the truths necessary for salvation from the other truths, and define as binding the bare minimum elements of faith that are necessary for salvation. –3. The council should then pursue dialogue with the separated brothers and sisters in the faith and seek to reach agreement on the bare minimum necessary elements of faith. Church bodies that hereby commit themselves to advocate no doctrine above and beyond the bare minimum of the Catholic faith, or commit to restrict themselves to that bare minimum of the faith in their body of doctrine, would be regarded as qualified for union with the Roman Church and would be properly fitted out for their own *ritus* [liturgical rite]. In doing so, the pope and council should give binding assurances that in the future no one will be forced to accept new truths of the faith as necessary for salvation that were unknown in the early church…, and so on." But, to my knowledge, these theses have found no resonance among the bishops and theologians of the Roman Church.

regrettable that in the publications of both sides the necessary restraint has not always been respected. The only possibility is to make clear the presuppositions with which both sides proceed and to ascertain the direction toward which the preparations on both sides are going.

a) If in the preceding analysis the ecclesiological structure of both of the councils and the limitations still existing today for drawing the churches closer together have been correctly presented, then one has to observe that at the moment the presuppositions for a joint council toward union have still not been given. If one considers the Roman Church's commitments to dogma and canon law and its widespread unfamiliarity with the ecumenical task, especially in Italy, Spain, and South America, then one should not be disappointed that the second Vatican council will take place as an internal council of the Roman Church.[xiv]

That the second Vatican council, in accord with the will of the pope, is above all to serve the Roman Catholic Church in examining itself and preparing itself for the unity of Christendom speaks to the fact that in convening this council Pope John XXIII has been moved by a genuine ecumenical impulse. Likewise it is entirely correct to note that contact between the Roman Church and the churches of the World Council is to be taken up in an unofficial manner for the time being, that is, in the form of collaborative theological work. It is not possible that in the encounter between the Roman Church and the member churches of the World Council the preparatory stages for drawing the churches closer together—which have proven themselves to be necessary in the ecumenical movement—will be skipped over before these churches could make a common witness to the world.

b) Despite this reticence on both sides, there are important movements and forces that have been noticed in both the Roman Church and in the World Council that are advancing in the same direction as the postulates that have been set down here in the previous sections of the third part of this essay.

As a matter of fact, powerful forces are at work in the Roman Church to give greater validity once again to the *koinonia*-structure of the church—be it by clarifying the position of bishops and of the lay apostolate or be it by developing the liturgy to allow for more diversity in terms of content and language. Corresponding to this, conversely, is a powerful movement in the World Council, which insists on moving from mere cooperation to a stronger integration (as in the case of the World Council of Churches and the International Missionary Council), from the very narrow Christological Basis to a fuller Trinitarian one, and from mere belief in unity to its visible and efficacious representation. From opposing starting points already here a moving toward each other is taking place.[xv]

Moreover, people are no longer content merely to let the various existing church traditions confront one another but both sides are endeavoring to interpret anew their own positions and those unfamiliar to them on the basis of the apostolic, biblical foundation held in common. The Eastern Church and the Reformation churches are already being understood differently today by important circles within the Roman Church than in past centuries, and also vice versa. The inter-church communication already existing in biblical-exegetical and in patristics scholarship is to be valued as highly as the mutual efforts to work through the historically transmitted dogmatic formulas in a new way to reach the reality of revelation attested to by these formulas. In this regard, the efforts of some Roman Catholic theologians deserve the highest respect. When one considers what little use today German Lutheran theologians in general make of the great ecumenical possibilities that the tradition of their church provides them with respect to dogma and church order, and compares that to the intensive use that various outstanding contemporary Roman Catholic theologians are making of the incomparably more limited ecumenical possibilities of their church, one can really question where today the greater intensity of intellectual effort for the unity of Christendom exists, yes, the intensity of that imaginative love and scholarly inquiry without which no ecumenical work can succeed.

All of this means, of course, that the fundamental barriers that exist between Rome and the other churches have still not been surmounted. Nevertheless, perhaps something new is heralded by the fact that there are also some in the Roman Church who are as perplexed as we are regarding the question about how the unity of divided Christendom can be realized. In this perplexity they join their voices with us in the same "*Kyrie eleison*," plead with us that the same Holy Spirit would descend, and are able to anticipate with us the unity of the separated churches only as a divine miracle that transcends all of our notions and expectations.

c) Just how much will be achieved now at the two councils and what particulars of the hopes and dreams will come to fulfillment—for example, those which Hans Küng has expressed with a sincere and lively ecumenical openness—no one can say in advance.[24] Without a doubt, it would already mean much for Christendom and the world if both councils would make clear in their respective resolutions that they are not convening in opposition to each other and that each of them seeks not to serve itself but wants only to serve the Lord Jesus Christ.

---

24 Hans Küng, *Konzil und Wiedervereinigung: Die Erneuerung als Ruf zur Einheit* (Freiburg: Herder, 1960). [*The Council, Reform, and Reunion*, trans. Cecily Hastings (New York: Sheed and Ward, 1961)].

Editor's Notes

[i] The genesis for this essay can be found in Schlink's earlier and much briefer article, "Ökumenische Konzilien einst und heute," which was published in *Die Zeichen der Zeit* 6 (1952), 407–410. That essay paved the way for a new analysis of the same topic, which was published as "Die altkirchlichen Konzilien und die Vollversammlungen des Ökumenischen Rates der Kirchen: Ein kritischer Vergleich" [Ancient Church Councils and the Assemblies of the World Council of Churches: A Critical Comparison], *Ökumenische Rundschau* 10 (1961), 139–48. Schlink later made this essay the first part of the present essay. That part was translated into English as "The Ecumenical Councils & the Assemblies of the World Council of Churches," *Dialog* 1, no. 1 (1962), 32–37. The complete three-part version of the essay was first published as "Ökumenische Konzilien einst und heute" in *Die ökumenischen Konzile der Christenheit* [The Ecumenical Councils of Christendom], ed. Hans Jochen Margull (Stuttgart: Evangelisches Verlagswerk, 1961), 393–428. It was included in KC under the same title (see KC 1.241–71). A translation of this essay, however, was not included in CC.

[ii] The Third Assembly of the World Council of Churches took place in New Delhi, India, between 19 Nov and 5 Dec 1961. There were 577 delegates from 197 member churches. The theme was "Jesus Christ—the Light of the World." The second Vatican council had been announced by Pope John XXIII on 25 January 1959 at the conclusion of a prayer service for Christian unity. The first session of that council began on 11 October 1962. Some 2,300 bishops attended, assisted by several thousand theologians, church historians, and experts in canon law. This first session lasted about ten weeks. The other three sessions also met in the fall of the year (1963–65) and lasted about the same amount of time. Because the Second Vatican Council had not yet been completed when Schlink wrote this essay, it will be referred to here as the "second Vatican council."

[iii] Schlink refers here to canons in the 1917 *Code of Canon Law*. Title VII is on "the supreme power and those who by ecclesiastical law are participants therein." The first chapter addresses the authority of "the Roman Pontiff" (Canons 218–221). The second chapter (Canons 222–29) concerns "the Ecumenical Council" (*De Concilio Oecumenico*). Canon 222 states that an "Ecumenical Council cannot be held that was not convoked by the Roman Pontiff." This Canon appears as Canon 338 in the 1983 edition (post-Vatican II). Canon 223 from the 1917 edition indicates who may deliberatively vote in such an Ecumenical Council. This Canon (slightly modified) is essentially re-stated in Canon 339 of the 1983 edition in the section on "The College of Bishops." Canons 224 and 225 from the 1917 edition, which are not found in the 1983 edition, address conditions and rules by which participants may be absent from the Council or leave early. Canon 226 ("The fathers can add to the questions proposed by the Roman Pontiff others, if they are approved beforehand by the President of the Council") is now a part of Canon 338 of the 1983 edition. Canon 227 ("The decrees of a council do not have definitive obliging force unless they are confirmed by the Roman Pontiff and promulgated by his command") is the current Canon 341. Canon 228 of the 1917 edition contains two statements: "§1. An Ecumenical Council enjoys supreme power over the universal church. §2. Appeal from a sentence of the Roman Pontiff to an Ecumenical Council is not given." This Canon was revised in the 1983 edition. §1 is now embedded in Canon 336, the first canon in the article on "the College of Bishops": "The college of bishops, whose head is the Supreme Pontiff and whose members are the bishops by virtue of sacramental consecration and hierarchical communion with the head and members of the college, and in which the apostolic body endures, together with its head, and never without its head, is also the subject of supreme and full power over the universal church." §2 is now embedded in Canon 333 (as §3): "There is neither appeal nor recourse against a decision or decree of the Roman Pontiff." Canon 333 is the third canon in the section on "the Roman Pontiff." For the 1917 edition, see *Codex Iuris Canonici*, issued and promulgated by Pope Pius X (Rome: Vatican, 1917; ET: *The 1917 Pio-Benedictine Code of Canon Law*, trans. Edward N. Peters [San Francisco: Ignatius, 2001]). For

the 1983 edition, see *Codex Iuris Canonici*, authorized and promulgated by Pope John Paul II, trans. Canon Law Society of America (Washington, D.C.: 1983), 119–23.

[iv] Conciliarism took a variety of forms in the late-medieval Western Church but all of them held that an ecumenical council is superior to the pope. Early forms, from the thirteenth and fourteenth centuries, taught that councils, as an assembly of autonomous bishops, are representative of the whole church and stand above the pope. The most famous proponent of this early version was Marsilius of Padua (ca. 1275–1342). Later forms of conciliarism emphasized the importance of individual bishops or their churches and were often linked to a nationalized form of the church (e. g., Gallicanism in France). Conciliarism was condemned at Vatican I.

[v] The Lactrocinium (i.e., "The Robber Synod") was held at Ephesus in 449. Convened by Theodosius II (401–450) the synod addressed issues that had arisen from the condemnation of Eutyches the year before at a synod in Constantinople. Eutychus opposed Nestorianism and had been accused of confounding the two natures in Christ. This Ephesian synod was dominated by proponents of Monophysitism, who taught that in the person of Christ there is but a single, divine nature after the incarnation. They declared Eutyches orthodox and reinstated him as head of his large monastery in Constantinople. The Roman legates present at the Ephesian synod (they had brought with them Pope Leo's "Tome") left insulted. Subsequently, in a letter to the Empress Pulcheria, Pope Leo described this synod as "*non iudicium, sed latrocinium*" ("not a trial, but a theft"). Its decisions were reversed at the Council of Chalcedon in 451.

[vi] Already in November 1518 Luther had called for a general council to address some of the pressing issues that had arisen, e. g., the question of restoring the chalice to the laity. In June 1520 he wrote his *Letter to the Christian Nobility* (LW 44.123–217), wherein he indicated his desire that the German secular estate, following the examples of the Roman emperors who had convened and presided over the first four ecumenical councils, should convene "a truly free council," that is, free of papal control. During the rest of his lifetime, imperial and ecclesial politics derailed the prospects of holding such a council. Nevertheless, every time it appeared the council might be convened (e. g., in the late 1530s, during the pontificate of Paul III), Luther turned his attention to this topic, most importantly in his 1539 treatise, *On the Councils and the Church* (LW 41.9–178). Here Luther indicated his willingness to compromise, even on significant issues, as long as such compromises did not undermine the essential matters of the faith. "We are not such accursed people (praise and thank God!) that we would let the church perish rather than yield even on major points, as long as they are not against God; on the contrary, if it depends on our knowledge and ability, we are prepared to perish leaving neither hide nor hair behind, rather than to see the church suffer harm or loss" (LW 41.16). The first session of the Council of Trent began in mid-December 1545, just a few months before Luther died.

[vii] Cf. endnote 10 in chap. 13 ("The Significance of Eastern and Western Traditions for Christendom") above.

[viii] An allusion to AC V.3: "[God] gives the Holy Spirit who produces faith, where and when he wills, in those who hear the gospel…" (BC 40).

[ix] In the Roman Catholic Church *concelebration* refers to the joint celebration of the Eucharist by several bishops and/or presbyters, one of whom functions as the presider. It is practiced as a sign of church unity in the local congregation and of union with other congregations when Eucharistic hospitality is offered to visiting clergy.

[x] In post-fourth-century Eastern Orthodox churches, the Holy of Holies is the sacred space containing the altar that holds the consecrated Eucharist. Patterned after the Jerusalem Temple's Holy of Holies, which contained the Ark of the Covenant and could only be entered once a year by the high priest, this Orthodox inner sanctum symbolizes heaven. Gradually there developed forms of a low partition (much later these developed into the iconostasis on which icons were hung) that divided and linked the nave and the Holy of Holies. Typically the iconostasis has three doors, one leading to the *diakonikon* (where the sacred vessels are kept

and cleaned by deacons), one leading to the *prothesis* (where the Eucharistic gifts are prepared), and one leading to the altar itself. Schlink is here alluding to reports that some Byzantine emperors entered the Holy of Holies through the central doors (the "Beautiful Door") and received the Eucharist directly from the altar. For such reports, see Gilbert Dagron, *Emperor and Priest: The Imperial Office in Byzantium*, trans. Jean Birrell (Cambridge: Cambridge University Press, 2003), 97 ff.

[xi] "...we issue the same decree and resolution concerning the prerogatives of the most holy church of the same Constantinople, new Rome. The fathers rightly accorded prerogatives to the see of older Rome, since that is an imperial city; and moved by the same purpose the 150 most devout bishops apportioned equal prerogatives to the most holy see of new Rome, reasonably judging that the very city which is honored by the imperial power and senate and enjoying privileges equaling older imperial Rome, should also be elevated to her level in ecclesiastical affairs and take second place to her..." (Canon 28, Council of Chalcedon, Tanner 1.100).

[xii] Canon 218, *The 1917 Pio-Benedictine Code of Canon Law*, 93–94.

[xiii] Cf. canons 542, 1131, and 2314, *The 1917 Pio-Benedictine Code of Canon Law*. The phrase "*sectae acatholicae*" is not found in the 1983 *Codex Iuris Canonici*.

[xiv] It bears underscoring that Schlink made this observation about the Roman Catholic Church in 1961. At that time he was only familiar with the ecumenical dialogues between Roman Catholics and Lutherans that had been taking place in Germany since 1946. Indeed, he was a key participant and leader in those dialogues, both before and after Vatican II. By contrast, other such dialogues did not begin until near the end of the council or shortly thereafter. For example, the official Lutheran-Roman Catholic dialogue in the United States did not begin until 1965.

[xv] A product of the 1910 World Missionary Conference (Edinburgh), the International Missionary Council was formally constituted in 1921. It served as a federation of Protestant mission councils and societies from Europe and North America. After major ecumenical conferences in Jerusalem (1928), Tambaram (1938), Whitby (1947), Willingen (1952), and Accra (1958), the IMC integrated into the World Council of Churches in 1961, where it became the Division (now Commission) on World Mission and Evangelism.

Chapter Fifteen:
The Resurrection of God's People

Sermon on the Text of Ezekiel 37.1–14[1]

Text: The hand of the LORD came upon me, and he brought me out by the spirit of the LORD and set me down in the middle of a valley; it was full of bones. He led me all around them; there were very many lying in the valley, and they were very dry. He said to me, "Mortal, can these bones live?" I answered, "O Lord GOD, you know." Then he said to me, "Prophesy to these bones, and say to them: O dry bones, hear the word of the LORD. Thus says the Lord GOD to these bones: I will cause breath to enter you, and you shall live. I will lay sinews on you, and will cause flesh to come upon you, and cover you with skin, and put breath in you, and you shall live; and you shall know that I am the LORD." So I prophesied as I had been commanded; and as I prophesied, suddenly there was a noise, a rattling, and the bones came together, bone to its bone. I looked, and there were sinews on them, and flesh had come upon them, and skin had covered them; but there was no breath in them. Then he said to me, "Prophesy to the breath, prophesy, mortal, and say to the breath: Thus says the Lord GOD: Come from the four winds, O breath, and breathe upon these slain, that they may live." I prophesied as he commanded me, and the breath came into them, and they lived, and stood on their feet, a vast multitude. Then he said to me, "Mortal, these bones are the whole house of Israel. They say, 'Our bones are dried up, and our hope is lost; we are cut off completely.' Therefore prophesy, and say to them, Thus says the Lord GOD: I am going to open your graves, and bring you up from your graves, O my people; and I will bring you back to the land of Israel. And you shall know that I am the LORD, when I open your graves, and bring you up from your graves, O my people. I will put my spirit within you, and you shall live, and I will place you on your own soil; then you shall know that I, the LORD, have spoken and will act, says the LORD."

Here we are shown a wide field, crisscrossed in every direction with bleached human bones. We can no longer recognize which of these bones once belonged to one and the same body. Was this a battlefield or a place of execution? Or was there here a cemetery, whose burial mounds of dirt have been blown away by a storm?

What Ezekiel saw was far more horrific than a place of those long dead. No, it was living people of his own time and place which he saw in this vision as bones of the dead—people who breathe, eat, drink, marry, work, and pray. Nevertheless, they are dead people, indeed, decomposed, for they are people

1 Delivered in August 1952 in the chapel of the Ecumenical Institute in the Château de Bossey, Geneva, at the end of the second session of the Commission that prepared the theme of the WCC Assembly in Evanston. ["Die Auferstehung des Gottesvolk(e)s. Predigt über den Text Hesekiel 37.1–14" was first published in KC 1.272–75. The translation by J. C. G. Greig appears in CC (330–33) as "The Resurrection of God's People." –Ed.]

who have lost hope. Ezekiel beheld in this vision the real situation of his people, the Old Testament covenantal people in the diaspora in part, banished to Babylon in part, miserable remnants in Jerusalem and Palestine. What is the hope that these people lost? The hope of becoming one again, of becoming the one people of God in the land, something God's promise had assured them.

This sight can suddenly come upon us, too, today—as we behold the condition of Christendom. We are, to be sure, living, intensely busy, holding worship services, instructing the youth. Our churches are engaging in mission and making manifold advances into the world. We consider these as workings of the Holy Spirit and think ourselves to be a new creature *in Christo*. But in the midst of all of this busyness the vision of the field full of dead bones suddenly comes upon us, for Christendom is not *one* people. The churches work alongside one another and against one another. Again and again, each one speaks for itself and the one talks past the others. Again and again, because of their disunity, the churches are the greatest hindrance to the salvation of the world, for through their disunity they refute the message about the sole Savior and Lord of the world, under whom all that is divided is one. Christians thus live as disconnected and scattered bones on the wide field of the earth, and to a great extent they have come to terms with this condition. Many have given up the hope that all who confess Christ will become members of one body and arise in joint praise of God.

The vision of Ezekiel was full of horrors. The field of bones that is Christendom is, however, even more profoundly shattering than that of the Old Testament people of God, for since that time God has redeemed his people in Jesus Christ from the lordship of death, and with him has powerfully established a new covenant. After all, at Pentecost God poured out his Spirit upon all flesh. But despite this, we are not one. Is it thus any wonder that some doubt whether we are in truth reborn and a new creature in Christ? After all, the new creature is only a reality as the fellowship of the body of Christ, which is *one* body. After all, the working of the Holy Spirit by its very nature creates the unity of God's people, since this people is gathered by the *one* Spirit of God.

"You, O son of man, do you really think that these bones will live again?" Just as God asked the prophet, so too he asks us.

In these days we have, for the second time, worked together on the theme of hope, and our hope has been strengthened through this joint work. Despite our origin in different churches, countries, and traditions, we have become one fellowship, in which the one has heartened the other through his witness to the Christian hope and in which we have all then been able to express in common—not alongside one another or against one another, but together with one another—the one hope in Christ, and to put this down also in writing. Truly, we have experienced in our midst something of the way the scattered bones can become joined together once again in one body, and we have every reason to thank God for this.

But the question that God directs to us goes still further. It is concerned not merely, as here, with a circle of twenty-five scholars, but with the people of God as a whole. It is concerned with Christendom as a whole, whose divisions and impotence are so vividly before our very eyes. Do you believe that these bones will live again?

Ezekiel's answer is neither "No" nor "Yes." He answers, "Lord, you know." And thereby he bows down to God, acknowledges him to be the Lord who works everything and can do everything. God alone can raise the dead. Ezekiel's answer is thus, despite all of its hesitancy, not without hope.

But it is decisive that God is not content with such an answer, neither back then nor today. God conscripts the one who hopes, places him into service, and makes him his instrument. He does not allow him to stand by, waiting inactively with his "Lord, you know," but sets him in motion, makes him to be his mouthpiece, and wants to accomplish his deeds through him. Thus he sends the prophet, and thus he sends also us, after he has awakened hope in us and has strengthened it.

The task of God is so enormous that he seems to demand simply an absurd action by humans. We are to call upon those who do not hear, who have no ears, whose sense organs have long since rotted away and have decayed into dust and ashes. We are to address dead and self-satisfied Christendom, which has come to terms with living alongside one another in separated churches, "You dry bones, hear the word of the Lord! Thus says the Lord about these bones, 'See, I want to put breath in you so that you may live. I want to give you arteries and to make flesh grow on you and to cover you with skin and to give you breath so that you may become alive again and you will experience that I am the Lord.'" We are not speaking about the dead—about those who seem to be living but who are in truth dead—but speaking to them. Is this not nonsense?

All words of God seem to us as foolishness as long as we do not obey them in faith, but we are to carry out this task of God and believe that God's word is an active and life-creating word. Through his word God gives at the same time the ability to hear it, through his word God brings about new organs. Through his word God has created the world, through his word God also brings about the resurrection of the dead.

Even more astonishing is what comes next: "Prophecy to the winds until they again become living!" Who is meant by the wind? Is it the spirits of the dead that are to return again? No, it is God's Spirit—the Spirit by means of which God gave life to the first human being, the Spirit by means of which God inspired the Old Testament prophets, the Spirit which God poured out on all flesh at Pentecost. This Spirit of God is the God who himself makes alive, the Lord. God bids us to call upon the Spirit in his name. To do this is not merely to ask and plead with longing uncertainty, but rather to call upon the Spirit in absolute certainty. Indeed, it is almost a command that God lays upon us, namely, that we bring him into alignment with his Spirit, for it is God's will to fulfill this calling according to his Spirit. However questionable some of our prayers may be, the petition for his Spirit is in every case well-pleasing to God. He wants to give the Spirit to those who ask him for it. So great is God's condescension that he permits us to call upon his Spirit in this certainty, the third person of the Godhead himself, and to expect from the Spirit what God has offered and promised us.

Ezekiel did not only hear and perceive the task but he also saw its fulfillment. The bones came together again, bone to its bone, and there grew arteries and flesh upon them and breath came into them and they became living again and stood up. "And it was a very great people."

Let us depart with this promise. Its fulfillment is the body of Christ, which rose from the grave and continues to grow as it unites in itself the believers from all peoples and periods—the body of Christ which fulfills all in all. Amen.

Book Two: After the Council

Preface

The Second Vatican Council came to its solemn close on 8 December 1965. An impressive multiplicity of topics was addressed by this council. Its resolutions now lie before us. But its history has not ended, for that history also entails the outcome of its effects. Translating the resolutions of the council into reality will take time, and, as the history of the council itself shows, it will not happen everywhere at the same time nor in the same way. In this respect the conclusion of the council is only "the beginning of the beginning" (Karl Rahner).[i] For the moment, nothing definitive can yet be said about its significance. That will only be possible after many years to come.

Nevertheless, the rest of Christendom cannot confine itself to awaiting further developments, for in this council the Roman Catholic Church has undertaken a surprising turn toward the other churches. In the Decree on Ecumenism it has opened up possibilities for mutual exchange and cooperative work with the "separated sisters and brothers" that had until now been denied to Catholic Christians. Realizing these possibilities, however, does not rest with the Roman Church alone but depends at the same time on how the other churches evaluate the changed situation and how they now engage the Roman Church going forward. They must study the resolutions of the council with great care, gain clarity about their implications, and attempt in a provisional way to gauge now the significance of this council for the living interaction of all Christians.

The observers at the council had the privilege of following the events in St. Peter's at closest range. After having participated in all four periods of the council as the official observer from the Protestant Church in Germany, I could not evade the task of reporting publicly, from a Lutheran perspective, about the results of these four years. In a manner understandable to the plenary participants and that does without scholarly footnotes, I seek to give here an introduction to the most important resolutions of the council, to attempt an analysis of the changed situation after the council, and then to consider how we are now to conduct ourselves in relation to the Roman Catholic Church. In doing so we cannot overlook the fact that the Protestant Church in Germany, as a member church of the World Council of Churches, is in an alliance with not only the other Reformation churches but also the Orthodox churches of the East. For this reason, some of their perspectives will also be expressed here. If in what follows I typically refer to the Roman Catholic Church as the "Roman Church," I'm using its self-designation merely to respect the fact that most other churches also understand themselves to be catholic churches and even refer to themselves as such.

The observers at the council were given the task of reporting on the events of the council to the church leaders who had delegated them and of sharing information about the position of their churches with the council fathers and theologians. A fruitful dialogue developed, above all in the setting of the joint sessions with the Secretariat for the Promotion of Christian Unity, in which the texts under examination at the council were discussed and criticism, which had been explicitly invited, was shared. Cardinal Bea[ii] is to be especially thanked for the fact that this dialogue could be led in an open and trusting manner. I would like the following expositions also to be understood as an expression of gratitude, for how else could we give thanks than by taking the resolutions of this council seriously as they affect us and by carefully testing— with the eyes of hope—which possibilities present themselves for future interactions among Christians.

Editor's Notes

[i] Karl Rahner made this famous remark in a lecture he delivered in Munich on 12 December 1965, just four days after the conclusion of the council. "The council has marked a beginning for *aggiornamento*, for renewal, yes, even for repentance—which is always overdue—and conversion: the beginning of the beginning. That is a lot. But it is only the beginning of the beginning…. The church has claimed responsibility for a task, but it has yet to be fulfilled…" (Karl Rahner, *Das Konzil – ein neuer Beginn* [The Council: A New Beginning] [Freiburg: Herder, 2012], 37 ff.). The term *aggiornamento*, which was explicitly linked to the council by Pope John XXIII, entails both the accommodation of the church to the changed situation of the modern world but also a renewed, deeper, spiritual inquiry into what God wills for the church today. Cf. sec. 2 of chap. 10 ("Post-Conciliar Possibilities of the Roman Church") below. This term will be left untranslated.

[ii] Augustin Cardinal Bea (1881–1968) was a German Jesuit who served as the first president of the Secretariat for Promoting Christian Unity (later called "The Pontifical Council for Promoting Christian Unity"), the Curial organization that is charged with the ecumenical affairs of the Roman Church.

Chapter I:
The Spiritual Awakening of Christendom

The outcome and significance of the Second Vatican Council cannot be understood if we isolate it and consider it only in relation to the history of the Roman Catholic Church, for events have occurred in the twentieth century that have changed the situation of all Christendom and have set before all of the churches new issues and decisions. Moreover, these changes have not at all come to an end. Rather, they continue to occur in rapid succession at a breathtaking pace.

1. Christendom's Loss of Its Security

The decades that lie behind us belong to one of the most dramatic periods in the entire history of the church. Structures by which Christendom had naturally become embedded in the surrounding culture and political order, forms that had been growing for centuries, had been called into question or even shattered. Through the tumult of events, entire churches have lost their public influence and have been forced into a nearly invisible existence. The infiltration into traditional Christian nations by forces that are enemies of the faith, whereby Christians have been reduced to a minority, can only be compared with the invasion of Islam into regions of the church in the Near East and North Africa since the seventh century, and the number of those who have been killed in the twentieth century because of their membership in the church far exceeds the number of Christians who were victims of persecution in the era of the ancient church. Many others have fallen away from the Christian faith in the situation of persecution. Churches of all confessions have been struck by these upheavals. Every church body has suffered great losses in people, influence, and freedom.

One would see these major changes only as preliminary if one thought that both world wars, and the revolutions that accompanied them, were responsible for them. These wars and revolutions had only a triggering effect; they were not the underlying cause. They simply revealed what had already been occurring beforehand through a long process of intellectual changes, without as yet having rescinded the legal safeguards of the churches. In the nineteenth century nearly all churches (apart from those in North America and the independent churches in England) still understood themselves in terms of the imperial church, a conception that had been brought to completion under Justinian and which had been maintained by the Byzantine and West-Roman empires after the schism between the Orthodox and Roman churches and also by the Protestant territorial princes after the division between the Roman Church and the Reformation churches.[1] But this conception of the unity of Christian faith, culture, and national order had already for a long time been called into question. Through the paradigm shift of the natural sciences and the Enlightenment, through the estrangement of educated people and laborers from the church, and through the church's reticence about new scientific, social, and political necessities, that unity, even where it was still formally maintained, had already become undermined and a mere façade—long before it became totally shattered by the tumult of the twentieth-century's events in world history. Where, however, a religion-less order replaced the old order, it became clear that the post-Christian person, who had once been familiar with the freedom in Christ but had then renounced Christ, could not in the long run persevere in the neutrality of agnosticism, but gave birth to new meanings and ideologies by which that person—in opposition to the Christian faith—sought to master the issues of the age and to develop and carry out comprehensive systems that ended up enslaving people in a way that is similar to the enslavement by the powers and authorities about which the New Testament writings speak. It is no accident that some leaders [Führer] of anti-Christian movements have come out of Christian schools and seminaries.

Corresponding to these processes in traditionally Christian countries are the profound transformations occurring in those regions of the world where Christianity first began to be spread. There was still in the nineteenth century such an intensive mission in Africa and Asia on the part of Europe and America that for the first time in its history Christianity had stretched across the whole world, and the goal of a Christianized humanity seemed to be close at hand. As a consequence of the two world wars, however, both of which appeared to the non-Christian world to be fratricidal wars among Christian nations, there developed such a weakening of moral repute and power that the non-Christian nations could rise up in revolt, free themselves from colonial domination, and constitute themselves as sovereign states. In the process they discovered a powerful resource in their own religions, especially Hinduism, Buddhism, and Islam, which many believed to be dead but which actually have renewed themselves with astonishing strength and are now turning to undertake a mission of their own into the world. Deprived of the protection of their legal and economic privileges under the colonial powers, and exposed to the assault of nationalism and the non-Christian religions, today the churches in these territories are isolated and their further expansion is made significantly more difficult. Entire regions are now utterly sealed off from the Christian message. In addition, thousands of syncretistic sects have burst on the scene, especially in Africa, where nationalistic-tribal groups are breaking away from the Christian churches.

Even taking into account these major changes, our considerations cannot end with the factors that triggered the two world wars and ended colonialism. Those factors, too, are only preliminary matters. Christianity got into this difficult predicament in those territories solely because its expansion had been too narrowly and unquestioningly associated with Western civilization, Western ways of thinking and living, and Western methods of education, and had by no means reached the real identity of the Asiatic and African peoples to the extent that it had seemed to under the pseudo-transformation in the colonial period. The Father of Jesus Christ, who is spoken of in the missionary message, came across to these people more like the powerful God of the white race than the universal Father of all human beings and thus also as *their* Lord and Father. So it was inevitable that, in the national awakening of those peoples, the Christian churches would be suspected of being representatives of foreign political powers, and for that reason restricted and in part also persecuted and killed.

Christendom today has thus lost its security in a particular way. In vast regions it has become a persecuted church, and in others it is barely tolerated, but even where it still seems to be determining the total life of a nation and is given legal protection by the state, its position is being undermined. This holds true not only of the Roman Catholic countries, such as Italy, Spain, and the South American nations, but also of West Germany, Scandinavia, and England. Deprived of cultural and political supports in their situation, Christians have in a new way again become strangers and pilgrims in this world. To be sure, the number of baptized is larger than the number of adherents in each of the other religions, and the number of Christians continues to grow. Nevertheless, in view of the rapidly expanding number of people as whole, Christendom today is a steadily declining minority, and its total number is even less if one figures it on the basis of the statistics for those who actually attend the worship services rather than merely the number of those baptized.

2. Renewal from the Source

Christendom has reacted very differently to its loss of security. Some saw those who took their security as opponents against whom they must fight with all their weapons. In a dogged struggle, they sought to save what they could from what was threatened, and aimed at clinging ever more tightly to what could not be saved. Even if their weak condition has now been exposed, they assert their claims with restorative power and seek to reestablish what was lost as soon as a new political situation permits it. Examples of this are not limited to the events in Spain.[ii]

Others recognized in this loss of security the working of God, who uses even the enemies of the church as his instruments. They recognized in the tempests of world history the power of God who shakes and jostles the tree of Christendom so that the dry leaves and barren branches will fall in the storm of his chastisement, and those parts of the tree that live from the powerful nourishment of his roots will be tested and strengthened. They recognized in the enmity of their environment and in that apostasy the activity of a church that had become secure and comfortable, which appeared to many to be less like the light of the world and the helper of the poor and more like a buttress defending antiquated ideological, social, and political systems. The losses suffered were interpreted by these individuals as vanished illusions, while in these tempests the real situation of the church came to light anew and its proper tasks were disclosed afresh. The church experienced that the power of Christ manifested itself in the weakness of Christians, and that the sufferings of those who bear witness to the faith are sufferings-with-Christ, through which his cross becomes victoriously present in this world. Here the church's loss of security was affirmed, as was its status as pilgrim and stranger. The dominant theme was no longer the battle against the enemies of the church, but rather it became the wrestling with God for his forgiveness and for his direction in the further walk of obedience.

Thus began, in the most disparate parts of Christendom, a new inquiry into Holy Scripture. With the ending of the Constantinian era the situation of the church in many regions had in a surprising way again become similar to that of the earliest Christian community. There thus developed a basic search for answers that the New Testament witnesses of the apostles and the earliest Christian community—because of their proximity to God's once-and-for-all act of salvation in Christ—could give to contemporary questions. As witnesses to the way in which God leads his people, the Old Testament Scriptures also became alive again and current, as warning, consolation, and direction for the present. There thus developed in many churches, for the most part independently of each other, one of the strongest biblical movements in the history of the church, wherein theologians and laity engaged in joint study of Scripture, a movement that led to many Bible translations and biblical commentaries.

The concern here was not only an historical interest in biblical writings, but rather it was about hearing what God wants to say to us today. The concern, in other words, was not only about reading the scriptural word but about expounding and proclaiming that word's assurance and claim and about its reception in faith, prayer, and worship. The concern was not only about the act of salvation that God has fulfilled once-and-for-all but about God's action of salvation today on the basis of that unique act. Jesus Christ is, after all, "the same, yesterday and today and forever" (Heb. 13.8). So there arose a liturgical movement in many churches that was not primarily determined by historical and aesthetic interests, but rather was rooted in a basic hunger for the living word of God and for the sacramental participation in Christ's death and resurrection, and in the desire of people to offer themselves as a sacrifice of praise to God in the fellowship of believers.

In this biblical and liturgical awakening there arose a new interest in the confession of the church, for in the confession the believer affirms the heart and center of the manifold statements in Holy Scripture. In confession believers transfer themselves over to the Christ who died once-and-for-all and is the present Lord. In the confession all statements of the faith are concentrated: witness and prayer, doctrine and worship. At the same time, those confessing do not remain isolated individuals but join in voicing the confession of the church—of the sisters and brothers who are living at the same time with them and of the ancestors who went before them in the faith. There thus developed a fresh awareness of church dogma, in its function of gathering, strengthening, and norming.

In the process of all of this, there developed a fresh thinking about the church, its nature, its mission, its form. Its former possibilities for action were widely changed. The more strongly, however, alien encroachments called the form of the church's existence into question or sought to destroy the church, the more significant the identity of the church of all ages became—its being called out from the world, the universal priesthood of all believers, and the unity of the sojourning people of God with the saints triumphant. In this way the ancient church became newly important, not only the pre-Constantinian church, which was persecuted in this world and, if need be, tolerated, but also the church that was temporally near the earliest Christian community, in which the abiding structures of the church began to assume their first comprehensive historical form on the apostolic foundation. In an unexpected way, the century in which the church lost its security became "the century of the church" (O. Dibelius),[iii] and it opened up a broader vista beyond the borders of one's own church body. Churches like the Russian Orthodox, which some in the West had regarded as petrified, began to emit a bright light through their martyrdom, and to shame and awaken other churches that had been considered strong.

Thus, in the midst of the loss of its security in our time, a renewal of Christendom from its source has begun.

3. The Responsibility for the World

These starting points could not be designated as renewal if they were only to serve the religious self-gratification of Christians and their self-centered security, in which they sought to compensate for the loss of their external security. What speaks to the authenticity of this movement of renewal is that, along with the biblical movement, the liturgical movement, and the new recognition of the nature of the church, which comes from what takes place in the worship service and from reflection on the mission of the church, there developed a new turning toward the world. The church is, after all, not only called out of the world by God; it is also the people of God sent back into the world. By its very nature, the church lives not only in movement out of the world but also in movement into the world.

The more intensively Christians reflected back on the source of the church, the more independent they were from the accustomed cultural and political bonds with which the church's tradition had entangled itself. Men and women stood up who, in view of the upheaval of our time, deliberately refrained from engaging the objections and attacks of the church's opponents with the usual weapons of apologetics. On the contrary, they paused and reflected, humbled themselves under the judgment of God's word, and by means of that same word carefully studied the catastrophes and upheavals of our time. They were not ashamed to confess the guilt of a Christendom that had turned the message of Christ into a system of Christian ideology and the Christian discipleship into an affirmation of traditional social and political orders, a Christendom which had thoroughly failed to understand the ethos of the modern sciences, the interests of the labor movement and of the colonial nations, and the dangers in the claim to sovereignty by the European nation-states. So, through the church's own sin and fault, many for whom the gospel is especially valid were pushed aside into unbelief, namely, those who hunger and thirst and are seeking after truth and righteousness. The obligation of servant ministry to the world was recognized anew.

This servant ministry at all times consists above all in bearing witness to Jesus Christ. Indeed, Christ has died for all, and as the risen one he has been established as Lord over all. Indeed, he has become a brother and Lord to everyone. Therefore, this whole message is to be called out to everyone, for Christ wants to come to everyone through the call of the gospel. While this message is not new, it had to be conveyed in a new way so that Christians would not cloak the universality of their Lord. Then it became true that Paul's statement had to be taken seriously anew: "Although I am free in relation to every person, I have made myself a slave of all so that I might win many. I became a Jew to the Jews in order to win Jews.... To the weak I became weak in order to win the weak. I have become all things to all people in order that I might by all means save some" (1 Cor. 9.19 ff.). Christians not only have to proclaim the message of Christ's self-humiliation, but they must also follow it. New approaches to witnessing were thus undertaken by pastors and laity in a great multiplicity of ways.

This witness could not remain restricted to the word but had also to be extended to places where the word could not yet be received or where it was forbidden. Moreover, entering into solidarity with labor, the circumstances of life, the needs and questions of others—all this can also become a witness to Christ, which gives rise to new questions and hopes. In manifold ways, living congregations have thus emerged in new forms, which are aware of their responsibility in their de-Christianized or even heathen surroundings.

This responsibility is also valid in respect to the upheavals in secular society, the conflicts between social strata, nations, and races, the problems of the developing countries, the population explosion, the oppression of the poor, and the arrogance of the mighty. The message of Christ is the primary mission of Christendom, but God does not want only the justification of the sinner through faith, he also wants secular righteousness, in which all people live together in peace. It is characteristic of the spiritual awakening of Christians that today many no longer defend their own security and the traditional order but have instead begun to think about their fellow human beings in a revolutionary way and to raise their voices with a new freedom on behalf of the oppressed, undaunted by disagreeable reactions to their public warnings addressed to their own government. They know, too, that their responsibility cannot stop at the borders of their own nation, but rather it obligates them to act on behalf of all nations and for peace among all people.

Thus, paradoxically, precisely through Christendom's loss of its security in the world, the reality of this world has opened up anew for Christendom. Through the breakdown of its traditional place of safety and security in European culture and the political order, Christendom has undergone a transition from the European epoch to the global epoch. The relationship of patronage between the European and American churches, on the one hand, and the mission fields, on the other, has now been supplanted by the fellowship of churches that share equal rights and that come from all parts of the world, all races, nations, and cultures.

This renewal from the source already determines in part the consciousness of entire regions of the church, whereas elsewhere it is only just beginning to do so. In most places it is occurring in tension with traditional forces in the church. In only a few churches, however, are the signs of this spiritual awakening entirely absent. It is not always the same people and groups who are supporting the biblical movement, the liturgical movement, missionary proclamation, social responsibility, and the cause of world peace. Yet wherever a true spiritual awakening has occurred, all these various commitments were not understood as opposed to one another but as cohering functions of the same church life that fulfills itself as a fellowship of differing charismata and servant ministries.

4. The Ecumenical Movement

In this spiritual awakening Christendom became aware of the shame of its divisions. How can the world recognize Christ as the one Lord if the churches bearing witness to him are not united? How can the world expect peace from Christ if he has not even brought peace among those who confess him? The shame of division was recognized as the guilt of Christendom in the presence of God and human beings.

The biblical movement, the liturgical movement, the responsibility for secular righteousness, and so forth, have, in general, come to life in the various churches spontaneously and independently of one another, but this parallel spiritual awakening which was taking place could not remain hidden from the separated churches. Those in the awakening recognized the working of the same Christ beyond the borders of their own churches, and the walls between the churches became transparent. This led to encounters between members of different churches, to study groups, to encounters between official representatives of the churches, to large conferences, and finally to comprehensive, formal arrangements in which the churches worked together.

The ecumenical movement of our time sprang from many sources and became then a flowing current, inclusive of all churches. Not surprisingly, the first strong impulses came from the Student Christian Movement and missions, for nowhere is the separation of churches so painfully apparent than in the missionary witness. Since no unification is possible without clarifying the differences regarding dogma, liturgy, and church law, already prior to the First World War a World Conference on Faith and Order was planned ("Faith and Order"), alongside the International Missionary Conference. However it was not until after the tumults of the First World War that a world conference could meet in Stockholm in 1925, one that engaged the burning issues related to the practical fellowship of the churches in prayer and worldwide service ("Life and Work"). At this conference very impressive statements were offered that expressed repentance for the church's failure to carry out its obligations correctly and to carry out its responsibility for bringing the gospel to bear on all domains of human life, statements that determined the further course of this work. Two years later, in Lausanne, the first of the world conferences on Faith and Order occurred, where, through careful comparisons, the churches became aware of the commonalities they shared within their differences. Both of these two ecumenical movements were united in 1948 in Amsterdam to form the World Council of Churches, and in 1961, at New Delhi, the International Missionary Council merged with the World Council.

The ecumenical movement began in the domain of the Reformation churches, but already early on it found its greatest reverberation in the Orthodox churches of the East. What opened the way for the creation of the movement and its initial formation and structuring was the encyclical letter of the ecumenical patriarch of Constantinople, dated 20 January 1920, and sent "to all churches, wherever they may be."[iv] In this letter he called upon them, despite their existing doctrinal differences, to create a federation for mutual assistance, to refrain from proselytizing one another, and to seek a fellowship of acting together. The Orthodox churches, with the exception of the Russian Orthodox Church, thus participated in the world conferences from the beginning. To be sure, after the Second World War, the other Orthodox churches in the Communist sphere of influence could also no longer participate for the time being, despite the fact that they—especially the Bulgarian and Romanian churches—had made very fruitful ecumenical contributions in the past. Since 1961, however, all of them, including the Russian Orthodox Church, as member churches of the World Council of Churches, constitute a living fellowship with the old non-Orthodox oriental churches (the Monophysite and Nestorian churches), together with the Lutheran, Reformed, Anglican, Methodist, and other Reformation churches, as well as the Old Catholic Church. All Christian church bodies on earth are today represented in the World Council, with the exception of the Roman Catholic Church.

"The World Council of Churches is a fellowship of churches which confess the Lord Jesus Christ as God and Savior according to the Scriptures and therefore seek to fulfill together their common calling to the glory of the one God, Father, Son, and Holy Spirit" (Constitution of the WCC, Art. 1).[v] Agreement with this Basis is the presupposition for membership. Within the work of the World Council the particular task of the Commission on Faith and Order is

to proclaim the essential oneness of the church in Christ and to keep prominently before the World Council and the churches the obligation to manifest that unity and its urgency for world mission and evangelism, [and also] to study questions of faith, church order, and worship, together with the relevant social, cultural, political, racial and other factors in their bearing on the unity of the church. (WCC Constitution, Art. 6.2)[vi]

The member churches of the World Council, to be sure, are not yet united, but again and again they have experienced and publicly borne witness to their being one in Christ, and on the basis of this oneness they seek unification. In this certainty of being one in Christ, the multiplicity of churches are less a matter of being against one another than a matter of being with one another, and—interpenetrating through the diversities of the church traditions—the abundance of the treasure of the same grace and the historical leading of the same Lord are beginning to be recognizable. The churches are thus helping one another to overcome the barriers of their differences so that the poor and threatened among them can further develop their individuality in freedom. In missionary engagement, the churches thus support one another in word and deed, taking a common position in relation to the problems of rapid social upheaval, the developing nations, racial tensions, economic and political oppression, and so forth, lending a helping hand to the harassed, and submitting appeals to governments and nations. Above all, however, the World Council of Churches is a fellowship of faith, prayer, and witness. Something great has happened when today churches—which for centuries had lived next to one another and yet had lived past each other and had not infrequently fought with each other—can say together:

We confess Jesus Christ as the Savior of humankind and the light of the world. Together we accept his command. We commit ourselves anew to bear witness to him among people. We offer ourselves to serve all in love, namely, the love by which he alone loves us. We acknowledge afresh the task to make visible before the world our unity in him. We pray for the gift of the Holy Spirit in order to fulfill our task. (The message from the Assembly of the World Council of Churches in New Delhi to be communicated in the worship services of the member churches)[vii]

5. The World Council of Churches

What resulted in the ecumenical movement is a conciliar happening that is taking shape in the assemblies of the World Council.

Here representatives of the churches come together from all countries, races, and peoples, and from the most diverse church traditions, and these are not merely the leaders and theologians of these churches but also *laity*, men and women. In these assemblies all churches have equal rights and all of their representatives are equally, without any differentiation, given a seat and a vote. These assemblies freely decide their constitution, order of business, the issues they will address, and they elect their presidents and the leaders and co-members of their committees. They freely deliberate the overtures and adopt resolutions. In this way there is a deep enrichment for the assemblies in that not only the church's officeholders but also the *laity*, with their spiritual gifts and ministries, are involved in the deliberations and resolutions, and also that *laity* can be elected to the office of president of the World Council—all because the spiritual experiences and impulses do not only come from the various churches and countries but also from the various areas of responsibility, from the official work of the church, free evangelization, education, social work, economic life, political activity, and so forth, in a mutual exchange and shared commitment to bear witness to Christ in the world.

All deliberations take place in the context of joint worship. They proceed from it and they aim toward it. The worship services—as in the councils of the ancient church as well as in the Roman Church—are not merely the external framework; rather, they decisively determine and permeate the entire process of deliberating and deciding as a whole. The issues for deliberation are above all the unity of the church in Christ and the joint witness to Christ in the contemporary world. Since the representatives of the churches come from the most diverse peoples, races, and nations, among whom there exist in part considerable tensions and oppositions, further issues ensue from the obligation to consider what responsibility God's will of love imposes upon the believers in the midst of the concrete tensions of today's world and which paths Christians must take for the sake of peace and helping the oppressed.

These assemblies are ecumenical, for one thing, in the sense that all churches on earth are invited to participate as full members of the World Council without any condition that an individual church change its dogmatic, liturgical, or constitutional character. These assemblies are also ecumenical in their common concern for the unity of all churches, in accord with the will of the Lord of the church. In this endeavor, however, no church can be forced by majority vote to deny its insights or change its character. If an assembly of the church can be called ecumenical only if all the churches on earth are gathered in it, then the assemblies of the World Council are not ecumenical, since the

Roman Church in particular is missing. Yet they are ecumenical as assemblies, since they are open to all churches and by the common faith in Christ seek the unity of all churches.

The assemblies of the World Council of Churches have some similarities to the structure of the synods of the ancient church. However, even apart from the fact that the ecumenical councils of the ancient church were convened by the emperor and hence were not free synods, there are such profound differences that the World Council has never claimed to be the continuation of the ecumenical councils. The most important difference consists in the fact that among a number of member churches in the World Council there is no fellowship in the Lord's Supper at all, or only a limited one, and no mutual acknowledgement of ministerial offices. In the assemblies of the World Council, some churches pray and deliberate with one another who in part do not acknowledge one another as church in the full sense. The synods of the ancient church, by contrast, were supported by a given, if also frequently imperiled, visible unity of the churches, and therefore they possessed a greater authority from the very start.

The assemblies of the World Council are thus a *novum* in the history of the church. What constitutes their newness? The synods of the ancient church proceeded from the visible unity of the church and sought to defend and strengthen this unity against threats to its doctrine and church order. The assemblies of the World Council, however, presuppose a divided Christendom. To be sure, they also proceed from a unity, namely, from the acknowledgment of the one Christ as God and Savior, but this oneness in Christ is still hidden beneath the disunity of the churches. The assemblies *seek* that unity in which this oneness is visibly manifested and comes to be realized in full church fellowship. They are thus a venture of faith, love, and hope. In this seeking, the assemblies of the World Council of Churches do not themselves already claim to anticipate and manifest the hoped-for unity. They do not understand themselves to be the instrument of light for the whole of Christendom. They want only to serve and assist in the growth of the unity that God brings about through his Holy Spirit, when and how it pleases him.

Editor's Notes

[i] Justinian I (483–565) was Roman emperor from 527. The traditional date that marks the final stage in the schism between the Eastern Orthodox Church and the Western Roman Church is 1054. Martin Luther was formally excommunicated by Pope Leo X on 3 January 1521.

[ii] Schlink is here referring to events in Spain that occurred after the fall of the monarchy in 1931, which brought about the end of state-sponsored Catholic education and state financial support for the Roman Catholic Church and its clergy. This period unleashed major acts of violence against Roman Catholic clergy by anarchists and socialists, a conflict that only intensified during the brutal three-year civil war (1936–39). After Francisco Franco (d. 1975), who was himself a Roman Catholic, and his fellow Nationalists were at last victorious, Pope Pius XII praised the measures that Franco took to make Spain once again uniformly Roman Catholic.

[iii] Otto Dibelius, *Der Jahrhundert der Kirche* [The Century of the Church] (Berlin: Furche, 1928). Between 1926 and his resignation in 1933 (due to conflicts with the National Socialists) Dibelius (1880–1967) served as the General Superintendent of the *Kurmark* in the Church of the Old Prussian Union. He later became active in the Confessing Church that opposed the *Deutsche Christen*. Between 1945 and the early 1960s he was the bishop of the Protestant Church of Berlin-Brandenburg. Between 1949 and 1961 he also served as the president of the Council of the EKD.

[iv] Cf. the "Patriarchal and Synodical Encyclical of 1920" by Germanus V (1835–1920), in *Orthodox Visions of Ecumenism: Statements, Messages and Reports on the Ecumenical Movement, 1902–1992*, ed. Gennadios Limouris (Geneva: World Council of Churches, 1994), 1–8.

[v] Cf. endnote 2 in chap. 1 ("The Task and Danger of the World Council of Churches") of *The Coming Christ and Church Traditions*.

[vi] "Constitution of the Commission on Faith and Order," in Gaines, *The World Council of Churches*, 1116. Cf. endnote 2 in chap. 1 ("The Task and Danger of the World Council of Churches") in *The Coming Christ and Church Traditions*.

[vii] *The New Delhi Report*, ed. W. A. Visser 't Hooft (New York: Association Press, 1962), 54 (translation slightly modified).

Chapter II:
The Conciliar Awakening of the Roman Church

The events that led to the loss of security had also affected the Roman Church. Here, too, many responded with new thinking about the church's source, which bore fruit in the liturgical movement, in the re-discovery of the Bible, and in new reflection about the church and its social responsibility. These movements were also supported in some ways by the church's teaching office. But with respect to the ecumenical movement, the official Roman Church, until a few years ago, took a position of rejection.

When a delegation of bishops from the Anglican communion (the Episcopal Church in North America) visited Pope Benedict XV on 16 May 1919 in order to extend to the Roman Church an invitation to participate in the planned first ecumenical conference for faith and order, he received them personally and in a friendly manner but then sharply declined their invitation: the doctrine and practice of the Roman Catholic Church regarding the unity of the visible church are well-known to everyone, and hence it is not possible for the Catholic Church to participate in a congress as the one planned. Then, after this world conference had been held in 1927, with all of the non-Roman church bodies participating, Pope Pius XI, in his 1928 encyclical *Mortalium animos*, renewed the Roman Church's rejection of the ecumenical movement:

But, all the same, although many non-Catholics may be found who loudly preach fraternal communion in Christ Jesus, yet you will find none at all to whom it ever occurs to submit to and obey the Vicar of Jesus Christ, either in his capacity as a teacher or as a governor. Meanwhile, they affirm that they would willingly negotiate with the Church of Rome, but on equal terms, that is as equals with an equal. But even if they could so act, it does not seem open to doubt that any pact into which they might enter would not compel them to turn from those opinions which are still the reason why they err and stray from the one fold of Christ. This being so, it is clear that the Apostolic See cannot on any terms take part in their assemblies, nor is it anyway lawful for Catholics either to support or to work for such enterprises; for if they do so, they will be giving countenance to a false Christianity, quite alien to the one Church of Christ.[i]

Corresponding to this "No" to the ecumenical movement were the statements from Pope Pius XII's encyclical *Mystici corporis Christi* (1943), in which the borders of the mystical body of Christ are identified with those of the legally constituted Roman Church.[ii] When, in 1948, several Catholic theologians—in whose hearts there was an ecumenical impulse for fellowship with non-Roman Christians—wanted to participate as guests and observers at the world conference in Amsterdam, where the World Council of Churches was constituted, they were forbidden by the duly authorized church authority to do so. A short time later, on 20 December 1949, the *instructio* of the Holy Office concerning the ecumenical movement explicitly warned against the dangers of an irenic spirit and indifferentism and permitted inter-Christian conferences only if there was a reasonable prospect of success, that is, of bringing the separated churches back into the Roman Church, and ordered that otherwise such conferences were to be adjourned in a timely manner. When, in 1954, several Catholic theologians had already arrived in Evanston to participate as observers of the world conference, they were forbidden even to enter the city limits. Hand in hand with such prohibitions were serious snubs against prominent Catholic theologians who had supported ecumenical ideas. This is all the more striking since the Roman Church also had suffered severe losses in influence, security, and members, and saw the same new issues as the other churches. Nevertheless, in spite of many parallels, the direct connection between the movements of renewal on both sides remained almost entirely restricted to personal relationships, which were generally regarded with suspicion by Rome. These relationships could not develop into official cooperative work. This basic position of rejection by the Roman Church was grounded in the conviction that it was in itself already the one, holy, catholic, and apostolic church.

A profound change in the position of the Roman Church in relation to the other churches was then brought about by Pope John XXIII, who is rightly remembered in reverence and love by many non-Roman Christians as well. He established the Secretariat for Promoting the Unity of Christians and under the leadership of Cardinal Bea gave it so many possibilities for positive results that non-Catholic visitors to the Vatican soon became aware of a change in atmosphere. In 1961 Pope John sent Roman Catholic observers to the assembly of the World Council in New Delhi. He assigned extremely important tasks to the Secretariat for Promoting the Unity of Christians in preparation for the second Vatican council, and he invited the non-Roman churches and the World Council to send observers to that council. He summoned ecumenically minded Catholic theologians who had previously been under suspicion to serve as council theologians, and he determined that ecumenism would be its theme. At the council he created an atmosphere of brotherly openness in which a substantively fruitful and personally cordial exchange took place among the observers and many council fathers and theologians.

1. The Announcement and Preparation of the Council

On 25 January 1959, a few months after his election as successor to Pius XII, Pope John XXIII announced, to the surprise of many, that he would convene an ecumenical council which, according to his intent, was not only to serve the edification of the Catholic Church but also to be an invitation to the separated fellowships to search for unity. This announcement was widely understood to mean that the non-Roman churches, especially the Orthodox churches, were to be invited to participate in a union council. It soon became clear, however, that this was intended to be only a council of bishops of the Roman Church and that, despite this restriction, the announcement labeled it an ecumenical council because, according to its self-understanding, the Roman Church designates all of its councils as ecumenical. Despite this limitation regarding who has an official seat and vote at the council, the council's vision with respect to the objective for the council was not directed only toward the Roman Church.

The task of the council, to be sure, was above all to renew and strengthen the Roman Church itself, and during the time of preparation John XXIII kept publicly reminding all participants of this task in ever new expressions. This renewal should unfold not in further dogmatic demarcations against false doctrines but in the positive unfolding of the faith, in turning toward people of the present day and adapting to them (*Aggiornamento*).

In the modern era of a world whose features have changed profoundly, a world barely standing vis-à-vis the fascinations and dangers of an almost exclusive striving for material goods... , there is more to be concerned about than retracing one or another item of doctrine or discipline back to the pure sources of revelation and tradition; at issue is the substance of human and Christian thinking and living, for which the church is the guardian and teacher, and which must again be made official and resplendent.[iii]

As a result of the joint worship services, deliberations, and resolutions of the council, however, John XXIII did not expect merely a new flowering of the spiritual life of the Roman Catholic Church—a new Pentecost for it—he also expected there to be positive effects on the other churches and the world. He anticipated that the council would be "a wonderful display of truth, unity, and love"—"a display the sight of which, we hope, will be understood, also by those separated from this Apostolic See, as a gentle invitation to seek and find that unity for which Jesus Christ prayed so ardently to his Father in heaven."[iv] So, the council was also directed toward the other churches.

Attempts have been made to find the reasons for the announcement of this council in the external situation of the Roman Church: in its extensive isolation from the modern world, in the social backwardness of many Catholic countries, in the threat of Communism, in its isolation over against the other churches, including the Orthodox churches, which had meanwhile joined the World Council. But the driving force for the announcement of the council was a different one. According to the words of John XXIII, the idea for the council was not the result of lengthy considerations, but rather it came to him as a divine stimulus during prayer, as an inspiration, which felt to him as if he had been suddenly touched by God.[v] Through this stimulus, his very loving inclination toward people, so characteristic of him, became effective in his determination of the tasks of the council and in his expectations of what the council would effect, namely, the creation of a new fellowship with the separated brothers and sisters and, beyond them, with all who are still far off.

The preparation of the council was immediately undertaken in a comprehensive manner. Bishops throughout the world, as well as the boards of the Roman Curia, the superiors of religious orders, and the Catholic faculties, were asked to identify the issues frankly, which in their view needed to be addressed by the council. These responses were published in many volumes—the responses of the bishops in eight volumes alone!—and were worked through systematically for the internal preparation of the council. In doing this, overlapping proposals were taken into consideration and an attempt was made to select the most comprehensive list of desired topics as possible. On Pentecost Monday 1960, ten preparatory commissions and three secretariats, including the Secretariat for the Promotion of Christian Unity, were established and the topics for the council were distributed among the commissions who would work through the proposals (schemata) for the council. These thematically determined commissions were subordinated to the Central Commission, through whose control the schemata, which had been worked through by the individual commissions, had to pass through before their distribution to the council fathers. Without doubt, in this way the council was prepared most comprehensively and carefully. Prior to the start of the council some seventy schemata had been worked through, yet only seven of them reached the council fathers as a basis for discussion before the first period of the council began. Then, in November 1962, there appeared a second volume with two additional texts.

2. The Structure of a Council of the Roman Church

The announcement of an ecumenical council by Pope John XXIII evoked such great surprise, primarily because of the widespread opinion, held since the end of the First Vatican Council (1870), that further councils of the Roman Church would no longer be necessary, indeed, perhaps even no longer possible, since that council had defined the primacy of the Roman bishop as consisting in his possession of the highest and plenary power over the church and in the infallibility of his definitive decisions on doctrines of faith and morals. According to Canon 218 of the *Codex Juris Canonici*, the Roman pontiff has "not only a primacy of honor, but the supreme and plenary power of jurisdiction in the universal church, both in matters of faith and morals and in matters that concern the discipline and government of the church scattered throughout the whole world."[vi] A council of the Roman Church had thus become fundamentally superfluous. If, however, such a council is convened, it is henceforth entirely dependent on the greater or lesser willingness of the pope to listen to the voice of the bishops, for the pope alone has the right to convene a council, to determine the topics treated and the order of business, to appoint the preparatory commissions and presiding officers, and to lend his weight to the resolutions of the council fathers. Only through his consent and his promulgation do these resolutions become resolutions of the council. On the basis of these considerations, there arose not only the question of whether a council of the Roman Church is still necessary but of whether under these presuppositions a genuinely conciliar action is still possible in the Roman Church, since one individual member of this church had been recognized to have such an all-embracing power over the whole church.

Because of this structure, grounded in canon law, a council of the Roman Church differs from the councils of all other churches. Indeed, for the councils of the ancient church such a domineering position on the part of the Roman bishop would have been strange. The presence of the Roman bishop or his legate was not constitutive for either the concept or the validity of an ecumenical council in the ancient church, as the Second Ecumenical Council at Constantinople (381) demonstrates.[vii]

In the more recent history of Roman councils a profound change has occurred also in the composition of the council. While in some medieval councils laity still participated in large numbers, since that time a complete clericalization has taken place. Those who participate in the council with "seat and vote" are now limited to the bishops, or more precisely, to the cardinals, patriarchs, primates, archbishops, bishops, certain abbots, and other representatives of the upper clergy. In contrast to the so-called Apostolic Council (Acts 15) and the synods of the first centuries, and in contrast to those of the Reformation churches and some of the synods of the Eastern Church, the laity of the Roman Church are completely excluded. Their voice can only be heard indirectly, namely, insofar as the bishops make the concerns of the Church's laity their own. The direct cooperation of the lower clergy is also excluded from the drafting of resolutions.

A council of the Roman Church also differs from the councils or synods of the other churches in that it designates itself an "ecumenical council," even though in it only the bishops of the Roman Church have a seat and vote, but not the bishops of the Eastern Church and those of the non-Roman churches of the West. This designation is made use of even when it is not a union council and when it does not in any other way concern itself with the theme of the unification of the separated churches. The Roman Church designates its general councils as ecumenical because it fundamentally acknowledges no other church as *church* in the true and complete sense of that word. According to its self-understanding, it is in itself already the one, holy, catholic, and apostolic church on earth. By contrast, all other churches—both the Reformation churches and the Orthodox churches—have refrained from designating their own synods as ecumenical councils because of the divisions in the church. Correspondingly, no other church acknowledges the general councils of the Roman Church as ecumenical. This is one of the reasons why the Orthodox churches were so hesitant to send observers to the Second

Vatican Council. Also, the Roman Church's self-designation of its councils as ecumenical councils differs from the ecumenical councils of the ancient church, which could rightly designate themselves as such because the Eastern and Western churches were united.

If one compares the councils of the Roman Church with those of the ancient churches, the former are also a *novum* in the history of councils. We must not allow our view of this to be clouded by thinking that the Roman councils have become what they are today through an historical process of development and that in this respect they have preserved the semblance of a continuity. Rather, this development, which underwent considerable zigzagging in the late Middle Ages, has resulted in profound changes that differ from the structure of the synods in the ancient church.

The councils of the Roman Church are indeed a *novum* in an entirely different sense, yes, almost the opposite sense, from the assemblies of the World Council of Churches. While the latter proceed from the situation of a divided Christendom, the Roman councils—disregarding all of the churches that are not subject to the pope—proceed from the premise of the internal, visible unity of the Roman Church. In contrast to the Roman councils, the assemblies of the World Council seek to embrace the whole of Christendom and, proceeding from the confession of Christ that is shared by all participants, to move forward to joint statements on issues of faith and church order and, beyond that, to cooperative work and visible unity. The Roman councils, however, have been determined by the intention to secure the Roman Church more and more through dogma and canon law, and to firm up its own existing visible church unity, which the non-Roman churches are then being invited to join. If the danger threatening the World Council consists in the fact that its member churches are content to occupy themselves in busyness, instead of achieving visible unity, the danger threatening the Roman Church is that it shuts itself up into a centralized solipsism, instead of recognizing the catholic fullness of the Christ who is working on earth.

3. The First Period of the Council[viii]

After the solemn procession of more than 2000 bishops through the portal of St. Peter's and after the mass, which was celebrated with the invocation of the Holy Spirit, Pope John XXIII opened the council with an impressive address, which gave the council fathers a significant orientation and at the same time allowed them complete freedom in treating the concrete topics of the council. Particular attention was given to the pope's warning against a pessimistic view of the present age and to his admonition "to distinguish between the substance of the ancient doctrine of the deposit of faith (*depositum fidei*) and the formulation of its wording."[ix] The Catholic doctrine is to be set forth "according to the methods of scholarly research and the literary forms of modern life," and above all with pastoral application.[x] In doing that, it "meets contemporary needs more by demonstrating the validity of its doctrine than by condemning (false doctrines)."[xi]

In the first session of business, on the following day, there was to be the election of the members of the council's ten commissions, based on the proposed slates that contained primarily the names of those who had served on the preparatory commissions. On the motion of Cardinals Liénart and Frings,[xii] the election was postponed so that the council fathers could themselves identify suitable persons prior to voting. New slates were then drawn up from the circles of the council itself, and the results of the elections demonstrated not only the independence of the council from the Curia and its proposed names but also its intention to secure for the progressive forces their proper place in the events of the council.

The reason for this step, which caused quite a stir, was, for one thing, the disappointment regarding the documents that had been developed by the preparatory commissions, especially by the Theological Commission standing most closely to the Holy Office. In view of the situation of Catholic theology, particularly in France and Germany, these documents were astonishingly retrogressive. Thus, for example, had the schema of the Constitution on the Sources of Revelation been carried out, it would have made further work of modern Catholic exegetes impossible, and the schema of the Constitution on the Purity and Preservation of the *Depositum Fidei*, with its undifferentiated string of rejections of various errors of our time, did not in any way correspond to the pastoral aim of the council. Equally retrogressive was the wording of a schema on marriage. Obviously, the representatives of a new Catholic theology had not been able to prevail against the dominating conservative forces in the preparatory commissions. Added to this was the fact that already prior to the council some of these short-comings had been objected to in the Central Commission, but then, despite these criticisms, the texts were not rectified before they were sent to the council fathers. A high-handedness was caught sight of in the circle of the Curia, to which one did not want to yield. Still other, older vexations about the Curia also played a role.

With this first independent decision by the council the path toward freedom was paved, in which then the deliberations of the council and the alignments among the council fathers occurred. To set forth a detailed history of the council is not our task here. Our particular interest focuses, above all, on the content of the council's resolutions and their significance for the rest of Christendom. In this chapter, however, we must represent the impressive dynamic of the whole process: the breakthrough by the progressive forces, their growth, and their restraint in view of the obligation to reach joint resolutions with the retrogressive forces.

The council's discussion began with the schema of the Constitution on the Sacred Liturgy. This schema was the most fully developed, its topic lay closest to the heart of every bishop, and for that reason it was most suited to create a synodical atmosphere quickly, since it was not at all obvious that the more than two thousand bishops would so soon experience such synodical fellowship. The questions raised here about the use of the vernacular and the liturgical privileges of the territorial conferences of bishops were already of great significance, especially since important questions about the understanding of the church were already heralded by the questions of liturgical practice, especially those regarding the understanding of unity, within which, until now, the unity in using the Latin liturgical language had also been a part. How are unity, uniformity, and multiplicity related to one another? The interest in the pastoral address to the person of today and such a person's capacities for understanding, which was so important for the further course of the council, soon began to grow and to make itself pertinent over against the traditional unquestioned assumptions about the liturgical order. The dramatic aspects of the discussion intensified with the schema on the sources of revelation [de fontibus revelationis], which was directed against modern Catholic biblical scholarship and moved along the lines of recent attacks in Rome against the work there by the Pontifical Biblical Institute.[xiii] This schema also rejected an interpretation of the Council of Trent, namely, an interpretation that attempted to raise the value of Holy Scripture by understanding it as the source of the whole of revelation, not merely of a part of it. Also highly dramatic were the objections—especially on the part of the Melchitic Patriarch Maximos[xiv]—against the schema of a Constitution on the Unity of the Church [de ecclesia unitate] that contained the conditions for the unification of the Orthodox churches with the Roman Church, conditions that were regarded by the Orthodox as offensive rather than as inviting.[xv]

There was more at issue in these and other discussions than only these texts. A spiritual awakening occurred in the council, whose dynamic has rightly made a profound impression also outside of the Roman Church. Through an impressive self-criticism there was strong pressure for a renewal of the Church. A dynamic working instead of the static self-understanding, a moving forward instead of the standing still, the courage to be poor instead of securing power and glory, the openness toward the separated sisters and brothers instead of the demarcations of self-vindication—all of these were called for, as was a new approach toward the world. This spiritual awakening deeply affected more and more of the council fathers, and soon the other council fathers appeared to be pushed back into the defensive position of a minority. It became clear that there are most basic spiritual forces alive in the Roman Church, which had often remained hidden under ritual, juridical, moralistic, and scholastic forms, and which were now breaking forth in the conciliar encounter and were shaking these barriers—in order to serve God and human beings in a new, direct way. The press has again and again spoken of a struggle by the "progressive" forces against the "conservative" ones, but these labels are misleading, for, aside from the fact that the discussions of the council, even during dramatic moments, were conducted in a dignified and objective manner, the "progressives" have very little in common with modernism or liberalism. On the contrary, they link in a new way to the theology of the fathers in the ancient church and are therefore in reality more like representatives of the old. Conversely, the "conservatives" are more like the modernists in the history of the church in that they advocate the positions of the newer Catholicism that have emerged since the time of the Counter-Reformation, positions that were then firmed up in the nineteenth century through neo-scholastic theology. In the awakening of the "progressives," therefore, the concern was about an ecumenically significant reconsideration of the biblical and ancient-church foundations that are shared by all the churches, in order to tackle in a new way the issues and tasks confronting Christendom today.

The rapid spread of this movement would not have been possible apart from the theologians who were assembled in Rome, either as council theologians or as theological advisers of their bishops. Pope John XXIII had not hesitated to call also the most prominent advocates of the new theology, individuals who had been hindered under his predecessor and who continue to be suspect by the Holy Office. Pope John thus made it possible for representatives of all theological orientations in the Roman Church to be present at the council. What such forward-looking theologians—as, for example, the Germans Karl Rahner, Hans Küng, and Josef Ratzinger, or the French Yves Congar, Jean Daniélou, and Henri de Lubac—had accomplished, can hardly be overestimated.[xvi] Their contributions, to be sure, could not be directly expressed in the council's *aula*[xvii] in St. Peter's, since there only bishops had a seat and a vote, but in many lectures at bishops' conferences, and in countless conversations, they set forth their perspective on the issues treated in the schemata; and many bishops who were still rooted in the scholastic school-theology of their student days recognized that the new theology, which at first seemed strange to them, opened up the possibility of tackling the issues of our time in a more appropriate way than could have been done by the school-theology with its conceptuality that is so foreign to contemporary thinking. Thus, in the course of the council, conversions in theological thinking clearly occurred, and increasingly the bishops, as they worked out their formal opinions in the discussion, entrusted themselves to the advice of precisely these "progressive" theologians.

This awakening also effected the relationship between the council fathers and the official observers from the non-Roman churches. There were, of course, cardinals, bishops, and theologians who shook their heads at the pope's ecumenical interests and consented only because of their duty of obedience to him. This consent was perhaps made easier when they considered that the presence of the official observers and guests from the various churches might appear in the eyes of the world to be a gathering of all the churches around the pope. They encountered the observers with a marked, if rather distant civility. There were others, however, who enthusiastically thought that the existing differences and the history of the divisions in the church could be jumped over and who expected that the impact of the council would awaken in the observers an irresistible pressure to return to the Roman Church. They encountered the observers with an embracing certainty of victory. There were also, however, those who took seriously the reasons for the church divisions and the commitments of conscience held by those Christians separated from Rome, and who perceived the existence of the other churches as a genuine challenge to the Roman Church. They had no firm conception of how unity could be brought about but began first by questioning in brotherly openness about the truth by which the others live, and then, in turn, witnessed to them the truth by which they themselves live. Here genuine encounters occurred and ecumenical insights developed that have the promise of bearing fruit. The number of those who sought such openness in conversation with the official observers increased, and there resulted a profound exchange concerning the council's proposals. The Secretariat for Promoting Christian Unity had achieved outstanding results in facilitating these encounters. Each week he invited people to a joint meeting with the official observers, in which the latter were expected to provide critical opinion on the texts of the council then under discussion. Some of the formal recommendations by the observers to the council were then referred by the Secretariat to the appropriate commissions for consideration, and more than once ideas of the observers were adopted in the official opinions of the council fathers in the *aula* or in the editing of the texts.

That the council could unfold in this freedom was due especially to Pope John. On only two occasions did his intervention in the events of the council become apparent: when—despite the still ongoing discussion about the liturgy—he instructed that St. Joseph be included in the canon of the mass and when he withdrew the schema on the sources of revelation as a basis for discussion. Here, however, he decided in favor of the majority of the council fathers, despite their not having reached a two-thirds majority. The council thus began as a force field with three poles: pope, council, and Curia; or, more precisely: the pope, the Curia alongside the "conservative" council fathers, and the "progressive" fathers, who included only a few representatives of the Curia. In contrast to the First Vatican Council and the Council of Trent, the pope and the Curia did not form a common pole of force. Only in this way was it possible for the forward-thinking majority of the council to be victorious over the retrogressive forces of the Curia in numerous ballots.

4. The Second and Third Periods of the Council[xviii]

Given how sincerely John XXIII had been revered and beloved far beyond the borders of the Roman Church, and given how profound the general grief was after his passing, anxious questions arose: Who will be his successor? Will he carry on with the council? And how will he do this? Paul VI[xix]—Cardinal Montini, who had served at one time as the Secretary of State under Pius XII and who had recently been the Archbishop of Milan—quickly endorsed the council, and in a letter to the chairman of the presidium of the council, Cardinal Tisserant,[xx] he instructed that the organization of the council's work be streamlined, an important step, and he also permitted several laity (initially only men, later also women) to be auditors (*auditores*) at the working meetings of the council.

In his address at the opening of the second period of the council the new pope whole-heartedly affirmed the task which his predecessor had set before the council. Speaking directly to the deceased he said:

Being conscious of the church's teaching office, you have revived the conviction that Christian doctrine is not only a truth which is investigated by a reason illuminated by faith, but also a word which creates life and action, and that the authority of the church must not confine itself to condemning errors that conflict with the faith, but must also extend to proclaiming the positive and essential doctrines by which faith is fruitful.[xxi]

Beyond that, Paul VI deepened the program of his predecessor. With great urgency he set Christ before everyone as the starting point, the way, and the goal of the entire conciliar work of the assembly. The four key issues of the council had to be handled in a Christocentric manner: the self-understanding of the church, its reform, the reuniting of all Christians in unity, and the dialogue with the contemporary world. In connection with the presentations on the third issue, the pope addressed the official observers from the non-Roman churches:

If we must acknowledge some blame for this separation, with humble supplication we ask God for forgiveness and we also ask forgiveness from those brothers who believe they have been wronged by us. As for us, we are ready to forgive the offenses against the Catholic Church and to forget the pain that has been inflicted upon it in the long course of disputes and divisions.[xxii]

The conditional way in which guilt was here expressed, as well as the fact that obviously the dogmatic decisions of the Roman Church were excluded from the confession of guilt, must not hinder us from recognizing in these words an echo of the Fifth Petition of the Lord's Prayer, and from responding in a corresponding manner. With great feeling the pope assured the observers of the sincerity of his approach to them and of his respect for "the original and common religious heritage that was preserved among the separated brothers and was in part also well developed by them."[xxiii]

This speech could be understood as an encouragement by the forces of renewal at the council. They thus continued to make progress in the discussions about the church and ecumenism, which, together with those concerning religious freedom and the state of Israel, were the focal point of this period of the council. In the criticism of the very conservative schema on the church [*de ecclesia*] and in the acceptance of ecumenical ideas that were new to most, the dynamic of the initial discussions reached its theological depth. More and more a salvation-historical and eschatological consideration of the church and its relation to the world became prominent, and biblical concepts were explicitly given preference over against the conceptuality of the scholastic school-dogmatics. From these presuppositions there resulted an increasing openness for God's salvific action beyond the borders of the Roman Church as well. From these new perspectives, the non-Roman churches were drawn into the deliberations and more and more there was an awareness of the dimensions of the multiplicity within the church's unity. The dynamic of the council began to have its effect in the thinking about foundations and methods.

Also during the second period of the council, the number of those who committed themselves to the progressive way for renewing the Roman Church grew larger, while the retrogressive forces seemed to have become an even smaller minority. At the same time, however, it became clear that this minority persisted in its position and could not be overcome, especially since it had a strong reserve in the Curia. Furthermore, especially in the discussions about the college of bishops, it became clearer than was the case in the first period that its authoritative obligations in terms of both dogma and canon law place limits on every renewal of that church, and that the forces of resistance could with some justification appeal to this fact. In addition, the slowness in the progress of the council's work was increasingly depressing. At the end of the second period, only the Constitution on the Sacred Liturgy and a rather superficial Decree on the Modern Means of Communication (press, radio, and television) could be released. Even though the original seventy schemata had been condensed to seventeen, there was still a large number of council proposals that had not yet been accepted as a basis for discussion or that needed to be reworked because of the widely divergent opinions in the discussion. Finally, there were proposals whose texts had not yet been handed over to the council fathers. These facts may well have also influenced the pope's speeches at the end of the second period and at the beginning of the third. Those speeches were more reticent than his first address and could no longer be understood as a supportive stimulus for the progressive forces.

The third period demonstrated that these forces had in no way grown weak. In the questions concerning the relationship of Scripture and tradition, and also, particularly, in the concern for a new relationship to the contemporary world, noteworthy advances were made. At the same time, however, there now began in increasing measure the search for compromises that would have the prospect of adoption. This became especially clear in the discussions about the subject of Mary. Despite the clearly negative impacts that it would have on the relationship with the non-Roman churches, "progressive" council fathers now began to minimize their objection to designating Mary as "mediatrix," which was demanded by the "conservatives," while the opposite side no longer seemed to insist on the additional demand that Mary be designated as "Mother of the Church." Through these and other compromises it became possible for the schemata on the church and ecumenism to be adopted by large majorities in the voting on their individual paragraphs.

At the end of the third period, however, it became clear that the minority sought to achieve its goals not only by its contributions to the council sessions and in the commissions but also through hidden influences on the procedures of the council and by appealing to papal authority. On 16 November, surprisingly, a *nota explicative praevia* [an explanatory note] to the third chapter of the schema on the church was distributed, which (with the claim of permanent validity) precisely defined the freedom of the pope in relation to the college of bishops and in this sense shifted the accents in the text that had already been voted on and adopted by the council. On 19 November, a previously scheduled vote on the schema concerning religious freedom was surprisingly set aside, and a petition to the pope, sponsored by the American bishops and supported by many hundreds of signatures in just a few hours [which called for a reconsideration of this action –Ed.], was rejected. Furthermore, the highest authority ordered nineteen textual changes to be made to the Decree on Ecumenism, which had already been adopted through voting on its particular details. Several of these changes clearly weakened the ecumenical openness that had been intended. These interventions caused great consternation and dejection among most of the council fathers, since a different "collegial" understanding of the relationship between pope and bishops had meanwhile been established. Thereupon, in the public closing session on 21 November, the pope proclaimed Mary as "Mother of the Church," even though in its text on Mary the council had deliberately avoided this title.

There can be no doubt that in accord with the structure of a council of the Roman Church the pope was justified to intervene in this way. Nevertheless, it is difficult to know why he intervened as he did since these interventions damaged the repute of the council in the eyes of the world and shattered its confidence in its synodical freedom. Did he want to come to the aid of the conservative minority and prevent a repetition of what happened at the First Vatican Council—now, however, involving not the opponents but the supporters of the definition of primacy at that time?[xxiv] Did he want to make concessions to the Curia because he saw himself as being reliant upon their work in a special way? Did he see the authority of his primacy endangered by the tendencies of the progressive fathers? In any case, at the end of the third period the constellation of powers had been changed in relation to the first period. The pope now seemed to be making common cause with the Curia and the conservative minority, and the tri-polar relationship of forces seemed to have become a bipolarity.

5. The Conclusion of the Council[xxv]

In the official discussions of the fourth period no new advances emerged, not even in the treatment of the still most controversial schema on the church in the contemporary world. It was now a matter of coming to a conclusion. Apart from the questions about celibacy and birth control, the pope imposed no limits on the discussions, and his wishes for changes were submitted by him— as some had heard—not as orders of the pope but as formal opinions of the bishop of Rome, who did not want them to be considered as different from the formal opinions of the other bishops. Nevertheless, he attached great public importance to a formulation of the definite texts in such a way that in the final voting there might be the fewest possible negative votes. In this way the conservative minority was given greater weight than its number warranted, and certainly some of the texts were thereby weakened, the significance of which, however, one must not overstate. If one compares the final officially authorized texts with the initial proposals, one cannot help but see what great advances were reached and also how many of the newly awakened progressive positions were retained in the compromise formulations. If in a joke—which, incidentally, did not originate among the official observers—the council was compared to a dance that moves one step forward, one step backwards, one step left, one step right, and then everybody turns himself around, it is only fair to add that the steps forward were much greater than those backward.

The fourth period was characterized especially by the editorial work of the committees and by many formal recommendations. In this period eleven proposals were adopted and proclaimed by the pope. Only with the greatest respect can one think of the excellent work that the commissions accomplished in these exceedingly difficult final revisions. For many of the schemata there were thousands of proposed changes, which in part were completely contradictory. Every proposed change had to be carefully examined in the light of the total thread of the previous discussion, and its acceptance or rejection had to be precisely established. All this was accomplished with remarkable care and in great loyalty to all the fathers so that until the very end further clarifications were attained.

That the proposals of the council were almost all adopted by an overwhelming majority must be credited to the work of the commissions. This consensus appears not to have been the result of weariness or an act of obedience in relation to a formal obligation to reach agreement, but the fruit of working together in the course of which objective arguments eventually established a *rapprochement*. Looking back on the fourth period one can say that, within the limitations of a council of the Roman Church, a genuine synodical event took place in Vatican II, indeed, to a greater extent than in Vatican I. That no one seemed to be vanquished at the end of the council was especially due to papal diplomacy.

Despite all of the advances, just how great the gap remains between the separated churches became clear shortly before the end of the council in the contributions regarding the issue of indulgences, which had been the historic cause of the Reformation and which are rejected also by the Eastern Church. Despite some in part very sharp, Catholic criticism against the practice of indulgences, one hardly heard a single voice that called indulgences as such into question. Corresponding to this were also the stipulations in the apostolic constitution *Mirificus eventus*, in which the pope announced a council jubilee in connection with the institution of the holy year.

On 7 and 8 December the council was brought to its resplendent close. Several days earlier a joint worship service was held in the Basilica of St. Paul Outside-the-Walls, in which the pope, the bishops, and the observers participated. Scripture readings and prayers were spoken alternately by Catholic theologians and non-Catholic observers, and the pope delivered a warm-hearted farewell speech to the representatives of non-Roman Christendom. On 7 December the pope proclaimed the last four resolutions of the council. In addition, a papal brief was read and presented to the delegate of the Ecumenical Patriarch Athenagoras.[xxvi] In this brief the pope expressed his regret concerning the excommunication of Patriarch Cerularius in the year 1054 and its consequences for the Roman and Orthodox churches—an impressive gesture of his desire to be reconciled.[xxvii] On 8 December the council was publicly and solemnly concluded by the pope in St. Peter's Square. All sixteen resolutions were put in force as official for all time, and the bishops promised to maintain them always. At the same time, the universality of the Roman Church was in view through multiple greetings to the sick, laborers, artists, and others.

Editor's Notes

[i] *Mortalium animos*, Encyclical of Pope Pius XI on Religious Unity (6 January 1928), Vatican.va, accessed 26 January 2016, http://w2.vatican.va/content/pius-xi/en/encyclicals/documents/hf_p-xi_enc_19280106_mortalium-animos.html (cf. Denzinger 3683).

[ii] *Mystici corporis Christi*, Encyclical of Pope Pius XII on the Mystical Body of Christ (29 June 1943), Vatican.va, accessed 26 January 2016, http://w2.vatican.va/content/pius-xii/en/encyclicals/documents/hf_p-xii_enc_29061943_mystici-corporis-christi.html (cf. Denzinger 3800–3822).

[iii] Address of Pope John XXIII to members and advisers of all commissions preparing for the council (14 November 1960), *Herder-Korrespondenz* 15 (1961), 167.

[iv] *Ad Petri cathedram*, Encyclical of Pope John XXIII on Truth, Unity and Peace in a Spirit of Charity (29 June 1959), Vatican.va, accessed 26 January 2016, http://w2.vatican.va/content/john-xxiii/en/encyclicals/documents/hf_j-xxiii_enc_29061959_ad-petri.html (This encyclical does not appear in Denzinger.)

[v] "As regards the initiative for the great event which gathers us here, it will suffice to repeat as historical documentation our personal account of the first sudden bringing up in our heart and lips of the simple words, 'Ecumenical Council.' We uttered those words in the presence of the Sacred College of Cardinals on that memorable 25 January 1959, the Feast of the Conversion of St. Paul, in the basilica dedicated to him. It was completely unexpected, like a

flash of heavenly light, shedding sweetness in eyes and hearts. And at the same time it gave rise to a great fervor throughout the world in expectation of the holding of the Council" (Pope John XXIII, "Opening Address to the Council" [11 October 1962], Vatican.va, accessed 26 January 2016, http://w2.vatican.va/content/john-xxiii/la/speeches/1962/documents/hf_j-xxiii_spe_19621011_opening-council.html]. For an English translation of this important address: vatican2voice.org, accessed 26 January 2016, http://vatican2voice.org/91docs/opening_-speech.htm

[vi]   "Romanus Pontifex, Beati Petri in primatu Successor, habet non solum primatum honoris, sed supremam et plenam potestatem iurisdictionis in universam ecclesiam tum in rebus quae ad fidem et mores, tum in iis quae ad disciplinam et regimen ecclesiae per totum orbem diffusae pertinent" (Canon 218 in the 1917 *Codex Iuris Canonici*).

[vii]   Theodosius I convened this Eastern synod in Constantinople in May 381 in order to unite the Eastern Church in the wake of the long conflict over Arianism. 150 Orthodox bishops took part and, at the behest of the emperor, Meletius of Antioch presided. The bishop of Rome was not invited. Apparently, only one Western bishop was present, and this by accident. Although no other Western bishops or Roman legates were present, this synod's outcome was sufficiently important that it came to be regarded in the East and in the West as the Second Ecumenical Council. Its primary theological significance resides in the fact that it applied to the Holy Spirit the Council of Nicaea's reasoning about the Son's relation to the Father.

[viii] The first period took place between 11 October 1962 and 8 December 1962. Unlike the other three periods, this one had only one session. Over the course of the four periods of the council (thirty-six weeks in total) there were nine sessions. Within these sessions there were 168 plenary working meetings and ten public assemblies. More than 2500 bishops participated in the council.

[ix]   "Est enim aliud ipsum depositum fidei, seu veritates, quae veneranda doctrina nostra continentur, aliud modus, quo eaedem enuntiantur..." [For it is one and the same deposit of faith, and the truths contained in our venerable doctrine are one thing and the manner in which they are annunciated is another...], (Pope John XXIII, "Opening Address to the Council").

[x]   "...ea ratione pervestigetur et exponatur, quam tempora postulant nostra" [...be rationally investigated and expounded in a manner required by our times] (Pope John XXIII, "Opening Address to the Council").

[xi]   "....magis quam damnando, suae doctrinae vim uberius explicando putat hodiernis necessitatibus esse consulendum" [rather than damning (false teaching), explaining the validity of its teaching to meet today's needs of society more fully] (Pope John XXIII, "Opening Address to the Council").

[xii]   Achille Liénart (1884–1973) was Bishop of Lille. Josef Richard Frings (1887–1978) was the Archbishop of Cologne.

[xiii] This schema was eventually withdrawn by Pope Paul VI.

[xiv]   Maximos IV Cardinal Saigh (1878–1967) was the Melchite patriarch of Antioch. At the start of the council, he was eighty-four years old. By its end he had proven to be one of its "most colorful figures" (Xavier Rynne, *Vatican Council II* [New York: Farrar, Straus and Giroux, 1968], 60). He usually spoke in French at the council, instead of using the stipulated Latin.

[xv]   The original schema *de eccelesia unitate* was drawn up by the Commission for the Eastern Churches in order to address the reunion of those churches with Rome. It was made available in November 1962. (This schema is not to be confused with the schema *de ecclesia*, the original proposal for the Constitution on the Church, which was drawn up by the Preparatory Commission, under the direction of Alfredo Cardinal Ottaviani (1890–1979), secretary of the Holy Office of the Curia and perhaps the leading voice among the "conservatives."). The Orthodox observers felt that *de ecclesia unitate* did not fully appreciate their reality as church. Moreover, the document affirms papal primacy and the supremacy of the Roman Church. The condition within the schema that the Eastern churches "return to the house they deserted" was

particularly offensive. This schema was eventually set aside by the council and its elements reworked and re-incorporated into other schemata.

[xvi] Karl Rahner (1904–84), a Jesuit priest and scholar, taught at the University of Innsbruck (after 1937), and was made a *peritus* (expert adviser) by Pope John XXIII in November 1962. Cf. endnote 1 in the preface above. Two years earlier Hans Küng (b. 1928) had been appointed to teach Catholic theology at the University of Tübingen. Like his colleague Joseph Ratzinger (later Pope Benedict XVI [b. 1927]), he also was appointed *peritus* by Pope John XXIII. Schlink had significant contact with all three of these Catholic theologians. Yves Congar (1904–95) served on the preparatory Theological Commission in advance of the council, and was one of the most influential of the *periti*. Jean Daniélou (1905–74) and Henri de Lubac (1896–1991) also served as *periti* at the council.

[xvii] The term *aula*, in this context, refers to the main nave of St. Peter's basilica, where the council fathers were seated and where all of the council's working sessions took place. Normally, this term is used for the main lecture hall at a European university.

[xviii] The second period (sessions 2–3) took place between 29 September 1963 and 4 December 1963. The third period (sessions 4–5) occurred between 14 September 1964 and 21 November 1964.

[xix] Pope Paul VI (1897–1978), born Giovanni Battista Montini, was ordained in Brescia and then undertook further studies in Rome. In 1922 he joined the staff of the Vatican's Secretariat of State. After a brief time of service in Warsaw, he returned to Rome where he continued his service in the Secretariat of State. In 1954, in the wake of political infighting in the Vatican, he was made archbishop of Milan. Pope John XXIII made him his first cardinal. Cardinal Montini was sixty-five when he became pope.

[xx] Eugène Tisserant (1884–1972) had been the Titular Archbishop of Iconium (after 1937) and was serving as the librarian and archivist of the Roman Church at the time of Vatican II. He had also served in a number of roles in the Curia, including president of the Pontifical Biblical Commission (1937–1946).

[xxi] Speech of Pope Paul VI at the opening of the second period of the Second Vatican Council (29 September 1963). For the Italian and Latin versions of this speech: Vatican.va, accessed 5 February 2016, http://w2.vatican.va/content/paul-vi/it/speeches/1963/documents/hf_p-vi_spe_19630929_concilio-vaticano-ii.html

[xxii] Speech of Pope Paul VI at the opening of the second period of the Second Vatican Council (29 September 1963).

[xxiii] Speech of Pope Paul VI at the opening of the second period of the Second Vatican Council (29 September 1963).

[xxiv] At the First Vatican Council, which began on 8 December 1869, the seven hundred or so bishops were divided into two opposing groups. On the one hand, there was an overwhelming majority of conservative bishops who favored a robust, definite statement on papal infallibility. They also wanted to reaffirm the *Syllabus of Errors* (1864). On the other hand, a liberal minority (never more than about 20% of the total) found itself more and more in the defensive position. The Curia made sure that none from the minority was placed on the committee that was to draw up the statement on infallibility. Other maneuvers on the part of the conservatives further alienated the liberals. Eventually, when deliberations appeared to be moving too slow to their liking, the conservative majority appealed to Pope Pius IX (1792–1878; pope from 1846) that he allow the issue of infallibility to be addressed first, ahead of the more general discussion about the nature of the church. The minority also appealed to the pope, who disregarded their objections and sided with the conservative majority. The final version, adopted on 18 July 1870 (during a thunderstorm), includes the famous teaching: "That the Roman pontiff, when he speaks *ex cathedra*, that is, when acting in the office of the shepherd and teacher of all Christians, he defines, by virtue of his supreme apostolic authority, a doctrine concerning faith or morals to be held by the universal Church, possesses through the divine assistance promised to him in blessed Peter the infallibility with which the Divine Redeemer willed his Church to be endowed in defining the doctrine concerning faith or

morals; and that such definitions of the Roman pontiff are therefore irreformable of themselves, not because of the consent of the Church" (Denzinger 3074; Tanner 2.816). Cf. Thomas Bokenkotter, *A Concise History of the Catholic Church*, rev. ed. (New York: Doubleday, 2004), 322–26.

[xxv]   The fourth period (sessions 6–9) occurred between 14 September 1965 and 7 December 1965. The solemn closing of the council took place on 8 December 1965.

[xxvi] Aristocles Matthew Spyrou (1886–1972), who as Athanagoras I had been the Greek Orthodox Archbishop of North America (1930–48), was the Patriarch of Constantinople from 1948 until his death.

[xxvii] Michael Cerularius (c. 1000–1059) was the Patriarch of Constantinople between 1049 and the year of his death.

Chapter III:
The Resolutions of the Council

The comprehensive task of *aggiornamento* that Pope John XXIII had set before the council and the comprehensive consideration of the questions that had been requested by the bishops to be taken up at the council correspond to the large number of conciliar resolutions, their thematic diversity, and their unusual scope as a whole. The scope of texts far exceeds that which was decided upon by any of the ecumenical councils of the ancient church or also by any of the later councils of the Roman Church, including even the Council of Trent, whose periods covered a span of eighteen years (1545–63).

1. Constitutions, Decrees, Declarations

As late as the third period, five different types of schemata were still being proposed to the council, namely, constitutions, decrees, declarations, propositions, and a *votum* [an authoritative opinion] on the sacrament of marriage. In the final results, however, only three types of conciliar resolutions are to be differentiated. The sixteen resolutions are here listed in chronological order within each type, including the Latin opening words by which they are named and the date of their solemn proclamation by the Pope (promulgation).

Constitutions:

a) Constitution on the Sacred Liturgy (*Sacrosanctum concilium*, 4 December 1963)
b) Dogmatic Constitution on the Church (*Lumen gentium*, 21 November 1964)
c) Dogmatic Constitution on Revelation (*Dei verbum*, 18 November 1965)
d) Pastoral Constitution on the Church in the Contemporary World (*Gaudium et spes*, 7 December 1965)

Decrees:

a) Decree on the Mass Media (*Inter mirifica*, 4 December 1963)
b) Decree on the Catholic Churches of the Eastern Rite (*Orientalium ecclesiarum*, 21 November 1964)
c) Decree on Ecumenism (*Unitatis redintegratio*, 21 November 1964)
d) Decree on the Pastoral Office of Bishops in the Church (*Christus Dominus*, 28 October 1965)
e) Decree on Priestly Formation (*Optatam totius ecclesiae renovationem*, 28 October 1965)

f) Decree on the Suitable Renewal of the Religious Life (*Perfectae caritatis*, 28 October 1965)

g) Decree on the Apostolate of the Laity (*Apostolicam actuositatem*, 18 November 1965)

h) Decree on the Mission Activity of the Church (*Ad gentes*, 7 December 1965)

i) Decree on the Ministry and Life of Priests (*Presbyterorum ordinis*, 7 December 1965)

Declarations:

a) Declaration on Christian Education (*Gravissimum educationis momentum*, 28 October 1965)

b) Declaration on the Church's Relation to the Non-Christian Religions (*Nostra aetate*, 28 October 1965)

c) Declaration on Religious Freedom (*Dignitatis humanae personae*, 7 December 1965)

How do these three types of conciliar resolutions differ from one another? The answer to this question is not easy if one tries to formulate definitions on the basis of how these terms have been used in the history of the church, since in the course of time the word *constitution* has been understood in different ways, and in the course of church history very dissimilar decisions and texts have been designated as *decrees* and *declarations*. In Vatican II the constitutions are those resolutions in which a principal issue, encompassing many particular questions, is treated in a fundamental way, while decrees give directives for specific topics, frequently with explicit reference to basic decisions made in the constitutions. The Declaration on Religious Freedom and the one on the church's conduct toward the non-Christian religions are basic explanations of specific topics, while the Declaration on Christian Education could also have been designated a decree.

Among the constitutions themselves there are further differences in terminology. The one on the church and the one on revelation are explicitly designated "dogmatic constitutions," and the one on the church in the contemporary world is called a "pastoral constitution," while the Constitution on the Sacred Liturgy, without further qualification, establishes the principles of liturgical reform. These last two constitutions also proceed from dogmatic explanations, the pastoral constitution, in particular, from the doctrine of human beings, and the Constitution on the Sacred Liturgy from the explanation of the ecclesiological significance of the worship service. On the basis of this foundation, then, the pastoral constitution provides fundamental instructions for living together in human community, while the latter constitution for further work in liturgical reform. The dogmatic constitutions concerning the church and revelation, however, do occupy a pre-eminent place in that each of them as a whole sets forth dogmatic teaching, something that was also the case in the dogmatic constitutions of Vatican I concerning the Catholic faith and the church (papal primacy). It is striking that, in contrast to the dogmatic decrees of the Council of Trent and the dogmatic constitutions of Vatican I, the dogmatic constitutions of Vatican II do not contain any canons against false doctrine, that is, any anathemas. There is no precedent for the concept of a pastoral constitution in the history of church councils, a matter which will be addressed later (chap. 8).

If one inquires into the issue of their obligating authority, both dogmatic constitutions have the highest rank, since the other two constitutions contain a higher number of statements that are subject to change—not with respect to their foundation, but doubtless the form of the liturgy and certainly the situation of the world are historically prone to change. This is also true regarding many statements in the decrees, while the declarations have only a limited significance compared to constitutions. Lending even further significance to both dogmatic constitutions is the fact that they—especially the Dogmatic Constitution on the Church—are repeatedly being used as the authoritative foundation for the decrees, but also for the pastoral constitution.

Are the dogmatic constitutions to be designated now as dogma in the strict sense? This question was raised repeatedly and then was answered by the authorized Commission for the doctrine of the faith and morals, which stated that "taking into account conciliar custom and the pastoral aim of the present council" only what was explicitly set apart by the council as properly defined dogma is to be acknowledged as such.[i] Thus, in no way are the dogmatic constitutions as a whole "dogma" in the solemn sense of an uncorrectable, infallible decision. Rather, they are specific statements which were explicitly emphasized as dogmatic definitions. Most of the council theologians are of the opinion that such definitions are generally incomplete, as indicated also by their lack of condemnatory statements. Consequently, the council held to the pastoral task that Pope John XXIII had set before it, and it avoided deepening the differences between the Roman Church and the other churches, which would have happened with the adoption of new dogmas. This is of particular ecumenical significance in view of the statements of the Dogmatic Constitution on the Church about Mary as mediatrix, for although this title goes beyond the official Mariological dogmas of the Roman Church, it is itself still not dogma. Naturally, this observation does not do away with the fact that the dogmatic statements of the council have a much greater significance and a greater binding authority than papal encyclicals.

2. An Attempt at Systematically Ordering the Council's Resolutions

At first glance, the topics that are treated in the conciliar texts and named in their titles appear to present a confusing multiplicity. This has to do with the large number of stated topics that the bishops wanted to be addressed and with the formation of the sixteen texts that were ultimately adopted out of the more than seventy original schemata. As impressive as the scope and multiplicity of the conciliar topics are, from this genesis there developed some overlapping and repetition, but also the separation of some things that belong together and their distribution into different conciliar texts, as seen, for example, in the juxtaposition of the Decree on the Mission Activity of the Church and the Declaration on the Church's Relation to the Non-Christian Religions. In a similar way, this is also true of occasional discrepancies. Thus, the definition of the relationship between the church and the world in the Dogmatic Constitution on the Church and in the Decree on the Mission Activity of the Church is closer to the New Testament statements than the corresponding statements in the Pastoral Constitution on the Church in the Contemporary World.

If one attempts to order systematically the various resolutions of the council on the basis of their content, one must keep in mind that it was no accident that the proposal on the sacred liturgy was the first to be discussed and adopted as a resolution. To be sure, the initial version of this proposal was already more developed than the other schemata, but, given its subject matter, it was also natural to discuss it first since the life of the church is uniquely concentrated in the event of the worship service. Occurring here is God's revealed salvific action for human beings, here people are built up to be the church through Christ's present activity, here ensues God's sending of those who have been called out of the world back into it. Here people respond to God's act of salvation as they praise him, call upon and confess him, give themselves over to him, and from here they proceed into the world in order to attest to him and to present their bodies to him in his service as "a living sacrifice, holy and pleasing to God" (Rom. 12.1). In the event of the worship service, the life of the church is concentrated as a fellowship of those assembled in a mutual receiving and serving and at the same time as a fellowship of all worshiping assemblies on earth with the liturgy of those who have reached the goal—those who have preceded us in the faith—and with the praise of the rest of creation.

If we take the Constitution on the Sacred Liturgy as our systematic starting point, we must then understand the Dogmatic Constitution on Revelation to be the result of reflection on God's revealed salvific action, and the Dogmatic Constitution on the Church to be the result of reflection on the worshiping assembly.

Some of the decrees must then be understood as an explication of the dogmatic statements in the Dogmatic Constitution on the Church regarding the arrangement of the people of God on earth. The Decree on the Catholic Churches of the Eastern Rite explains statements from the second chapter of the Dogmatic Constitution on the Church concerning the individual churches, while the Decree on the Pastoral Office of Bishops in the Church explains Articles 18–27 in the third chapter, and the decrees on the education and ministry of priests do that for Article 28 in the same chapter. The Decree on the Apostolate of the Laity explains that constitution's fourth chapter and the Decree on the Suitable Renewal of Religious Life does so for its sixth chapter, while the Declaration on Christian Education is of a more general nature.

The systematic ordering of the rest of the council's resolutions is suggested by an image that Pope Paul VI repeatedly used, namely, that of concentric circles in which the Roman Catholic Church is to carry out its dialogue with others: the innermost circle—the Roman Church with the pope as its center—is surrounded by the circle of non-Catholic Christians, which is surrounded by the circle of the non-Christian religions, which is surrounded by the circle comprising the whole of humanity (so, for example, in the encyclical *Ecclesiam suam*).[ii] Corresponding to this schema of the three concentric circles surrounding the Roman Church are the three secretariats established by the pope in recent years: the Secretariat for Promoting Christian Unity, the Secretariat for the Non-Christian Religions and Non-believers, and the proposed Secretariat for the Promotion of International Social Justice. Also corresponding to this same schema are the surprising trips that Pope Paul VI undertook during the council: the trip to Jerusalem (after the conclusion of the second period) led to a meeting with the Ecumenical Patriarch Athenagoras of Constantinople; the trip to Bombay (after the third period) led to an encounter with non-Christian religions; and the trip to New York (during the fourth period) took him to the United Nations.[iii]

Within the council's resolutions one finds directives for the conduct of the Roman Church with non-Roman Christendom in the Decree on Ecumenism, directives for the encounter with non-Christian religions in the Decree on the Mission Activity of the Church and in the Declaration on the Church's Relation to the Non-Christian Religions, and directives for the church's conduct in relation to the basic issues of humanity as a whole are found in the Pastoral Constitution on the Church in the Contemporary World and in the Decree on Mass Media, while the Declaration on Religious Freedom is of significance for all three concentric circles, that is, not only for the dialogue with non-Roman Christendom and the non-Christian religions but also for the fundamental relationship between the Roman Church and state authority.

This inner systematic ordering will determine the structure of the following chapters, in which, however, we will make a minor adjustment: the Dogmatic Constitution on Revelation will be placed at the end because we will also make summary observations there about the use of Holy Scripture in the other resolutions of the council. We will thus take up in the following order: (1) the reform of the worship service (chap. 4); (2) the self-understanding of the Roman Church (chap. 5); (3) the council and the non-Roman churches (chap. 6); (4) the council and the non-Christian religions (chap. 7); (5) the council and the contemporary world (chap. 8); and (6) Holy Scripture, tradition, and the teaching office (chap. 9).

3. Preliminary Hermeneutical Remarks

This is not, to be sure, intended to be a commentary on the resolutions of the Second Vatican Council nor is it an *Examen Vaticani secundi* of the type produced by Martin Chemnitz in his day, in the situation of the Counter-Reformation, when he subjected the resolutions of the Tridentine Council to an examination (*Examen Concilii Tridentini* [1565–73]).[iv] What is intended here is only a general overview of the events at the council so as to engage the question of what significance they have for the non-Roman churches and how these churches ought to conduct themselves toward the Roman Church in the wake of the council. Despite this restriction of the task, an overview of the texts still requires a preliminary consideration of the principles according to which the adopted and promulgated texts are to be interpreted. Such a consideration of hermeneutics is all the more important since the evaluations of the council's resolutions are very different, both in and outside the Roman Church. At one extreme, on the one hand, there are the optimistic utterances, according to which all essential hindrances have now been eliminated and the unification of Christendom is imminent. On the other hand, there are the pessimistic judgments, made by those who are of the opinion that basically nothing has changed, who even think that the relationship among the churches has been made more difficult by the ecumenical program of the Roman Church. Between these two extremes there is a great multiplicity of opinions, which are more or less confident or also reserved. Doubtless, this great diversity of judgments about the resolutions of the council is due to a considerable degree to the lack of clarification about the principles of interpretation. Since non-Roman Christendom is naturally interested particularly in the Decree on Ecumenism, we will begin our hermeneutical considerations at this point and attempt from here to secure several general criteria, which are also important for the interpretation of the other resolutions.

a) The Decree on Ecumenism is often interpreted in isolation, as if it were itself the sole theme of the council. But ecumenism is merely one of the council's topics alongside many others. The Decree on Ecumenism is surrounded by numerous other constitutions, decrees, and declarations, which were taken no less seriously by the council fathers. The subject of these other conciliar texts is in part so tightly bound to the Decree on Ecumenism that the latter cannot be rightly interpreted apart from the former. This is above all true with regard to the dogmatic constitutions on the Church and on revelation, and the Decree on the Catholic Churches of the Eastern Rite (*Catholic* = "those united with Rome"). But even the decrees on the apostolate of the laity and the mission activity of the church, the Declaration on Religious Freedom, and the one on the church's position toward the Jews and the non-Christian religions, and, not least, the extensive proposals regarding the presence of the church in the contemporary world—all of these are also of great ecumenical significance. The connection between the Decree on Ecumenism and these other texts must in no way be overlooked, for the answers which the same council gives or does not give in these other texts—for example, with respect to the question of religious freedom or marriages between Catholics and non-Catholics or the cooperation of Christians on the mission field—must be regarded as authentic interpretations of the ecumenical program. Obviously, of particular ecumenical significance are the statements in the Dogmatic Constitution on the Church regarding the position of the pope and of his relationship to the bishops. In general, this rule must be applied, namely, that the individual text is rightly understood and interpreted only in the context of all of the resolutions of the council.

b) The Decree on Ecumenism is widely accorded greater weight than the other resolutions of the council. This is especially true with respect to the Dogmatic Constitution on the Church, which is still to a greater degree under the influence of the conservative theologians and of those whose understanding of the church is narrower than that of the Decree on Ecumenism. During the second period, the argument for according a higher valuation to the Decree on Ecumenism was often based on the fact that it was unclear which of the two had the greater binding authority, a constitution or a decree. Meanwhile, from the beginning, many said that a dogmatic constitution is to be ranked higher than a decree, and in the third period the relationship between the Decree on Ecumenism and the Dogmatic Constitution on the Church was clearly decided in favor of the latter, for the *relatio* [report], which was submitted with the second version of the schema *de oecumenismo*, designated the dogmatic statements of the constitution as the authoritative presuppositions for ecumenism. Likewise, the text of the decree that was then adopted explicitly refers to the constitution (see Art. 1 [Introduction] of the Decree on Ecumenism, final sentence). Hence the Decree on Ecumenism is to be interpreted in the light of the Dogmatic Constitution on the Church, and not vice versa. When interpreting each of the conciliar texts, one must inquire about its relationship to and dependence upon the other texts that were adopted, especially those in which dogmatic principles are to be found.

c) The resolutions of the council are the result of a wrestling in the council, whose outcome is reflected in the various versions of the relevant schemata. No first draft of any of the schemata was adopted. The disputing occurred in the *aula* of St. Peter's during the voting of the council fathers, and it continued in the council's commissions which, after working through a given set of official opinions, produced a new text in which the objections and wishes of every preceding opinion had to be taken into account. The new version of the text that had been produced was then resubmitted to the plenary, along with published responses and an introductory report on the most important perspectives in the revision. Even during the voting, it was still possible to submit amendments, and these then in turn had to be considered by the commissions. This work, which in the case of several texts went through all four periods of the council (for example, the Dogmatic Constitution on Revelation), must certainly be considered in the interpretation of the resolutions. Since the earlier proposals, the official opinions, and the reasons for textual revisions had not yet been released, they can be adduced here only insofar as they were made public by the council's theologians and especially in the daily reports of the council's press corps.

d) The council is more than merely its resolutions. The one who only knows its resolutions has not yet comprehended the conciliar event as a whole, for a dynamic breakthrough occurred at the council, a breakthrough that is more comprehensive and more forward-leaning than what is expressed in the council's resolutions. Since the majority of delegates to the council were open to the progressive impulses, not a few caught sight of the significance of the resolutions—especially since they are not solemn dogmatic definitions that are incapable of being corrected—in that the resolutions opened hitherto closed doors and have established an official right of existence for further new advances in the Roman Church. The wording of the statements in the texts as such appears to be less significant for such an understanding of this dynamic breakthrough, since that wording in part lags considerably behind the far more progressive impulses, as well as the insights and goals of the ecumenical avant-garde, and of the Roman Church's youth, who are following those same progressives. The caution and reticence, for example, of the Decree on Ecumenism, is then clarified by saying that for the moment its only concern is to win the whole Roman Church for the idea of ecumenism. In this sense the decree is understood less as a text than as an historical passage on the way toward a wider ecumenical unfolding.

Undoubtedly, the resolutions of the council are rightly interpreted only if they are interpreted against the background of the event of the council as a whole. But it is not easy to comprehend precisely the power and the trend of these progressive impulses, and it is impossible to say with any certainty how these impulses that have newly arisen will have their effect after the council and how much support the conservative minority will receive in the wider church and in the Curia.

When we reconsider the Decree on Ecumenism, we see clearly how the newly arisen impulses have led to numerous improvements in the original text. Altogether, four versions of this decree were presented to the council for consideration and adoption, the second and third of which grew out of previous discussions and official opinions. In the process of working through these many thousands of official opinions, the Secretariat for Promoting Christian Unity acted superbly, and in both the second and third versions it introduced many noteworthy improvements over against the original text.

On the other hand, however, one cannot overlook the fact that already in the second version—alongside these improvements (in the sense of a greater ecumenical openness)—there were also several not unimportant attenuations that showed the originally less-precise and therefore more ecumenically open

understanding of the church in the Decree on Ecumenism was accommodated to and subordinated to the narrower concept of the church in the
Dogmatic Constitution on the Church. Moreover, there was a great stir
among many council fathers and official observers when the third version—
whose individual elements the council had already voted upon and whose
three chapters the council had already adopted by an overwhelming
majority—at the last minute, by means of an intervention that appealed to
the highest authority of the pope, received several amendments, which
disillusioned ecumenical expectations. This was particularly true regarding
the weakening of statements concerning the Lord's Supper in the Reformation churches and concerning the fruit of their biblical research. Other
surprising interventions in the events of the council during the last days of
the third period also made it clear that the conservative forces were stronger
than many had assumed.

Thus it is true that the resolutions of the council are to be interpreted in the
context of the whole conciliar event, and yet the context must be viewed not
only in the awakening of the progressives but also in the determined struggle
of the regressive forces. If one has followed the course of the council's actions,
one gets the impression with regard to most of the resolutions that in carefully
balanced formulations the council said the utmost of what could be said jointly
by the council fathers. The statements in the resolutions of the council cannot
be devalued in favor of hopes or fears for further developments after the
council. Rather, in any case, the textual statements must be taken seriously on
the basis of their wording. By conciliar resolution and by papal promulgation
the official texts have received an authority that determines the further action
of the Roman Church.

e) No text can be interpreted apart from its significance for the interpreter.
This is true also of the council's resolutions, although it is obvious that not all
resolutions are significant in the same way for each of their interpreters. Thus,
for the non-Catholic reader, the dogmatic constitutions on revelation and on
the Church, as well as the Decree on Ecumenism and the Declaration on
Religious Freedom are perhaps more significant than the Decree on the
Suitable Renewal of Religious Life. However, in order to do justice to the
resolutions of the council, it is necessary to distinguish between their
significance for the Roman Church and their significance for the other
churches. There are numerous resolutions which appear to be nothing less
than revolutionary for the Roman Church itself, so much so that their
implementation within the church is bound up with not insignificant
problems. These same resolutions, such as, for example, the introduction of
the vernacular in the worship service or the acknowledgment of religious
freedom, have nothing new to say to most of the other churches. Their
significance lies in the fact that here the Roman Church is changing its former
practice. It is therefore necessary, when interpreting the council's resolutions,
to consider the position of the Roman Church on these issues in the time

before the council. Only then will the significance of the resolutions for the Roman Church become clear.

In the following chapters, on the basis of the above considerations, we shall seek first of all to evaluate the resolutions of the council against the background of the presuppositions of the Roman Church itself and to restrict ourselves for the moment to the immanent critique of these resolutions on the basis of these presuppositions, among which Holy Scripture and the ancient church occupy a special position. Only then (in chaps. 10 ff.) will the significance of the council be considered for the non-Roman churches.

By taking these hermeneutical perspectives into account, it is to be hoped that one escapes the tangled knot of the very different assessments of the council by the enthusiastic optimists and the skeptical pessimists, and thus come closer to recognizing the council's true significance.

Editor's Notes

[i] This phrase was part of a statement that the Theological Commission that was responsible for drafting the Dogmatic Constitution on the Church made on 6 March 1964. "Taking into account conciliar custom and the pastoral aim of the present council, this holy synod defines as binding on the church only those matters concerning faith and morals which it openly declares to be such. The other matters which the synod puts forward as the teaching of the supreme magisterium of the church, each and every member of the faithful should accept and embrace according to the mind of the synod itself, which is clear either from the subject matter or from the way it is said, in accordance with the rules of theological interpretation" (Denzinger 4350–4359; Tanner 2:898). The purpose of this clarification was to shed light on how the constitution, especially its third chapter, is to be interpreted. The secretary general of the council quoted from this theological statement on the evening before the final vote (16 November 1964). His announcements to the council, part of the official Acts of the Council, were published as an appendix to the constitution.

[ii] *Ecclesiam suam*, Encyclical of Paul VI on the Church (6 August 1964), Vatican.va, accessed on 13 February 2016, http://w2.vatican.va/content/paul-vi/en/encyclicals/documents/hf_p-vi_enc_06081964_ecclesiam.html

[iii] Paul VI, who was given the nickname "the Pilgrim Pope," traveled to Jordan, Israel, and Palestine 4–6 January 1964. On this trip he met with Ecumenical Patriarch Athenagoras I in Jerusalem. This meeting led to the rescinding of the excommunications that had been officially promulgated in 1054. Paul VI attended the Eucharistic Congress in Bombay 2–5 December 1964. He addressed the General Assembly at the UN on 4 October 1965.

[iv] Martin Chemnitz [1522–86], *Examen Concilii Tridentini* (1565–73); ET: *Examination of the Council of Trent*, 4 vols., ed. and trans., Fred Kramer (St. Louis: Concordia Publishing House, 1971–86). Chemnitz was a German Lutheran Reformer, theologian, and co-author of the Formula of Concord, but he is perhaps best known for this careful analysis of the doctrinal decrees of the Council of Trent, as the latter had been interpreted by the southern prelates who had participated in the Tridentine discussions.

Chapter IV:
The Reform of the Worship Service

The Constitution on the Sacred Liturgy is a fruit of the liturgical movement. This movement arose in Benedictine monasteries in Belgium, Germany, and Austria, had a very strong reverberation especially in the German Catholic youth movement, and was brought to numerous congregations through younger priests. Flowing from this movement, which was grounded in diligent theological, historical, and musical scholarship, were also strong impulses toward non-Roman Christendom. After popes since Pius X—but especially Pius XII—had promoted this movement through important individual reforms (as articulated in a series of encyclicals), while also occasionally setting limits on it, the task was given to the council to adopt the fundamental principles for a future universal reform of the Latin rite. Thus the task was not to carry through the liturgical reform itself with respect to its details, but rather to determine the principles according to which a special liturgical commission is to carry out this reform. Naturally this does not exclude the fact that the newly developed principles already contain some direct changes to the previous liturgy and that thus, already before the conclusion of the post-conciliar work of that Commission, these changes began to have their effect in the congregations. The renewal of the liturgy is based on the distinction between "a part [of the liturgy] that cannot be changed, insofar as it has been divinely laid down, and those parts that are subject to change" (Art. 21).[i]

It is a matter here of dealing with a liturgical constitution, not a dogmatic one. The dogmas of the Roman Church, especially the doctrine about the sacrifice of the mass, continue to be unalterably presupposed. Since, however, the liturgy may be understood as an interpretation of dogma, the question arises whether the liturgical constitution has perhaps brought about shifts in accent or even additions to the former understanding of dogma, especially the dogmatic statements about the mass. We must here restrict ourselves to the chief worship service, the mass, and to focus our attention especially on those elements of renewal that at the same time signify structural changes in the life of the Roman Church.

1. The Salvific Action of God

The first chapter of the Constitution on the Sacred Liturgy begins with God's universal saving will and his once-for-all completed act of salvation in Jesus Christ.

The wonderful works of God among the people of the Old Testament were but a prelude to the work of Christ the Lord in redeeming human beings and giving perfect glory to God. He achieved his task principally by the paschal mystery of his blessed passion, resurrection from the dead, and the glorious ascension. (Art. 5)

To accomplish so great a work, Christ is always present in his church, especially in its liturgical celebrations. He is present in the sacrifice of the mass, not only in the person of his minister, ... but especially under the Eucharistic species. By his power he is present in the sacraments, so that when anyone baptizes it is really Christ himself who baptizes. He is present in his word, since it is he himself who speaks when the Holy Scriptures are read in the church. He is present, lastly, when the church prays and sings, for he promised: "Where two or three are gathered together in my name, there am I in the midst of them" (Matt. 18:20). (Art. 7)

The constitution is thus concerned with the present working of Christ who has brought about salvation in his death and resurrection. He is the one who is presently acting in the liturgical action of the priest and the congregation. In the following we shall focus our attention especially on the statements about Christ's presence in the Eucharist and in the word.

a) The Tridentine doctrine distinguishes in the Eucharist between the administration of the sacrament (communio, Session 21) and the sacrifice of the mass (sacrificium, Session 22).[ii] This distinction is not only a dogmatic one but to a large extent a liturgical one. A large number of masses, indeed the majority of them, are celebrated in the Roman Church without anyone—except the priest who is celebrating—receiving the sacrament. Conversely, the sacrament can be offered in other worship services without the consecration being done in them; previously consecrated wafers are distributed. Such a separation between the sacrifice of the mass and the communion is rejected by the Eastern Church and the Reformation churches, since it does not correspond to the character of the meal instituted by Jesus. According to the liturgical constitution, low masses may also be permitted without communion, but the accent has shifted. Thus, with regard to all liturgical rites, it is taught "that a communal celebration, with a congregation present and actively taking part... is to be preferred, as far as possible, to a celebration that is by one person alone, as it were in private" (Art. 27). And additionally: "This applies especially to the celebration of the mass" (Art. 27). "That more perfect form of participation in the mass whereby the faithful, after the priest's communion, receive the Lord's body from the same sacrifice, is strongly commended" (Art. 55). In this connection the directives for the joint celebration of the mass by several priests (concelebratio) should also be mentioned (Art. 57), for thereby the number of simultaneous masses in the same church is reduced and then, even when the congregation does not receive the sacrament, there is at least a communio of the participating priests.

The extremely lively and fruitful discussion, which the mystery theology of Odo Casel stimulated in the 1920s and 30s, especially in German-Catholic theology, found no further expression in the constitution.[iii] But perhaps it exerted some influence in that it directed its attention to the whole course and implementation of the worship service. Also, the mass is here understood not as a representation of Christ's death on the cross, but rather it is understood in the context of both his death and his *resurrection:* "The victory and triumph of his death" are represented in it (Art. 6).[iv] Without contradicting the Tridentine statements, the constitution also goes beyond them, in that it points to the eschatological character of the Eucharist.

In the earthly liturgy we take part in a foretaste of that heavenly liturgy which is celebrated in the holy city of Jerusalem toward which we journey as pilgrims, where Christ is sitting at the right hand of God, a minister of the holies and of the true tabernacle.... [In the worship service] we eagerly await the Savior, our Lord Jesus Christ, until he, our life, shall appear and we too will appear with him in glory. (Art. 8)

The eschatological connection of the Lord's Supper is today also more fully seen again in the Reformation churches. Through these shifts in accent, in accordance with its institution as the Lord's Supper, the New Testament character of the Eucharist is again more fully prominent.

The Council of Trent had taught, "If anyone says that all Christ's faithful should receive both forms of the most holy sacrament of the Eucharist by command of God or as necessary to salvation: let him be anathema (*anathema sit*)" (Session 21, *Doctrina de communio*, Can. 1).[v] Accordingly, the distribution of the sacrament in both kinds—which had been customary up to the twelfth century—although it certainly was not excluded in principle, nevertheless was in actual practice prohibited, despite some passing concessions that had been made in the sixteenth century. Withholding the cup from the communing laity has been rejected by both the Orthodox Church and the Reformation churches. Without retracting the validity of the cited Tridentine position, the liturgical constitution specifies that "communion under both kinds may be allowed at the discretion of bishops, both to clergy and religious, and to laity, in cases to be determined by the apostolic see" (Art. 55). To be sure, the only example for such a reception by the laity specifically mentioned by the constitution is that of the newly baptized in a mass following their baptism; yet the constitution does in principle also open up the possibility of permitting the distribution of the sacrament under both kinds in other cases. Although this distribution is not foreseen as the rule, still there is a shift in accent here, which again comes closer to the Lord's two-fold words of institution, as it has been handed down in the New Testament.

b) "The importance of Holy Scripture in the celebration of the liturgy is of paramount importance. For it is texts from Scripture that form the readings and are explained in the homily, and Scripture's psalms that are sung; the prayers, collects, and liturgical songs are scriptural in their inspiration; and it is from Scripture that actions and signs derive their meaning.... [For this reason], it is necessary to promote a heartfelt and living love for Holy Scripture..." (Art. 24).

Thus, there is to be "a fuller, more varied and more appropriate approach"

(Art. 35.1) to the reading of Scripture. "In order that believers can be provided with a richer diet of God's word, the rich heritage of the Bible is to be opened more widely, in such a way that a more representative portion of Holy Scripture will be read to the people over a set cycle of years" (Art. 51). This makes possible a revision of the order of scriptural readings (pericopes) for the worship service and also a greater number of ways to arrange the pericope cycles in relation to one another.

In the structure of the mass, the sermon is to take a set place and its ministry is to be faithfully carried out (Art. 35.2), both in the mass and in special services of the word (Art. 35.4). "Through the homily the mysteries of the faith and the guiding principles of the Christian life are to be explained from the sacred text over the course of the liturgical year. The homily is strongly encouraged as part of the liturgy itself" (Art. 52).

The Constitution on the Sacred Liturgy, therefore, gives special weight to the connection between sacrament and word, not only in the sense that the sacrament becomes what it is by the consecrating word but also in the sense that the reading of Scripture and the sermon go together with the sacrament. To be sure, private masses and masses without a sermon are not coming to an end in the Roman Church, but the accents are shifted in a direction that can be warmly greeted by both the Reformation churches and the Eastern Church. In this connection, it is significant that Scripture reading and the sermon are not only accorded importance in teaching about Christ's presence in the sacrament; rather, there is explicit mention of Christ's presence in the word. Of course the constitution here only stated that "[Christ] is present in his word since he himself speaks when the Holy Scriptures are read" (Art. 7). That the gospel is by its very nature not Scripture and reading but living word and concrete assurance—that is, a sermon, and precisely in this way "power of God" (Rom. 1.16)—is here overlooked. In addition, according to the weight that the constitution assigns to the word and the sacrament, the formula would not read "word and sacrament" but rather "sacrament and word." Yet even the significance of the word in the sacrament itself still remains weakened when the words of institution are spoken softly over the elements of the bread and wine so that the congregation cannot hear them. Nevertheless, it is significant that the constitution has said not merely of the sacrament but of the liturgy as a whole: in it "God speaks to his people; in it Christ is still proclaiming the good news" (Art. 33). The Council of Trent had not taught about the word in this way, alongside the sacraments as the instrument of the present and working Christ.

2. The Participation of the Congregation

Since the early Middle Ages the congregation had begun to be silent in the worship service and was itself no longer speaking the liturgical responses and doxologies. More and more the congregation's participation was reduced to the adoration and reception of the consecrated host. In general, what happened at the altar and what took place in the worship by the congregation separated from one another: everyone prayed alone. This was not only a de facto development; rather, there were theologians who championed the fundamental opinion that the responses in the service were the exclusive task of the priest's attendant in the mass. From the beginning, however, the modern liturgical movement has taken a position against this view, and by translations of the missal it has made it possible for the congregation to follow the worship service. Also, already in 1903 in a *motu proprio*,[vi] Pope Pius X had called for the "active participation" of the faithful in the mass as an indispensable source of the spiritual life. Since then, this insistence has been raised again and again, but actually realizing it has been a difficult problem. What does "active participation" mean? Is it sufficient to enable an understandable but mute participation in the mass, in place of a disconnected praying by each individual? Or should the congregation go beyond this and become an active, speaking participant in the worship service?

The constitution teaches emphatically:

Liturgical services are not private functions, but are celebrations of the church, which is the "sacrament of unity," namely, the holy people united and ordered under their bishops. Therefore liturgical services pertain to the whole body of the church; they manifest it and have effects upon it; but they concern the individual members of the church in different ways, according to their differing rank, office, and actual participation. (Art. 26)

The church, therefore, earnestly desires that Christ's faithful, when present at this mystery of faith, should not be there as strangers or silent spectators; on the contrary, through a good understanding of the rites and prayers they should take part in the sacred action conscious of what they are doing, with devotion and full collaboration. They should be instructed by God's word and be nourished at the table of the Lord's body; they should give thanks to God; by offering the Immaculate Victim, not only through the hands of the priest, but also with him, they should learn also to offer themselves. (Art. 48)

The worship service is to be conducted in such a way that within the make-up of the congregation everyone present will participate in his or her own proper way in the service (Art. 28). This participation should not merely be a faith that is listening but one that is heard: "To promote active participation, the people should be encouraged to take part by means of acclamations, responses, psalmody, antiphons, and songs, as well as by actions, gestures, and bodily attitudes" (Art. 30). Only then should "a reverent silence... be observed at the proper time" (Art. 30). Such active participation belonging to "the Christian people, 'the chosen race, the royal priesthood, the holy nation, God's own people' (1 Pet. 2.9; compare 2.4–5) is their right and duty by reason of their baptism" (Art. 14).

Of special significance in this connection is the re-introduction of the general intercessory prayer in the mass. In the course of streamlining the mass and shifting increasing importance to the sacrifice of the mass, this prayer had disappeared from the Roman mass, in distinction from the liturgy of the Reformation churches and the Eastern Church. The sacrifice of the mass had essentially taken the place of the general prayer of the church, except for a few silent intercessions by the priest during the sacrifice, something the congregation could not do with him. Now, however:

[E]specially on Sundays and feasts of obligation there is to be restored, after the Gospel and the homily, "the common prayer" or "the prayer of the faithful." By this prayer, in which the people are to take part, intercession will be made for the holy church, for the civil authorities, for those oppressed by various needs, for all people, and for the salvation of the entire world. (Art. 53)

With all this emphasis on the active participation of all the members of the congregation in the worship service, it is to be noted that their verbal expression can only be voiced in a liturgically set manner. That expression is limited to responses, prayers, and acclamations prescribed in the liturgical formulas. Here there thus continues a fundamental difference over against the statements of the Apostle Paul regarding the multiplicity of spiritual gifts through which every member of the congregation receives in the freedom of the Spirit a special servant ministry in the congregation—and a fundamental difference with Paul's statements regarding the manner in which these spiritual gifts manifest themselves in the worship service of the congregation, in the free word of prophecy, of teaching, and so forth (1 Cor. 12 and 14). But this difference is also found in the other churches where the worship service follows set liturgical forms, and there also one must ask whether sufficient space is allowed for the free witness of the spiritual gifts.

3. Enabling the Vernacular

Can the congregation actively participate in the worship service if the liturgy is in a foreign language?

In lively discussions the point was made that the Latin liturgical language belonged to the unity of the Roman Church and that this unity would be weakened if the vernacular were permitted. In the background there was still the persuasive idea that the very inability to understand the words was appropriate to the holiness of the mystery. However, in order to make possible the active participation of the people in the liturgy, it was resolved that the vernacular "would be given greater scope, especially in the readings and directives and in several prayers and chants" (Art. 36.2). In addition, permission was granted to use the vernacular when saying the general prayer of intercession, which had been newly inserted into the liturgical order.

At first glance, these directives seem to contradict the Tridentine instructions: "Although the mass is full of instructions for the faithful people, the council fathers did not think it advantageous that it should be celebrated everywhere in the vernacular" (Session 22, *Doctrina et canones de sanctissimo missae sacrificio* [Teaching and Canons on the Most Holy Sacrifice of the Mass], Canon 8).[vii] Thus, the missal of unity from 1570, which was constructed on the basis of this Tridentine decision, called for the exclusive use of the Latin language. But the basic dogmatic decision of Trent merely says: "If anyone says... that the mass *has to be* celebrated only in the vernacular, let him be anathema" (Session 22, *Canones de sanctissimo missae sacrificio* [Canons on the Most Holy Sacrifice of the Mass], Canon 9).[viii] Accordingly, with its introduction of the vernacular, Vatican II does not contradict the fundamental principles of the Council of Trent but merely transcends the latter's de facto rejection of the vernacular. In this way, the former rule is respected to the extent that the use of the Latin language is to be maintained in the Latin rites (Art. 36.1), that the introduction of the vernacular has indeed been made possible and encouraged by the council but not demanded, and to the extent that the parts of the liturgy in which the use of the vernacular is explicitly recommended do not include the words of consecration and the prayers in the canon of the mass. Moreover, "steps should be taken so that the faithful may also be able to say or to sing together in Latin those parts of the Ordinary of the mass which pertain to them" (Art. 54). Despite this concern to respect the former usage, the statements concerning the vernacular signify a very important step.

4. Enabling Further Accommodations

In order to enable the participation of the congregation, the constitution goes still further:

Even in the liturgy, the Church has no wish to impose a rigid uniformity in matters which do not implicate the faith or the good of the whole community; rather the Church respects and fosters the genius and talents of the various races and peoples. Anything in these peoples' way of life which is not indissolubly bound up with superstition and error the Church studies with sympathy and, if possible, preserves intact. Sometimes in fact the Church admits such things into the liturgy itself, so long as they harmonize with its true and authentic spirit. (Art. 37; compare Art. 38)

Thus "accommodations" [*Anpassungen*] are to be made, "especially in the case of the administration of the sacraments, the sacramentals, processions, liturgical language, sacred music, and the arts" (Art. 39). In the scholarly research within the liturgical movement, it has been clearly recognized how strongly the liturgy is marked by late antiquity and the Middle Ages, and how ever more urgently the question has been raised regarding whether and to what extent this liturgy is suitable for Christians in entirely different cultures, whose religious and philosophical ideas are so foreign to the rites of Greco-Roman late-antiquity and of the European Middle Ages. Very difficult problems arise here, including the question about the use of the elements of bread and wine, since their symbolical significance is not evident in countries where they have no role in the daily nourishment. While the constitution excludes any change in the sacraments with respect to this question, it does allow room for an accommodation of the rites to the presuppositions of other peoples and cultures. This is especially true for baptism: "In mission lands it is found that some of the peoples already make use of initiation rites. Elements from these, when capable of being adapted to Christian ritual, may be admitted along with those already found in Christian tradition" (Art. 65). It is also true for marriage: "the competent territorial ecclesiastical authority... is free to draw up its own rite suited to the usages of place and people" (Art. 77). Moreover, the national traditions of music (Art. 119) and art (Art. 123) are to be given their place in the liturgy, and "the materials and form of sacred furnishings and vestments" may be adapted "to the needs and customs of their different regions" (Art. 128; compare Arts. 107 and 110).

In light of Pope Benedict XIV's 1742 veto of the very far-reaching accommodations that the Jesuits had made in eastern Asia, the council once again took up this exceedingly difficult but inescapable problem and created the presuppositions for new endeavors at its solution.[ix] How pressing this problem is felt within the Roman Church is shown by the fact that again and again one hears people express the opinion that east Asia would be Christian today if in the eighteenth century the pope had not prohibited the accommodations made by the Jesuits.

5. Liturgical Rights of the Conferences of Bishops

But who is responsible for the introduction of the vernacular and for the accommodations? Previously, questions about the liturgy in the Roman Church had been decided in a centralized manner. Here the council brought about a relaxation of this restriction: "In virtue of power conceded by the law, the regulation of the liturgy within certain defined limits belongs also to various kinds of competent territorial bodies of bishops legitimately established" (Art. 22.2) This decision is the basis for letting questions about the vernacular and accommodations be decided by the conference of bishops in a country or larger territory. They have "to decide whether, and to what extent, the vernacular is to be used" (Art. 36.3) and to "consider which elements from the traditions and culture of individual peoples might appropriately be admitted into divine worship" (Art. 40.1). Resolutions of the conferences of bishops concerning the introduction of the vernacular "are to be approved, that is, confirmed, by the Apostolic See" (Art. 36.3; compare

40.1). The "Instruction for the Orderly Implementation of the Constitution on the Sacred Liturgy," published on 26 September 1964, then gave precise directives concerning the composition of the resolutions, the procedure for voting on them, and their presentation to the Holy See. The right of the conferences of bishops is thus restricted. But even though the ultimate decision rests with the Apostolic See, it is still significant that the conferences of bishops will now be generally constituted and accorded rights that go beyond a mere right to make proposals.

6. New Structures

The worship service is the heart and center of the church's life, and it is no accident that the most important terms in the New Testament for the church (*ecclesia*, people of God, body of Christ, temple of the Holy Spirit) have been shaped by the worshiping assembly. The constitution expresses this central function of the worship service in that it calls the liturgy "the summit toward which the activity of the church is directed; at the same time it is the font from which all its power flows" (Art. 10). It is "a sacred action surpassing all others; no other action of the church can equal its efficacy by the same title and to the same degree" (Art. 7).

Because of this central importance a reform of the liturgy cannot fail to have abiding consequences for the total life of the church. This is not true for each detail of such a reform, but it is true of the fundamental structures of the worship service to the extent that they have been newly accentuated or changed through such a reform. What are the most important structural changes in the liturgical constitution of Vatican II?

a) The word of Holy Scripture and its interpretation in the sermon are emphasized in a new way in relation to the other parts of the traditional liturgy and are given greater weight next to the sacraments than was formerly the case.

b) In the directives for the active participation of the congregation the mouth of the laity is opened for Christian witness in a new way and the universal priesthood of all believers is accorded a new significance. When the constitution explicitly accords to the laity "the right and duty to participate fully, consciously, and actively in liturgical celebrations," by reason of their baptism (Art. 14), to be sure, it does not annul the difference between the laity and the priestly office of the ordained, but all Christians are active in the priestly office. In this the laity actively encircle the priests.

c) By giving basic permission to use the vernacular and to make accommodations to the ideas, customs, and rites of the nations, uniformity in the liturgy is replaced by other structures of unity in the worship service in the multiplicity of rites.

d) By permitting the national conferences of bishops and giving them the right to make liturgical decisions over against the centralism, a structural shift occurs in the direction of understanding church unity as a fellowship. No longer alone but in fellowship with the bishops does the pope govern the worship life of the Roman Church.

These structural changes are of great ecumenical significance, since a unification of the churches is not possible apart from regaining the ancient-Christian structure of fellowship and of unity-in-multiplicity. Above all, it is of fundamental importance for all endeavors toward unification that Holy Scripture, as the authentic tradition of the prophetic and apostolic witness, which is common to all churches, is given new respect.

The principles of liturgical reform first had an effect in those masses celebrated in the *aula* of St. Peter's every morning at the start of the council's business. To be sure, from the beginning, value was laid upon the fact that the multiplicity of the Latin and Eastern rites was honored, and it was a joy for the Protestant and Orthodox theologians that in the Eastern liturgies the Eucharistic words were spoken audibly and the sacrament was distributed in both kinds to a circle of communicants. As a rule, however, the mass was celebrated according to the Roman rite. Again and again the same two biblical texts of the Mass of the Holy Spirit were read, the words of institution were inaudible, the assembly hardly participated actively in the liturgy, and (apart from the celebrating bishop) there was no communion. After the promulgation of the liturgical constitution, however, matters were increasingly different. The assembly took a more active part in the liturgy through the responses, there was more variety in the scriptural readings, and the sacrament was regularly distributed to the laity, who were allowed to participate in the council as auditors (*auditores*). In addition, on special occasions there was a joint celebration on the part of the pope and several cardinals, bishops, or priests. But, to be sure, a joint communion service of all the council fathers never took place, and in none of the masses during the entire council was there ever a sermon on a biblical text, since the public papal addresses at the beginning and closing of each of the four periods had a different character and were not an exposition of a given biblical text.

Since the liturgical constitution validly established new structures, their effects cannot, however, remain restricted to the worship service. Rather, in the course of theological reflection on the renewal of worship life, the consequences for the dogmatic understanding of revelation and of the church must be drawn. One must ask, however, whether the structural changes in worship life have already been fully brought into a dogmatic understanding by the council, or if its dogmatic statements come up short.

Editor's Notes

[i] All quotations from the Constitution on the Sacred Liturgy, *Sacrosanctum concilium* (promulgated by Pope Paul VI on 4 December 1963), are here based on the English translation that is given on the Vatican's website, accessed between 15 February 2016 and 23 February 2016, Vatican.va, http://www.vatican.va/archive/hist_councils/ii_vatican_council/docu ments/vat-ii_const_19631204_sacrosanctum-concilium_en.html (cf. Denzinger 4001–4048 [Tanner, 2.820–43]).

[ii] Cf. Denzinger 1725–1760 (Tanner 2.726–28, 732–37).

[iii] Odo Casel (1886–1948) was a German-born priest and Benedictine monk (Herstelle, Westphalia) who became perhaps the leading figure in the liturgical movement. Through his "mystery theology" he attempted to articulate how Christ is present in the Christian worship service.

[iv] The Constitution on the Sacred Liturgy here quotes from the fifth chapter of the Tridentine Decree on the Eucharist (Council of Trent, Session 13, 11 October 1551). See Denzinger 1643–1644 (Tanner 2.695–96).

[v] Cf. Denzinger 1731 (Tanner 2.727).

[vi] A personally signed letter to the Roman Church at large.

[vii] Cf. Denzinger 1749 (Tanner 2.735).

[viii] Cf. Denzinger 1759 (Tanner 2.736). Schlink places emphasis here by his introduction of italics into the original.

[ix] In 1742 Pope Benedict XIV (1675–1758) promulgated two bulls, *Ex quo singulari* and *Omnium solicitudinum*, which explicitly condemned the Jesuit missionary practice in India and China that allowed local converts to continue to "worship" or venerate their ancestors, in keeping with their cultural traditions, a practice that the Jesuits likened to the Catholic practice of venerating the saints. Benedict also ruled on how God's name is to be rendered in Chinese, an issue that had been debated since the early seventeenth century. As a result of these two bulls, many converts in East Asia left the Roman Church.

Chapter V:
The Self-Understanding of the Roman Church

The church is a strikingly late topic in the history of dogma. To be sure, in connection with faith in the Holy Spirit, the ancient church's creeds confess "the holy catholic church" (the Apostles' Creed), "one, holy, catholic, and apostolic church" (the Nicene Creed), "the communion of saints." In addition, the church is the subject of all dogmatic statements ("we believe," the Nicene Creed). But in the ancient church the Trinitarian and Christological dogmas were the first to be more precisely defined, and then in Western Christendom, under the influence of Augustine, the dogmas of grace. Of course there was always theological contemplation about the church. Moreover, elements of an understanding of the church are found in other dogmas, at least insofar as they contain statements about the borders of the church, as well as determinations concerning the ordering of the church in canon law. Nevertheless, until now the dogma about the church has not been comprehensively and firmly settled, neither in the Eastern Church nor in the Roman Church nor in the Reformation churches. Even the important seventh article of the Augsburg Confession constitutes teaching about the marks of the church rather than a doctrinal description of the reality of the church in its full range. It is self-evident that the initial topics in the history of dogma would be the triune God's encounter with the church and his gracious working. Dogmatic teaching about the church is a later stage of reflection. Here the receiving and confessing fellowship of the believers was itself the topic of their statements. To be sure, the First Vatican Council had introduced a comprehensive schema on the church, consisting of fifteen chapters and twenty-four dogmatic statements containing anathemas (canons), but only the second chapter, on papal primacy, together with a supplement on the infallibility of the pope, was discussed at the time, revised, adopted, and promulgated as the constitution *Pastor aeternus*.[i] The topics that were left unfinished at that time were again taken up at the Second Vatican Council. However, in contrast to Vatican I, the second council—in its *de ecclesia*—did not strive to develop a dogmatic definition of the church nor a formula for anathematizing but restricted itself to describing the church.

1. The Starting Point in Salvation History

The Dogmatic Constitution on the Church begins with the "completely free and hidden decree" of the eternal Father.[ii] "Before time began," God "'foreknew and predestined all the elect to become conformed to the image of His Son, that he should be the firstborn within a large family' [Rom. 8.29]"

(Art. 2). According to the free "decree of his wisdom and goodness" God created the world and "decided to raise people to a participation in his divine life. Fallen in Adam, God the Father did not leave people to themselves, but ceaselessly offered the means to salvation, in view of Christ, the Redeemer 'who is the image of the invisible God, the firstborn of every creature' [Col. 1.15]" (Art. 2). "Already from the beginning of the world the fore-shadowing of the church took place. It was prepared in a remarkable way throughout the history of the people of Israel and by means of the Old Covenant. In the present era of time the church was constituted and, by the outpouring of the Spirit, was made manifest" (Art. 2). It was instituted through the sending of the Son who inaugurated the church through the proclamation of the good news of the coming of God's kingdom (Arts. 3 and 5), and was awakened to life through the Holy Spirit whom Jesus, after his death and as the risen one, poured out on his disciples (Arts. 4 and 5). "Thus, the church has been seen as 'a people made one with the unity of the Father, the Son and the Holy Spirit'" (Art. 4).[iii] "While it slowly grows, the church strains toward the completed kingdom and, with all its strength, hopes and desires to be united in glory with its king" (Art. 5). "At the end of time it will gloriously achieve completion, when, as is read in the fathers, all the just, from Adam and 'from Abel, the just one, to the last of the elect,' will be gathered together with the Father in the universal church" (Art. 2).[iv]

Through the sacraments the faithful are "[f]ortified by so many and such powerful means of salvation" (Art. 11). Taking part in the Eucharistic sacrifice is "the fount and apex of the whole Christian life" (Art. 11). "As often as the sacrifice of the cross in which Christ our Passover was sacrificed (1 Cor. 5.7), is celebrated on the altar, the work of our redemption is carried on, and, in the sacrament of the Eucharistic bread, the unity of all believers who form one body in Christ [1 Cor. 10.17] is both expressed and brought about" (Art. 3). In the faithful the Holy Spirit awakens prayer and witness and the manifold gifts for service in the fellowship. "By the power of the gospel he rejuvenates the church, continually renewing it" (Art. 4).

Consequently, "the church, equipped with the gifts of its founder and faithfully guarding his precepts of charity, humility and self-sacrifice, receives the mission to proclaim and to spread among all peoples the kingdom of Christ and of God and to be, on earth, the initial budding forth of that kingdom" (Art. 5). As the Son is sent by the Father, so the church is sent by the Son for the unceasing proclamation of the gospel so that "God's plan may be fully realized, whereby he has constituted Christ as the source of salvation for the whole world" (Art. 17). This mission is not added to the activities of the church as one alongside many others; rather it necessarily follows from the essence of the church, specifically from the essential attributes of its catholicity. The church thus strives "to bring all humanity and all its possessions back to Christ, its one head, in the unity of his Spirit" (Art. 13).

"Just as Christ carried out the work of redemption in poverty and persecution, so the church is called to follow the same route that it might communicate the fruits of salvation to humanity" (Art. 8). The church in this world is thus on a pilgrimage through a foreign land (Art. 6). "All the members ought to be molded in the likeness of him, until Christ be formed in them (compare Gal. 4.19).... On earth, still as pilgrims in a strange land, tracing in trial and in oppression the paths he trod, we are made one with his sufferings, like the body is one with the head, suffering with him, that with him we may be glorified (compare Rom. 8.17)" (Art. 7).

This starting point and framework of the Dogmatic Constitution on the Church in salvation history signifies an important advance beyond the schema on the church at the First Vatican Council but also beyond the encyclical *Mystici corporis Christi* by Pius XII (1943). The conceptuality and lines of thought are now determined far more strongly by the Bible, and accordingly the Dogmatic Constitution on the Church is not concentrated on a timeless definition of the nature of the church and its characteristics but on an understanding of the church as the advancing, saving, all-encompassing working of the triune God. In doing so, the line of thought from the beginning is carried through again and again with a stronger emphasis on the future consummation. In addition, the eschatological expectation is the special theme of the seventh chapter, in which, however, the accent lies above all on the unity that already exists between the pilgrim church on earth and the heavenly fellowship of the glorified. If the Constitution on the Sacred Liturgy has already understood the mass not only in connection with Christ's death but, beyond that, with his resurrection, then the Dogmatic Constitution on the Church represented the reference to salvation history in its full range and thereby incorporated, and even largely replaced, the traditional ontological schema of nature and super-nature into a historical way of thinking. This new starting point has also had an influence on other resolutions of the council. It is most welcome and opens up new possibilities for ecumenical dialogue, for the mighty deeds of God are the common foundation of all Christian churches. Only on this basis can the differing doctrines and rites that deal with the realization of God's act of salvation in the separated churches be opened up in a new way for on another. It is worth noting, too, the ecclesiological declarations of the World Council of Churches in Amsterdam, Evanston, and New Delhi are also largely determined by this starting point in the Trinity and salvation history.

2. Body of Christ and People of God

The statements in Vatican I's schema on the church and in Pius XII's encyclical on the church were determined by the concepts of the *corpus Christi mysticum* and *societas*. The latter concept had received its character—in the sense of a complete, supernatural, and spiritual society—from the post-Tridentine analysis of the Protestant notion of the state church and modern theories of the state. By contrast, Vatican II's Dogmatic Constitution on the Church surprisingly deemphasizes the concept of society in favor of biblical concepts and images, which are expressed in a remarkable variety of ways: as flock (sheepfold), vineyard (planting, farm, olive tree), God's building (house, temple, city), bride of Christ, mother of believers (Art. 6). While these biblical concepts and images are linked together more than they are exegetically developed and made systematically fruitful, there is a thorough development of the terms *body of Christ* (especially in Art. 7) and *people of God* (especially in chap. 2). The concept of *societas* is, to be sure, not missing (compare, for example, Art. 8), but it does not play a controlling role. In that connection, it is noteworthy that both of these fundamental ecclesiological concepts of the body of Christ and the people of God are used next to one another in the constitution—naturally, not without reference to one another but without allowing the one to merge into the other or treating the one merely as a clarification of the other. In bringing these two different kinds of concepts and images together, the document attests to the mystery of the church.

In the statements about the church as the body of Christ the decisive elements of the New Testament statements are treated to a far greater degree than in the encyclical *Mystici corporis.* If in this latter document the statements about the body of Christ proceed from a presupposed social-philosophical conception of a hierarchically structured society, into which conception the biblical statements have been inserted, then the constitution is focused on New Testament statements and has given clear expression to building up the church as the body of Christ through Christ's sacramental body (Art. 7). If it was characteristic for the encyclical to minimize the statements about the exaltation of Christ and the outpouring of the Holy Spirit so that a temporal gap arose between Christ and the church, which then had to be bridged by the church's ministerial offices in their succession, then, by contrast, the statements of the constitution are determined much more strongly by the presence of the exalted Christ and the ever new working of the Holy Spirit in the church. The manifold sacramental, physiological, eschatological, and also cosmological relationships that are indicated in the New Testament statements about the church as the body of Christ are given incomparably greater attention in the constitution than in earlier texts.

The biblical designation of the church as the people of God helps us to see the special connection in salvation history between the Old Testament nation of Israel and the church, the messianic-eschatological people of God. The reason that chapter two of the constitution treats the people of God is, however, not only the concern for salvation history expressed in chapter one but also the insight that, before considering the doctrine of the hierarchy (as originally planned), the constitution ought to present doctrinal statements in which—without denying the difference between task and authority—the unity of the hierarchy and the laity and the religious orders is expressed. "Though they differ from one another in essence and not only in degree, the common priesthood of the faithful and the ministerial or hierarchical priesthood are nonetheless interrelated: each of them in its own special way is a participation in the one priesthood of Christ" (Art. 10). Corresponding statements follow that treat the participation of the whole people of God in the prophetic office of Christ (Art. 12). By adopting New Testament statements about the church as a prophetic people and a royal priesthood, there opens up for the following chapters—which treat bishops, priests, deacons, laity, and religious orders—the fruitful possibility of starting with the threefold office of Christ, namely, the prophetic, priestly, and royal office, in order to define the specific character of the ministerial offices and members of the church, that is, as a specific kind of participation of each and every member and ministerial office in this three-fold office. On the basis of this starting point as a matter of course, the possibility has been gained for a systematic grouping together of the various levels of the hierarchy, the laity, and the religious orders. Hence, this application: "The obligation of spreading the faith is imposed on every disciple of Christ, insofar as he or she can" (Art. 17). The proclamation of the message to all people is an essential manifestation of the life of the church as a whole on the basis of the sending of the whole people of God and therefore of each of its members. This important idea is further emphatically developed in the decrees on the apostolate of the laity and the mission activity of the church.

Both in the statements about the church as the body of Christ and in those about the people of God attention is given to the multiplicity of gifts and servant ministries which the Holy Spirit brings about for the good of the church (Arts. 4, 7, 12). However, not only the multiplicity of individual members but also the variety of the different "parts" and "orders" of the church is acknowledged within the unity. Within the church different orders are merged together. "Moreover, within the church particular churches hold a rightful place; these churches retain their own traditions, without in any way opposing the primacy of the chair of Peter, which presides over the whole assembly of charity and protects legitimate differences, while at the same time assuring that such differences do not hinder unity but rather contribute toward it" (Art. 13). This fundamental acknowledgment of the member churches is the presupposition for the decree on the catholic (that is, united with Rome) Eastern churches, which "solemnly declares":

[T]he churches of the East, as much as those of the West, have a full right and are in duty bound to rule themselves, each in accordance with its own established disciplines, since all these are praiseworthy by reason of their venerable antiquity, more harmonious with the character of their faithfull, and more suited to the promotion of the good of souls. All members of the Eastern rite should know and be convinced that they can and should always preserve their legitimate liturgical rite and their established way of life, and that these may not be altered except to obtain for themselves an organic improvement. All these, then, must be observed by the members of the Eastern rites themselves. Besides, they should attain to an ever greater knowledge and a more exact use of them....[v]

Corresponding to this is the acknowledgment of the special rights of the patriarch of the Eastern Church (Arts. 7 ff.), the orders of the sacraments (Arts. 12 ff.), and the liturgy (Arts. 20 ff.). Of course the acknowledgment not only of papal primacy but also of all the dogmas of the Roman Church is maintained as the limit to the above multiplicity. The constitution does not make provision for easing up on uniformity in dogmatic statements in favor of a mutual acknowledgment of differing dogmatic formulations of the one faith, something that was characteristic in the first centuries of church history.

Corresponding to the concern for the multiplicity of church traditions is a greater emphasis on the structure of fellowship than on centralization, of course without the "pastoral guidance of the Roman pope" being diminished by the acknowledgment of special rights and orders of particular churches (compare the Decree on the Catholic Churches of the Eastern Rite, Arts. 3, 4, 9, and others).

3. Arranging the Members of the Church

The church is a fellowship of many diverse members. The Dogmatic Constitution on the Church teaches that this arrangement is a hierarchical ordering, which encompasses all of the faithful and consists of levels of authority, tasks, and obligations of obedience, and of course it begins with the topmost level. With great care it thereby develops the relationships which connect each level with the others within the unity of the people of God.

a) Pope and Bishops

In its dogmatic constitution *Pastor aeternus*, the First Vatican Council had taught in its adoption of a formulation from the Council of Florence that to the Roman bishop, "in the person of St. Peter, was given by our Lord Jesus Christ the full power of feeding, ruling, and governing the whole church," and then added: "The Roman bishop is the supreme judge of all the faithful."[vi]

No one may lawfully pass judgment on this judgement. And so they stray from the genuine path of truth who maintain that it is lawful to appeal from the judgments of the Roman pontiffs to an ecumenical council as if this were an authority superior to the Roman pontiff.

And so, then, if anyone says that the Roman pontiff has merely an office of supervision and guidance, and not the full and supreme power of jurisdiction over the whole church, and this not only in matters of faith and morals, but also in those which concern the discipline and government of the church dispersed throughout the whole world; or that he has only the principal part, but not the absolute fullness, of this supreme power, ... let him be anathema. (*Pastor aeternus*, chap. 3)

When the Roman pontiff speaks *ex cathedra*, that is, when in the exercise of his office as shepherd and teacher of all Christians, in virtue of his supreme apostolic authority, he defines a doctrine concerning faith or morals to be held by the whole church, he possesses, by the divine assistance promised to him in blessed Peter, that infallibility which the divine Redeemer willed his church to enjoy in defining doctrine concerning faith or morals. Therefore, such definitions of the Roman bishop are of themselves, and not by the consent of the church, irreformable. (chap. 4)

Although this same constitution had declared that this power of the pope "in no way detracts" from "the power of ordinary and immediate episcopal jurisdiction" of the bishops (chap. 3), there was still the widespread impression that the bishops would henceforth be nothing more than instruments and representatives of the pope.

The third chapter of Vatican II's Dogmatic Constitution on the Church begins where Vatican I had left off. That chapter teaches "that by divine intention the bishops have succeeded to the place of the apostles as shepherds of the church" (Art. 20). To them "is conferred through episcopal consecration the fullness of the sacrament of order" (Art. 21; compare Art. 26). The power of pastors "is proper, ordinary and immediate, although its exercise is ultimately regulated by the supreme authority of the church" (Art. 27). "[Bishops] are not to be regarded as vicars of the Roman pontiffs, for they exercise an authority that is proper to them, and are quite correctly called 'prelates,' heads of the people whom they govern" (Art. 27).

"Episcopal consecration, together with the office of sanctifying, also confers the office of teaching and of governing, which, however, by its very nature, can be exercised only in hierarchical communion with the head and the members of the college" (Art. 21). The tasks of the bishops are set forth in the constitution and especially in the Decree on the Bishops' Pastoral Office in the Church, which unfolds the bishops' threefold prophetic, priestly, and royal office, whereby, it should be especially noted that priority is accorded to the task of proclaiming the gospel (Art. 25). Their tasks in relation to their dioceses, the priests, and the laity, and in relation to the pope, the other bishops, and the whole church, are set forth in detail. Many of these prudent pastoral directives can be described as exemplary, also for domains beyond the Roman Church.

Calling upon the fact that Jesus established the apostles in "a kind of college or a tight fellowship," the constitution teaches that the bishops also form a college.

In the structure of this college the bishops, faithfully recognizing the primacy and pre-eminence of their head, exercise their own authority for the good of their own faithful, that is, of the whole church.... The supreme authority with which this college is empowered over the whole church is exercised in a solemn way through an ecumenical council. (Art. 22)

Not the individual bishop, but the college of bishops together with its head, the Roman bishop, is "the bearer of the supreme and full power over the whole church" (Art. 22). In addition, the infallibility "dwells... in the college of bishops when it exercises the supreme teaching ministry, together with the successor of Peter" (Art. 25).

   With that, however, the statements of Vatican I about the primal authority of the pope are in no way to be impugned. With numerous repetitions the constitution reaffirms that the pope has "full, supreme, and universal power over the church and is always able to exercise it freely" (Art. 22). The college of bishops, however, can exercise it only when the pope calls it to a collegial action or confirms such an action (Art. 22). The same is true for the infallibility of the pope. As usual, "his definitions, of themselves, and not from the consent of the church, are justly styled irreformable.... Therefore they need no approval of others, nor do they allow an appeal to any other judgment" (Art. 25). The college of bishops, however, can exercise the infallible supreme teaching office (Art. 25) only at the behest of the pope and in agreement with him. The *Nota explicativa praevia* [Preliminary Note of Explanation] added to the constitution by the supreme authority, makes this completely clear:

The distinction is not one between the Roman pontiff and the bishops taken collectively, but a distinction between the Roman pontiff taken separately and the Roman Pontiff together with the bishops. Since the Supreme pontiff is head of the college, he alone is able to perform certain actions which are not at all within the competence of the bishops, for example, convoking the college and directing it.... (Sec. 3)

The Roman pontiff, taking account of the church's welfare, proceeds according to his own discretion in arranging, promoting and approving the exercise of collegial activity. (Sec. 3)

Corresponding to this are also the regulations concerning the synod of bishops that the pope published on 15 September 1965 in the apostolic letter *Apostolica sollicitudo*, issued *motu proprio*.[vii] The decision regarding whether, when, and where the synod of bishops (consisting of elected representatives of the regional bishops' conferences) is to meet, which topics are to be treated, and whether the council is to be purely advisory or also authorized to pass resolutions, rests exclusively with the pope.

   This determination of the relationship between the pope and the bishops is grounded in the presupposition that they are the successors of Peter and the apostles and that the latter also governed the church as a college with corresponding degrees of coordination and subordination. Yet neither the discussion in the council nor the constitution gave further attention to the historical contents of the New Testament texts and the issues arising from them. Neither was the basis for Peter's predominant function among the apostles and in the original community in the earliest period examined more closely, nor was the fact taken into consideration that already during Peter's lifetime James took over the leadership of the Jerusalem congregation. Nor was the historical problem of the boundary lines of the apostolic circle investigated, nor was sufficient historical support provided for transferring the concept of a college to that circle. In addition, there is no historical clarification for understanding the pope and the bishops as successors to Peter and the apostles. Without a doubt, a much, much later concept of succession was here projected back into the New Testament texts, whereby in them some particular starting points were generalized in an unhistorical manner.

b) Bishops and Priests

The bishops, in turn, "have legitimately handed on to different individuals in the church various degrees of participation in their ministry" (Art. 28). "Priests, although they do not possess the highest degree of the priesthood, and although they are dependent on the bishops in the exercise of their power, nevertheless they are united with the bishops in sacerdotal dignity" (Art. 28). They share in the episcopal office on a lower level. They are "helpers" (*adjutores*, Art. 20 and others), "co-workers," "instruments" (Art. 28) of the bishops; they support the bishops (*assistunt*, Art. 21). "They make [the bishop] present in a certain sense in the individual local congregations, and take upon themselves, as far as they are able, his duties and the burden of his care, and discharge them with a daily interest" (Art. 28). "In the name of the bishop, [they] gather the family of God together into one fellowship enlivened by one spirit" (Decree on the Ministry and Life of Priests, Art. 6).[viii] They can thus be understood to be representatives of the bishop in the individual congregations of his diocese.

"On the level of their ministry" the priests also "participate in the office of Christ the sole mediator" (Art. 28). Also their task is unfolded as a participation in the office of prophet, priest, and king. This unfolding occurs briefly in the Dogmatic Constitution on the Church and in detail in the decrees on the ministry and life of priests and on priestly formation. With great prudence these documents treat the different relationships of the priests' ministry to their congregation and the whole church, to the laity, to the other priests, to their bishop, and the leadership of the universal church. The directives for the priestly life and the training of priests are models of pastoral care. Noteworthy is the priority that is given in the Decree on Priestly Formation to the study of the Bible and salvation history over the study of scholastic theology. In the midst of the contemporary issues related to theological education this decree deserves careful study in other church bodies as well.

"In virtue of their common sacred ordination and mission, all priests are bound together in intimate brotherhood" (Art. 28). They constitute "one priesthood with their bishop although bound by a diversity of duties" (Art. 28). The bishops

gladly listen to their priests, indeed consult them and engage in dialogue with them in those matters which concern the necessities of pastoral work and welfare of the diocese. In order to put this into effect, there should be—in a manner suited to today's conditions and necessities, and with a structure and norms to be determined by law—a body or senate of priests which represent the presbytery. This representative body by its advice will be able to give the bishop effective assistance in the administration of the diocese. (Decree on the Ministry and Life of Priests, Art. 7)

There is no mention here of an administrative authority that the presbytery or senate of priests has over this diocese. In this respect, the presbytery in fellowship with its episcopal head does not correspond to the college of bishops in its fellowship with the pope, for not only can the bishops be called in for consultation but, as a college with the pope, they have the same authority as he has by himself. The difference in the levels of consecration between bishops and priests could be worked out here.

If the office of bishop has been elevated in its dignity by the Second Vatican Council, then the gap between bishops and priests has been enlarged, for this difference will now no longer be primarily understood as a difference in jurisdictional power but as a difference in consecration. With this emphasis on the difference in consecration, the Roman Church has indeed moved closer to the Eastern Church's understanding of episcopal consecration, but at the same time it has moved further away from the understanding of ministerial office in the Reformation churches, since the latter do not understand the difference between the office of pastor and that of bishop to be a fundamental difference of ordination, but rather a difference of jurisdictional authority. In this respect the Reformation churches are closer to the predominant view in scholastic theology, including Thomas Aquinas, who rejected a difference between the sacramental nature of the consecration of bishops and that of the consecration of priests. In other respects, however, the Dogmatic Constitution on the Church moved away from the Eastern Church's understanding of the office of bishop to the extent that the possibility of exercising that office without the acknowledgment of the pope is denied (compare the *Nota explicativa praevia*, final paragraph).[ix]

The basis for this determination of the relationship between bishops and priests is the installation of bishops by the apostles and the transmission of the office by the bishops to "different office bearers" "in varying degrees" (Art. 28). Here, too, the council did not give more detailed attention to the historical factual situations and problems. The priests are too unquestionably equated with the elders mentioned in the New Testament. In those writings there is a variety of titles for the functions of church government and also a variety of structures for church leadership. By no means can one presuppose the presence of a bishop in every place. Nor can one assume that in the earliest period the leadership of the congregation was carried out only on the basis of a transfer of office through the laying on of hands. Where the New Testament writings do speak of bishops, they are leaders of a local congregation, and thus correspond more closely to the priests than to the bishops in the constitution. The title "priest" is applied in the New Testament not to a particular officeholder but only to the people of God as a whole. In turn, the presbyters were the elders, the first to come to faith, the old and trusted members of the congregation, and it cannot be proved from the New Testament texts that they had been made presbyters through ordination by a bishop. Here, too, a later conception of offices and the transfer of office have been projected back into the beginning of the church.

c) Priests and Deacons

Alongside the priests, the deacons are called "helpers" of the bishops. Here the council made an important decision in opening up the possibility of restoring the diaconate, which had been preserved as a solemn step in the process toward priestly consecration but is now restored "as a proper and permanent rank of the hierarchy," with specific tasks of ministry (Art. 29). The reason for this decision was the shortage of priests in many areas and the impossibility of providing congregations with pastoral care.

It is the duty of the deacon, according as it shall have been assigned to him by competent authority, to administer baptism solemnly, to be custodian and dispenser of the Eucharist, to assist at and bless marriages in the name of the church, to bring Viaticum to the dying, to read the Sacred Scripture to the faithful, to instruct and exhort the people, to preside over the worship and prayer of the faithful, to administer sacramentals, to officiate at funeral and burial services. (Art. 29)

In addition, deacons have "duties of charity and of administration" (Art. 29). Hence, deacons may assume important priestly tasks but they are not permitted to offer the sacrifice of the mass, and may only distribute the host consecrated by the priest.

This provision deserves special attention: "With the consent of the Roman bishop, this diaconate can, in the future, be conferred upon men of more mature age, even upon those living in the married state. It may also be conferred upon suitable young men, for whom the law of celibacy must remain intact" (Art. 29). On the basis of discussion in the council, this last provision appears to be more a concession to the emergency that exists because of the shortage of priests than a positive opinion about the help which the spouse can provide in ministry to the church. Here the constitution lags behind the ordering of the Eastern Church (as well as parts of the same that are united with Rome), which permits priests, including *young* priests, to be married, as long as the marriage occurred before consecration to the priesthood, and it lags completely behind the ordering of the Reformation churches, which, consistent with New Testament tradition, permits pastors and bishops to be married.

d) Hierarchy and Laity

The term laity is here understood to mean all the faithful except those in holy orders and those in the state of religious life specially approved by the church. These faithful are by baptism made one body with Christ and are constituted among the people of God; they are in their own way made sharers in the priestly, prophetical, and kingly functions of Christ; and they carry out for their own part the mission of the whole Christian people in the church and in the world. (Art. 31)

The mission of the laity is called an apostolate. In the Dogmatic Constitution on the Church and especially in the Decree on the Apostolate of the Laity, but also in many other resolutions, such as, for example, the Decree on the Mission Activity of the Church and the Pastoral Constitution on the Church in the Contemporary World, the interest of the council was intensively directed toward the concern that the general priesthood of all believers not remain an empty title but become effective in active apostolic service. It impressively unfolds how the laity are to be effective in the prophetic, priestly, and royal office in the midst of this world. "[T]he laity, by their very vocation, seek the kingdom of God by engaging in temporal affairs and by ordering them according to the plan of God.... It is therefore their special task to order and to throw light upon these affairs in such a way that they may come into being and then continually increase according to Christ to the praise of the Creator and the Redeemer" (Art. 31). Moreover, the laity are called to witness, to confess, and "to evangelize the world" (Art. 35). Through their activity they are to participate actively "in the salvific mission of the church itself" and "in a special way to make the church present and operative in those places and circumstances where only through them can it become the salt of the earth" (Art. 33). "The Lord wishes to spread his kingdom also by means of the laity" (Art. 36). In a comprehensive and exemplary way the tasks of the laity are unfolded in all directions. "Because of the very economy of salvation" the laity should learn to distinguish carefully between the rights and duties which they have insofar as they belong to the church and those which they have as members of human society (Art. 36).

In all directions the apostolate of the laity is allied with the servant ministries of the various levels of the hierarchy.

And if by the will of Christ some are made teachers, pastors and dispensers of mysteries on behalf of others, yet all share a true equality with regard to the dignity and to the activity common to all the faithful for the building up of the body of Christ. For the distinction which the Lord made between sacred ministers and the rest of the people of God bears within it a certain union.... Pastors of the church, following the example of the Lord, should minister to one another and to the other faithful. These in their turn should enthusiastically lend their joint assistance to their pastors and teachers. (Art. 32)

Within such an alliance and cooperation, however, the difference between the laity and the clergy consists not only in that the laity lacks the authority of the consecration for offering the mass but also and especially in that for the exercise of its apostolate the laity are subject to the clergy and obedient to them. "Let the consecrated shepherds recognize and promote the dignity as well as the responsibility of the laity in the church.... Attentively in Christ, let them consider with fatherly love the projects, suggestions and desires proposed by the laity" (Art. 37).

The laity have the right... to receive in abundance from their consecrated shepherds the spiritual goods of the church.... They should openly reveal to them their needs and desires.... The laity should... promptly accept in Christian obedience decisions of their consecrated shepherds, since they are representatives of Christ as well as teachers and rulers in the church. (Art. 37)

This obedience applies not only to their activity as members of the church but also to the exercising of their rights and obligations in the midst of human society, insofar as the pastors interpret for them in the light of the gospel the natural law that is binding for human society.

As impressive as is the intensity with which the general priesthood of all the faithful is emphasized, it is nevertheless remarkable, in view of the line of demarcation between clergy and laity, that the New Testament statements have not been fully taken into consideration. This is true especially regarding the Pauline teaching about the spiritual gifts. To be sure, an excellent opinion by Cardinal Suenens[x] called this teaching to mind and there is an unmistakable intention to incorporate it (Art. 7), but on the basis of a more careful exegesis of 1 Cor. 12.1–11 and 27–31; 1 Cor. 14; Rom. 12.3 ff., and the historical reality of the Pauline congregations which is recognizable here, it is impossible to distinguish between the hierarchical offices and the charismata of the laity, as was done already in the first two chapters of the constitution and especially in the third and fourth chapters. While fully acknowledging the preeminent position of the apostles, the multiplicity of spiritual gifts and servant ministries in the New Testament is not grounded in a corresponding multiplicity of commissionings and sendings by the apostles but in the freedom of the Holy Spirit who works these gifts and ministries "as he wills" (1 Cor. 12.11). At the same time, the kerygmatic ministries, especially the prophets, stand in first position after the apostles (1 Cor. 12.28), the leaders of congregations only at a later position (1 Cor. 12.28; Rom. 12.8), while the gift of discerning the spirits is in turn a special charisma (1 Cor. 12.10). Thus, through the awakening of the manifold spiritual gifts the message of Christ is brought into the world in a variety of forms, and through this working of the Spirit new congregations come into being. In that connection, the ordering of the offices in the congregation, and especially their mutual coordination and subordination, is the topic of later historical developments, the starting points of which are barely present even in the book of Acts and the Pastoral Letters.

e) Religious Orders

After the chapters on the hierarchical structure of the church (chap. 3) and the laity (chap. 4), a special chapter addresses the religious orders that have pledged themselves through a solemn vow to chastity, poverty, and obedience. As in the teaching about the hierarchy, there is in this chapter the same significant tendency toward drawing the religious orders more strongly into the totality of the church. Just as the chapter on the church as the people of God (chap. 2) precedes the one on the structure of the hierarchy, so the chapter on the religious orders (chap. 6) is preceded by a chapter "on the general call to holiness in the church" (chap. 5). After forcefully stating that "all believers in Christ are invited to strive for the holiness and perfection of their own proper state" (Art. 42), the constitution does not understand the religious orders as being an isolated state of holiness but as a form of the general holiness of all the baptized and as "a sign which can and ought to attract all the members of the church to an effective and prompt fulfillment of the duties of their Christian vocation" (Art. 44). "The religious state of life is not an intermediate state between the clerical and lay states" (Art. 43) but rather a gift, help, and stimulus for both. Here, too, the grouping of this state and servant ministry with the other parts of the church has been thought through with great care and developed further in a special decree.

If we summarize the statements of the constitution concerning the arrangement of the church, it is clear that every member receives his or her place in a pyramidal system of superior and subordinate orders, of comprehensive and limited authorities, and of the corresponding obligations to obedience—in a system whose apex is the pope in the full range of his governing authority.

If one were only to see this, however, one would fail to recognize an important aim of the constitution, for its interest lies not only in the existing superior and subordinate order but also in the grouping of the different levels in the fellowship of the one people of God: All of them, each in his or her own way, participate in the threefold prophetic, priestly, and royal office of Jesus Christ. According to their particular commission, all are to serve one another, not only the laity serving the hierarchy but also the hierarchy serving the laity and likewise mutually serving the different levels of the hierarchy. Moreover, it is clear that each person, within the context of his or her mission, is encouraged and even obligated to take his or her own initiative and is by no means expected only to be obedient to his or her superiors. The aim of bringing all members of the church into closer cooperation and uniting them in a common mission and thus easing up on the system of superior and subordinate orders in the direction of the fellowship structure of the church constitutes the new perspective in this teaching about the parts of the church.

At the same time, however, it is true that the space for the individual working of each person, that is, the space for the servant ministry of the spiritual gift bestowed on the individual, is granted and limited by the superior office. Even as the bishops already have no right to assemble as a college and pass resolutions but must wait for the pope to grant them this possibility, still less are the priests as such given a right to lead the diocese in fellowship with the bishop, and the laity have even less authorization to lead the congregation together with the priest or the diocese together with the bishop or the whole church together with the college of bishops and the pope. They remain dependent upon the degree to which the hierarchy invites their counsel and help and is attentive to their wishes. Naturally, this does not exclude the possibility that the posture of the members of the hierarchy may in fact lead to a genuine synodical fellowship on the different levels, but the structure of fellowship, in contrast to the hierarchical centralization, is not guaranteed in canon law. Without a doubt, here the council lagged behind expectations that were also circulated in the Roman Church itself.

It is therefore no accident that the constitution did not consider more carefully the New Testament statements about the apostles, teachers, prophets, bishops, pastors, presbyters, and so forth, or the New Testament relationship between charisma and the laying on of hands, and that between succession and tradition. To be sure, one cannot derive a complete and comprehensive church order from the New Testament. The starting points for that in the earliest Christian congregations are too varied. Yet every ordering of the church will have to remain true to the historical apostolic foundation and the fundamental structures in the earliest Christian community. Here, however, there are profound differences between the Dogmatic Constitution on the Church and the New Testament writings. The New Testament witness to the freedom of the Holy Spirit, who works charismata and servant ministries as he wills, together with the witness to the fellowship of charismata and servant ministries, breaks up the conception of hierarchical centralization.

4. The Borders of the Church

In the version of the Dogmatic Constitution on the Church that was submitted in the second period of the council there was—in addition to an introduction that gave rise to the expectation that the document would aim at a solemn dogmatic definition—the statement that the one church, as a constituted and ordered fellowship in this world, is "the Catholic Church that is governed by the Roman pontiff and the bishops in fellowship with him."[xi] The one, holy, catholic church was thus identified with the Roman Church. To be sure, an ecclesiological identification in itself need not be understood in an exclusive sense. In principle it is entirely possible for a church to confess its identity with the only holy church and at the same time to reckon with the possibility that the one holy church is a reality in the other churches, too. In this version of the schema, however, the identification of the one holy church with the Roman Church was obviously intended to be exclusive since the discussion was not about the churches beyond the Roman Church. Rather, the discourse was only about non-Catholic Christians, that is, non-Catholic individual persons, and not about non-Catholic churches. Despite acknowledging, then, that such individual non-Catholic Christians are connected with the church, that acknowledgment did not mean that they, as members of their non-Roman church, belong to the one, holy, apostolic church. Rather, it meant that such Christians are connected with the Roman Church, which claims to be the one, holy, catholic, and apostolic church. It remains an open question, however, whether this connection is intended to say that the non-Catholic Christians are members of the church or if they are only oriented toward the church. This connection with the church was established through baptism, which—although it was received outside of the Roman Church—is nevertheless identical with the baptism administered by the Roman Church. This connection was further grounded through the "*votum ecclesiae*," that is, through the desire for the one church. This longing desire which moves the hearts of Christendom beyond Rome was thereby interpreted as a longing for the Roman Church governed by the pope. Because of this relationship of the non-Roman Christians with the Roman Church, the possibility of salvation and the reception of grace was accorded to them.

The final version of the constitution indicates a considerable change. The statement that the one church in this world "*is* the Catholic Church (*est ecclesia catholica*) which is governed by the Roman pontiff and the bishops in communion with him" was replaced by this formulation: the one church "*subsists in* the Catholic Church (*subsistit in ecclesia catholica*) governed by the successor of Peter and the bishops in communion with him" (Art. 8).[xii] This change permits the understanding of an identity that is less exclusive. To be sure, occasionally council theologians were heard to say that this loosening up with regard to the church's exclusivity was merely taking into account the fact that the church is not only on earth in the Roman Church but also in the heavenly communion of the reality of the glorified saints. But the context of this textual change as well as the basis for it, as stated in the council, makes clear that the exclusivity of identifying the one, holy, catholic, and apostolic church with the Roman Church should be loosened up in its actual earthly existence. The phrases that were added show, however, that the possibility of openness given with the concept of *subsistere* [to subsist] will be used only with the greatest reticence: "...many elements of sanctification and of truth are found outside of its visible structure. These elements, as gifts belonging to the church of Christ, are forces impelling toward catholic unity" (Art. 8). The language here does not refer to the church or to the churches beyond the borders of the Roman Church but only to "elements of sanctification and of truth."

To understand this *"subsistit in,"* the explanations concerning the different ways of relating or coordinating believing Catholics, those who believe in Christ, and finally all people who are called to salvation by God's grace need to be drawn in. In this context it is asserted:

[For there are many non-Catholics] who honor Sacred Scripture, taking it as a norm of belief and a pattern of life, and who show a sincere zeal. They lovingly believe in God the Father Almighty and in Christ, the Son of God and Savior. They are consecrated by baptism, in which they are united with Christ. They also recognize and accept other sacraments within their own churches or ecclesiastical communities. Many of them rejoice in the episcopate, celebrate the Holy Eucharist and cultivate devotion toward the Virgin Mother of God. They also share with us in prayer and other spiritual benefits. Likewise we can say that in some real way they are joined with us in the Holy Spirit, for to them too he gives his gifts and graces whereby he is operative among them with his sanctifying power. Some indeed he has strengthened to the extent of the shedding of their blood. (Art. 15)

Although the concept of "elements" is here clarified in many respects, avoided still are dogmatic statements regarding the churches that are outside the Roman Church, and the only statements that are made are about persons. Adding that they receive sacraments "within their own churches or ecclesiastical communities" does not constitute a dogmatic statement about the ecclesiological status of these churches, but is simply a phenomenological statement about where they receive the sacraments. Beyond that, here too the working of the Spirit outside of the Roman Church is understood as an awakening of the longing for unity with the Roman Church.

The "elements" of the church beyond the borders of the Roman Church receive then further elucidation through remarks on the Jews and Muslims.

Nor is God far distant from those who in shadows and images seek the unknown God.... Those also can attain to salvation who through no fault of their own do not know the gospel of Christ or his church, yet sincerely seek God and moved by grace strive by their deeds to do his will as it is known to them through the dictates of conscience. (Art. 16)

To be sure, these statements have indeed weakened the original significance of Cyprian's phrase, "[there is] no salvation outside of the church" [*nulla salus extra ecclesiam* –Ed.].[xiii] And yet the understanding of the borders of the church has remained so narrow that the phenomenological recognition of the reality of other churches is hindered, but above all the mystery that is hidden in church history, namely, that the body of Christ is indissolubly one despite the divisions in the church, is being improperly rationalized and the encompassing expanse of the *una sancta* is being recognized. In its statements about the earthly reality of the church, the Dogmatic Constitution on the Church makes a claim for the Roman Church that all other churches dismiss.

The reasons for this narrow concept of the church are to be found, on the one hand, in the temporal proximity to the encyclical *Mystici corporis*, which in a strict sense had equated the borders of the mystical body of Christ with those of the legally constituted Roman Church. Since, however, the Dogmatic Constitution on the Church adopted at Vatican II goes beyond that encyclical in other essential points, the narrow concept of the church is not only caused by that encyclical. Rather, the reasons lie also in the methodological and substantive shortcomings of the constitution itself.

a) Neither in the different versions of the schema of the Dogmatic Constitution on the Church nor in the discussions at the council was there mention of the historical fact of the multiplicity of witnesses, confessional statements, traditions, and church orders within the earliest Christian congregations and those of the ancient church. Correspondingly, the understanding of church unity which emerges from the New Testament writings and which underwent extensive changes in the course of the first three centuries, up to the formation of the imperial church, has not been given sufficient attention. The understanding of unity in the constitution was not formulated on the basis of the Jewish-Christian, Jewish-Hellenistic, and Hellenistic congregations existing side by side in earliest Christianity nor on the basis of the ancient-church structure of mutually acknowledging ministerial offices and baptismal creeds that showed considerable variation from one territory to another. Rather, this understanding is determined by the unity existing today within the Roman Church, whose understanding of unity in faith and of jurisdictional order differs considerably from the understanding in the earliest Christian community and the ancient church. This is also true with respect to the definition of the relationships among pope, bishops, priests, and laity. In taking steps to loosen up uniformity in respect to multiplicity, and thus in respect to understanding unity as fellowship, biblical and ancient-church elements were incorporated into the constitution, but its understanding of unity and the structure of the Roman Church were not actually confronted with the historical-factual situation of the reality on the ground in the earliest Christian community and the ancient church, let alone critically evaluated by it.

b) Despite the clear exposition of the ecclesiological significance of the worshiping assembly in the Constitution on the Sacred Liturgy, and despite the statements that are emphasized in the Dogmatic Constitution on the Church regarding the elevation of the baptized into the fellowship of the body of Christ through the reception of the sacramental body (Art. 7; compare

Art. 11), the local congregation plays only a subordinate role. From the beginning, the focus is directed toward the universal church on earth and it remains fixed there, which creates the impression that the statements about particular churches and local congregations must be derived deductively from what is said here. When in the New Testament writings both the local worshiping assembly and the universal church are designated as *ecclesia* and as body of Christ, that is because one and the same Christ and one and the same Holy Spirit working in the local worshiping assembly and in the universal church is present as the one who is giving himself. Since the unity of the local churches in the universal church is given by this presence of the one Lord, both paths of thinking about the church must be taken in a systematic-theological way: from what occurs in the local worshiping assembly to the unity of the universal church and vice versa. If the latter path is one-sidedly preferred, then the danger arises that in the understanding of unity, in contrast to the New Testament witnesses, priority is given to the jurisdictional-hierarchical ordering over against the Lord who is bestowing himself in the worshiping assembly, and there is the danger of ecclesiologically disparaging the local church in favor of the cathedral churches of the hierarchy.

c) Out of the great multiplicity of relationships between Christ and the church, the constitution one-sidedly favors those of solidarity, fellowship, and unity, namely, those relationships which are given in the designation of the church as the body of Christ, while the designation of the church as the people of God, already found in the Old Testament witnesses, contains not only the relationship of fellowship but also that of the Lord as Judge over against his people. While it is true that the constitution alludes to the fact that those members of the church who do not persist in love, and whose thinking, speaking, and acting are not consistent with the grace of Christ, "will be the more severely judged" (Art. 14), it does not speak of Christ as the Judge of the *church.* According to the New Testament witnesses, however, his judgment will not be restricted to individual persons who regarded themselves as his followers and even prophesied in his name and performed great deeds, to whom the Lord will nevertheless say, "I never knew you. Depart from me" (Matt. 7.22). On the contrary, his judgment is proclaimed also against *entire churches,* as for example in the letter to the church in Laodicea, "Because you are lukewarm, and neither cold nor hot, I will spit you out of my mouth" (Rev. 3.16; compare also 2.5, 16). The constitution did, indeed, incorporate the designation of the church as the people of God and thus the relationship between Israel and the church, but nevertheless, despite acknowledging the salvation-historical identity of the Old Testament covenant people and the church as the true Israel, the constitution nowhere echoes the prophets' proclamation of judgment against the covenant people. God has indeed established a new covenant in Christ, created a new creation, and given to the church the promise that it will never be destroyed, but we cannot overlook the fact that the promise of an abiding remnant was given to the Old Testament covenant people, and that the difference between both of the covenants does not annul the identity of the people of God in the midst of the threats and temptations of this world and under the warnings of God. Thus the ancient-church fathers and the medieval theologians earnestly and entirely correctly understood the prophetic preaching, for example, of Hosea and Ezekiel, as God's word to the church (compare the extensive material in Hans Urs von Balthasar, *Wer ist die Kirche?* [Who is the Church?] [Freiburg i. Br.: Herder, 1965], 55 ff., "Die heilige Hure," [The Holy Harlot]).

d) It has already been pointed out that the constitution's teaching about the hierarchical ordering of the church did not do full justice to the New Testament statements concerning the freedom of the Holy Spirit and especially the Pauline teaching about the fellowship of the spiritual gifts and servant ministries. Since the constitution in its understanding of the church still is determined in a special way by the legal structure of the hierarchy, which subordinates the free charismata to itself, it is hindered from recognizing in its necessary expanse the working of the Holy Spirit and his gifts, servant ministries, and ministerial offices beyond the borders of the hierarchically governed Roman Church.

e) The narrowness of the concept of the church in the constitution may also be determined, furthermore, by the fact that its statements about the church proceed too one-sidedly from the substantive concepts and images that the New Testament uses to designate the church, while too little is said about the assurance and the claim with which the Lord and the apostles encountered the church and still encounter it today. We can think, for example, about the fact that in the Gospel of John the terms *church*, *people of God*, and *body of Christ* do not appear, and that the very significant ecclesiological statements in John 13–17 are stated almost exclusively (apart from the parable of the vine) in terms of promise, consolation, indicative, imperative, warning, threat, and intercession ("you are clean," "abide in me," love one another," and so forth). One should in no way fail to recognize that the constitution, in contrast to the older dogmatic texts, has given due weight to the multiplicity of biblical concepts and images and to the comprehensive context of salvation history. And yet, one cannot overlook the danger which otherwise is often bound up in one's consideration of salvation history, namely, that in place of actually listening to the Lord who encounters the church one substitutes a description of the relationship between the Lord and the church, and thus the gathering and edifying but also the critical and judging activity of the Lord is displaced by substantive and attributive statements about the nature of the church, as occurred in a similar way in the Tridentine decree on justification, in which doctrine is taught through objectifying description rather than in the manner of being encountered existentially. The Dogmatic Constitution on the Church says too little about Christ's *encounter* with the congregation that occurs in the worship service, about his address in the word, and about his administration of the sacrament, and too quickly subsumes the worship event as a means of a universal process.

Thus, in its teaching about the hierarchical structure and the borders of the church, the constitution is more apologetic than it is dogmatic, that is, it is more concerned with the need to justify the existing Roman Church than it is to evaluate critically the present Roman Church on the basis of the norm of the historical, apostolic, and earliest Christian tradition. Nevertheless, the forces which are here seeking to overcome the centralistic uniformity cannot be overlooked.

5. Mary and the Church

The Dogmatic Constitution on the Church closes with an eighth chapter, "The Role of the Blessed Virgin Mary, Mother of God, in the Mystery of Christ and the Church." Its history belongs to the most dramatic moments of the council. Surprisingly, in November 1962, the schema of an independent constitution, On the Blessed Virgin Mary, was distributed. It aimed at a further development of Mariology by suggesting that Mariological statements from the encyclicals of the most recent popes should be elevated to the rank of a dogmatic conciliar resolution, and especially that the title "mediatrix" should be explicitly acknowledged. The title "co-redeemer" (*corredemptrix*), as it was stated in a note, was indeed not included, out of deference to the Protestants, but the substance of this title was included. On 29 November 1963 a narrow majority at the council resolved not to treat the topic of Mary in an independent Mariological constitution but rather within the Dogmatic Constitution on the Church. In September 1964 the discussion about including the completed text on Mary as the final chapter in the Dogmatic Constitution on the Church reached its climax, as the dogmatic acknowledgment of Mary as mediatrix and as Mother of the Church was demanded by the maximalist side, while the opposing side rejected such a development of Mariological dogma as theologically unripe. The end result represents a compromise: The title "mediatrix" was cautiously adopted, but not the title "Mother of the Church." The closing chapter is therefore not maximalistic, since it defines no new Mariological dogma, but it is also not minimalistic, since it explicitly took up the dogmas of the Immaculate Conception (1854) and Mary's bodily assumption into heaven (1950) and, in addition, acknowledges Mary as mediatrix.

Fundamental for the determination of the relationship between Mary and the church is the section "On the Role of the Blessed Virgin in the Economy of Salvation" (Arts. 55–59). Corresponding to the salvation-historical starting point in the doctrine of the church, this section treats first the Old Testament witness, then the earthly life of Mary, and finally her assumption into heavenly glory, as the presupposition for her present activity on behalf of the church and her veneration by the church. In what follows we proceed from the New

Testament statements about Mary but cannot enter into a discussion of matters relating to history and the history of tradition.

a) On the basis of the Gospels all churches are mindful of Mary, the mother of Jesus, as the chosen member of God's people who was used by God in a unique way to carry out his work of redemption, namely, to realize the incarnation of his Son, and who in the obedience of faith assented to this service. Beyond that, however, the council understands Mary as "entirely holy and free from all stain of sin" "from the first moment of her conception," "fashioned by the Holy Spirit into a kind of new substance and new creature" (Art. 56).

b) According to the New Testament witnesses, Mary's "Yes" of faith did not remain self-evident during the public ministry of Jesus. According to the Synoptic Gospels, Mary did not belong to the circle of disciples. Although she was a highly favored mother, she did not understand Jesus when he stayed behind in the temple (Lk. 2.50). Although she was his mother, Jesus let her stand outside and, turning away from her, said to his disciples, "Here are my mother and brothers! Whoever does the will of God is my brother, and sister, and mother" (Mk. 3.34 ff.). That the relatives of Jesus thought him to be out of his mind was handed down in the same context (Mk. 3.21). To be sure, according to the Gospel of John, Mary accompanied Jesus to the wedding at Cana, but there she was rebuffed by him (Jn. 2.4). The Gospels thus present Mary as a woman assailed in her faith and who experienced grief, not only because of the suffering of her son but also because of her inability to understand his path. This characteristic inability of Mary to understand Jesus (apart from a formal reference to Lk. 2.41–51) is overlooked by the Dogmatic Constitution on the Church (Art. 57 f.).

c) In the New Testament reports about the passion, there is no indication that Mary recognized in the death of Jesus the redemptive act of the Christ, God's Son. She seems to have suffered the same shock as the disciples. The first confessions of faith are handed down in the reports of the passion as statements of the one malefactor on the cross and of the centurion. Admittedly, Mary did not flee, according to the passion narrative in John, and she remained beneath the cross. But even if the figures of Mary and John are understood symbolically, the words of Jesus (Jn. 19.26 f.) are not an acknowledgment of her faith in him but a loving provision and directive addressed to Mary and John, that is to say, to the Jewish- and Gentile-Christian church of the future. The Dogmatic Constitution on the Church, however, teaches a co-working of Mary in Jesus' sacrifice on the cross, "in that she lovingly consented to the immolation of this victim which she herself had brought forth" (Art. 58).

d) As with the faith of the apostles, so with Mary it was the work of God's grace that despite these spiritual attacks and trials she was, along with the other women and brothers after Jesus' resurrection, united in faith and in prayer with the apostles, and she awaited the coming of the Holy Spirit (Acts

1.14). There is no indication in the New Testament that she occupied a special place in the earliest Christian community. There is no tradition that the risen Jesus appeared to her (as he did to Peter, James, and others), nor that she had hastened to the disciples with the message of the empty tomb or of Jesus' resurrection (as Mary Magdalene and others had done), nor that she later had proclaimed to others the message of God's act of salvation in Jesus Christ, as the apostles did. Corresponding to this, the New Testament designates the apostles and prophets, not Mary, as the foundation of the church (Eph. 2.20; compare Mt. 16.18 and Rev. 21.14). Those same New Testament writings, even those that were written at the end of the first century or in the second, report nothing about the end of her earthly life. But the Dogmatic Constitution on the Church teaches: "Finally, the Immaculate Virgin, preserved free from all guilt of original sin on the completion of her earthly sojourn, was taken up body and soul into heavenly glory, and exalted by the Lord as Queen of the universe" (Art. 59). This teaching is without historical foundation, since neither the New Testament nor the church's tradition of the first five centuries attest to an ascension of Mary.

e) Accordingly, because Mary "in this singular way cooperated by her obedience, faith, hope and burning charity in the work of the Savior in giving back supernatural life to souls," she is our mother in the order of grace" (Art. 61), and she "is invoked by the church under the titles of advocate, helper, counselor, and mediatrix" (Art. 62). The title of "mediator" is used in the New Testament most exclusively for the one sent by God to proclaim and fulfill the once-and-for-all historical act of salvation. Now there are other titles of Jesus which in the New Testament are transferred to members of the church: son of God, servant of God, holy one, shepherd, bishop, and so forth. Such transfers are called analogies and are explained in this way, for example, that Jesus Christ alone is the Son of God by nature, while the believers are sons of God through adoption. The analogical use of such titles of honor for Jesus remains intelligible only when the difference is completely clear. The New Testament safeguards the difference by refusing to transfer some titles, such as, for example, Christ, Lord, mediator, Savior. Only when some titles are not transferred to members of the church can it be clearly maintained that the transfer of other titles is intended to be merely an analogy. The exclusivity of the mediatorship of Jesus Christ is attested to most decisively in the New Testament: "There is *one* God and *one* mediator between God and humankind, namely, Christ Jesus, himself human" (1 Tim. 2.5). The Dogmatic Constitution on the Church cites this verse, too (Art. 60) and declares that the Mariological title of mediatrix "neither takes away from nor adds anything to the dignity and efficacy of Christ the one mediator" (Art. 62; compare Art. 60). But this sentence is already largely contradicted by Catholic piety, wherein people are often not aware of the theological distinction between worship, which belongs to God alone, and veneration, which belongs to Mary. In addition to the Christological title of "mediator," the Dogmatic Constitution on the Church transfers other titles to Mary that correspond to the New Testament statements about the working of the Holy Spirit: "advocate," "helper," "counselor." While the constitution's statements about the working of the Holy Spirit are truncated, its Mariology is excessive by the transfer of Christological and pneumatological titles to Mary.

What does the mother of the Lord signify for the understanding of the church? That significance lies precisely in the fact that the New Testament writings attest to these two things: Mary as the physical mother of Jesus and the unpretentious member of the earliest Christian community; and Mary as the one uniquely chosen for service and the one subject to spiritual attacks and trials—both of which make remembrance of her precious and consoling. Precisely in this way is she an exemplar of faith and a *typos* [image –Ed.] of the church. In both respects, in her being chosen to be "the bearer of God" and in the spiritual trials of the suffering mother, her life is an unforgettable doxology of God's grace. The Dogmatic Constitution on the Church, however, teaches that Mary is not so much a member of the church but rather the mother who stands opposite the members of the church. When she is taught to be a member of the church, it is in such a way as to distinguish her from all of the other members of the church, and she is distinguished by no means only through her having conceived and given birth to the Son of God. Rather, going beyond the New Testament statements, claims are made for her sinlessness, her cooperation in the sacrifice on the cross, her ascension into heaven, and her abiding mediatorship, on the basis of which she is exalted above all believers and venerated in a cultic way. In this sense she is a *typos* of the church. The church, "contemplating [Mary's] hidden sanctity, imitating her charity and faithfully fulfilling the Father's will, by receiving the word of God in faith becomes herself a mother.... The church herself is a virgin" (Art. 64). While "the followers of Christ still strive to increase in holiness by conquering sin," in the "most holy Virgin the church has already reached that perfection whereby she exists without spot or wrinkle (compare Eph. 5.27)" (Art. 65). In a corresponding manner other privileges and titles of Mary are also transferred to the church. Thus the Dogmatic Constitution on the Church truly closes with a Mariological compromise but also with a glorification of the church that is grounded in Mariology.

Editor's Notes

[i] Cf. Denzinger 3050–3075 (Tanner 2.811–16).

[ii] All quotations from the Dogmatic Constitution on the Church, *Lumen gentium* (promulgated by Pope Paul VI on 21 November 1964), are here based on the English translation that is given on the Vatican's website, accessed between 23 February 2016 and 3 March 2016, Vatican.va, http://www.vatican.va/archive/hist_councils/ii_vatican_council/documents/vat-ii_const_19641121_lumen-gentium_en.html (cf. Denzinger 4101–4179 [Tanner, 2.849–900]).

[iii] The constitution is here quoting from Cyprian's treatise, *On the Lord's Prayer*, 23 (PL 4.553).

[iv] The constitution is here quoting from Gregory the Great's *Homilies on the Gospels*, 19.1 (PL 76.1154).

[v] From Articles 5 and 6 of the Decree on the Catholic Churches of the Eastern Rite, *Orientalium Ecclesiarum* (promulgated by Pope Paul VI on 21 November 1964), based on the English translation that is given on the Vatican's website, accessed on 23 February 2016, Vatican.va, http://www.vatican.va/archive/hist_councils/ii_vatican_council/documents/vat-ii_decree_ 19641121_orientalium-ecclesiarum_en.html (cf. Denzinger 4180–4183 [Tanner 2.900–907]).

[vi] Chapter three of the First Dogmatic Constitution on the Church of Christ, *Pastor aeternus* (promulgated by Pope Pius IX on 18 July 1870). See Denzinger 3059–3064 (Tanner 2.813).

[vii] See the English translation of *Apostolica sollicitudo*, the apostolic letter of Pope Paul VI (issued *motu proprio* on 15 September 1965), on the Vatican's website, accessed on 25 February 2016, Vatican.va, http://w2.vatican.va/content/paul-vi/en/motu_proprio/documents/hf_p-vi_ motu-proprio_19650915_apostolica-sollicitudo.html. The phrase, "*motu proprio*," means that this apostolic letter was written on the pope's personal initiative and with his personal signature.

[viii] Art. 6 of the Decree on the Ministry and Life of Priests, *Presbyterorum ordinis* (promulgated by Pope Paul VI on 7 December 1965), Vatican website, accessed on 25 February 2016, Vatican.va, http://www.vatican.va/archive/hist_councils/ii_vatican_council/documents/vat-ii_decree_ 19651207_presbyterorum-ordinis_en.html (cf. Tanner 2.1042–1069; This document is not included in Denzinger.).

[ix] "It is clear throughout that it is a question of the bishops acting in conjunction with their head, never of the bishops acting independently of the pope. In the latter instance, without the action of the head, the bishops are not able to act as a college: this is clear from the concept of 'college.' This hierarchical communion of all the bishops with the supreme pontiff is certainly firmly established in tradition. N.B. Without hierarchical communion the ontologico-sacramental function [*munus*], which is to be distinguished from the juridico-canonical aspect, cannot be exercised" ("Preliminary Note of Explanation" to the Dogmatic Constitution on the Church; cf. Denzinger 4358–4359 [Tanner 2.900]).

[x] Leo Joseph Suenens (1904–1996) was born in Belgium. Between 1961 and 1979 he was the archbishop of Mechelen-Brussel, the primatial Belgian see. He was made a cardinal by Pope John XXIII in 1962. Cardinal Suenens was one of the major figures at Vatican II. He played a key role in setting its agenda. He had significant influence on the content of both *Lumen Gentium* and *Gaudium et Spes*.

[xi] Cf. Xavier Rynne, *Vatican Council II* (New York: Farrar, Straus and Giroux, 1968), 175–88.

[xii] The emphases here are by Schlink.

[xiii] This famous phrase of Cyprian of Carthage (d. 258), part of a longer sentence, is found in his letter to Jubaianus concerning the baptism of heretics (Cyprian, Ep. 72, sec. 21).

Chapter VI:
The Council and the Non-Roman Churches

The Dogmatic Constitution on the Church is the basis for the council's statements about the relationship of the Roman Church to the other churches, to the non-Christian religions, and to humanity as a whole, in other words, for the relationship of the Roman Church to the three concentric circles, of which it considers itself to be the center. Among these statements, the Decree on Ecumenism is especially significant for the rest of Christendom. This decree was adopted in the closing session of the third period of the council by an overwhelming majority of 2156 council fathers to only eleven contrary votes, and then promulgated by Pope Paul VI. The significance of this decree becomes clear as soon as one thinks about the earlier, negative relation of the Roman Church to the ecumenical movement. In this chapter we shall first examine the content of this decree and then later, in the seventh and eighth chapters, inquire into the extent to which its determinations have influenced the other decisions of the council, for it makes a difference whether the thoughts in the Decree on Ecumenism merely stand next to the other decisions of the council, or whether the former permeate the latter.

1. Openness toward the Non-Roman Churches

Originally, the schema of the Dogmatic Constitution on the Church had viewed the problem of the non-Roman churches only as a matter concerning *individual* non-Catholic Christians who had a connection with the Roman Church because of their baptism and their longing for the Roman Church. In contrast, the initial version of the Decree on Ecumenism, whose first chapter treated the principles of ecumenism and thus also the subject of the understanding of the church, was from the beginning far more open. The statements about the one, holy, and catholic church were initially made without referring to the Roman Church and without identifying the two in an exclusive way. Hence from the start there was here a great openness for the reality of the church, even beyond the borders of the Roman Church and at the same time a greater respect for the mystery of the church, which we can attest to correctly only if we know that it transcends human ascertainment and articulation. There was, furthermore, no explicit mention of the pope, but only of Peter, whom the Lord had chosen from among the twelve to preside over the college of his brothers by strengthening each one in the faith and shepherding the whole flock. Certainly, this statement was not intended to be merely historical, but in these investigations into the unity of the church the emphasis rests primarily on the historical, apostolic foundation and not so much on the form of Roman primacy as it had developed in the course of Western church history. Undoubtedly, from here significant possibilities arose for ecumenical dialogue on this topic, which is especially controversial among the churches.

But it was precisely this ecclesiological basis for the schema on ecumenism that was sharply criticized in the council's *aula*. Cardinal Frings demanded that clear expression had to be given to the idea that we need not look forward to one church of Jesus Christ, but that this one church, founded by the Lord and built on Peter, was already there in the Roman Catholic Church. He held that it is this church that will be brought to consummation at the end of time. Other voices, too, demanded that greater clarity be given to what constitutes the oneness of the church and the unity of faith and government so that no misunderstanding would arise among the separated sisters and brothers. There was criticism of the fact that the schema did not maintain the complete identity of the mystical body of Christ with the Roman Catholic Church, as it had been taught in the encyclical *Mystici corporis Christi*. Love for the separated called for the complete truth and the avoidance of any and every irenic approach. By failing to mention the primacy of the *successors* of Peter in the schema on ecumenism, out of a false irenic approach, the fundamental truths of the unity of the church were being concealed. Biblical citations, given their indeterminacy, are not to become the cause for imprecision in issues of controversy.

It is probably because of such objections that the final version of the Decree on Ecumenism expresses more strongly and frequently that the unity, fullness, and treasures of the one, holy, catholic, and apostolic church are a reality only in the Roman Church and thus under the successor of Peter as its head. It is "through Christ's Catholic Church alone, which is the all-embracing means of salvation, that the fullness of the means of salvation can be obtained" (Art. 3).[i] The final version of the Decree on Ecumenism thus has in some measure accommodated its statements on the principles of ecumenism to the more reticent Dogmatic Constitution on the Church.

In the council's discussions concerning the first version of the decree there were also voices, to be sure, that were heard in favor of going even further than its statements. Numerous council fathers were especially dissatisfied that the Reformation churches were designated merely as "communities." While one group of council fathers was critical of the fact that "the communities that came into being in the sixteenth century" were being evaluated too positively and that the difference between the Orthodox and the Protestants was not being stated plainly enough, another group (Cardinal König and others) emphatically demanded that these "communities" should in any case be designated "ecclesial communities."[ii] Thirty Indonesian bishops went so far as to insist that not only the Orthodox churches but also the churches of the Reformation should be spoken of as "churches." Other council fathers also supported this demand.

On this issue the definitive text of the decree went beyond the first version. It speaks explicitly of "churches and ecclesial communities" alongside the Roman Church. Admittedly, the decree does not define in what sense non-Roman churches are to be designated as "churches" or as "ecclesial communities"—surely these designations imply more than merely an accommodation to these churches' own self-designation and imply a certain ecclesiological acknowledgment, but hardly in the same sense as the Roman Church understands itself as church, and surely only in an analogical sense. That the terms here are not further clarified need not necessarily be regarded as a defect, for new ecclesiological problems have emerged with the ecumenical movement, for which all churches today still lack adequate terms and concepts. On the basis of the council's discussions it should be clear that the changed designation for the non-Roman churches is to accord them a larger ecclesiological significance, and this intention should be acknowledged by them.

The decree here therefore goes beyond the statements in the Dogmatic Constitution on the Church, which in its definitive form speaks only of "elements" of the catholic church beyond the borders of the Roman Church, and thus the decree shows a greater ecumenical openness to the non-Roman churches. Such a step beyond the Dogmatic Constitution on the Church was necessary if the ecumenical problem was to be tackled at all, for it truly is only taken seriously as a problem dealing with separated *churches*. To be sure, the more narrow Dogmatic Constitution on the Church continues to take precedence in rank and binding significance over the more open Decree on Ecumenism, and the ecumenism of the Roman Church will be able to step over the limitations of the Dogmatic Constitution on the Church only insofar as it can make believable that already in its statements about the "elements" of the catholic church in the other churches—because of the communal character of some of these elements (for example, baptism and the Lord's Supper)—the Dogmatic Constitution on the Church is speaking implicitly of communities, yes, even of churches outside of the Roman Church.

2. Directives Regarding Ecumenical Conduct

The second chapter of the Decree on Ecumenism bears the heading "*De oecumenismi exercitio*" [on the practice of ecumenism]. In the impressive simplicity of its instructions it contains the most ecumenically progressive expositions of this decree. Since the drafting of the first version, the material had been continually improved. Newly added, for example, is the reference to the church on its pilgrim way being called "to that continual reformation" (Art. 6). Also new is this paragraph:

The words of St. John hold true about sins against unity: "If we say we have not sinned, we make him a liar, and his word is not in us" (1 Jn. 1.10). So we humbly beg pardon of God and of our separated sisters and brothers, just as we forgive them that trespass against us. (Art. 7)

While the directives of this chapter are indeed directed to members of the Roman Church, they ought, in my opinion, to be acknowledged as valid in their essentials and taken to heart by the other churches, for they in fact are formulating the first requirement for discourse among the separated sisters and brothers, something that should be self-evident among Christians but unfortunately is not everywhere self-evident. If these fundamental principles of ecumenical conduct are translated into practice, we may expect that a lot of soil that has been hard and barren for a long time on both sides of the ecclesial borders will be plowed anew. In a special way, this chapter permits the earnestness of ecumenical desire to become clear, a desire that defines the Secretariat for Christian Unity and also many council fathers. Brought especially to the forefront for each member of the Roman Church are the following necessary points:

a) The spiritual renewal of the heart (Arts. 7 f.). Without conversion, without sanctification, without self-denial, humility, willing service and generosity toward the separated, without growth in love and the longing for unity, ecumenism is not possible. In fact, a genuine ecumenical movement is always a movement of repentance. It does not begin with the demand to the separated that they repent, but with one's own repentance; not with the demand to others that they change, but with one's own readiness to do so.

b) The prayer for unity (Art. 8), and to be sure, where it is possible, together also with separated sisters and brothers. Of course in the council's discussions the objection was raised that joint prayer for unity would be a deception in that everyone prayed according to his or her opinion. The Catholic understanding of the prayer for unity, however, could only have the intention of praying for the return of the separated sisters and brothers. To this Cardinal Bea replied (in the sense of Couturier, the French ecumenical pioneer)[iii] that it was sufficient if each person praying would leave it up to God to decide when and how a more complete unity is to be achieved than the mind of the ones praying now recognizes. Joint prayer, which is recommended, is distinguished from joint worship services, which may be permitted by the bishops only under certain circumstances.

c) The careful concern for truly understanding the separated sisters and brothers, their doctrine, their worship life, their piety, and their historical and cultural presuppositions. Toward this end, there was also a call for the broadening within theological education (Art. 10).

d) Dialogue with the separated sisters and brothers on an equal footing (Arts. 9 and 11). In this dialogue Catholic doctrine is to be presented clearly to them and accommodated to the presuppositions of their understanding, without diminution (avoiding an ideologically irenic approach), but also without polemics. Here the emphasis could primarily be thought of as an academic dialogue among theologians, not yet a dialogue between churches. To be sure, the first version of the schema *De Oecumenismo* left unspecified in the statement about dialogue to what extent dialogue is here only concerned with an explanation of Catholic truth with thoughtful empathy for the presuppositions of the dialogue partners, or is concerned also with a common and joint wrestling for the truth. It cannot be ignored, however, that every presentation in a genuine dialogue becomes a joint seeking, inquiring, and researching, for we human beings do not have the truth but the truth lays hold of us. In the *aula* of the council there were, in fact, voices which called for joint research with the separated sisters and brothers. Particularly impressive in this regard were the criteria for a genuine ecumenical dialogue that were set forth by Auxiliary Bishop Elchinger (of Strasbourg).[iv] The final version of the decree then also speaks explicitly of "joint research with the separated sisters and brothers," the task of which is "to investigate the divine mysteries," with the goal that "the way will be opened by which through friendly rivalry all will be stirred to a deeper understanding and a clearer presentation of the unfathomable riches of Christ" (Art. 11). Especially helpful in this connection is the directive: "When comparing doctrines with one another, they should remember that in Catholic doctrine there exists an order or 'hierarchy' of truths, since they vary in their relation to the fundamental Christian faith" (Art. 11). This order can, however, according to the Roman Catholic understanding of dogmatic validity, be understood solely *substantively and systematically*, but not in the sense of differing degrees of *binding validity* between the central and less central dogmas.

Let us pause here for a moment. In view of the most extreme reticence of the Roman Church that existed until recently in relation to the other churches, these instructions already mean more than perhaps appears at first glance. They receive their special importance, however, from the fact that they are not merely words on a page but words that have to be heard in the context of the council itself. They are not simply demands but an expression of what had already begun to become a reality in the work of the council and what we as official observers had experienced in numerous encounters with the fathers and theologians of the council. A new dialogue had already begun there, with mutual respect, love, and openness, and through a common and genuine wrestling for the truth.

e) To be emphasized then is the injunction to cooperate with the separated sisters and brothers (Art. 12), especially in social issues, in problems relating to technological advances, in the commitment to overcome existing emergencies and needs, for example, in the elimination of illiteracy. These examples are at present confined within the boundaries of natural law. Yet the discussion in the council made progress insofar as it pointed to the necessity of cooperation among the churches' relief programs in developing countries, such as the cooperation of Catholics and Protestants in solving the problems of Christian Africa. Moreover, an ecumenical collection, once proposed by Oscar

Cullmann, was recommended.[v] This collection is to be announced and collected in the worship service by a Protestant congregation for a Catholic emergency, or vice versa.

f) Beyond all this, the final version of the decree also explicitly mentioned the task of jointly witnessing to the faith:

> Before the whole world let all Christians confess their faith in God, one and three, in the incarnate Son of God, our Redeemer and Lord. United in their efforts, and with mutual respect, let them bear witness to our common hope which does not disappoint us. (Art. 12)

The readiness of the council to bear joint witness to Christ with non-Roman Christendom is of extraordinary ecumenical significance.

g) If we inquire further with respect to what the Decree on Ecumenism says about the removal of particular hardships that make it difficult for separated Christians to live together, such as, for example, the non-recognition of a marriage of a Roman Catholic and non-Catholic performed by a Protestant pastor, or the redoing of a properly administered Protestant baptism *sub conditione* (because of its invalidity), or the rivalry among churches on the mission field—about these burning issues the decree says nothing. At a later point we will have to ask if these issues are dealt with in the other resolutions of the council. But already here we must draw attention to the long and fiercely debated Declaration on Religious Freedom, which provides the presupposition for abolishing such distressing situations as exist, for example, for the Protestant Church in Spain, and that, far beyond Spain, place a heavy burden on the relationship between the Roman Church and Protestant Christendom.[vi] The motives for this recent commitment to the freedom of faith on the part of the Roman Church are certainly quite varied. The Roman Church itself today needs this freedom in areas where it is being suppressed. Yet the demand for the freedom of faith has also been made quite consciously by many for a new relationship to other churches in areas where the Roman Church predominates. Expressed in various official opinions was the valid point that understanding another's faith and being respectful to it—and thus, religious freedom—is the necessary foundation of ecumenism. To be sure, there was strong opposition in the council to the Declaration on Religious Freedom, and attention was rightly called to the Roman Church's tradition, including the explicit rejection of religious freedom in the Syllabus of Pius IX (§ X).[vii] Against this opposition the declaration could prevail only by unilaterally going beyond the final version of the Decree on Ecumenism and assuming that the Roman Church is the only true religion, by taking up the limitation of religious freedom through the less precise concept of the "common good" (*bonum commune*) and, in addition, by making a special provision for those countries where *one* religion predominates and is acknowledged in a special way through the legal order of the state (Art. 6). But even in this case there is the demand that religious freedom be granted not only to the consciences of the individual adherents of the other religious communities but also to these communities themselves. Here, too, the concern is no longer only about tolerance but about the right of religious communities to act freely— something that the *declaratio* unfolds in its details (worshiping assembly, religious education, election of officeholders, administrative independence, and so forth, Art. 4)—and about the obligation of the state to defend this right. Despite those restrictions, the *declaratio* thus signifies a noteworthy step forward, which is designed to make the encounter with the separated churches possible on a new basis.

Initially, to be sure, the decree's directives regarding ecumenical conduct confine themselves to the very first steps. These directives are undoubtedly of great significance; indeed, for many Catholic theologians and laity they are nothing short of revolutionary significance. But between these first steps and the desired-for unification there still remains a huge gap. For the unification of the separated churches cannot truly be expected without first removing the heaviest burdens to living together so that the joint witness to Christ, which the baptized owe to God and the world, may become possible.

3. The Goal

The goal of Roman Catholic ecumenism is the unification of the separated churches, more precisely, their unification with the Roman Church. Unification, to be sure, is not the immediate and direct goal of the council—that goal is the renewal of the Roman Church—but it was already an express goal during the council, if only as an expected outcome of the renewal. The renewal of the church should take place so that the countenance of the Roman Church might shine more convincingly on the separated sisters and brothers and a wider door to this Catholic house of the church be opened for all. In this sense it was already the expectation of Pope John XXIII, which was also expressed by his successor, that the council become "a wonderful spectacle of truth, unity, and charity. For those who behold it but are not one with this Apostolic See, we hope that it will be a gentle invitation to seek and find that unity for which Jesus Christ prayed so ardently to his Father in heaven."[viii] The goal of ecumenism consists, therefore, in a succession of coordinated goals. That the council focused on the renewal of the Roman Church itself as the first goal is in line with what other churches in their endeavors toward unification found to be necessary. Only with the highest respect can one acknowledge the seriousness and humility with which this renewal has been undertaken by numerous council fathers.

a) The Renewal of the Roman Church

The demand for inner renewal expressed in the Decree on Ecumenism is directed not only to individual members of the Roman Church but also to the Roman Church as a whole (Arts. 4 and 6):

Christ summons the church to continual reformation as she sojourns here on earth. The church is always in need of this, in so far as it is an institution of human beings here on earth. Thus if, in various times and circumstances, there have been deficiencies in moral conduct or in church discipline, or even in the way that church teaching has been formulated—to be carefully distinguished from the deposit of faith itself—these can and should be set right at the opportune moment. (Art. 6)

The demand for church renewal was discussed in a number of formal opinions and explicitly affirmed and given concrete shape in a variety of ways, even going so far as to demand a new theological vocabulary, a new church structure, and a renunciation of the display of ecclesial ostentatiousness—so that in these words one can catch sight of not merely a set of postulates but also clear indications of a renewal that has already begun. Deeply moving expressions of a change of heart and a new mindset were voiced, which, without any attempt to gloss over the history of the church, spoke of the church's ongoing failure in what it owed the world and the separated Christians. A number of formal opinions explicitly took over the words from Pope Paul's opening address concerning the necessity of mutual forgiveness. Yet, there was an objection, namely, that the statements concerning the Catholic Church's share in the guilt for the divisions of the church were creating discomfort in the council and that those who cannot rid themselves of a guilt complex should go to their father confessor (Bishop Muldoon, Sydney).[ix] However, this objection was most emphatically rejected by the council: A public and truthful admission of guilt is the first step in all efforts to restore unity (Abbot President Butler, England).[x] It is unmistakable that in the council a movement of renewal broke forth, despite all of the impeding factors.

This renewal of hearts and minds had its effect in a special way in the struggle over the form of the church's order. The council was thus vigorously engaged in relaxing the centralization of the church through the promotion of collegiality and in permitting the multiplicity within the church to become evident again in place of uniformity. Bearing in mind also the struggle about the collegial understanding of church government, a renewal in the direction of the fellowship-structure of the church shows itself in the area of the liturgical and legal order of the church. In addition, there is the noteworthy intensity with which—in a critical examination of former ideas and forms of conduct—a new dialogue was taken up with the world.

This renewal, of course, reaches its limits with dogma. As has already been stated, the liturgical reform in no way signifies a change in the Tridentine teaching about the sacrifice of the mass. The Mariological dogmas of 1854 and 1950 also remain unchanged. In their conciliar oath the council fathers explicitly committed themselves to all of the dogmatic decisions of the Roman Church in its history and hence also to all repudiations (anathemas) contained therein against the doctrines of the non-Roman churches. But the antitheses in the statements of faith that are contained in the dogma, along with the anathemas that are bound up with them, are the deepest hindrance to unification. As far as the doctrinal differences among the churches are concerned, the council repealed none of the existing anathemas to help bring about unification. To be sure, in both Protestant and Catholic theology today we see the task of translating dogmatic statements from the way in which they were formulated and conceptualized in their historical setting, as well as their particular structure of thought and expression, into contexts, concepts, and structures of our time that are in part entirely different. In this we see the possibilities of a new interpretation of dogmatic statements and of their development toward a consensus among the separated churches. But the council made hardly any use even of this insight into the historical character of dogmas nor of this possibility for a new interpretation, as it seems to me. Nor was there an attempt to distinguish between the greater or lesser binding weight of the various dogmatic decisions in light of the perspective of the confession of Christ.

b) The Unfolding of the Roman Church's Catholicity

The unfolding of catholicity also serves to prioritize the goal of unification. That unfolding is closely connected to the renewal.

The demand for this unfolding signifies, first of all, the task of securing the greatest freedom to the various forms of Roman Catholic spiritual life, theological work, and so forth. Beyond that, however, it points to the necessity of acknowledging "the riches of Christ and virtuous works" in the lives of the separated sisters and brothers (Art. 4). As long as the Roman Church understands itself exclusively as the catholic church, it can acknowledge as a means of grace and working of grace in the other churches only what it recognizes as elements of the Roman Church still present in them. Increasingly, however, there is also a greater openness toward that spiritual reality in the other churches which has not unfolded in the Roman Church but that nevertheless belongs to a fully unfolded catholicity. More and more one recognizes that the catholicity effected by God is greater than that which is realized in an individual church body, even in the Roman Church itself, for through the divisions it has become "difficult" for the Roman Church "to express in actual life the fullness of catholicity in every aspect" (Art. 4).

Thus more and more one recognizes the obligation to make space within the

Roman Church and to give hospitality there to all that has been discovered in other churches as a true expression of spiritual life, an advance in biblical insight, an experience in social action, and so forth. Already prior to the official adoption of the topic of ecumenism, in past years, for example, chorales of the Reformation churches were taken over into Catholic song-books, as were methods and results of Protestant biblical scholarship and ways of framing issues in systematic and ecumenical theology (for example, the topic of lay activity). In a similar way this has also been true for a long time with respect to the liturgy, patristic theology, and the mysticism of the Eastern Church. This opening up toward others is now to be deliberately actualized. The virtual catholicity of the Roman Church must be unfolded as compre-hensively as possible in an actual catholicity. In this connection there was, for example, strong criticism voiced against the practice of standardizing and Latinizing that had been insisted on earlier in those parts of the Eastern Church that are united with Rome.

It is also true, of course, that the possibilities of this expansion of the structure of the Roman Church, in terms of canon law and especially dogma, are indeed limited. But perhaps here there will be more extensive expansions than may be logically deduced from the existing presuppositions about dogma and canon law.

c) The Unification of the Separated Churches

Despite all of the differences in Rome's evaluation of the separated churches, the council fathers shared the common conviction that the unity of the church is a reality in the Roman Church and that unification is to be achieved by bringing about the full fellowship of the non-Roman Christians with the Roman Catholic Church. This is the goal of ecumenism: that "all Christians will at last, in a common celebration of the Eucharist, be gathered into the one and only church.... We believe that this unity subsists in the Catholic Church as something it can never lose" (Art. 4).

Belonging to this complete fellowship is the confession of the one faith, the common celebration of the divine *cultus* (hence, fellowship of the sacramental life), and concord in church government, that is, acknowledging the full primatial authority of the bishop of Rome in matters of faith and discipline, in accordance with Vatican I.

This goal is not new, and yet one does not do justice to the decree if one sees in it only the invitation to return to the Roman Church, an invitation that is repeated by other methods and under a different name, for we dare not overlook the fact that this ultimate goal of ecumenism can mean quite different things. The approach to the unity existing in the Roman Church is not the same if it is a matter of the present situation or of a renewed Roman Church of the future; nor is it the same if the primacy is administered only in the sense of

Vatican I or in cordial fellowship with the leaders of other churches; nor is it the same if it is about the return to the Roman Church or a mutual reconciliation between the Roman Church and other churches; nor is it the same if, according to the Roman Church's understanding, non-Roman churches become true churches only by first returning or if churches which mutually acknowledge one another establish full fellowship. To be sure, the concept of "return" [*Rückkehr*] has thus far not disappeared, either from the formal recommendations of the council or from papal pronouncements. If it is, however, today consciously avoided by important council fathers and theologians, then one cannot only look for practical considerations lurking between the lines, but rather presuppose the insight that the concept of return is not adequate for the desired unification, for both historical and ecclesiological reasons.

The goal of unification thus presents itself in various ways, depending on the depth of the renewal and how comprehensive the unfolding of catholicity is held to be necessary. This situation, in turn, depends on whether the renewal and the Catholic openness toward others is understood as already having been realized in the council or if it is only something taken up by the council but remains an unfinished task for the future:

(1) The stronger the assumption is that the Roman Church has already renewed itself in its present state through the council and unfolded its catholicity, the more the unification will be understood as a return. Already possessing unity and catholicity, the Roman Church is waiting for the conversion of the others and is ready to give them from its own treasure what they lack. One might suspect that several council fathers voted for the decree because they thought they could interpret it in this way. In this attitude, however, there is the danger that some believe the renewed invitation to return, as expressed in the council's decree, is all that is necessary and that the inevitable disappointment that will then follow will freshly deepen the sense of separation.

(2) But the more the people within the Roman Church will look upon the events of the council as a beginning, though not yet the required realization of renewal and catholic unfolding, the more they will expect the unification to be a result of a mutual change, of a mutual conversion [*Bekehrung*] of the separated toward one another—not as a return [*Rückkehr*], but rather as a reconciliation; not as a submission, but rather as a mutual acceptance of fellowship; not as a one-sided giving, but rather as a mutual giving and receiving. In this understanding of unification a way is opened up for further mutual spiritual discovery, reconciliation, and cooperative work, a way whose length and the individual steps on it cannot be determined in advance, a way on which both sides must entrust themselves to the guidance of the Holy Spirit. Here, too, Roman dogma and papal primacy remain untouchable, but that does not exclude a new interpretation by means of a changed form of church teaching and activity.

(3) Within the Roman Church there are also theologians and laity who regard the future shape of a united Christendom as far less settled from the outset than is the case in the Decree on Ecumenism and, even more so, in the Dogmatic Constitution on the Church. These individuals keep themselves consciously open (not merely in view of the goal itself) to the action of the unifying Holy Spirit, which cannot be calculated in advance nor circumscribed by thinking that is governed by canon law. Also, in this perspective, changes in dogmatic understanding and in the centralized order are considered possible, changes that would in fact not be merely new interpretations but rather corrections of existing dogmas. In this refusal to insist on a conception of unification predetermined by dogma and canon law, the way is open most freely and directly for the dimension of fellowship among the separated churches in mutual spiritual giving and receiving, a fellowship which in its essence also longs for the realization of unity in the confession of faith, in the sacraments, and in ministerial offices, and in this longing prays for God-pleasing ordering.

The Decree on Ecumenism permits various possibilities of understanding the unification that is to be worked toward. Above all, however, the text points toward the second position cited above, without entirely excluding the first one. In the decree, and especially in the Dogmatic Constitution on the Church, the third conception above is the least defensible, even though on the basis of the decree's presuppositions its advocates can be tolerated for a part of the way toward unification. Consistent with these three different possibilities is that from the council's documents no complete clarity can be gained on precisely what the difference is between ecumenism and the work of gaining converts, which is also affirmed in the same decree (Art. 4).

There is no need to give up hope for a future greater expansion of the possibilities for understanding unification. For the time being, however, the non-Roman churches can only deal with the present reality of the Roman Church, and they must see with all cool-headed realism that the acknowledgment of *all* Roman Catholic dogmas, including the dogma of *papal primacy* in the *full* significance of the infallibility declared at the First Vatican Council, is the Roman *conditio sine qua non.*

4. Possibilities and Limits of Ecumenism

The ecumenism of the Second Vatican Council springs from an elementary urge for fellowship with the separated sisters and brothers, a desire which in the course of the council gripped more and more of the council fathers. The directives for ecumenical conduct, which set forth an excellent clarification of what is initially necessary, provide guidance for the steps that are to be taken toward the separated churches as a result of this desire.

At the same time, the decree also clearly indicates the limits to which the council knows itself to be bound in its understanding of ecumenism.

a) The goal of ecumenism is limited by the decisions about dogma and canon law that were pre-set for the council, for dogmas are regarded as irreformable, as are also the provisions in canon law to the extent that they are regarded as God's law. These limits remain comparatively narrow, not only because the Roman Church feels very strictly obligated to its dogma and its understanding of God's law—that is also true of other churches—but because in its dogmas and canon law this church has firmly specified its position so comprehensively, and by its numerous anathemas has so decidedly marked itself off from other churches as no other church has done. Consequently, this church also has less room to maneuver, with respect to ecumenical activity, than the other churches.

In addition, there are the limits which this council itself, through the Dogmatic Constitution on the Church, has added to the dogmatic commitments that were in place already before the council. Although this constitution is not regarded as dogma in the strict sense of a solemn dogmatic definition, nevertheless it has a very high rank of binding authority as a decision of the council. Considering that the doctrine of the church—except for papal primacy—had not hitherto been firmly settled through a conciliar decision, the statements of the Dogmatic Constitution on the Church concerning the borders of the church, for example, as well as the ascription of the title of mediatrix to Mary, signify an additional restriction to the Roman Church's freedom of movement in ecumenical dialogue. The ecumenical openness of the Roman Church is thus limited not only by the dogmas already in place prior to the council but also by the dogmatic statements of the council itself. This raises the question: Was it necessary at this time to decide and promulgate a definition of the nature of the church? Have not many new problems and aspects of ecclesiology become evident, also in the Roman Church, through the ecumenical movement, for which adequate concepts are still lacking? Did it not constitute a hope for ecumenical dialogue that in the questions surrounding ecclesiology in all the churches there were far fewer settled dogmatic positions than, for example, in the doctrine of justification or in the doctrine of the sacraments? Was it not possible to wait and see what would come out of the possibilities created by the Decree on Ecumenism for theological cooperation among the separated churches in providing *common* answers to the new ecclesiological questions that have arisen? It makes some sense, to be sure, in view of this council's temporal proximity to Pius XII's pre-ecumenical and narrow encyclical on the church, *Mystici corporis*, that it could not now say much more about the other churches than what was said in the Dogmatic Constitution on the Church. Nevertheless, was it necessary to restrict ecumenical dialogue by means of the latter document in the very moment when it was made possible by the decree?

b) These presuppositions determine the understanding and the evaluation of the various non-Roman churches which are dealt with in the third chapter of the decree under the title "The Churches and Church Fellowships Separated from the Roman Apostolic See." At this time one need not inquire into the decree's concrete statements about these churches but rather to inquire about the criterion by which they are assessed in these statements, for the concrete judgments which one church applies to another are not as important for the encounter of the separated churches as is the criterion by which they are mutually to assess one another. What, then, is the criterion which was applied to the rest of Christendom in the various versions of the decree and in the discussions about them?

Corresponding to the self-understanding of the Roman Church as the one, holy, catholic, and apostolic church, the primary criterion is the Roman Church itself, that is, its present reality as it has been determined in history through dogma and canon law. The criterion is not the earliest church, nor the church of the first centuries as such, but only to the extent that it is identical with the contemporary Roman Church, that is, only to the extent that the former is manifested in the latter. In a certain sense this criterion corresponds to the rule that the first source of Roman Catholic dogmatics is not Holy Scripture but the Church, specifically the Church's teaching office. Since the ecclesiological reality of the non-Roman churches is thus measured by the reality of the Roman Church, a characteristically quantifying way of evaluating them occurs. They are evaluated according to the quantity of those elements that are constitutive of the Roman Church and are also present in the other churches, that is to say, according to the quantity of dogmas, sacraments, and ministerial offices which they have in common with the Roman Church. The order of preference of these non-Roman churches is determined by this quantifying way of thinking. In this way the presence of a hierarchical ordering in the apostolic succession of consecration plays a special role. Corresponding to this starting point, when in the discussion individual council fathers called for the start of dialogues toward unification, only the Orthodox Church was mentioned, and then, in view of the Anglican Church, it was recommended that, first of all, the question of the validity of Anglican ordinations, which had been answered in the negative under Pope Leo XIII, be reexamined.[xi] Naturally such a quantifying way of thinking makes it exceedingly difficult to understand the other churches from the center of their life, and it was clear that particularly the special spirituality of the Eastern Church remained to a large extent hidden to this way of thinking.

There are, however, statements in the decree De oecumenismo and also statements in the formal opinions that were offered in the discussions that break through this quantifying way of thinking, statements which are determined by the direct and immediate impression of the witness to Christ, of prayer, of worship life and sacramental piety, of servant ministry to the world, and of martyrdom in the areas of the separated churches. The criterion here is much more directly Christological and pneumatological, and thereby the biblical one that is common to all churches. The experience of the mystery of unity in Christ is here being spoken of, which cannot be grasped by means of traditional ecclesiological concepts. Here hearts meet in the certainty of the same faith, even if the form of the faith statements and of church activity is different. Breaking through that kind of quantifying thinking also occurs when effects of grace are discovered and acknowledged in the non-Roman churches, effects that did not develop in the Roman Church yet are regarded as necessary for the full realization of the mystery of Christ in the church and hence for the full realization of the catholicity of the church. The quantifying way of thinking in the schema was even explicitly criticized in individual formal opinions, since the center of all the elements of the church is Jesus Christ himself. Corresponding to this was the demand of the American Cardinal Ritter (St. Louis), namely, that all thinking about unity must proceed more strongly from Christ.[xii]

On the basis of the very lively discussion it is difficult to say which basic attitude predominates. In view of the majority of votes it is quite possible that it is the first one mentioned, namely, that the separated churches are understood primarily not as churches that have grown up on apostolic ground and live by the power of Christ and the Holy Spirit but rather as churches that have split off from the Roman Church, whereby the pressing question for evaluating them is about what they still have in common with the Roman Church after their separation. Entirely apart from the historical question, which seems not to have been considered here—namely, that the Roman Church itself, after all, has also undergone further development in dogma and canon law, both since its separation from the Eastern Church and since its own exclusion of the Reformation churches—one must still consider the fact that, according to all other ecumenical experiences, a deeper mutual understanding only begins when it proceeds on the basis of the common historical apostolic foundation of the church and the separated churches encounter one another anew in a joint listening to the witness of Holy Scripture, by which each church allows itself to be judged and its view of the other churches is opened up. But this is possible even without first working out an ultimate clarification of the relationship between Scripture and tradition, since Holy Scripture has *in fact* remained common to all the separated churches.

c) Let us inquire further into the concrete evaluations that are made about the non-Roman churches in the third chapter of the decree, which takes into consideration the multiplicity of those churches that has developed histor-ically. The first part of the chapter deals with "the Eastern churches," while the second part deals with "the separated churches and ecclesial communities in the West."

What is quite noteworthy and new here is the consistent tendency to seek and lift up what is positive in the separated churches. Undoubtedly this represents a new tone over against early official pronouncements of the Roman Church regarding other churches. Attention is directed, above all, to what the Roman Church and the other churches have in common, and the effort to avoid offensive expressions is unmistakable. This chapter thus avoids the terms *schismatics* and *heretics*, and left undecided is the question of whether the Orthodox churches may still be labeled schismatic or whether, in view of their rejection of papal primacy as dogmatically defined by Vatican I, they have become heretical. Meanwhile the classic distinction between schismatics and heretics seems not to have been simply put aside but, without using these terms, lives on in the distinction between churches and ecclesial communities, although without specifying which non-Roman churches, with the exception of the Orthodox, are to be labeled as "church" or merely as "ecclesial fellowship."

Joined to the positive statements about the non-Roman churches are references in each section to the differences that exist between them and the Roman Church. In characterizing the Eastern churches, these differences are viewed almost exclusively from the perspective of a permissible and mutually complementary multiplicity, while in characterizing the Reformation churches the differences are presented more strongly as oppositions. From the determination of the differences, the topics will arise that will be assigned to future dialogues. Here too the other churches can only applaud this process, for a fruitful ecumenical dialogue can begin only when the participating churches are made aware not only of the commonalities but also of the existing differences, or, stated more precisely, "the commonalities in the differences" and "the differences in the commonalities" (Karl Barth),[xiii] and then proceed on this basis to formulate the questions that must be carefully and jointly clarified from the perspective of each side. This method has also proved effective in other ecumenical work.

Nevertheless, observers at the council from the most diverse churches, even some of the council fathers and council theologians, have felt that precisely this third chapter does not make much of an advance, mainly for two reasons:

First, many felt that they were not really understood because of the groupings and characterizations that were imposed upon them. Thus—to mention only a few examples—in the preamble (Art. 13) there is a brief reference to the rise of the non-Chalcedonian churches (the Copts, Nestorians, and so forth) but the first main section of this chapter actually speaks only of the Eastern Orthodox churches, which was all the more surprising since the heterodox Eastern churches were more strongly represented at the council than the Orthodox. Yet the Orthodox were also irritated because they could not consider the Decree on Ecumenism in isolation from the Decree on the Catholic Churches of the Eastern Rite (that is, those united with Rome), a decree which was discussed, adopted, and promulgated by the council at that same time and which also made very clear to them the difference between the juridical Roman understanding of Orthodoxy and the latter's pneumatic self-understanding. The second main section overlooks the medieval divisions in the West, of which, indeed, only the Waldensian Church and the Bohemian

Brethren eluded extermination. The characterization of the Reformation churches remains colorless and seems to be controlled by a general concept of Protestantism that may be convenient but does not do justice to the real situation, as if there were no church bodies with dogmatic stipulations and a legal ordering of ministerial offices. If the situation were reversed, would the Roman Church have felt itself correctly understood if it had been characterized on the basis of a general concept of Catholicism in which the more or less common marks of the Roman, Old Catholic, Orthodox, Monophysite, and Nestorian churches, and perhaps also the ancient apostolic church, were included?

Second, to others it appeared strange that the characterization of the non-Roman churches was still linked—even before the opening of the ecumenical dialogue—with judgments concerning God's action taking place in them, which judgments are difficult to reconcile with an ecumenical openness for inquiry into the spiritual reality of another church, if indeed such judgments should not be entirely taken away from human hands and left to God. What can the praise accorded to the Orthodox Church mean if the same decree decisively clarifies that the fullness of the church is to be found only and exclusively in the Roman Church? Or what should the Church of the Lutheran Reformation think about the courtesies in the statements about the Reformation churches when at the same time it is denied that they receive the body and blood of Christ in the Lord's Supper? What right has the council to judge that the Reformation churches "have not preserved the genuine and total reality (*substantia*) of the Eucharistic mystery" (Art. 22), even though the Evangelical-Lutheran Church confesses the true and substantial presence of the body and blood of Christ in the Lord's Supper? What right did the pope have to delete a statement already adopted by the council concerning the use of Scripture in the Reformation churches, namely, that "moved by the Holy Spirit, they *find* God who speaks through Christ in the Holy Scriptures," and to reduce it to the statement, "They call on the Holy Spirit and *seek* God in the Holy Scriptures"? Would it not be more accurate to begin an ecumenical dialogue with at least an initial openness for God's activity in the other churches rather than passing judgment on them? It is natural that the churches in question repudiate such judgments.

d) It is surprising, moreover, that in characterizing the Eastern and Western churches that are separated from Rome the decree completely overlooked their membership in the World Council of Churches. Oddly enough, there is no mention in the entire decree of this fellowship which was legally constituted in Amsterdam in 1948 and which now embraces more than two hundred non-Roman church bodies. The decree speaks only of the ecumenical *movement* and its confession of the triune God. However, it is impossible today to do justice to the reality of the Eastern and non-Roman Western churches if one looks upon them as isolated groups, and if one ignores the fact that these churches, as member churches of the World Council, live together in a fellowship which in numerous ways has proved worthwhile and is steadily growing, a fellowship of giving and receiving that results in new openings and in new impressions.

This ignoring of the World Council of Churches is all the more surprising since the Secretariat for Unity maintains contacts with the World Council and made use of its offices in the process of inviting observers from the non-Roman churches. One can, however, account for this unusual silence of the decree by the fact that the World Council represents a *novum* in church history, something that in a peculiar way escapes the standard by which the Roman Church evaluates the others, for the World Council cannot in any way be understood as a breaking away from the Roman Church. If it were, one could measure what elements of the Roman Church it had retained since the break. The World Council is rather the means of a movement that seeks to overcome the separation through the cooperative work of the separated churches. In this, membership is open also to the Roman Church. Moreover, the failure to mention the World Council in the Decree on Ecumenism may rest on the claim of the Roman Church that unity is already a reality in that church and therefore need not first be sought. No one thus rose in the council's discussions to propose that the Roman Church participate in the existing fellowship of the various Orthodox, Evangelical-Lutheran, Reformed, Anglican, Methodist, and other churches in the World Council.

5. Roman Ecumenism

In summary, the result is that the ecumenism of the decree is a specifically Roman ecumenism. It is an attempt at a characteristic synthesis between the exclusivist concept that is grounded solely in canon law, as it is present in the Roman Church's designation of its own general synods as ecumenical councils, and the broader concept, as it is employed today in the ecumenical movement to designate the efforts toward unification and the growing fellowship of the separated churches. The Roman Church designates its councils as ecumenical because it believes that it is itself already the one, holy, catholic, and apostolic church, and it therefore uses this designation regardless of whether or not such a council is dealing with the issue of reunion. Without giving up this narrow concept of ecumenism, the Roman Church has taken up an entirely different one, namely, the one which has generally established itself in the course of the unification efforts of the non-Roman churches, and it has sought to combine the two concepts. That this concept of ecumenism, both in its relation to its exclusive notion in canon law and in its relation to the ecumenical movement of the non-Roman churches of the East and of the Reformation, still requires further clarification was also something repeatedly stated by the council fathers.

Editor's Notes

[i] All quotations from the Decree on Ecumenism, *Unitatis Redintegratio* (promulgated by Pope Paul VI on 21 November 1964), are here based on the English translation that is given on the Vatican's website, accessed between 7 March 2016 and 15 March 2016, Vatican.va, http://www.vatican.va/archive/hist_councils/ii_vatican_council/documents/vat-ii_decree_19641121_unitatis-redintegratio_en.html (cf. Denzinger 4185–4194 [Tanner 2.908–920]).

[ii] Franz König (1905–2004), a native of Austria, was the Archbishop of Vienna from 1956 until his retirement in 1985. He was particularly interested in ecumenical issues and played a significant role in the formulation of the Decree on the Church's Relation to the Non-Christian Religions.

[iii] Paul Irénée Couturier (1881–1953) was a French priest who was instrumental in helping to establish the Week of Prayer for Christian Unity. Educated at Lyon and ordained a priest in 1906, he later worked at the Institut des Chartreux at Lyon. Throughout his life he was in frequent ecumenical conversation with non-Roman Christians, both Orthodox and Protestant. He wrote many tracts on prayer for unity and was in close contact with leaders of the WCC.

[iv] Léon Arthur Elchinger (1908–98) was a French priest (ordained in 1931) and bishop. He was the Auxiliary Bishop of Strasbourg (1957–67) and then Bishop of Strasbourg (1967–84).

[v] Oscar Cullmann (1902–1999) was a Lutheran professor of the New Testament and early church history at the Sorbonne and in Basel, Switzerland. Born in Strasbourg, where he went to seminary, he later was very active in the ecumenical movement. He was one of the official observers at the Second Vatican Council.

[vi] Schlink is here alluding to the persecution of Protestants in Nationalist Spain during the Franco dictatorship (1939–1975). This included violence against Protestant clergy and laity, violence against Protestant chapels and churches, the confiscation of Protestant Bibles and literature, propaganda against Protestants, and so on. Cf. endnote 2 in chap. 1 ("The Spiritual Awakening of Christendom") above.

[vii] The Syllabus of Pope Pius IX (1792–1878), published on 8 December 1864, sets forth a collection of errors that had been proscribed by him between 1846 and 1864. The tenth section presents four propositional statements that are identified as "errors relating to present-day liberalism." These errors include the following opinions: (1) that the Catholic religion should not be "the only State religion, excluding all other forms of worship"; (2) that immigrants to Catholic regions should be allowed "to exercise publicly their own form of worship"; (3) that "civil freedom of worship and the full right granted to all to express openly and publicly any opinions and views" does not "lead to an easier corruption of morality and of the minds of people" nor "help to propagate the plague of indifferentism"; and (4) that "the Roman pontiff can and should reconcile and adapt himself to progress, liberalism, and the modern culture" (Denzinger 2977–2980).

[viii] Pope John XXIII, *Ad Petri Cathedram*, sec. 62.

[ix] Thomas Muldoon (1917–1986), a native of New South Wales, Australia, was ordained in Rome in 1941, where he also completed a doctorate in theology. He returned to Australia to teach dogmatic theology (in the pre-modern tradition of scholasticism) at St. Patrick's College. He was appointed auxiliary bishop of Sydney in 1960, where he also served as a parish priest. Schlink is here alluding to Bishop Muldoon's public remarks at the council against other Christian church bodies and against the "tearful and tedious laments" of those bishops who deplored some of the Catholic actions during the Protestant Reformation. Cf. John Carmody, "Muldoon, Thomas William (1917–1986)," *Australian Dictionary of Biography*, National Centre of Biography, Australian National University, http://adb.anu.edu.au/biography/muldoon-thomas-william-15785/text26977, published first in hardcopy 2012, accessed online 11 March 2016.

[x] Basil Christopher Butler (1902–86) was a convert to the Roman Church from the Church of

England. In 1929 he became a Benedictine monk at the Downside Abbey. In 1933 he was ordained a priest. During the time of the council he was the Abbot President of the English Benedictine Congregation. In 1966 he was made auxiliary bishop of the Diocese of Westminster. At the council he was perhaps the leading English-speaking participant.

[xi] In his apostolic letter, *Apostolicae curae et caritatis* (13 September 1896), Pope Leo XIII (1810–1903) ruled that Anglican ordinations were invalid. Cf. Denzinger 3315–3319.

[xii] Joseph Elmer Ritter (1892–1967), a native of Indiana, was ordained in 1917 in Indianapolis. He later served as auxiliary bishop and bishop of that city. He was appointed archbishop of St. Louis in 1946, a position he filled until his death. He was created a cardinal by Pope John XXIII in 1961. Cardinal Ritter participated in all four periods of Vatican II.

[xiii] Schlink has here slightly modified Barth's original phrasing. Prior to the constituting assembly of the World Council of Churches in 1948 Barth had encouraged participants in the Faith and Order movement to go beyond merely elaborating what the divided churches have in common and to focus more on *"die Übereinstimmungen in den verschiedenheiten"* ("the agreements in the disagreements") and *"die Verschiedenheiten in den Übereinstimmungen"* ("the disagreements in the agreements"). In his October 1951 address, "The Task and Danger of the World Council of Churches" (included as the first chapter in book one of this present volume; cf. endnote 7 in that chapter), Schlink renders the phrases slightly differently. See also Hanns Lilje, "Der gegenwärtige Stand der ökumenischen Bewegung, Kritische Ergebnisse der Dritten Weltkonferenz für Glauben und Kirchenverfassung in Lund (15.–28. August 1952)" [The Present Condition of the Ecumenical Movement: Critical Consequences of the Third Conference on Faith and Order], *Theologische Literaturzeitung* 78, no. 2 (1952), 69, where Lilje also refers to Barth's role in developing this dialectical thesis.

Chapter VII:
The Council and the Non-Christian Religions

The council also examined the relationship to the non-Christian religions. Here, too, there was an effort to resume the conversation in a new way. This second concentric circle, by which the Roman Church sees itself and the rest of Christendom encircled, is treated in the Declaration on the Church's Relation to the Non-Christian Religions[i] and the Decree on the Mission Activity of the Church.[ii] It is noteworthy that one and the same topic is treated in two different resolutions, of which the first teaches a positive evaluation of the religions and due respect for them, while the second stresses the necessity for missionary proclamation on the basis of their deficiencies. Even though the two resolutions of the council place the accents differently, they do not contradict one another. It is surprising, furthermore, that the Declaration on the Church's Relation to the Non-Christian Religions does not refer to the Decree on the Mission Activity of the Church, and that the latter does not refer to the former. But with respect to their topic, they belong so close to one another that the one text cannot be isolated from the other and neither can be correctly understood apart from the other. A misleading picture would ensue if the adherents of the non-Christian religions would take note of only the declaration and if Catholics would take note of only the decree. Both texts want to give members of the Roman Church directives for their conduct in relation to the non-Christian religious world. The juxtaposition of these two conciliar resolutions is perhaps best understood in the light of the declaration's historical genesis, that is, how it was originally specified to be a conciliar message regarding the Jews, and then, because of objections from the Arab world and the bishops from Arab countries, it was gradually enlarged and developed into a declaration concerning non-Christian religions in general. In addition, the statements about the conduct toward the non-Christian religions are imbedded in general statements about the unity of the human race and the necessity of engaging every person with the attitude of a brother or sister. Thus the Declaration on the Church's Relation to the Non-Christian Religions flows then into the thoughts of the Declaration on Religious Freedom and the Pastoral Constitution on the Church in the Contemporary World.

No foundation therefore remains for any theory or practice that leads to discriminations between people, between nation and nation, with reference to human dignity and the rights flowing from it. The Church reproves, as foreign to the mind of Christ, any discrimination whatsoever between people, or harassment of them because of their race, color, condition of life, or religion. (*Nostra aetate*, Art. 5)

1. The Opening toward the Non-Christian Religions

Just as it did in relation to the non-Roman churches, the council also brought about an openness toward the non-Christian religions. The systematic starting point for this, too, is given in the Dogmatic Constitution on the Church, particularly in its statements about "many elements of sanctification and of truth" that can be found beyond the borders of the Roman Church (*Lumen gentium*, Art. 8), for the presence of such "elements" is taken into account not only in the case of non-Catholic Christians but also of non-Christian religions. Even non-Christians "are related in various ways" to the Roman Church— above all, the Jewish people, "but also those who acknowledge the Creator. In the first place among these there are the Muslims, who, professing to hold the faith of Abraham, along with us adore the one and merciful God, who on the last day will judge humankind"—and even "those who in shadows and images seek the unknown God" (*Lumen gentium*, Art. 16). This basis provides the grounding for the directives in the declaration and the decree concerning the conduct toward the non-Christian religions.

The religions are understood as answers to the unsolved riddles of the human condition, which today, even as in former times, deeply stir the hearts of people: What is a human being? What is the meaning, the aim of our life? What is moral good, what is sin? Whence suffering and what purpose does it serve? Which is the road to true happiness? What are death, judgment and retribution after death? What, finally, is that ultimate inexpressible mystery which encompasses our existence: whence do we come, and where are we going? (*Nostra aetate*, Art. 1)

While the Decree on the Mission Activity of the Church speaks only generally of the religions, the declaration examines several historical religions: Hinduism, in which people "contemplate the divine mystery and express it through an inexhaustible abundance of myths and through searching philosophical inquiry"; Buddhism, which recognizes the radical insufficiency of this changeable world and teaches a path by which people can either reach a state of freedom or obtain supreme enlightenment (*Nostra aetate*, Art. 2); and above all Islam, where mention is made of characteristics it has in common with the Christian faith, such as the adoration of the one God the Creator, the calling of Abraham, reverence for Jesus, to be sure, not as God but nevertheless as a prophet, honor for the Virgin Mother Mary, and the expectation of the Day of Judgment. In all of this, the document is concerned above all with providing descriptive observations.

But the declaration does not stop there, since it recognizes that the religions, "though differing in many particulars" from what the church holds and sets forth, "nevertheless often reflect a ray of that truth which enlightens everyone" (*Nostra aetate*, Art. 2). It recognizes what is "true and holy" in the religions, their "spiritual and moral goods and also the values in their socio-cultural values" (Art. 2). It regards them, especially Islam, "with esteem" (Art. 3). In addition, the Decree on the Mission Activity of the Church acknowledges that "grace and truth are to be found among the nations" (*Ad gentes*, Art. 9) and that there are "seeds of the word" lying hidden in their traditions (*Ad gentes*, Art. 11). To that extent the religions are not only witnesses of searching but they also contain true answers.

The declaration accentuates above all what the non-Christian religions have in common with the Christian faith and refers to their differences only in passing. The religions are above all evaluated positively, whereby the descriptive observations and the theological statements concerning the truth in them flow into one another. The Pauline statements about the thorough-going perversion of the heathen's knowledge of God attested to in creation (Rom. 1.18–32; 3.8–20) are not brought into the declaration. In addition, there seems to be no consideration that the advanced monotheistic religions especially, despite their commonalities with Christianity, have in a special way closed themselves against the gospel. Also, the declaration has not examined the strengthening of these religions and their missionary advances in our time. The question must be raised here whether the declaration's evaluation is not too optimistic concerning the "grace and truth" in the non-Christian religions, indeed, whether on the basis of a phenomenological comparison such evaluations concerning the truth there can be made at all. Does not the truth hidden in the religions become perceptible only when the gospel encounters them and when their adherents again recognize the truth of the proclaimed message concerning Christ as the truth that obligates them? In any case, both of these conciliar texts remain reticent vis-à-vis the theories of the "anonymous Christianity"[iii] of non-Christians and the "cosmic Christ"[iv] who is effective among them—theories that make the dialogue with non-Christian religions more difficult to the extent that they do not take the self-understanding of these religions seriously. The council is right, however, in not limiting the freedom of God's working of salvation that is hidden from us.

2. Israel

From the outset, the council had foreseen saying a word about the relationship of the Roman Church to the Jews, in which the council wanted to highlight the unique position of the Jews, which has no parallel in any other non-Christian religion, and to exhort the members of the Roman Church to conduct themselves toward the Jews in a brotherly and sisterly manner. The *relatio* [report], in which Cardinal Bea supported the first version of this text, which was initially given to the council fathers as an appendix to the Decree on Ecumenism, constitutes one of the most impressive and most thoroughly biblical formal opinions that was heard in the *aula* of St. Peter's.[v] The Pauline ideas in Romans 9–11 formed the foundation and were clearly given their due.

At that time the presentation ran into resistance, not only from the bishops from Islamic countries, who had reason to fear retaliation from their respective governments (because of their opposition to the state of Israel), but also from a conservative minority from Italy and other countries independent of Islam, who objected to any mitigation of the collective guilt of the Jewish people. Out of regard for this two-fold opposition, several statements in the final version were toned down so that many of the former opponents were able to vote affirmatively in the final ballot. Thus in the title of the declaration, which was itself separated from the Decree on Ecumenism, the Jews are no longer named, the statements about the other religions, especially Islam, were strengthened, the statements about the Jews now appear simply as remarks about one religion among others, and the whole discussion is circumscribed by statements about the universal brotherhood of all people. By contrast, many expressed the view that the Dogmatic Constitution on the Church was a more appropriate place for a word about the Jews than the Declaration on the Church's Relation to the Non-Christian Religions.

The essential content of the section was retained, however. Indeed, the statements that were presented offer an excellent, biblically grounded opinion and directive. The most important paragraphs read as follows:

Thus the church of Christ acknowledges that, according to God's saving design, the beginnings of its faith and its election are found already among the patriarchs, Moses and the prophets. It professes that all who believe in Christ—children of Abraham according to faith—are included in the same patriarch's call, and likewise that the salvation of the church is mysteriously foreshadowed by the chosen people's exodus from the land of bondage. The church, therefore, cannot forget that it received the revelation of the Old Testament through the people with whom God in his inexpressible mercy concluded the ancient covenant. Nor can the church forget that it draws sustenance from the root of that well-cultivated olive tree onto which have been grafted the wild shoots, the gentiles. Indeed, the church believes that by his cross Christ, our peace, reconciled Jews and gentiles and made us both one in himself.

The church keeps ever in mind the words of the apostle about his kinsmen: "and to them belong the adoption as children, the glory and the covenants and the law and the worship and the promises; theirs are the patriarchs and from them is the Christ according to the flesh" (Rom. 9:4–5).... The church also recalls that the apostles, the church's main-stay and pillars, as well as most of the early disciples who proclaimed Christ's Gospel to the world, sprang from the Jewish people....

True, the Jewish authorities and those who followed their lead pressed for the death of Christ; still, what happened in his passion cannot be charged against all the Jews, without distinction, then alive, nor against the Jews of today. Although the church is the new people of God, the Jews should not be presented as rejected or accursed by God, as if this followed from the Holy Scriptures. All should see to it, then, that in catechetical work or in the preaching of the word of God they do not teach anything that does not conform to the truth of the gospel and the spirit of Christ.

Furthermore, in its rejection of every persecution against any person, the church, mindful of the patrimony it shares with the Jews and moved not by political reasons but by the Gospel's spiritual love, decries hatred, persecutions, displays of anti-Semitism, directed against Jews at any time and by anyone. (*Nostra aetate*, Art. 4)

3. Directives Regarding Conduct in Relation to the Non-Christian Religions

The declaration exhorts the members of the Roman Church above all to acknowledge, preserve and promote "the spiritual and moral goods as well as the socio-cultural values which are to be found among them" (Art. 2), to hold the religions, especially Islam, in esteem (Art. 3), to "act like brothers and sisters" (Art. 5) and to keep peace. In addition, the Decree on the Mission Activity of the Church contains corresponding instructions.

At the same time, however, the conduct of every Christian in relation to the non-Christian religions must be determined by the missionary obligation. Though only alluded to in the declaration, this is the topic of the Decree on the Mission Activity of the Church. The endeavors of the non-Christian religions "need to be enlightened and purified." "The sainted fathers of the church firmly proclaim that what was not taken up by Christ was not healed" (*Ad gentes*, Art. 3). As "words of judgment and grace, of death and life," the words of Christ must be proclaimed to all religions. "For it is only by putting to death what is old that we are able to come to a newness of life" (Art. 8). Here, too, Paul is cited: "'All have sinned and have need of the glory of God' (Rom. 3.23)." The Christian message liberates

whatever truth and grace are to be found among the nations, as a sort of secret presence of God, ...from all taint of evil and restores to Christ its maker, who overthrows the devil's domain and wards off the manifold malice of vice. (Art. 9)

The riches which "the bountiful God has distributed among the nations" are "to be illumined through the light of the gospel, to set them free, and to restore them under the dominion of God the Savior" (Art. 11). Here the language is by no means only about supplementing a partial truth by the fullness of Christian truth but also of the necessity of conversion. As the Dogmatic Constitution on the Church already taught, this missionary activity among the religions grows out of the very nature of the church, and in this activity God's plan of salvation for humankind, which Jesus served, is realized. This missionary task "was inherited from the apostles by the order of bishops, assisted by priests and united with the successor of Peter and supreme shepherd of the church" (Art. 5) and, beyond that, also concerns the laity. The declaration presents very circumspectly the tasks of the missionaries (chap. 4), the direction of missionary work—whereby provision is made for a reorganization of the Curial Congregation for the Propagation of the Faith by involving bishops from all over the world—the leaders of missionary institutes, and the papal mission work (chap. 5), and the task of the whole church to assist the mission (chap. 6).

This large-scale missionary offensive seems to contradict the admonition to conduct themselves peacefully with the religions. But a form of missionary activity is called for that differs from many practices well-known from history. For one thing, the Declaration on Religious Freedom forbids the use of political power. For another, there is the admonition to lay bare "gladly and reverently" "the seeds of the Word" which lie hidden in the religions and "by sincere and patient dialogue" to look for the "treasures" which God has given to the nations (Art. 11). Finally, it is demanded again and again that there be a kind-hearted accommodation to the special forms of thinking and acting in the nations to be missionized, to the point of a corresponding reshaping of the church's rites. Christians are to strive to live together peacefully with the non-Christian religions in one and the same love, and to proclaim to them the sole salvation in Christ.

4. The Goal

On the one hand, the goal of this conduct is peace between the church and the non-Christian religions. Perhaps in the background here is the thought of working together in the future in a common defense against atheism.

At the same time, the goal is the expansion of the Roman Church, not by dominating the peoples through foreign influences but by liberating the truths and values contained in their religions, philosophies, and rites so as to allow them to develop on their own. Particular churches will thus strive to have local bishops, priests and deacons—churches which "through their being endowed with the riches of their own nation's culture" are "deeply rooted in the people" and whose members "should be true and effective patriots" (Art. 15). In the education of the clergy special value is to be placed "on the points of contact between the traditions and religion of their homeland and the Christian religion" (Art. 16). "They borrow from the customs and traditions of their people, from their wisdom and their learning, from their arts and disciplines, all those things which can contribute to the glory of their creator, or enhance the grace of their savior, or dispose Christian life the way it should be" (Art. 22). Forcefully, this "goal of accommodation" (Art. 22) is again and again brought into view. The limits of this accommodation, however, are the dogmas of the Roman Church and papal primacy, together with canon law insofar as it is taught as God's law. Thus every young church, despite all of its independent growth, is to be a faithful representation of the Roman Church.

Now of course it cannot be overlooked that through such a far-reaching accommodation, if it is not to lead to syncretism and particularism—and this was explicitly denied by the council (Art. 22)—the tension which by its very nature exists between the goal of peace with the religions and the goal of the expansion of the Roman Church among the religions cannot be removed, for the latter goal has the priority. But the non-Christian religions see in the Christian mission a threat to their future survival.

5. Mission and Ecumenism

If we compare the ecumenical and the missionary programs of the council, numerous analogies emerge: There is an opening toward both the non-Roman churches and the non-Christian religions. In both, "elements" of truth and grace are acknowledged. In contrast to both, the statement of Cyprian, namely, "Outside of the church there is no salvation," is not maintained in its original strictness. In contrast to both, the members of the Roman Church are summoned to a kind-hearted, new understanding and to dialogue, in which they are to set forth the Catholic teaching unabridged. In both cases the goal is to live together in peace and unity, which is already a reality in the Roman Church. In that connection, it is foreseen that there will be an unfolding of the Roman Church's catholicity through accepting the special gifts that are characteristic of the non-Roman churches and the non-Christian religions. Neither the non-Christian religions nor the non-Roman churches can remain as they are. By analogy there is also the tension between the goal of peaceful co-existence and the goal of the expansion of the Roman Church. Is there in the background here the widespread traditional view, according to which the separated Christians are as far removed as non-Christians, indeed, even further removed than a pious heathen, since, in distinction to the latter, the Christians consciously separated themselves from the Roman Church?

Despite these analogies it would be an error to understand the decisions of the council as if ecumenism were only a specific aspect of missionary activity. The Decree on the Mission Activity of the Church quite clearly sets forth what all Christians have in common over against the non-Christian religions, and it frequently calls on the church's members to strive for fellowship with non-Roman churches in missionary activity. "Thus, missionary activity among the nations differs from pastoral activity exercised among the faithful as well as from undertakings aimed at restoring unity among Christians" (Art. 6). Missionary activity and ecumenism are indeed "most closely connected" because this separation among Christians harms the mission proclamation and hinders its credibility. The missionary task makes the ecumenical task of the union of all the believers into one flock all the more urgent (Art. 6). Even before this union, however, the instruction stands: In coordination with the Secretariat for Promoting Christian Unity, the Congregation for the Propagation of the Faith should search out "ways and means for bringing about and directing cordial cooperation as well as harmonious living with missionary undertaking of other Christian communities, that as far as possible the scandal of division may be removed" (Art. 29). "This living witness will more easily achieve its effect if it is given—in accord with the norms of the Decree on Ecumenism (Art. 12)—when it is made in common with other Christian communities" (Art. 36). To be sure, here there is no mention of a partitioning of mission fields among the churches, but the Decree on the Mission Activity of the Church pulls the basis out from under the Roman Catholic mission work among the young churches of the other church bodies.

Editor's Notes

[i] All quotations from the Declaration on the Church's Relation to the Non-Christian Religions, *Nostra Aetate* (promulgated by Pope Paul VI on 28 October 1965), are here based on the English translation that is given on the Vatican's website, accessed between 20 March 2016, and 25 March 2016, Vatican.va, http://www.vatican.va/archive/hist_councils/ii_vatican_council/documents/vat-ii_decl_19651028_nostra-aetate_en.html (cf. Denzinger 4195–4199; Tanner 2.968–971)

[ii] All quotations from the Decree on the Mission Activity of the Church, *Ad Gentes* (promulgated by Pope Paul VI on 7 December 1965), are here based on the English translation that is given on the Vatican's website, accessed between 20 March 2016 and 25 March 2016, Vatican.va, http://www.vatican.va/archive/hist_councils/ii_vatican_council/documents/vat-ii_decree_19651207_ad-gentes_en.html (cf. Tanner 2.1011–1042).

[iii] For Karl Rahner's theory of the "anonymous Christian," see especially his essays, "Christianity and the Non-Christian Religions" (April 1961), in *Theological Investigations*, vol. 5 (London: Darton, Longman & Todd, 1966), 115–134; and "Anonymous Christians," in *Theological Investigations*, vol. 6 (London: Darton, Longman & Todd, 1969), 390–98. "Therefore no matter what a man states in his conceptual, theoretical and religious reflection, anyone who does not say in his *heart*, 'there is no God' (like the 'fool' in the psalm) but testifies to him by the radical acceptance of his being, is a believer. But if in this way he believes in deed and in truth in the holy mystery of God, if he does not suppress this truth but leaves it free play, then the grace of this truth by which he allows himself to be led is always already the grace of the Father in his Son. And anyone who has let himself be taken hold of by this grace can be called with every right an 'anonymous Christian'" (Rahner, "Anonymous Christians," 395).

[iv] The notion of the "cosmic Christ" was primarily developed in modern Roman Catholic theology by Pierre Teilhard de Chardin (1881–1955), who used this phrase more than thirty times in his early works (1916–24). In his later writings he used a synonymous expression, "the universal Christ." See, for example, Pierre Teilhard de Chardin, *The Divine Milieu* (New York: Harper and Row, 1960), 56–62. See also J. A. Lyons, *The Cosmic Christ in Origen and Teilhard de Chardin* (Oxford: Oxford University Press, 1982), 38–39.

[v] The term *relatio* refers to the ten-minute speech (maximum) that a bishop or council father would be permitted to give on a given council text in one of the working sessions of the council. There were typically ten to fifteen of these speeches per working session.

Chapter VIII:
The Council and the World

Beyond the circles of non-Roman Christendom and the non-Christian religions that encircle the Roman Church, the council turned its attention also to the outermost concentric circle, which encompasses the whole of humanity, and engaged the issues that are placed before humanity as a whole in the world of today. These issues are treated comprehensively in the Pastoral Constitution on the Church in the Contemporary World.[i]

By taking up this daunting task the council took a courageous step, unprecedented in the history of the councils. For the concern here was not, as in the usual decisions of a council, about establishing the doctrine and order of the church in delimitation from heresies and schisms and about removing internal ambiguities and contradictions within the church, but rather about devotion to humanity as a whole and about clarifying the pressing social issues of today. The concern is also not about making a decision that the council expects to be binding for all time, like a dogmatic decision, but rather about clarifying and instructing precisely for the present situation, which will already be different in many respects in ten years and will then require once again new reflection and instructions. Recognizing the ominous situation of today, the council gave itself the task of speaking concretely in this situation about what faith in Christ can offer to help.

Corresponding to the significance which the council granted to this task, the Pastoral Constitution on the Church in the Contemporary World addressed itself directly to all people. The council here desires to turn itself "not only to the daughters and sons of the Church and to all who invoke the name of Christ, but to the whole of humanity. For the council yearns to explain to everyone how it conceives of the presence and activity of the church in the world of today" (Art. 2 and elsewhere). This distinctive feature is all the more remarkable since the Decree on Ecumenism, although it deals with non-Roman Christians, does not address itself to these but to the members of the Roman Church, just as the Decree on the Mission Activity of the Church and the Declaration on the Church's Relation to Non-Christian Religions are not directly addressed to the adherents of these religions but aim to instruct the members of the Roman Church. While these texts concern non-Catholics and non-Christians to a high degree as far as their content is concerned, that content is brought only indirectly to the attention of those people. The Pastoral Constitution on the Church in the Contemporary World, however, wants to address these people directly, whose "salvation" [*Rettung* = "rescue"] and social "renewal" [*Aufbau* = "construction"] are its concern (Art. 3). It wants to engage in direct dialogue with these individuals. (Art. 3 and elsewhere.).

This two-fold task—clarifying the contemporary situation of human beings and addressing all people—naturally brings forth numerous difficulties. The obvious presupposition of this conciliar text is the Dogmatic Constitution on the Church (Art. 2). For one thing there is a difficulty in that the Dogmatic Constitution on the Church speaks of the church in a general and timeless manner, while the declaration deals with an entirely conditioned, historical situation of the church in the world, one that is new and that did not exist either at the time of the formation of the biblical writings or during the period of the earlier dogmatic decisions. But given that it is not easy to grasp the exceedingly complex situation of the world today, it is altogether a difficult task to arrive at concrete answers to contemporary problems by means of settled general dogmatic statements that largely came into being under completely different historical circumstances. Secondly, the task of addressing non-Christians is also difficult. From what common presuppositions can they be addressed and which arguments will make the best sense to them? In addition, there was the technical difficulty that this text—in distinction from all of the others—had not already been prepared by a pre-conciliar commission, but had to be worked out during the council, even though it could also make use of individual pre-conciliar elements. Thus there was little time to allow it to become fully mature and to make final systematic and stylistic adjustments to the individual sections that had been prepared by the various sub-commissions. Furthermore, there were so many historical, sociological, sexual-ethical, political, and other types of issues that there was hardly a council father or council theologian who could be viewed as being competent in all of these problem areas at once. Accordingly, it was necessary to consult with competent laypeople, indeed more extensively than was the case with other conciliar texts, but these laypeople were not entitled to share their voice or give their vote in the council's *aula*.

Until shortly before the final vote, the *novum* of this procedure induced in many of the council fathers an uncertainty about whether the matter under consideration had really matured sufficiently and was ready for action, or whether it might not perhaps be better to restrict themselves to general principles or merely to a declaration on the question of world peace and to turn over the remaining questions or even the whole matter to a post-conciliar synod of bishops that the pope would launch. In addition, there was embarrassment regarding how such a new type of conciliar text should be designated, given that in ten years it would probably have to be considerably revised in view of further changes in the world situation. The term *constitutio* suggested itself because of the scope and substantive weight of the text, but on the other hand that designation seemed too weighty for such an attempt which, because of many of its statements, could not from the beginning claim to have the abiding significance of a fundamental exposition. For this reason, consideration was given to titles that implied less of a claim, such as "conciliar letter" or "declaration" (*declaratio*) or "exposition" (*expositio*). But here too, the text appeared to be too significant and also too large in scope with respect to its topic. Thus in the end the new type of title "*constitutio pastoralis*" was chosen, whereby the designation *pastoral* sought to give expression to the church's concrete attention to the people of today.

No one can maintain that the council solved all of the methodological and substantive difficulties that were given with this task. This was clear to most of the council's fathers and theologians themselves when the document was drawn up, and it is therefore no disparagement of their achievement if some of the questions that remain open are identified here; for it is obvious that not all of these new issues could be solved during the few years of the council's duration, nor have they been solved in other churches, since they are instead constantly changing and being reconsidered. Thus the council is to be highly praised given that, despite these difficulties, it undertook to deal in the broadest scope with the theme, "the church in the contemporary world," and turned its attention directly to all human beings. The fact that for the sake of the urgency of many issues the council was willing to take some unresolved textual inadequacies into the bargain is not only an impressive indication of the council's sense of responsibility in relation to the contemporary human situation, but also a proof that it was ready to take seriously the dogmatic statements in the Dogmatic Constitution on the Church concerning the pilgrim people of God. The church in this world is in fact sojourning, in which it must continually reconsider its next concrete steps by faith in the act of salvation that has been accomplished once and for all. In this conscious tentativeness and open-endedness which characterize the pastoral constitution, the council came quite close to the dialogical way of working that is customary in the World Council of Churches and, in a fuller measure than is explicit in this constitution, has become a partner in the common striving of the churches, one which none of them can avoid in the midst of this rapidly changing world.

After a preface concerning its goal, this constitution treats the following topics: "the situation of human beings in the contemporary world" (the Introduction); "the church and the vocation of people" (Part One); and "some problems of special urgency" (Part Two).

In the first part, the Church develops its teaching about humanity, on the world in which human beings live, and its own relationship to both. In part two, the Church gives closer consideration to various aspects of modern life and human society; special consideration is given to those questions and problems which, in this general area, seem to have a greater urgency in our day. As a result in part two the subject matter which is viewed in the light of doctrinal principles is made up of diverse elements. Some elements have a permanent value; others, only a transitory one. (Explanatory footnote appended to the title)

Thus the first part offers above all the abiding dogmatic presuppositions, while the second part sets forth the relevant consequences.

It is therefore difficult and even often impossible to determine in individual cases which of the constitution's statements claim an abiding fundamental significance and which are to be understood as time-bound accommodations to the contemporary situation. This question is all the more important since this conciliar text in some statements—for example, concerning the freedom of scholarship, the freedom of religion, the distinction between church and state, and the autonomy of secular domains—goes beyond earlier decisions of the Roman Church, and, yes, even contradicts them. Are these statements universally valid as fundamental decisions for the future as such, or could the older decisions against the freedom of religion, against the autonomy of the state, and so forth, be made newly valid again as binding in another historical situation? Questions of this kind no doubt also cause difficulties for Catholic interpreters. There is, moreover, the difficulty of interpretation which resulted from the dramatic genesis of the text out of heterogeneous impulses and proposals which were not brought into full systematic alignment in the official formulation. The history of this text is perhaps the most interesting of all, and if all of the preparatory and preliminary proposals for the text will be published, it could become clear with what intensity the council wrestled here, not only for new individual insights but also for a new fundamental orientation. Especially praiseworthy is the fact that the council avoided the danger of assembling a set of condemnations against erroneous opinions about sexual ethics, science, and politics, in other words, the danger of creating a new Syllabus of Errors, and instead gave expression to what is substantively necessary in the completely different, dialogically determined form of positive statements.

1. Openness toward the Contemporary World

Following the preface, the constitution begins with a description of the present situation of humanity. This description is further elaborated in the next two main chapters, for example, in §19 f. of part one, in the remarks concerning atheism, and then at the beginning of each of the chapters in part two, which in turn proceed from the present situation in the light of special thematic perspectives. "We must therefore recognize and understand the world in which we live, its explanations, its longings, and its often dramatic characteristics" (Art. 4).

"Today, the human race is involved in a new stage of history. Profound and rapid changes are spreading by degrees around the whole world." These changes come from "the intelligence and creative energies of human beings," and they in turn have an effect on them. This social and cultural transformation "has repercussions also on the life of religion" (Art. 4). Special attention is thus directed to the development of the natural sciences, anthropology, and sociology, which make possible a technology which is changing the earth and advancing into the solar system, and is bringing about a plan for addressing population growth (Art. 5). Moreover, attention is also directed to the development of industrial society and its impacts on rural communities and the growth of large cities.

With circumspect vision the text is pointing to the manifold issues which have arisen through these developments, issues not only between individuals or professional groups but also, for example, between technologically advanced nations and developing countries, between nations that have atomic weapons and those that do not, and between economic and political systems and power blocs that infringe upon one another. The text shows both the general issues of depersonalization and the very special issues, such as, for example, the structure of leisure time. Special note is then taken of the outcomes that the indicated changes have had on religious life, and attention is drawn to the various forms of atheism that are being propagated today, whose root cause also includes the failure of Christians who "neglect their own training in the faith, or teach erroneous doctrine, or are deficient in their religious, moral or social life, [and thus] must be said to conceal rather than reveal the authentic face of God and religion" (Art. 19).

As with the establishment of dialogue with the non-Roman churches and the non-Christian religions, so also here too there occurred a *positive* opening up toward the contemporary world. To be sure, the text clearly points to the manifold "tensions," "contradictions" and "inconsistencies," "imbalances," "antitheses," "conflicts," and "dangers" in the contemporary world, and neither the decline of religious commitment nor the rise of atheism are in any way overlooked. And still, the presentation in the constitution completely avoids an atmosphere of catastrophe and holds to the line in Pope John XXIII's opening address to the council, when he warned against those who can see "nothing but night and ruin in the modern age": "We feel we must disagree with those prophets of gloom, who are always forecasting disaster, as though the end of the world were at hand."[ii] Without overlooking the difficulties and dangers of the contemporary situation of the world, the constitution affirms the present world and, if anything, sees in the "difficulties," "contradictions," and "antitheses" a transitioning to a better state of affairs for humanity. Particularly characteristic is its positive engagement with the idea of progress. Without overlooking the difficulties that accompany cultural, technological, and economic progress, such progress is explicitly affirmed in all these areas and its furtherance is made obligatory. Similarly, the Decree on Mass Media also oddly minimizes the dangers connected with mass communication in contrast to the potential benefits they thereby provide the church. Advances in the sciences and technology are understood above all as a divinely willed unfolding of the creaturely capabilities that are given to human beings, and in this context the political and economic difficulties in the international arena are viewed as a growing awareness of the unity of humanity. Thus the severity of the conflict between the ideologies of atheism and freedom, and between the political blocs determined by these ideologies, is embraced by an overall hopeful perspective, as is the strength of the new nationalism of the former colonial nations and the conflicts among the races. This perspective fits with the fact that the constitution specifies with equal emphasis the repercussions of these world changes on the religious life as, "on the one hand," the purification of the religious life and the intensification of a more personal and active commitment to the faith and, "on the other hand," atheism and the decline of religious commitment (Art. 7), without fully appreciating the new forms and epochal impacting force of the steadily growing spread of atheism and the experience of God's remoteness that shatters religious commitments. Also striking is how the dispute with atheism has been loosened from the dispute with Communism, which is undertaken almost only indirectly. Despite the text's frank acknowledgment of the circumspect manner of its presentation and the absence of depicting things in black and white, the question arises whether the intention to engage all people in dialogue has not led to minimizing the harsh conditions of reality. This question was also raised by several council fathers, and not only by those whose dioceses are directly involved and who maintain that a dialogue with those who hold power is impossible.

Hence the pastoral constitution does not begin with a biblical or dogmatic understanding of the world, which would only be understandable to Christians, but rather with the empirical reality of this world as it stands for all to see. The concern here is not so much to analyze the deeper historical causes of the world's contemporary situation as it is to line up the phenomena. To be sure, modern natural science is identified as a cause of the technological and social changes, but there is no further counter-questioning about the complex reciprocal effects of the various factors or about the intellectual roots of modern science. This would in fact have gone beyond the possibilities of this constitution. It does, however, pursue the repercussions of these phenomena on humanity: the perplexity, angst, and questions that surface in people's minds in view of the contemporary situation of the world. These questions are, first of all, concrete questions about the relation of the sexes, about the legal social order, about overcoming the danger of war, and so forth. Yet they are not only penultimate questions about overcoming external difficulties. Rather, in their desperate needs, perplexities, and anxieties, human beings have themselves been called into question:

[I]n the face of the modern development of the world, the number constantly swells of the people who raise the most basic questions or recognize them with a new sharpness: what is a human being? What is this sense of sorrow, of evil, of death, which continues to exist despite so much progress? What purpose have these victories purchased at so high a cost? What can people offer to society, what can they expect from it? What follows this earthly life? (Art. 10)

Perhaps the extent to which this last question is a live issue among contemporary people is overestimated. Perhaps today it has been driven out of human consciousness to a greater extent than the constitution assumes. To be sure, faith is still able to recognize this last question again as the driving force of atheism and the pathos of nihilism in our time, but for the consciousness of these people it is generally no longer an open question.

The constitution, therefore, does not begin with the questions that God addresses to contemporary human beings through his revelation but rather with the contemporary world situation and the questions that surface in the minds of people in view of that situation.

2. The Starting Point for Dialogue with the World

The pastoral constitution addresses itself to all people. It desires to engage them all in dialogue—whether they are members of the Roman Church or other Christians, whether they are adherents of the non-Christian religions or skeptics or atheists—and it wants to answer for them all the penultimate and ultimate that have surfaced in the contemporary world situation. Which arguments does it use and on which presuppositions that are common to all human beings does it make these arguments?

a) The common starting point is the empirical reality of our time, as it appears to everyone in cultural, scientific, social, and political phenomena.

b) Presupposed then as being common to all are the anxieties, longings, and questions that the contemporary situation triggers in human beings— concrete questions and ultimate questions of meaning.

c) Presupposed then is a "divine seed" (Art. 3), a "seed of eternity" (Art. 18) in every human being, God's "voice… in the depths," God's "law" in the inner conscience (Art. 16), the natural law which God has given to all human beings and which reason can recognize as a demand (*passim*), as well as the self-attestation of God through creation that encounters all human beings.

d) Contact is also established with the knowledge, even if it is shaken, that humans have about values (*valores, bona*)—"eternal values" (Art. 4), "traditional values" (Art. 7), "positive values" (Art. 57). "Insofar as they stem from endowments conferred by God on human beings, these values are exceedingly good" (Art. 11). Also engaging ideas concerning "truth, goodness, and beauty" (Art. 57) and "the wisdom of the ancestors" would seem to belong in this same context.

e) Beyond the possibilities given to all human beings for knowledge of God and God's law as well as knowledge of values, the constitution presupposes that grace is effective not only in Christians but invisibly in all people of good will, and that the Holy Spirit offers not only Christians but all human beings the possibility of "being associated" with Christ "in a manner known only to God" (Art. 22).

f) Finally, the biblical statements about creation, about God's act of salvation in Jesus Christ, about the church and the eschatological fulfillment are set forth as arguments, whereby the Christological and eschatological statements frequently appear at the end of individual lines of thought.

Thus the arguments that the pastoral constitution makes use of in addressing contemporary human beings are quite manifold, quite different in their philosophical and theological origins, and often imprecise in their conceptuality (for example, regarding values). Concepts from phenomenology, natural law, the philosophy of values, and salvation history are used side by side without fusing them into a systematic unity. It is clear that the constitution seeks to attach itself as comprehensively as possible to the presuppositions of those being addressed in order to enter into dialogue. It is also clear, however, that the council did not restrict itself to those presuppositions that all people have in common. Rather, by employing arguments that are by no means self-evident to everyone, the council transitions from dialogue to teaching. This is especially the case with the biblical statements on salvation history (f), but also of the assertion that all people of good will are spiritually associated with Christ in a hidden manner (e). But even where the argument refers to the address of God in every conscience and to the natural law that is given to everyone (c), it is not presupposed that this command of God is actually recognized by all people in truth. Repeated reference is thus made to the fact of the erring conscience. In addition, values (d) "are often wrenched from their rightful function by the taint in the human heart, and hence stand in need of purification" (Art. 11). The questions that human beings raise will accordingly be unveiled in truth only in the light of the revelation of Christ. Natural law must be interpreted in the light of the gospel (*passim*), and only thus are the "principles of justice and equity demanded by right reason" recognized in truth (Art. 63). Values are to be evaluated in light of the Christian faith and connected to their divine source (Art. 11).

The multiplicity of arguments is encompassed by the notion of agreement between revelation and human experience, especially the experience of oneself (Art. 13), and of the correspondence between the church's message and "the most secret desires of the human heart" (Art. 21). However, the questions and most secret desires of human beings will ultimately be unveiled only in the light of the revelation of Christ. Thus in the pastoral constitution the church encounters humanity as the teaching church, not only in the statements concerning Christ but also in the argumentation involving conscience, natural law, and so forth, which all have in common. The question arises whether it is sufficient for the constitution to make use of God's act of salvation in Christ as one argument alongside others in the dialogue with humanity. How are non-Christians to understand this argument? Since faith alone is able to understand the foolish word of the cross as the revelation of God's wisdom, we must ask whether the constitution as an address to all people should not be more strongly directed toward the awakening of faith? Should it not move toward proclaiming Christ?

Substantively, the responses to contemporary questions begin with a doctrine about human beings. "It is around humankind therefore, one and entire, body and soul, heart and conscience, mind and will, that our whole treatment will revolve" (Art. 3). By not starting with the doctrine of God but with the doctrine about human beings, the constitution has its point of contact in the fact that in the conscience of contemporary human beings the question about God has largely been replaced by the question, "What is a human being?" The first major part deals in the first chapter with the dignity of the human person, in the second chapter with human society, and in the third with human activity in the world. Accordingly, ultimate questions concerning the meaning of human existence are, to begin with, answered in the first part, and then, on this basis, answers to the concrete penultimate questions of our time are given in the second part.

The doctrine about human beings developed here contains many familiar elements of philosophical anthropology that the Roman Church has taken over from the ancient heritage and the new philosophy and incorporated into its fundamental theology and dogmatics. This is true, for example, of the statements concerning the reason, conscience, freedom, and personal dignity of human beings as well as the equality of all people and their personal fellowship.

But the doctrine about human beings is at the same time developed in a biblical, salvation-historical manner. Thus it does not begin with a philosophical statement but with the creation of humankind "in the image of God"—"with the capacity to know and love its Creator, and was divinely appointed with authority over all earthly creatures to subdue them and use them to God's glory" (Art. 12). Also, humankind's being intended for personal fellowship is inferred from the biblical statement concerning the creation of humankind as "male and female" (Art. 12). Through the influence of evil, humankind revolted against God and sought to find its goal apart from God. Thereby, in contradiction to its original calling, humankind has fallen into misery (Art. 13). "In Christ, 'the image of the invisible God,' light is again shed on the mystery of humankind. He has restored to the offspring of Adam the likeness of God which had been deformed since the first sin. In his death Christ has merited life again for us" (Art. 22).[iii] Through his Spirit he has fulfilled the intended design of creation for personal fellowship in the fellowship of the church, which he will one day bring to consummation (Art. 32). Both the understanding of the church in the Dogmatic Constitution on the Church and the understanding of human beings in the pastoral constitution are determined in a special way by salvation history.

The philosophical and salvation-historical understandings of human beings (here again shaped more by creation and the centrality of Christ) have not been brought into a complete systematic unity. On the whole, however, the accents appear in some respects more biblical than is usually the case in Roman Catholic theology. Over against the widespread understanding of human beings as "rational beings" (*animal rationale*), consisting of body and immortal soul-spirit [*Geistseele*], the emphasis here is aimed more strongly toward the wholeness of the person, and human dignity is based not only on human rationality/spirituality but also on human corporality. In this way the fellowship between man and woman appears in a new light, and the significance of corporality in personal fellowship is elsewhere also clearly lifted up. Over against the widespread attempt to differentiate between nature and supernature in human beings, and to interpret the succession of original state, fall, and redemption as the possession, loss, and restored reception of supernatural grace (while the "pure nature" of human beings remains unhistorically the same), the constitution keeps its focus more definitely on the historicality of human beings (in the structure of its reflection on salvation history). In this way the changes in the ordering of human social-communal life and human dominion over nature are seen more clearly.

3. Directives for Servant Ministry in the Contemporary World

Under the heading "Several Specially Urgent Problems" the five chapters of Part Two draw concrete consequences from the theological anthropology and give directives for practical conduct. Each of these chapters is so interesting that it deserves to be respectfully and thoroughly analyzed by experts from the scholarly disciplines that study sex, culture, society, and economics, as well as political science. In doing that it would be very interesting to make a careful comparison with the earlier positions of the Roman Church and with the answers given today outside the Roman Church. Because of space constraints we must confine ourselves to lifting up those statements that are of special significance for human social-communal life today. We will follow the sequence of the five chapters.

a) Marriage and the Family

After a presentation on the contemporary situation, the document begins with the following foundational principles:

The intimate partnership of married life and love has been established by the Creator and qualified by his laws, and is rooted in the conjugal covenant of irrevocable personal consent. Hence by that human act whereby spouses mutually bestow and accept one another a relationship arises which by divine will and in the eyes of society too is a lasting one. For the good of the spouses and their off-springs as well as of society, the existence of the sacred bond no longer depends on human decisions alone. For, God himself is the author of matrimony, endowed as it is with various benefits and purposes. (Art. 48)

In that connection, the document shows that Christ encounters Christian spouses through the sacrament of marriage, which corresponds to the understanding of marriage in the Catholic tradition. At the same time, however, there has been a significant shift in accent. Moral theology in the past taught that the primary goal of marriage is the creation of offspring and the second is mutual assistance, and that its intended purpose is to be a remedy against sexual desire (concupiscence). This desire is thereby understood to be a rebellion against the spiritual powers. By contrast, the constitution teaches that the first goal of marriage is the union of the marriage partners in personal love (Art. 49) and only then the procreation of offspring (Art. 50). Marital love "is uniquely expressed and perfected through the appropriate enterprise of matrimony" (Art. 49) and it is aimed at "cooperating with the love of the creator and the savior, who through them will enlarge and enrich his own family day by day" (Art. 50). Marriage is thus a union in personal self-giving, which is crowned by the procreation and raising of children (Art. 48).

Without damaging the essence of marriage and the "autonomy" [*Eigengesetzlichkeit*] (Art. 48) given to it by God, this shift in accent allows us to see the issue of responsible parenthood (Art. 50) and to acknowledge that there are situations in which "at least temporarily the size of their families should not be increased" and in which "the faithful exercise of love and the full intimacy of their lives is hard to maintain" (Art. 51). "[W]here the intimacy of married life is broken off, its faithfulness can sometimes be imperiled and its quality of fruitfulness ruined, for then the upbringing of the children and the courage to accept new ones are both endangered" (Art. 51). That this issue is recognized is highly significant, even though the constitution suggests no concrete ways for permitting contraception. It demands only that no methods of birth control be undertaken "which are found blameworthy by the teaching authority of the church in its unfolding of the divine law" (Art. 51), and it points to the ongoing studies of a papal commission (footnote 14). In addition, terminating a pregnancy is strictly prohibited. While the issue of the population explosion that is occurring in many parts of the world has not been solved, through the council the dialogue concerning this problem has received an altered presupposition on the part of the Roman Church.

b) Cultural Progress

After marriage and the family, the document asserts that culture is "the cultivation of the goods and values of nature" in their significance for "a true and complete realization of the human essence" (Art. 53). The term "culture," as understood by the constitution, refers to:

everything whereby we develop and perfect our many bodily and spiritual qualities; applying ourselves through knowledge and labor to bring the world itself under our control; rendering social life more human both in the family and the civic community through improvement of customs and institutions. Throughout the course of time we express, communicate and conserve in our works great spiritual experiences and desires so that they might be of advantage to the progress of many, even of the whole human family. (Art. 53)

Here, too, the document proceeds from the contemporary situation and then sets forth a fundamental determination of the cultural task. In their cultural work "human beings carry out the design of God, revealed at the beginning of time, of subduing the earth and completing creation, and we are cultivating ourselves while at the same time observing Christ's great commandment to devote ourselves to the service of the sisters and brothers" (Art. 57). This engagement takes place with the confidence that "the mystery of the Christian faith furnishes them with an excellent stimulant and aid to fulfill this duty more courageously and especially to uncover the full meaning of this activity, one which gives to human culture its eminent place in the integral vocation of humankind" (Art. 57). Over against earlier authoritarian claims by the Roman Church, it is striking to what high degree the constitution acknowledges the "autonomy" [*Eigengesetzlichkeit*] of culture, the awareness of contemporary people that "they themselves" are "artisans and creators of culture," and the significance of culture for the maturing of the human race. In spite of the danger of a "purely this-worldly and even anti-religious humanism" (Art. 56), the autonomy [*Autonomie*] of culture is expressly affirmed, as are the freedom which it demands to be able to unfold itself and the "legitimate possibility of exercising its autonomy according to its own principles" (Art. 59). This acknowledgment of the "legitimate autonomy of culture and above all the sciences" is expressed despite the difficulties which can arise for the relationship between culture and Christian education.

These difficulties do not necessarily harm the life of faith, rather they can stimulate the mind to a deeper and more accurate understanding of the faith. The recent studies and findings of science, history and philosophy raise new questions which have consequences for life and which demand new theological investigations.... The deposit of faith or the truths of faith are one thing and the manner in which they are enunciated, in the same meaning and understanding, is another. (Art. 62)

For such tasks the constitution acknowledges that "all the faithful, whether clerics or laity, possess a lawful freedom of inquiry, freedom of thought and of expressing their mind" (Art. 62). Truly striking over against the well-known tendency of the Roman Church toward a cultural monism stamped by the church is the affirmation of a cultural pluralism (Art. 53) and a "universal form of human culture" that embraces Christians and non-Christians, "one that promotes and expresses the unity of the human race to the degree that it preserves the particular aspects of the different civilizations" (Art. 54).

According to the teaching of the council, the autonomous progress of culture is limited by "the ethical order" (Art. 59), "the preservation of the rights of the individual person and community, whether particular or universal, within the limits of the common good" (Art. 59). Furthermore, it is impossible without the church to recognize the "full meaning" of culture or "the innermost reason of being," since the methods of the empirical sciences are inadequate for this (Art. 57). The freedom of theological research is limited by the church's teaching office. Thus both the affirmation and the limitation of culture are spoken of side by side. The mutually supportive relationship between the Christian faith and the sciences is maintained but not really clarified, as little as the historical fact that the natural sciences frequently had to fight for their advances against the church. Various opinions expressed in the council *aula* went much further and called, for example, for a rehabilitation of Galileo. Nevertheless, new presuppositions for a dialogue about these questions are given through the constitution.

c) The Socio-Economic Life

After a presentation on the "disquieting" situation of the given time and the necessity for "many reforms in the socioeconomic realm and a universal change of mentality and attitude" (Art. 63), the third chapter proceeds to set forth the "principles of justice and equity demanded by right reason" and as the church has worked them out "down through the centuries and in the light of the gospel" and has "put them forth especially in the most recent period" (Art. 63). Hence, the expositions in this chapter refer especially to the social encyclicals of the popes since Leo XIII, above all the encyclical *Mater et magistra* (1961) of John XXIII, but without thereby stopping there. We cannot here go into the very interesting comparison between the encyclicals and the constitution but must restrict ourselves only to the most important instructions of the council's text. Determinative for the whole is the strong affirmation of economic progress that comes at the start:

Today, more than ever before, attention is rightly given to the increase of the production of agricultural and industrial goods and of the rendering of services, for the purpose of making provision for the growth of population and of satisfying the increasing desires of the human race. Therefore, technological progress, an inventive spirit, an eagerness to create and to expand enterprises, the application of methods of production, and the strenuous efforts of all who engage in production—in a word, all the elements making for such development—must be promoted. (Art. 64)

All people should participate in this progress. Therefore, not only does each person have the "duty to work faithfully" but also "the right to work," that is, circumstances of work that respect human dignity (Art. 67), the right to a wage that makes a worthwhile life possible (Art. 67), the right "to have a share of earthly goods sufficient" for oneself and one's family (Art. 69), whereby

private property is regarded "as an extension of human freedom" and
"constitutes a kind of prerequisite for civil liberties" (Art. 71). To safeguard
these rights "the active participation of everyone in the running of an
enterprise should be promoted" and the workers' right to strike as a
"necessary, though ultimate, means" is acknowledged (Art. 68). All people
have the right, "in extreme necessity, to take from the riches of others what
they themselves need" (Art. 69); "for in this situation the old principle holds:
'In extreme need all goods are common, that is, to be shared'" (Art. 69,
footnote 11). In addition, expropriations in the interests of the general welfare
is envisaged, provided there is fair compensation. Corresponding demands for
the participation of all in economic progress are also made for the coexistence
of nations. The immense economic inequalities that now exist among the
nations, and which are often still increasing and linked to discrimination,
"must be removed from the world as soon as possible" (Art. 66). The
obligation to struggle together against hunger and to provide assistance to
underdeveloped regions is expressly enjoined upon the people (Art. 69 and
elsewhere).

In this way socio-economic progress is affirmed as a service to people,
"viewed in terms of the full range of their material needs and the demands of
their intellectual, moral, spiritual, and religious life" (Art. 64), and whereby
the individual or political abuse of economic development in the name of "a
false liberty" must be repudiated (Art. 65). In engaging socio-economic
progress, Christians should take the lead in promoting justice and love and let
their lives "in faithfulness to Christ and his gospel" be marked "by the spirit of
the beatitudes, above all by the spirit of poverty" (Art. 72).

d) The Life of Political Communities

Also in evaluating opposing systems of political order the constitution
upholds the rights of the human person. Their protection is the necessary
condition for an active participation in political interactin with one another.
The political community is derived not from power but from the common
good.

Individuals, families and the various groups which make up the civil community are
aware that they cannot achieve a truly human life by their own unaided efforts. They
see the need for a wider community, within which each one makes his specific
contribution every day toward an ever broader realization of the common good....
The political community exists, consequently, for the sake of the common good, in
which it finds its full justification and significance, and the source of its inherent
legitimacy. (Art. 74)

The divinely ordained authority of the state, "primarily as a moral force," must
direct the energies of all citizens toward the common good, in the course of

which "the choice of government and the election of leaders is left to the free will of citizens" (Art. 74). When governmental authority oversteps its bounds, the citizens have the right, "within the limits of natural law and the gospel," to resist for the sake of promoting the common good. "It is inhuman for public authority to fall back on dictatorial systems or totalitarian methods which violate the rights of the person or social groups" (Art. 75). Rather, that form of political order to be aspired to is one that gives freedom to all its citizens "to participate actively in the establishment of the juridical foundations of the political community and in the direction of public affairs, in fixing the terms of reference of the various public bodies, and in the election of political leaders" (Art. 75), whereby a separation of powers is to be anchored in the law.

Over against the history of the Roman Church and its former claim to both the spiritual and secular sword, the constitution's explicit acknowledgment that the political community and the church are "mutually independent and self-governing" is important (although the issue of the Pontifical State, whose secular sovereign is at the same time the head of the Roman Church, is of course ignored). This mutual independence corresponds to the fact that "there be a correct notion of the relationship between the political community and the church, and a clear distinction between the tasks which Christians undertake, individually or as a group, on their own responsibility as citizens guided by the dictates of a Christian conscience, and the activities which, in union with their pastors, they carry out in the name of the church" (Art. 76). Yet church and state must work together. In this way the church must promote political freedom and the political responsibility of citizens by "preaching the truth of the gospel, and bringing to bear on all fields of human endeavor the light of its doctrine and of a Christian witness" (Art. 76), by interpreting the universally valid natural law in the light of the gospel, and by "giving up the exercise of certain rights which have been legitimately acquired, if it becomes clear that their use will cast doubt on the sincerity of its witness or that new ways of life demand new methods" (Art. 76). The state, for its part, is obligated to grant to the church the freedom to proclaim the gospel and its social teachings and "to pass moral judgment in those matters which regard public order when the fundamental rights of a person or the salvation of souls require it" (Art. 76). The Declaration on Religious Freedom also corresponds to these statements concerning the differentiation and the coordination of the political and ecclesial tasks.

e) Peace and the Community of Nations

The council here wants "to point out the authentic and most noble meaning of peace and to condemn the frightfulness of war" (Art. 77). Peace is "not simply the absence of war" but rather "the enterprise of justice," "the fruit of that order structured into human society by its divine Founder, and actualized by individuals as they thirst after ever greater justice"—indeed, peace is "the fruit of love, which goes beyond what justice can provide," "the symbol and fruit of the peace of Christ who proceeds from God the Father" (Art. 78). Peace is ultimately rooted in the reconciliation of humanity with God through the incarnate Son of God (Art. 78). Because of human sins the danger of war threatens until the Second Coming of Christ. Aggressive war is condemned in a traditional way, but the right of legitimate defense is acknowledged, without, however, conceding that all means are permitted in time of war. The observance of the natural law of nations and of international conventions aimed at humanizing military activity is recommended, as are humane provisions for those who object to war for reasons of conscience and who are to be placed into some other kind of service to society. In addition, however, in view of the threat of nuclear war, the council felt compelled to face the issue of total war and to condemn it as a crime against God and humanity, since it destroys indiscriminately entire cities and countries with their populations (Art. 80). It takes no comfort in the stalemate of the mutual atomic threat as a way of securing peace but demands that there be a progressive disarmament, "not unilaterally indeed, but proceeding at an equal pace according to an agreement" so that we "can agree to a complete ban on all war" (Art. 82). "This goal obviously calls for the establishment of a universal public authority, recognized by all, which will possess the effective means on behalf of all to safeguard security, the observance of justice and respect for rights" (Art. 82).

The council here forcefully urges an end to strife and hatred and to intensify cooperation among international organizations in the various social fields concerning nutrition, health, education, and labor, as well as care for refugees and the advancement of developing countries (Art. 84). To be aimed at is "a truly universal economic order" without all too great a profit-motive, national ambitions, the will to political domination, etc. (Art. 85), and in a responsible way to strive for a progressive social settlement, and in this way the causes of military conflicts will be removed at the roots. In addition, the problems of population explosion must be addressed through international cooperation, in the course of which the council leaves the decision regarding the number of children to have entirely up to the parents, not to the judgment of the state. There can be no violation of the moral law. There is, however, no mention here regarding which methods of birth control correspond to it (Art. 87).

In its answers to the various cultural, economic, social, and political issues of our time—apart from the emphasized peculiarity of the Catholic understanding of marriage and its restraint concerning contraceptives—the council brought about a far-reaching accommodation, which many recognize to be necessary today. Some former positions that the Roman Church had adopted, for example, with respect to the natural sciences, progress, the sovereignty of the state, conscientious objection, labor strikes, and so forth, against which modern development could in part be achieved only through hard struggles, have now been given up and instead there is an extensive affirmation of the autonomy of the sciences, the fundamental principles of the social market economy, of democratic government, and the principles and goals of the United Nations. To be sure, the council teaches that there is a different (namely, theological) basis for this than what is customary today in, for example, scientific research and the United Nations, but the concrete instructions themselves come very close to what is accepted today and contain little that is new. Naturally, the council's instructions are not invalidated by this extensive agreement. Their value, however, consists less in their suggestion of new and special ways than in their support and strengthening of the threatened forces for order in this world. Of course these chapters of the constitution, which reflect the composition of the authorized commission of the council, are stamped to a high degree by Western, particularly European thinking. Their directives thus correspond more closely to the practical possibilities of people who live in the Western part of the world rather than in the Eastern and African parts.

Now the constitution addresses itself not only to all Christians but to all people. Are the non-Christians able to understand it? Certainly they can understand several of the concrete directives. But these are grounded in a theological doctrine about human beings and this in turn is ultimately grounded in a doctrine about Christ. But Jesus Christ can only be known in faith. Hence, once again, questions arise: In view of non-Christians, is it sufficient merely to cite the Bible repeatedly? Should it not be interpreted in a more up-to-date manner? Is it sufficient merely to cite Jesus Christ repeatedly as one argument among others for action in the world? Should he not be proclaimed and conveyed to non-Christians in a more direct form of address by the constitution? For "faith comes from preaching" (Rom. 10.17). What, then, are non-Christians to think of Jesus Christ, if the constitution, in citing him to provide concrete instructions for the contemporary world situation, then says little more than what many reasonable people today also hold as necessary without this faith? Does Jesus Christ really encounter the non-Christians as Lord in the pastoral constitution, that is, in the one conciliar text that expressly addresses itself to them?

4. Christ and the World

Thus the pastoral constitution begins by considering the contemporary world, by elaborating on the questions that have arisen today, and by answering these questions, first of all, on the basis of the doctrine of human beings and then by concretely dealing with the most burning individual issues. This structure corresponds to a widespread apologetic method. The danger in this procedure, however, is admittedly that the conversation partners too obviously presuppose the questions for which they already have an answer, and the opposite danger is that some tailor the answers to fit just so with the questions of the conversation partners that the Christian witness is weakened. Obviously, both dangers can also occur at the same time.

For this reason, we will follow the reverse procedure in the following two sections by beginning with the New Testament witness to revelation and then from there to inquire about the extent to which the statements of the pastoral constitution concerning the relationship between Christ and the world and between the church and the world correspond to it. We must restrict ourselves to the following theses.

a) According to the witness of the Pauline letters and the Gospel of John, the world, especially humanity, is God's creation which, through rebellion against God, has come under the dominion of the powers of destruction and is subject to God's judgment. This judgment will come to the world as its end: "The substance of this world is passing away" (1 Cor. 7.31), "the world passes away, together with its lust" (1 Jn. 2.17). That the world still continues to exist, despite its being subject to judgment, has its basis in the patience of God the Preserver and in the love of the Redeemer.

b) Out of love for the world God sent his Son and gave him up to death. In Jesus Christ God's salvation has broken into this lost world. Through his message about the in-breaking kingdom of God, through his blessings and woes Jesus has placed people before a decision, and in the encounter with his person their future salvation and judgment are decided. In his death on the cross he has taken the sins of the world upon himself. Yet not simply by the fact of his death but by faith in the crucified one is deliverance from the judgment of God's wrath bestowed.

c) Having been raised from the dead and exalted to the right hand of God, Jesus is Lord. All things have been made subject to him so that he might make them all subject to God. But in the New Testament writings Jesus is not called "Lord of the world." Christ is the Lord of the church, of the fellowship of those who have been called out of the world and who, through faith, he has delivered from the bonds and decay of this world. He is the head of the new creature [*Kreatur*]. "Whoever believes in the Son has eternal life. Whoever does not believe the Son will not see life but the wrath of God remains over him" (Jn. 3.36).

d) Christ will come as Judge of the world—of the living and the dead. "We must all appear before the judgment seat of Christ so that each may receive recompense for what he has done in the body, whether good or evil" (2 Cor. 5.10). Then Christ will receive some and reject others. Then all will acknowledge Christ to be the Lord. His coming will be the end of the world and the fulfillment of the new creation, which has dawned in his resurrection and is growing in a hidden way in the church. The New Testament writings, however, do not speak of a "new world" but of a "new creation," "a new heaven and a new earth."

These biblical statements are also the basis for the pastoral constitution. Nevertheless, there are shifts in it which cannot be overlooked.

The world is above all understood as creation and as loved by God in Christ, while the rule of sins, the forces of corruption, and the world's having fallen under judgment appear strangely faded, and there is no mention of God's wrath upon the world. In addition, it should be asked whether, in the context of the New Testament's understanding of the world, more should have been said about the brokenness of human worth and freedom and the autonomy of culture.

In the constitution Jesus Christ is taught less as the Redeemer of the world than as the Preserver of this world. His work of salvation is claimed above all for the task of overcoming the world's cultural, economic, and political difficulties of our time. This is not always a sufficiently clear distinction between redemption from the world's difficulties and redemption from God's judgment, between justice in the human community and God's justice for believing sinners, between the peace of the world and the peace that comes to believers through God's act of reconciliation in Christ, as well as between human freedom in the secular sense and the freedom of the children of God.

The impending coming of Christ is understood less as the end of the world than as its fulfillment. There's no mention of the sufferings and catastrophes which, according to the statements of the New Testament, must precede his coming, nor is there any mention of the Antichrist, in whom the world's rebellion against Christ is concentrated. The "signs of the times" (Art. 4) are not put forward as omens of the end and the coming Christ. Through the ideas of development and progress the conflict between the world and Christ and the nearness of his sudden in-breaking are downplayed, and the progress of this world is tied to the coming kingdom of God in a way that does not equate them but that nevertheless recognizes earthly progress to be "of great significance for the kingdom of God" (Art. 39) in a way that is foreign to the New Testament writings.

As alien as the New Testament understanding of the world may initially appear, the question should be raised whether the constitution would not have viewed the threatening character of the contemporary world situation more realistically if it had avoided weakening the New Testament statements by its accommodation to modern ideas of development. This would seem to have been a result less of American influences than of French, that is, due to the evolutionary-cosmic conception of Teilhard de Chardin.

5. The Church and the World

a) The church is the people of God who have been called out of the world, who believe in Jesus Christ, who have been given into his death through baptism, and who are built up as his body through the Lord's Supper. They are in the world, but as the ones who through Christ have been set free from earthly bonds they are exhorted: "Do not be conformed to this world" (Rom. 12.2),

"Do not love the world nor what is in the world" (1 Jn. 2.15). Rather, faith is the victory that overcomes the world (1 Jn. 5.4).

b) As the people of God who have been called out of the world, the church is sent by God back into the world in order to proclaim to all people the sole redemption in Christ. This word of the cross is a foolish and offensive message for the world, one that contradicts the wisdom of this world and calls for faith. Thus, wherever the gospel is proclaimed authoritatively, a parting occurs, on the one side to life and on the other to death. Just as Jesus came "not to bring peace but the sword" (Mt. 10.34), so also the gospel brings about contradiction and conflict, for the world resists the lordship of Christ. In the midst of the conflict, however, the peace of God is given to those who by faith hand themselves over to Christ as their Lord, give glory to him, and go out to meet his coming. As the witness to Christ, the church is thus the instrument of God's in-breaking kingdom.

c) Faith in Christ recognizes that God preserves the world, despite its being subject to judgment, so that the gospel can be proclaimed to it and many be saved through faith. Hence the church is not only sent to pass on the message of Christ but also to bear a responsibility for preserving the world. This responsibility is expressed in the New Testament writings in the admonitions to obey political power and to disobey it if obedience to God demands it, in the admonitions to slaves and masters, and in other statements in the catalogue of vices and virtues and the "table of duties" [Haustafeln]. In these admonitions the church has rightly recognized the systematic starting point for its support of a just and peaceful order of interacting with one another that embraces both believers and unbelievers.

d) These two tasks of the church—proclaiming the saving message of Christ and contributing to the preservation of the world—need to be distinguished. They do in fact belong together, for one and the same God is the Preserver of this world and the Deliverer from its chains, and the expectation of the coming kingdom gives an ultimate urgency to every engagement with one's fellow human beings. Yet the proper and first mission of the church is the message of Christ, not the ordering of the world. Jesus Christ himself was after all sent to proclaim the lordship of God, not to be a "judge and arbitrator" over quarreling individuals (Lk. 12.13 f.). Through the message of Christ the lordship of Christ comes into the world. The church must above all serve as the instrument of the lordship of Christ.

e) Thus the church in this world is in foreign territory. "We have here no continuing city, but we seek that which is to come" (Heb. 13.14). Hence, the church is sojourning in this world, and its way of following Christ leads through disdain, persecution, and suffering unto glory. This is its way, one that comes out of the same divine necessity as the way of Jesus. In this worldly insecurity and weakness of the church the power of the risen Lord wants to manifest itself. "Do not be surprised at the fiery ordeal that is taking place among you to test you, as though something strange were happening to you. But rejoice insofar as you are sharing Christ's sufferings" (1 Pet. 4.12–[13]).

Such New Testament statements are of course given their due weight in the Dogmatic Constitution on the Church and in the Decree on the Mission Activity of the Church, but in the Pastoral Constitution on the Church in the Contemporary World they are strangely faded.

To be sure, the latter states: "Christ gave his church no proper mission in the political, economic or social order. The purpose which he set before her is a religious one" (Art. 42). But then the constitution goes on to speak above all about questions concerning the world order. The New Testament relationship between the two tasks of the church appears to have shifted out of place. The foreground is occupied not by the scandal of the word of the cross, the message concerning the redemption of believers from the world, but rather by a concern for the preservation and progress of the world. To this end, Christ is primarily appealed to, and he appears here more as an argument than that his act of salvation and his judgment are announced and spoken directly to all people.

Corresponding to this is the fact that the New Testament understanding of the church has also experienced a change here. Though the title is "The Church in the Contemporary World," little is said in the text concerning the concrete situation of the church. Instead, in a peculiar sort of timelessness, the church seems to be placing itself over against the changing world and instructing it. In this way the existence of the church appears as normal when its freedom is secured constitutionally, and it is abnormal when its situation is not secured or even when it is persecuted. But does it really help when those who are oppressed and deprived of their freedom are given directives for the social and political order, the realization of which is impossible for them to carry out? Does the church owe them merely a model for an ordered human society? Or does it instead owe them above all the consolation of Jesus: "Blessed are you when people revile you and persecute you and utter all kinds of evil against you falsely. Rejoice and be glad" (Mt. 5.11); "Consider it nothing but joy whenever you face various trials" (Jam. 1.2); "Rejoice that you suffer with Christ" (1 Pet. 4.[13])? Not the complaint about the injustice that is experienced but the acknowledgment of the privilege of being permitted to suffer with Christ— that must be the first word of the church, for in the sisters and brothers who are suffering with him is manifested the glory of the risen Christ in the midst of the world. Only incidentally does the pastoral constitution speak of the large parts of Christendom whose commitment and faithfulness is the glory of the church today.

These criticisms would be less important if the title of the pastoral constitution read, "The Church and the Order of the Contemporary World" or "The Contribution of the Church to the Preservation of the Contemporary World." However, the title "The Church in the Contemporary World" or, as it was originally proposed, "The Presence of the Church in the Contemporary

World," presents a far more comprehensive task. Of course we cannot overlook the fact that much of what is missing here is expressed in the Dogmatic Constitution on the Church and in the Decree on the Mission Activity of the Church. But those texts offer direct instruction only to members of the Roman Church. Even though the Dogmatic Constitution on the Church wants "to clarify more precisely for the faithful and the world the nature and comprehensive mission of the church" (Art. 1 of the Dogmatic Constitution on the Church), it does not, in fact, address non-Christians directly and explicitly. Thus the council has remained strangely reticent in its direct witness to Christ in the world, unless we understand the way the Roman Church presented itself at the council as such a witness to Christ. While fully acknowledging the courageous advance that the council has taken with its pastoral constitution, in the language of Reformation theology it would need to be said that here law and gospel are not distinguished in the right way.

6. Servant Ministry to the World and Ecumenism

The pastoral constitution has engaged questions which also confront the rest of Christendom and for which the World Council of Churches since its general assembly in Amsterdam (1948) has offered similar and in part identical answers. Thus we must add the admission that in many respects the World Council has not sufficiently clarified the theological foundations for the church's mission in relation to the ordering of this world (issues of natural law, the two kingdoms, the reign of Christ, and so forth). The pastoral constitution does not refer explicitly to any concrete proposals of other churches or of the World Council, but restricts itself to this general statement: "The Catholic Church gladly holds in high esteem the things which other Christian churches and ecclesial communities have done or are doing cooperatively by way of achieving the same goal" (Art. 40). For the future it desires "that Catholics, in order to fulfill their role properly in the international community, will seek to cooperate actively and in a positive manner both with their separated sisters and brothers who together with them profess the gospel of charity and with all who are thirsting for true peace" (Art. 90; compare Art. 92). The connection between this constitution and the Decree on Ecumenism thus remains rather general, and that the latter's instruction to work together in the social domain was not further specified in the constitution.

To what extent did the Decree on Ecumenism generally have an impact on the other resolutions of the council? Does it merely stand next to them, or do its ideas permeate the other resolutions? The Decree on Mass Media does not refer to ecumenical cooperation, even though that would suggest itself here. Otherwise, the ecumenical obligation is mentioned in numerous texts, such as the decrees on bishops, priests, and laity. While the ecumenical idea is thus introduced into various areas of church activity, most of the references are formal. They do not lead beyond the Decree on Ecumenism and fall short of the urgency of the latter's directives. The strongest echo of that decree occurs in the Decree on the Mission Activity of the Church.

Editor's Notes

[i] All quotations from the Pastoral Constitution on the Church in the Contemporary World, *Gaudium et Spes* (promulgated by Pope Paul VI on 7 December 1965), are here based on the English translation that is given on the Vatican's website, accessed between 25 March 2016 and 31 March 2016, Vatican.va, http://www.vatican.va/archive/hist_councils/ii_vatican_council/documents/vat-ii_const_19651207_gaudium-et-spes_en.html (cf. Denzinger 4301–4345; Tanner 2.1069–1135).

[ii] Pope John XXIII, "Opening Address to the Council," [11 October 1962], Vatican.va, accessed 29 March 2016, http://w2.vatican.va/content/john-xxiii/la/speeches/1962/documents/hf_j-xxiii_spe_19621011_opening-council.html

[iii] Schlink has here elided material from article twenty-two in the constitution.

Chapter IX:
Scripture, Tradition, Teaching Office

At the beginning of every session of the council there was a solemn procession in which the Gospel in the form of a priceless manuscript was carried down the aisle of St. Peter's Basilica and enthroned on a golden throne atop the altar where the mass had just been celebrated. During this procession the council fathers sang the hymn, "*Christus vincit, Christus regnat*" [Christ conquers, Christ reigns].[i] This chant, together with this symbolic acknowledgment of the gospel as Lord and judge of the deliberations and resolutions of the council, corresponds to the ancient church's and the Reformation's understanding of Christ as the center of Holy Scripture and of his presence in the word of Scripture.

This impressive ritual acknowledgment of the governing function of the biblical word of God found its echo in numerous solidly biblically based opinions in the council's deliberations, whereby in the course of the sessions biblical arguments were increasingly emphasized. This acknowledgment was also reflected in the council's resolutions, not only in important details but beyond that in a general preference for biblical conceptuality over against that of scholastic dogmatics, and it was reflected in the decision to adopt a biblically based conception of salvation history as the repeatedly asserted foundation for treating the various topics of the council.

On the other hand, despite the enthronement of the gospel manuscript, one needs to note that during the entire council no sermon was preached in which a previously read biblical text was expounded. To be sure, biblical words and ideas were expressed in the papal addresses, but the topics and structures of these addresses were not determined by a biblical text but instead by the situation of the council at that particular time. It was likewise noteworthy that the biblically shaped opinions in the council were delimited by the pertinent dogmas of the Roman Church. The biblical lines of argumentation were unfolded only within what could be stated theologically in those areas uninhibited by dogma.

This raises the question: What authority has the council accorded to Holy Scripture? The answer can be reached not only indirectly, from the actual use that the council made of Holy Scripture; rather, the answer has also been given by the council directly and fundamentally by the Dogmatic Constitution on Revelation.[ii] One must ask how the fundamental coordination of Scripture and tradition relates to the actual appeal to Scripture and tradition in the official opinions of the council fathers and in the council's resolutions.

The most important reasons for this fundamental inquiry were, on the one hand, the unrest that had entered into part of the Roman Church through the new Catholic scholarship on the Bible, and, on the other hand, the discussion concerning the interpretation of the Tridentine statements about the relationship between Scripture and tradition that was provoked above all by the Tübingen theologian Geiselmann.[iii] Previously, the Tridentine decision was generally understood to mean that the apostolic teaching was partly contained in Holy Scripture and partly in oral tradition, but now Geiselmann had shown that it was possible to understand that the sum total of apostolic teaching may be found in both Holy Scripture and in oral tradition—a possibility which broadened the basis for ecumenical dialogue. In addition, it is evident in the various versions of this dogmatic constitution that a genuine struggle occurred at the council, in the course of which the initial rejection of the new biblical scholarship and of Geiselmann's thesis was overcome.

1. The Revelation of God in Jesus Christ

Just as we were only able to evaluate the Dogmatic Constitution on the Church when we compared it with the schema on the church at the First Vatican Council, so the significance of the Dogmatic Constitution on Revelation becomes evident only when it is compared with Vatican I's Dogmatic Constitution on the Catholic Faith (especially its second chapter).[iv] In addition, the newer constitution's starting point, when compared with that of the older text, is strikingly determined by Holy Scripture.

While Vatican I's statements on revelation were determined by the relationship between the natural knowledge of God and supernatural revelation, and were insisted upon so formally through this distinction between nature and supernature that (apart from the one citation of Heb. 1.1 f.) God's historical act of salvation in Jesus Christ was not really considered, this act of salvation is the central focus of Vatican II's Dogmatic Constitution on Revelation. The preface of the latter text begins with the prologue of the First John: "We proclaim to you the eternal life which was with the Father, and has appeared to us…" (1 Jn. 1.2–3). The first chapter begins with these words:

In his goodness and wisdom God chose to reveal himself and to make known to us the hidden purpose of his will (see Eph. 1:9) by which through Christ, the Word made flesh, people might in the Holy Spirit have access to the Father and come to share in the divine nature (see Eph. 2:18; 2 Peter 1:4). (*Dei Verbum*, Art. 2)

The same paragraph closes with this sentence: "By this revelation then, the deepest truth about God and the salvation of humankind shines out for our sake in Christ, who is both the mediator and the fullness of all revelation" (Art. 2).

This revelation of God in Christ is not placed over against natural revelation, in the one-sided manner of Vatican I, but is understood as the completion of God's entire activity of revelation in history. This revelation is prepared through God's continuous witness in creation, through the inauguration of supernatural salvation for humankind's first parents and, after their fall, through the promise of redemption, the call of Abraham, and the ministry of Moses and the prophets to God's people (Art. 3). All of this pointed to the revelation of God in Christ (Arts. 3, 4). The constitution's starting point in salvation history is repeated here.

"This plan of revelation is realized by deeds and words having an inner unity: the deeds wrought by God in the history of salvation manifest and confirm the teaching and realities signified by the words, while the words proclaim the deeds and clarify the mystery contained in them" (Art. 2). While the understanding of revelation as a disclosure of knowledge content stood in the foreground of the statements from Vatican I, revelation is now taught much more emphatically as God's saving activity toward human beings.

Such salvation-historical and Christocentric shifts in accent give rise to fruitful approaches for a new dialogue between Reformation churches and the Roman Church.

In common with all churches the council teaches the finality of the revelation of God in Jesus Christ.

With words and deeds, signs and wonders, but above all through his death and glorious resurrection, yes, simply through his presence and appearance, and finally through his sending of the Spirit of truth, Christ has perfected and fulfilled revelation and confirmed it through the divine testimony.... The Christian dispensation, therefore, as the new and definitive covenant, will never pass away and we now await no further new public revelation before the glorious manifestation of our Lord Jesus Christ. (Art. 4.)

2. Scripture and Tradition

Because revelation is completed in Jesus Christ there is a permanently fundamental significance to the proclamation of the apostles as the eye-witnesses who were commissioned by Christ and there is also an abiding necessity to preserve their message through the church (Arts. 7, 8). The commission to proclaim that Jesus gave was fundamentally carried out

by the apostles who, by their oral preaching, by example, and by observances handed on what they had received from the lips of Christ, from living with him, and from what he did, or what they had learned through the prompting of the Holy Spirit. The commission was fulfilled, too, by those apostles and apostolic men who under the inspiration of the same Holy Spirit committed the message of salvation to writing. But in order to keep the gospel forever whole and alive within the church, the apostles left bishops as their successors, "handing on their own teaching function" to them. (Art. 7)

The constitution did not pay detailed attention to the important fact that Paul addressed all believers as his successors (1 Cor. 4.16; 1 Thess. 1.6). "This sacred tradition, therefore, and Sacred Scripture of both the Old and New Testaments are like a mirror in which the pilgrim church on earth looks at God..." (Art. 7).

The statements concerning Holy Scripture, its inspiration, and its divine authorship through chosen and commissioned individuals who made use of their abilities and powers—these are traditional. Important for historical research is the fact that no overall inerrancy is asserted of Holy Scripture; rather, "the books of Scripture must be acknowledged as teaching solidly, faithfully and without error that truth which God wanted put into sacred writings *for the sake of our salvation* (Art. 11; emphasis added). Thus it is explicitly said of the Old Testament books that they "also contain some things that are incomplete and time-bound" (Art. 15). The historical reliability of the four Gospels is emphatically affirmed. Yet here, too, it is acknowledged that the writers made a selection from the oral and written traditions that were available to them, that they condensed some things and explicated others "in view of the situation of their churches" (Art. 19). It is surprising that no detailed consideration was given to the historical motives behind the formation of the biblical canon, which are so important for the understanding of tradition.

Alongside the preservation of the New Testament writings is the apostolic proclamation conserved through oral tradition. The concept of this tradition is very broad in the Dogmatic Constitution on Revelation. Here nothing is stated about the concrete contents of oral tradition.

[This] includes everything which contributes toward the holiness of life and increase in faith of the peoples of God; and so the church, in its teaching, life and worship, perpetuates and hands on to all generations all that it itself is, all that it believes.... The words of the holy fathers witness to the presence of this living tradition, whose wealth is poured into the practice and life of the believing and praying church. (Art. 8)

The constitution also lacks any instructions concerning the criteria that might assist in ascertaining the apostolic tradition in the midst of other existing expressions of the life of the church, as, for example, the age and breadth of certain teachings or church regulations. Since the concrete contents of the oral apostolic tradition are not obvious in the constitution, it is good that "the practical life of the church," the "doctrine, life, and worship" of the church are recognizable, that tradition lies close at hand, that it "bears" the life of the church and "flows into" this life, and is to be identified with the life of the church. But in every case, however the theological schools may give more definition to the content of oral tradition, the collected dogmas of the Roman Church claim to be the authoritative definition of apostolic teaching. Special difficulties are here created by the bodily assumption of Mary, since this is attested to neither by the New Testament nor the tradition of the first centuries. Because of this dogma the former understanding of tradition as the uninterrupted historical transmission of apostolic teaching was called into question, and the attempt was made to base this dogma on the present faith-consciousness of the Roman Church. The concept of tradition in the Dogmatic Constitution on Revelation is so broad that it encompasses the faith-consciousness of later periods of the church itself, even when its content is not demonstrable in Holy Scripture and the tradition of the first centuries.

How does the constitution now define the relationship between Scripture and tradition? When the third version of the text was presented, it was explicitly clarified that the debated question would be left open, namely, the question about whether revelation is transmitted only in part by Holy Scripture and in part by oral tradition, or if it is transmitted as a whole by Holy Scripture and as a whole by oral tradition. If the former is the case, then Holy Scripture is insufficient to provide complete knowledge of revelation, but if the latter is the case, then tradition may be understood as a history of the interpretation of Scripture. This latter view comes close to that of the Reformation churches. To be sure, here too the definition set forth at the Council of Trent is upheld, namely, that both oral tradition and Holy Scripture are to be acknowledged and honored "with the same sense of devotion and reverence" (Art. 9). Since oral tradition is presupposed to be a correct interpretation of Scripture, even this second way of defining the relationship does not permit Holy Scripture to serve as a critical norm in the strict sense over against the tradition. The difficulty with the first position ("in part... in part") lies in the fact that the anti-Gnostic church fathers and also the medieval scholastic dogmaticians emphatically regarded themselves as scriptural theologians. The difficulty with the second position ("as a whole... as a whole") lies in the fact that many dogmas of the Roman Church cannot be grounded in the historical sense of Holy Scripture. For that reason, there are today Catholic biblical scholars who, because of their historical conscientiousness, reject the biblical-exegetical burden of proof for the whole of the dogmatic tradition and despite the intensity and fruitfulness of their biblical-theological work prefer the first position.

At the request of the pope the final version of the text included the following sentence: "Consequently it is not from Sacred Scripture alone that the church draws its certainty about everything which has been revealed" (Art. 9). Accordingly, the conservative definition of the relationship ("in part... in part") appears to have won out in the end. However, this sentence is also meaningful even if one understands the tradition as the normative interpretation of Scripture that is necessary for the correct understanding of Scripture. Nevertheless, this sentence goes against the scriptural principle of the Reformation. One could indeed try to challenge this by pointing out that the Protestant faith does not live by Scripture alone but by the proclaimed gospel, but the constitution does not grant to the living, proclaimed gospel the central significance that it had, for example, for Paul.

In other respects it is noteworthy that, in relation to the formulations of Trent, many of the statements in the Dogmatic Constitution on Revelation invert the Tridentine order of Scripture—Tradition and mention tradition first (Arts. 7–10). Beyond that, the constitution uses "tradition" as an overarching concept that encompasses both oral and scriptural traditions (Art. 8). To this extent, the concept of tradition has become more important compared to the Tridentine statements.

3. The Interpretation of Holy Scripture

Whether the one or the other determination of the relationship between Scripture and oral tradition is taught, the principles of the interpretation of Scripture are in any case highly significant.

The constitution emphatically demands that the interpreter carefully investigate "what meaning the sacred writers really intended" (Art. 12). "The interpreter must investigate what meaning the sacred writer intended to express and actually expressed in particular circumstances by using contemporary literary forms in accordance with the situation of his own time and culture" (Art. 12). Differing "literary genres" are to be distinguished which were used from time to time by the authors of the biblical writings (Art. 12). In addition, one must distinguish between the oral and written traditions then available to the authors, on the one hand, and the way those traditions were reworked by them, on the other (Art. 19). In this way the methods of form criticism and redaction criticism are affirmed. This exegetical engagement with the historical sense of the text is of greatest significance. In the results of this historical work far-reaching agreements have emerged today across the separated churches.

To ascertain the right sense of the biblical texts, "serious attention must be given to the content and unity of the whole of Scripture" (Art. 12). This demand, too, is to be affirmed since the same God has revealed himself in historical sequence, and since his final revelation in Jesus Christ was proclaimed by its very nature through a multitude of human witnesses. To be sure, comprehending the unity of Holy Scripture is already a systematic task and it is possible to do in various ways. Here the constitution emphasizes that "the living tradition of the whole church must be taken into account along with the analogy of faith" (Art. 12).

"According to these rules" exegetes are to work "toward a better under-standing and explanation of the meaning of Sacred Scripture, so that through preparatory study the judgment of the church may mature" (Art. 12). This could seem to indicate a meaning of Scripture that goes beyond what the authors intended to say, and to suggest that historical research is inadequate when it comes to comprehending that meaning. This kind of going beyond the intended meaning is frequently found in the interpretation of Old Testament texts in the New Testament. It is justified there to the extent that the salvific activity of God in the Old covenant is ultimately unveiled only in Christ. Such an approach is questionable, however, when the interpretation also goes beyond the historical meaning of the New Testament witnesses concerning the ultimate revelation in Jesus Christ. Although the church is hastening to meet the coming revelation of Christ, it is after all expecting the same Christ who has revealed himself already in glory as the risen one. Although the "tradition which comes from the apostles develops in the church with the help of the Holy Spirit" (Art. 8), the working of the Holy Spirit consists by its very nature in "bringing to remembrance" all that Christ has said (Jn. 14.26). Hence the Spirit points back to the historical, original witness and makes it present. The constitution provides no criterion for comprehending the deeper sense of Holy Scripture. Thus, for example, the possibility remains open to appeal to Gen. 3.15, Rom. 5 and 6, and 1 Cor. 15.21–26, 54–57 in order to teach that Mary was assumed body and soul into heavenly glory (as does Pius XII's 1950 apostolic constitution *Munificentissimus Deus*), even though these biblical texts do not speak of Mary.

4. The Church's Teaching Office

In view of the indeterminate breadth of the concept of tradition and the indeterminate possibility of going beyond the historical sense of Holy Scripture, the necessity of securing the unity of the faith arises. The constitution grants this task to the church's teaching office. "The task of authentically interpreting the word of God, whether written or handed on, has been entrusted exclusively to the living teaching office of the Church, whose authority is exercised in the name of Jesus Christ" (Art. 10). To be sure, it is explicitly added that the teaching office is not above the word of God (as handed down in the tradition and Holy Scripture) but serves it, "teaching only what has been handed on, listening to it devoutly, guarding it scrupulously and explaining it faithfully in accord with a divine commission and with the help of the Holy Spirit, it draws from this one deposit of faith everything which it presents for belief as divinely revealed" (Art. 10). But the papal teaching office in fact infallibly determines what counts as apostolic tradition in the midst of the church's life and what counts as the deeper sense of Holy Scripture, without the members of the Roman Church being permitted to call this into question on the basis of the historical sense of Scripture and the historically demonstrable tradition of the ancient church.

So to the non-Catholic the principled determination of the relationship of Scripture, tradition, and the teaching office appears in many respects to be more an apologetic presentation than a dogmatic one, for it defends the way the Roman Church is constituted and upholds the possibilities of its development in the future. But it does not clearly and distinctly subject this church and its teaching office to a norm that stands opposite it, namely, the norm of the historical, apostolic tradition.

5. Directives for the Use of Holy Scripture

The Dogmatic Constitution on Revelation closes with a chapter on "Holy Scripture in the Life of the Church." To be sure, here also it is stated that the church has always viewed Scripture together with sacred tradition to be the highest rule of faith, but in fact in the admonitions of this chapter a weight is given to Holy Scripture that goes beyond the foundational determination of the relationship between Scripture and tradition.

This occurs not only in the urgent admonitions to produce new translations on the basis of the original texts ("in cooperation with the separated sisters and brothers as well"), to engage in research of Holy Scripture (in the course of which study of the church fathers is not mentioned as something independent of Scripture but as serving the interpretation of Scripture), to preach and to undertake every form of instruction (especially in the liturgical homily), as well as to undertake in a regular and prayerful way deeper immersion into Holy Scripture, and so forth (Arts. 22–25). There are, furthermore, very important foundational statements expressed here that ground these admonitions. Holy Scripture is thus mentioned alongside the Lord's body as an object of veneration. "From the table both of God's word and of Christ's body" the church "unceasingly receives and offers to the faithful the bread of life" (Art. 21). Here the meaning of the ancient designation of the word as "audible sacrament" comes alive again. The word of Holy Scripture is a present and active word: The sacred writings "impart the word of God himself without change, and make the voice of the Holy Spirit resound in the words of the prophets and apostles" (Art. 21). Through the word of Scripture God acts presently: "For in the sacred books, the Father who is in heaven meets his children with great love and speaks with them; and the force and power in the word of God is so great that it remains the support and energy of the church, the strength of faith for its children…" (Art. 21). Consequently, "like the Christian religion itself, all the preaching of the church must be nourished and regulated by Sacred Scripture" (Art. 21). These impressive statements concerning the power of God's word go beyond the weak Tridentine statements, where the gospel had been granted only a preparatory significance for the reception of justification. Of course these statements fall short of Paul since they do not have the living voice of the proclaimed word of God primarily in view, but rather the written word. Here, too, there remains a difference in relation to Reformation theology.

The effusive appreciation which is in fact accorded to Holy Scripture in this chapter, going far beyond what is said about oral tradition, is extremely important. If these admonitions are followed, the word of Scripture will in fact be able to exert itself in the Roman Church as a norm and power to a far greater degree than the foundational determination in chapter two concerning the relationship between tradition and Scripture leads us to expect.

Looking back from the statements of the Dogmatic Constitution on Revelation to what took place in the council as a whole, we observe a far-reaching correspondence between them both.

The dogmatic determination of the relationship between Scripture and tradition corresponds to the fact that among the theologians of the council the dogmaticians and experts in canon law and liturgy were by far in the majority, while experts in biblical scholarship were consulted surprisingly little. This determination of the relationship, moreover, corresponds to the fact that the statements of Scripture could be unfolded only in those areas left open by dogma, while Scripture was elsewhere utilized only to support and clarify dogmatically defined statements. But the latter were not subjected to the critical norm of Holy Scripture and corrected by means of new insights from historical exegesis. The special position of the church's teaching office made its impact not only in the papal intervention in the proceedings of the council, as mentioned earlier, but also in the fact that the explanatory notes added to the schemata quite often contained more citations from the encyclicals of recent popes than from the Bible, a state of affairs that was lamented also by some of the council fathers. In light of this weakening of biblical authority in favor of the teaching office one may also understand the fact that in the Pastoral Constitution on the Church in the Contemporary World the New Testament understanding of the world and the expectation of judgment were noticeably weakened in the process of making accommodation to the world of today as demanded in the fulfillment of the papal program of *aggiornamento*.

However, the effusive element in the statements of the sixth chapter of the Dogmatic Constitution on Revelation, that is, the statements concerning Holy Scripture in the life of the church, has its correlation in what happened at the council: There was thus an increasing variety of scriptural readings in the conciliar masses, there was in the council's opinions the growing importance of biblical evidence over against merely appealing to tradition, and, beyond that, there was the increasing preference for biblical concepts over neo-scholastic ones. In addition, corresponding to the instructions in the Dogmatic Constitution on Revelation, there were impressive exhortations in numerous other resolutions of the council, for example, as in the Decree on Priestly Formation, to study the Bible, to engage in biblical instruction, and to give biblical sermons.

6. The Ecumenical Significance

The Dogmatic Constitution on Revelation has been evaluated by the other churches in a generally reticent manner. Some recognized its considerable significance for the intra-Catholic discussion and welcomed the possibilities that it secured for Catholic theologians. There was less significance found in its bringing about clarifications going beyond the traditional teaching than in its resisting the attacks of the conservative forces against modern biblical scholarship who are also opposed to a new dialogue on the issues regarding Scripture and tradition. The document's significance for ecumenical dialogue, by contrast, was widely estimated to be quite low.

Yet one must not overlook that the understanding of revelation in this constitution is already of considerable significance. If one thinks further about revelation as God's historical act of salvation in the Word, new aspects of the disputed understanding of dogmas as "revealed truths" are bound to surface, and here a more careful distinction between revealed truth and its attestation by the church is needed. In addition, the peculiar indeterminacy in the concept of tradition and in the determination of the relationship between Scripture and tradition is of positive ecumenical significance, for not only in the Roman Church but also in the Reformation churches the issue of tradition has been newly set in motion. Both the research on the history of traditions in the Old and New Testaments and the discussion of the hermeneutical issues of scriptural interpretation, together with investigations into the history of scriptural interpretation, have raised perspectives that the older controversy among the churches had not yet recognized in their significance in this way. The indeterminacy in the statements of the constitution makes room for a new ecumenical dialogue on these questions that are so divisive among the churches. But especially to be welcomed are the impressive instructions for the use of Holy Scripture. Holy Scripture after all—apart from some rather insubstantial differences regarding the limits of the biblical canon—is still the foundation that is common to all the churches for their dialogue. It is to be hoped that, as these instructions are followed, Holy Scripture will *in fact* have greater weight in the general consciousness of Catholic theologians and laity than the theoretical determination of the relationship between Scripture and tradition leads us to expect, and that on this basis many traditional doctrinal disagreements among the churches may be discussed and clarified in a new way. All of these possibilities cannot in any way be underestimated.

Ultimately decisive in every ecumenical dialogue is, of course, the common norm that is acknowledged by the participating churches as the guiding authority before which they jointly kneel. But even though all churches have Holy Scripture in common, it is, as presented in the Dogmatic Constitution on Revelation, so in the grip of tradition—that is, not only in the tradition of the ancient church but also in the special tradition and even the present life of the

Roman Church, as well as in the church's teaching office—that its authority is reduced to the point where it hurts. The authentically transmitted historical witness of the apostles and the earliest Christian community in Holy Scripture is not clearly given its due in its primary normative and thus also critical position over against the contemporary Roman Church and the pope. But as long as this does not take place—even though Holy Scripture is held in common by the Roman Church and the other churches—the commonly acknowledged basis for the dialogue between them that has been in place from the beginning, will remain only quite narrow.

Editor's Notes

[i] This long hymn, also known as *Laudes Regiæ* [Royal Praises] or *Laudes Imperiale* [Imperial Praises], has been sung at papal and imperial coronations since the early middle ages.

[ii] All quotations from the Dogmatic Constitution on Revelation, *Dei Verbum* (promulgated by Pope Paul VI on 18 November 1965), are here based on the English translation that is given on the Vatican's website, accessed between 11 April 2016 and 30 April 2016, Vatican.va, http://www.vatican.va/archive/hist_councils/ii_vatican_council/documents/vat-ii_const_19651118_dei-verbum_en.html (cf. Denzinger 4201–4235; Tanner 2.971–981).

[iii] Josef Geiselmann (1890–1970) taught Catholic dogmatics and historical theology at Tübingen University (after 1934). See especially his book, *Die Heilige Schrift und die Tradition* [Holy Scripture and Tradition] (Herder: Freiburg im Breisgau, 1962).

[iv] The Dogmatic Constitution on the Catholic Faith, *Dei Filius*, was adopted in the third session of that council, 24 April 1870. See Denzinger 3000–3045 and Tanner 2.804–811. The second chapter of this constitution is specifically about the doctrine of revelation.

Chapter X:
Post-Conciliar Possibilities of the Roman Church

The preceding chapters could not treat all of the individual questions that the council engaged. We had to restrict ourselves to those conciliar answers which are of special significance for the rest of Christendom. We shall now attempt to understand the resolutions of the council as a whole.

1. Openness and Concentration

However one systematically arranges the sixteen resolutions of the council, it will become clear in every case that a remarkable openness and concentration took place simultaneously at the council.

a) First of all, the openness of the Roman Church toward the outside, beyond its own borders, needs to be emphasized. Thereby the council has in many ways corrected the Roman Church's former attitude toward the non-Roman churches, the Jews, and the other non-Christian religions, as well as toward the social issues of humanity in general. These corrections in the council's resolutions did not, of course, take the form of explicit criticism of earlier conduct, but they do in fact go far beyond that conduct. In all areas of the surrounding world, which we distinguished according to the schema of the concentric circles, the council strove in a positive way to become aware of what the members of the Roman Church have in common with other people in their various Christian, world religious, and political-social areas of life.

At the same time, in its Dogmatic Constitution on Revelation and especially its Dogmatic Constitution on the Church, the council has carried out an inner concentration that in many respects constitutes a narrowing. Formerly, the Roman Church did not have a comprehensive conciliar doctrine of the church, and various possibilities for understanding the church remained open. However, a narrowing here refers above all to the doctrine of the hierarchy, which is henceforth fully articulated and whose systematic rigor has, if anything, increased the gap between the Roman Church and the Reformation churches. A narrowing also refers to the supplement of Mariology by the acknowledgment of Mary as mediatrix.

b) The council's openness was directed not only toward the outside but also, if one may say it this way, toward the inside, namely, over against the realities which are suppressed or encysted in the Roman Church. After a long epoch of increasing centralized uniformity in the liturgical rites and the stipulations in canon law, the council consciously turned to remnants of early non-Roman liturgies which had still been preserved in the West in several places within the Roman Church, and especially honored the variety of liturgies in the Eastern churches united with Rome, churches which can look back on a hard struggle against the tendencies toward uniformity. In addition, in the explanations of the Dogmatic Constitution on the Church regarding particular churches and their special traditions, the tendency to relax the uniformity in the Roman Church and to move in the direction of multiplicity within this church was clear. Pointing in this same direction is the prominence given to the patriarchs of the Uniate Eastern churches in the council's seating arrangements, by assigning them privileged seats opposite the cardinals and in front of the bishops' gallery.

But this inner openness also cannot be seen in separation from the simultaneous concentration and delimitation which the council accomplished, both dogmatically and in terms of canon law. Together with all established dogmas, the unlimited power of the pope over the church was explicitly confirmed, and the actualization of the college of bishops' authority to lead and teach the whole church was made entirely dependent on his will. Thus the limits with respect to how much multiplicity is possible are clear.

c) Beyond that, there is also an openness toward the past, namely, a new concern for the historical foundations of the church in its biblical and ancient-church witnesses. This shows itself in several important details, for example, in the adoption of the manifold New Testament concepts and images for the church, in the salvation-historical understanding of the church as the people of God, in the emphasis on the universal priesthood of all believers (Dogmatic Constitution on the Church), in the understanding of revelation (Dogmatic Constitution on Revelation), and in the use of New Testament and Old Testament statements regarding human beings created in the image of God (Pastoral Constitution). Likewise, in the struggle over the determination of the relationship between Scripture and tradition, as well as between the pope and the college of bishops, arguments from the ancient church played a role, even if they were implemented only in part. In any case, it is clear that a stronger preference for biblical concepts secured a greater freedom of possibilities for theological statement.

Nevertheless, even this openness could extend only insofar as permitted by established dogmas and other established elements of the tradition which could not be given up. Even papal encyclicals from the past century have limited this openness in some conciliar texts.

2. Aggiornamento

This threefold openness and concentration is summed up in the concept of *aggiornamento*. It means more than merely the accommodation to the changed situation of the world. It means at the same time a renewal of inquiring into what God commands today. In this sense *aggiornamento* means not only accommodation but spiritual awakening. This renewal, to be sure, cannot be designated as *reformation* in the sense of that which resulted from the spiritual awakening of the church in the sixteenth century, for in contrast to that reformation, the Roman Church at the Second Vatican Council did not subject itself to a comprehensive critique through the historical apostolic message, as it is authentically transmitted in Holy Scripture, but instead it essentially excluded its traditions of dogma and canon law, as well as other traditions, from such a critique. Thus the plea of Pope Paul VI for forgiveness on the part of the separated sisters and brothers, a plea that was connected with this renewal, would also be misunderstood if one interpreted it to mean that the dogmatic repudiations of the doctrines of the non-Roman churches, which had deepened the rift between the Roman Church and the other churches, would be retracted. A change in the dogmas of the Roman Church remained beyond discussion throughout the entire council. The Reformation's principle, *ecclesia semper reformanda est* [the church ought always to be reformed], which was taken up by the council, has a different meaning there from what it has in the Reformation churches themselves, which follow the axiom of continually subjecting even their confessional writings, along with their dogmatic statements, to the judgment of Holy Scripture.

Nevertheless, one would underestimate the council if one spoke only of individual reforms which it accomplished. Rather, a process of renewal took place that reaches further than the individual resolutions—a movement that has captured many hearts in the Roman Church so that they long to serve God and their fellow human beings with greater faithfulness, devotion, openness, and love.

3. The Dialectic of the Council's Resolutions

If a church firmly holds to its tradition and at the same time wants to engage new problems and tasks, it is inevitable that unsettled issues and tensions appear in its statements, tensions not only in terms of conceptuality but also in content. This holds true also for many statements in the resolutions of the Second Vatican Council.

Among such tensions between the new and the old—whereby the new is often the old in church history and the old is the modern from the Counter-Reformation—the following, for example, are striking:

a) On the one hand, a strong, new emphasis on Holy Scripture; on the other hand, its being classified with tradition and the subordination of its interpretation to the papal teaching office;

b) on the one hand, a strong, foundational emphasis on the church's unity as a unity in multiplicity; on the other hand, holding to the uniformity of dogmatic formulas and the basic hierarchical structure;

c) on the one hand, a strong emphasis on the structure of fellowship and a new understanding of church unity as a fellowship of particular churches; on the other hand, a renewed guarantee in dogma and canon law of papal primacy in the sense of Vatican I;

d) on the one hand, the positive statements in the Decree on Ecumenism concerning the non-Roman churches and fellowships; on the other hand, merely acknowledging in the Dogmatic Constitution on the Church the "elements of sanctification and truth" beyond the borders of the Roman Church;

e) on the one hand, the understanding of the unification of the church as a reciprocal reconciliation; on the other hand, the elements in the concept of return and submission;

f) on the one hand, the acknowledgment of effective grace far beyond the flock of the baptized; on the other hand, holding to the tenet that "outside the church there is no salvation";

g) on the one hand, the promotion of religious freedom and its being secured through constitutional law; on the other hand, limiting this freedom through the general moral law as it is interpreted by the Roman Church, and by means of consideration of the common good and for those nations in which a specific religion predominates;

h) on the one hand, the emphatic acknowledgment of the autonomy of the sciences, of culture, and so forth; on the other hand, the claim that the church's teaching office has a theocratic responsibility for these domains;

i) on the one hand, the clear distinction between the tasks of the church and those of the state; on the other hand, the continued recourse to the political possibilities at the pope's disposal as sovereign of the Papal States. One could continue to make further such comparisons.

If one considers the various versions of the schemata, the diverging opinions in the discussions of the council fathers, and the reasons their proposed amendments were in part accepted and in part rejected by the respective commissions, it becomes clear that such tensions within the council's resolutions are largely about compromises that were to have made the acceptance of the proposals possible, also by the conservative minority. Yet at the same time one gets the impression that these tensions have their origin not only in such tactical necessities and also in no way felt only to be a burden but rather were affirmed as an fitting expression of the catholicity of the Roman Church, for by combining the various possibilities through a "both... and" construction, space is kept open for further joint unfolding of the various forces that had struggled with one another at the council. While the "conservatives" now believe that they have rescued for the future many a thing about which they had been anxious, many of the "progressives" understand those disagreements and tensions as a dialectic of an historical advance which has been made possible by the council. Indeed, many see precisely in these unresolved issues the expression of the conciliar dynamic that is pointing to the future. Thus one will need to evaluate these tensions not only as a weakness in the council's resolutions but also as a symptom of a spiritual awakening of the Roman Church, whereby everything will depend, of course, on how these unresolved issues are overcome in future steps forward.

4. Possibilities of Post-Conciliar Activity

On the basis of such unsettled issues, after the council one will have to reckon with differing interpretations of various statements in the texts to the extent that specific interpretations are not authoritatively decreed. Not everyone will see and hold to the dialectic in the statements. On the contrary, some will understand the one or the other side as the actual meaning of the council and will seek to make it authoritative. Such differences in interpretation were visible already during the council itself, in the opinions, conversations, and essays. The ecumenical dialogue partner will very carefully have to keep in mind the whole of the council's statements and the full extent to which they can be variously interpreted, if the ecumenical dialogue is not to lose the ground of reality under its feet.

The extent of possible interpretations that exists in some points cannot remain without effect on the theological thinking. Already at the council itself, Roman Catholic theology was by no means a monolithic block. There were representatives of neo-scholastic "school theology," representatives of an ontology modified by a philosophy of existence and salvation history, and also some theologians whose thinking was so strongly determined by biblical theology that in some respects they could be called Protestant theologians. It was, in that connection, remarkable that these differing theological orientations were not represented by specific religious orders (as, in contrast to earlier councils, the fronts here were generally not drawn up between the orders) but ran through the orders. The variety in Catholic theology will further increase after the council. Already during the council it was not easy to recognize in the statements of some bishops and theologians the Catholic theology that has been well known up until now. One could, for example, come upon specific issues and starting points in neo-Protestantism that have now arisen in the domain of Catholicism as a result of the attempt to accommodate itself to modern thinking, and Karl Barth's thesis concerning the kinship between Catholicism and neo-Protestantism received some confirmation. In the future one will probably have to reckon with still further surprises, and it will become more difficult than before to say wherein the peculiarity of Catholic theology resides.

Because the council's resolutions contain various tensions, the post-conciliar behavior of the Roman Church is also not firmly settled in every respect. Rather, the resolutions leave room to move, in which quite different ways of acting are possible, depending on which side of the resolutions is emphasized. Thus, on the basis of the Dogmatic Constitution on the Church, the co-responsibility of the bishops to govern the whole church can be put into action to a large extent, but the former centralized form of government can also be maintained. On the basis of the council's statements about the laity room has been given to them to participate spontaneously in the church's life on various levels, whether in the local congregation, the diocese, or the whole church, but the laity can also be hindered by insisting on their obligation to obey the clergy and be deprived of responsible effective action. From the pastoral constitution's emphasis on the autonomy of the secular domains, it follows that the church's proclamation should restrict itself to the principles of political and social ethics, but the same constitution could also be appealed to in support of a political Catholicism. Also, the decrees on ecumenism and religious freedom permit a variety of practical outcomes.

Which forces will prevail in the future? At this point no one is able to make a sure prognosis. This is impossible because the "conservatives" and the "progressives" do not constitute neatly specified groups, and because already at the council it became clear that, depending on the topic, many who were thought to be conservative could vote progressively and vice versa.

There is some evidence that initially there will be a period of slowing down, for the bishops now face the difficult task of implementing the council's reforms in their dioceses. It is well known what difficulties among the church's people the reform of the liturgy has already encountered in some places, for example, in France. For many regions of the church the new ecumenical program will appear even stranger, as will the acknowledgement of religious freedom. Back in their home dioceses the bishops are no longer borne up by the *élan* of the elite of the Roman Church assembled in Rome, and the different situation between the council and the home diocese will have an effect on many bishops. At the same time, however, greater possibilities for influence will present themselves to the conservative forces in the Roman Curia after the dissolution of the council, and one must reckon with the possibility that by way of administration they will attempt to slow down or even reverse some of the things set in motion by the council.

It should certainly be ruled out that the dynamic that burst forth at the council will be hampered in the long run, especially since the theological youth has widely been affected by it. Even if a standstill sets in initially, it should be merely a transition. Doors have in fact been opened that no longer can be closed. A re-establishing of the pre-conciliar situation is unthinkable.

Chapter XI:
Pope and Curia

If one sets forth expectations about which of the possibilities laid out in the council's resolutions will be realized and about which of the forces visible at the council will prevail in the future, one cannot, of course, forget that in the Roman Church, less than in any other, what is decisive is not the free interplay of forces in the church but ultimately the pope.

1. The Post-Conciliar Position of the Pope

In the discussions of the first period it occasionally seemed as if the concentration of power in the pope to govern the whole church and the concentration of the infallible teaching office in him—matters that were dealt with at the First Vatican Council—might be weakened, and as if the concerns of the minority, then suppressed, at that council might yet still gain sway. The strikingly strong manner in which Pope Paul VI presented himself to the world, for example in his audiences, as the Vicar of Christ and the successor to Peter, and the unusual number of references in the Dogmatic Constitution on the Church to Vatican I's definition of papal primacy suggest that such reform tendencies were present in the council, or at least were feared to be there: Did Vatican II revise the decisions of Vatican I? Has the pope's position now been weakened?

If we look at the council's resolutions, especially to the third chapter of the Dogmatic Constitution on the Church (compare sec. 3 in chap. 5 ["The Self-Understanding of the Roman Church"] above), it is unambiguously clear that here indeed a supplement to, but not a revision of, Vatican I's definition of primacy has been made, and that the position of the pope has not been weakened through the statements about the college of bishops. Some even assume that his position has been further strengthened, since now the *freedom* of the exercise of papal power is being taught. "In virtue of his office, that is, as Vicar of Christ and pastor of the whole church, the Roman Pontiff has full, supreme and universal power over the church. And he is always free to exercise this power" (Dogmatic Constitution on the Church, Art. 22). In terms of substance, however, this statement was already included in the Dogmatic Constitution of Vatican I.

To be sure, many hope that, as a result of the dogmatic statements concerning the college of bishops and the stipulations concerning the synod of bishops, the weight will shift in practice, and that the former centralized governance of the church will be loosened by a governing that the pope exercises in fellowship with the bishops. There is some reason for this hope.

But the statements of the Dogmatic Constitution on the Church have unambiguously secured, both dogmatically and in terms of canon law, that the free decision lies solely with the pope, namely, whether and to what extent he will permit the bishops to participate in the exercise of the universal power to govern the church. He can govern the church alone, as well as make space for a synodical governing of the church, and in the succession of pontificates sometimes the one, sometimes the other form of governing can predominate.

In addition, many expect that the doctrine of the Roman Church will in the future be more strongly determined by Holy Scripture. A reason for this hope lies in the fact that the importance of the historical sense of Scripture will increase in the Roman Church. But apart from the fact that it is up to the pope's free decision whether he wants to exercise his infallible teaching office alone or in fellowship with the bishops, it is also up to him whether he wants to ground the decisions of his teaching office in biblical statements and their historical sense, on the historically ascertainable tradition of the ancient church, or on the present faith-awareness of the Roman Church. He has authority to define in a binding way also such contents of this awareness that cannot be demonstrated through historical research—what the authors of the biblical writings intended to say—nor can be shown in the tradition of the ancient church, and to define them as being implicitly contained in the Bible and as part of the oral apostolic tradition. Pius XII made use of this authority with the dogmatic definition of the bodily assumption of Mary into heaven. Without a doubt, the pope will still have this authority after the Second Vatican Council.

In the preceding chapters repeated use was made of the picture of the three concentric circles which surround the Roman Church in the center: non-Roman Christendom, the non-Christian religions, and finally the whole of humanity. This picture now needs to be clarified in regard to the fact that the pope is the center of these three circles insofar as he is the center of the Roman Church. He sees himself surrounded by four circles, the innermost of which became evident at the council. He devoted himself to the second circle in his meetings with the patriarch of Constantinople and the other church leaders, to the third circle in his encounters in Bombay, and to the fourth in his speech to the United Nations in New York. This conception corresponds to the fact that Paul VI addressed the United Nations not only in his own name "and the name of the great Catholic family but also in the name of Christians who share the feelings we express here."[i]

When we consider all of this, it is clear that the pope is of decisive significance for the interpretation and implementation of the council's resolutions. To be sure, every pope knows that he is obligated to carry out these resolutions, yet it is ultimately up to him, given the resolutions' tensions and unresolved aspects, to determine which of the important possibilities of doctrine and action will be realized, and which of the forces active today in the Roman Church will be given room so to move. In which direction will Pope

Paul VI determine the interpretation and implementation of the council's resolutions?

Through his intervention in the proceedings of the council, during the third period, he supported the conservative forces, and through the changes he prescribed for the text of the Decree on Ecumenism its openness in relation to the Reformation churches has been weakened. His proposals for changes to the Dogmatic Constitution on Revelation in the fourth period were likewise a weakening in a conservative direction. In the encyclical *Mysterium fidei*, which appeared just before the fourth period,[ii] the pope, in contrast to the liturgical constitution, laid greater stress on low masses, votive masses without Communion, and the adoration of the elevated sacrament, and he rejected the attempt of Dutch theologians to reinterpret the doctrine of transubstantiation, which rests on antiquated philosophical presuppositions, and their attempt to express the presence of Christ in the Lord's Supper in a more modern conceptuality (*transfinalisatio*).[iii] This encyclical elicited deep consternation in the circles of the council fathers and council theologians since the distinction between the unchangeable substance and the changeable form of the church's doctrine had been part of the program of John XXIII for the council and had opened up new possibilities for dialogue with the other churches. In addition, the apostolic constitution *Mirificus eventus*, which on 7 December 1965 announced a council jubilee, remained entirely conservative in its directives concerning the plenary indulgence.[iv] Furthermore, in this document, as in no document of this council, non-Catholic Christians are again called heretics and schismatics and are mentioned in the same breath with apostates, atheists, and freemasons. On the basis of these actions one would expect that after the council the pope will dampen the "progressive" forces. But it is difficult to say to what extent the pope's own theological conviction or the voice of his theological advisers and the Holy Office or even a tactical, balancing perspective, influenced these actions.

In contrast, there was nothing conservative about the intensity with which Pope Paul VI personally devoted himself to the non-Roman churches. His meeting with the ecumenical patriarch in Jerusalem, his reception of the same patriarch's delegation at the last session of the council and the paper he delivered there, in which he expressed regret for the excommunication of Patriarch Cerularius in 1054 and its consequences, and assured them of his loving efforts to remove the remaining hindrances to unification—also his meetings with other church leaders, such as the recent one with the archbishop of Canterbury—all these are a complete *novum* in the history of the Roman Church. In addition, Paul VI devoted himself to the official observers from the non-Roman churches in a manner no less friendly than his predecessor. Thus at his initiative a joint worship service of bishops and observers, which was criticized by the conservative side, took place at the end of the council in his presence. In this service Catholic and non-Catholic theologians took turns reading the Scripture lessons and speaking the prayers. To be sure, one could say that all of this need not contradict the conservative theological conviction of the pope, inasmuch as in these encounters the pope was concerned about establishing initial contact, but not about clarifying the existing dogmatic differences among the churches, and that the primatial position of the pope remained completely protected in terms of protocol. But here Paul VI did meet the "separated sisters and brothers" with a warmth and cordiality that broke through the conventional barriers and expressed his longing for fellowship with them in a manner that permits one to expect further spontaneous steps that are foreign to the conservative way of thinking. Also supporting this is the first council address that Paul VI delivered at the beginning of the second period, in which he had impressively defended and deepened the progressive tendencies of the council.

If one considers all of this, one will be reticent about making prognoses, especially since Paul VI knows that he is obligated to his so very different predecessors, John XXIII and Pius XII, both of which are at the same time his role models. It is, however, completely impossible to predict which consequences later popes will draw from the resolutions of Vatican II.

2. Objections of the Non-Roman Churches

It is well known that Vatican I's dogmatic definition of papal primacy and the infallibility of his teaching office was rejected by all non-Roman churches, including the Orthodox, although the latter acknowledges the preeminence of the bishop of Rome in principle. This rejection was not based on the remembrance of some unworthy representatives on the papal see and of the times when popes misused worldly power in the struggle against these churches, but rather it was based on principle. The plenipotentiary power and infallibility granted to the pope can be supported neither by New Testament statements concerning Peter nor by the ancient church's position of the bishop of Rome in the fellowship of the patriarchs. To be sure, one will have to take into consideration that every ordering of the church is subject to historical changes. In this understanding of primacy, however, people generally saw a violation of the basic spiritual structure of fellowship that belongs to the very nature of the church—quite apart from other weighty dogmatic differences.

These objections against papal primacy have not been removed by Vatican II. Even if there is cause for hope that in fact the structure of fellowship will gain importance, the pope's position of power is still not changed dogmatically or in canon law.

Beyond the historical and dogmatic objections, which we here cannot consider in detail any further, there are also substantial practical misgivings. Without a doubt the plenipotentiary power accorded to the pope is incomparably greater than what any one person can exercise. Although in this century a number of unusually outstanding personalities succeeded one another on the papal throne, not one of them was equally outstanding as a theological teacher and as pastoral care-giver, liturgist and arbiter of canon law and diplomat, to name only a few areas in which the pope must constantly set forth normative decisions. It cannot be otherwise. According to the New Testament statements, after all, the various spiritual gifts of teaching, prophesy, congregational leadership, and so forth, are distributed among the various members of the body of Christ, and only in the fellowship of their mutual service does the spiritual abundance manifest itself. Already this variety of gifts gives rise to practical limits for the independent activity of every pope, while the authority granted to him, and hence also his responsibility, is universal. In addition, there are other reasons why he remains dependent on co-workers, for in view of the worldwide size of the Roman Church it is quite impossible for him to be himself informed about all areas, issues, and personalities, so that he could on the basis of his own concrete way of looking at things make the required decisions, even if it were only the appointment of bishops. He remains dependent on the information, proposals, and outlines of his co-workers, including their elaboration of his encyclicals and addresses.

This gives rise to the issue of the Curia. It is not mentioned by the Dogmatic Constitution on the Church in the doctrine of the hierarchy (pope, bishops, priests, deacons), for dogmatically it has no special existence. It is to be nothing more than the executive instrument of the pope. In point of fact, however, the pope does not rule alone but with the Curia; indeed in many decisions the Curia rules in the name of the pope. Thus, in fact, the Curia participates in the papal plenipotentiary power and stands with the pope over against the bishops and the whole Roman Church.

3. The Reform of the Curia

In the council there was frequent, at times extremely sharp, criticism of the Curia, and not only by bishops of the Eastern churches united with Rome, to whose tradition the Curial centralization is particularly strange and offensive. Objections were raised that the manner of the Curia is antiquated and still entangled by the courtly forms from the time of its origin; that the Curia knows too little about the real situation of the church in different parts of the world and rules in a way that is bureaucratic, complicated, and out of touch with reality; that it is staffed one-sidedly by Italians, and that the other areas of the church, both in their personnel and with respect to their substantive concerns, are insufficiently represented; and that the Curia treated bishops as "inferiors," and so forth. There were demands that the Curia be subject to a council of bishops, that the tasks of the Curia be reduced to carrying out the decisions of the pope and the council of bishops, and that the number of Curial bishops and the priests employed there be sharply decreased and that many functions of the Curia be fulfilled through the laity, and so forth. Cardinal Frings was especially severe in his criticism of the Holy Office: No one could be condemned by this governing body in questions of faith without first granting the individual and his bishop a hearing and an opportunity to clarify and amend his remarks. Behind all this criticism was the bishops' desire for unmediated fellowship with the pope in the governing of their church and the whole church.

Pope Paul VI did not close himself off to this criticism. At a meeting of all the members of the Curia on 21 September 1963 he announced a thoroughgoing reform of the Curia. In his speech he clothed obvious criticism of this body—a body that is inclined toward autocracy, but which is also extremely sensitive— in words of appreciation and thanks for a job well done. He began the reform itself cautiously and gently. He created the legal basis in canon law for a synod of bishops, in which, to be sure, only the leading Curial cardinals are foreseen to be permanent members, while the elected representatives of the territorial conferences of bishops will constantly change. He voiced his approval of a reorganization of the Congregation for the Propagation of the Faith (*de propaganda fide*) by adding bishops and advisers from the mission fields. He implemented a change of name for the Holy Office, which will now be called the "Congregation for the Doctrine of the Faith." To be sure, it will have the same functions as before, but henceforth it is no longer to act in the manner of a court but is also to stimulate theological dialogue in the church. Furthermore, going forward, every accused person is to have the right to defend himself. In addition, the pope confirmed the Secretariat for Christian Unity as a permanent institution and established the secretariats for non-Christian religions and for non-believers. Further reforms are to be expected. Much will depend on whether these reforms will enable the bishops to work together directly with the pope and whether they will permit the pope to gain a more realistic understanding of the issues in the various areas of the church.

There is no doubt that much can be improved in the Curia's scope of responsibility, in its personnel, and in the way it works. The question remains, however, whether some of the expectations of those who vehemently demand reform are not unrealistic, for even if thoroughgoing reforms should be carried out, the necessity of a large Curial governing body remains bound to the former centralization, whose functions, for practical reasons, cannot be reduced merely to implementing the decisions of the pope and the synod of bishops. Such a reduction would most likely occur only if the pope, following the model of the ancient church, would organize the Roman Church into relative autonomous patriarchates and restrict himself to the exercise of his primacy of jurisdiction within the fellowship of patriarchs in the form of an honorary primacy with clearly defined legal limits, for he could then exercise such a primacy directly to a much greater degree. But there are no indications that this will be done.

Editor's Notes

[i] Pope Paul VI, Address to the United Nations (4 October 1965), An English translation of this address is available on the Vatican's website, Vatican.va, accessed 23 April 2016, http://w2. vatican.va/content/paul-vi/en/speeches/1965/documents/hf_p-vi_spe_19651004_united-na tions.html

[ii] This encyclical on the Holy Eucharist was published on 3 September 1965.

[iii] The term *transfinalization* was apparently coined by the French Marist, Joseph de Baciocchi (d. 2009), but it was also used by the important Dutch Catholic theologians, Piet Schoonenberg (1911–1999) and Edward Schillebeeckx (1914–2009). Schlink is here alluding primarily to the latter two.

[iv] The Latin and Italian versions of this apostolic constitution, which celebrated the close of the council and announced an extraordinary jubilee (that took place between 1 January 1966 and 29 May [Pentecost] that year), are available on the Vatican's website, Vatican.va, accessed 23 April 2016, http://w2.vatican.va/content/paul-vi/la/apost_constitutions/documents/hf_p-vi_ apc_19651207_mirificus-eventus.html. The constitution states, for example, that a plenary indulgence would be granted to all faithful Catholics if, during the jubilee, they would hear three sermons on the council's resolutions or attend a solemn mass that is celebrated by the local bishop or solemnly renew their faith at the local cathedral.

Chapter XII:
The Significance of the Council for the Other Churches

The Second Vatican Council is of greatest significance for the Roman Church. Without a doubt the council signifies a considerable strengthening for this church. One aspect of this strengthening is already evident in the fact that at the council Roman Catholic bishops from around the world came together for lively exchange of opinions. Another aspect of this strengthening, accomplished in large measure through the deliberations, is the movement away from a defensive posture toward concern for the issues of the present, and also, especially, the wide consensus by which the council's resolutions were ultimately adopted. Those assembled in Rome thus had every reason to return with new joyousness to their work at home.

To inquire about the significance of this council for the non-Roman churches is a different matter. Here the responses in part diverge considerably. Naturally, this difference resulted from the different expectations that people had for the council at its start. Those who originally held that, because of Vatican I, a genuine conciliar event would be impossible in the Roman Church were happily surprised. Those who had hoped, on the other hand, that through the council essential hindrances to the unification of the church would be removed were disappointed in their expectations and were in danger of failing to see at the end of the council what progress had been achieved. In what follows we cannot discuss the full range of the manifold evaluations of the council. Instead, by engaging only a few of the widespread critical responses we will here seek to clarify the question about the significance of the council for the non-Roman churches.

1. Unchanged Differences and New Starting Points

What can the council signify for the other churches since no dogma and no dogmatic condemnation by which the Roman Church once demarcated itself were rescinded or explicitly mitigated at the council? This holds true, for example, for the definition of the infallibility of the pope. This also holds true of the condemnations of the Reformation teachings concerning justification and the Lord's Supper. The council explicitly pledged its loyalty to the resolutions of Trent, not only by means of the solemn oath that all the council fathers made in the opening session but also through the council's observance of the 400th anniversary of that earlier council. This also holds true for the Mariological dogmas of Pius IX (the immaculate conception of Mary) and of Pius XII (the bodily assumption of Mary into heaven), through which the Roman Church deepened the rift between itself and all other churches, since the Orthodox churches also reject these dogmas, although, in distinction from the Reformation churches, they make similar statements in their piety. But they refuse to turn such statements of piety into dogmatic statements, the acceptance or rejection of which involves the salvation of the individual and the borders of the church. The council also explicitly prohibited an irenic weakening of the dogmas that are authoritatively binding. The dogmatic foundations of the historic Counter-Reformation, as well as the mission work of the Roman Church among the Orthodox, are thus maintained. In view of the central significance of the dogmas many judge that everything remains as it was before and that the council has no significance for the non-Roman churches.

But the council is not rightly evaluated if one looks only at the dogmatic differences that have in fact remained unchanged, because a series of new starting points have become manifest, and these can have consequences also upon the fundamental structures of the Roman Church. It is a matter here of shifts which become more obvious in the practical directives than in the basic dogmatic explanations but which are also not missing in the dogmatic constitutions. These changes in accent, which were exemplified through numerous examples in the earlier chapters, have opened up new possibilities that must be taken into consideration in any evaluation of the council and that justify a hopeful outlook. These changes in accent, for all that, are so important that the traditional descriptions of the Roman Church in the textbooks that set forth the teachings of the various church bodies are today no longer adequate. It must be further noted, however, that this council consciously renounced the establishment of new dogmas in order not to increase the oppositions among the separated churches. This fact ought to be appreciated in a positive way by the rest of Christendom, given that at the council there were definitely forces that pressed for new dogmatic definitions and condemnations and that could appeal to the history of councils for support.

The new tendencies, accents, and starting points signify, of course, nothing new for many non-Roman churches, to the extent that much of this new material has for a long time been self-evident to them. Not only in the Reformation churches but also in the Eastern Church, the Bible in the hands of the church's people, together with the sermon, has always played a greater role than in the Roman Church, which at times had even forbidden the use of the Bible by the laity. The Eastern churches and the Reformation churches have always distributed the Lord's Supper under both kinds and celebrated the liturgy in the vernacular. Moreover, the Orthodox and the Reformation churches have always maintained the fellowship structure of the ancient church to a much greater degree and have rejected a centralization that stresses uniformity. Also, the statements concerning the priesthood of all believers and the acknowledgment of religious freedom signify nothing new for most other churches. Thus many judge that the council merely satisfied the need of the Roman Church to catch up, but that it offered nothing new to the other churches, and that, at the most, one should be astonished that the Roman Church was so late in deciding for this new material, that there was so much reluctance about it, and so much timidity.

This evaluation, however, does not do justice to the council, and it would be wrong to conclude that the new conciliar starting points have no significance for the other churches, for the reasons that have been given. Certainly we have every reason to be thankful that through the Reformers the Bible, worship in the vernacular, the cup in the Lord's Supper, and other things were restored to us. But it cannot be a matter of indifference to us that through the introduction of the vernacular in the worship service, the biblical message also encounters the members of the Roman Church in a more understandable and personal way and makes it possible for them to participate in the worship service in a much fuller way. Should this not be for us a reason for joy and also a new incentive to take up with renewed enthusiasm that which we have inherited from our forebears? Without a doubt, it will signify a change in relationships between the churches when the Bible and biblical proclamation will play an increasing role in the consciousness of the people in the Catholic Church, and when one day, after the introduction of the vernacular and the further liturgical reforms that are still being prepared, the Roman mass will appear to the laity at first glance as hardly indistinguishable from the word-and-sacrament worship of the Reformation churches. Furthermore, it is of great significance for the shared life of the churches that this council treated the same questions and in part offered the same answers given by other churches in the fellowship of the World Council to questions of Christian responsibility in the world of today, particularly to the questions of rapid social change, atomic war, and racial tensions. Is it not also a cause for joy that in this way the scandal which a divided Christendom presents the world is mitigated?

2. The Significance of Roman Ecumenism

Furthermore, however, at the council, especially in its Decree on Ecumenism, there was a conscious turning toward the other churches that encountered their own longings. In this encounter areas of agreement between the ecumenism of the Second Vatican Council and the World Council became visible, which are of great significance. On both sides the source of this encounter were basic spiritual impulses that opened the eyes for brothers and sisters and awakened the longing for unity. The origin of the ecumenical movement at the beginning of the twentieth century did not spring from the external situation of the churches, and its progress in the last decades is not to be derived from increasing secularization, totalitarian atheistic systems, and the persecution of Christians. Rather, there occurred here a spiritual awakening in which the separated churches became certain of their unity in Christ and perceived their division as a sin and disgrace. So the ecumenical movement is a movement of repentance that grips hearts in a way that disturbs and blesses, destroys and builds up. I have no doubt that basic spiritual impulses also led Pope John XXIII to assign ecumenism as the theme of the second Vatican council and that just such impulses were effective in the council's discussions.

Now one can, of course, here object: What do these commonalities mean in view of the differences that exist between the ecumenism of the Second Vatican Council and the ecumenism of the World Council of Churches? For, without a doubt, the goal of ecumenism is, after all, not the same on both sides. To be sure, in either case the goal is the visible unity of the churches that are now divided, that is, the unity of faith, fellowship in the reception of the Lord's Supper, and also fellowship of the church's ministerial offices. But in this consensus there is the significant difference that the World Council explicitly leaves the form of this desired unity open, while the ecumenism of the Roman Church seeks to achieve unification in the form that is already existing in the Roman Church, in other words, in the acknowledgment of the Roman Catholic dogmas and papal primacy. To a much greater degree the World Council leaves room for the structure of fellowship found in the New Testament and the ancient church and for the churches' growing together in mutual conversion [Bekehrung] toward one another. These differences in understanding the goal can then also hardly fail to have repercussions for the use of ecumenical methods. The ecumenism of Vatican II is, then, a specifically Roman ecumenism. It is a synthesis between the narrow concept of ecumenism—as when the Roman Church designates all its own general councils as ecumenical councils because it claims to be already in itself the one, holy, catholic, and apostolic church—and the understanding of ecumenism commonly used today, namely, as the endeavor to draw the churches closer together and as the concern to unify the separated churches. In view of this present situation it should come as no surprise that some churches—for example, the Greek Orthodox Church—have not lost their fear that Roman ecumenism ultimately still strives only for submission and not fellowship. This mistrust was also awakened by the fact that the Decree on Ecumenism did not engage the World Council of Churches and that the interest of the Roman Church is largely aimed at bilateral negotiations with individual non-Roman churches.

The specifically Roman limitations of the Decree on Ecumenism are indeed self-evident. One must consider, however, that each church can be open to the other churches only on the presupposition that the one, holy, catholic and apostolic church is a reality in it. The Toronto Declaration[i] of the World Council likewise assures each member church the freedom to retain its self-understanding and its evaluation of the other member churches. In addition, within the World Council there are various kinds of ecumenism converging on one another. To be sure, most churches do not teach about their identity with the one, holy church with the same exclusivity as does the Roman Church, but one should not, at the outset, compare the presuppositions of the various churches with one another, but should instead focus attention on the intensity with which a church sets out, on the basis of its own presuppositions, to open itself up to the other churches. From this perspective, however, a thoroughly impressive ecumenical breakthrough is noticeable in the Roman Church within the short span of the last four years—a breakthrough that is all the more impressive since it came about despite the well-known rigidities of dogma and canon law in this church. Moreover, one cannot forget that the churches of the World Council also do not only all consult and make joint decisions with one another, but that within this fellowship a variety of bilateral negotiations between individual churches takes place.

3. The Practical Consequences

Now the members of congregations on both sides are interested less in the concept of ecumenism than in its practical effects. They judge the value of the Decree on Ecumenism and the significance of the council in general on the basis of the removal of burdens that impede living together as Christians. There are still areas of the Roman Church (also in Germany) where the baptisms of other churches, which are administered in the name of the Triune God, are not acknowledged, even though the Decree on Ecumenism has its basis in the common baptism. Mixed marriages consecrated by a Lutheran pastor are still declared invalid by the Roman Church and the Catholic spouses excluded from the sacrament, even though, according to the Decree on Ecumenism, the Lutheran Christian has become a member of the body of Christ through baptism. There are still mission fields of the Protestant churches, indeed, even national churches, as in Indonesia (NIAS), where the Roman Church is undertaking counter missionary work at great expense in terms of personnel and materiel, even though the decrees on ecumenism and the mission activity of the church call for a joint witness to the faith. There has still been no change in the legal situation of the Protestant Church in Spain, despite the Declaration on Religious Freedom. Admittedly, in individual cases the laws are no longer applied with their former severity, and yet the Protestants are still not permitted to call their church buildings "houses of worship" or to announce publicly the times of their worship services. But even in the realm of the Orthodox churches complaints are still voiced, despite the special accommodation of the council over against these churches and despite the prescribed softening about treating Roman-Orthodox mixed marriages that have been solemnized in the Orthodox Church.

It would, however, be premature in view of such facts to deny that already now the council and its ecumenism have a positive significance for the other churches, for in its resolutions the council was exclusively concerned with elaborating and enacting the basic principles that are to determine the concrete actions of the Roman Church in the future. Thus the Secretariat on

Unity is presently occupied with creating an "ecumenical directory" that will contain the directives for implementing the Decree on Ecumenism, directives, for example, concerning the acknowledgment of baptisms administered outside the Roman Church and concerning the possibility for joint worship services between Catholics and non-Catholics. In addition, despite the disappointing and inadequate *instructio* of 18 March 1966, the definitive regulation on the issue of mixed marriages is still pending.[ii] A change to the conditions in Spain depends not only on the Spanish episcopate and the Curia but also on the Spanish government.[iii] We must therefore await with attentiveness and patience the practical consequences that the Roman Church will draw from its fundamental resolutions at the council. Much will, of course, depend on these consequences. If they are not drawn, the Decree on Ecumenism will become discredited and meaningless for many Catholics and non-Catholics. The same will occur with the conciliar Declaration on Religious Freedom if the Protestant Church in Spain does not receive its due freedom. Some would then see in this decree only the claim of the Roman Church to its own freedom.

4. The Council as a Challenge to the Other Churches

What does the council mean for the other churches? The answers discussed here thus far are the product of a critical inquiry into the council and its outcomes. We are obligated to undertake such critical inquiry. But non-Roman churches would miss something most decisive if they were not to understand the council also as a critical challenge to themselves. Only then can its significance for them be really grasped.

If one considers the course of the council, the emergence of the manifold antitheses among the council fathers, and the completion of the deliberations down to the final votes, then one can have only the deepest respect for the care with which they listened to one another and learned from one another, for the openness of most of the bishops to the far-sighted issues and insights of the theologians, for the perseverance in struggling for common formulations, and for the outstanding accomplishments that the commissions and their sub-commissions achieved in their processing of the widely divergent opinions of the council fathers. The consensus that emerged in the final voting was, therefore, the result of an exemplary synodical effort, whereby especially to be highlighted is the fact that these resolutions contain many statements that would have been impossible prior to the council, and the fact that the consensus extends to the most differentiated issues and statements. That such a consensus, so differentiated and henceforth binding, is possible only in a general synod of a confessional church, but not in a general assembly of the World Council of Churches, is self-evident. Different church bodies, after all, are never able to speak in as differentiated and binding a manner as a single

church, and actually it is amazing what important decisions the churches of
the World Council have nonetheless already made together. If, however, we
compare the Second Vatican Council as the general synod of the Roman
Church with the corresponding general synods of the Lutheran or the
Reformed churches, or also with the Lambeth Conference, then we cannot
avoid the question about whether an equally far-reaching and differentiated
consensus would be possible in these churches with respect to new dogmatic
decisions concerning the relationship between the church and the church's
ministerial offices and with respect to questions concerning the relationship
between the church and the world.

Especially striking was the fact that despite all of the drama in the council's
deliberations a fracturing of groups and formal opinions into false alternatives
was almost entirely avoided—an outcome that has taken place in some areas of
the Reformation churches—for instance, alternatives regarding the church, of
understanding it as either being called out from the world or being sent back
into it. The council viewed both of these alternatives as belonging together,
just as the New Testament does as well. Likewise, the council avoided the false
alternative of either liturgy or service to the world. Both were viewed together,
while if elsewhere one emphasizes responsibility for the world, then one
suspects any emphasis on liturgy as liturgicalism. The sacrament and the
sermon too are now more correctly coordinated in the Roman Church than it
had been in the past, more so than is the case in Protestant circles, where some
neglect the sacrament for the sake of a relevant sermon. Nor did the council
permit the church's ministerial office and lay activity to fracture into two
alternatives, something that not infrequently occurs among us today, namely,
that those who want to take the universal priesthood seriously think they must
reject the church's ministerial office as clericalism. This is true correspondingly for the relationship between mission and the world come of age, and one
could continue with additional examples. This strange fracturing, which one
can observe not infrequently in Christendom, was noticeably avoided at the
council, without neglecting to take seriously either side of the alternatives as a
topic.

That the Reformation churches cannot affirm important doctrinal statements from the council is self-evident, for a reappraisal of the issues of the
faith that caused the division of the church in the sixteenth century did not take
place in the council—but neither have the synods of the Reformation churches
yet engaged these questions by means of the new methods of historical and
systematic research available today. Despite the divisive dogmatic differences
that continue to exist, we cannot avoid the question about whether the Roman
Church has not maintained basic Christian statements of faith—statements
also indispensable for the Reformers—about which there is no consensus
today among Protestants, such as the bodily resurrection of Jesus Christ and
his return at the end of history or the incarnation of the eternal Son of God
and, with that, the confession of the eternal Trinity of God the Father, the Son,

and the Holy Spirit. We are unable, of course, to approve of the Roman definition of the relationship of Scripture, tradition, and teaching office. But should it give us pause to reflect, that the belief in Holy Scripture as word of God has often been more unquestioning in the Roman Church than for many theologians and laity in the contemporary Protestant Church? And should not the persistence in prayer, the firmness of commitment, and the willingness to make sacrifices—encountered so impressively at the council—be felt as a question addressed to us?

Perhaps such counter-queries will be offensive to this or that reader. But in the council *aula* many a humble and fearless voice of criticism was raised about the situation of the Roman Church by the council fathers, so that it would be pharisaical if one wanted to suppress such critical questions to one's own church. I have no doubt whatsoever that the council has not relieved the Reformation churches of the mission that God has given them. But I do have serious doubts whether the Protestant Church is fulfilling the mission today in the way that God expects it to do.

The Second Vatican Council will be taken seriously only when non-Roman churches understand it as a challenge addressed to them. Here some of the questions already mentioned arise especially for the Protestant Church, and it will be left up to the representatives of the other churches to articulate to what extent the council signifies a question addressed to their churches. That the council is a challenge also for them cannot be doubted—in a similar way for the Anglican communion, especially with respect to the issue of the *consensus de doctrina*, and in a different way for the Eastern churches, especially with respect to the issues of *aggiornamento*. The council also constitutes a challenge to the World Council, which is in danger of being content with cooperative work among the separated churches. But the council, with its doctrine of the church and its ecumenical program, despite the inherent weaknesses contained in it, has unmistakably called for visible unity, and has rightly warned against being satisfied with mere cooperative work.

Editor's Notes

[i] Cf. endnote 1 in chap. 1 ("The Task and Danger of the World Council of Churches") of *The Coming Christ and Church Traditions*.

[ii] Schlink is here referring to the "Instruction on Mixed Marriages" that was promulgated on 18 March 1966 by the Sacred Congregation for the Doctrine of the Faith. This document is available on the Vatican's website. See http://www.vatican.va/roman_curia/congregations/cfaith/documents/rc_con_cfaith_doc_19660318_istr-matrimoni-misti_en.html (accessed on 5 May 2016).

[iii] Cf. endnote 2 in chap. 1 ("The Spiritual Awakening of Christendom") and endnote 4 in chap. 6 ("The Council and the Non-Roman Churches") above.

Chapter XIII:
Anxious Christendom

Before we proceed further to inquire into how the non-Roman churches should conduct themselves toward the Roman Church after the council, we need to set forth several fundamental considerations concerning both their relationship to the Roman Church as well as the relationship of the non-Roman churches to one another.

Ever since Karl Barth delivered his sensational 1929 lecture on "Roman Catholicism as a Challenge to the Protestant Church" and the Catholic theologian Robert Grosche, for his part (in the journal *Catholica*, founded by him), began to deal with issues of Reformation theology in an exemplary new way by engaging in theological dialogue about areas of controversy—as also the formal opinions of the council fathers demonstrate—the number of those taking other churches seriously as questions addressed to their own church has indeed significantly increased.[i] And yet the fear is still widespread that the position of one's own church is weakened and that other churches are given arguments against it when one identifies weaknesses in one's own church and discovers exemplary things in other churches, and publicly points to them. To be sure, this does not hold true to the same degree in all churches and with respect to their relationship to one other. In the history of the ecumenical movement some things in this regard have changed. But this fear can be observed again and again not only vis-à-vis the numerically superior Roman Church but also in the relationship of the member churches in the World Council of Churches with one another. One will have to say that a peculiar angst still characterizes contemporary Christendom, despite its ecumenical awakening. But where the conduct of Christians toward one another is determined by angst, their engagement with the world is also inhibited. The angst about one another heightens the angst about the world.

1. Grounds for Angst

This anxious reticence has a number of causes. To inquire in detail about them would not only be an historical and theological task but also one of depth psychology, in which it would become evident that the reasons in one's present awareness are in no way always the actually dominant ones. Furthermore, in the relationship of the individual churches to one another the same kinds of reasons are in no way always in the foreground.

One important reason for the angst is the memory of the historical sequence of events in the church separations, which continue to have an effect like a trauma in the subsequent relationship of the separated churches. Not infrequently was the separation bound up with violence and bloodshed but always with conflicts and pain, which then in the further course of history continued to have an effect, especially in the efforts to force the others to return. This memory continues to have an effect as angst about further threats, although most of the churches no longer have at their disposal the resources of secular power. The significance of such a memory becomes clear when, for example, one compares the relationship between the Reformation churches and the Eastern Church, on the one hand, to each of their relationships with the Roman Church, on the other. Their separation from the Roman Church was first-hand and direct, while the separation between the Eastern Church and the Reformation churches was only inherited and not carried out by them directly and was therefore less burdened. The memory of the sufferings that had been mutually inflicted in their history can only be detoxified through mutual forgiveness.

Another reason is evident in the portraits of the other church, which have been created in the conflict of separation in order to justify the special status of one's own church by means of the most persuasive presentation of the differences and to counter the attacks of the other church. Arising in the painful process of separation, these portraits on both sides tend to bring with them an exaggeration of the differences and a minimizing of what both sides still retain in common after the separation. These portraits have a characteristic shaping effect and demonstrate themselves, beyond the time of their origin, to be characteristically constant in the awareness of every church, even when in the meantime changes have taken place in the thinking and life of both churches and many abridgments and biases from the time of the separation have been remedied. In an unhistorical manner, every church is inclined to maintain these portraits in their catechisms and in their disputes about other church bodies. But these must be re-examined and corrected through study of the past and present of the churches.

If one begins, however, to study the present reality of the other churches, there arises as a further reason for the angst, namely, the experience of their foreignness, and this is all the more, the more one is rooted in the piety and in the dogmatic, liturgical, and legal framework of one's own church. Even when both churches have overcome much that was one-sided in the time of their separation, their further development nevertheless proceeded in each case from the special presuppositions of the particular church and therefore frequently appears at first glance not so much as the churches' drawing nearer to one another but as a further differentiating. Here a great care in research is required. It is insufficient merely to search for elements of the dogmatic formulas, rites, and so on, of one's own church that can be rediscovered in the other church; here translations are necessary. Often one rediscovers in the other churches the same elements present in entirely different forms. Thus, for example, the content of the Reformation's formula "righteous and sinner at the same time" is rediscovered within the domain of the Roman Church, though not in the dogma, but rather in the piety, especially in the believing reception of absolution in the face of death.

In addition, there is the concern that confusion will arise among the people of one's own church if one relinquishes the current portraits of the other churches and becomes too deeply involved in ferreting out what is held in common. Remembering the historical sequence of events in the separation and clinging to the portraits that arose at that time mean, after all, an aid to preserving the institutional church body. Angst about the dissolution of the doctrine and ordering of the church plays a far smaller role among Christian young people and many active laity today than among those who bear a responsibility for church leadership. This angst is heightened by the appearance of ecumenical enthusiasts who think that the differences among the churches today have become meaningless. But these enthusiasts are not only losing their own church roots but they are also leading others into an uncertain "no man's land" between the churches, and thus they are hindering the churches from drawing closer together more than they are promoting it. Such enthusiasts are today a peripheral phenomenon in almost all churches. Careful consideration is, in fact, required so as to avoid the danger of confusion and chaos when the necessary corrections to the self-understanding of one's own church and to the understanding of other churches are undertaken. There is a risk, however, that remains connected with every correction of one's own church, and that must be acknowledged.

The one sound reason for reticence over against other churches can ultimately only be the concern about departing from the revealed truth, namely, denying the Lord to whom the church belongs and whom it must serve. Where this danger exists, the issue is not only about remembering the history of the separation but also about validating the fathers' witness to the truth, and not only about the portraits of the other churches but also about the separation between truth and error. It is not simply a matter of preserving a closed sociological organization but a matter of salvation. When it is a matter of confession or denial, then separation is not only permitted but commanded. It is, therefore, not an accident that church separations which resulted originally from other reasons—for example, from political or jurisdictional ones, as in the case of the separation between Rome and Byzantium—then came to be understood, in the course of the conflict, as differences about the truth.

Since a separation is ultimately only justified for the sake of the truth, every church seeks to justify its special existence by means of the truth. The reasons for the separations, however, are undoubtedly quite multilayered and they still have in no way been thoroughly clarified in a systematic way. Thus separations also arose, for example, because a church, hardened in terms of both dogma and church order, did not make space in its framework for newly emerging charismata and insights about the faith, but rather excluded vital forces and forced them into a special church existence. Therefore, we must today inquire anew whether and to what extent the delimitation against false teaching really was and yet still is in every case the reason for the separation. In any case, the longing for unity demands new questions and research, a renunciation of comfortable notions and an intensive pastoral engagement.

2. Church Tradition as Protection and Hindrance

The heart of all faith statements is the confession. It is founded on the message of God's act of salvation in Jesus Christ. In the confession believers transfer themselves to Christ's ownership as Lord and thus give glory to God the Father, the Son, and the Holy Spirit. The confession is made before God and people. In it are concentrated the statements of prayer and worship, which are addressed to God, and the statements of witness and doctrine, which are addressed to one's fellow human beings. The confession is voiced by the fellowship of believers, and by joining one's voice to their confession one lives as a member of the church. As a confession of the church it thus determines the praying and the witnessing, the worshiping and the teaching of every individual member. In that way, the confession is of central importance for the unity of the church.

The confession in its roots is confession of Christ. In the course of the history of dogma it has been made more precise and thematically expanded over against various historical threats to the faith. In the process, there were shifts in the structure of the statement, depending on whether the dogma was formulated more in the structure of doxology (the Eastern Church), or of doctrine (the Roman Church), or of proclamation (the Reformation churches)—also shifts in understanding the validating of the dogmas and in the establishing of them, all the more so ever since the emergence of the Constantinian imperial church, which considered uniformity in dogmatic formulas to be necessary for the unity of the church, and dogmas were made into set, constituent parts of the state's legal order. Above all, however, differences in content came about as a result of differences in historical fronts, over against which the confession was made more precise, resulting in further dogmas, whereby the substantive and structural shifts reinforced one another. In addition, these later dogmatic statements assume a central position in the life of the church. They determine both the extemporaneous personal prayers and testimonies of the believers as well as the ordering of the church and of the constituent parts of the liturgy of the congregations. Beyond that, they determine the ordering of church activity and of the church's ministerial offices, for in all of its speaking and acting the church wants to abide in the truth to which its confession bears witness, and all of the church's orders and customs are intended to help it abide in this truth. In this way, dogma, piety, church order, and life are experienced as a whole.

If we designate this whole as church tradition, then the separated churches exist side by side as different traditions. These traditions can be more or less explicitly established in church law, down to individual details, or room can be made for the freedom of faith expressions. They can also become more or less the object of theological reflection, and even be fundamentally validated as a principle of tradition. Individual believers are, however, always members of the totality of activity in the church, and they live within the totality of a given tradition, whether they are clearly and completely aware of this or not. Also, those constituent parts which the separated churches still hold in common exist now in different wholistic structures; and in times of crisis—as history shows—calling into question such decisions that had previously been a matter of adiaphora, would be understood as harming the truth, such decisions as, for example, making use of the concepts of a given philosophy, or using leavened or unleavened bread in the Lord's Supper, or even making the sign of the cross in a certain way or placing crosses on the altar.

Tradition is without doubt an important defense for preserving the churches. The more tradition is explicitly formulated and secured in church law, the more it becomes an important aid in protecting and further securing the fellowship of believers as a fellowship of the brothers and sisters who live today together with the fathers and mothers who have gone before them in the faith, that is, an aid in protecting and securing the continuity of the church in the flux of history and its unity in all places in the present. And especially the identity of dogmatic formulas and juridical church orders make it easy to establish and protect the reality and borders of a church. With this in mind, one can understand that the Roman Church at the council proceeded so carefully with its innovations and that the council fathers themselves, even when an earlier position was corrected, made an effort to prove that the position in question had always been held by the church—as, for example, in the issue of religious freedom, where the Church had always stepped in for religious freedom (as in the *relatio* [presentation] of Bishop de Smedt regarding the first version of the relevant declaration).[i] Comparable processes can also be noticed in other churches.

The more comprehensively the tradition embraces the thinking and living of the believers, all the more, however, it is also a hindrance to the life of the church. One need only consider, for example, how much the Aristotelian philosophy that Thomas Aquinas once employed in service to a missionary advance has in the modern era hindered both Roman Catholic theology and post-Reformation Protestant Orthodoxy from coming to grips in a timely manner with the issues raised by the thought processes in the natural sciences and then also in historical thought. One can also consider, how much the tenacious adherence to the imperial-ecclesial conception of the ecclesial, cultural, and political unity of the church has hindered the churches from recognizing how its tasks have changed in the midst of the social and political upheavals that have occurred most recently. Or one can consider how the traditional understanding of ministerial office stood in the way of the awakening of the universal priesthood of believers from the slumber of a mere designation to an active and effective responsibility. Far too often preserving the tradition resulted in churches being unable to reach their contemporary life-world, but instead they merely replaced the positions of the day before yesterday with yesterday's position, while the church, as the eschatological people of God, is called to be the advanced guard of humanity. In no way does this hold true only of those churches that explicitly advocate the principle of tradition but it is also true of those who reject this principle and who, for lack of reflection about tradition, in many cases remain captive to it, in fact, more self-evidently than the former, and thus they close their eyes over against changed situations.

This two-fold dynamic of church tradition becomes especially apparent in the encounter of the separated churches with one another. In that the tradition encompasses and protects the whole of the church's vitality, at the same time it hinders every church from understanding another one as a living whole and from breaking through its own limiting borders. Tradition holds understanding captive and hinders one from taking another church seriously, fully and completely, as a challenge to one's own church. This then results in angst and the dilemma between longing for the unity of the separated churches and clinging to the inherited unity of one's own church, the dilemma between the will to be fully open to other churches and the concern about losing the story of one's own church.

3. The Relationship between Past and Future

The relationship to the historical past for the churches today is different from what it was for the congregations to whom the New Testament letters were written and about which the Acts of the Apostles reports.

The faith is grounded on God's historical act of salvation in Jesus Christ. The eyewitnesses of the words, deeds, and fate of Jesus, above all, of the appearances of the risen one—on the basis of which his death was thus recognized as an act of salvation—had from the beginning a foundational significance for the congregations. From the start it was necessary to preserve this witness and to pass it on. The traditions served to maintain as abiding God's act of salvation in Jesus Christ, which then led to the writing of the Gospels and the kerygmatic formulas contained in the New Testament letters and, beyond that, to the whole of the New Testament proclamation and exhortation. The interest rested completely on the content of the tradition, which had to be maintained. There was at that time, however, still no further pondering the process itself of transmitting the tradition, for the temporal distance to the foundational salvific act was small, and the apostolic eyewitnesses and their immediate disciples were still present or still temporally close.

The greater the temporal distance between the church's present and its historical origin, the more tradition had to become an issue. With the advance of the gospel into ever new regions, the necessity arose to make use of new ideas and terms and still to maintain the identity of the original message of Christ. There arose the necessity to demarcate the original tradition from other traditions that falsely made the same claims, to gather the original written witnesses, and to add a canon of New Testament writings to the Old Testament Scripture. The greater the distance from the beginning, the more urgent became the task of making the identity of the message of Christ secure by means of further statements of confession and by the ordering of the church's ministerial offices. The history of this tradition, that is, the multiplicity of interpretations that the original tradition encountered on its way through history—in preaching and teaching, in liturgy and the ordering of the church's ministerial offices, and so on—joined the foundational historical act of salvation that had been transmitted. Even though the church is always concerned only with abiding by the salvific act that took place once and for all time, and with preserving its original witness, the necessity arose to take into consideration this process of transmitting the tradition, which traversed many centuries, in order to understand the origin of the tradition. Thus the process itself of transmitting the tradition, together with its history, received a weight of its own, which comes to gain more and more weight since this process took place in different areas of the church, in different historical situations and intellectual confrontations, and was embodied in various church traditions, which then stood in part next to each another and in part in opposition to one another. In this way, the relationship of the churches today to the past, in contrast to the relationship of the first congregations to their past, is changed, because of both the history of the tradition of one's own church and because of the ongoing dispute with the traditions of other churches.

But also the relationship of the church to the future is largely different today from what it was in the early period. Paul had written to the Roman congregation, "Salvation is nearer to us now than when we first believed; the night is far gone, the day is at hand" (Rom. 13.11 f.). He expected this day of the Lord to be not only a day of salvation but also as a day of judgment, that is, not only as judgment concerning the world but also as judgment concerning Christians. "We must all appear before the judgment seat of Christ, so that each one receives according to how he has acted in the body, be it good or evil" (2 Cor. 5.10). For that reason, Paul toiled in "the fear of the Lord" (5.11) and exhorted the believers to work out their salvation "with fear and trembling" (Phil. 2.12). This corresponds to Jesus' announcement about the separation of the good from the evil, which the returning Son of Man will undertake, and about his exhortation to be watchful. "On that day many will say to me, 'Lord, Lord, did we not prophesy in your name, and cast out demons in your name, and do many deeds in your name?' Then I will say to them, 'I never knew you; go away from me you doers of evil'" (Mt. 7.22–23).

If, for Paul, the day of the Lord had already drawn nearer in the course of a few years since his conversion, it would have to be even more distressing for the consciousness of later Christendom that that day has drawn nearer still in the course of centuries. To be sure, all churches confess Jesus Christ as the one who "shall come to judge the living and the dead," but as a rule they no longer firmly expect him to come soon. Apart from special times of crisis, in which this expectation erupted anew, the day of the Lord has faded into the distance, and its troubling closeness has waned. The dual emphases within the original dialectic of "already" and "not yet" shifted as the expectation of the in-breaking of God's kingdom was largely supplanted by statements about the presence of God's kingdom, and church history was understood as the history of God's kingdom. By and large, the eschatological message of Jesus and Paul did not establish itself, but rather the Lukan starting points in the Acts of the Apostles determined the further unfolding of that message. It was thus possible to incorporate the coming day of the Lord—a day that in judging and completing will, as the end of the world and of the form of the church and as a comprehensive new creation, break through and transcend all notions—into comprehensive theological systems of the mighty deeds of God. Neither systems of salvation history, as in modern Protestantism, nor the conception of salvation history, as in the Second Vatican Council, are free of the danger of leveling the Lord's imminent in-breaking into a comprehensive view of the total course of church history and world history.

The tradition of the first congregation was tightly enclosed by the history of the earthly Christ, which was temporally close to them, and by his soon expected return in glory: Then all people will see the one whose act of salvation is now being transmitted and proclaimed in words. By contrast, through the progress of church history the process of transmitting the tradition, together with its outcomes, has taken on an increasing weight of its own, which through the waning expectation of the Lord's nearness and the settling in for a longer-lasting history of the church, gained even more weight. Thus the vision of the church is more often directed backwards rather than forwards. While God's act of salvation accomplished in the death and resurrection of Jesus calls us into the future and exhorts us to live on the basis of this future, the fear of losing the past—that is, not only its origin but also the outcomes of the centuries of church history—is often greater than the fear of the coming day of the Lord. Instead of eagerly hastening out to meet the Lord, the churches, burdened with the whole framework of the traditions, often move ahead at no more than a snail's pace.

If the various traditions of the separated churches are to encounter one another, it will be necessary for them not only to look backward on the history of their development but also to look forward to their ending, for the apostolic message exhorts not only the preservation of what was transmitted but also the expectation of the one who is breaking in at the end of history.

The normative priority of the original message of the eyewitnesses must be unconditionally maintained over the witnesses of every later period of church history, and the primacy of the decision of the coming Christ over all decisions that were made or are still to be made in the history of the church. Indeed, the expectation of the coming Lord belongs so much to the apostolic message that it is not being maintained without this alert expectation. On the basis of this remembrance, together with this expectation, the excessive weight of the church traditions is reduced and their being side-by-side and their being opposed to one another is being opened up. The remembrance of Jesus makes it impossible not to hear his "woes" against the scribes and Pharisees, "woes" that also fall upon our theology and piety. The expectation of the coming one makes it impossible not to hear the threats that the Lord addresses to entire churches in the seven letters of Revelation, because the coming Christ will carry out separations, which will cut more deeply than the separations of this age. His separations will cut straight across all the existing separations in this world. The expectation of the coming Christ makes it completely impossible to view the weaknesses and sins in one's own church as more harmless than those in the churches separated from us. The actual issue is not the self-preservation of the churches in the rivalries of this time, but rather being able to stand on the Day of Judgment.

4. The Common Norm

When the various traditions of the separated churches begin to call one another into question, it is of decisive importance that this calling into question be determined by the origin and the future they hold in common. If every church were simply to compare the other church with itself, such a dialogue would not go any further. If churches would do nothing more than call one another into question, without giving glory to the Lord who calls them all into question, that would not have a cleansing and edifying effect but only a relativizing and destructive one. But where is the message about the act of salvation, accomplished once and for all, together with the promise of God's act that is still coming, being transmitted in a binding manner for all churches? Does a norm exist that is being commonly acknowledged by all the churches?

All churches fully agree that the apostolic message and its echo in the first congregations are of foundational importance for the church of all times. They fully agree in acknowledging this irreplaceable norm for all further words and deeds on their part. But they diverge on the question of where this norm encounters them, and they give different answers about the relationship between Holy Scripture and tradition; and here there is controversy not only about the relationship between these two but also about the limits of the biblical canon, and above all about the concepts as well as the concrete contents of the tradition. Moreover, there are various definitions of the relationship among Scripture, tradition, and teaching office.

Faced with this factual situation, however, one cannot overlook the fact that, despite existing differences, Holy Scripture is held in common by all churches, and that the differences in the limits of the biblical canon have hardly any weight that they play no urgent role in the disputes among the churches. Even though the churches are moving apart from one another in the way that they define the relationship between Scripture and tradition, and do not therefore accord the same normative position to Holy Scripture, in the worship of all churches the Scripture readings occupy an incomparably prominent position. Even where one tries to derive apostolic tradition not only from Holy Scripture but also from church tradition, Scripture enjoys the unchallenged advantage that here it transmits the authentic words of the apostolic and earliest Christian witnesses without change, while the oral apostolic tradition has entered into the church's life, participates in its historical changes, and can therefore no longer be recovered in its authentic wording. In addition, the separated churches are linked by the fact that even where tradition is acknowledged as normative next to Scripture, the principle that there can be no contradiction between Scripture and tradition is valid. This principle of the absence of contradiction is of great importance precisely for the dialogue between the Reformation churches and the Roman Church. That principle makes possible a continuation of the common argumentation more than the opposition between the Scripture principle and the tradition principle—no matter how both principles may have been modified in contemporary theology—lets one expect. An arbitrariness with respect to the contents of the tradition is also excluded by the principle of the absence of contradiction, even when it leaves room for a very diverse developing of the witnesses in Holy Scripture.

Thus, it lies close at hand—in this process of mutual asking and permitting oneself to be asked—to submit to Holy Scripture, and in fact in the ecumenical dialogue over the course of the last decades Scripture has more and more established itself as the common norm. With this actual acknowledgment of Holy Scripture as the norm held in common by all churches, nonetheless the controverted fundamental issue about the significance of tradition and teaching office alongside Scripture is not settled. The issue whether, in what sense, and to what extent oral apostolic tradition is acknowledged in church tradition is left open, and very likely requires further clarification. But also in the history of theology and the history of dogma the clarification of the *content* of the *credo* preceded reflection on the *act* of believing, and it fully preceded the clarification of the issues concerning the teaching of dogmatic principles. The witness to Christ in Holy Scripture is, however, clear and overwhelming. Thus, an acknowledgment of Scripture as the actual common norm is making possible an exceedingly fruitful reciprocity of questioning, a new mutuality of understanding, and, indeed, a common witness.

The Decree on Ecumenism has also pointed to this great actual significance of Holy Scripture. To be sure, the churches move apart with respect to the fundamental determination of the norm, but what the decree says is valid: "But the sacred Scriptures provide for the work of (ecumenical) dialogue an instrument of the highest value in the mighty hand of God for the attainment of that unity which the savior holds out to all" (*Unitatis redintegratio*, Art. 21).

In this respect, modern historical-critical research is highly significant, for it has uncovered a far greater multiplicity of starting points in Holy Scripture than had hitherto influenced the individual church traditions. Thus this research has discovered a far greater multiplicity of theologies within the biblical writings than was known in earlier times. This same salvific act in Jesus Christ is attested to in the New Testament writings in ways that make use of very diverse conceptualities and contexts of meaning. We are therefore recognizing within Holy Scripture far more starting points for possible dogmatic developments than had been evident before to the theologians of the separated churches and also than had actually come to be developed in the prior history of dogma. We see clearly that a selective decision has taken place in the dogmatic formulations, through which individual biblical concepts were lifted out of a great multiplicity in order to systematically summarize this multiplicity. Thus inevitable differences arose when, for example, the saving activity of God was made more precise in the Eastern Church under the New Testament concept of sanctification, whereas in Western Christendom it was made more precise under the concept of justification, and here, the Reformation churches made it more precise as a declaration of righteousness, whereas in the Roman Church it was made more precise as renewal. In their being located together in the New Testament, these various concepts bear witness to one and the same saving activity of God, but in the dogmatic preference for one of them the danger arises that a narrowing enters in and the differences among the dogmatic statements will ultimately be understood as differences and contrasts in the faith.

Correspondingly, this holds true with respect to the multiplicity of starting points for the ordering of the church, which are contained in the very diverse statements of the New Testament concerning prophets, teachers, adminis-trators, pastors, bishops, and so on, as well as concerning the freely emerging spiritually gifted ministries, and about the sending into ministry by means of the laying on of hands. Here, too, there are more starting points than are actualized in the church law of individual churches. We need to investigate in which historical fronts this or that starting point further developed and became secured in church law.

The manifold starting points for later dogmatic and church-law decisions are not found in the New Testament writings in a timeless co-presence with one another, but in these starting points historical developments become visible that have already taken place in early Christendom. We must keep in view not only the content of the New Testament witnesses but also the historical and forward-moving acts of bearing witness—not only the church orders of the congregation but also the carrying out of serving, leading, and ordering. Furthermore, we must work out the basic structures in which the life of the church, its address to God and to fellow human beings, as well as its other ministries, are carried out. Thus only knowledge of the basic structures of worship will yield a clear understanding of the unity in various liturgies, and only from the knowledge of the basic structures of the theological statement can the issue of the unity of dogmatic statements be undertaken in depth, which is not satisfied simply by comparing the wording in the dogmatic formulations.

If we proceed from the common foundation and from the common future of all churches rather than from the particularity of one's own tradition, then the various church traditions will not be marginalized, but they will undoubtedly be understood anew and will be opened up for one another. It is impossible in any case to skip over the church traditions since, in fact, every church—with or without a principle of tradition—lives in a given tradition and, above all, since the apostolic gospel must by its very nature necessarily be preserved not only as letter but as further oral proclamation and that will have to be addressed in new words to changing historical situations. The New Testament writings would not be truly honored as norm if in the encounter of the separated churches people were to deny everything that cannot be documented in so many words in the witnesses and directives of the Bible. The word of God is "a light unto our path." In this light we must endeavor to understand anew the multiplicity of the churches' paths through the changes of the ages.

5. Overcoming the Fear

If we examine ourselves under the evidentiary claim of Holy Scripture, all of us without exception are called to account. We are called to account both by the warnings with which the earthly Jesus encountered the pious and the righteous of his time and by the end that they prepared for him on the cross, as well as by the acknowledgment of the coming Christ who will also judge the Christians. The security with which we draw boundaries between ourselves and other churches will be shattered and all self-glorification will be annihilated. "If we say we have no sin, we deceive ourselves, and the truth is not in us" (1 Jn. 1.8). Every church, indeed, has every reason to plea, "Lord, have mercy!" Instead of our fearing the other churches and the loss of our own particular church tradition, we should be fearing the Day of the Lord.

Jesus' *proper* mission, however, was not to judge, but to save, to forgive, to heal. He addressed his "woes" to the pious, the righteous, the rich, and the satiated, so that they might recognize their poverty and sin and receive salvation together with the sinners, prostitutes, and tax collectors, along with the poor, the hungering, and the thirsting. Thus, he will come not only as Judge but also as Redeemer. In that he overthrows and ends the rebellion of human self-righteousness, he will redeem the wretched, the poor, the yearning, and those who are hungering and thirsting for righteousness, and he will make all things new. Not the judgment according to works but the justification of the sinner through faith in Jesus Christ is the proper message of the gospel. That is, the gospel not only announces the sentence of acquittal in the coming judgment but it declares and makes the believer righteous now and grants him the new life. "If we confess our sins, he is faithful and just, and will forgive our sins and cleanse us from all unrighteousness" (1 Jn. 1.9). Thus the ultimate position of the believer is not fear of the judgment but rather confidence, "joy for the Day of Judgment" (1 Jn. 4.17). This joy is revealed to those who in repentance say "yes" to their deserved judgment and who believe in Jesus Christ, who has borne the sins of the world and was judged in the place of sinners.

If the hardened borders between the churches have been shattered by fear of the judgment, so by joy for the Day of Judgment hearts will be made wide for the love that seeks not its own but seeks the brothers and sisters and encounters them in reciprocal self-giving and receiving. This love is grounded in God's deed of love, who has given his Son for the world. It is at the same time grounded in the confidence permitted for the future on the basis of God's deed of love. In repentance and faith we can know ourselves to be embraced by this love. Consequently, "there is no fear in love, but perfect love casts out fear" (1 Jn. 4.18).

But who are the sisters and brothers that we are to love? The answers that the New Testament writings give to this question are as precise as is the shaming expanse for the churches standing side by side one another today: "No one can say 'Jesus is Lord' except by the Holy Spirit" (1 Cor. 12.3). "Every spirit who confesses that Jesus Christ has come in the flesh is of God" (1 Jn. 4.2). "He who confesses the Son has the Father also" (1 Jn. 2.23). Paul could even transcend envy and rivalry and say, "What then? Only that in every way, whether in pretense or in truth, Christ is proclaimed; and in that I rejoice. Yes and I shall rejoice" (Phil. 1.18 f.). Surely there is also misuse of the name of Christ, but greater than such misuse is the Christ who is himself at work.

But if the angst of the churches in their conduct toward one another yields to love, then their angst before the world will also dissipate. How much energy the churches waste in drawing boundaries between one another and in disputing with one another! Love for the brothers and sisters, however, liberates for servant ministry in the world. Because God loved the world, such love cannot be kept unto itself but must make its way into the world.

Editor's Notes

[i] Robert Grosche (1888–1967) was a German Roman Catholic priest and theologian. He was also a friend of Karl Barth. In the 1930s, when Barth was teaching at Münster, Grosche and Barth belonged to a circle of theologians who engaged in "controversial theology," a form of polemical theology that took theological differences seriously. As a way of encouraging further efforts at this new way of engaging in ecumenical dialogue, Grosche founded the journal *Catholica* in 1932.

[ii] Émile-Joseph Marie de Smedt (1909–1995), bishop of Bruges, Belgium, gave a celebrated speech on religious freedom in the second period of the council, on 19 November 1963. In this period he served as the official spokesman (*relator*) for the commission that composed the Declaration on Religious Freedom. He thus defended its continuity with established Catholic doctrine, contrary to several "traditionalists" who held that it departed from Catholic doctrinal tradition.

Chapter XIV:
Necessary Steps

How should the non-Roman churches conduct themselves toward the Roman Church after the council? In answering this question we must keep in mind the fact that in our century a basic longing for unity has awakened in all the churches on the part of all who believe in Christ. This longing is the work of the Holy Spirit, for the will of the Lord that "they may all be one" has become for Christendom a great and inescapable obligation. But that is the work of the Holy Spirit, that he opens up hearts to the will of Christ. For this unity of those belonging to him in love, Jesus has prayed to God that "the world may know that you have sent me and have loved them even as you have loved me" (Jn. 17.23). The Lord wills that no mission and no spiritual gift that he has given to the individual churches be lost, but that all these gifts come to fruition in the fellowship of the worship service and in servant ministry to the world.

1. Wrong-Headed Reactions

If we take this seriously, then certain types of conduct toward the Roman Church, which one encounters here and there, are not possible.

Under the impact of the council, anxiety has sprung up in some Protestant Christians that they will be overwhelmed by the Roman Church and that they will suffocate in its ecumenical embrace. For this reason, they react with an frequently unconscious tendency to belittle what has newly emerged in the Roman Church, to become more critical, to set forth as Protestant what the Protestants and the Roman Church do not have in common, and to adopt an anti-dogmatic, anti-liturgical, anti-sacramental stance. In this way, however, the whole of the biblical message cannot be brought to bear, and the special mission of the Reformation churches to the rest of Christendom cannot be realized. The ecumenical obligation would thus be denied.

Others permit themselves to be so impressed by the council that they equate the avant-garde leading group in the movement of renewal there at the council with the Roman Church as a whole and thus misjudge the real situation. In their enthusiastic expectations they overlook the limits that the council has imposed on ecumenical activity in the Roman Church, and thus they neglect the obedience to the mission that God that has given them as members of the Reformation Church—a mission that is also valid with respect to the Roman Church.

The way between these two extremes must be sought and taken in openness and sober clear-headedness.

There is yet a third attitude toward the Roman Church that is quite widespread and that does not do justice to the present situation—an attitude which guards itself against any engagement, an attitude of being a mere spectator and a dispassionate critic of what is taking place today in the Roman Church. Here one is nothing but a detached observer. But the role of being a mere spectator toward another church should be impossible for a Christian. Bearing the name of Christ in common calls in any case for a decision. It is, to be sure, easy to note that the council did not create the presuppositions for a unification of the separated churches; for already the fact that the council maintained, as a condition for church unification, the affirmation of all the dogmas of the Roman Church, together with all their accompanying condemnations of the doctrines of other churches, means a narrowness in the understanding of unity, a narrowness which makes it impossible for the other churches to include in this unity everything that God has given to them in the knowledge of faith as well as the other gifts he has entrusted to them. If they were to accept this condition, this would lead to an impoverishment of Christendom, which would ultimately be of no benefit to the Roman Church either.

The unification of the churches, however, can only be the result of a preceding and progressing approach toward one other. But in respect to this, the council has provided a series of highly significant starting points in its Decree on Ecumenism, which coincide in large measure with what the ecumenical movement of the non-Roman churches has come to recognize in recent decades as the necessary first steps. These possibilities now opened up in the Roman Church are not merely to be observed critically, but rather they are to be actively engaged. The ecumenism of the Roman Church that is barely born can unfold in a truly ecumenical way only if it finds an echo in the other churches.

What steps need to be taken here? The answer to this question will be voiced differently by the non-Roman churches with respect to the details, depending on the historical, dogmatic, and church-law presuppositions by which their relationship to the Roman Church is determined. But despite these differences, fundamental requirements can be identified for further steps, which apply to all churches. These steps are to be elucidated here by using the Protestant Church as an illustration.

2. The Necessary Presuppositions

The first condition for drawing closer is self-examination in repentance. Not the demand of repentance directed at others, but our own repentance must stand at the beginning. We cannot evade this repentance by boasting of the spiritual awakening that occurred in the sixteenth-century Reformation—the rediscovery of the message of the justification of the sinner by faith, the restored reception of the Lord's Supper under the forms of bread and wine, the opening of the whole Bible for the church's laity, the spiritual awakening of the priesthood of all believers, and so on. We must rather examine the real situation of our church *today*. How is it going with the preaching of the pure gospel, with attendance at the worship service, reception of the Lord's Supper, and the actual use of the Bible in Protestant Christendom today? We cannot answer this question concerning our real situation by reciting the slogan "Christ alone, grace alone, Scripture alone" any more than we can answer the question concerning the *real situation* of the universal priesthood by pointing to the *principle* of the priesthood of all believers. And how is it going today with respect to the consensus of all believers, which was so important for the Reformers? But in such a self-examination, we must not stop with the comparison with the Reformation, but must press through the tradition of our church to the historical, apostolic, early-Christian foundation. In light of the word of Scripture, we must examine our present state and the history of our church. We cannot expect the New Testament message merely to confirm the Reformation, but rather we must also inquire whether this message in the fronts of that time has perhaps been made relevant in a one-sided or an abridged manner. We must also inquire, for example, whether the ordering of the church's ministerial office, as it developed during the Reformation period in the conflict with the Enthusiasts [*Schwärmer*],[i] let the universal priesthood of the believers have space for the activity that Paul acknowledged in his statements concerning spiritual gifts and ministries. How is it going with the spiritual gifts today and with the power of the universal priesthood to awaken again those who have become estranged from the faith? Do we not have many reasons for a conversion and a renewal on the basis of the church's origin?

In connection with our self-examination in repentance we must strive for a new understanding of the Roman Church and seek the truth also there where its witness encounters us as hidden under strange forms. When focusing on the Roman Church, one cannot stop with legalistic, ritualistic, and superstitious phenomena but must be focused on the whole of its life and especially the renewal being carried out within it: in the worship service, in biblical scholarship and dogmatic work, in its conduct toward the rest of Christendom and toward the world. Similarly, in looking back on history, one must not stop merely with the form of the Roman Church when it encountered the Protestant awakening at the time of the Reformation and in the Counter-Reformation, but rather the great historical breakthroughs that have at various times taken place in the Roman Church's piety and theology and in its reforms and missionary advances need to be kept in view. It is ultimately important, however, that we not observe the past and the present of this church in isolation but that we go back to the New Testament witnesses and, on the basis of the multiplicity of Christologies and ecclesiologies as well as the liturgical starting points and church orderings found there, try as far as possible to interpret Roman Catholic church tradition. With eyes of love and with the humility of inquiry we must strive for a new understanding of the Roman Church, discover the treasures hidden there for us under strange forms, and thank God for the knowledge of truth, faithfulness, and devotion that he has produced also there through the Holy Spirit. Undoubtedly, we have to get rid of many misunderstandings, caricatures, and all too convenient schemata, by means of which we tend to evade the question that the Roman Church poses for our church.

Repentance before God and the search for brothers and sisters under the word of Holy Scripture is the indispensable presupposition for all further ecumenical steps. When we in repentance are wrestling for our renewal, the encounter with the Roman Church will be genuine, that is, free from anxiety and fanatical enthusiasm. Then we can speak of our own shortcomings openly and without fear of losing our prestige, and likewise we can testify openly in humility and freedom to the truth that lies hidden in the other.

3. The Ecumenical Dialogue

The next step is taking up the dialogue with the Roman Church. This dialogue already had its beginning many years ago at various places through the spontaneity of individual Christians, and it has since been kept alive among the youth, especially in university campus associations, and in other study groups of laity and theologians. The time has now come to take up this dialogue also in official encounters of church leadership and in various levels of church work.

For an ecumenical dialogue it is essential that all participants consciously encounter one another as members of their own church. Only when they know themselves to be obligated to the doctrine and ordering of their own church can there be an encounter between the churches. The dialogue is fully ready to take place, the partners to listen to one another as brothers and sisters who know themselves to be obligated to the same Lord. Thereby, all minimizing of existing differences is to be avoided. Certainly, however, the depth and weight of these differences must be examined anew, and through their common faith in Christ and through joint study of Holy Scripture the participants must strive to overcome the differences.

More than enough topics are set for the dialogue, given that the churches are side-by-side in the midst of the same world situation. It might be especially near at hand to begin with a joint analysis of the Decree on Ecumenism and the Toronto Declaration of the World Council of Churches, as well as the Pastoral Constitution on the Church in the Contemporary World, along with the reports and resolutions of international church conferences that correspond to the various topics. Hereby, the Catholic dialogue-partners should be asked to explain what, in their understanding, these resolutions of the council mean for the interactions of the separated churches, and in turn we should let them ask us what conclusions are to be drawn from the documents of the World

Council. Not only the traditional differences among the churches but also the spiritual climate of the life-world in which the churches are doing their ministries, as well as the problems of proclamation and church instruction, call for joint clarification. In doing this, of course, church history cannot be skipped over. If in the treatment of relevant contemporary issues one ignores church traditions and thinks that results will thereby be achieved more quickly, this will sooner or later prove to be a mistake. Church tradition will eventually speak up for itself and will call into question the results of that type of dialogue. The traditions must be included in the dialogue; they must be understood anew and opened up to one another in the light of Holy Scripture. The central theme of the dialogue must remain the unity of the church.

At the beginning, every dialogue has an informative character and seeks to promote better understanding. The dialogue, however, cannot stop at one's own self-understanding, nor at understanding other churches, nor restrict itself to practical matters. Rather, research must be done in order to arrive at a deeper self-understanding and on the basis of the common foundation to bring to light the commonalities contained in the oppositions.[ii] Alongside the dialogue of church leadership, therefore, the cooperative work of task forces is necessary, which are established by the church leadership to devote themselves to the long-range clarification of given dogmatic issues as well as sexual and social-ethical ones (such as, for example, concerning the understanding of marriage and the laws pertaining to marriages between Catholics and non-Catholics) that divide the churches, and they are also to work up common translations of biblical and liturgical texts. As important, however, as the dialogues carried out or sponsored by the church leadership have become in our time, they cannot by any means try to quench the ecumenical spontaneity of the church's members or even to supplant it. It must not be forgotten that the ecumenical dialogue in most cases owes its origin not to church leadership but to unusual spiritual awakenings in the churches.

On whichever private or official levels the ecumenical dialogue is carried out, the principle of "*par cum pari*" ["peer to peer"], recognized also by the Decree on Ecumenism, must in every case be maintained.[iii] That is to say, the participants in the dialogue must have equal rights in alternating those who lead as chairs, the choice of meeting place, the selection of topics, the corresponding makeup of the groups with respect to interested laity, experts, bishops, theologians, and so on. Adhering to the principle of "*par cum pari*" does not mean distrust of the one against the others, but it signifies the form in which the exchange can take place in the most untroubled and free manner.

Moreover, it cannot be overlooked that the non-Roman churches have long been in dialogue with one another as member churches of the World Council. To be sure, the churches of the World Council are still not united. They are, however, on the way toward unification, and through joint worship services, deliberations, resolutions, and activities have grown together into a spiritual fellowship, which, to be sure, could not yet be grasped in dogmatic terms but which has nevertheless become an undeniable reality. It would not be consonant with this reality if the ecumenical dialogue with the Roman Church were led in isolation, that is, as a bilateral dialogue in an exclusive sense. The presence of the other churches today belongs to a fruitful bilateral dialogue. This is all the more true of churches that share the same confession, as they are united in confessional world federations, the pan-Orthodox Conference, and the Anglican Communion. For this reason, it is important that the dialogue between the Roman Church and the World Council of Churches has been taken up and that here an attempt is being made to establish a common formulation of the nature and guidelines of ecumenical dialogue.

4. Joint Prayer

The ecumenical dialogue is more than merely a discussion using rational arguments. It is here all about an encounter that embraces the totality of Christian existence, since it is about the encounter between the churches in all of the dimensions of their spiritual life. So the dialogue cannot be divorced from prayer, since in surrendering to God we are also opened up to his working in the sisters and the brothers.

Even the presuppositions for the dialogue are to be asked for in prayer. How could a repentant self-examining and a seeking for the truth in another church be possible without the Holy Spirit, who opens our eyes to our own reality and bestows a new understanding of the separated sisters and brothers?

Prayer must also accompany the dialogue itself. How could we ourselves keep this dialogue from sliding back again into contentious and fruitless arguing, in which all seek only their own self-justification? How could we by our own powers break through the unfamiliarity and bring to light the truth by which we all live?

Many people—both individuals and congregations—are praying for the unification of the churches. This prayer should also be prayed jointly by the separated. For a long time all churches have been praying simultaneously for unification during the Week of Prayer for Christian Unity.[iv] Where Christians come together for ecumenical dialogue, however, there is the opportunity also to hear the word of Scripture in joint worship services and to thank God for what he has already bestowed and to ask him to supply what is still lacking. Every church knows the prayer, "Lord, have mercy!" and the doxology, "Glory to God in the highest!"; for that reason, Christians should also jointly sing them. Every church prays the Lord's Prayer; for that reason, Christians should also pray it jointly. The high-priestly prayer of Jesus for the unity of his own has been given to all churches as promise that God will hear their prayers for this unity. Jointly calling upon God should always be the first shared word before the partners in the ecumenical dialogue mutually address one another.

5. Easing Catholic and Non-Catholic Interaction

Ecumenical dialogue cannot be an end unto itself. It must result in changes in the conduct of the churches toward one another. A first important step beyond the dialogue would be the removal of the heaviest burdens in the interactions of the separated Christians with one another.

This holds true especially for the existing stipulations of canon law regarding marriages between Catholics and non-Catholics, which stipulations have painful repercussions, by no means only in Germany. The council, unfortunately, produced no change in this matter. It is true that the council considered a draft outline that would have mitigated the matter in the spirit of the Decree on Ecumenism and submitted it to the pope with the request that a new regulation be put in force, but, according to reports, objections were voiced by the conferences of the English and American bishops. This could account for the fact that the *instructio* of 18 March 1966 fell considerably short not only of the expectations of the Reformation churches but also of the draft considered by the council, and it caused extensive disappointment in Catholic circles in general. This problem is, after all, also a burning issue for many Catholic Christians and an occasion for being embittered with and alienated from the church. The council created important presuppositions for establishing a new regulation in the treatment of such marriages: The Decree on Ecumenism recognizes also non-Catholic Christians on the basis of baptism as members of the body of Christ, and the Declaration on Religious Freedom emphases most emphatically a person's personal dignity, whose free decision in religious matters is to be respected. Also important is the revision that the council undertook with regard to the practice affecting marriages between Catholics and members of the Orthodox Church: Henceforth the validity of such a marriage performed by an Orthodox priest is acknowledged, even though the Orthodox Church (like the Protestant Church in Germany) affirms, in contrast to the Roman Church, the possibility of divorce and the marriage of divorced persons by the church. Hence the issue of divorce cannot be a hindrance to a new treatment in canon law of marriages between Protestants and Catholics. On the basis of these presuppositions it should be impossible for the Roman Church to continue to declare Protestant-Catholic marriages invalid if they were performed by a Protestant pastor. Rather, on the basis of the aforementioned new presuppositions, the conclusion appears to me to lie close at hand, that the churches involved might well continue to emphatically warn their members about the special dangers of such a marriage, but ultimately leave it up to the consciences of their members to decide whether they want to be married in a Catholic or a Protestant ceremony and how they want their children baptized and raised, and that the churches should acknowledge these marriages and refrain from imposing penalties. This view is shared by the council theologian Hans Küng and several other Catholic theologians, who at the moment constitute only a very small minority. One may, however, assume that the *instructio* of March 1966 does not represent the definitive regulation.

For the churches' drawing together much depends also on the removal of the other burdens to interaction between Catholics and non-Catholics that have already been mentioned. This is true especially of proselytizing that one church promotes among other churches and of resorting to governmental force in the suppression of another church. Both ways of acting not only hinder the ecumenical approaching of the churches toward one another but also promote agnosticism among those who were converted by material means and self-interested propaganda and those who are hindered by state power in the free exercise of their faith.

The removal of existing burdens cannot, of course, be expected only of the Roman Church. There are burdens to which the Roman Church knows itself to be subjected from our side. Every church will have to do its part to make possible the interaction among brothers and sisters in Christ.

6. Joint Work

A further step is the coordination of the charitable and social work of the churches in their native countries, in developing countries, and in disaster areas. Several starting points for such coordinating already exist. Beyond that, the churches should develop forms of joint work in planning and implementing. There are also situations that call for decisions in the history of individual nations and of the world where the churches cannot remain silent. They should then consult one another, coordinate their steps, and strive for a common message in which to proclaim God's command in a warning, exhorting, and comforting manner. Also, in cultural activity, especially in the educational system at home and in the developing countries, the churches should strive for a greater level of joint work in planning and implementing than has hitherto been the case. How much has been neglected or done only halfway, to the detriment of the needy, which could have been accomplished with joint work! How much more, therefore, has also remained ineffective because the church leaders, both Catholic and Protestant, entrusted too little to the responsibility of the laity and expected too little of their initiative and joint work!

7. The Joint Witness to Christ

The Decree on Ecumenism exhorts Catholic Christians not only to do joint work with the separated sisters and brothers in social, cultural, and other areas but also to bear joint witness to the faith: "Before the whole world let all Christians confess their faith in God, the one and the three, in the incarnate

Son of God, our redeemer and Lord. United in their efforts, and with mutual respect, let them bear witness to our common hope which does not disappoint us" (*Unitatis redintigratio*, art. 12). It does say here *how* this confession of faith is to be made jointly—whether every Christian is to confess the same God and Savior *for himself or herself* or whether, beyond that, the separated Christians are to confess him *together.* The churches united in the World Council—the Orthodox, Lutheran, Reformed, Anglican, and others—have repeatedly done the latter in public declarations and messages and also in the constitution of the federation. It would be an impressive witness to the one Lord before the world if it were possible on special occasions for all Christian churches, including the Roman Catholic Church, to confess Christ jointly and to voice the good news to the world.

These might be the first steps in drawing the Protestant Church and the Roman Church closer together. These steps do not mean the unification of both churches. That would still require many other steps. These are, however, the inescapably necessary first steps if the will of the Lord "that all may be one" is taken seriously. Even if the Roman Church is not a member of the World Council, it will be welcomed as partner in the joint endeavor for unity.

Editor's Notes

[i]   Cf. endnote 7 in the introduction ("The Task") of *The Coming Christ and Church Traditions.*

[ii] Cf. endnote 13 in chap. 6 ("The Council and the Non-Roman Churches") above.

[iii] Schlink is here alluding to the ninth section of the Decree on Ecumenism (*Unitatis redintigratio*): "We must get to know the outlook of our separated sisters and brothers. To achieve this purpose, study is of necessity required, and this must be pursued with a sense of realism and good will. Catholics, who already have a proper grounding, need to acquire a more adequate understanding of the respective doctrines of our separated sisters and brothers, their history, their spiritual and liturgical life, their religious psychology and general background. Most valuable for this purpose are meetings of the two sides – especially for discussion of theological problems – where each can deal with the other on an equal footing [*ubi unusquisque par cum pari agat*] – provided that those who take part in them are truly competent and have the approval of the bishops. From such dialogue will emerge still more clearly what the situation of the Catholic Church really is. In this way too the outlook of our separated sisters and brothers will be better understood, and our own belief more aptly explained."

[iv] Traditionally this is celebrated between the 18th and 25th of January.

Chapter XV:
The Mystery of Unity

All Christians believe that the church is God's act, not as if they had joined themselves together but only through his action of gathering has it come into being and is being preserved. All Christians confess the church to be the "one, holy, catholic, and apostolic church": made one, as belonging to the one Lord Jesus Christ who gifts himself to it; made holy through the one Holy Spirit who prepares it for servant ministry; sent into the world by him who has overcome the world; built on the foundation of the apostles. As a member of the church, every Christian is certain—through whose message he has come to faith in Christ, through whose baptism he was buried into Christ's death and resurrection and at whose table he receives Christ's body and blood—of being a member of the one, holy, catholic, and apostolic church. Indeed, he is certain that this church, in which he has received and is receiving these gifts, is the one, holy, catholic, and apostolic church.

This church in its historically conditioned existence is the self-evident center from which every Christian looks at other churches and evaluates them. When Christians look at other churches, they seek first of all for what they have in common with their own church, and they look for people in these other churches who think and act as they do. This starting point also suggests itself for the individual churches. However a church thinks about the possibility of *church* beyond its own borders—whether it will exclude this possibility or leave it open—it normally proceeds in these considerations from the point of view of its own reality. In the certainty that Christ is working in it and that the Spirit is alive in it, it looks for the same results and gifts in the other churches. So a quantitative evaluation of the other churches is evidently somehow taking place, their knowledge of the truth, their means of grace, and the grace that has been allotted to them. In doing so, "traces" [*Spuren*] and "elements" [*Elemente*] are noted as parts of the "fullness" [*Fülle*] present in the certain wholeness of one's own church.

But just as obvious as this manner of considering seems to be, so little do the other churches feel they are being understood by it. As a matter of fact, this interpretation does not do justice to the self-understanding of the other churches, since *every* church lives in the certainty that Christ is working in it and that the spiritual gifts are alive in it. It understands itself not primarily from the point of view of another church but rather from the point of view of the origin of God's historical act of salvation in Jesus Christ and of the outpouring of the Holy Spirit through whom Jesus Christ is today present in its midst. Thus, through this manner of considering, the churches mutually confirm their separation.

1. The Turning-Point in the Understanding of the Church

The first chapter proceeded from Christendom's loss of its security, from its being torn out of its traditional embeddedness in its cultural and political life-world, from the shattering of the traditional form of its existence.

But the self-awareness of the church as *church* was also shaken, that is, the self-evident way by which the church to which one belongs is identified with the one holy church and then from this point of view evaluates the rest of Christendom. Precisely in times of upheaval and oppression it becomes evident that in other churches not only elements of our church are present but also that Christ himself is at work in their midst and manifests himself to the world through them. The interpretation of other churches from the perspective of one's own church as the center does not correspond to the spiritual experiences that we have today as we encounter other churches, because there we are encountered by Christ, who in the freedom of his grace is bound to no presuppositions regarding the borders that humans make. In his freedom he is able to make weak and despised churches the light of the world, and to expose strong and esteemed churches as powerless constituent parts of this world.

The self-awareness of the church as church has also been shaken through the short-comings of one's own church, which come to light in the loss of its security. Precisely in times of upheaval and persecution one's own indolence and smugness become manifest, which have hindered us from multiplying the talents entrusted to us[i] and from serving others before they turned away from Christ in disappointment or despair.

So the shaking of the self-awareness of the church as church signifies both shame and blessing. The number of Christians grows who are dissatisfied with the traditional condition of their church. At the same time the number is growing of those who live spiritually no longer only from the traditions of their own church but at the same time from the spiritual gifts that have emerged in the other churches. Thus the witness of suffering in the Russian Orthodox Church after the First World War, or the liturgical movement in the Roman Church, or the fruit of biblical scholarship in the Protestant churches became gifts for all churches. This shaking of the self-awareness of the church as church is today moving more or less strongly through all churches, including the Roman Church.

Without these shakings the council's statements about the other churches also cannot be understood. While the first version of the Dogmatic Constitution on the Church had exclusively identified the one, holy, catholic, and apostolic church with the Roman Church, the final text (by substituting *subsistit in* for *est*; compare "The Borders of the Church" in chap. 5 ["The Self-Understanding of the Roman Church"] above) opened up the possibility of thinking of the one, holy, catholic, and apostolic church that reaches beyond the borders of the Roman Church. The constitution itself, of course, makes the most reticent use of this possibility in that it speaks only of "elements of sanctification and of truth" outside the borders of the Roman Church. The constitution is less reticent, however, in enumerating the items that interpret how this statement concerning the "elements" is to be understood: baptism, acknowledging Holy Scripture, religious zeal, faith in God the Father and in Christ, the Son of God, in some places also other sacraments, the episcopate, and devotion to Mary.

They also share with us in prayer and other spiritual benefits. Likewise we can say that in some real way they are joined with us in the Holy Spirit, for to them too he gives his gifts and graces whereby he is operative among them with his sanctifying power. Some indeed he has strengthened to the extent of the shedding of their blood. (Dogmatic Constitution on the Church, Art. 15)

As "elements or endowments" that "can exist outside the visible borders of the Catholic Church," the Decree on Ecumenism lists "the written word of God; the life of grace; faith, hope, and charity, along with other interior gifts of the Holy Spirit and visible elements" (The Decree on Ecumenism, Art. 3). This enumeration is supplemented by numerous other references in the first and third chapters of the decree. "It is right and salutary to recognize the riches of Christ and virtuous works in the lives of others who are bearing witness to Christ, sometimes even to the shedding of their blood" (The Decree on Ecumenism, Art. 4). While the Dogmatic Constitution on the Church had spoken only of persons who share in such elements outside the Roman Church, the Decree on Ecumenism goes further and speaks of "churches and ecclesial communities" beyond these borders (compare the section "Openness toward the Non-Roman Churches" in chap. 6 ["The Council and the Non-Roman Churches"] above).

All these statements, to be sure, were made by the Roman Church unambiguously as the center. The reality of the Roman Church is the norm for evaluating the other churches (compare section "b" of "The Possibilities and Limits of Ecumenism" in chap. 6 above). What is acknowledged as elements of the church in the other churches are elements of what is present in the Roman Church in abundance. In this sense it can be said of these elements that "as gifts properly belonging to the church of Christ" they "possess an inner dynamism toward Catholic unity" (Dogmatic Constitution on the Church, Art. 8), and in the same sense it can be said of the non-Roman churches that "their efficacy is derived from the very fullness of grace and truth entrusted to the Catholic Church" (The Decree on Ecumenism, Art. 3). In this sense also the jurisdictional claim of the Roman Church over every baptized person beyond its borders is to be understood. But in the same conciliar texts there is an unambiguous acknowledgment of the working of Christ and the Holy Spirit beyond the borders of the Roman Church, even though these Christians do not resort to the mediation of the Roman Church: by baptism "they are united with

Christ," and the Holy Spirit with "his gifts and graces" is "operative among them with his sanctifying power" (Dogmatic Constitution on the Church, Art. 15), "the riches of Christ" are present in their lives (The Decree on Ecumenism, Art. 4). If one compares these statements with the encyclical *Mystici corporis Christi* of Pius XII, and if one remembers the council's explicit emphasis on the necessity of renewal for the Roman Church, one sees clearly that the shaming and the blessing of the shaking of the self-consciousness of the church as church, which has occurred in our time, has had an effect also on the resolutions of the council.

If one goes as far as the council went, then the question is to be raised, of course, whether the starting point in one's own church is to be maintained in this way, and whether it is sufficient to acknowledge "elements" of one's own church in other churches. The concern is no longer only whether such statements do justice to the way other churches understand themselves but whether they are appropriate to the working of Christ and the Holy Spirit in the other churches, a working that is, after all, explicitly acknowledged. Surely "all those justified by faith through baptism are incorporated into Christ" (Decree on Ecumenism, Art. 3). Surely the reception of "the riches of Christ" (The Decree on Ecumenism, Art. 4) is not merely the reception of one part of Christ. Surely sanctifying grace (Dogmatic Constitution on the Church, Art. 15) is not merely a preparatory grace. Surely, if such a working of Christ in the power of the Holy Spirit is acknowledged outside of the Roman Church, should this not bring about a change in thinking about the church? Surely, instead of beginning with one's own church and understanding Christ's working in other churches as an "element" of one's own church, should not one begin with Christ's working and understand one's own church as a portion of this, his working?

Every church is in danger of understanding itself as the center around which the other churches orbit as planets. This lies so close at hand because all Christians are certain that the church whose message brought them to faith— in which church they were incorporated into Christ through baptism, and through word and sacrament they are again and again nourished anew—is the one, holy, catholic, and apostolic church. But the working of Christ is not restricted to this one church. He works in freedom without being bound by the borders of our churches. We cannot be content to measure other churches in respect to ourselves, but we have to take our starting point with Christ, by whom we are measured along with all churches. He is the sun around whom we, together with other churches, orbit as planets and from whom we receive light. A kind of Copernican revolution is necessary in ecclesiological thinking.

Now, to be sure, any one church might retort that it is one with Christ and that therefore there is no difference between its self-understanding as the center of all churches and its acknowledgment of Christ as the center. Here, however, the great multiplicity of relationships between Christ and the church, about which Holy Scripture attests, must with care be taken seriously. We cannot unilaterally claim God's covenant with his people for ourselves, for God can raise up children for himself from stones, and he can call those his people who were not his people. Nor can we unilaterally claim the unity of Christ with our church, nor his being in it and it being in him; we must at the same time take Christ seriously as the one who encounters our church in a forgiving, exacting, and judging way, and who is free "to spit" [*auszuspeien*] out of his mouth churches that make their appeal to him (Rev. 3.16). Taking seriously the biblical multiplicity of relationships between Christ and the church (compare section "c" of "The Borders of the Church" in chap. 5 above) will make the security of a quantitative evaluation of the grace that he has given other churches impossible.

2. The Mercy of Christ

What happens if we see the "elements and endowments" mentioned by the council as the deeds of Christ, and if we seek to understand our own church and other churches from the perspective of Christ's working?

Although Christ desires the unity of all believers, he is working in separated churches. Even if they dispute their power to forgive sins, he still forgives their sins. Even if they do not acknowledge one another as the body of Christ, he incorporates them into his body through their baptism. Even if they do not conduct themselves toward one another as members of one body, he gives them his sacramental body. Even if they dispute over the full range of spiritual gifts, he is working in these gifts in the power of the Holy Spirit. And even if they dispute the authority and legitimacy of one another's ministerial offices, he makes use of these offices in order to build up the churches and to lead them. So low does the Lord stoop down to the churches that he serves them even when they are not one. As the exalted one, Jesus Christ has not ceased to be the same one who had humbled himself, became the servant of all people, and died for them on the cross. If we catch sight of the working of Christ in the separated churches, then his mercy becomes overwhelmingly great to us.

There are separations that God commands. Here the concern is the borders between salvation [*Heil*] and damnation [*Unheil*], between the confession of Christ and the denial of him. There are also, however, separations that have arisen from lovelessness, lust for power, contentiousness, and narrowness among those who confess Christ as Lord and yet fail to see the universality of his working. If we cannot refrain from acknowledging "the riches of Christ" and "the gifts of the Holy Spirit" beyond the borders of our church, then this means that Christ will not permit every separation brought about by the churches to be a separation from him. Through the working of this same Lord a unity of the separated is kept intact, a unity into which their division does not penetrate and which is not dissolved by their division. Through the reception of the gifts of the same Christ there remains a unity, which is hidden under the divisions—hidden from the eyes of the churches and from the eyes of the world. So low does Christ stoop down to the churches that he takes their divisions upon himself and permits the separated to be one in him.

This hidden unity is beginning to come to light in our generation. We are beginning to sense it. We are overwhelmed by the riches of the gifts of Christ, which encounter us where formerly we had neither seen them nor expected them. We are beginning to sense how oppositions that we regarded as irreconcilable belong together, and how biases that seemed intolerable to us are necessary correctives for our own bias. From the oppositions, the riches of the one Holy Spirit's work begins to emerge, and we begin to sense that even through the scandal of divisions God has preserved a universal whole—a whole that has not been fully unfolded in any one church—and continues to unfold it.

If, thus, the present of Christendom is seen in a new light, the same is also true of its history. We are beginning to sense how puzzling—in a manner surpassing all our imagination—the working of Christ and the guilt-laden actions of Christians permeate one another. Through the scandals of church history he has held fast to his salvific will. Through the pain and suffering of the divisions he has judged the church and at the same time has not ceased calling, admonishing, and gifting it, and placing it into servant ministry for the salvation of the world. Again and again, his grace was greater than his judgment. Indeed, even through divisions he has let insights and gifts unfold that before were suppressed and had withered. Even through the churches' oppositions to one another he has attested to the riches of his grace and has increased the number of his people. Just as God's omnipotence appears to be an impotence in the face of the crimes and catastrophes of world history, so Christ's lordship appears utterly futile in the face of the history of the divisions, the fights, and the failures of Christendom. But just as God himself by his governance of the world encompasses even the evil and causes it to serve the welfare of his own, so Christ takes even the divisions into the service of his lordship.

In that way, the mystery of unity is the mystery of the mercy of Christ. In that he does not cease to have mercy on the churches and through their dubious servant ministry to carry out his work of salvation for the world, its unity has been decided. If the mystery of unity is beginning to come into view today in the midst of a divided Christendom, in the way of both shaking and blessing, it does not cease to be a mystery. On the contrary, it comes into view precisely as a mystery, for the mercy of Christ transcends all our boundaries and imaginings. Just as the church came into being as a result of God's action and not because human beings decided to join together and establish the church, so it is also with the church's unity. Just as the church is indestructible, so also is its unity. The church may be oppressed and hindered from expanding, its membership may be reduced, indeed, it may be pushed back into being hidden; nevertheless, God will preserve it in the midst of this world so that it cannot perish. So its unity may be disfigured by the disunity of its members and hidden by its divisions; nevertheless, in spite of its contentions God will not cease to be the one who will deal with it in a redeeming, purifying, and judging way, and he will preserve its unity even though it be hidden under divisions.

Does acknowledging Christ's working in the separated churches justify the separations? No. The scandal and the guilt of separation become completely clear precisely when Christ's working becomes visible beyond the borders of one's own church. Is the certainty of a unity that is hidden under the separations a comfort? No, just the opposite. If we are one in Christ, then it is impossible to remain disunited. "Are we to continue in sin that grace may abound? By no means! How can we who died to sin still live in it?" (Rom. 6.1 f.). Precisely the greatness of the lovingkindness with which Christ bestows himself upon the separated churches is the most powerful impetus for unification. Such unification cannot mean that we would have to create the unity, it is given in Christ. But we have to make space for this unity and get rid of all that disfigures and hides it. This command for unification is as valid as all New Testament imperatives: God demands nothing that he had not already given in Christ.

3. The Recognition of Unity

Where, however, is this unity to be found for which we are to make space? We are sensing it more than we clearly recognize it. We are certain that Christ is working beyond our own church, but we do not yet recognize clearly wherever it is that he is working. We know there are church separations that are not a separation from Christ, but we cannot yet distinguish them clearly from those other separations necessary for the sake of salvation. Christendom lives today in a time of surprising discoveries, but we are not yet able to distinguish clearly among impressions, hopes, illusions, and realities. Clarity is made more difficult by the fact that, together with the "riches of Christ" and the "gifts of the Holy Spirit" outside one's own church, dimensions of the one, holy, catholic, and apostolic church are beginning to open up, for whose comprehension past doctrines of the church are inadequate and the appropriate concepts are still lacking. In this situation there is not only the danger of anxiously retreating into one's own church in the face of Christ's universal working, but also the opposite danger, namely, of losing the reality of the church on earth in the fanatical manner of the enthusiasts.[iii] But the concern here is precisely the visibility of the universal church. Where should we start off in order to move from our inklings and impressions to a clear recognition of the unity concealed by the divisions? Where is the one church on earth beyond the borders of one's own church to be found?

We proceed here, too, from the concrete references by which the "elements and endowments" outside the Roman Church have been explained in the council's resolutions: Holy Scripture, religious zeal, faith, baptism, the episcopate, the life of grace, virtuous works, and so forth. In comparing the sequence of such references in the Dogmatic Constitution on the Church (Art. 15) and in the Decree on Ecumenism (Art. 3), and by adding further scattered statements, one is struck by a certain element of randomness in the arranging. Assembled here were various items of what was noticed in other churches, and in the course of the council's deliberations this data was added. One may perhaps rediscover in the randomness of the listings the element of amazed discovery that today is characteristic of the churches' mutual observing of one another anew. These "elements" rest on very different levels. This holds true, for one thing, in view of their capability of being recognized; not all of them are visible in the same way. What is visible, for example, is the use of Scripture, the administration of baptism, and the office of bishop. This does not hold true, however in the same way with regard to religious zeal, faith, love, virtues, and so on, and especially the "life of grace" and the "inner gifts of the Holy Spirit" characteristically elude empirical verification. Even the actual determination of a genuine martyrdom must ultimately be left to God, even if a person visibly and publicly suffered martyrdom. The listed elements rest on different levels also in view of their functions. Some are means of grace through which Christ is working in the power of the Spirit. Others are workings, spiritual gifts that are imparted through the means of grace. But where must we start off in order to achieve a clear recognition of the working of Christ and thus achieve a clear recognition of the unity of the church?

Now one notices that in lining up a variety of references, both in the Dogmatic Constitution on the Church and in the Decree on Ecumenism, special prominence is given to *baptism:* "Through baptism" the Christians separated from the Roman Church "are honored with the name of Christian" and are "united with Christ" (Dogmatic Constitution on the Church, Art. 15). They are "justified by faith through baptism" and are "incorporated into Christ" (Decree on Ecumenism, Art. 3). "By the sacrament of baptism, whenever it is properly conferred in the way the Lord determined, and received with the appropriate dispositions of soul, a person becomes truly incorporated into the crucified and glorified Christ and is reborn to a sharing of the divine life…" (Decree on Ecumenism, Art. 22). In this way one such "element" is given prominence, one that is at once visible and a means of grace. Especially honored is also *Holy Scripture:* "For there are many who honor Scripture as a norm of faith and of life" (Dogmatic Constitution on the Church, Art. 15). "The written word of God" is also mentioned by the Decree on Ecumenism at the beginning of its enumeration. Both of these emphases suggest the following reflections.

Since in regard to the issue of unity, the concern is about the visible church, more precisely, about the recognition of the only holy church that is becoming visible also outside our church, we must start off with the *visible* "elements" through which Christ bestows the inner gifts. The council rightly gave prominence to baptism as a visible means of grace through which the faithful are justified, incorporated into the body of Christ, and reborn to the new life. Equal prominence must be given to the gospel, for it is "the power of God unto salvation to everyone who believes" (Rom. 1.16). Through the proclaimed message of Christ's act of salvation God not only *summons* to faith and *announces* justification and the new life but *creates* faith and *bestows* righteousness and new life on the believers. Further prominence is to be given to the second chief sacrament of all the churches, the Lord's Supper, in which, under the visible forms of bread and wine, Christ grants participation in his body and blood and thus builds up the believers as his body. In whatever manner in the life of the churches these means of grace may be unfolded in the various forms of preaching, absolution, benediction, or also further "sacraments," here Christ is working in a clearly recognizable way—in such a way that we can hear, see, and taste his working.

But wherein can we recognize that here the pure gospel is preached and the sacraments are administered in truth?[iii] In their enumeration of the "elements" the conciliar texts have rightly given precedence to Holy Scripture "as norm of faith and of life," because the historical act of salvation in Jesus Christ and its attestation through the apostles and the earliest community is of foundational and normative significance for the speaking and acting of the church of all ages. The gospel and the sacraments are to be recognized by their agreement with Holy Scripture. Now, the gospel in its very nature is not a book but an oral message. Not the biblical baptismal texts but the administration of baptism, not the New Testament texts on the Lord's Supper but the reception of the Lord's Supper—this administration and reception grant participation in the body of Christ. Even though Holy Scripture is given normative precedence over all of the speaking and acting of the church, it points beyond itself insofar as its statements must be proclaimed and realized ever anew in the historical situations that are constantly changing. In that regard, evaluating the proclamation and the sacraments is not to be done in a biblicistic-legalistic way. It must take into account the full range of possibilities that are contained in the biblical witnesses and that have been realized in one way or another in the history of proclamation and of the administration of the sacraments. The question concerning conformity to Scripture has often been answered in an unhistorical way, and thus activity of Christ in the other churches has often gone unrecognized.

Through the gospel and the sacraments Christ justifies, sanctifies, and renews the faithful, takes them into his death and resurrection, and builds them up as his body. Through the gospel and the sacraments he gives them the Holy Spirit in manifold gifts and produces the "virtuous works" as fruit. The inner life of Christians is hidden from us. We are forbidden to distinguish between believers and hypocrites and to pronounce final judgment on their works. God knows the heart and the works, and he will one day make them manifest. But the gospel and the sacraments are to be clearly recognized on the basis of Holy Scripture, and we may be sure that believers are there where the gospel is preached and the sacraments are administered,[iv] because the gospel is not an empty word and the sacraments are not empty signs. Christ is working in them to awaken and to renew. The unity of the church is thus recognized by the gospel and the sacraments.

In the midst of the differences and contrasts in the church traditions one's gaze must be directed toward this word and sacrament event through which Christ builds up the church. The weight of the individual constituent parts in the church traditions is to be measured from this perspective. The significance of the dogmas and the necessity of clarifying dogmatic differences cannot be underestimated. Salvation, however, does not come through dogmatic statements about word and sacrament but rather through the proclamation of the word and the administration of the sacraments. Dogmatic statements are in the service of this word and sacrament event, but they are not yet the event itself. Also, the significance of ministerial offices and the clarification of existing differences here are very important. But the ministerial office is designed to serve the working of Christ through word and sacrament and cannot be called a means of grace in the same sense as word and sacrament. The various constituent parts in church tradition and in the present life of the churches cannot simply be connected and compared with one another. Rather, the structure of the contexts of the effects has to be considered, a structure in which each of these constituent parts is designed to serve the working of Christ through word and sacrament. Then the unity will be recognized that encompasses the many differences. That unity will be recognized when the one Christ is recognized, who, through word and sacrament, builds up the one church in the multiplicity of church traditions.

4. The Manifestation of Unity

If the unity of the church is recognized, the unity that encompasses the borders of the individual churches and their traditions, then one cannot stop with that recognition. Rather, the unity that has been recognized must be manifested, and the separations by which it is distorted and obscured must be eliminated. No matter how well developed the mutual respect of the separated churches has become and, beyond that, no matter if a cordial affection has emerged, and if the understanding of another church has led to a spiritual participation in its life, yet neither tact nor friendship nor joint spiritual experiences, nor even working together in certain areas, can replace the unity of all believers given by God that is to become visible in this world. This bodily unity in full fellowship cannot be treated as a distant goal or even only as an idea. With great emphasis the council has rightly pointed to the urgency of this unity.

Because the believers in Christ are one, they must struggle for unification. It is not up to them to establish unity, but they must make room for it. Because we are one in Christ, we must become one. This task of making space for unity means intensive working together in asking, researching, and answering. Here we must make use of the most diverse methods of exegetical and historical scholarship, but also the most up-to-date framing of the issues and the most incisive knowledge from the fields of logic, linguistics, depth-psychology, sociology, and anthropology in the broadest sense. In rethinking the dogmatic differences anew, we must push forward to the point where the churches can jointly confess the mighty deeds of God. In the process of rethinking the issues of jurisdiction, autonomy, autocephalism, and so forth, we must find the form of fellowship in which the unity of the churches will become visible. But of what value is all this researching if it does not take place in the love that knows itself responsible for making sure that nothing of what God has entrusted to another church is lost? The believers must work for this unification with "fear and trembling" (Phil. 2.12), just as for their salvation.

Nevertheless, this unification will not be the result of human will, work, and accomplishment. Just as the unity in Christ is given by God, so too can the unification of the churches be produced only by him, who "is at work in you, both to will and to work for his good pleasure" (Phil. 2.13). For this reason, in the midst of all ecumenical work, the churches pray that God would grant unity in the freedom of his grace. In the first period of the ecumenical movement various models of a united Christendom and its ordering were outlined, but in the course of time there has been less and less talk of such proleptic constructs. It has been increasingly recognized that the unification of the churches and the form of the unified church is to be expected only from God. Thus in the annual week of Prayer for Christian Unity, Christians from churches all over the world pray at the same time—and often also in joint worship—for "the unity of the church of Jesus Christ, as he wills it and when he wills it."[v] In this prayer, composed by the Catholic priest Couturier, all glory is given to God, since the praying Christians do not act proleptically but await everything from God. More than ever the churches today are aware of their dependence on the miracle of God's guidance, which is able to show the way even there where human efforts come up against insurmountable barriers.

In this praying and working, it is nevertheless clear to all that—whatever form God has foreseen for a unified Christendom—the unity of the message of Christ, the unity of baptism, the fellowship of the Lord's Supper, and the mutual recognition of one another's ministerial offices are indispensable elements for unity. This is not a humanly devised notion but a divine necessity preset for the churches from their origin. In the assembly of the World Council of Churches in New Delhi (1961), the assembled churches expressed this concern in the following words:

We believe that the unity which is both God's will and his gift to his church is being made visible as all in each place who are baptized into Jesus Christ and confess him as Lord and Savior are brought by the Holy Spirit into one fully committed fellowship, holding the one apostolic faith, preaching the one gospel, breaking the one bread, joining in common prayer, and having a corporate life reaching out in witness and service to all and who at the same time are united with the whole Christian fellowship in all places and all ages in such wise that the ministry and members are accepted by all, and that all can act and speak together as occasion requires for the tasks to which God calls his people.[vi]

The statements of the Augsburg Confession, the most important confession of the Reformation, share this understanding of unity:

For this is enough for the true unity of the Christian church that there the gospel is preached harmoniously according to a pure understanding and the sacraments are administered in conformity with the divine word. It is not necessary for the true unity of the Christian church that uniform ceremonies, instituted by human beings, be observed everywhere. As Paul says in Ephesians 4[.4–5]: "There is one body and one Spirit, just as you were called to the one hope of your calling, one Lord, one faith, one baptism."[vii]

Here, too, one could attempt to point to the first steps that will not only lead to drawing the churches closer together but, beyond that, are necessary for unification. We must here restrict ourselves to a few basic principles, and in view of the great significance of the confession we emphasize the issue concerning the dogmatic consensus that by its very nature belongs to unity:

a) Unification will be impossible if each church insists on all its dogmatic statements, regards them all as equally binding, and demands their full acceptance by the other churches as prerequisite for unification. The Second Vatican Council's Decree on Ecumenism has rightly pointed to the fact that the dogmatic statements constitute a kind of hierarchy and must be interpreted from their controlling center. All dogmas are in fact and ultimately an unfolding of the central confession of Christ. The distinction between central confessional statements and their further concrete unfolding is of great importance not only for *understanding* the dogmas of other churches but also for *unification*. Then, indeed, this hierarchy must be understood not only as a hierarchy of contents but also as a hierarchy in the claim of obligation in the various dogmatic statements. As surely as the unity of the faith is the condition for unification, just as surely the indiscriminate acceptance of all the dogmatic statements is not the condition, since in the course of church history the one confession of Christ has been expounded in different statements as it met a variety of special fronts and conceptualities, which are not important for the whole of Christendom in the same way and which cannot be imposed on all in the same way. Within the structure of canon law a distinction is made between what is "by divine right" and what is "by human right," that is, between the unalterably valid command of God and the alterable concrete application of canon law. Similarly the central dogmas should also be distinguished from the variableness of their concrete expression.

b) But even if the *substantive* unity of the central dogmatic affirmations holds as indispensable for the unification of the churches, the same dogmatic *formulas* do not necessarily have to be required for the unity of the church. It cannot be forgotten that in the ancient church numerous territorial baptismal creeds were used side by side and that the unity of the church is not confessed by having the same creedal formula, but it is confessed in the same Lord and in the mutual acknowledgment of different confessional formulas. In its statements on the liturgy, the council rightly moved away from a centralized uniformity in the direction of the structure of fellowship.[viii] Similar starting points are found in the council's statements concerning theological traditions and the stipulations of canon law for the particular churches. However, the understanding of unity as fellowship in mutual acknowledgment must, in addition, be expanded also to embrace the understanding of dogmatic unity, if in the process of unification the riches of that which God has granted the churches in knowledge and doctrine is to be included.

The Roman Church could perhaps agree to the second principle, because it is only an expansion of the dogmatic statements regarding that church's affirmation of the multiplicity of rites and theologies. The Decree on Ecumenism thus states with regard to the Eastern Church, "that these various theological formulations are often to be considered as complementary rather than conflicting" (Decree on Ecumenism, Art. 17). To be sure, the document is here speaking only of a different way of proclaiming doctrine, not specifically of solemn dogmas. In any case, when the Roman Church attempted union with the Greek Orthodox Church at Florence (1439), it did not demand that the Greek Church insert into the text of its creed the previously rejected *filioque* but contented itself with an expression of consensus with the content of the Western formula. The first principle would, however, practically mean a correction of the Roman Church's traditional demand that all its dogmas be universally and equally binding.

c) Beyond that, however, it is correct to say that none of the churches can remain exactly as it is; in every case a renewal and an unfolding of catholicity, that is, a return to God and a turning toward the other churches, is needed. One-sided positions must be lifted, impoverishments must be supplemented, errors must be corrected, and anathemas must be canceled. Church history shows that all attempts at achieving unification by having one church absorb the others have come to ruin. They had to come to ruin because no church as it is can make space for everything that God has done in the others. Unification will not be possible without sacrifice. But where the sacrifice is offered to God, there is no loss but only the self-sacrifice unto a treasure which is greater than what one previously possessed.

Editor's Notes

  [i] Cf. Mt. 25.14 ff. and Lk. 16.1 ff. (esp. vv. 8–10).
 [ii] Cf. endnote 7 in the introduction ("The Task") to *The Coming Christ and Church Traditions*.
[iii] Cf. AC 7.
 [iv] Cf. AC 5, 7, and 8.
  [v] The French priest Paul Couturier was instrumental in helping to establish the Week of Prayer
       for Christian Unity.
 [vi] *The New Dehli Report*, 116.
[vii] AC 7. Schlink cites the German text.
[viii] Cf. Schlink's analysis of this *koinonia-structure* in chap. 14 ("Ecumenical Council's Then and
       Now") of *The Coming Christ and Church Traditions*.

Index of Biblical References

Old Testament

New Testament

Index of Persons

Index of Subjects

Edmund Schlink: Schriften zu Ökumene und Bekenntnis

Herausgegeben von Klaus Engelhardt, Günther Gaßmann, Rolf Herrfahrdt, Michael Plathow, Ursula Schnell, Peter Zimmerling.

Band 1: Der kommende Christus und die kirchlichen Traditionen. Nach dem Konzil

Mit einer biografischen Einleitung von Jochen Eber. Herausgegeben von Klaus Engelhardt. 2004. Unveränd. Nachdruck d. Ausg. v. 1961 u. 1965. 529 Seiten, kartoniert
ISBN 978-3-525-56701-2

Im erstem Band wurden Schlinks seit langem vergriffene Ökumenische Schriften gesammelt wieder zugänglich gemacht.

Band 2: Ökumenische Dogmatik. Grundzüge

Mit einem Vorwort von Wolfhart Pannenberg. Herausgegeben und mit einem Nachwort versehen von Michael Plathow.
3. Auflage 2005. 828 Seiten, kartoniert
ISBN 978-3-525-56186-7

Die »Ökumenische Dogmatik« ist Schlinks Buch gewordenes Lebenswerk, Frucht eines jahrzehntelangen Engagements, das auch für den gegenwärtigen ökumenischen Dialog nichts an Aktualität eingebüßt hat.

Band 3: Die Lehre von der Taufe

Herausgegeben und mit einer Einleitung versehen von Peter Zimmerling.
2. Auflage 2007. 174 Seiten, kartoniert
ISBN 978-3-525-56935-1

Schlink verfasste das Buch nicht nur in ökumenischem Horizont, sondern in dezidiert ökumenischer Absicht.

Band 4: Theologie der lutherischen Bekenntnisschriften

Herausgegeben und mit einer Einleitung versehen von Günther Gaßmann.
4. Auflage 2008. 272 Seiten, kartoniert
ISBN 978-3-525-56716-6

Das streng systematisch aufgebaute Buch, das dogmatische und pastorale Reflexionen verbindet, ist Ausdruck der Theologiegeschichte des 20. Jahrhunderts und reicht in seiner Bedeutung ins 21. Jahrhundert hinein.

Band 5: Ausgewählte Beiträge. Kirchenkampf – Theologische Grundfragen – Ökumene

Herausgegeben und mit einem Vor- und Nachwort versehen von Ursula Schnell.
2010. 327 Seiten, kartoniert
ISBN 978-3-525-56718-0

Der fünfte und letzte Band der »Schriften zu Ökumene und Bekenntnis« enthält zehn Beiträge Edmund Schlinks zu Kirchenkampf, theologischen Grundfragen und Ökumene.

Weitere Informationen / further informations: www.v-r.de

V&R Academic
Verlagsgruppe Vandenhoeck & Ruprecht | V&R unipress

www.v-r.de

A guide for comprehending Pannenberg's Systematic Theology in the context of his most relevant writings

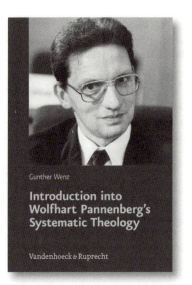

Gunther Wenz
Introduction to Wolfhart Pannenberg's Systematic Theology
2013. 267 pages, softcover
ISBN 978-3-525-56014-3

eBook: ISBN 978-3-647-56014-4

As one of the great thinkers of our time, Wolfhart Pannenberg has influenced the history of Christian theology and philosophy of religion since the second half of the 20th century. His Systematic Theology and many of his other works have become classics in the theological science.

In this introduction Gunther Wenz examines the main pillars of Pannenberg's theology: the self-manifestation of God, the Trinitarian God, the creation of the world, Christology, anthropology, pneumatology, eschatology and ecclesiology. The book thereby offers a valuable guide to comprehending Pannenberg's Systematic Theology in the context of his most relevant writings.

V&R Academic
Verlagsgruppe Vandenhoeck & Ruprecht | V&R **unipress**

www.v-r.de